DESKFORD

A LOWER BANFFSHIRE PARISH

JOHN AITKEN

*To Sarah & Mick
with best wishes
John*

1880

Copyright ©John Aitken 2016

Published in Great Britain by the Banffshire Field Club, a Registered Scottish Charity (SC015944). Revenue from all books published by the BFC is used for the continuation of its non profit-making publishing programme.

Email: bfc.1880@gmail.com
Website: banffshirefieldclub.org.uk

ISBN 978-0-9524239-2-8

First published 2016

A catalogue record of this book is available from the British Library.

The right of John Aitken to be identified as the author of this work has been asserted by him in accordance with the Copyright, Designs and Patents Act, 1988.

All rights reserved. No part of this publication may be reproduced, stored or transmitted in any form without the express written permission of the publisher.

Publication of this book has been made possible by significant funding from The Banffshire Field Club. In addition, the publishers wish to acknowledge the financial assistance given by Deskford Community Association, The Rotary Club of Keith and The Cullen, Deskford and Portknockie Heritage Group.

Printed in Keith, Banffshire, by MMS Almac Ltd.

ABOUT THE AUTHOR

John Aitken has been a resident of Deskford since 2001. He was formerly Rector of Keith Grammar School. He is currently a committee member of The Banffshire Field Club and is a committee member and former President of the Cullen, Deskford and Portknockie Heritage Group.

ABOUT THE BANFFSHIRE FIELD CLUB

The Field Club was established in 1880 by a group of prominent locals "to explore the District...inquiring into the Geology, Botany, Natural History, Archaeology, etc".

The Field Club has an archive of lectures presented since its foundation. These papers, or 'Transactions', recorded the business at each meeting along with a lecture given by an invited expert. They were printed in booklet form by the Banffshire Journal for issue to the members until the practice ceased in 1939. The subjects cover all aspects of interest relating to Banffshire, covering archaeology, astronomy, biology, botany, excursions & field trips, geology, geography, nature, science and social history. These papers are available for sale and are listed on the Club's website at banffshirefieldclub.org.

It is still going strong in 2016, with an annual programme which includes monthly talks over the winter and excursions to places of interest in the summer. It has recently begun publishing and republishing books of local interest, of which this volume is one.

CONTENTS

CHAPTER		PAGE
1.	Foreword	ii
2.	Introduction	1
3.	Physical Environment	4
4.	Mists of Time	15
5.	Infrastructure and Services	33
6.	Agriculture and Industry	74
7.	Religion	150
8.	Education	216
9.	Military, Politics, Land Ownership and Aristocracy	267
10.	Law and Order	318
11.	People	380
12.	Celebrations	434
13.	Society	467
14.	Folk Beliefs and Superstitions	498
15.	Appendices	528
16.	Sources	586
17.	Index	
18.	List of Subscribers	

FOREWORD

My neighbour Brian from Hollanbush said "I suppose you'll start your book about Deskford with *'Once upon a time'*". We both laughed, but later, when thinking about it, I realised that what he had said summed up well what I hoped to do. This book is a mainly factual account of Deskford's history but also contains a number of beliefs, stories, suppositions and deductions as well as displaying a number of old and new photographs which together may go some way towards explaining and describing the "once upon a time" of this area.

Any history is a collection of many once upon a times based on the different sources of information available. However, just as these four words had an unexpected relevance for me, another oft-quoted maxim, "the past is a different country; they do things differently there", does not really bear examination. In fact, to characterise the past in this way is to place it within the rigid parameters of a single entity, juxtaposed against and equal to a mono-dimensional present. The past is much more varied, and to continue the country analogy, is more akin to an entire United Nations of countries, as different to each other as can be imagined, and as different to each other as each is to the present. They present continuous surprises and eccentricities, especially if viewed solely through the prism of our today.

Though making use of a number of academic publications, this book is not one. Formal standards of academic evidence have not been applied, permitting the use of evidence which is almost certainly accurate but which is for example not explicitly linked to Deskford or which is only available anecdotally. Where there is widely accepted evidence that particular languages or farming methods or social attitudes and structures or house building specifications, or forms of worship were universal across Lower Banffshire or the North East, it is presumed that these also applied in Deskford. While I have attempted to be accurate across a range of specialisms in which I am not an expert, it is inevitable that I will have made some mistakes, for which I accept full responsibility. I would be grateful if readers would let me know of these and let me have their corrections. Similarly, if any reader has additional information which I have not uncovered about this area I would be grateful if they would let me know of it.

A local history such as this is bound to be influenced by the nature and extent of local sources which have survived or which are available. While I have tried to take account of apparent over emphases such as the focus on fornication in Kirk Session minutes, or the zeal of C18th antiquarians whose wish to believe in a local Roman presence outweighs the evidence available to them, I am aware that what I have written is inevitably affected by the nature and balance of information available. Though the amount of documentary evidence in existence is substantial, it is frustrating to think of the sources which have disappeared, including school registers and early log books, Turnpike Trust minutes, School Board minutes and Poor Law registers, together with C20th Deskford Parish Church documents and the many primary sources referred to as extant by C19th antiquarians such as Dr Cramond, but which are now lost.

The reasons for some of these losses are crass. In 1746 retreating Jacobites, in a malicious spree of destruction against the Earl of Seafield, who was a Government supporter, ransacked Cullen House and caused a blizzard in the streets of Old Cullen comprising ancient documents from it. In the C20th many of Banff's earliest documents were used to fuel the boiler for the central heating of Banffshire County Council offices. As late as the mid 1970s, on the dissolution of Cullen Town Council, many historic documents were thrown out in skips, including, for example, several volumes of the Protocol Books of George Duncanson, Notary Public in Cullen in the C16th, in which all civil legal transactions including land transfers and purchases were recorded. More recently, on the closure of New St John's church in 2004, a number of its records were disposed of.

Information for this book has been obtained from original documents, newspapers, websites, maps, short papers, books, local and national archives and interviews with local people. Institutions and individuals approached were universally helpful, with a special mention due to Ruaraidh Wishart and his colleagues at Aberdeen City Archive and Graeme Wilson and his colleagues at Moray Heritage Centre. A full list of sources and those who have helped is recorded at the back of this book. My grateful thanks to all of those mentioned and if I have missed anyone out, my sincere apologies.

In particular I should like to thank John Rennie for his unrivalled knowledge of Deskford and his proof reading, Alistair Mason for his detailed proof reading and academic input, Colin Brown and Allan Robertson at MMS Almac for their patience and advice, and Sue Ritchie for her cover design. Above all I should like to thank Roy Milligan for the hundreds of hours he has spent helping with the book, applying his IT skills and expertise on layout and presentation, and offering advice from his previous experience of publishing. His input and his advice have been invaluable. The responsibility for accuracy is however mine alone, and any mistakes or misrepresentations must be laid solely at my door. If any are noticed I would appreciate being appraised of these.

As Richard Rolle de Hampole (1290/1300 - 1349) is quoted:-

"And if any man that es clerk
Can fynde any errour in this werk
I pray hym he do me that favour
That he wille amende that errour
And if men may here any errours se
Or if any defaut in this tretice be
I make here a protestatacion
That I will stand til the correccion
Of ilka rightwyse lered man
That my defaut here correcte can"

John Aitken, Little Skeith, Deskford. 2016.
01542 840476, jaskeith@btinternet.com

INTRODUCTION

Deskford is one of a small group of self-effacing parishes in Lower Banffshire which also includes Fordyce, Cullen, Ordiquhill, Grange and Rathven. Their fame is limited, their history largely unexceptional and punctuated by only occasional excitement, usually in a minor key. Perhaps the points of greatest interest and pride in this area are Cullen Auld Kirk, Fordyce Academy, Ordiquhill as the home of the Kerr's Pink tattie, and, perhaps approaching European significance, that Celtic war trumpet, the Deskford Carnyx, the bi-centenary of the finding of which is celebrated this year.

This book attempts to give an account of the history of Deskford, five miles north to south and three miles east to west if measured as a parish and somewhat larger if measured as an estate. Whilst it is a history of Deskford and of the people who have lived here over the centuries, it will hopefully also give a flavour of life in the past in other similar areas in the North East, and perhaps more widely across Scotland.

The area provides evidence of the existence of inhabitants in pre-history and of their artefacts and structures, but most of what has been recorded is of the more recent past. I have nevertheless attempted to explore the entire history of the area as fully as possible. Apart from the first chapter on Deskford in the Mists of Time, I have chosen to organise the book on a thematic rather than on a chronological basis.

For the greatest part of of its existence the most important activity in Deskford has been farming, while the most important sense of structure in the past 450 years has been provided by the Kirk. Each of these has been allocated its own chapter as have education, infrastructure, law and order, and the physical environment amongst others.

Throughout its history the people of Deskford have had the same basic needs, those of food, shelter, clothing, security and a social and regulatory framework within which to live their lives and which they understand and accept. The specifics of how these needs have been addressed vary significantly over the years, but at all times the lives of the inhabitants have been directed towards meeting these needs. Over the years the people of Deskford have held beliefs which were embraced, sometimes with enthusiasm and sometimes less so. Usually there was an overarching system of morality and appropriate conduct to which almost all adhered.

This does not in any way suggest that the oft-used local saying, "Its aye been that wye" is correct. Those of us born in the middle of last century were born into the last few decaying years of a society which placed great emphasis on decency, rectitude and decorum, but this really only existed from mid-Victorian times. At other periods in the past six or seven hundred years, and probably before that, attitudes towards crime, sobriety, sex and other aspects of society changed regularly and often quite dramatically. As a counterpoint to this, amongst the people there has perhaps also been an identifiable leaning towards resistance to change, particularly in terms of agricultural methods, housing and education. Another oft used local saying, "It'll dae", has a long history.

In the past most of the people born in Deskford lived out their lives in Deskford. There was a stability about the population which fed through into folk memory. Some individuals or even families were industrious. Some were lackadaisical. Some were relatively prosperous and others could never overcome poverty. Some were thrifty and others had no money sense. Some lent money to the kirk and others were on the poor roll for generation after generation. Some were good neighbours and others were disputatious.

Some were intelligent or wise whilst others were stupid or glaikit. Some were placid when others were emotional. The individuals from every period in the past were the same mix as we see nowadays. They did not have access to the knowledge or technology of recent times but they dealt with the circumstances they encountered in whatever era they lived. Were it possible for our ancestors, the Deskford inhabitants of the past, to be reborn today,

BANFFSHIRE FIELD CLUB

The Banffshire Field Club was founded in 1880 by a small enthusiastic group of men interested in all aspects of the County of Banff and beyond. Among them was Thomas Edward, the internationally renowned and self-taught naturalist from Banff, and William Cramond, Cullen schoolmaster and local historian.

Over the past 135 years, the Field Club's interests have covered a wide range of topics relating to the County - natural history, social and political history, its major families, its great houses and castles, literature, architecture, agriculture, famine, railways, politics, religion and even murder and mayhem. All of this research is available in the form of small printed booklets and are known as the 'Transactions' of the Banffshire Field Club.

The age of the Transactions means that *'Agriculture in Banffshire 150 years ago'* from 1902, actually takes you back to the 1750s. The story of the creation of Macduff is fully described in *'The Making of a Banffshire Burgh'* from 1893. All are a fascinating read.

The membership of the Field Club has always been drawn from a wide variety of the County's population with enquiring minds.

The Club meets on the second Saturday of each month from September to April (except January) in the form of a lecture about some area of Banffshire interest and occasionally, neighbouring Counties. Talks usually last for about an hour, followed by tea and biscuits and an opportunity to meet others with similar interests.

Location: St. Rufus Church Hall, Turner Street, Keith, AB55 5DJ
Time: 2:15 p.m.
Cost: £2 for members; £3 for visitors (per meeting).
Membership: £5 per year.

www.banffshirefieldclub.org

The Carnyx, an iron-age Celtic war trumpet discovered in Deskford in 1816 (Museum of Banff copy)

PUBLICATIONS

'The History of the Banffshire Field Club 1880-2015'
by Monica Anton & Roy Milligan (A5, 48 pages): £7 (free to members)

'Banffshire Churches' - revised and updated
by Donald Findlay (A5, 48 pages): £7

'Deskford, A Lower Banffshire Parish'
by John Aitken (B5, 650 pages): £25

Forthcoming Publications:
'Whitehills and its Four Harbours' by Andy Strachan
'Cullykhan and the Story of Troup' by Alex. McKay

ARCHIVE

The Field Club has an archive of lectures presented since its foundation. They were printed in booklet form by the Banffshire Journal for issue to Field Club members, until the practice ceased in 1939.

TRANSACTIONS IN-STOCK:

Some titles are available for sale from stock as original printed booklets and usually range from £1.00 to £15.00 according to the number of pages (plus a minimum of £1 p&p). Most titles are available for under £5.

Individual papers on various subjects were often printed and stapled together in sets, resulting in more than one paper with the same reference number. Regardless of the subject required, you would receive and be charged for the complete set of originals as they are not easily divisible.

TRANSACTIONS OUT-OF-STOCK:

Out-of-stock titles can be scanned and re-printed on demand. Prices are quoted on application and may be slightly higher than originals.

These digitised Transactions are re-printed with a 10-11pt font size and are much easier to read than the originals. Unless already digitised and thus available immediately for re-printing, they will be supplied as soon as possible.

A list of Transactions indicating the above availability is available on our website:
www.banffshirefieldclub.org.uk

If you require Transactions, contact the **Publications Secretary** for a quotation incl. p&p.
e-mail: **bfc.1880@gmail.com**

Banffshire Field Club is a registered Scottish charity, No. SC015944 some would be successful in the world of the present while others would struggle badly.

This then is the story of the people of Deskford over the millennia, their successes and their failures, their good luck and their bad luck, their joy and their sadness. There are now very few people living in the area who can trace their ancestry back locally for more than one or two generations. Whether they can or cannot is irrelevant. The most recent resident incomers may feel an affinity with their predecessors in the Howe o' Deskart, while those whose families have lived here for a long time may have little interest. I hope this book helps everyone who reads it to identify in some way or another with the people who lived here in the past, and that everyone who reads it can find a moment or two to think about long-lost Deskford and the people who lived there.

PHYSICAL ENVIRONMENT

TOPOGRAPHY AND GEOLOGY

The shape of the land in Deskford is caused by small streams, and earlier by glaciations which moved over the area from west to east. These have left a wide"Howe" surrounded by hills on all sides. Altitude varies from 100ft in the north of the parish to nearly 1000ft at the top of Lurg Hill.

On the east side, near Cultain, lies Cotton Hill at 556ft, then, moving south along the watershed which forms the eastern boundary between Deskford and Fordyce parishes and Deskford and Grange parishes, we pass Standingmanhill near Ardicow, the Hill of Summertown, Greenhill, the Hill of Inverkindling and

The east side of Deskford from the south with Lurg Hill to the right and Cotton Hill in the distance, centre left, showing Clochmacreich in the centre of this view.

Lurg Hill. Chapel Hill is a low outlier between Backies and Clochmacreich.

On the west side, and shielding Deskford from the north, lies Clune Hill, with the Gallows Knowe on its flank being at a height of 353ft. Further south the hills on Aultmore are not as steep as those on the east side but include the substantial Clashmadin at 871ft, together with the Old Fir Hill and Lomond Hill. Faichyhill is an outlier rising immediately to the west of Mosside.

The First Statistical Account states that in the lower land of the valley the soil is loam resting on strong deep clay, whilst on the hills it is a light black mossy soil resting on clay and gravel. Much moorish and waste ground on the western hills was improved for agriculture in the late C18th and early C19th. Rocks include almost vertical strata of mica slate with fragments of quartz embedded and a rich north-south bed of fine compact limestone. Having excellent supplies of water, wood, moss and lime made Deskford a very attractive location.

WATER COURSES

Deskford occupies the valley of the Deskford Burn as it flows north, from its source on the watershed near the boundary with the parish of Grange, to the sea at Cullen. The burn starts as a trickle emerging from field drainage near Tillybreedless Bridge. Some of its early course near Clochmacreich has been cut and straightened as an artificial channel, but from there onwards it increases significantly in volume from the addition of tributary burns throughout its length, and long before it leaves the parish it is able to support small trout. In a couple of places it has cut deep gorges, and by its lower course could almost be described as a very small river. As it passes through Cullen its name changes to the Cullen Burn. There are many tributary burns on both sides of the Deskford Burn, most named but some unnamed, some long and some short and some containing a significant volume of water and some not.

On the east side of the valley, travelling from south to north, the first tributary burn we meet is a short unnamed one just north of Clochmacreich. The second one is also unnamed, but is much longer, coming off Lurg Hill and passing 50m south of Upper Skeith behind which, what used to be a ford on the old Cullen to Portsoy road can still be identified. It joins the Deskford Burn near a major ford on the old main road between Keith and Cullen at a spot known as Three

Burns Meeting or Three Waters Meeting (this tributary, the Deskford Burn and the Tack Burn entering from the west) by the old entrance to Craibstone Quarry. Next there follow three unnamed burns, the first being a short one which runs downhill from Mid Skeith to Lower Craibstone. This is followed by a longer one which runs downhill 100m south of Little Skeith and which may have been known at one time as the Stotfauld Burn and then another very short one. The next burn on the east side is a short and fairly insignificant looking one, just south of Mains of Skeith, called the Kil Burn which, together with the Stotfauld Burn, appeared on a land transaction of 1542.

After this we meet the Hoggie Burn, one of the main tributaries on the east side of the valley. It originates in the moss above Kintywaird and flows between Lower Broadrashes and Hollanbush then immediately north of Mains of Skeith through a deep gorge into the Deskford Burn. Until around 2004 when mains water became available it provided the Lurg Hill water supply for a number of properties. The course of the burn downstream from Lower Broadrashes occupies a deep wooded valley which is carpeted with snowdrops in February. For a brief time in the C18th this burn was known as the Burn of Skeith.

Next comes the Flake Burn, a short burn which travels north-west from Ordens and had the Priest's Well on its bank. In 2013 Pam and John Robertson found some industrial slag on the banks of this burn. It is followed by Alton (Old Town) Burn, another short burn which flows down opposite Kirktown.

The same burn which is called the Blackspot Burn above Oathillock becomes the Linn Burn below it. On this lower portion lies the scenic rocky gorge of the Linn from which a few minute specks of gold were panned in 2012. The next burn on the east side of the valley is known as the Whitestrype Burn as it runs parallel to and just south of the Ardicow road. As it passes Little Knows it becomes the Herd's Burn and flows into the Deskford Burn to the south of Carestown.

There were two further burns on the east side, which were recorded around 170 years ago. The Clay Strype entered the Deskford Burn opposite Clune and the Boggie Strype ran through Leitchestown steading and then down to the

Deskford Burn. The flow of many of the burns on the east side has been reduced by the extensive planting of trees in recent times, some on what was good farmland.

On the west side of the valley there are a greater number of burns and some of them are considerably longer, since the watershed on the west side is much further away from the Deskford Burn than is the one on the east side.

Travelling south to north the first burn encountered is the Quean's Strype, a small trickle between Bossy Hillock and Tillybreedless Bridge, which for most of its course runs through Grange parish but for the last short stretch forms the parish boundary between Grange and Deskford. On its north bank, level with Myreside, just inside Deskford parish, stood the large Grey Cairn, of which no trace remains. There next follows a burn just to the south of Langlanburn. Modern maps and other sources attribute no name to it, but it must be likely that it is the Langlan Burn after which the farm was named.

The Tack Burn just east of the B9018 at Craibstone.

A fairly large but unnamed burn crosses under the main road beside the layby by means of a substantial bridge, and this is followed by the Tack burn which flows to the south of the site of the former Aultmore Lodge then between Craibstone and Craibstone Cottages where the banks are covered in snowdrops in March. It then crosses under the main road and enters the Deskford Burn at Three Burns Meeting.

The Ely Burn is a short one which passes to the south of what was Wairdleys croft and under a fairly large bridge just west of the former Woodend smiddy. Next, still travelling north, is the Waird Burn, which runs down the northern boundary of the former Wairdleys croft and is culverted under both the main road and the Berryhillock road where the gap between the two roads is narrowest. Thereafter the remaining four burns on the west side of the valley are all long and substantial ones.

The Creichy Burn flows north for some distance to Muir of Squaredoch where the Poors Houses used to be sited, and then east and downhill to a point immediately north of Berryhillock. Next comes the Lornach Burn which flows from the moss, near the former site of Lornachburn Farm, then between

The Ha' Burn immediately before joining the Deskford Burn showing Milton Mills and the field in front of it where Milton village lay.

Stripeside and Bloomfield down to the West Manse. At this point it changes its

name to the Mosside Burn which runs for much of its course through what used to be a moss, by means of a cut channel, to Ardoch Farm which is now South Lissens pottery. After Ardoch it again changes its name, this time to the Ha' Burn, passes round Ha' Hillock, goes under the main road by means of a substantial bridge and enters the Deskford Burn just north of Milton Mills.

The Burn of Blairock delineates the parish boundary between Deskford and Rathven for much of its course. It travels from west of Bogrotten, is culverted under the minor road on the corner near Greens of Blairock, passes under the Blairock road on a well causeyed ford, runs past Burnsford after which it is known as the Broxy Burn, and thence to the Cullen Burn at Lintmill Lodge.

The final burn, the Burn of Aultmore, lies outside the parish of Deskford, but is in an area which has always considered itself part of the community of Deskford. For much of its course it has been subject to slate quarrying, at Slateheugh, below Burnside of Aultmore and at Darbreich. Here it becomes known as the Darbreich Burn. It flows past Briggs of Darbreich and north of Braidbog, goes through the plantation just west of Davie's Castle becoming the Glen Burn, and joins the Cullen Burn just west of Lintmill Lodge.

WELLS AND DAMS

Almost every farm had a well and, from around 1800 many had a mill dam, though few of the latter remain, one exception being the one at Backies. It is sometimes difficult to distinguish between what is a burn and what is a drainage ditch and in some cases small burns were converted into drainage ditches. Additionally, channels were often cut from small burns to mill dams and then back into the burns. The largest of the mill dams were those which served Berryhillock and Milton Mills, each of which had two mill dams.

FLOODS, BOGS AND MOSSES

Two hundred years ago the banks of these tributary burns were recorded as being cloaked with birch, hazel, alder and gean, but despite being small with limited catchments, they, together with the Deskford Burn, caused considerable damage during the Muckle Spate of 1829 which devastated much of the North East. In Deskford it caused significant flooding and erosion of banks, though fortunately few houses lay close enough to the burns to be damaged, except at Berryhillock and Milton Mills.

Within Deskford historically there were a number of wet or boggy places, most of which have been lost due to drainage associated with agricultural improvement. Pum's Pot, on the parish boundary just south of Tochieneal Brick and Tile Works, and halfway between the turnpike road and Deskford Burn, had been filled in by the 1860s. It had been thought to be a bottomless water-filled pit but was probably a sinkhole associated with an old course of the burn.

Coyll Moss, a dangerous swamp near the top of the Green Hill.

In 1771, just as the Green Hill improvements, which encompassed the later farms of Greenhill and Kintywaird, were being made, several features were identified on this land. These included the "bogs and myres called Knock Stables", 200m north-east of Greenhill Farm, and the "wet and spouty ground called the Black Banks", 300m north of this. 300m east of Greenhill and 100m south of the road to Bogmuchals School lay "Rottenhillock, a wet place", not to be confused with the farm of Rottenhillock later established on the Aultmore Improvements. Coyll Moss still exists today in the forestry plantation uphill from Greenhill farm. It is a dangerous swamp round the margins, and mostly covered in water. It was named Coal Moss on a C18th plan, by which time it was largely worked out as a moss. Great care should be taken if viewing it, and no attempt should be made to walk on it. On the east side of the valley two small lochans were to be found north of the present Blairock road, but both were drained over 200 years ago.

Deskford was a favourite destination of crofters and cottars displaced by agricultural improvements elsewhere in the late C18th. This was largely because of its ample peat mosses, available to poor new crofting tenants taking into agricultural use what had previously been moor, moss and myre on Aultmore. Some of the peat mosses on Aultmore were not named, but many were, the largest of them being Milkwell Moss and Cranloch Moss, both above Langlanburn and to which some old peat roads can still be traced. Other peat mosses on Aultmore included Sheilmuir Moss, Linny Moss, Bossies Moss, Blackgutter Moss, Greensinks Moss and Chaddo Moss.

The much more limited mosses on the eastern side of the valley included Cottonhill Moss, Moss of Bognagight and Lurghill Moss. By 1770 some of the mosses had already been exhausted and were being taken in and cultivated by new crofters. All mosses were carefully regulated with particular ones being allocated for the exclusive use of tenants in particular parts of Deskford, as well as for Cullen House and for the residents of Cullen whose own mosses were, by the mid C19th, completely exhausted.

VEGETATION AND ANIMALS

After the last Ice Age retreated in about 12000BC-11000BC, tundra would have developed in Deskford, with grasses, sedges, dwarf willow and birch establishing themselves. As the temperature rose, mugwort, sorrel, dock and meadow rue arrived followed by a dense forest of birch, oak, elm, hazel and elder, much of which had been cut down and replaced by moorland by 1000BC. By 1750, just before agricultural improvement, half of Deskford was said to be "a mossy, heathery, benty, treeless, watery, stony expanse".

Certainly until 1000AD in all cases, bears, beavers, wolves and wild boars had existed in Deskford, and at an even earlier time there were possibly aurochs. The only species which seems to have increased substantially in number in the past 200 years is the midge, while wild birds and hares are examples of wildlife which have reduced significantly in number.

WEATHER

Since the last Ice Age Deskford, like the rest of the country, has experienced fluctuations in climate, with much of the Bronze Age being milder and much of the Iron Age cooler. From 1100AD till the mid C14th the climate was mild, but it deteriorated after this. The climate of the C18th was considered cold and wet. However, even in the midst of milder periods there could be short interludes of extremely cold and wet weather, leading to crop failure and many people dying of starvation.

Deskford is cooler than Moray but milder than Buchan, and is wetter than Moray but drier than Buchan, with an average rainfall in the C20th of 32" (800mm). Throughout its history the west-facing slopes of the eastern hills, particularly Cotton Hill, had a notorious reputation for lightning. In addition to this, extreme conditions were not infrequent. The Muckle Spate has already been mentioned. In the early 1880s the Wilson family, who were tenants at Little Knows, dug 100 cartloads of snow out from the farm close on one occasion, which was about half of what lay there. In June 1888 there was 2" of snow and a heavy frost, and at the end of May 1891 there were heavy snowfalls and severe frosts. Snow was also recorded in some years in September.

Even in the first half of the C20th the widely-held folk belief that in those times schools never closed and pupils struggled in to attend in all weathers is clearly contradicted by the Deskford School Log which records frequent closures for the sort of weather which would not have closed a school in the early C21st. On days of poor weather when the school did stay open some very low attendances are recorded.

SIZE AND BOUNDARIES

Deskford parish occupies just over 8,000 acres and is bounded by the parishes of Cullen, Fordyce, Grange and Rathven. It is about five miles north to south by about three miles east to west. Deskford Estate, held by the Earls of Seafield, was larger than the parish, and incorporated the lands of Myreside, Marchbank, Wester Windyhills, Goukstone, Nethertown, Over Windyhills, Lurgbrae and Greens of Lurgbrae, all of which are in Grange parish, as are the two largest of Deskford's peat mosses, the Milkwell and Cranloch mosses.

On the west side, many farms which are part of Deskford Estate and which have always considered themselves part of Deskford, are in fact in Rathven parish. These include Braidbog, Easter and Wester Darbreich, Briggs of Darbreich, Rashiehill, Greens of Blairock, Whiteknowes and everything to the west of them. In this area the Blairock burn is the boundary between the two parishes.

In the C19th the Earl of Seafield's Deskford Estate marched with the lands of Strathisla and the Moor of Balnamoon (both Lord Fife) in the south, Burnside and Myretown (Lord Fife), Hills of Edingeith (Innes) and Bogmuchals (Abercrombie) in the east, Towie and Birkenbog (both Abercrombie) in the north east and Letterfourie, Darbreich, Rannas and Corrydown (all the Duke of Gordon) in the west.

It was not uncommon to straighten marches, both between different farms on the same estate and between different estates, the latter usually by excambion. For example, in 1841/42, marches between the farms of Knappycausey, Squaredoch, Mosside, Faichyhill, Upper Blairock, Ardoch, Nether Blairock, Mousehillock (now Burnsford), Corbiecraig and Clunehill, all within Deskford Estate, were straightened. In 1829 the march between the

Seafield and Abercrombie Estates on the east side of Deskford, which had been very crooked, was straightened by means of exchanging small areas of land totalling two acres in a line going north from the Ardicow road. In 1860 Seafield and Abercrombie lands totalling about four and a half acres on either side of the Deskford Burn between Leitchestown and Towie were exchanged, making the course of the burn the new boundary.

There were five standing stones in the Slack of Standingman, south of the road beyond Ardicow, of which the westernmost one was in Deskford as was the single one to the north of the road, on the Birkenhill track. The Black Cairn and the Cat Cairn are small piles of stones marking the boundary between Deskford and Fordyce, the latter on the Hill of Summertown. The Tomb of the Lying Horse, south-south-west of the Hill of Inverkindling, was a large stone forming the boundary between Deskford, Fordyce and Grange. There were three cairns and one large stone on its end on the boundary between Deskford and Grange east of the farm of Lurgbrae and near Greens of Lurgbrae. In the second half of the C19th the boundaries between different farms were marked by dry stane dykes and hawthorn hedges. Bands of travelling dry stane dykers worked on some Deskford farms.

THE MISTS OF TIME

The further back one looks the less definite one can be about the history of any particular place. However it is possible to make deductions about Deskford and its people based on evidence found both within the parish and in the wider North East. Some of the oldest references in Scottish history are in the form of legend. For example the very name Scotland is reputedly derived from Scota, an Egyptian Pharaoh's daughter, who is supposed to have sailed here with her husband Geytholos, both having been exiled. She was contemporary with Moses, is credited with having brought the Stone of Destiny here, and founded the tribe called the Scots.

THE MESOLITHC

Though there is evidence of human existence in Happisburgh, Norfolk 800,000 years ago and in Cheddar Gorge 400,000 years ago, evidence in Scotland occurs only after the country's emergence from the last ice age, within the last 12,000 years. The first people to live in the North East were small groups of hunter-gatherers who moved around the area in bands of four or five families. At this time the total population of Scotland may have been as little as several thousand but they were evenly spread and it is likely that some of them passed through Deskford or even had one of their temporary animal-skin tented settlements here. There would certainly have been nuts, berries, game and even fish, including both brown trout and sea trout from the Deskford Burn, for them.

If any of them were in Deskford around 6100 BC it is possible that they would have been wiped out by the enormous tsunami which struck the east coast of Scotland and was caused by a two hundred mile long undersea landslip off the coast of Norway. It penetrated fifty miles inland along the River Forth and would have also penetrated up the course of the Deskford Burn, scouring lower-lying areas near the burn where any encampments might have been. Anyone camped at Cullen at that time would certainly have had no chance. Unfortunately this event helped to eradicate much of whatever faint evidence of these people's presence may have existed.

After this catastrophic flood the area, which was heavily afforested, recovered and would have been repopulated by hunter-gatherers, still living in hide tents, wearing fur and skins, using simple tools and taking advantage of the easily available wood for fires both for cooking and for personal comfort.

THE NEOLITHC

The above is assumption based on what is known and postulated about the wider North East, but from now on we start to be able to add vestigial and fragmentary local evidence to enhance the picture. Between 6000BC and 4000BC there was a gradual change from Mesolithc hunter-gatherer to Neolithc farmer. These latter people would have grown wheat and barley in very small enclosed fields with stone or turf walls, and kept cattle and sheep. They were either immigrants from north-west Europe or, more likely, were locals who adopted the lifestyle which spread north. It is from this period that we have the first evidence of human activity in Deskford with the find of a flint scraper in Dr Fraser Hunter's dig at the site of the carnyx (NJ522637), near Leitchestown, in 1994.

By just after 4000BC the Neolithc farmers had completely supplanted the Mesolithc hunter-gatherers in this area, however they still moved about within the locality between one area of small fields and another when the soil became impoverished. Gradually, as the population increased, permitted by surpluses in food production, in turn made possible because of improving climate, permanent settlements were established. The people in these are likely to have been the first permanent inhabitants of Deskford. They continued deforestation both for fuel and to provide more land for farming.

BRONZE AGE

In this early Bronze Age period, swords, knives and axes were produced, and as recently as 2013 a metal detectorist, Gordon Hay, who had been born and brought up in Deskford, uncovered a Bronze Age bronze axe head between Inaltrie and Careston (NJ515626). By the later Bronze Age, buckets, horse harnesses and sickles were also being made.

Bronze Age bronze axe head found by Gordon Hay near Careston in 2013.

It was during this period that, for the first time, conflict between different tribes took place and the concept of a tribe owning land emerged. By 3000BC a society existed which developed its own rules and customs and which had both tribal chiefs and priests. For the first time they produced pottery. By 2500BC the total population of Scotland may have risen to as much as 50,000 or more. Life expectancy was less than thirty and the average person was not as tall as today. By 1000BC there had developed a military aristocracy.

IRON AGE

In the Bronze Age the climate had been very good, but as the Bronze Age turned into the Iron Age between 800BC and 600BC the weather deteriorated, which caused cultivation on the higher land to be abandoned and which in less exposed places such as Deskford led to competition for land. After 600BC the climate again improved. An iron industry focussed on the production of everyday tools and other items developed, different from the often ceremonial metalwork of the Bronze Age.

It was at this time that hillforts were built. This happened because there was increasing competition between tribes which often spilled over into armed conflict. Some of these hillforts were used through to Pictish times. Local examples include Green Castle at Portknockie, Durn Hill behind Portsoy, Castle Hill in Cullen and Davie's Castle between Deskford and Cullen.

Following a deterioriation, the climate again improved from about 400BC, which led to increased crop yields which in turn led to a greater intensity of conflict. This was more deadly than previously because of improvements in the technology of war. In addition tribal leaders were now primarily war leaders and this increased the status of warriors. Life expectancy was still less than 40. However progress was also being made in other aspects of life. Rotary querns replaced saddle querns for grinding cereals. This was also a period in which Celtic art and culture flourished, probably not as has previously been believed by immigration, but more likely by the adoption of these by the indigenous population.

Celtic tribes, led by warrior chieftains, were ubiquitous by 200BC, and by 300AD had evolved into the Picts. For these Celtic tribes kinship was vital, status was important and war the way in which both were demonstrated. Much of the warfare was directed towards taking slaves, many of whom were traded to Europe.

In the Iron Age, from about 700BC onwards, inhabitants of Deskford would have lived in wooden round houses with thatched roofs. Their lives were prosperous and well ordered. Celtic languages replaced older ones, though a few echoes of these older languages can still be heard in placenames, for example those of rivers such as the Deveron and the Findhorn.

By 150AD the Romans identified two Celtic tribes occupying the North East, the Vicomagi in what is now Moray and the Taexali in what is now Buchan. Not for the last time Deskford lay in the debateable lands between powerful tribal strongholds. The Deskford Carnyx, a Celtic war trumpet, discovered in 1816, dates from this period. The millennia up to the emergence of the Picts about 300AD left evidence of human existence in lower Banffshire, including Deskford and surrounding areas, but much of this is now deduced only from cropmarks or from the records of visitors or keen antiquarians of between 100 and 250 years ago. Much has now disappeared entirely.

ARCHAEOLOGY

Within Deskford, excavations by Dr Fraser Hunter at Leitchestown in the mid 1990s uncovered evidence of a ceremonial site which had existed for several thousand years and from which were retrieved a Mesolithc flint scraper, a Neolithc or Bronze Age scraper, a Middle Bronze Age bone toggle, an Iron Age stone palette, a C1stAD shard of high quality samian ware pottery and a cremated adult woman from 1600-1100BC. The Carnyx itself was a C1stAD war trumpet, possibly left as a votive offering. It was five feet long from mouthpiece to swine's head, was played vertically giving it a total height of around ten feet, and could be heard four miles away. It was constructed from beaten bronze with brass fittings perhaps made from reworked Roman metal, and had enamel eyes and a wooden clapper for a tongue.

Other scattered archaeological finds have been made in Deskford. Industrial slag has been found by Pam and John Robertson near the Flake Burn and by Stuart Black near a burnt mound at Cultain, where he also discovered an Iron Age round house. A food vessel dated 3000BC was found at Carestown and is held in Banff Museum, to which it was presented by the Earl of Seafield in 1858. Also at Carestown a Bronze Age beaker was found in 1888. These are both near the site where a Bronze Age bronze axe head was found in 2013. In

1908 a carved stone ball, just over two and a half inches in diameter, and with four projecting discs, was found on the Hill of Aultmore. In 1874 a barbed and

Re-enactment of the playing of the carnyx using replicas.

tanged arrowhead of buff coloured flint, with one barb broken, and measuring almost two inches by just over one inch, was found on the moor. Dr Gordon Noble found much Pictish hack silver at Gaulcross in 2013.

ROMANS

In the neighbourhood of Deskford many urns and flint arrowheads have been found at the Bauds and in the grounds of Cullen House, and a Roman coin of Emperor Claudius Gothicus of the C2nd AD was found buried at Lintmill. Within Deskford, in 1726, a hoard of Roman coins equated in importance by Dr Fraser Hunter to the recent finds at Birnie and Clarkly Hill was found "near the old bridge a little below the Tower of Deskford". These were preserved by the Earl of Findlater and are thought to represent, similarly to the Birnie and Clarkly Hill hoards, bribes paid by the Romans to keep good relations with local Celtic chieftains. The coins were of Emperor Antoninus Pius, his wife Faustina, and Otho and others. This bribery would have been to contain any conflict with the warrior chieftains in the North East, who were becoming more powerful and more prosperous and who focussed much of their efforts on aggressive warfare and personal and tribal prestige.

Possibly the most eagerly wished-for connections with the distant past are with the Romans. From the C18th to the present day various individuals with a Deskford connection have proposed a variety of these. Unfortunately most are a triumph of hope over reality.

With the existence of Roman Camps at Auchenhove and at Bellie, and a possible Roman fort at Boyndie, it is likely that, either in the late C1st AD or during Lollius Urbicus' military expedition to the Moray Firth in 140AD, Roman soldiers did pass through Deskford, using an older north south route which legend claims passed from Grange through Deskford to Rannas.

Of the remaining speculation, much is fanciful, and perhaps the most fanciful was by Rev Lawtie, Minister in Fordyce in the late C18th. He was an enthusiast for finding Roman evidence. He suggested that the name Deskford was derived from "Decius' Fort", named after the victor of the Battle of Mons Graupius. This is extremely unlikely as there is no evidence whatsoever of a Roman fort in Deskford, and the name Deskford pre-dates the arrival of the English language in the area. It is probably of Gaelic or earlier Celtic derivation.

Rev Lawtie proposed a Roman station incorporating Kirktown, but the Deskford Minister, Rev Morison, stated that he remembered the banks and ditches being built. Rev Lawtie then proposed as Roman, a paved road extending half a mile from Kirktown, but Rev Morison stated that he remembered it being improved and paved as it had been in such a poor and boggy condition that it could not be used for half the year.

Some early C19th maps show the road from Bellie to Rannas, then over the hill to Deskford and on to Grange Kirk, Nethermills, Aberchirder and central

Aberdeenshire as a Roman road. This attribution again seems fanciful; there is no evidence of it and the route bears no resemblance to known Roman roads elsewhere in Britain, though the route named may be that of an earlier Iron Age trackway.

TRIBAL BOUNDARIES

A tribal structure was well established in the North East by the early Bronze Age and continued through the Iron Age, Celtic and Pictish times, only disappearing with the advent of feudalism in the C12th. Thus for thousands of years Deskford would have existed as a tribal land or part of one, though unfortunately little is known about the lives of the inhabitants. In 100AD Deskford lay in the border lands between the Vacomagi and Taexali tribes. In Pictish times, recent research suggests that it lay in the border lands between the Fortriu Pictish kingdom in Moray and the Cé Pictish kingdom in Buchan. Even in mediaeval times Deskford was positioned near the border between the earldoms of Moray and Buchan and the thanages of Boyne and Enzie.

THE PICTS

From the time that the Picts became established, around 300AD, the entire country was split into large tribal groups, one of whose main purposes was conducting warfare against other tribes. Each tribe comprised several smaller local groups and there were also semi-autonomous small local groups which, while not part of a tribe, were affiliated to one. Deskford may have been within the lands of the Cé or occupied by one of these semi-autonomous groups. It is a clearly defined area, the Howe O' Deskart, surrounded as it is on all sides by hills. The earliest identifiable placename in the area is Pattenbringan. The first part of the name is the Pictish "pett" word meaning a piece of land, and the second part is a Gaelic personal name, perhaps Brendan. The name probably dates from the C10th when the newly introduced Gaelic elite retained the land boundaries and systems of tenure of the Picts whom they replaced.

Caledonian is a term which predates Pict and is probably indigenous while Pict is thought to be Roman slang for "painted people". A Roman dice tower found in Germany is inscribed "The Picts are beaten, the enemy annihilated, let us play without care", although this may well just be propaganda. The Picts remained pagan after most of northern Britain had become Christian, and even when they were converted to Christianity by St Ninian, St. Columba and others, their Christianity was not secure.

The Pictish inhabitants of Deskford shared the common system of land ownership known in later Gaelic speaking times as duthaich which meant homeland with hereditary rights. By early Christian times the tuath meant both the tribe and its territory. The head of kin was the kinkynie and beneath him were the mormaer or governor and the toisech or war leader, from which the surname McIntosh is derived. Each tribe had three free dignitaries, the eclais (church), the flaith (lord) and the file (poet). The words toath fold, in use until agricultural improvement in the C18th, for the great fold for all the beasts of a fermtoun or wider area comes from the word tuath.

Throughout their existence Picts were involved in wars, and individuals would come to fight for the tribe or the kingdom from across its lands. Men from Deskford possibly fought against Aedan mac Gabrain of Dal Riata when he brought his armies into the North East in the late C6th to fight the local Picts. They may also have been represented in the Pictish army which defeated Ecgfrith the Northumbrian king at Nechtansmere in 685. The great tribal leaders ensured that all their small local groups and affiliated groups contributed men and supplies for their armies. Some Deskford Picts may have been present in 729 at Burghead when the Pictish navy was attacked and 150 of their ships wrecked. The Iron Age fort at Green Castle, Portknockie, which was reused by the Picts, would have been well known to them as a stronghold. Even after the Picts had been subsumed into the Scottish kingdom it is almost certain that Deskford men were part of the Scottish army of King Indulf which defeated the Norsemen at the Battle of the Bauds near Cullen in 962, if this event is indeed fact and not myth.

The Picts were at their most powerful between the mid C8th and early C9th but rapidly thereafter fell under the control of a Scots elite, though retaining a largely Pictish social and legal system. This would have happened in Deskford as in the rest of the Pictish territories and led over time to the Pictish p-Celtic language being replaced by the Gaelic q-Celtic one. By and large pre-existing tenure and land division systems were retained as has been mentioned in relation to Pattenbringan.

The new Scots elite adopted many aspects of the tribal and leadership customs of the Picts and in the C12th, with the introduction of feudalism in Scotland, many of these tribal leaders became feudal superiors. As the tribal chiefs were given feudal titles they often found these preferable to their old tribal titles, since the feudal system gave them power and wealth as individuals rather than as an integral part of the tribe. Though this was a major change from the social system which had existed for several thousand years, the change was made much easier with the old leaders under the old system becoming the new leaders under the new system.

THE LAW

We do not know a great deal about tribal laws during Pictish and earlier times though they certainly existed, interwoven with tribal customs. In 697, Adomnan, Abbot of Iona, wrote the Law of the Innocents which was accepted by the King of Picts, the King of Scots and over fifty Irish Kings. Under this law penalties were prescribed for attacks on non-combatant women, children and priests. Even into the C12th and C13th, under feudalism, we only have fragmentary evidence of a legal framework, largely because of the theft of many official Scottish documents by King Edward 1st in 1296 when he attempted to eradicate any evidence of Scotland operating as an independent country.

Some elements of tribal law were preserved in Deskford as across the country by Birlay Courts which persisted into the C17th. These decided on disputes over matters such as farm boundaries, dates on which all tenants within a multiple tenancy would begin ploughing and other common tasks which required cooperation. Almost no evidence of their processes or outcomes survives anywhere as these were purely oral. Nevertheless Birlay Courts were very important and powerful in reguLating many aspects of rural life.

The first laws introduced under the feudal system were the "Leges inter Brettos et Scottos", (Laws of the Brits and the Scots) which were put in place by King David 1st in the C12th, and which incorporated much tribal tradition. Fines were fixed for two types of slaughter, cro and kelchyn, and also for "blude drawn". These varied according to the status of the victim. Cro for the killing of the king was 1000 ky (cattle) or 3000 ore (ounces of gold), and his kelchyn was 100 ky. The amounts specified fell through various levels of society from the king's son (equal to an earl), an earl's son (equal to a thane), a thane's son, a thane's nephew or grandson (equal to an ochethern or free tenant), down to a carl (slave or serf), the cro for whom was 16 ky and the blude drawn 1 cow. If the wife of a free man was killed, her husband received the kelchyn but her family from before her marriage received the cro and the blude drawn. If the wife of a carl was killed, the lord of the land in which she lived received the kelchyn and her family the cro and the blude drawn.

Merchet was the maiden fee paid to the feudal superior on the marriage of the daughter of any dependent. If the daughter of a serf, the merchet was a calf or 3/- (shillings), if the daughter of a free man it was a cow or 6/-, if the daughter of the son of a thane or of an ochethern it was two cows or 12/- and if the daughter of an earl it was twelve cows.

Anyone attempting but failing to strike another person in the King's Court as it moved round the country had to pay four cows to the King and one to the victim. If contact was made but no blood drawn it was six cows to the King, and two to the victim. If blood was drawn it was nine cows to the King and three to the victim. Anyone drawing a knife in the King's Court would have it stuck through his hand, and if he had drawn blood his hand would be cut off.

A thief should not escape punishment either by paying for what was stolen or because of friendship with the lord. The cost of injuring anyone was, on the foot 1 merk, an eye ½ merk, a hand 1 merk, an ear ½ merk and a tooth 12d (old pennies). Each inch of the length of a wound cost 12d as did each inch of its breadth. A stroke under the ear cost 16d and a stroke with a staff cost 8d, but if the victim fell to the ground the fine was 16d. A wound on the face cost a gold coin. These are only a few examples from the fragments of these laws which survive, but they are enough to show that the legal system which applied to the people of Deskford in the 1100s was very detailed.

Under King Alexander 2nd in 1220 anyone who held land from the King but failed to respond to a summons to join up with the army, had to pay a fine according to status. A thane had to pay six cows and a gillot, an ochethern fifteen sheep or 6/-, half each to the King and the thane, and a carl one cow and one sheep, but if he had absented himself with the permission of his thane the whole fine went to the King,

Under the Regiam Majestatum of 1200 to 1230, if a lord had carnal intercourse with the betrothed of a servus or slave then the latter was freed. There were also defined punishments for the theft of a calf or ram or any beast which could be carried off on the back, for rape and for trampling to death with a horse.

Tribal tradition was often absorbed into the feudal system of laws, for example with the different degrees of bondage or serfdom. However King Edward 1st when he had proclaimed himself overlord of Scotland, passed a law forbidding wergild as contained in the Law of the Brits and the Scots, though he was not immediately successful in ensuring this change was applied. As the feudal system developed, responsibly for applying and interpreting the law was devolved to local lords, in Deskford firstly by means of the Barony Court and then the Regality Court.

PHYSICAL STRUCTURES

Deskford contains a number of ancient structures which either still exist or which have been demolished but which are recorded as having existed at one time. At the site of the find of the Deskford Carnyx there has also been uncovered evidence of continuous occupation since about 5000BC. Dr Fraser Hunter considers it likely to have been a ceremonial site of some significance, used for meetings and ceremonies and also used as a central location for storing grain. An aerial photographic survey showed evidence of crop marks including a ring ditch at Milton (NJ517632) and crop marks and evidence of Bronze Age activity near the site of Law Hillock. All of these sites lie very close to one another towards the north end of Deskford. They also lie very close to the sites of the Roman silver coin hoard and the Pictish silver hoards found at Gaulcross on Ley farm in the early C19th and in 2013 by Dr Gordon Noble.

Law Hillock itself, (NJ517630) was a moot hill, a site at which justice was handed out. These were common in the North East, but many shared the same fate as Deskford's Law Hillock which was ploughed in by the tenant farmer in the 1840s. It had been conical, of a fair height and comprised mostly stone, which was used by the farmer to help with the construction of a steading. By 1866 there remained a small circular eminence of a different colour from the surrounding ground. By 1961 there was a slight swelling of the ground, marked by darker coloured grass. By 2013, the farmer, Jimmy Stewart, observed that there was a patch of very sandy soil there.

Deskford contained many standing stones and cairns, often marking boundaries, but many of these have been removed and a few may be lost in forestry plantations. Grey Cairn (NJ486575) lay on the boundary between Deskford and Grange parishes, on the tiny burn of Quean's Strype, about 100m north of Myreside farm. It was carted away for building and no sign of its existence remains, though its site was shown on the 1867 1st edition 25" OS map. It was used as a boundary marker between Deskford (originally Fordyce) parish and Grange parish but may well have been much earlier and only reused for this purpose. On the other side of the public road, on Clochmacreich land, there were two unnamed cairns which were swept away by agricultural improvements, probably towards the end of the C18th. On the boundary between Deskford and Grange parishes, on the flank of Lurg Hill, there was another large marker stone, this time lying on its side.

On the long eastern boundary of Deskford, where it marches with Fordyce parish, there were several cairns and also individual stones, some of which may have been only one or two hundred years' old estate boundary markers, but some of which may have been older. From the north the named ones are Standingmanhill Stones (NJ535608), Black Cairn, Cat Cairn (NJ528596) and the

Cairn of the Lying Horse (NJ517581). On the west side of Deskford, on Aultmore, were a series of boundary stones between Deskford and Rathven parishes. In recent research and field investigation Peter Mason and Steve Liley have discovered many other boundary stones in the locality.

On the estate plan of 1771 the Stone of Marliter is shown about 200m north-east of Greenhill farm. There are also two large horneblende blocks amongst the remains of Pattenbringan (NJ515645), which was demolished in the early C19th. These remains lie about 200m north of the Deskford parish boundary with Rathven and a similar distance from the route of the pre-turnpike main road from Cullen to Keith. Pattenbringan is one of the oldest domestic sites in

Cat Cairn on the parish and estate boundaries above Greenhill farm.

the area, though it has been disputed whether the two stones are ceremonial or geological.

Immediately south of Pattenbringan and just within the parish of Deskford lie the Gallows Knowe and Gallows Well (NJ513639), rediscovered in 2012 by Pam and John Robertson. They lie in a forestry plantation quite near the summit of Clune Hill and adjacent to the clearly identifiable old Cullen to Keith road. The gallows were erected in 1698 to serve the newly created Regality of Ogilvie of which Deskford was the burgh. The knowe, which is barely recognisable, has two probable graves on it, while the well, about 50m to the north of it, has a revetted wall, is about 1 metre in diameter and 1 metre deep with shallow stone steps leading down the open side. It is in excellent condition.

On the top of Cotton Hill (NJ530625) there were many stone cairns as commented on by Pennant in his *Tour of Scotland in 1769*. These were

One of the disputed stone blocks at Pattenbringan.

removed around 1870 when the hill was planted with trees. It is most likely that they were ancient field clearance piles but a persistent legend claims that they commemorated the dead from the Battle of the Bauds.

About half a mile north east of Cotton Hill, and just into the parish of Fordyce, two stone circles were recorded, and a hoard of silver jewellery was found in the early C19th at Gaulcross near Ley farm. Silver chains, buckles, pins and brooches were found in a ring cairn there, but only three of the fifty or so items discovered are now known to exist, in Banff Museum. The stone circles were demolished using gunpowder. The Gaulcross site was revisited in 2013 by a team led by Dr Gordon Noble of Aberdeen University and around one hundred further, mainly small, silver items were discovered. They were widely spread and were probably part of the C19th hoard, scattered by ploughing. Many of them were hack silver probably kept as a form of wealth or for reuse as Pictish jewellery. It is likely that there is some significance in the proximity of the Gaulcross hoard to the sites of the Deskford carnyx and the C18th Deskford hoard of silver Roman coins.

A mile further north cairns and coffins were found at Kilnhillock and Brankanentham, but these were destroyed in the C18th. Within half a mile to the north of the parish boundary and close to the Deskford Burn, three tumuli were found on a field just north of Smithstown farm, which later became the site of Tochieneil Brick and Tile Works, and a stone circle was found on Towie farm, just over the burn. Davie's Castle (NJ497643) lies beside the track from

Ha' Hillock.

Shirralds to Braidbog, which was once the main road between Old Cullen and Aultmore. It is an Iron Age fort which was probably reused in Pictish times. The name was often attributed to Bishop Davie Stewart who built Davie's Tower at Spynie Palace, but he was active in the mid C15th which seems too late a date. It has a commanding defensive position and a prominent ditch and earthwork.

Immediately west of the main road, just opposite where the minor road to Kirktown branches off, can be seen Ha' Hillock (NJ509628), a small C12th motte in a crook of the Ha' Burn, a tributary of the Deskford Burn. There were many such small mottes throughout the North East, for example Gallowhill in Grange, Ha' Hillock in Alvah and the Ha' Hill of Minonie, some of which were built on previous defensive sites. They tended to be built by smaller local lords under feudal obligation to Norman magnates who either had been planted by the King, or were tribal leaders who had adopted feudal titles. In 1865 Deskford's Ha' Hillock was measured as an ellipse of 18 feet by 30 feet, and in 1961 it was identified as having originally been 28m in diameter. On top would have been a wooden hall surrounded by a wooden defensive stockade. It gave the name to the nearby Ha' Burn.

Stone castles were being built by the C13th, but the Ha' Hillock site is too constricted and insubstantial for this purpose. The remains of the C13th stone Castle of Inaltrie (NJ518631) lie about half a mile away immediately adjacent to the site of the Law Hillock. It is conceivable that the local lord moved from Ha' Hillock to Inaltrie at this time. The Castle of Inaltrie was built around the same time as the substantial castles of Elgin and Forres, so it may well have been of some importance. However it did not survive for a great time, already being referred to in the early 1500s as "the auld Castle of Inaltry". A legend developed that it may have been a religious establishment because of an iron cross found there in the late C18th, but this is almost certainly inaccurate, and reflective of the enthusiasms and lack of evidence required by a few local antiquarians of that period when stating their beliefs. The name Inaltrie is of Gaelic derivation and this mitigates against another suggested reason for it having been a religious establishment, that the name incorporates the English word "altar" within it.

This was the first of three castles to be built in Deskford, Its ruins being filled up with rubbish to form a kailyard by the then tenant in the early C19th. The two other castles in Deskford were the Tower of Deskford at Kirktown

(NJ509617), which was possessed by the Sinclairs and then the Ogilvies, and the Castle of Skeith (NJ504604), further south and adjacent to the present farm of Mains of Skeith, which was possessed for much of its existence by the Abercrombies. There is also mention made in historical documents of there

Existing fragment of the Castle of Inaltrie

having been a manor house at Ardoch (NJ508625), which was certainly one of the oldest land holdings in Deskford. No evidence exists as to the precise site the manor house occupied, though the last built farmhouse of the name does contain some unusually thick walls.

INFRASTRUCTURE AND SERVICES

PLACENAMES

Most of the placenames of farms in Deskford are very old, being of Gaelic or old Scots derivation. In itself this is not the full picture as some of the Gaelic or Scots names may be translations of earlier Pictish or Celtic names which described the physical location of the farm. A number of unfortunate fallacies have been perpetuated, including one about the likely meaning of the name Deskford itself. Another is the assertion in the First Statistical Account that Clochmacreich is the only placename of Gaelic derivation in the parish and the claim by Rev Lawtie of Fordyce that Inaltry means "place of the altar".

The most likely meaning of Deskford is from the Gaelic "deas gart" meaning south field or garden. This explanation is given strong support by the persistent local pronunciation, "Deskart". Earlier writers proposed a variety of other possibilities, some of which, such as "the ford on the dark stream" and "Decius' Fort" are extremely unlikely or impossible. The proposed meaning which gained most popularity was "Chess fure" meaning cold place to the south. Its popularity was however more due to uncritical repetition than the credibility of the claim, originally made by Rev Walter Chalmers around 1790. The same meaning is also claimed for Fordyce, with the syllables reversed, though this is also likely to be false.

Many of the oldest names in the parish have a Gaelic derivation, but one local name, Pattenbringan, has a clearly Pictish first element, though almost certainly adopted by the Gaelic speaking settlers who came after the Picts. It lies just outside the parish to the north and for many centuries comprised the Constabulary Lands of Cullen. Its "pett" first element relates to the Pictish land tenure system which was continued by the Gaelic-speaking elite who formed the next hierarchy. It means "piece of land" and its presence was usually followed by a Gaelic personal name, in this case possibly a corruption of

"Brendan", giving a meaning of "Brendan's estate". Skeith is a prominent local placename whose meaning is unclear. It might be from the Pictish or Brettonic for "woodland", but might equally be from the Gaelic for "windy place" or the old Scots for "shadow".

Gaelic names became attached to prominent natural features such as Aultmore (big burn), Milkwell (rounded hill from maol) and Cranloch (tree place). Adjacent settlements also have names derived from Gaelic, such as Findlater (white slope), Cullen (place of the holly bush) and Fordyce (portion of tribal land allocated to a tribal sub-chief).

Gaelic farm names within Deskford include Blairock (field), Clune (meadow), Ardoch (the field on the height), Darbreich (upper part of the wood), Inaltrie (hill pasture, supported by the persistent local pronunciation "Nyattery"), Ardicow (wooded height), Clochmacreich (settlement at the boundary stone) and Bognageith (windy bog).

Tillybreedless is probably a composite Gaelic/Scots name. Tilly (tulach) is Gaelic for a small hill of assembly and is also found in Tullywhull, the older name for Ordiquhill. Breedless is old Scots for narrow (breadthless). A few of the Scots placenames which began to be introduced in the late C12th or early C13th refer to early tenants, for example Craibstone (Craib's Toun, possibly referring to a Flemish immigrant), Careston (Kerr's Toun) and Leitchestown, but others refer to features. Wairdleys means the pasture beside the calves' enclosure, Faichyhill means fallow hill, Knappycausey means the road through the knapperts (heath pea), Backies, originally Backies of Over Skeith, means peat bank, Hoggie means the place where the hogs (sheep) are penned and Hollanbush means holly bush. Swailend means end of the bog or seasonal loch and Coyll Moss, above Greenhill, and pronounced "quile", refers to the bog coal which was found there.

Many of the placenames of this period have obvious meanings, Knows, Broomhaugh and Bogrotten among them. Ha' (hall) Hillock refers to the C12th motte there and Law Hillock to an ancient tribal moot hill location where judgments were handed down. Broxy Burn refers to the badger. Langlanburn, though no earlier than the C17th, is probably named from the adjacent burn, which seems to have lost the name when this transferred to the farm.

Though pronunciation in the local dialect gives strong supporting evidence for the meanings of certain placenames such as Deskford and Inaltrie, it can also cause confusion. Clunehill in Deskford is the same name as Cleanhill in Drybridge, the confusion being caused by the local pronunciation of "u" as "ee". Indeed Over Clune (Clunehill) is referred to as Over Clean in the Deskford Kirk Session minutes of 1743. Some of the earlier agricultural improvements attracted names which described their location, Braidbog, Rashiehill and Tod (fox) holes being some of these.

Amongst the last of Deskford's farms to be given individual names were those which were in the final phase of new croft establishment on Aultmore. These came into existence from moor and moss in the first half of the C19th. Until the 1861 census they were known collectively as Aultmore Crofts, but by 1871 all had gained individual names. Many, such as Stripeside, Braehead, Poolside, Cottar Clump, Rottenhillock and Gateside described their precise location. Others either took the tenant's name, such as Duffushillock and Bellcroft, or were fanciful inventions such as Bloomfield. These individual names were probably required by the surveyors of the 1st edition 25" OS map, surveyed in 1867.

Most placenames in Deskford have been established for hundreds of years, but some changes continue to be made. In the mid C19th, for reasons of aspiration to gentility, Upper Bogrotten was renamed Whiteknows. In the early C20th Hoggie Croft was renamed Hollanbush in place of the original farm of that name, which had lain 200m further downhill and which was demolished. In the late C20th Upper Squaredoch was renamed Hillview in order to avoid confusion, and in 2012 a redevelopment of the Poors House site re-adopted the older name, Muir of Squaredoch.

VILLAGES

In the mid C18th five identifiable villages existed in Deskford, of which only two remain as villages today, Kirktown and Berryhillock. The other three were at Cottartown of Inaltry, Cottartown of Ardoch and Milton. Cottartown of Inaltry lay high up the hill above Inaltrie farm and began as the cottartown for Inaltry Castle, but had ceased to exist by the end of the C18th. Cottartown of Ardoch, where the tearoom is now, was still an identifiable cottartown in the late C19th, but by 1900 had been remodelled into a single farm. Milton ceased to be a village as cottages were gradually abandoned in the mid C20th. Most of these lay just to the north of Duncan McLean's garage.

Milton village, to the north of what is now Duncan McLean's garage

Kirktown developed as a village serving the Tower of Deskford and the Church, and also contained the manse and the school. Berryhillock may have initially developed as the cottartown for the Castle of Skeith, though there was an earlier farm of the name. Certainly, by the mid C19th, together with Aultmore and Cottartown of Ardoch, Berryhillock was where the poorest people in Deskford tended to live. In 1771 Kirktown was the largest of the villages, closely followed by both Milton and Berryhillock. By 1881 there were twenty-three houses in Berryhillock, fourteen in Kirktown and ten in Milton. Cottartown of Ardoch had eight houses in 1841, five in 1871 but only three by 1891. In the 1950s, Berryhillock had fifteen houses and Kirktown eleven.

Kirktown from the south, showing Dominie, Old St John's and the Muckle Hoose, all to the right of the road.

Although it had eight houses in the late C19th, Muir of Squaredoch was never considered a village.

Kirktown is almost certainly the older of the two remaining villages, with its links to St John's Church, which predated the Tower. Until the 1880s much of

Cottages in Kirktown around 1900, with Keills in the foreground. The two blocks of semi detached cottages nearest the camera are now individual detached houses, but without front porches.

the village, including the manse, the school and several cottages, lay in what is now the central and western sections of the graveyard. Before about 1750 the present road through the village and the cottages on it did not exist. Kirktown Farm lay on the other side of the road to where it is today. There were several cottages on the site of the present Kirkton farm and there were two cottages in the Orchard. Many of the inhabitants held crofts or smallholdings in the area between the present main road and the Kirktown road, towards the north end of the village. In 1830 Kirktown comprised the Kirk, the manse, the combined school and schoolhouse, a dame school, the ruined Tower, a few slated houses called the nunnery and several thatched cottages. However, as shown in the 1867 OS map and a drawing by James Spence in 1873, part of the northern range of the Tower of Deskford was still occupied at this time.

For most of the last two hundred years Berryhillock was the most populous

Berryhillock today from the West Manse road.

village in Deskford, and housed many of its poorest inhabitants. In addition to the present front row of cottages there were many in the backlands between the front row and the road to the mill. There had previously been two rows of cottages, one behind the other near the foot of the street. The front row of three was sold to Banffshire County Council not long after World War II by Ian McLean's uncle, for £15. The Council built the present council houses on the site. At the start of the C20th almost every house in Berryhillock had been either thatched or had a corrugated iron roof.

Milton was more dispersed though at one time it had been the largest village

Berryhillock around 1900 with several thatched cottages.

in Deskford. When the the Cruden houses at Bleachfield were built in the late 1940s, they were considered part of Milton but this was just about the same time that many of the cottages on the other side of the burn began to be abandoned. In 1871 Cottartown of Ardoch was described as "a number of scattered cottages consisting of dwelling houses, outhouses, gardens and crofts of land attached".

OLD ROADS

For the majority of the period of human occupation of Deskford, local people travelled on foot or with pack animals or farm animals. Paths and tracks evolved along the driest and most convenient routes between sites used for farming or for ceremonial or ritual activities. Some would be paths worn by sheep or other domesticated or wild animals. None except the old main roads from Keith to Cullen and to Portsoy, and possibly from Squaredoch to Rannas via Darbreich, was designed, planned or built.

Almost all tracks were local, with very few long-distance ones. It may be that the earliest long-distance routeway locally was an Iron Age track which it is suggested came from what is now central Aberdeenshire via Aberchirder through Nethermills, Grange Kirk, Goukstone and Deskford then over the Hill of Maud to Rannas and thence on to Bellie. On its route through Deskford it paralleled currently existing roads, most of the way from Goukstone to Squaredoch, but about two to three hundred metres east of the present road and the same over the Hill of Maud. Other early routes in Deskford included those from Kirktown to Cullen via Clune Hill, from Kirktown to Fordyce and from Squaredoch to the Enzie.

Until around 1800 roads throughout the North East were in very poor condition. Before 1700 there were hardly any wheeled vehicles of any type. Acts of Parliament of 1617, 1671 and 1699 gave power to Justices of Peace to mend roads and bridges using tenants, cottars and farm servants for labour. Each of these groups had to give up to six days a year, but instead could pay 20/- Scots. If they had additionally to provide a horse they were required to pay 30/- to be excused. The money could be used to pay other individuals to do the work, but the system was not successful.

1718 was the first year in which the authorities gave serious attention to the public roads and bridges in Banffshire. A meeting of JPs stated that "The highways within the shyre of Banff are generally neglected and in many places in ye winter impassible.....They appoint the JPs of each parioch to survey all the public roads within the hail parioches and when the said roads are not 20' (feet) broad or where the repairing of the calseys and ridges are needful, to report the same and in what condition they are presently and what money will be required for making them sufficient.......(They should) cause the constables oversee and sett about mending such of the said highways as can be repaired by the services due the parishes by law".

John Gordon of Drumwhindle was appointed the Deskford Parish Overseer. In 1725 £40 was voted to the tenant of Ardoch for repairs to the bridge near the Kirk at Deskford, "to be expended at the sight of Drumwhindle, Wm Ord and yr overseir". In 1726 the Commissioners of Supply appointed "John Gordon of Drumwhindle, Walter Ogilvie of Ardoch, Thomas Innes of Muiryfold, John Innes of Edengeith and William Ord in Kirktown of Deskford, or any three of them, to call workmen and make ane estimate of ane bridge to be build at the Three Burns Meeting in the head of Deskford". This would have replaced the ford which still exists on the track between Lower Craibstone and Backies today, however three hundred years later the replacement bridge has still not been built.

At that time two major roads passed through Deskford, the Keith to Cullen road and the Keith to Portsoy road. They left Keith as a single road along what are now Union St. and Drum Rd, before crossing the River Isla by the still extant stone bridge just off the A95, opposite Grange Church, and proceeding from there to Goukstone. At this point it angled up the hillside to Over Windyhills where even today an area of rough ground at the top of the field shows its route. It then paralleled the present road 200m east of it and at the top of the steep wooded slope as it progressed to Nethertown and Clochmacreich before it became the present Backies Farm track. About 100m north of Backies the Cullen and Portsoy roads split at a shop and croft, Backies Croft, which lay between the road and the Deskford Burn.

The ford at Three Burns Meeting on the track to Upper Skeith and Backies.

The road to Cullen continued down the Backies track and crossed from the east side to the west side of the Deskford Burn by means of the ford which still exists at the Three Burns Meeting. It then ran along about 100m of the present public road at Lower Craibstone before crossing what are now fields to join the Berryhillock road where it forms a T junction with the Mains of Skeith track.

41

The public road through Berryhillock is the old main road, but it continued through what is now Caroline Cottage and the fields beyond to emerge into the drive of the manse. From here it continued along the route of the present public road into Kirktown, down the drive of "Dominie", through the central section of the present graveyard and back on to the public road, hard along the western wall of "The Muckle Hoose" and out its entry gate. After about 1750 the main road followed the route of the current public road through Kirktown.

It left Kirktown and followed the public road along to the junction with the present main Keith to Cullen road opposite Ha' Hillock. It followed the course of this road till branching off up the Clune Hill farm track and entering the

The old Cullen to Keith main road near the Gallows Knowe on Clune Hill.

plantation on top of Clune Hill, within which a perfectly preserved section of this pre-1800 main road can be seen close to the Gallows Knowe and the Gallows Well. On leaving the plantation it went through the middle of what is now the Pattenbringan fields along a line that is shown on a 1794 estate plan, annotated "As the road from Keith to Cullen is intended to be shutt up, the breadth thereof is included in the measure of the severall fields lying contiguous to it". It crossed the Cullen Burn near Lintmill Lodge and proceeded into Old Cullen.

The old main road from Keith to Portsoy left the Cullen road at Backies Croft and crossed a ford behind Upper Skeith which can still be seen. It went directly from here to and behind Mid Skeith, then followed the present public road past Lower Broadrashes, Hoggie, Little Knows and Cultain and then on to Portsoy via Fordyce. Both the Keith to Cullen and Keith to Portsoy main roads were replaced by the present routes when these were built as turnpikes around 1826.

Ford immediately behind Upper Skeith on the line of the old Keith to Portsoy road.

Nowadays we tend to think that only public tarred roads should be classified as roads and that everything else is a farm, estate or forestry track. In the C18th and C19th there was no such distinction, and there were many more roads in Deskford than there are now. The road from the Darbreich and Braidbog area to Cullen was the present forest track passing east of Davie's Castle and through Shirralds, the present Braidbog to Nether Blairock road only being built in the early C19th.

There was no road on the line of the present main road between the bottom of the Clunehill track and Clune, until the turnpike was built in the 1820s. A road did run south from either Lintmill or Tochieneal to Clune, and then it followed the line of the present minor road to Milton. The line of the old road can still be seen on the bend at Clune, several feet below the level of the public road. The Crooked Roadie from Milton to Ha' Burn Bridge did not go all the way up but crossed the Ha' Burn approximately where the trees now begin, and went directly up to the old main road which is also the present main road. There was a road from the Kirktown road at Ardoch, following the line of the present green track, crossing the present main road at the pottery and going up the track to the tearoom. It then proceeded uphill to Upper Blairock and beyond.

There was a road from Cottartown of Ardoch, where the tearoom is now, to Muir of Squaredoch by way of Mosside, and well into the middle of the C20th there was a road from Muir of Squaredoch, past Cottar Clump, passing between Bloomfield and Stripeside and on to Duffushillock. This may originally have been a peat road. The old road from Squaredoch to where the West manse is now went from the present B road along a route immediately south of Squaredoch and Hillview before crossing the present road and paralleling it about 5m to the north all the way to the bridge at the West Manse. New roads being built alongside old roads was common practice.

The other roads on the west side of the valley were by and large peat roads to Milkwell Moss, Cranloch Moss, the Old Fir Hill and other mosses. One of these followed the present minor road west from the Mains of Skeith track, over the main road which it predated, past the site of Carrothead and past Swailend and the site of Blackhillock, and followed the existing track south from the 90 degree bend in the present road above the site of Aultmore Lodge. Another was the track which bears south from the site of Duffushillock and which was probably an extension of the Cottar Clump to Stripeside road mentioned above. Yet another was the present track which goes south from the crossroads near Rosebank. A short peat road also ran west from Langlanburn to good peat mosses.

The road pattern on the east side of the valley, serving longer-established farms, and adjacent communities has survived relatively well even though some individual roads have not. There was the Fishwives Road or Fisher Road which went uphill from the Lythe, over Cotton Hill, to cross the present road just south of Little Cultain, before going on to Auchip and Slackdale in Fordyce parish. Another road was an extension of the present Meikle Knows track across to Careston. This was ploughed in by the estate about 1980, not many years after some local residents had unsuccessfully petitioned Banffshire

County Council to adopt the road and tar it. A solid masonry bridge remains to mark the route, halfway between Meikle Knows and Careston.

The road from Oathillock to Kirktown, the old route from Fordyce, used to go round the north side of Kirktown Farm after crossing the bridge and before entering Kirktown. Briefly, in the early C19th, a well-made road linked Mains of Skeith and Croftgloy, and it has left a masonry bridge with a very high arch over the Hoggie Burn near Mains of Skeith. More than 200 years ago there was a direct road from Inaltrie to Leitchestown, passing to the east of Bleachfield and joining the route of the minor public road half way between Bleachfield and Leitchestown. There was also a road directly uphill from Inaltrie to Cottown of Inaltrie. The present three-way junction near Little Knows used to be a five-way junction, with additional roads going from the junction to the top of Cotton Hill and to Cottown of Inaltrie. The road to the top of Cotton Hill may have been a short peat road to the moss there.

Bridge over the Hoggie Burn at Mains of Skeith on the short lived road between Mains of Skeith and Croftgloy.

A road came north from Edingight, round the east of Lurg Hill, past the Lying Horse at the Hill of Inverkindling, then immediately west of Coyll Moss and onward to Deskford and Cullen. Present day forest tracks and forest breaks east of Greenhill Farm may replicate part of its route. At the Lying Horse it formed a crossroads with the limestone road between the quarry at the Elbow Doups in Deskford and Binnuchars (Badenyouchers) in Bogmuchals. Slightly later, in 1771, there was also a road between the Elbow Doups quarry and the main Keith to Portsoy road between Mid Skeith and Little Skeith.

In the second half of the C18th Rev Lawtie, Minister of Fordyce felt that he had identified 450 yards of surfaced Roman road near Kirktown. Amongst others Mr Morison, Minister of Deskford disagreed, as he remembered the road having been surfaced forty years earlier because it had been impassable in winter.

At the start of the C19th, but before the Deskford Turnpike, the present B9018, had been built, the Roads Commissioners were very active in repairing the old main road and in repairing minor roads and building new ones. To this end between 1805 and 1830 they employed a number of contractors including Malcolm McBean, James Lobban, John McHattie, William Smith, William McIntosh, James Ritchie, James Stewart, Alexander Runcie, William Cumming, John Wilson, Walter Allan, Duncan McPherson, George Legg, Peter Gamie, William Riddoch, Alexander Peterkin, James Gordon, R. Gray, Joseph Stevenson, John Taylor, Alexander Geddes and A. Coull.

The main work undertaken included cleaning, making, repairing and gravelling existing roads, making new roads, covering drains, building bridges and cutting ditches. The old Keith to Cullen road was the one on which most effort was expended, but other roads which received attention included the Portsoy road, the Greenhill road, the new Inaltry road, the Milton Mill road, the Backies to Greenhill road, the Old Moss road, the Broxy Burn to Deskford road, the Old More (Aultmore) road, the Mid Skeith road, the Craibstone road and the Carrothead road.

Bridges were built or rebuilt at Milltown and near Kirktown, both of which were washed away during the last fifty years and replaced by new ones. Others were built at Oathillock and at Berryhillock. Most of the contracts were for less than £10, and the Collector of the Assessments from both heritor and tenants was Alexander Stables.

THE DESKFORD TURNPIKE

Between 1750 and 1844, 350 Turnpike Acts were passed in Scotland. The Deskford Turnpike was one of the last of these to be completed, in 1825 or

1826, and established the route of the present B9018. It incorporated only short stretches of the previous Keith to Cullen road. Detailed specifications and regulations governed the building of what was a step change in the quality of roads in the area. The length of the turnpike from Cullen Toll Bar to Auchinhove was 10 miles, 2 furlongs and 207 yards, as can be observed from the milestone which can still be seen at Auchinhove. Though most of the cost was contributed by the Earl of Seafield and the Earl of Fife, all householders in Deskford except parochial clergy, parochial schoolmasters and paupers were assessed and had to contribute to the cost.

The metalled bed was 14' wide and 12" deep. It was dug out then filled with irregular shaped stones of 2" or 3", with blinding laid on top. On either side of the metalled bed 13' was laid with earth, giving a total width of 40', however these specifications were not always adhered to. The cost of making the road was £300 - £500 per mile.

The charges to be levied were laid out in a very detailed and precise way. A coach, berlin, landau, chariot, chaise, calash or other such carriage with four wheels, drawn by six or more horses or beasts of draught, was charged 6/-. If there were four horses the charge was 3/-, if two horses, 1/6d and if one horse 8d. A chaise, gig, curricle or other like carriage with two wheels, drawn by two horses or other beasts of draught was charged 1/- and if drawn by one horse, 6d. A wagon, wain, cart or other like carriage, drawn by six horses, oxen or other beasts of draught was charged 7/-, if five horses 5/-, if four horses 3/-, if three horses 1/6d, if two horses 8d and if one horse 4d. A horse, mare, gelding or mule, with or without rider, laden or unladen, was charged 2d. A drove of oxen, neat cattle, asses, horses or fillies, unshod, was charged 10d per score (20) and a drove of calves, hogs, sheep, lambs or goats was charged 5d per score.

The maximum weight for wide wheeled four wheelers was eight tons in summer and seven tons in winter between November 1st. and April 30th. Medium wheeled vehicles were six tons and five and a half tons respectively and narrow wheeled vehicles were three tons and two and three quarter tons respectively. Tolls could be temporarily reduced by up to 50% for carts drawn by oxen or transporting lime or other manure.

If tolls were not paid the Trustees could seize horses, cattle and carriages and, after six days, sell them. Anyone avoiding toll houses could be fined from 40/- to £5. There was no charge for using the turnpike for less than 200 yards, for going to church or to a funeral, for a Minister visiting the sick or carrying out other duties, for horses or cattle going to pasture or to water, for horses going to blacksmiths, for horses or carts carrying mail, for horses or carts carrying soldiers, their arms or baggage, for sick, wounded or disabled soldiers or for carts carrying vagrants or criminals with legal passes. Any abuse of the above could attract a fine of up to £5.

Trustees were permitted to build fences, to shut up and suppress old and useless roads and even plough them in to become farm fields. This happened at several places within Deskford, for example between Lower Craibstone Cottage and Berryhillock and between Berryhillock and Kirktown. Trustees could take stone or gravel from anywhere they liked, on giving six days' notice, with compensation being paid. They could erect milestones and require landowners to lop existing trees and refrain from planting new ones within six feet of the new road. No new buildings were to be built within thirty feet of the centre of the new road. No one was allowed to leave dead horses, carrion, dung, carts or loads on the road. If fines were not paid, Sheriffs or JPs could send offenders to prison.

Toll houses at Cullen Toll Bar, Goukstone and Auchinhove were let out. It was intended to build another toll house, probably somewhere in Deskford, but if this actually happened, no evidence as to its location exists. In 1848 Robert Scott and William Taylor paid £80 rent for the Cullen Toll Bar and Mr Henderson £26 for Goukstone. They then kept the tolls collected, however the Goukstone toll house may not have been profitable as it was regularly rouped. Toll keepers were banned from selling beer, ale or spirits without special permission, and they could be fined up to £5 for neglect.

The northern end of the turnpike was convenient for the new town of Cullen, and the northern section appears to have been completed before the southern section. Within Deskford there were milestones between Ha' Burn Bridge and Ha' Hillock, at the school, at the foot of the Raemore track and at the foot of the Langlanburn track. Of these, the only one which can be seen in situ is the

Raemore one which was five miles from the Cullen Bar. All the milestones were buried for security reasons at the start of World War II and the Raemore one is the only one which has been subsequently uncovered and replaced.

Stevenson & Co, contractor, was paid £36 for building bridges at Nether Blairock (Ha' Burn), Berryhillock and Wairdleys. George Lobban was paid £47:10/- for building bridges at Craibstone and "over the burn betwixt Craibstone and Langlanburn" and James Rannie and Francis Sellar were paid £15 for building the Tillybreedless Bridge. Various contractors were paid respectively £13, £80, £6, £217, £200, £60 and £100 to build particular sections of road.

The milestone at the foot of the Raemore track.

An arbiter fixed compensation for damage done by construction of the turnpike on the farms it passed through. Most awards of compensation ranged from 3/- to £1:5/-, but Mr Forbes at Raemore got £3:8:10d and Mr Black at Ardoch £6:14:3d. In 1838, Mr John Wilson was paid £1:19:5d for clearing the road of snow, and tenants of toll houses were

Tillybreedless Bridge on the B9018.

not charged rental for one month because the road was blocked with snow. Ongoing expenditure was incurred around this time for repairs to roads and bridges, for administration costs, postage, overseer's salary, snow clearing, audit of accounts, cutting roadside weeds and scouring ditches.

In 1835 William Anderson, Accountant, reported that he had received £400 from the Earl of Seafield, being one third of the money subscribed by him, £200 from the Earl of Fife's Trustees, £200 from Alexander McDonald and smaller amounts from other individuals. Later that year he received the remaining £800 from the Earl of Seafield. In 1836 a total of £735 was borrowed from the Earl of Seafield to allow the road metal to be widened and deepened in sections and some repairs to be carried out. A further £149 was subsequently borrowed from the Earl against the credit of the tolls.

In 1859 the assessment on individuals was between 6d and 8d per £ of valued property. Mr John Thomson, Cullen, was Clerk and Treasurer to the Deskford Turnpike. The revenue from the tolls in 1857/1858 was £121 and the expense of maintenance £202:1:7d. The surveyor's salary was £7:10/- and the Clerk's £5. The debt was £9,719:6:5d, and the only subscribers were Lord Seafield and Lord Fife.

In 1867, C. Michie, a contractor, submitted his invoice for erecting fences along the sides of the turnpike :-

844 larch posts @4d	£14:1:4d
32 larch straining posts @2/-	£3:14/-
72 stayes (braces) @3d	18/-
1723 yds nos 4, 5 and 6 wires and staples	£19:13/-
1723 yds erecting @ 1¼d per yard	£8:19:5¾d
36 bars for barways @6d	18/-
36 ironwork for the above	£3:6/-
Total	£50:19:9¾d.

MODERN ROADS

That same year, 1867, tolls were abolished on the turnpike. During the late C19th money no longer required for the toll road, now a turnpike, was used to improve the minor side roads. In 1879 the Tenant Road Trustees met, including Alexander Hay representing Deskford and John Cowie, Inaltrie, representing Fordyce. In that year a bridge was built over the Hoggie Burn at Lower Broadrashes. In 1887 the Backies Bridge on the Deskford Burn was built, presumably the bridge on the Backies Farm track, south of the farm and just before it joins the main road. Before these bridges were built, roads crossed burns by fords, some of which were very well constructed, of large regular blocks of stone, and which can still be seen, for example at Three Burns Meeting and under the bridge between Upper Blairock and Braidbog.

Despite these improvements, in 1899 it was reported that although the surface of the main road was good from Auchinhove to Grange Crossroads and also near Cullen, the part in the middle, mostly in Deskford, was rather poor. However less than ten years later, Mr McGregor, the Deskford roadman, who lived in Kirktown, was considered excellent, and better than those in adjacent areas. The Grange roads were not in nearly such good condition and it was possible to tell where the Deskford roads stopped and the Grange ones started. When there were snowdrifts, Mr McGregor organised all local farms to send men with spades. They cut a cart's-width passage through what were often very deep drifts. In 1900 there was a sign at the school corner, pointing to Buckie, "Buckie by Hill of Maud, 6 miles, 2 furlongs".

The last of the roads in Deskford were built as recently as the very end of the C19th, for example the road from Lornachburn to Rosebank. Previously there had not even been a track there. During the C20th there was little change to the road system except for a very gradual programme of surfacing with tar and the abandonment of some roads. Decisions on both of these were not always taken on a rational or democratic basis. "Who you know" had a significant influence. The first road in the parish to be tarred was the main Keith to Cullen road, which was done in the late 1920s. The hill road to Buckie was one of the first of the side roads to be tarred, in 1938, but the route which was tarred at that time was from Rosebank via Briggs, Greens of Blairock and the West Manse to Squaredoch. This was not the shortest route but Willie Fordyce remembers using it to cycle from Rosebank to Deskford school because the surface was smoother than the untarred but shorter alternative.

Several roads were tarred during World War II, and more in the years after the war, for example the road from Craibstone past Aultmore Lodge. However the Swailend road was not tarred till much later. None of the roads radiating from Milton Mills, the Crooked Roadie, the road to Clune and that to Leitchestown and Fordyce were tarred till after the war. Jean Allan (nee McLean) remembers the surface of the road to Fordyce being very poor for school pupils cycling from Deskford to Fordyce Academy. The Todholes to Lornachburn road was tarred in 1946, but onwards to Rosebank not till much later. Braidbog to Nether Blairock had been completed around the start of the war. Progress continued until the last road in Deskford to be tarred, the one past Tod's Cottage and Braehead to Duffushillock was done in 1961. Jimmy Stewart remembers being annoyed that the County Council waited till just after he and his family flitted from Braehead to Knows before they tarred the road.

In the mid 1950s the Ha' Burn Bridge was reconstructed to reduce the sharpness of the bend and to widen the road over it, and the resultant mismatching parapets can still be seen. In the mid 1950s the bridge between Milton Mills and Bleachfield was washed away in a spate and replaced by a modern one, and around 1980 the bridge on the road from Kirktown to Oathillock was washed away and replaced by the present culvert and embankment at a much higher level and on an easier alignment. The fact that a narrow and precarious strip of the old bridge was all that remained in place for several weeks did not stop Jack Stewart cycling over it on his way to get the school bus.

BUSES AND CARS

Buses between Keith and Cullen began in the early 1920s with the first being called the "Golden Arrow". These proved to be a great boon to the people of Deskford who up to that time had relied on the trap, the gig, the boxcart, the bicycle or Shanks's pony.

Alexander Johnson in the Todholes farm gig.

The bus driver would deliver groceries and butcher meat to the end of farm tracks to be collected, the butcher meat for Mrs Duncan at Clochmacreich being left on top of a high post after the dog got an earlier delivery. By the late 1930s there were two buses a day in each direction between Cullen and Keith and by 1950 there were three buses a day. However, as car ownership rose and the population of Deskford declined the service ceased to be viable. Buses were provided by Ross of Huntly and Glennies of Newmill, which became Stables some time after World War II.

As early as 1930 cars were owned by several individuals in the parish, including Messrs Cumming at Upper Blairock, Milne at Burnsford, McConnachie at Ardoch, Park at St John's manse, Morrison at the West manse, Gordon at Berryhillock and Taylor at Mains of Skeith. In the early 1920s, Mr McConnachie, Ardoch, had become the first man in Deskford to have a car, a Ford. He was quickly followed by Mr Muiry, the Berryhillock shopkeeper, who hired out his car for a variety of purposes including transporting inmates home from Ladysbridge Lunatic Asylum on their release. By the early 1930s Mr Gordon, Berryhillock, also had a car. Mr Kitchen, Clune, had an Armstrong-

Siddeley. By 1939, in addition to these, JA Beveridge, the schoolmaster, had an Aston, Mr Craib of Mosside a Ford, Mr Currie of Greenhill a Riley, Mr Simpson of Craibstone a Triumph, Mr Taylor a Morris and Mr Ross of Kirktown a car of unknown make. Mr Simpson also had a Dodge and a Bedford lorry for carting lime and Mr McConnachie the earliest tractor in Deskford.

In 1962 petrol cost 4/6d a gallon (5p a litre) and could be purchased from Finnie's shop in Berryhillock which had a pump. Most locals bought their petrol there and many, such as Jackie Smith, had an account. In November of that year the price fell to 4/5d a gallon.

Somewhat surprisingly, given the relatively easy terrain there was never any serious proposal to build a railway from Keith to Cullen through Deskford, and indeed before the opening of Tochieneal station in 1884 Deskford folk had to walk to Portsoy, Cornhill or Keith in order to catch a train for Aberdeen or Elgin. In 1919 there was great excitement in Deskford when the first aeroplanes to be seen in the area passed overhead.

SERVICES

By the 1950s almost every farmer had a car, and there were now twenty private telephones in the parish, plus one public telephone kiosk at Berryhillock. In 1945 there had only been six private telephones. Whilst most households had obtained wirelesses in the 1930s, by the late 1950s and early 1960s many were getting television sets. Also in the 1950s a weekly refuse collection began in Kirktown and in Berryhillock. The Minister hoped that this would reduce the "unsightly dumps of tins, slops and other rubbish to be seen near these villages, and which were a source of nuisance and possible infection".

Toilet facilities were very basic until the 1950s. Farmworkers would just use the midden and houses would have a small wooden shed at the foot of the garden. Government grants became available in the 1950s for the installation of baths, and many locals took advantage of this.

As in much of the rural North East the standard of housing in Deskford was very poor. Just after World War II the four Cruden houses were built at

The Cruden built County Houses at Bleachfield.

Bleachfield as part of a scheme to provide better quality houses for farm workers, and a row of single storey council houses was built in Berryhillock. In the 1950s and 1960s when many croft houses were being abandoned, there was a great strength of feeling locally that the Council should compulsorily purchase them and let them as council houses. Despite a packed and angry public meeting supporting this idea, it never happened.

ELECTRICITY

The electricity supply came to Cullen and Portsoy in 1936/37, but Deskford had to wait until the 1950s before it slowly, in a number of separate phases, began to spread throughout the parish, most of which was connected by the 1960s, except for a small area round Braidbog, which Willie Taylor remembered did not get a public electricity supply till the 1980s. While waiting for the public supply to be provided by the North of Scotland Hydro Electric Board many farmers had their own generators.

Towie, Clune, Shirralds and Inaltrie got electricity in the late 1940s because Cullen House wanted it and got it cheaper if some farms were included. In 1952 it extended to Nether Blairock, Ardoch, Mosside and the school and schoolhouse. The main reason for this was to provide power for the new electric lathes in the Technical Room of Deskford Secondary School, now the Jubilee Hall. The school's outside lights used ordinary incandescent 40 watt bulbs. Both Berryhillock and Kirktown got street lighting in the 1990s.

Almost all of Deskford was on the public electricity supply by the 1960s, but by this time many farm houses were being abandoned, so the poles and wires to them were removed. In the 1990s and 2000s, when some of these farm houses were being renovated and reoccupied, the electricity supply had to be reconnected, at great expense. Rural and Calor gas were also widely used, and Tilley lamps and paraffin lamps gave light.

WATER

The main well serving Berryhillock, located at the entrance to the Mill track.

Traditionally most of the parish obtained water from private wells, with Berryhillock having public wells and Kirktown a "spootie" near Mary Anne's Cottage. The difference was that wells were still while spooties spouted. By the end of World War II most crofts and farms still used wells, often by now supplying rotary pumps in the kitchen, but Seafield Estate installed piped water to others from sources on Lurg Hill and Bogrotten. This led to the installation of baths and WCs, though many families still lacked these. There was no public sewage system.

The first houses in Deskford to have a public water supply were the four Cruden County Houses at Bleachfield, and it was intended to provide a public supply to Berryhillock and Kirktown by 1957, using the existing Kirktown supply pumped to a cistern at Squaredoch, with a gravity feed from there to the two villages.

In the not too distant future these three housewives will no longer have to go to the springs at Kirkton of Deskford for their water. A new scheme is planned to bring running water to each household. The three women are, left to right, Mrs Coull, Mrs Reid and Mrs Rumbles.

This cistern was built and was subsequently fed by a branch from the coastal main, running up the east side of the main road. In the early 2000s, the Lurg Hill supply was replaced by a pumped main from Cullen to Grange which supplied the east side of Deskford. There were some initial problems connecting this as the pressure was so high. When Inaltrie was being connected the alkathene connections kept being blown apart by the pressure which was measured at 23 bars. Old brass fittings had to be obtained to secure the connection.

In the early C20th the Cullen water supply from Bin Hill was inadequate, providing only 55,000 gallons per day. In the early 1920s some water was taken from the Deskford Burn to augment the supply. In 1928 it was proposed to supply Cullen, Lintmill, Tochieneal and Ellyside with water from a source at Leitchestown via ¾ inch lead pipes. This was not carried out as Leitchestown would have lost its own supply, and the water was in any case heavily impregnated with iron. There was an angry exchange in the P&J between Rev Robertson of Cullen and the Trustees of Seafield Estate in which each questioned the other's honesty and integrity over this proposal.

Finally, in 1932, the Cullen Water Scheme, which cost £30,000, was built, providing 150,000 gallons of water per day from three wells in Deskford and Grange, the Milkwell, Loanhead Well and Rumbling Wells. The supply opened in 1933 and flowed via a 5½ inch cast iron pipe from cisterns on Aultmore through Deskford along the western verge of the main road. There was a station in a now demolished cottage at Ardoch to aerate the water and to prevent build-up of pressure. Despite repeated requests, Deskford was given no access to this supply, even though it passed through the centre of the parish. This supply was stopped in 1980 when Cullen was connected to the new coastal main which uses water from the River Deveron.

All farms, cottages and villages in Deskford were supplied with water from wells from which it was carried in pails. Some of these wells were one or two hundred metres from the houses. In Kirktown the spootie was opposite the Muckle hoose and there was also a well at Orchard Cottage. At Berryhillock the main well, which can still be seen, was at the back of the village in the bank at the side of the minor road beside the junction with the track to Berryhillock

Mill. There was also one at Caroline Cottage and another halfway down the back road to Berryhillock Mill. The village of Milton was supplied by a well between the low road and the burn.

OLD WELLS

There were a number of well-known healing wells in the parish from which it was common to drink the water. St. John's Well, which appeared to rise from under the church and which was considered effective against eye complaints, disappeared entirely when it was piped around 1880. The Blindwell was at the side of the old road from Ha' Hillock to Kirktown and was reputed to cure rheumatic complaints. A field between the old and new roads, Blindwell Park, was named after it.

In a letter to the *Aberdeen Journal* dated 17/09/1776 and signed Rusticus F, the mineral wells at Blairock in Deskford are lauded highly. The writer complains that they are now "utterly neglected and so full of insects and vegetables of different kinds". He states that it is the strongest mineral well in the county, judging by the "quantity of rusty mineral stuff discharged from the water". The well was on a moor and "until lately was remote from all houses, and unfrequented, and had a well grounded fame for being effective in treating gravellish disorders". The location is now lost, but may have been in what is now mature forest between Upper Blairock and Braidbog.

Deskford people also visited St Mary's Well at Ordiquhill, though this was discouraged by the Kirk. Some also made pilgrimages to the well at Tarlair and to Jenny's Well on the shore between Portknockie and Cullen on May 1st when pins and small offerings were left.

There are or were other wells in Deskford for which no domestic, ritual or medical use is recorded. The Priest's Well lay on the side of the Flake Burn between Ordens and the Deskford Burn. It was still in existence in the first half of the C20th and the tenant, Mr Merson, spoke of it to his family. In 2013 Pam and John Robertson found some industrial slag there. The Well of the Elbow Doups was at the extreme south west corner of the Greenhill improvements, near Mid Skeith and the limestone quarry of the same name. There was a well on the bank of the Deskford Burn between Milton Mills and the bridge over the burn. In the 1950s an old filled-in well, which had last been recorded in the early C18th, was found beside the lade to Milton Mills. Fishers Well was also recorded in the area, perhaps near the Fisher Road.

The Gallows Well can still be found beside an intact fragment of the old main road between Old Cullen and Keith as this passes through the modern plantation on top of Clune Hill. It lies about 50m from the site of the gallows and is well preserved, being a circular stone revetted well about three feet in diameter and the same depth, with shallow steps leading down to it.

The Gallows Well.

FUEL

Peat, coal and wood have all been used as fuel in the past in Deskford but, of the three, peat was by far the most commonly used. When wood was used it was often bog fir or illegally acquired green wood. To buy, it was more expensive than coal. Some bog coal, a type of lignite, was obtained from Coyll Moss, but the most commonly used coal came from Brora to Cullen in two stone barrels. A barrel cost 2/- in 1800 but had fallen to 1/1d or 1/2d by 1836. In new farm houses built in the early C19th coal could be burned in the iron fire grate in the good room but could not be used on the flat slate hearth in the kitchen. Peat was the only fuel which could be used there.

Deskford had peat mosses on both sides of the valley, but those on the east side, from Cotton Hill to Lurg Hill, were largely exhausted by the early C19th. Those on the west side were far more extensive and had not been exhausted by the time peat cutting went out of fashion and ceased. When it was used by everyone there was constant concern that the available supply would be used up.

In the early C18th which tenants could use which mosses was comprehensively and rigidly ordained by the Regality Court. And towards the end of that century the amount of limestone being processed at Craibstone was reduced because of the fear of over extraction of peat. The most extensive deposits in the west were at Sheilmuir, Milkwell and Aultmore. In 1771 areas of the Milkwell Moss were reserved for the Chamberlain and for Cullen House, and by 1842 Cullen had exhausted its own local mosses and had to import supplies of peat, including significant amounts from Deskford. In 1900 places as distant as Fordyce and Bogmuchals obtained peat from Aultmore. Use of peat persisted well into the C20th with some being sold door to door from lorries in the 1960s. Possibly the last peat to be dug in the area was by Jackie and Gladys Smith in the mid 1980s from the moss above Sheilburn School.

Mossing took place after the turnip seed had been sown but before the harvest. Each tenant was allocated a section of the peat moss at a nominal rent, and the whole process was supervised by the moss grieve appointed by the Estate. It was essential that this individual was well respected and that his decisions would be accepted as final. Moss lands were carefully regulated by agreements known as moss tolerances and tenants paid a "moss marl" for the peat which they dug. The job of the moss grieve was to enforce regulations and adjudicate on disputes about the mosses. In the mid to late C19th William Bremner who had been born in Grange in 1821 was moss grieve for Seafield Estate and by the end of the century the job was being carried out by

Alexander Taylor, the retired tenant of Little Skeith who by then lived in Little Skeith Cottage.

In the C19th peat spades were wooden, iron shod and with an iron "tusk". The fauchter spade was used for tirring the peat banks. Peat cutting was hard work, especially during a wet summer, though the midges were worse during a dry one. Sometimes clocks were put forward by an hour in good weather to take advantage of morning daylight. The surface of the bank was removed in divots then one man would cast the peat and two would row the brick-like pieces some yards away from the bank on an open slat sided barrow. Here it was couped. When the peats had dried sufficiently they were spread, turned over and laid flat, and after a few weeks were ready to be set. Four pieces were placed on end, apart at the bottom and together at the top, with a fifth peat laid flat across the top to keep them in position, the whole thing being called a rickle. When dry they were barrowed a bit further to where they could be loaded onto a cart and taken home to be built into stacks capped with turf. Twenty score of peats would last the winter on a small farm.

Building a peat fire was also a fine art for it was generally kept alive day and night and never allowed to go out. The brick shaped peats were built into a pyramid, leaning towards each other and meeting at the top. Last thing at night, or if the occupants left the house during the day, the fire was covered by a divot. Later, even if it seemed the fire had gone out, it could be brought back to life by using the bellows which each house kept beside the fire.

Because peat cutting was fairly labour intensive there were problems in getting enough during both world wars. In 1916 the Deskford Parish Council had difficulty getting peats for those on the Poor Roll. The man who for the previous five years had carted them in at a charge of 5/6d per load was refusing to do so that year. Three paupers were informed that if they could get a load or two anywhere, the Parish Council would pay for them. In 1941 June was perfect weather for casting peat, but cutters could not be got anywhere.

LIGHT

Candles and lamps of various types were used to provide light. Some of the poorer households who could not afford other forms of light would go to the moss with a long auger-like probe to search for bog fir tree trunks which were to be found up to six or eight feet deep and had a diameter of up to twelve inches. These were taken home, cut into splints, dried, and used as fir candles when they were stuck into the "peer man" lamp. In the early C19th cottars still used oil cruisies or home made dip candles. The cruisie was a triangular lamp hung from the wall. By the mid C19th small tin cruisies were carried about. They were shallow dishes with a beak carrying a wick made of rush pith and using mainly colza (rapeseed) oil. Around this time paraffin lamps were introduced, taking the place of mould candles just as these had taken the place of dips. Paraffin lamps and naphtha lamps and later tilley lamps meant that "reekie peters" went out of use. For many years after its opening in the 1840s the Deskford Free Church used candles, before these were replaced by lamps.

COMMERCE

For much of its history Deskford had a flourishing commercial sector but shops were not limited to the villages, with grocers being recorded at Backies, Squaredoch and Whiteknowes at different times. In August 1811 there was advertised in the *Aberdeen Journal* a roup of the stock of John Stewart, merchant in Hoggie, on behalf of his creditors. His stock included cloths, corduroys, printed cottons, cambrics and groceries, etc. In 1790 there had been 18 weavers, eight shoemakers and four tailors in Deskford.

Most of the shops were in Berryhillock and Kirktown and the numbers expanded in the late C19th. In 1841 there were grocers in Squaredoch, Kirktown and Backies. By 1851 there were a merchant, a grocer and a clothier in Berryhillock, and a clothier/grocer and a bookseller in Kirktown. 1861 saw a tailor, a dressmaker, a grocer, a clothier and a cooper in Berryhillock and a tailor, a general merchant and a shoemaker in Kirktown, who were joined by a grocer and spirit merchant in 1871. In the 1860s there was a bakehouse attached to one of the Berryhillock shops where they baked "bread, harvest baps and fascinating biscuits with raised curly edges". The general merchant at Backies was Ann Bidie and she was still operating in 1881.

In the 1850s it was the custom to buy each item separately, get the change, then purchase the next item. When a jug was brought in for treacle it was put on the scales empty and balanced by bits of old broken clay pipes, before the treacle was poured in and balanced by the weights. In Berryhillock there was a shoemaker, Auld John, his son Johnny and his wife, Mistress Reid, who kept a little shop which sold everything.

In the late C19th, anyone living in Deskford would be able to purchase almost any item they required within Deskford. In 1881, local farmer Willie McWillie bought one pair of strong boots from Harper and Dow, Berryhillock for 15/- and a suit of clothes from Mitchell, tailor, Berryhillock for £2:10/-. Though some shops remained in operation for many years others had only a brief existence. In 1886 Miss Ingram started a dressmaking business in Kirktown, and that same year Alexander Brander, shoemaker, Berryhillock ran away, leaving a wife and considerable debt. In 1888 there was a roup in a merchant's in Berryhillock as he was emigrating to the USA.

Towards the end of the C19th, *Slater's Directory* listed three boot and shoe makers in Deskford, John Benzie, James Lorimer and George Taylor, one grocer and general dealer, John Reid, one vintner, James Watt and two tailors, Alexander Reid and Alexander Shepherd.

In earlier years, but persisting well into the C19th there were regular visits to Deskford from packmen and chapmen with packs of cloth, cutlery or books etc. If given accommodation they might well sell napkins, scissors or dresses at low prices. One such packman was Huntly Johnnie who sold cutlery. He was considered to be a very sullen individual.

In the 1860s in Deskford "packwives came round carrying large wicker baskets covered by American cloth. Inside the lid there were ties, handkerchiefs, chains, beads, lace collars, dollies, dollies' hats and frocks. Inside the basket were babies' hoods and bonnets, frocks, sunbonnets, pinafores of dotted muslin and sprigged print, blue ribbons for sashes, wincey aprons and petticoats, eis wool and worsted mutches, crossovers, fascinators, shawlies, cuffs and hummlies. Coloured reels were 1/2d. There were Berlin wool hanks in soft shades of green, crimson, pink and fawn. A large leather pouch or purse hung from her waist under her skirt and accessible through a slit. Packwives were important at that time".

A variety of shops persisted well into the C20th. In 1900 there were two joiners' shops, one in Berryhillock and one in Miltown, two shoemakers, Lorimer in Kirktown and Gray in Berryhillock and three grocers, one in Kirktown and two in Berryhillock. In the 1930s there were two shops in Berryhillock, one run by James Muiry, a tailor turned grocer who had a shop at

Muiry's shop near the top of Berryhillock.

the top of the village from 1923. It also had a petrol pump and he owned an Austin car which he hired out. During World War II, every Friday, he took a few local ladies to Buckie for shopping. After the war the car hire business was operated by a Mr Milton. Mr Muiry also sold bottles of beer unofficially, "under the counter". Dry goods were sold loose and syrup draft. When the roads were blocked with snow he sent a horse sled to Cullen for supplies.

The other shop was run by the Misses Reid, whose Post Office at the bottom of the village sold paraffin, candles, matches, tobacco and sweets. In April 1959 the Postmistress, Miss Annie Reid, died aged 72 in the house adjoining the Post Office. Her family had run the shop for many years and she had taken over before World War II. She had played the organ in the church for over forty years, giving up in 1955, and had also taught Sunday School. Mr Finnie, Mr Muiry's son-in-law, took over from Miss Reid. Dovey Legge was a souter at 10, Berryhillock, between the two shops. Here he worked in a wooden outbuilding till his business closed just after the war. Jimmy Simpson at Craibstone sold paraffin and cigarettes from a machine at the entrance to the farm, beside the bridge on the main road.

In the early part of the C20th there was a small "jenny-a'-thing" shop in Kirktown called Mary Anne's. James Lorimer, "Jim the Souter", in Kirktown died at the age of 84 in 1939, leaving Kirktown without a shoemaker. During the 1930s he had employed two men at Rose Cottage, and concentrated on making and repairing shoes, while Dovey Legge concentrated on repairing boots for farmers and farmworkers. During the 1930s James Mitchell, Kirktown, still had a tailor's shop, and Findlay the tailor in Kirktown made suits which were sold by Mr Muiry from his shop in Berryhillock. Between the two world wars, shops in Deskford often stayed open in the evenings as this was the only time farmworkers could get to them.

In addition to these shops many other businesses operated in Deskford. There were two smiddies, at Woodend and at Cottartown. There were two meal mills, at Milton and at Berryhillock. There were joiners, builders, engineers and Jimmy Gordon ran a carpenter's and undertaker's business in Berryhillock.

In the C20th local shops were supplemented by many vans which criss-crossed the parish. Some of these, before World War II, were horse-drawn while others were motors, but after the war they were all motors. Different areas in

Deskford were served from different towns, but all the vans had disappeared by the 1960s. Many different businesses started rounds, but some of these did not last very long. Amongst the more successful were the Co-op drapery, hardware and grocery vans.

Before World War II Sheilmuir was served by vans from Lipton's the grocer and by the Co-op butcher, both from Buckie. Elsewhere a van came round from Slater the grocer in Cullen and Jim Garden, a grocer's salesman from Keith, did a round in the southern part of Deskford in a horse-drawn van.

The heyday of vans was in the 1950s, when there was a wide variety. Grocers' vans came from Robertson's of Fordyce, Patterson's of Buckie and also from Cullen. Bakers' vans came from Reid of Cullen, McKenzie of Cullen, Donald of Portsoy, Wallace of Buckie, Young of Cullen, Stevenson of Keith and Fletcher of Cullen. A butcher's van came from Bruce of Cullen and another from Petrie of Portsoy. Drapers' vans came from Robertson of Cullen and Gray, previously Simpson, of Keith. Fish vans came from McKay of Sandend, Smith of Sandend, Sutherland of Portsoy and Downie of Whitehills. A hardware van came from Robertson of Fordyce and a shoemaker's also came from Portsoy.

Reid of Cullen baker's van with driver, Johnnie Pirie, and two Deskford girls, Kathleen and Margaret Simpson, in the 1950s.

POSTAL SERVICES

In 1860 Cullen was the post town for Deskford and mail from the south reached there by coach from Portsoy at about 6:00pm, having come as far as the railway terminus at Portsoy by train. Deskford letters were brought by the post runner the following morning to the little shop in Berryhillock, after which he continued another seven or eight miles through Grange, before calling back at Berryhillock at 4:00pm or 5:00pm en route to Cullen. He walked between 22 and 24 miles a day, six days a week. It was very rare for mail from the south not to get through, and even if the train got stuck in snow, mailbags were put on horses or even taken forward on foot.

The Post Office occupied two different premises in Berryhillock at different dates, but for most of this time it was in the bottom house in the front row of cottages. By coincidence it was in Squaredoch from about 1860 to 1880 and again in 1988 when, after the parish had been without a Post Office for three months, following the death of the sub-postmaster, Michael Marshall of Squaredoch was appointed. For much of its existence in Deskford the Post Office was run by the Reid family who were originally from Broadrashes.

In 1886, Mr RW Duff, MP, succeeded in having a post runner appointed for a run between Berryhillock and Drybridge on Mondays, Wednesdays and Fridays. Local residents hoped to have this increased to daily but, if that wasn't possible, would prefer Tuesdays, Thursdays and Saturdays. The newly appointed post runner was Alexander Geddes, who left Berryhillock around 10:00am on the arrival of the post runner from Cullen, and proceeded via the Free Church manse and Wester Greens of Blairock (there were three Greens of Blairock Farms) where he left mail for Braidbog and Wester and Easter Darbreich. He then went in by Briggs and Lower Bogrotten and several other farms en route to Drybridge. His return was by Rosebank, Hillhead, Rottenhillock, Whiteknowes, Bloomfield, Cottarclump, Craighead, Wellcroft and the Poors Houses, arriving back at Berryhillock around 2:00pm. The run took in more than one hundred farms and crofts.

In 1912 Miss Reid, Berryhillock, was Postmistress. Mail arrived each day from Cullen at 8:30am and then three auxiliary postmen took it in different directions before they returned to Berryhillock for the return 1:15pm mail to Cullen. In 1891 there had been only two auxiliary postmen and the mail for Cullen had left at 1:30pm. In the 1930s two postmen from Cullen delivered mail in Deskford on bicycles, but were often late. Around 1950 there were two postmen, both from Cullen, John Sudden and Mr McAllie. One came in the morning and the other in the afternoon. However by the 1960s local farms had only one delivery per day, often at lunchtime, firstly by bicycle and later by van. If the school closed early because of adverse weather, local schoolchildren would sometimes get a hurl in the post van.

Surrounding areas also had postal deliveries, with a route having been established from Portsoy to Bogmuchals in the late C19th, and Sheilmuir being served in the 1950s and 1960s by Willie Fraser from Drybridge.

ALEHOUSES AND ILLICIT STILLS

There were taverns and alehouses in rural areas of Scotland from the C13th. They sold mainly ale and beer with a little wine. Whisky was only introduced in the C15th and was often made from oats. Over the years there have been alehouses in Deskford in Kirktown, Berryhillock and Squaredoch as well as many informal howffs.

In 1727 the Deskford Kirk Session was of the view that the Lord's day was very much profaned by drinking in alehouses after the church service, and till late on the Sabbath night. It decided to prosecute both keepers of alehouses and their customers if there was any profanation of the Lord's Day. In 1770, Walter Syme ran an alehouse in Berryhillock which sometimes came to the attention of the Kirk Session for "scandalous diversions" such as dancing, playing on the fiddle and playing cards as well as the routine drunkenness and swearing.

Also around 1770 a widow and the mother of a poor Deskford cottar's son who rose to be the owner of a large firm of attorneys and conveyancers in London ran an alehouse in the parish. The son was known locally as "carroty Sandy".

By 1836 Rev Innes was able to bemoan the fact that although there were now fewer alehouses in Deskford, one remained, which "is quite unnecessary, and affords facilities and temptations to intemperance". He felt that certificates from Ministers and Kirk Sessions should be obtained before any alehouse was licenced. This alehouse closed down soon afterwards, and was the last in the parish.

There were many illicit stills in Deskford, but by their nature records of their existence were not kept. Rev Innes, writing in 1840, stated that there were now none in the parish, but that until recently they had been very common and that their effect was still felt. Whisky had become more popular than beer in the late C18th because of the imposition of the malt tax on beer and ale. The average whisky-drinking man drank one pint of whisky a week.

The period between 1780 and 1835 was when they were at their most common, small stills having become illegal in 1779. Records are sketchy but it is believed that there were illicit stills in the Milkwell area, on a hill towards Keith and one on Aultmore, run by a tenant called Bremner, an ancestor of Alison Smith. He was tried and fined a large sum at Banff, though his offence was not stated. It is thought however that he kept an illicit still.

NEWSPAPERS

Newspapers, mainly the *Aberdeen Journal*, were widely read in the late C18th in Deskford, with perhaps half a dozen neighbours clubbing together for a subscription. The paper was delivered by arrangement, someone meeting the stagecoach on a Wednesday, the day of publication. Each of the joint subscribers kept it for one night before passing it on to their nearest fellow subscriber. Once each of the joint subscribers had had an opportunity to have the paper for one night, they would all meet in the home of the "Header", the first person delivered to, in order to discuss the news. The paper was often read aloud first. The *Aberdeen Journal*, now merged as the *Press and Journal*, was the oldest newspaper in Scotland.

MEASUREMENT

Throughout the last thousand years there was an enormous complexity surrounding every type of measurement. A measure of weight could vary according to the commodity being measured, and measures of volume were different in different places. On many occasions Parliament attempted to impose a clear and sensible system only for the population to continue with their old and incoherent practices.

Land measure was particularly important in farming areas such as Deskford, and from the C13th the following system was used:-

    13 acres = 1 oxgang
    26 acres = 2 oxgangs = 1 husbandland
    52 acres = 4 oxgangs = 1 auchtenpart
    104 acres = 8 oxgangs = 4 husbandlands = 1 ploughgate
    416 acres = 32 oxgangs = 4 ploughgates = 1 davoch

This was further complicated by the use of different names for the same measure. An oxgang was the same as an oxgate, a carucate and a bovate. In some parts of Banffshire a davoch equated to 8 oxgangs, not 32. In Deskford the use of husbandland and oxgate have been recorded. For example in 1671 there was reference to "The lands of Little Skeith, extending to 4 oxgate". There were also smaller measures. There were, for example, 4 roods or rigs in a Scots acre, which itself was bigger than an English acre. A davoch is variously claimed to be the amount of land able to be ploughed by the old ox plough or alternatively the area of land which generated a standard vat of grain in tax.

Another vital type of measure was that of the volume of cereal crops. It was not until 1457 that the size of the pint, firlot, half firlot and peck etc were fixed. Over the next hundred years or more these increased until they settled down as:-

    4 lippies (or forpits) = 1 peck
    4 pecks = 1 firlot
    4 firlots = 1 boll

16 bolls = 1 chalder

The number of bolls in a chalder was subsequently reduced to 8, and there was also confusion with one heaped corn firlot being equal to 1.45627 imperial bushels. In 1578 it had also been decided that victual and salt from foreign countries must contain 18 pecks to the boll instead of 16. In the time of King David a gallon measure was determined as 6½ inches deep, 8½ in diameter, 27in circumference at the top and 23in circumference at the bottom, and to contain 4lb each of standing, running or salt water.

From 1624 weights were determined as:-

1 pickle of wheat from the middle of the ear = 1 grain
36 grains = 1 drop
16 drops = 1 ounce
8 ounces = 1 mark
2 marks = 1 pound
16 pounds = 1 stone

Many years later, at the time of the Union of the Crowns, this changed to 14lbs = 1 stone. However the tron stone of 19lbs Paris standard was used for butter, cheese and tallow. A stone of wool weighed 15 lbs and a stone of wax 8lbs.

In measuring liquids there were two mutchkins to the chopin and two chopins to the pint. However a gallon of ale was a different size from a gallon of wine. In measuring length, 1 inch was the determined as three barley or bere corns without their tail, or the length of the thumb of a man of middle stature, measuring to the root of the nail. An ell measured 37 inches. In 1663 the foot of twelve inches was introduced and in 1685 the yard of 36 inches was added, however the ell continued to be used into the C19th.

Much of the confusion over measurements began to be eradicated after the Union of the Parliaments in 1707, but it took a long time for the official standardised measurements to be adopted everywhere. Local measurements, together with some of the commoner standards such as Paris measure, Amsterdam measure and Linlithgow measure were adhered to tenaciously. It perhaps puts into context the fear in the early 1970s that the change from imperial to decimal measurement would be confusing.

AGRICULTURE AND INDUSTRY

For almost all the time that people have lived in Deskford, agriculture has been the most important activity. On its success or failure rested the viability of the community. The biggest and most persistent threat was from poor harvests caused by bad weather. For example in 1630 there was a great drought and the corn was parched and dried up. Weather was however not the only threat. In 1693 too many men in service to farms in the parish had taken to trades, particularly in Cullen, without the consent of the Justices, and therefore "the husbandmen (tenant farmers) in the countrie are now rendered destitute of their servants". The farm servants were ordered to return from their new trades to the farms they were legally obliged to be working on or face imprisonment.

There was a great deal of community involvement and cooperation. A new tenant was given great help, for example with ploughing. He also went round his neighbours after they had sown some of their own fields and was given seed corn. This was known as "thiggin' the seed". Seed corn was also given to any crofter who had suffered a failed crop. The new tenant also went round thiggin' at harvest time when he was given a few sheaves by every established farmer. He went to different farms at seed thiggin' and at harvest thiggin' and offered snuff to each donor. When going round his neighbours like this it was vital for the new farmer to appear a decent individual. This system operated right up till the Poor Law Amendment Act of 1845, which many locals felt undermined the sense of community. Under the Act responsibility for supporting the poor was transferred from the Kirk Session to the new Parochial Board.

Soil fertility was important in maximising yield. Soil from end rigs, road verges and dug-out ditches was used as the base for middens. It absorbed cattle urine and was used as a base for cattle dung. It was then mixed with lime in the dunghill on the field. Use of lime had begun in the C17th in Deskford where it was readily available. It was very effective but over-use made fields sterile and its use was stopped for a while, before being gradually reintroduced in sensible amounts. Marl from Enzie was also used. For a time Sunderland lime at 2/2d a barrel was preferred to local lime at 2/1d a barrel. Sea Dogs (dogfish), which are small sharks, were also used as fertiliser. They cost 1/6d to 2/- per 100, with a cartload holding 800 to 1,000. One cartload of sea dogs was mixed with six cartloads of earth before spreading. Fermented weeds were also considered a good fertilizer. At Cultain in relatively recent times lime was mixed with clods of earth which fell off drying tatties and neeps and used as a fertiliser.

Deskford has always been considered a particularly good area for farming as the fields never became too dry in time of drought or too wet in time of continuous heavy rain, though the west-facing slopes of Cotton Hill were notorious for lightning. In the C17th Deskford farms were mainly arable unlike the farms round the slightly wetter Keith, where they were more mixed.

In 1769, when Thomas Pennant made his "Tour in Scotland", he passed through Deskford and was of the opinion that "the country round Cullen has all the marks of improvement, owing to the indefatigable pains of the late noble owner in advancing the art of agriculture and planting and every other useful business [probably the bleachfield which Lord Seafield had recently opened], so far as the nature of the soil would admit. His success in the first year was very great; the crops of beans, peas, oats and barley were excellent; the wheat was very good, but, through the fault of the climate, will not open till it is late, the harvest being in these parts in October. The plantations are very extensive and reach to the top of the Bin Hill".

Dr Johnson, who toured with Boswell around the same time, was highly critical of Cullen, but passed no comment on Deskford as he kept the curtains on his coach closed when passing through.

The success of the agricultural community in Deskford involved a far larger number of roles than just the farming. For example William Bremner became Moss Grieve, a very important job, on Seafield Estate in 1862, and was responsible for agreements known as moss tolerances, and tenants' moss marls (payments). He was also responsible for settling disputes relating to moss lands. Another example was James Ingram, crofter in Upper Craibston, who died in 1862 at which time he was also a drainer and a mosser. In 1936, Miss Jane Moggach, Todholes, won £10, a fortune at that time, as the prize for the farm servant in the County of Banff longest in his or her current job. She had served with Mr Johnston there since 1908. Brief interludes from toil could be had for all tenants and farm servants at the Peter Fair at Rathven and the Hallow Fair at Fordyce where, in addition to the sale of beasts, there would also be a large number of sweetie stalls, showies, entertainments and other "catchpennies". Though fairs were legislated for in Deskford they never took off and were soon abandoned.

Labour on farms was always heavy and involved long hours. In the C18th, between March and October, the farm servant worked between 4:00am and 8:00pm with one hour off for breakfast and another for "twal 'oor". When, forty or fifty years later, ploughmen worked from 6:00am till 6:00pm, old retired farm servants called these the "easy 'oors". Even just before World War II farm servants worked a sixty-hour week with no paid holiday.

Some trends in farming resulted from circumstance. Before the 1880s neeps were usually overwintered in the field, but around this time they were badly eaten by rabbits and hares, so from then on they were lifted at the back end and stored in the neep shed in the steading. In the mid C19th tile drains replaced old stone drains in the fields because of a ready supply from Tochieneal Tile Works. In the mid C20th all steadings were re–roofed with 8' by 4' sheets of grey asbestos, reputedly because the Countess of Seafield was very friendly with an American businessman who was involved in their manufacture.

Some of the vast changes between pre- and post-improvement farming in Deskford can be shown by the example of Burnheads. In 1762 it was a joint tenancy held by James Dougal and James Milne. Rent was paid in meal, barley, poultry and cash. In 1794 James Dougal was the sole tenant with a new 19-year lease. By 1831 his son-in-law, Walter Sim, had taken over the tenancy at the much increased annual rent of £18:11:2½d, in cash only, because of the new farm buildings which had been built. In 1851 it was 66 acres, and held by

James Mitchell, and in 1861 his son, John Mitchell employed two ploughmen, one cattleman, one domestic servant and his sister Jane as housekeeper. By 1871 it had increased in size to 104 acres and was held by Charles Milne who had four farm workers. In 1908 it was tenanted by Andrew Reid, in 1942 by William McPherson and now, in 2016, by Sammy Miller.

AGRICULTURAL SOCIETY AND TENURE

The system of tenure in place at any particular time has had a great influence on the nature of society. There have been many different systems, all of which caused both benefits and problems for the inhabitants of Deskford. In the pre-feudal, pre-C12th period there were a number of grades of peasant sub-tenant including both slaves and serfs. There were four ways in which a tenancy was paid for. Cain was the rent in cattle, grain and pigs, Conveth was the obligation to give hospitality to the overlord and Feacht and Sluaged were obligations on members of the tribe to follow their chief in battle. All four were absorbed into the feudal system and by the late C13th Cain and Conveth had been partially replaced by cash rent, obtained by selling surplus produce in Cullen or Keith. Over the next four or five hundred years a variety of forms of tenure went in and out of favour.

The Black Death in 1350 caused an increased availability of rented farmland as landowners found it difficult to get hired labour, and serfdom ceased by 1400. Rents fell as land became more easily available, and some touns fell vacant. Husbandmen were the most common type of major tenant, each holding between one and four oxgangs. However much more numerous were the crofters and cottars who were either sub-tenants or tenants at will with no security of tenure.

By the late C15th the large ferm touns had been replaced by smaller touns and some individual farms. Toun splitting took place because of increasing demand for land. Examples of this include the various Skeiths, Nether and Upper Blairock and Meikle and Little Knows. The pattern developed of longer tenancies, and many of these were kindly tenancies under which relations of the lord were permitted to continue in their tenancy year after year. In the C16th many farmers in Deskford were named Ogilvie or Abercrombie.

For smaller farmers in places such as Deskford tenancies were difficult to obtain and in the C14th and C15th most held short-term verbal tenancies of between one and six years, which made the tenants vulnerable, but not as vulnerable as their sub-tenants who were tenants at will. Wadsetters were creditors of the landowner who had free tenure while the debt remained, though this was not common. Kindly tenancies disappeared and were overtaken by more commercial tenancies when population increase caused greater demand for land. The eviction of kindly tenants in the late C16th caused some turmoil. Farms were rouped to the highest bidder, which did not encourage continuity, but the first 19 year leases appeared in the early C18th by which time around 50% of farms in Deskford had multiple tenancies, whereas previously the vast majority had been individual tenancies.

Nineteen year leases were the norm for many years, but by the middle of the C20th most had become 14 year leases, with a possible break at seven years. Now there is a rent review every three years, but with an inclination towards continuity. Seafield Estate operates a mixed system, cultivating some land itself, leasing some to tenants and renting some on an annual basis to contractors. It has also, over the last 50 years, sold off a number of farms in Deskford.

Before improvement, sub-tenants and herds only received meal and a plot of land, but no cash, for their labour. Boys, halflins and the landless were paid in cash but this was not thought to be so advantageous. Amongst sub-tenants the crofter was slightly superior to the cottar. Almost at the bottom of the scale were the grassmen and grasswomen, often widows, who herded livestock, but below them even were the landless labourers. Cottars' wives were required to help with many of the specific activities related to farming but few labourers had wives.

By 1950 there were still a few tied cottages in Deskford but the numbers were declining rapidly. The chaumer system, which operated locally, had a rigid hierarchy. In one farm in Deskford where the chaumer was a considerable distance from the farmhouse, the farm servants walked between the two for meals in rigid order of precedence, foreman followed in turn by second horseman, third horseman, cattleman and finally orraman.

The relationship between tenants and Seafield Estate varied over the years. In the 1850s tenants' views diverged from those of the Estate, particularly after the Law of Hypothec gave landowners preferential security over their tenants' stock and crop, even when these were sold to a third party. During the century many tenants felt that Seafield Estate was guilty of rack-renting, and, when, in the difficult times of 1887, Lady Seafield agreed to reduce rents by 10% it was pointed out that other large estates were reducing their rents by between 15% and 25%. Much of the friction and conflict centred on the role of the Factor. By the 1950s there was a generally good relationship between the Estate and its tenants, but the attitude of individual Factors varied. Some were more interested in the shooting than in farming.

In 1511, within the Bishopric of Aberdeen, the average rent of a ploughgate of land was £3:7:9d Scots in money, one year's rent as grassum (an initial payment), 20d for commuted service, 1 firlot of oats, 1 firlot of meal, 1 firlot of malt, 1 sheep, ½ of a kid, 5 capons, 5 fowls, 4 moorfowls and one pig from the mill, plus 2 stones of cheese from every holding. Crofters were bound to build one rood of the fold for every cow possessed and pay 9/9d in money, 1 firlot of bere and 10 fowls.

By 1790 rent of arable land in Deskford was 12/- per acre, paid partly in money and partly in barley and oatmeal. Money rent was always paid at Martinmas, after harvest. Barley and oatmeal rent was paid between Christmas and Candlemas. Entry to a farm, house, garden and meadow was Whitsunday and to arable land after harvest. Farm houses and offices were valued on entry and had to be maintained by the tenant. They were valued again when he left and he had to pay any loss in value to the incoming tenant.

The proprietor had the right to cut ditches through a farm in order to drain any other farm or part of the Estate. He could also plant any moor or rough pasture within a farm with trees without any reduction in rent, though from 1750, in order to stop cattle damaging trees, tenants got, at the end of their lease, every third tree planted during their tenancy. Multures was effectively a local tax, and included thirlage to the landowner, knaveship to the miller and abstracted or dry multure. Bondages, customs and multures were gradually and randomly abolished over a number of years, though, rather shockingly, feudalism was only abolished in Scotland, the last country in Europe where this happened, in 2004.

In the 1840s in Deskford there were 2,800 acres cultivated or occasionally in tillage, 5,100 acres of waste or pasture, of which 250 acres could be cultivated and 600 acres were under wood. The average rent was 17/6d per acre. In 1950 all holdings in Deskford were between 6 and 146 acres and they averaged about 80 acres. Rents were about £2 per acre, but by 1960 had increased by up to four times, contributing to the large number of farms and crofts which were abandoned or merged with another around this time. In 1953 in Deskford there were 2,306 acres of arable, 1,625 acres of temporary grass, 226 acres of permanent grass, 416 acres of rough grazing, 44 horses, 166 dairy cattle, 1,731 beef cattle, 346 sheep, 575 pigs and 20,149 poultry. There were 73 holdings of over 1 acre and there were 75 tractors.

Individuals were important in the different kinds of agricultural society which existed in Deskford at different times. In addition to the changes, expansions, contractions and economic conditions which existed, the attitudes and ambitions of individuals also played their part. For example, in 1772, George Miln, who had a 19-year tack (lease) in Squaredoch wrote to the Earl of Findlater asking in addition for the land in Faichyhill recently vacated by James Huie. In the 1870s Charles D Forbes, Tochieneal, introduced a steam plough, possibly a static one. In 1906 Brodie Taylor, the new tenant of Swailend, presented an exhibition of a new threshing machine, fitted up by Messrs Wright, Millwrights, Boyne Mills, Portsoy. He was complimented on his enterprise as a farmer.

A different example of the culture befell Jimmy McBeath, who was later considered King of the Cornkisters for his singing of bothy ballads. Many of these were recorded for posterity by the School of Scottish Studies at Edinburgh University in the early 1950s. He had left school at 13 before World War I and had feed at Brandane's Fair to a farm in Deskford where he was beaten savagely by the farmer with the back chain of a cart for not being in proper control of his horses. He described the farm servants of that time as being "a very sad-crushed people, very sair crushed doon". Perhaps mercifully neither the farm nor the farmer in Deskford where he was so cruelly treated is named. During World War I he enlisted in the Gordon Highlanders.

In the difficult years before World War I there was a reduction in the cereal acreage in Deskford, and lower yields were accepted, compensated for by the lower costs of less liming. There was also more hay production at the expense of turnips, because hay meant lower labour costs. In 1915 the Deskford Farmers' Supply Association applied to register as a Society under the Industrial and Provident Societies' Act 1893. The committee was WW Kitchen, Clune, Secretary, Alexander Ross, Kirktown, William A Stewart, Nether Blairock, Alexander Milne, Burnsford, John M Morrison, Clunehill, George McConnachie, Ardoch, and Alexander Shepherd, Craibstone. Its registration was cancelled in 1919 for wilfully failing to submit an annual return, despite being reminded, and the cancellation was advertised in the *Banffshire Reporter* of 12/02/19. However in 1924 the Deskford Agricultural Cooperative was formed with 27 members. Its secretary was William Currie, Greenhill.

In 1935 John Milne left Burnsford for a larger farm near Banff, taking a cottar man with him. That same year George Morrison took over Clunehill which he had jointly tenanted with his mother since his father died. His mother bought the lady teachers' house in Kirktown. In 1941 Jessie and Bella Taylor gave up Bellcroft but remained in the house. The land was taken over and farmed by Geddes Rumbles of Cottar Clump.

Some aspects of agricultural life remained static for a very long time, such as the use of sickles from Roman times till 1805, whilst others changed fairly rapidly, such as the transition from walking or using the gig to bicycles and then cars, over a period of fifty years from 1880.

Oats was by far the most common crop, and a farmer's prosperity was judged by his cornyard. There was a certain smugness in Deskford that its harvest was always two or three weeks earlier than that of Bogmuchals. Finishing the stacks was the high point of the farmer's year and was an occasion of great satisfaction if the crop was good. The social changes which came with the introduction of a capitalist system in the early C19th were not always foreseen, such as the baking of two different qualities of oatcake, a superior one for the farmer and his family and an inferior one for the farm servants. This is recorded on an unnamed Deskford farm.

The farming year was organised round the quarter days, with the year beginning with Martinmas in November, and moving round Candlemas in February, Whitsun in May and Lammas in August These were the same dates as those of the much earlier four pagan festivals, which had been Christianised.They were used as term days though the Church of Scotland did not recognise them as feast days.

Life and death was always close, with despair being caused by the regular cattle deaths from anthrax in the 1930s and the death of horses from grass sickness in 1938, which led indirectly to the introduction of many tractors in Deskford. There were also different attitudes to wildlife, demonstrated in 1880 when the first reaction of a local farmer on seeing a heron was to run home to get a gun to shoot it.

DECISION-MAKING

Farming was a precarious existence and from early times control and regulation were felt necessary. In 1214 laws were passed to control the time of ploughing and of sowing. Those who owned fewer than five cows were not to use them for ploughing but should dig using a spade instead. Those who had oxen were obliged to sell them to those who had land to plough and sow, and there were fines for those who did not cultivate the land they occupied. Those who failed to plough in winter because it was too cold, and as a result had to beg for food in summer, should not be given any. Instead they should be made to work for others in exchange for meal. King James 1st passed a law which stated that every man "tillan with a pleuch of aucht oxen" had, in addition, to sow a certain quantity of pease and beans.

In 1457 tenants, by Act of Parliament, were required to plant broom for thatching and for bedding for cattle, and in addition, hedges round their fields and trees near their steadings. The Act of 1503 prohibited oxen and horses from being poinded for debt if the debtor had any other goods, lands or possessions. Between 1563 and 1565 all corn had to be threshed immediately because of shortages. Any stacks found standing on the 10th of July would be confiscated. The Act of 1587 made the maiming of cattle, the cutting or injuring of ploughs or ploughing gear and the destruction of growing corn or wood punishable by death.

An Act of 1621 laid down the duties of farm servants. It outlined the evils which had arisen from them refusing to be hired unless paid "great and extraordinary wages", or engaging only from Martinmas to Whitsunday and then "casting themselves loose" from their engagements at a time when much work, such the cutting of peats, had to be done. No farmworker should leave his employment at Whitsunday unless he could prove he was fee'd to some other job. If he could not, he could be compelled to return to the farm and serve for such wages as had formerly been agreed on.

As early indications of future improvement, in 1661 Parliament passed the General Enclosure Act and in 1695 the Division of Runrig Act. However neither had any great effect as landowners could not afford to implement them, even though the Act allowed landowners to enforce enclosure against the tenant's will. In the late C17th a law was passed prohibiting the cutting of turf on the outfield for use as manure.

In addition to frequent legislation, tight regulation was maintained in local areas such as Deskford by Birlaymen and Birlay Courts. Landowners appointed officials and tenants appointed their representatives, the Birlaymen, who decided how many animals each tenant with rights to common grazing could have. This depended on the size of the holding. 1½ cows equated to 8 sheep or 40 goats, because the last mentioned were not selective grazers. Despite this there was much overgrazing. Birlaymen, especially where there were joint tenancies, could prevent argument by deciding what rotation should be used, or when ploughing, sowing or harvesting should begin. They also adjudicated on boundary disputes and accusations of illegal activities. Unfortunately, in

Deskford, as in almost all other areas, written records of their discussions and decisions were not kept so we have no details of their operation.

FIELD PATTERNS

For much of its Bronze Age, Iron Age and Pictish history, agriculture in Deskford was concentrated lower down the valley and comprised very small fields, worked with handtools. By the C12th this was still how cottars and crofters operated, but, ahead of England, larger farms had by this time introduced the rig and furrow system of large open fields cultivated by eight or twelve ox ploughs. These open fields were worked by individual ferm touns of perhaps four families. The new system may have resulted from the arrival of Norman and Flemish incomers, influencing the indigenous inhabitants. Rigs were formed in a long reverse "S" shaped ploughing pattern in order to allow the cumbersome ox ploughs to turn to the left at the end of rigs. There were also short rigs called butts and temporary enclosures for beasts called faulds (folds).

This infield/outfield system lasted until the second half of the C18th, though in some large Deskford farms such as Croftgloy, Oathillock and Ordens it had already been amended from a runrig system of scattered strips to a composite runrig/rundale system. Under rundale, rigs were consolidated into blocks, intermingled with those of other joint tenants.

Rundale reduced the requirement for all tenants on these farms to agree precise dates for the main activities such as ploughing and harvesting, as on farms where tenants had scattered strips these had to be cooperative activities. This need for cooperation had led to rigid adherence to tradition which reduced the number of arguments, but which suppressed innovation or change. Enclosure in the late C18th further reduced this requirement for cooperation.

When rigs and furrows were first ploughed up and converted into enclosed fields, good soil from the ridges filled the baulks between them, leaving what had been the fertile ridges as bare, stony, barren strips which could still be seen fifty years later. To begin with, the enclosed fields were too small which wasted land round the edges of the fields, though initially this waste was limited because the sickle was still used for harvesting. Over the intervening 240 years fields gradually became larger and larger, to suit the needs of increasing mechanisation, until we have the situation which exists in Deskford today in which single fields occupy what had previously been several farms.

In the C17th, before improvement in Deskford, there were no hedges or dykes, excepting the head dyke which was built of feal (turf) to separate the infield from the outfield. Deskford was mostly rough moorland which reached as far down the hillside as immediately above Raemore farmhouse and steading on the west side. There were no planted woods or other trees except on the banks of burns and round kailyard dykes. Because there was no artificial field drainage, only sloping land, which drained naturally, could be cultivated. At this time it was still common to leave the "Gudeman's Croft" (devil's portion of land) uncultivated.

The system was controlled by the Baron Baillie who ran the Baron Court, and later the Court of Regality, assisted by the Birlaymen. Between them they resolved disputes, laid down rules for such activities as cutting peat, building head dykes and the planting of pease. They also imposed punishments for offences such as non-payment of rent or debt, trespass by cattle and boundary disputes. The introduction of the post of factor in the early C18th undermined what had been a relatively well-accepted system, and led to greater hostility between landowner and tenant.

In the last decade of the C17th there was repeated crop failure, leading to starvation, destitution and the abandonment of some farms, which were not worked for up to 50 years in Deskford, a shorter time than in some areas.

Field names were used extensively from early times though they did not always persist, and were liable to being changed. Some old abandoned farms, such as Tillybreedless and Bognageith survive as field names on Langlanburn and Backies respectively. Some fields were named after previous sub-tenant crofters and some identified on the 1771 Estate Plan are still in use today, such as Gushet on Gowkstone. At the time of improvement, boundaries between previously existing farms in Deskford were often subject to significant alteration. Examples of this include Squaredoch and Knappycausey. In 1871, 30 acres of the lower fields of Ardicow were removed and added to Knows.

In the second half of the C18th all fields carried names, many of which were descriptive such as den, croft, acre, shank, scabbies, morass, brae, claylands, outfield, intown, gushet, yaaval, meadow, loaning, hillock, kilnhillock and thornybauks. Newly taken-in farms often did not have a name and were just known by the tenant's name and a description of the quality of each field. Some farmers seemed more imaginative in their field naming. For instance, on Carestown there were Black Gutters, Crumblands, Polished Neuk and Over Wynding, while on Ardoch there were Clayholes, The Tarries, Toash Acre, Back o' the Yard and Whey Tails.

Some field names were common. Butts were short rigs in blocks and in Deskford we find, amongst others, Butts on both Meikle and Little Knows, Drowned Butts at Hellensland (Lower Broadrashes), Watery Butts at Clochmacreich, Claybutts on Gowkstone, Butts o' the Broom on Carrothead, Green Butts on Langlanburn and Moddy Ward Butts on Ardicow.

Another common field name was fold, meaning a temporary field enclosure for beasts. Some of the many in Deskford included Bearfold and Bogfold on Leitchestown, Redfold on Little Ardicow, Backfolds on Inaltry, Little Fold on Little Knows, How Fold on Meikle Knows, Sandy Fold and Flake Fold on Croftgloy, Whities Fold and Hill Folds on Ardicow, Brae Folds on Upper Skeith, White Fold, Long Fold and Cow Fold on Over Windyhills, Herd's Fold on Raemoir and Hill Folds on Craibstone.

Others were less common, but still used on several farms. For example we had Balnahaugh on Clochmacreich, Ball Haugh on Carrothead, Blackland Haugh and Bog Haugh on Smithstown, Long Haugh on Nether Clune and Haugh of Milltown. All of these were of course near the Deskford Burn.

Ley, which means pasture, was present in Longley, Broadley and Backley on Ardoch, Longley on Oathillock and Stony Ley on Langlanburn. Waird, an enclosure for calves, appears several times. In addition to the croft called The

Wairds, there were Wairds of Croftgloy, Broomwaird on Mains of Skeith and Meikle Waird on Meikle Knows.

By the late C20th most fields in Deskford were fenced. Some had had dry stane dykes as field boundaries and a few had had hedges. By 1840 most moor, moss and waste had been improved, but improvements continued, for example with the laying of Tochieneal tile drains from that time onwards. As late as the 1970s there was still draining, ditching and the taking in of land on some farms such as Cultain, Langlanburn and Whiteknowes.

FARMS

Some farms in Deskford have been in existence for about a thousand years, and in some cases perhaps even longer. The land has certainly been farmed

Ordens, Croftgloy, Hoggie and Greenhill from the west side of the Howe 'o Deskart

since the Bronze Age. Concepts of ownership and tenure were not the same as those to which we are accustomed. There was a form of tribal communal ownership under the Picts and this was at least partially retained under the succeeding Scots elite who were responsible, between 900 and 1100, for the naming of farms such as Clochmacreich, Raemore, Skeith, Ardoch, Inaltrie, Ardicow, Clune, Cultain and Blairock, all of which have a Gaelic derivation.

Ownership and tenure became clearer under the feudal system from the early C12th onwards, and as the Scots language displaced Gaelic from about 1200, farms with Scots names came into being, such as Croftgloy, Ordens, Craibston (Craib's Town), Carestown (Kerr'sTown) and Leitchestown.

The Annals of Cullen mention a number of farms in Deskford in the C16th, including Easter Skeith (1521), Ordecow (1531), Echinaltry (1541), Meikle Knows (1545), Clochmacreich (1562), Leitchestown (1586), Aithillock (1587), Ower Blarayacht (1587) and Squaredoch (1588). During this period there were many land transactions of different types, purchase, mortgages and tenancies, and it is difficult to distinguish small estates from farms; indeed they were often one and the same thing.

Black and white copy of prizewinning colour slide "Deskart Hairst" by George Sinclair. Harvest at Mid Skeith in 1992 on fields now covered by mature trees. The land behind the steading is also now under trees.

All of these farms survived until the time of agricultural improvement in the late C18th as did other very old farms such as Tillybreadless, Bognageith and Bognabrae, though these three were abandoned as individual holdings together with Burns and Nether Clune in the middle of the C19th. Another farm which went out of existence around this time was Knappycausey, the land of which had moved about, but on some of which New St John's Church was built in 1871. At different times the farm had been on different sides of the new turnpike. Many holdings survived as separate farms until the middle of the C20th, when there was a significant number of mergers to produce larger farms. Many which ceased being separate farms still exist as private houses. Examples of these include Raemore, Swailend, Upper Skeith, Mid Skeith, Little Skeith, Lower Broadrashes, Hoggie, Hollanbush and Kintywaird. Some, such as Upper Broadrashes and Carrothead have disappeared completely, as have many on the west side of the valley.

Before agricultural improvement there were several farms under multiple tenancies. These included Squaredoch, Ordens and Oathillock. Where there is now just Nether Blairock as a working farm there had previously been Nether Blairock, Upper Blairock, Wester Blairock (always known as Wyvers, because of the weavers who lived there in the C19th) Easter Blairock, Little Blairock, possibly one of the three farms at Greens of Blairock and Blairock Croft. Clune was split into Clunehill, Mid Clune, Nether Clune and Clune Croft. In addition there were small crofts and cottar houses on most of the medium and large

Johnny Sutherland at work at Bloomfield

farms. For example in 1771, Cottar Croft and Quaint's Croft both lay at the upper end of Mid Skeith Den, James Wilson's dairy was in the north and east of Little Knows, Croft of Cairnley was on Leitchestown, and Parks of Smithstown lay between Inaltrie and Leitchestown, east of Bleachfield.

Whilst there had been continuous change throughout history, the late C18th improvements brought unprecedentedly rapid and major changes. Farms such as Croftgloy and Ordens, on each of which there had been several fermtouns plus crofts, were enclosed and became single tenancies with single farms and steadings. Over the 90 years from 1760 onwards a very large number of new farms and crofts were taken in from the moor and moss on the west side of Deskford. The last to be taken in, the smallest and poorest, did not have individual names until the 1860s. Before that they had been known collectively as Aultmore Crofts, but when the surveyors for the Ordnance Survey arrived, each croft became named individually.

New farms on the west side, taken in from the moor, were established in several phases, with some of the earlier ones such as Braidbog, Rashiehill, Greens of Blairock, Upper and Lower Bogrotten, Weston and Todholes being of a fair size. Even amongst these however changes took place. Upper Bogrotten was renamed Whiteknowes and the house and steadings moved 300m further from the public road. There were three farms named Greens of Blairock, the one which still exists and two others about half a mile further down the Blairock Burn and on the other bank.

Robert Cruickshank sen. with a load of hay at Little Mosside.

Of the later, smaller crofts, none is still worked, and in many cases no evidence of their existence remains. The roll call includes Bogetra, Blackhillock, Aultmore Wood, Upper Craibstone, Poolside, Poolhead, Braeside, Upper Braeside, Braehead, Bell Croft, Greystone, Bloomfield, Stripeside, Wellcroft, Cottar Clump, Craigie Croft, Todside, Crofthead, Craighead, Duffushillock,

Rottenhillock, Lornachburn, Comb's Croft, Bogside, Barone, Gateside, Bell Croft, Greystone, Bloomfield, Stripeside, Aikenhillock, Headroom of Swailend, Little Raemore, Upper Burnheads and the inevitable Newtown. There were a few other small crofts spread elsewhere across the parish including Corbie

From a painting of the Cruickshank family croft at Little Mosside

Craig, Brigend, Craigloy, Blackheath, Little Mosside, Mosside Park, Upper Mosside, Back Park of Ardoch and Cross of Ardoch. Legg's Brae was a croft near Clune. There were in addition many in the area of Shielburn, including Povitic, Slatehaugh, Slateheuch, Hillhead, Rosebank, Bankhead, Burnside of Aultmore, Backburn, Badenhannan, Quarryhead, Rosehead and Wellheads. This list is not exhaustive.

In the C18th or C19th there were also brief existences on the east side for Harder, Bogs of Ordens, Smithyhillock, Hellensland, Bogs of Inaltry, Croft of Forder's Acre, Kemp's Croft, Viewfrith, Broom-haugh

The former Ardoch Cottage, perhaps on the site of a previous croft, either Back Park of Ardoch or Cross of Ardoch.

91

and Rathillock. Hollanbush lay 200m further down the Hoggie Burn than its present namesake which was originally called Hoggie Croft. Burnsford was originally known as Mousehillock. Greenhill was known for a short period in the mid C19th as Earlstoun and Backie's Croft was known as Croft Riddoch, also for a brief time. Upper Craibstone has the distinction of having been abandoned twice and re-occupied between each.

According to James Wilson, writing around 1880, there were 65 separate holdings of between 6 and 200 acres in Deskford. This would also have included farms outside the parish to the south, but within Seafield Estate, such as Marchbank, Wester Windyhills, Nethertown, Myreside, Lurg Brae, Greens of Lurgbrae, Over Windyhills and Goukstone. Just outside the parish to the north were Pattenbringan, Swallowhillock, Smithstown, Ellyside and Malthouse Croft.

The derelict farmhouse of Craigie Croft with Cottar Clump behind it.

The vast majority of farms and crofts went out of use in the 1950s and 1960s, their land combined with that of other farms or left to become rough grazing. One example would be Slatehaugh, Slateheuch, Povitic, Quarryhead and Rosehead in Sheilmuir being combined into a single 124 acre unit by Jackie and Gladys Smith. As leases expired in the 1960s Mid Skeith was amalgamated with Upper Skeith, Little Skeith and Upper Broadrashes, though only the last named house and steading was demolished. The land was later afforested.

This type of process had a major impact on the population and social structure in Deskford. A way of life abruptly disappeared for many people, and by 2014 even the memories are disappearing fast. Jimmy Stewart, Meikle Knows, found a quern stone in a pile of large stones. These had been used into the C20th by some farmers' wives. There are cheese presses in the garden dykes at both Clune and the ruin behind Braidbog, and until very recently there was one at Upper Blairock. In living memory there were rats in every grain loft and every farmer had a terrier. Poolside was considered the wettest farm in Deskford, and Bloomfield, tenanted by Mr Sutherland, was considered the garden of Deskford. Billy Murray remembers his father running down from the mill dam at Little Skeith after opening the sluice to start the mill, as the dam only held enough water for 15 minutes milling. Willie Fordyce remembers his mother saying she had been born in Bogetra which went out of use and was amalgamated with Blackhillock in 1887.

Farmyard at Berryhillock Mill

There are no really old farm buildings left in existence in Deskford. Before improvement they were very insubstantial, with turf, or clay and bool walls and thatched roofs, similar to those at the Highland Folk Museum at Newtonmore. These did not last long and were frequently rebuilt, with the old turf and thatch being added to the midden. Even the first generation of post-improvement rebuilding has generally disappeared with the exception of a few houses such as Leitchestown and Langlanburn. Most of what are now considered as "old" farmhouses were built between 1880 and 1910, for example Inaltrie in 1880, Mid Skeith in 1890 and Oathillock in 1905. Around the late C19th a new byre was built at Backies which was tiled, and had a cement floor. It had required 2cwt of iron nails, bought from Cullen at 15/- per cwt. A new byre for 20 cattle and stables for horses might cost £70. Tenants ambitious to increase their stock levels might build temporary wooden byres and cartsheds roofed with turf.

As farms were rebuilt their precise location often moved about the area close to the steading. For example both Cultain and Inaltrie had occupied positions on both sides of the public road but were rebuilt to lie on one side only. At Carestown a new stretch of road on the present alignment was built to stop the public road going through between the farm buildings.

Rentals increased as the years passed. Alexander Taylor had Little Skeith between 1904 and 1922 when the annual rental rose from £24 to £31. William Murray Jr took it over in 1925 at £35, but by 1965, when W Beattie Jr took it over and farmed it and Mid Skeith as a single unit, the rental had risen to £514:10:2d.

In the C21st, many old farm houses have been sold as private houses and others are rented. Most of the land is still owned by Seafield Estate, though in the 1960s it sold Langlanburn and later also Clochmacreich to Sandy Strathdee. Around 2000 it sold Craibstone with Backies and more recently it sold Marchbank, Myreside, Wester Windyhills and Nethertown. Of the remaining Seafield Estate land, much is farmed by the Estate, some by remaining tenants and some in partnership between the Estate and contractors.

CROPS

In Pictish times farming in this area comprised both the cultivation of crops and the rearing of animals. Barley had been grown for thousands of years but oats were only introduced around 100 AD. Bere, a primitive kind of barley, which grew in four rows in the head instead of barley's two, was preferred to barley as late as the C18th as it grew more quickly and produced a bulkier crop. It was the last crop planted and the first harvested on infield and gave a yield of 4:1 or even 5:1. Both bere and barley were used in early subsistence agriculture in the North East, mainly for ale and broth, though bere meal bannocks were occasionally made. In Deskford more bere than barley was grown up till about World War I.

The rotation on outfield areas was as follows. In year 1 there was the "ley" crop of oats, followed in year 2 by the "yaavel" crop, also of oats. Sometimes in year 3 it was manured and bere was grown. This was followed in years 4 and 5 by the "bar reet" crop of oats and in year 6 by the "warsche" crop, also of oats. After this there were several years in which the land remained fallow. Oats, pease and beans were sown from the beginning of March to the middle of April and bere or barley from the beginning of May.

Till the C17th the only oats which were grown on either infield or outfield were the hardy grey and black types, but after this time the higher yielding white oats were grown on the infield. Oats was the staple food crop, being used for porridge, brose, sowens and breid (oatcakes). It had also been used to make whisky. The oat-based food made up the greatest part of the diet for 600 years into the C20th. It was commonly the only food crop grown on the outfield, where it was rotated with fallow areas on which animals were grazed and gave some dung. It was sown at four firlots of Linlithgow measure to the acre, with a return of 6 or 7 bolls on average to the acre, a yield which could be as low as 3:1, which was described as "Ane to graw, ane to gnaw an' ane to pay the laird witha'". Much early oats was sown. By 2012, Sammy Miller at Burnheads was the only farmer in Deskford who still grew a "park o' corn (oats)" each year, but European Union regulations mean that in 2015 several farms are doing so once more. Willie Fordyce at Mid Skeith had stopped in 1986 and Jimmy Stewart at Meikle Knows around 1990.

Before 1500 the only vegetables which were grown were leeks, onions, kale, cabbage, fat hen (colewort), beans and peas. Cabbage was the most important of these, and together with leeks was grown as far back as 400 AD. Pease and beans were introduced around the C10th or C11th and by the late C17th and early C18th Acts of Parliament were passed encouraging farmers to grow them, but the yield on pease could be as low as 2:1. In the C17th mashloe, a mixed crop of pease and beans, was grown.

Hemp was also introduced about the C10th or C11th, and by the early C18th both flax and hemp were grown on every farm, often as a single, heavily dunged rig. Hemp was grown for sacks, ropes, canvas and nets, while flax was used for shrouds, priests' robes, and later, for clothing. Alfalfa, otherwise known as lucerne, had been introduced by Norman landowners. Heather and broom were treated as crops for use as thatch and as bedding for overwintering cattle in the byre. Hay was introduced as a crop for the first time in the mid C18th, and at the same time, with the big changes to farming methods, the number of thistles fell significantly, but dockens appeared for the first time. Vetches, known as tares, were grown to feed cattle.

Potatoes were introduced in Deskford for the first time around 1745 and neeps (turnips) in 1748, and soon both were being cultivated very extensively. The potatoes, a white kidney variety, were grown on every farm, croft and garden and proved their value by preventing starvation when the cereal crops failed in 1783. Before their introduction up to 33% of cattle might die each winter from starvation.

Turnips replaced a hard red cabbage, now lost, as animal feed and white cabbages replaced both curly kale and the tougher (difficult to believe) rough kale, for human use. Potatoes were planted by hand until the 1930s, and until 1860 they were lifted using the graip. After this mechanical means were increasingly used. Though turnips were a great improvement in allowing far greater overwintering of cattle with fewer dying, the work involved in their cultivation was heavy. Turnip fields were ploughed in November, cross ploughed in March or April and harrowed to break up clods and remove weeds. They were then twice ploughed in May or June and harrowed again. Sowing took place in June using bobbin johns, seed barrows and later, horse-drawn two-drill seeders. Hoes were used to single plants and to weed the drills and they were lifted during autumn or winter.

Throughout history there have been many crop failures, some of them catastrophic. These happened for example in 1308, 1309, 1310, 1315, 1318 and 1337, with many people dying, especially in the countryside as they relied entirely on the food they grew. There was another countrywide series of very poor harvests in 1782, 1783, 1796, 1800, 1801 and 1811. During the last of these, fortunately for Deskford, on a narrow strip of land near the Moray Firth coast, there were bumper crops which could be sold for high prices. Though figures are not available for Deskford, they are likely to be similar to those in the adjoining parish of Grange where almost half the population died of starvation in the 1690s. In 1850, on some newly reclaimed and damp ground in Deskford, the crops never ripened at all and were cut green and fed to the cattle.

In 1800 there were few orchards around Banffshire though those beside the Tower of Deskford and the Castle of Skeith still existed. Fruit such as apples, pears, plums, cherries, red and black currants and gooseberries were grown in private gardens.

From 1790, on the large improved farms in Deskford, rotation was used. A large part of the farm would be fallow, or under turnip or green vegetables. One third would be under sown grass at 8lb of red clover, 8lb of white clover, a small amount of rib grass and two bushels of rye grass per acre. This was cut as hay in the first year then left as pasture. Oats was the main cereal. Previously barley or bere had been more important but became less so when turnips and sown grass were introduced. For both oats and barley, yields were much improved, and some pease and beans were still grown. In 1885 Burnheads had 24½ acres of oats, 17 acres of new grass, 17 acres of turnips, 6 acres of barley, 12 acres of second year grass and ¼ acre of tares, plus another 14 acres unidentified.

By the 1930s, farms in Deskford each grew about one acre of potatoes, some to eat and some to sell. Corn (oats) was the main crop but there would be some barley and a field of neeps. Wheat, when tried, was unsuccessful. There might be ½ acre of cabbages or Brussels sprouts. By 1970 silage had largely taken over from neeps and by then barley had taken over as the main crop from oats as combine harvesters were introduced. Farms began to focus on barley and cattle, though as time passed barley became more and more important because of the good prices which could be got from the distillers for malting barley.

By the 1950s a six year or seven-year rotation was used. The six year rotation had three of grass, one of ley, one of turnips and one of oats, whilst the seven year rotation had an extra year of oats, the yaavel. Wheat was carried manually in 2¼ cwt bags (115 kilos), barley in 2cwt bags (102 kilos) and oats in 1½ cwt bags (76 kilos). The hundredweight (cwt) of 112 lbs was the universal measure.

As always, throughout the C20th, yields were variable year on year. For example 1927 was a disastrous year while 1934 produced an excellent oat crop and an excellent hay crop but only an average turnip crop. In 1941 the hay crop was much lighter than usual. Weather conditions and the consequent quality and quantity of barley crops are essential in the C21st to ensure they are purchased at good prices by the distillers rather than at low prices as animal feed.

The finances of farming were closely observed and in 1840, Deskford raised grain worth £3,234, potatoes worth £485, turnips worth £809, hay and pasture worth £1,502 and flax worth £33. Haymaking, using a three-toed fork, lasted till just before harvest. When machinery was introduced there was a constant search for greater efficiency, and individual farmers would host trials of a new reaper or binder, which many other local farmers attended, and which often became social occasions. One example, in 1906, was the trial of a new threshing machine at Swailend. Careful calculation of farming methods was made. For example, in the late C19th, using fertiliser, it was reckoned that a farmer could get one stack of lea corn from one acre, whereas without fertiliser it would take between two and two and a half acres. However the cost of fertiliser then had to be factored in. Experiments were constantly being carried out. For example Siberian wheat was tried in 1812, but was not successful.

HARVEST AND THRESHING

The harvest in a good year would start in early September and last for about seven weeks, but often, in poorer years, it lasted into November.

For well over a thousand years oats and bere were cut by women, using a saw-toothed heuk (sickle). In the C18th this was replaced by a larger smooth-bladed heuk, used by both men and women, though men demonstrated greater productivity. This was in turn replaced, almost at a stroke, in the North East in 1805, by the scythe, which had already been used for many years for cutting hay and grass. It was introduced more slowly in other parts of Scotland and indeed was not used commonly in the South West till 1850. Scythes could not operate on stony ground so their introduction required greater stone clearance from fields.

In pre-improvement times, harvesting by sickle involved a team of seven, six of whom operated sickles across two rigs, with one man stooking. Each shearer did a five or six feet wide cut and managed about one third of an acre per day. Scythes were used by men with women lifting, gathering and binding sheaves, and an old man tying and stooking them, followed by a male or female raker, raking up loose heads of corn. Three scythers needed one raker and a scythesman could cut two acres per day. In addition scythe cut sheaves were more open and therefore dried more quickly. Scything also produced more straw than the sickle as it cut closer to the ground.

George Stewart, Braehead, with his binder.

By the 1850s the routine of harvest on Deskford farms required five or six scythesmen cutting in echelon and in time with each other, so that the cut corn all fell in one direction. Behind each scythe came a woman gatherer who made sheaves, held together with a band, and behind them came an older and less fit man who set up stooks of five or six pairs of sheaves.

Harvest was always started near the end of the week so that Sunday's rest came after not too many days of labour. If the harvest was backward, work might be resumed at midnight on the Sunday, if it was a moonlit night. Cutting and stooking usually took between ten days and a fortnight, and the Sunday by which almost all of it had been cut, but before any had been carted home was called "Stooky Sunday". Taking clyack was still a major ritual.

Reapers pulled by horses were introduced in the 1870s, and by 1880 they were cutting as much as was being done by scythe. By 1885 the vast majority of the harvest was being done by reaper, or the newer and more efficient binder, though scythes were still used for small awkward areas, head rigs or where the crop had been flattened by the weather. Not all reapers were equally effective. In 1879 a Hornby reaper on Oathillock did not do a good job, but on nearby

Ian Morrison, George Morrison, Clunehill, William Johnston, Todholes and Unknown, possibly at Clunehill

Knows a different machine did do a good job and particularly where scythes were not effective because the crop was wet.

Knows was typical in having thirteen stacks of oats and two of barley, and clyack was taken by the end of October. In 1888 the harvest extended into

November, with Greens of Blairock only taking clyack on the 11th, but this was much earlier than in neighbouring Bogmuchals where Barnyards of Badenyouchars still had a park to cut on the 27th. Combine harvesters replaced binders in the 1960s, and barley gradually took over from oats as the main crop.

In pre-improvement times sometimes a rig was left unsown to allow wild oats to grow, which gave an earlier crop and which bridged the food gap between old and new corn. Harvest was the one time of year which required a long and hard day's work over many weeks by every person available. The last sheaf cut on each farm was called the clyack sheaf, which was always cut by the maidens, and under no circumstances was allowed to touch the ground. It was dressed up in womens' clothing (rags by the late C19th), carried home in

Jean McLean, aunt of Duncan, in the stackyard at Milton Mills around 1930.

triumph and kept till Christmas or New Year when some of it was fed to the best milk cow. On the day that clyack was taken there was a feast which must include cheese, the "clyack kebback", which must be cut by the farmer. Later that day was held the "meal an' ale", with food and a dance. In earlier times some farmers had left some stalks uncut, for the Gudeman or Devil, a similar gesture as leaving the Gudeman's Croft uncultivated.

In the early C18th sheaves from the stooks were taken back to the farm from the field by pack horse, but by the end of the century carts were used, piled high, and with one man on top, directing the horse by voice only, "hie" to turn to the near side and "weesh" to turn to the off. Pre-improvement stacks in the cornyard were small, seven feet high and five feet in diameter, with pointed tops. Stone bases for stacks were introduced about 1780, and post improvement stacks were much bigger, around fifteen feet in diameter. Finished stacks were thatched and tied down with, originally, straw ropes, the making of which was a skilled task done under cover in winter or in bad weather.

Hand threshing with a flail had been carried out over the winter for centuries. Sometimes sheaves were lashed against a protruding stone or an open frame, with iron cross bars. Sometimes it was done by treading to protect the straw for thatching. It was carried out in the barn where the roof couples were high enough not to get in the way. The threshing floor was clay, just to the side of the area used for winnowing, which was carried out between two open doors.

Threshing mills were a warmly welcomed innovation when they were invented around 1800 and farms throughout Deskford built mill dams and associated lades and water wheels to power them about this time. These mill dams on many farms had a very small capacity and were only used for a weekly thresh for day-to-day needs of the farmer's family and beasts. Travelling steam mills were introduced around 1870 and were used for the main thresh. This required a team of at least six men, and usually more, so farmers helped on neighbouring farms and this was reciprocated. Older boys took time off school, with or without permission. Travelling steam mills were replaced by belt drives on tractors on individual farms and eventually by combine harvesters, the use of which meant stack yards being abandoned and Dutch Barns being built.

The rucks (stacks) in the cornyard were often built on a tripod in the middle with a vent in the side, and were thatched. Both of these helped drying. In Deskford the practice was to take some corn to be ground into meal in Milton

Mills or Berryhillock Mill in November, to be used by the family and any farm servants and their families. The rest of the rucks were threshed in the spring for seed or for sale. Oats were sold to one or two merchants based in Buckie or Portsoy respectively, and while some barley was also sold to them, much was sold directly to the distilleries.

In the 1750s the flail was used daily over the winter and twice on Saturdays, because no work was permitted on Sundays. After it had been cut by heuk, brought in in currachs and stacked the corn was ready for threshing and winnowing, which was done using winnowing riddles between two open doors. This was later replaced by a winnowing fan. Every farm had its kiln with an open fire called a "kiln logie". Grain was dried on straw which lay on top of a wooden rack, though grain which fell through the rack did not produce good meal. Kilns were dangerous and often went on fire.

After drying, grain was stored in a dry bed and then was carted to the mill in long narrow boll sacks across a horse's back and tied under its belly. A line of horses was tied together for this journey. Even though tenants were thirled to the mill, the quern, like the one found by Jimmy Stewart at Meikle Knows, was still used unofficially into the C20th by farmers' wives for home use, since the costs of using the mill were resented and it was claimed that the meal produced by a quern was of better quality. Corn was shelled on the shelling knowe by farm servants (eg Shilling Hill in Portsoy) and meal was separated by hand from the sids which were used for sowans. From the early 1500s some graddaning was done instead of threshing. It was a job for women and involved the careful burning off of stalks and chaff, leaving grain. This process however died out in the early C18th.

BEASTS

In Pictish times cattle were the main animal kept, but there were also sheep, pigs, geese and fowl. Horses, dogs and cats had been domesticated. Right through into the early C19th the cattle were small, light animals which might only produce 2 pints of milk a day. From 1750 cattle were driven from

Deskford, south to Falkirk Tryst. This flourished in the first quarter of the C19th with, for example, in 1810 1200 beasts worth £150,000 moved south on droves from Aberdeenshire and Banffshire. From 1827 steamships began to transport local fat cattle to London, and later, the railways did the same with prime Scotch beef.

The native small black cattle however were so small that they could not be used for the plough, and work oxen were bought at three years old from the Lothians, and worked for eight to ten years. By the second half of the C19th selective breeding had achieved much superior breeds such as Aberdeen Angus and Shorthorn. By the 1950s in Deskford, beef cattle were usually Aberdeen Angus or Hereford, with the small number of dairy cattle being Ayrshire or Friesians.

In pre-improvement times beef cattle and sheep spent the summer on rough pasture and moorland on the hill, outwith the head dyke, and then on stubble fields after the harvest. Milk cattle and horses were kept nearer the fermtoun, or tethered on the weedy baulks between the rigs. Herding was done communally, and each tenant and subtenant had an allocated number of beasts they were permitted to graze, counted in soumes. One soume equalled half a horse, or one cow, or ten sheep or twenty lambs or eighty four goats. The large number of goats allowed was because they were not selective grazers and would eat almost anything, unlike cattle or sheep.

Before turnips were introduced in the 1740s there was little in the way of winter fodder and many cattle and sheep were sold just before the winter. For the beasts which were kept overwinter there was only some straw and coarse grass. Sprotts and broom were used for bedding. By spring those animals which had survived were very weak and often had to be lifted out to the field, being too weak to stand or walk. The day on which this took place was known as "lifting day". From the C14th stirks were kept for three years before slaughter.

In 1750 horses were small pot-bellied beasts of 12 – 14 hands, good for a pack saddle, but not needed for carts, of which there were few, or for ploughing, which was done by oxen. The number of sheep had increased dramatically until by the late C13th there were around 2 million in Scotland with a high demand and good prices for wool, though the demand fell in the C15th and C16th. The North East did not suffer too badly as it was an area of mixed farming. The traditional breed had been a small, light, whiteface which produced very fine wool, but these were replaced in the early C19th, first by Blackface and Linton, then by Northumberlands. Before 1800 ewe's milk butter was so foul that it was used only for greasing farm machinery such as axles. However ewe's milk cheese, set using the stomach of a calf, lamb, hare, deer or sow, or the gizzard of a fowl, was very highly regarded and preferred by many to cow's milk cheese. Sheep were widely kept on Deskford farms till about 1970, after which the focus was strongly on barley and beef cattle.

George Stewart with his bull at Braehead

In the early C20th draff was obtained from Glenglassaugh distillery, and bruised oats were also fed to cattle, with hashed oats to pigs. All that were bought in were bulls and rams, with home-bred heifers and ewe lambs kept for breeding. The travelling stallion covered the mares to produce young foals, which replaced broken-in young colts which were sold to horse breeders.

Neighbouring farmers sometimes agreed that one would buy a Shorthorn bull and the other an Aberdeen Angus one, perhaps every six years or so, and then they would swap and share. Cattle were often multi-suckled as calves, then kept on a maintenance diet for a second year. In the third year they were fed on hay, supplemented by neeps, bruised oats and linseed cake, giving good, natural, three-year-old beef. During World War II locust beans were fed to ewes at lambing which increased their milk production.

Some farms kept pigs, but these were more often found at mills and distilleries, and as pork and bacon were so unpopular locally, butchers from Aberdeen would come to the area, gather a herd of two or three hundred animals and drive them to Aberdeen. Throughout history farms in this area also kept fowls (hens), ducks, geese, and in later days, turkeys. They were often kept by the farmer's wife and seen by the farmer as a nuisance. However, starting in the 1930s and accelerating rapidly in the 1950s most farms kept hundreds of birds in the deep-litter system, and made excellent profits from them. In the 1880s several Deskford farmers had trapped or shot rabbits and sold them to Cullen butchers for 9d each, and others diversified into keeping bees and selling honey.

The life of farm animals has often been dangerous. In the C17th around 15% of overwintered sheep died and 10% of lambs died under gelding. Many cattle, sheep and deer died in 1268 and 1272 and in 1300 there was much sheep scab, known as pluk. In 1344 almost all poultry died from pestilence, and so grotesque and horrible was its effect on the birds that most people refused to eat them. Over many centuries deadly diseases such as foot rot, liver fluke, brucellosis and grass sickness took their toll.

An example which shows what a serious problem animal diseases could be, occurred in 1887. Blackhillock, tenanted by Mr Benzies, had an attack of pleuropneumonia amongst its cattle, which was investigated and reported on by Sergeant Morrison, Buckie. Six beasts were shot and buried in a hole nine feet deep, but four or five others survived, being kept in a separate byre. Both those slaughtered and those which survived were valued by Mr Finlay, Banff. The local authority then declared Blackhillock an infected place. Of the remaining cattle, some were owned by Mr Benzies and some by Mr Mair, flesher, Buckie. Both gentlemen wished all the cattle to be slaughtered so long as they were paid full value for uninfected beasts and three-quarter value for infected ones. The local authority ordered any infected animals to be slaughtered immediately, in the sight of Mr Cooper, Inspector. The premises at Blackhillock were old, very low and dilapidated, and difficult to disinfect, and the local authority asked Inspectors Cooper and McGillivray to report on how this might best be done. An epidemic of pleuropneumonia developed in many parts of Lower Banffshire at this time, but fortunately Deskford was relatively unscathed, other than in the case of Blackhillock.

In Victorian times communities such as Deskford had specialists who would be able to cover every requirement locally, and farm income was supplemented by a number of farmers who trapped rabbits or kept bees and sold the honey. Many sold hens to Cullen or Keith. In the late C19th William McLean, Berryhillock, was summoned whenever anyone had a pig to be killed, and Lorimer the farrier was brought in to castrate colts.

PRE-IMPROVEMENT AGRICULTURE

There is fragmentary evidence of farming in Deskford as far back as 5,000 BC. In prehistoric times there were small fields surrounded by stone walls. Of these it has been stated that there is or was evidence at Milton Mills, Ardoch and on Cotton Hill. These were only replaced by large open fields, ox ploughs and shared tenancies from the C12th. In the C8th all local farms had been mixed, with meat, dairy and cereals being produced, to which was added the produce from hunting, fishing (trout were caught in the Deskford Burn till the middle of the C20th) and foraging for nuts and berries. Each farm would support from one to four families.

In the Iron Age and Pictish times land was distributed amongst free tribesmen, though strangers could also join a tribe and be given a portion of land. There were serfs who went with the land and cottars and then husbandmen above them. Many Iron Age settlements were abandoned and then reoccupied as the climate changed, but there was an established settlement pattern in Deskford at the time of changeover from a tribal to a feudal society about 1100. This was in large part centred on those farms which lay fairly close to and mainly to the east of the Deskford Burn in its lower reaches within the parish.

Between 1000 and 1300 the climate improved and this caused increased cultivation. There was little assart (arable farming permitted within forests) except in areas such as Bogmuchals, and these areas may also have seen some pannage (pasture for pigs within woodland). It is probably during this period that the first farms with Scots rather than Gaelic names emerged. Examples of these include Craibstone, Croftgloy, Carestown, Oathillock, Squaredoch and Knows. Not all fields were ploughed every year, with some being allowed to remain fallow. Some of the early toun splitting, such as Blairock, Skeith and Clune may have taken place around the end of this period, the average toun size in the North East being between 25 and 100 acres, but it is more likely to have taken place later, up to the C16th.

By the end of the C10th the davoch had been established as a measurement of the land of a tenant farmer or farmers and was later used in the name Squaredoch (Square Davoch). Farmers lived in turf dwellings which they shared with their animals, surrounded by the even smaller huts of their dependant cottars or serfs. Each davoch contained fishing rights, timber rights, arable and pasture land and moor grazing. A davoch comprised 32 oxgangs or oxgates. In 1671 Little Skeith is recorded as being four oxgates in size.

After 1300 the amount of land cultivated fell because the climate had become worse, and in 1350 the population fell by about 25% locally due to the Black Death. The pattern of farming however which had been established before 1200 persisted till the second half of the C18th with minor evolution. Only naturally draining sloping ground could be cultivated while rashes and sprotts were gathered for thatching and bedding for cattle. Runrig was introduced around 1200 though in Deskford some farms later changed to rundale. There were large areas of commonty or common grazing which in the earlier part of this period were not considered part of any landowning or estate. These included Aultmore and Greenhill. In the late C19th Sheriff Cosmo Innes criticised land owners of previous centuries for bringing such areas into their own land-holdings, using self-interested legislation which they had passed in the Scottish Parliament which they dominated.

From around 1200 the most wealthy of the peasants rented ferm touns, often on a communal basis, and they often had land in more than one farm. This persisted in Deskford in farms such as Ordens, Oathillock and Knows into the second half of the C18th. Those who held one part of a multiple tenancy were known as portioners. In the C13th and early C14th there was an annual verbal rental, which was not very secure and which favoured the landlords when the population was high and increasing, but which, after the catastrophic population reduction caused by the Black Death in 1350, favoured tenants. Landowners rented out land at nominal rents rather than have it revert to moorland, and tenant holdings doubled in size while rents halved. There was a shift from arable to livestock farming which was less labour-intensive which suited a period in which the population had fallen.

When feu ferme tenancies were introduced, which required a large initial payment for a life tenancy, this favoured tenants with drive and ambition, but drove many existing tenants from the land and into becoming beggars and vagrants. Both short-term leases and feu ferme tenancies were often passed on to sons or brothers of deceased tenants. In the C16th there were many kindly tenancies which could be inherited or sold. In Deskford there were many Ogilvies and Abercrombies in such tenancies. However as the population rose in the C17th most tenancies were reorganised in a more formal, structured and written manner. Rent in kind often included "mairts", beasts killed just before winter at Martinmas.

From the C15th leases might contain conditions requiring open drains, crop rotation, remaining sober and keeping a kindly and lawful neighbourhood. Leases could be terminated for breaches such as theft, adultery, reset, having too many cottars, intemperate conduct, failure to rotate properly, allowing weeds to thrive and non-payment of rent or services. Such matters were usually resolved in the Birlay Court or, failing that the Baron Court and later the Court of Regality. Any tenant not the joint owner of at least one ox had to dig by hand at least seven feet square of ground per day. Stacks of corn were not permitted to be kept in the cornyard beyond December 25th and in 1452 all farmers had to have threshed all their grain by the end of May. Many of the regulations were to prevent profiteering in time of shortage.

By 1450 rents were rising again and by the 1500s the population was rising, which is probably what caused the toun splittings at Skeith, Blairock and Clune among others. During the C17th and early C18th methods of farming remained relatively unchanged, though there were improvements in productivity. One change which did happen early in Deskford was the use of lime. This took place locally from the C17th because of ample local supplies, and was responsible for the many small lime-kilns dotting the flanks of Lurg Hill in particular. As late as the 1740s creels on horses were used to transport both peat and dung as well as lime.

Farmers were suspicious of and highly critical of any suggested changes. Improvements were strongly resisted. The mantra which has been heard over the years, "We've aye done it this wye" certainly restricted progress. The four man, eight or twelve ox plough was ubiquitous from the mid C15th till the late C18th. It was effective in the rig and furrow system but could only plough about half an acre a day. The rigs were 15' to 18' wide. Ox ploughing, sowing by hand and harrowing were carried out as a single continuous activity in order to prevent birds getting the seeds. Sowing took place from mid April, with a one-handed cast which covered half the rig. This was gradually supplanted by a two-handed cast from a hopper carried on the chest. From 1750 this in turn was overtaken by the use of seed drill machines which required heavy harrowing before sowing. Rotation of rigs between tenants gave little incentive to improve, and the rig crowns were often parched while baulks between them were waterlogged.

Tenants were responsible for erecting their own houses and steadings and had the power to sub-let to crofters and cottars. Farms were largely self-sufficient. Each had a kailyard, a cornyard, a peat stack, a midden, trees on yard dykes and sometimes a broom park for thatch and winter bedding for beasts. Outfield cultivation was not introduced until the C15th, and feal (turf) dykes were used to prevent the outfield being cropped. Head dykes were very important to prevent livestock invading and destroying crops on arable land.

A 100 acre farm might have two unmarried ploughmen, a boy as a herd, a thresher and two or three maid servants, all living with the farmer's family. Married ploughmen had their own cottages and cottars were employed for particular activities during the farming year. They were sometimes hired for a year at Martinmas, and had to undertake all work at their own expense, and keep a labourer, usually a family member, to assist. In addition to having to cut corn, the cottar's wife would also have to assist in drying peat and hay, spreading manure, feeding animals, cleaning byres and stables and winnowing corn. In return he received a cottar hoose, a kailyard of about 1½ acres, enough pasture rights for 2 or 3 cows, and 15 bolls of meal a year. Widows could serve as grasswomen and get accommodation and some subsistence in exchange for feeding livestock.

Unmarried men and the farmer's sons slept in the low loft if there was one, and if not, in the stables. Female servants and the farmer's daughters slept in the kitchen, except if a strong wind made it too smoky, when they would sleep with the cattle in the byre. Cottars had to provide a woman to shear with the heuk at harvest time and carry at threshing time. This was usually about forty days per year in total and was unpaid. When she was employed for other tasks she was paid 1d per hour. Cottars' young sons could be compelled to work as herds for 6d per day or less.

Though tenants were much better off than cottars and farm servants there was a strong social cohesion which disappeared when improvement occurred. In 1750 wage earners were as well off as small tenants. The lifestyle was often harsh, but work was only hard and over long days at particular times of the year. At other times there was not a lot to do. Children of cottars left home before puberty to work for and live in the household of a local farmer. The greatest social gap was between cottars and even the poorest tenant or sub-tenant.

Cattle and sheep were put to the hill after calving and lambing, and whilst there were milked for cheese which was a large part of the rent paid in kind. Little was wasted. Slack times were used to make ropes from horsehair or from rushes from which the pith had been stripped for wicks for lamps. Much of the heavy lifting was done by women who in many ways were treated as beasts of burden. Cattle, having been tethered in the byre overwinter to staves by ropes made from peeled strands of bog fir or sprotts, were half starved by spring when they were carried out into the fields to begin grazing. This "lifting day" occasioned great celebrations.

Strong beliefs were still in existence. Farmers did not like to see trees being planted, as they felt this encouraged birds which ate the crops, threw shade which killed the grain and grew roots which spoiled the ground. In summer oxen were worked for four hours in the morning then, after a rest, for four hours in the afternoon. However in winter they only worked a total of about four or five hours. Well into the C18th winnowing was carried out using fans and a "wecht", a piece of cured sheepskin stretched over a narrow hoop.

The fermtoun was one of the main ways in which the agricultural community was organised in Deskford before about 1770, but because these were not solidly or robustly built, little or no evidence of their existence remains today. When improvement occurred some tenants lost their land, and, though they were subsequently no worse off financially as day labourers, and sometimes had better housing and diet, they were unhappy as they felt they had lost their freedom and their position in society. Those who got the new, long, improving leases became much more prosperous.

Before 1750 Scottish agriculture was much poorer and more backward than was the case in England, and English farmers were sometimes brought in to demonstrate better methods. After 1780 there was a complete turnaround and English farmers often came to learn from the superior, more efficient and more productive methods now being used in Scotland. This short period between these dates was one of enormous change.

1771

A large scale plan of the Earl of Findlater's Deskford Estate, drawn up in 1771, provides a fascinating insight into a period of great change in the parish in terms of roads, industry, location of houses etc, but particularly agriculture.

There was as yet almost no development on Aultmore or Shielmuir. Most farms had single tenants, cultivating unenclosed but consolidated blocks of land, and sub-letting one or two crofts. A few farms such as Knows, Carestown, Oathillock, Ordens, Squaredoch and Croftgloy were still worked under a multiple tenancy system, and also had some crofts. Many of the multiple tenants on these farms were portioners on several of them. Rig and furrow was still used and there were many fermtouns in locations where no evidence of their existence now remains. The proposed boundaries of new enclosed farms are superimposed in crayon, presumably waiting for the expiry of existing leases.

By this time there were already improvements near Bossyhillock, at Myretown, Marchbank and Wester Windyhills, tenanted by Alexander Morison, Mr Wood, Walter Spence and James Mellis. Tillybreedless, by this time a very old farm in decline, was tenanted by Andrew Littlejohn, with John Marquis, a crofter, also there. Longlandburn, a relatively new farm, was occupied by James Murieson, and also had a crofter, William Imlach. Goukstone was long established, was tenanted by John Bremner, and had two sub-tenanted crofts, Mid Croft and John Kerr's Croft. Part of it was called twenty penny land, one of the few references in the North East to a land measurement system common on the west coast.

Craibston was tenanted by Mr Copland who had sub-let five crofts, George Wright's, George Wilson's, Andrew Mellis's, a limer's croft and the Croft of the Tack. These crofters were also probably employed in Craibstone Lime Quarry. The tenant of Ramore is not recorded, but James Anderson had a croft here. Swellend was a small farm, tenanted by John Donald, and Carrothead was tenanted by Walter Andrew with a croft occupied by a man named Watson. Wardley existed, but the tenant is unknown, while Burnheads was a joint tenancy of James Dougal and James Milne. Many Berryhillock cottar houses were in the backlands of the present village, and the land worked by the residents extended well to the west of the present main road, the turnpike, which did not exist at that time, though the proposed route throughout the estate has been pencilled in. Charles Russel had 3 acres, James Milne 4 acres, James Dougal 2 acres and John Robertson 10 acres.

Knappycausey was tenanted by John Duffus and Squaredoch was a multiple tenancy involving George Donald 10 acres, George Shepherd 12 acres, William Chalmers 10 acres and Walter Reid 8 acres. Faichyhill was tenanted by William Reid. Kirktown was tenanted by Alexander Taylor and the area between the village and the route of the present main road was split into plots, of which the Minister had two of 3 acres each, as part of his glebe, Elspet Stables had two of one acre each, James Smith had the 6 acre Bank of Squaredoch, and William Wilson, John Morison, John Burges, William Murray and Walter Steinson had 1 acre each.

There were a few very recent, small, remote, isolated improvements near the slate quarries in the Shielburn area, tenanted by James Grant, Robert Watt and Robert Murray, and there was a regular line of, as yet unnamed, crofts along the route of what would later be the Blackhillock to Muir of Squaredoch road. These were tenanted by James Sutherland 3 acres, George Coke 3 acres, Andrew Longmore 7 acres, John Davidson 4 acres, Alexander Keir 8 acres, Donald Murray 6 acres, John Riddoch 8 acres and William Duffus 7 acres.

There were several improvements on what are now Todholes and Weston. James Huie had 9 acres, Peter Mathieson 6 acres, George Milne 9 acres, William Murray 9 acres and Alexander Huie 3 acres. There were four 6 acre proposed improvements beyond Weston, on what became Rashiehill. Alexander Wilson had a 30 acre improvement on what is now Briggs and William Bremner had an improvement of 12 acres arable plus 20 acres moor on what is now Braidbog. It is probably a descendant of his who was fined £10 at Banff Sheriff Court for what is believed to be operating an illicit still. Mosside was small and as yet uncultivated, probably because of the difficulty in draining it and channelling the Mosside Burn.

Ardoch was one of the oldest holdings in Deskford. It was tenanted by James Wilson and also had a croft sub-let to a man Browster, plus 7 acres of cottar crofts, mainly to the north of the present Cottartown track. Upper Blairock was an old established and large holding, tenanted by Thomas Duncan, who had one sub-tenanted croft occupied by James Nicol. Nether Blairock was tenanted by James Black, with one croft, occupied by George Craib. There was a small lochan on the boundary between Nether Blairock and Mousehillock (now

Burnsford), which was occupied by an unnamed tenant as was Corbie Craig, over the burn from it. Burns was tenanted by A Wilson.

Upper Clune (now Clunehill), was occupied by William Watt and had a subtenanted croft which can still be seen as the ruins of Clunehill Croft, occupied by John Scott. Mr Rainnie tenanted Mid Clune (now Clune), and James Watt tenanted Nether Clune which lay between Mid Clune and the site of the later tileworks. Milltown Farm, a large farm, lay south of the Mill, and there was also a separate 4 acre Mill Croft to the north. The tenants of neither are named.

On the east side of the Deskford Burn the farms were almost all long established. Cultain was tenanted by a Mr Murray, Leitchestown by James Reid who had one subtenanted croft, and Cairnley by Thomas Smith. Inaltry, which also had an orchard, was one of the oldest possessions in the parish. It was tenanted by James Nicol and had a croft occupied by Andrew Longmore. Cottown of Inaltry, uphill from the castle to which it doubtlessly related, was on the point of extinction and about to be enclosed.

Carestown was long established and had a dual tenancy, held by W Sim and James Morrison. Meikle Knows had a multiple tenancy held by James Reid, William Riddoch, Charles Russel, Alexander Taylor and William Watt, with a croft occupied by James Hay and also a cottar hoose. Oathillock had a multiple tenancy held by James Wilson, William Riddoch, and Alexander Hay, with three subtenanted crofts occupied by Alexander Milne, James and William Morison and Thomas Lawrence. Ordens was tenanted by Walter Morison and had three crofts, subtenanted by John Morrison, James Keir and James Cruikshank. Croftgloy had a multiple tenancy held by James Lawrence, James Watt, James Smith, James Reid and John Duffus, much of it in very small plots. Hollandbush was a dual tenancy held by John Nicol and Charles Russsel, plus a croft occupied by George Taylor. Hoggie comprised several lots occupied by labourers on the Greenhill improvements.

Both Ardicow and Little Ardicow, to the north of it, appear to have been tenanted by Alexander Murray. The improved enclosures of Greenhill were planted with oats and grass in 1771, but the oats were not successful, and the area became improved pasture. Broadrashes (later Upper Broadrashes), lay on both sides of the Portsoy road, and had a triple tenancy held by Alexander Reid, John Peterkin and John Lawrence. Little Skeith had a dual tenancy held by Andrew Black and Walter Milne with a croft occupied by Andrew Keir. Mid Skeith had a sole tenant, William Milne plus four crofts, Cottar Croft, Quaint's Croft and those occupied by E Mitchell and James Reid.

Upper Skeith was tenanted by John Reid, with Scot's Croft on the boundary with Bognageith. Backies, properly Backies of Over Skeith, was tenanted by John Wright and uphill from it was Bognageith, with an unnamed tenant and one croft, Scot's Croft. Mains of Skeith, long established and associated with the Castle of Skeith, by now ruinous but still showing turrets, garden and orchard stretching down to the Deskford Burn, was tenanted by John Peterkin. Broomhaugh, tenanted by John Smith, lay north of the ford over to the castle and on the east bank of the Deskford Burn, opposite the site of the Chapel of Our Lady of Pity.

Clochmacreich was tenanted by Alexander Thain and Nether Windyhills (now Nethertown) had a dual tenancy held by Alexander Morison and Alexander Wood and son. Over Windyhills was tenanted by James Mellis and had a subtenanted cottar hoose on the line of the present main road. Lurgbrae, originally known as Newlands of Deskford, was occupied by an unnamed tenant.

IMPROVEMENT AND POST IMPROVEMENT

The fashion for agricultural improvement hit Scotland with the energy and impetus of a tornado. One of the earliest and most successful improving landlords was the 6th Earl of Findlater and 3rd Earl of Seafield who began improvements in 1754 when he consolidated small holdings into single, larger, farms on long leases, probably of 19 years. He required tenants to divide the land with stone or turf fences, and pursue a new style of cropping. On his estate in Deskford about half the existing farms had been improved by the late 1770s, but only moderate progress had been made in taking new land under cultivation. Most tenants had nothing but contempt for the new ways and for those who supported them, but when agricultural prices rose rapidly after 1780, the increased yields and greater efficiencies on improved farms was seen to be very profitable and opposition quickly declined.

While before 1760 there had only been weak demand for tenancies, after 1780 there was very strong demand. The Earl of Findlater established the town of New Keith to accommodate tenants who had lost their land through improvements, but in Deskford many of these individuals obtained crofting tenancies on Aultmore, bringing moorland and bog under cultivation for the first time.

Improvement involved a number of processes. Waste land was reclaimed, fermtouns broken up, new steadings built and factors employed. As the advantages were seen, the Earl no longer had to force improvement on tenants, instead these tenants now took the initiative and forced the pace. Fields were enclosed, rigs broken down, strips consolidated, mosses drained, common land taken in and crops and rotations changed. The traditional style of farming was totally eradicated in a very short time, and practices which had been used for hundreds of years disappeared.

In Deskford the gentle and piecemeal changes which had taken place in the early C18th, such as consolidating rigs into large unenclosed blocks of land, and a gradual move towards individual tenancies, were submerged under a tsunami of comprehensive change. Farming changed from being an essentially subsistence, peasant cooperative system into a capitalist one. A very distinct class system developed for the first time with rigid demarcation between tenant farmer and his family and farm servant and his. As late as the 1920s, at a dance in the Parish Hall, a young farm servant finally worked up the courage to ask a local farmer's daughter for a dance, only to receive a slap in the face for his temerity in asking this of someone "better" than him.

Labourers and cottars easily evolved into farm servants, as did some crofters who did not get new crofting tenancies in Aultmore. The availability of these Aultmore crofting tenancies did however mean that the population of Deskford did not fall as much as in some places. Farm servants were wage earners with perquisites such as meal and milk in addition. In 1820 half of a farm servant's pay was in cash, up to £15 per year for a highly skilled ploughman.

A new enclosed farm supported as many people as the old shared tenancies and fermtouns, but peasant society ceased. Individual farms in Deskford operated the chaumer (chamber) system, under which farm servants were fed in the farmhouse kitchen, rather than the bothy system under which they cooked for themselves. The cottages which were provided for married farm servants after 1800 were of a better standard in Banffshire than in Moray. Some new farmhouses and steadings were built throughout the C19th, but the high point for this was the period between 1880 and 1910.

Between 1750 and 1825 there was a significant increase in the acreage of land cultivated in Scotland, and a 100% increase in yields. In the words of "Johnny Gib o' Gushetneuk", "there's been grun' made oot o' fat wasna grun' ava". One of the early developments in Deskford was on the Greenhill, which had previously been communal grazing on rough grass and moorland. Around 1770 it was enclosed, ditched and hedged, with Scotch fir and elder shelter belts planted. Fences were built which comprised a 5' high earthen wall, surfaced and capped with turf and with a 3' deep ditch on the inside. These were not steeply sloped.

A large number of labourers was employed on the Greenhill Improvements, and each was given a small plot of land at Hoggie to grow food for themselves. Unfortunately the improvement failed because of the bleak situation, the poor exposure and the wetness of the soil, all of which prevented the crops from filling and ripening. The hedges thrived but the shelter belts did not. The area was instead let for pasture, and it was not until the following century that increasing mechanisation allowed the farms of Greenhill and Kintywaird to be successful on this land.

By 1770 a few plots were let as crofts on Old More Hill (Aultmore), but the majority of crofts established in this area were later, even into the middle of the C19th. One of the last uses in Deskford for the "auld Scotch plough", the 8 or 12 ox heavy plough, was for the breaking up of virgin moorland for the first time. A few small areas of uncultivated land were still being taken in during the first decade of the C20th, when Mr Longmore, Cottartown, the father of Mrs Beveridge, later the schoolmaster's wife, drained Mossy Park by spade and then did the same with Rashy Park. At the start of the C19th improving crofts on Aultmore of 8 to 20 acres were let free for the first seven years, and thereafter for 19 years at a token rent of not more than 27/- a year. The population increased significantly as a result.

In the 1780s the Earl of Findlater was trenching and draining large areas of Deskford at his own expense. Rev Chalmers was of the opinion that "this is a substantial and advantageous mode of improvement. It not only gives bread to the industrious, and beautifies the face of the country, but perhaps proves more lucrative to the landowner than an extension of property". The famine of 1782 gave additional impetus to the accelerating enthusiasm for improvement. By 1790 the decline in the population of Deskford was attributed to the fact that there had previously been "a great number of crofters and sub-tenants in the parish who subsisted chiefly by manufacturing limestone. Since that time many of the crofts have been added to the adjacent farms and the tenants restricted to one, two or three sub-lets according to the extent of their possessions". However the amount of lime produced was reduced to prevent the "too rapid consumption of the moss".

In 1790 in Deskford, improvements were continuing to make progress. Horse hoeing had recently been introduced successfully, with 20,000 cabbages having been grown the previous year. In the parish there were 150 acres of sown grass, 30 acres of turnips, 15 acres of potatoes and 10 acres of lint. Cattle were of the small native Scotch breed, but had been considerably improved by the cultivation of green crops for fodder. There was a focus on rearing young cattle, not on fattening them. There were few sheep because improvements had reduced the area of rough pasture. Some English and some cross-bred sheep were kept on farms, but those kept on the hill were very small. The largest farm had 100 acres but most had between 30 acres and 60 acres. Rents went from 2/- per acre to £1 the acre with the average 9/-.

Despite the introduction of modern improvements, tenants were still required to perform services for the landowner, such as casting, winning and leading peat, ploughing and harrowing, making hay and harvesting corn in addition to various carriages. The Minister felt that "these services, though not exacted with rigour, are detrimental to the interest of the tenant, and consequently to that of the landowner. They often occasion interruptions to urgent domestic concerns, sometimes prevent the seasonable cultivation of the fields, and not unfrequently hazard the safety of their produce. It is astonishing that heritors, in many respects liberal minded and indulgent to their tenants, still continue this pernicious vestige of feudal slavery".

The mill dam at Backies in 2014.

By 1800 farmers had replaced the hand riddle for winnowing, rollers were used instead of hand mallets to break up clods, and leather replaced horsehair for harnesses. Threshing mills were introduced in the early C19th together with mill dams, few of which still remain, one exception being at Backies. Where there was insufficient or no water for a dam to be constructed, horse mills were built instead. These existed at Kirktown, Cultain, Little Knows, Clunehill, Burnsford, Todholes, Squaredoch, Hoggie and Lower Broadrashes. .

Tile drainage was introduced for the first time just before 1840 and was eventually laid across most of the farmland in the parish, and improved ploughs allowed even more unpromising land to be put under cultivation. By 1840 rent of arable land in Deskford was 17/6d per acre on average and agricultural labourers were paid 10d to 1/- per day in winter and 1/- to 1/3d per day in summer. Lime, bone meal and fish meal were all used extensively and guano was introduced from the middle of the century. Leases were still for 19 years but many farm buildings were poor, with little inducement to build new improved farm houses or steadings, though those which were built were of a distinctly higher standard than those they replaced. Some farmhouses were now slated, and there were few old turf houses remaining. All new build

Jimmy Kelman and his pair, perhaps at Puttingbrae, Drybridge.

was of stone and mortar. New fields had stone dykes or turf fences, many of which were replaced by wire fences later in the century.

Improvements continued to be made throughout the C19th, but these were limited in comparison to those made in the 1750s when potatoes, turnips, rye grass and clover were introduced, runrig and rundale eradicated and long leases of 2 times 19 years or life introduced. Carts were used to transport peat

Fordyce and Deskford Young Farmers' visit to Orkney, 1954

and corn instead of creels or currachs. More cattle could be overwintered which meant more dung, which meant in turn greater fertility, a virtuous circle.

The C19th brought increased mechanisation which reduced the increase in demand for labour as the cultivated acreage increased. In the 1880s land, for example that on the south side of Tillybreedless, was still being drained, and sown grass fields were being limed at 12 to 15 bolls per acre. From early in the century fallowing to make hay, and increasing use of dung were in evidence.

Hoeing neeps at Little Mosside.

Had the crofting legislation of the 1880s, as was proposed, applied to Banffshire, then Deskford might be a different place today, with a higher population and a higher number of small holdings, particularly on Aultmore. It might still have a school and a shop, and the villages of Kirktown and Berryhillock might be more populous. It might even have been considering a community buy-out of the land.

The system continued, with minor changes, well into the C20th, with what would be seen today as very heavy physical labour. For example growing turnips in the 1930s involved the use of the single furrow plough, then the grubber, then the harrow. After this, weeds, mainly couch grass, knot grass and string grass were pulled to be burnt, followed by drills being put up and filled with dung, carted from the midden and loaded by graip. Then the drills were split and the dung covered, followed by sowing. As the turnips developed, a major task was singling, usually done by male farm workers, but sometimes women were brought in for this and paid 5/- a day. Finally there was lifting and storage though sometimes the crop was left in the field.

One of the few remaining farming tenancies . Father and son, Jimmy and Jack Stewart, Meikle and Little Knows.

A major change, similar in impact to that of improvement, took place about 1960. Many farms were given up as they were too small to support a family, and government grants were available to both landlord and tenant for this purpose. By the 1950s large farms in Deskford no longer used horses. Geordie

Smith, Easter Darbreich, remembered buying Greens of Blairock's horses when they changed to tractors, and using them into the 1960s. He was one of the last to use horses.

As combine harvesters were introduced, barley replaced oats as the main cereal crop, and we arrived at the situation which exists today, of a very few, very large, farming enterprises, a barley monoculture in enormous fields, interrupted by an occasional small field of potatoes or turnips and, by 2013, the one remaining "park o' corn" at Burnheads. The majority of the new farmhouses of 1880 to 1910 have been sold or are rented, and the steadings are left unused, slowly deteriorating. Most of the crofts have been demolished.

How very different it is from the early C19th years of expansion. An 1824 plan shows two existing areas of improvements on Aultmore, with proposals for a third area to infill the land between them. The first area covers Upper and Lower Bogrotten, Hillhead, Badenhannen, Backburn, Kemp's Croft, Sleepy Green, Briggs, Greens of Blairock, Rashiehill and Braidbog. The second area included Todholes, Wat's Rhives and Weston, together with additional improved land for Craibstone, Raemore, Carrothead, Swailend and Burnheads. The third area, waiting to go, would be filled with the smallest, poorest crofts, stretching from Bogetra, Blackhillock and Braehead in the south to Craigie Croft and Gateside in the north. This group of the poorest crofts survived barely 100 years, but the positive, "can do", attitude of the C19th was reflected in the vibrant society that Deskford became then.

WAGES, PRICES AND COMMERCIAL TRANSACTIONS

Rents for farms changed over the years from being largely in kind, till by the 1800s they were all in money. By 1775 small farms in Deskford were rented for 20/- to 100/- per year. In 1880 most rents were under £100 per annum, with very few over £200, and by 1920 the rent for a good farm was about £1 per acre, with farms higher up the hillside about 15/- per acre. Crofts leased for 10/- per acre. By 1990 farms were rented for around £35 per acre. Backburn in

Shielmuir was rented to John Simpson for £22 in 1904, by 1918 George Taylor was paying £25 and by 1928 William Donald McKay was paying £32. This was reduced to £27 in the early 1940s, but by 1953, when it was included with Rosebank, the rent for William Fordyce was £100.

Wages also changed, from being largely or all in kind in distant times, to being paid in money for a six month or yearly engagement, to an hourly rate in the 1930s. In 1735 ploughmen earned 35/- per year plus a pair of shoes, coarse linen "harn" for a shirt and one or two yards of plaiding. Female farm servants got 13/4d in money plus a pair of shoes and an apron. By 1760 men earned £3, women £1 and married ploughmen £7, all per annum and half in money, half in kind. If engaged for the six or seven weeks of the harvest, a man received £1:10/- and a woman £1. A day labourer got 10d per day plus victuals for cutting peat, cutting hay or harvest work and 6d or 7d plus victuals in winter. In 1830 a casual female labourer earned 7½d per day. For comparison sugar at this time cost 8½d per pound and tea 6d per ounce. Turnip hoeing was the only piece-work done, at 12/- to 15/- per acre. By the 1950s the average farm worker's wage was £7 per week plus overtime.

In the mid C19th the cottar first horseman earned £22 to £26 per annum plus perquisites. The chaumer-living second horseman got £16 per half year and the orraman £11 per half year. By 1930 a married horseman's fee was £1 per week plus perquisites, and wage controls introduced in World War II guaranteed £2:8/- per week. In the 1930s, a cottar wife, milking twice a day, seven days a week, could add 5/- to her ploughman husband's weekly wage.

Records were kept at Kirktown Farm over an extended period. In 1845, for a six month engagement, the first horseman received £7:10/-, the second horseman £3:10/-, the cattleman £2:5/-, the young lad £1:5/-, the housekeeper £2:7:6d and the servant girl £1:5/-. By 1900 the first horseman was getting £15, the second horseman £12:5/-, the cattleman £12, the young lad £7 and the servant girl £6:10/-. In 1931 the first horseman got £21, the second horseman £18, the cattleman £15 and the servant girl £10. By the 1950s the ploughmen were getting £10 per week, an enormous increase over the 1931 pay rates.

Markets and fairs, together with cadgers, chapmen and pedlars, were responsible for much of the commerce which took place. The Hallow Fair in Fordyce, which took place on the last Wednesday in October, was a feeing fair at which cattle and sheep were also sold, while the fair at Ordiquhill was famous for horses. The Peter Fair at Rathven was always well attended from Deskford. By the early C19th the main Feeing Mart was at Keith in May.

Prices in the C18th were as follows

	1748			1798		
ITEM	£	s	d	£	s	d
1 draught ox	1	13	4	15-25	0	0
20 small sheep	4	0	0	12	0	0
1lb of beef or mutton			1-1½			5½-6
1 hen and a dozen eggs			4			-
1 dozen eggs			1			4-6
1 hen			0		1	0-3
A pair of geese		2	0		5	6
A pair of turkeys		3	0		7	0
A pair of pigeons			5½			6
14 haddocks			1½		1	6
1 bottle of claret		1	0		6	0

In 1750 draft horses cost £10-£12 and in 1784 they were £18-£20, and a good young horse for the cart cost £8-£9.

Fat bullocks realised £20 in 1850 and this remained roughly the same to the 1930s. By 1960 it had risen to £65 and by 1990 it was as much as £700. Grain prices in the 1930s were £5 per ton for oats and £7 for barley. By the 1960s it was £15 for oats and £20 for barley, and by the 1990s it was £110 for oats and £115 for barley. Farmers' earnings were further increased as yields per acre increased from 1 ton per acre in 1960 to around 2 tons in 1990. A binder in 1920 cost £20 to £25 in contrast to the hundreds of thousands of pounds for a combine harvester in the 1990s.

Farm workers had their own expenses, and in the 1920s a new pair of farming boots of "excellent indestructibility", purchased from Berryhillock or Kirktown, cost £2. After World War II most farms kept hens with the eggs being sold to the egg-packing station at Banff or to Robertson's of Fordyce.

When farms changed tenants a precise and detailed valuation was carried out, as with this one from Ordens in 1936.

ITEM	£	s	d
GRASS			
1st grass @ 50/- per acre	34	9	8
2nd grass @ 40/- per acre	29	16	9
3rd grass @ 30/- per acre	25	17	11
FALLOW			
Reccl. and labour @ 38/9d per acre	26	13	0
DUNG			
303.74 cubic yards @ 5/- per cubic yard	75	18	8
Green dung in field	2	5	0
SUNDRIES			
Cattle	1	7	0
Water troughs		7	6
All grates in the house	5	0	0
Threshing mill	30	0	0
FENCING			
2 hives @ 18/- per 100 yards	1	10	0
5 hives @ 15/- per 100 yards	25	3	1
4 hives @ 12/- per 100 yards	4	2	8
3 hives @ 9/- per 100 yards	1	2	6
2 hives @ 5/- per 100 yards		14	10
	1	4	0
Sub-Total:	263	12	7
Less Grass:	88	4	4
TOTAL:	175	8	3

When a farmer died a roup was usually held of his possessions, which could be varied in the extreme. On the death of Alexander Wood, Mosside, a roup was held on May 9th 1894, at which the following were for sale. 10 one year old cattle, 7 two year old cattle (in good condition), 5 excellent dairy cows, 4 calves, 1 brown heavy mare, 1 brown heavy horse, 2 mares, 3 box carts, single and double ploughs, 3 sets of harrows, 1 set of link harrows, 2 drill harrows, 1 iron grubber, 1 stone roller, 1 turnip sowing machine, yokes and swingle trees, 1 turnip cutter, 1 grindstone, 1 box, barrows, 1 Victory reaper with rake, 1 horse rake, 1 dog cart, 1 barn fan, bushel measures, corn sacks, beams and weights, scythes, spades, shovels, graips, forks, hoes and picks, wire fencing posts, cart and plough harness etc and the usual complement of tools about a farm. Also a few kitchen utensils.

Similarly at the roup at Swailend in 1905 for the late John Reid, a four year old horse made £37:10/-, an eight year old mare £27:10/-, a seven year old chestnut pony £17:10/-, 5 dairy cattle, calved and to calve £15 - £19:15/-, a six year old cow with two calves at foot £30:2:6d, 4 fat bullocks, two year old £10 - £22:15/-, 6 six quarter old bullocks £14 - £16:5/- and 6 yearlings, £8:10/- - £14:10/-.

In March 1921, a displenish sale was held at Gateside, occupied by Mrs Wood, who was giving up the tenancy, to be succeeded by Mr William Pirie Jr, Bogside. Good prices were realised, calving cows to £50:10/-, yearlings to £19, poultry from 1/9d to 4/9d, turnips 4/- per load and straw about 14/- per quarter.

TOOLS AND MACHINERY

Throughout the millennia, as technology advanced, so did its application to farming. Sometimes these advances were eagerly adopted and sometimes they were resisted. Though the pace of mechanisation increased at the time of improvement, there had been many advances before then.

In the C14th weeding was done with tongs, before these were replaced by hoes. From the 1720s winnowing fans or "fanners" were introduced into Scotland from Holland and spread fairly quickly as they made winnowing a less arduous task. In 1750 iron-shod wooden spades called "pyke spades" were used for casting feals and divots and also for digging stones. Peat spades were also iron-shod wooden tools, but they had an additional iron tusk. The "flauchter spade" was used for "tirring" the peat banks. Ploughs and harrows were wooden and ropes were made from horsehair, broom roots or heather.

By 1812 the old Scots ploughs pulled by oxen were only used for breaking up moor and rough land. They had been replaced for ordinary ploughing first by

Rotherham ploughs then by Small's ploughs, which had cast iron mouldboards and which cost £3 to £4. The Brake Harrow was used on rough ground, on new improvements, but also on cultivated ground. It cost between £3 and £6. A roller of granite or of "peasy whin", about five feet long and 8" to 14" in diameter, was now necessary on every farm because of the introduction of the scythe for harvesting, which required flatter fields. It cost £1:10/- to £3. New one-horse carts could carry twice as much as the old two-horse carts, as the road surfaces became much better. These new carts were five feet long and three-and-a-half feet wide, with an axle tree of iron and wheels of 4' to 4'6" in diameter. They cost £12 - £14. Turnip drills for smaller farms cost £1:6/-

Threshing machines were introduced in the 1790s and became common. They required a mill dam, lade and mill wheel, but they were very popular as threshing with a flail was a backbreaking task. By 1830 eight farms in Deskford had water-driven threshing mills. Those which had no suitable water supply built horse mills.

The reaper, and then, from about 1890, the binder, were inventions which dramatically changed farming when they were introduced. They were much more effective in fields in which tile drains had been laid, and most farms in Deskford laid these from the late 1830s when Tochieneal Tile Works opened. The box cart was the standard harvest cart in Deskford.

Screw-operated cheese presses, which can still be seen at Braidbog and Clune, were introduced in the first half of the C19th. Before them, all that was used was stone weights on a wooden plank. Hen houses were only introduced about 1900. Prior to that hens just roosted on the joists in the byre, and farmers often considered them as

Old cheese press against a gable of the ruin of the previous farmhouse at Braidbog.

Dodo Stewart and young friend at Braehead.

a nuisance.

The first tractor in Deskford is believed to have been an International, bought by Jimmy Simpson, Craibstone. By the mid 1930s there were only three, the others owned by George Taylor from Mains of Skeith, and also by McConnachie, Ardoch. Grass sickness in horses in 1938 caused more tractors to be purchased and during World War II there was a government scheme to help farmers buy them. Their numbers increased rapidly and the last horses in Deskford were used in the 1960s. The first combine harvester in the area was seen at Tochieneal in 1952, though binders did not finally go out of use till the mid 1960s. In the first half of the C20th, Sandy Lamb from Fordyce had two steam mills which were used in Deskford.

Throughout the past 200 years, individual farmers have sought to innovate and become more efficient. One of these was Walter Keir in Ordens, who in 1909 was reported as having made significant improvements on the farm since he became tenant. His most recent improvement was the introduction of a threshing machine of 8 to 10 quarters per hour capacity, driven by a 12" bucket water wheel. The mill was erected by Mr Brown, Newmill.

TRANSPORT

Till the later C18th, horses with panniers or currachs were used as pack animals. Currachs were creels of wickerwork hung from the crook saddle. For greater distances packets were used, made of wooden rungs, with a bend for holding the "birn". These could be used for transporting kegs of whisky or purchases from Cullen. Currachs had to be balanced to keep their position, so had to be filled simultaneously on each side. They were used for carrying peat in from the moss, or dung out to the fields, while long sacks over the horse's back carried grain to the mill.

Wooden sleds were also used, and in snowy weather they were used well into the C20th. For example, when the farmer's wife at Burnheads died in the early years of World War II, her body, because of snowdrifts, could not be got down to the undertakers in Berryhillock. Eventually the old black mare was harnessed to the sledge and she was got down in this way. Sleds had a simple harness. In the old days there was no collar, just a "breacham" of straw or sprotts.

When wooden carts pulled by horses were introduced, they were tiny by today's standards, holding the equivalent of four or five wheelbarrows, but this was still more efficient about the farm than the currachs had been.

PLOUGHING

Until the late C18th cottars and crofters with the least land usually used spades to till it. Larger crofters and farmers used the eight- or twelve-ox plough. There was great reluctance to change to the lighter, quicker and more efficient two-horse plough, because oxen gave more dung, were cheaper to feed and could be sold on easily when their working life was over. If a small farm only had one horse it was sometimes harnessed with an ox on the lighter plough, a practice which lasted into the C20th locally.

The ox plough, the "old Scotch plough", with its mould board, iron coulter and sock made locally in one day for 10/-, was pulled by oxen, was cumbersome and dictated the shallow S shape of the rigs. The oxen were driven by the gaad man (goad man), who prodded the beasts to keep them to task. There was also in the team a lead man, a ploughman, a fourth man and a boy to whistle to keep the oxen happy. The oxen were yoked to the plough by the soun (common rope), and the cheek lone (bridle) was attached to the yoke by the rack baan.

The tenant with two oxen was the lowest of the rent-paying class. He joined with three or five others to get a full team for a plough. Each position in the ox team had a particular name. On a twelve-ox plough the lead pair were the wyner on the right and the on-wyner on the left, followed by the steer-draught and on-steer-draught, the fore-frock and on-fore-frock, the mid-yoke and on-mid-yoke, the hin'-frock and on-hin-frock, and finally, nearest the plough, the fit-yoke and the on-fit-yoke. To turn oxen to the hamp (right) the gaad man put his gaad in front of the wyner's nose, and to turn wyre (left) he put it below the on wyner's tail.

Alexander Humphrey, writing from Keith as a visitor in the 1790s, commented that a team of eight or ten oxen pulling the clumsy Scotch plough were still often to be seen when two or four horses, pulling a modern light plough could do the same work in a much shorter time. In Grange, he stated, one quarter of the 167 ploughs were still of the old type.

As improvement progressed, so the classic image of the skilled horseman and his pair became universal. He had the highest status amongst farm servants, and this system of ploughing remained largely unchanged from about 1800 to about 1950 or 1960, when tractors took over. This change was made, often reluctantly, for the sake of efficiency, and despite much affection for the horses. In the 50 years since, the small tractors have themselves given way to today's monsters which plough multi furrows in a single pass.

In Victorian times ploughing usually started in February or March, governed by the weather, but it was not uncommon to plough in lying snow. There was also a sense of community connected to ploughing and it was always done without being asked for those in need, such as those with small crofts, widows and the infirm. This practice persists to the present day.

MILLING

For as long as cereals have been cultivated, some method of grinding the grain was required. In an area like Deskford querns were used from at least as far

Members of the Cruickshank family at Berryhillock Mill around 1920. (L to R) John Stephen (miller), Robert Cruickshank, Mary Ann Topp, Unknown, Bell, Margaret and Mrs Topp, nee Cruickshank.

back as the early Iron Age. Initially the less efficient saddle querns were used, and then the more efficient rotary ones took their place. These were used, occasionally into the C20th, to avoid using the Estate mill. From Pictish times ungeared small horizontal mills were used. These were small buildings which had a small capacity and were replaced by small vertical mills from the C12th. Until the C18th there were many of these small mills in Deskford, and it was only at this time that mills capable of grinding barley were introduced, such as the large ones at Miltown and Berryhillock which were built by the landowner to increase profit. Till then bere was bruised by using knocking stones, till the "knockit bere" was fit for making broth. All mills were undershot or horizontal until the C19th.

In the late C18th, when improvements in farming were in full flow, the compulsion on tenants to have their corn ground at either Berryhillock Mill or Milton Mills was fully enforced. For this service the tenant paid the miller one twelfth of what was produced. Tenants or their servants were also obliged to assist the miller in milling and to provide labour to repair the fabric of the mill and to keep drains and water courses connected with the mill in good order. Each tenant was also required to erect a kiln on his farm in order to dry corn. Both the system and the miller were unpopular. Initially the millstones used were of Pennan sandstone, but in the C19th this changed to French burr.

Into the C20th, both Milton and Berryhillock mills had crofts attached to them together with the associated steadings. The land of Berryhillock Mill Croft lay between new St John's Church and the manse, plus two fields between Kirktown village and the main road. The Milton Mill Croft was adjacent to the

Milton Mills showing one of its two mill dams.

mill, between it and Clune, but there had also been, in the C18th, a much larger Mill Farm on the south side of the mill. The mills dried oats and milled them into meal, most of which was taken home for domestic use, though latterly some farmers sold it from a meal cart round Cullen. With the increased cultivation of barley after World War II, the mills also dried this for farmers, before farmers got their own driers. This was necessary for the grain to be acceptable to the distillers for malting, for which the best prices were obtained. Milton Mill closed in the 1950s and Berryhillock Mill around 1965.

CROFTING

Before the late C18th each crofter had a small cottage or hut, a kailyard, a milk cow, a small amount of fertile land on the infield and the right to graze a few animals on the hill. Rent was paid in the form of labour to the tenant farmer on whose land the croft lay. Many crofters were also shoemakers, tailors or weavers. The croft of Wester Blairock is known to the present day as "Wyvers" as it was occupied by a family of weavers in the C19th. Amongst the other skills undertaken by crofters were tanning, rendering tallow and making candles. While crofters' wives spun and dyed wool it was later left to professional weavers to make it into cloth.

By 1900 crofters would help each other with many of the routines such as harvesting or tattie-picking. Only a few had a reaper, while others might borrow one or just use the scythe. Though the steam mill had been used on larger farms for some considerable time, it was not until about 1900 that it replaced handmills on crofts.

FORESTRY

After the last Ice Age there was a natural afforestation of Deskford with birch, oak, elm, hazel and elder, but from Neolithc times onwards this was gradually cleared for farming, building, fuel and other purposes. By the middle of the last millennium the area was largely treeless, with the only exceptions being the banks of some of the tributary burns and the orchards attached to the Tower of Deskford and the Castles of Inaltry and Skeith. All these orchards dated to about 1500, when it became fashionable for landowners to plant them.

So valuable were trees that tenants were required to plant them round their yard dykes, and in 1752, tenants, at the end of their lease, were entitled to every third tree or its value in money. New specimen trees were introduced to Scotland in the late C17th and early C18th, such as the lime in 1664, the silver fir in 1682, the maple and walnut in 1690, the laburnum in 1704 and the larch in 1727. Beeches and chestnuts were very rare and all of the above mentioned were considered exotic.

All of this changed dramatically in the mid C18th. The Earl of Findlater, in addition to being an innovatory agricultural improver, was also a keen afforester. By 1752 he had planted 32 million trees. Hedges were also planted round many of the newly enclosed fields during the second half of the C18th. The 7th Earl of Seafield also planted 60 million trees between 1853 and 1881. Between these periods of intense activity the Earl of Findlater made a successful trial of larix fir for shelter around 1780. In 1830, 250 acres of the Cotton Hill was enclosed and planted, which involved enclosure by six miles of dykes and ditches and the laying of nineteen miles of drains. In 1840 the Green Hill was planted with larch and common fir. During the second half of the C19th there was an average of 800-850 acres of plantations in Deskford.

Many of the plantations in Deskford were felled during the two World Wars, and during World War II members of the Women's Timber Corps, or Lumber Jills, worked on Green Hill and were accommodated at Greenhill and Oathillock farms. In 1941 it had been recorded that many of the largest strands of high forest in Banffshire had been in Deskford and Fordyce. The violent gale of 1953 destroyed many more. In clearing up after the gale many of the remaining woods were felled, all of which changed the appearance of the valley significantly. However replanting was already under way by 1955. Cotton Hill was planted in 1960, Green Hill in 1969, Smiddy Wood in 1962, Longwood in 1962 and part of Mid Skeith/ Little Skeith/Upper Broadrashes about 1965.

From 1923 very heavy timber of outstanding quality had been felled on Bin Hill by George Auld and Son, who installed a sawmill at Braidbog which gave employment to 20 men. In 1929 it was moved to Burnlevnit on the edge of the Hill of Maud, and a year later to Woodside. The whole area round the Bin Hill was felled and replanted, and to help with this George Auld built a narrow gauge railway all the way along the High Glen. Bogies were pulled by horse to a point directly below the sawmill, and from there were hauled by a steel hawser up the slope to the sawmill, a steam engine producing the power. The trees were all cut by hand-operated crosscut saws, and the sawn timber hauled to Aberdeen by a Sentinel steam lorry with solid rubber tyres.

A number of individual specimen trees were famous in Deskford. In the churchyard stood an ash tree called St John's Tree, which in 1790 had a circumference of over 24 feet. There was also another ash called Young St John's which had a circumference of over 12 feet. In addition there was a holly which was thought to be perhaps the largest in Scotland, with a circumference of over 8 feet. Young St John's was cut down around 1820 and only a small remnant of St John's remained by 1840. By this time the holly had rotted and was almost dead.

Also by this time the fruit trees in all three orchards had disappeared, with that at Skeith becoming a meadow and that beneath the Tower of Deskford having been replanted, mainly with young ash trees. There were also a holly of over 5 feet in circumference and a hawthorn of over 4 feet in circumference. Further down the Deskford Burn was a hawthorn of over 8 feet in circumference. On Clune Hill what was believed to be the original 1698 gallows was the only beech tree on the entire hill.

INDUSTRY

Throughout most of Deskford's agricultural past, individual farmers, crofters and cottars undertook most of the necessary related ancillary activities themselves, from building their houses to

"Dapple" in the shafts of the Cottarton smiddy gig.

spinning to making clothes and footwear, ropes and harnesses. The list is almost endless and it is difficult to be precise about when specialist activities such as weaving and iron working became focussed on a few members of the community.

Cottartown smiddy with Upper Blairock on the skyline.

Similarly it is difficult to differentiate between these specialist activities as part of a peasant community and as part of the capitalist system which later developed. One specialist occupation which was very important was that of the blacksmith.

At its peak in the C19th it is said that the Deskford Burn supported thirteen different industrial concerns over a length of three miles. Certainly the main

Posed photograph at Cottartown smiddy around 1900

activities such as the Craibstone Lime Works, the two meal mills, the Bleachfield and the Tochieneal Tile and Brick Works all relied on the power of the Deskford Burn, though not all activities did. Recently Pam and John Robertson found industrial slag near the Flake Burn below Ordens.

Quarrying is located where the raw material is found and usually as near as possible to where the product is to be used. Limestone has been quarried and processed in Deskford since at least the early C17th when its value in improving agricultural yields was first recognised. This was a big advantage and Deskford was well ahead of most of the country in using lime, because of the excellent local supplies.

Woodend smiddy, just south of Berryhillock.

By far the largest quarry was that at Craibstone, which continued operating till the 1950s and which was considered to produce a superior quality of lime. When limestone was first quarried however there were many small quarries in Deskford, mainly on the western flanks of Lurg Hill, for example between Mid Skeith and Upper Skeith, at the Elbow Doups and on Lurgbrae. A limestone road is shown on a C18th plan going between the Elbow Doups and Binnuchars (Badenyouchars) in Bogmuchals, via the Lying Horse.

Before local farmers started buying processed lime from

Craibstone limestone quarry in 2014.

139

Craibstone, they produced lime for their own use in the many limekilns which were scattered round the parish. Examples included those at the roadside above Nether Blairock, on the bank of the Whitestripe Burn south of Ardicow, where the Meikle Knows track turns 90 degrees to go up to the farm, in the field below the Meikle Knows track where it leaves the public road, where the burn crosses the public road between Weston and Greens of Blairock, where the upper track at Todholes joins the public road, on the roadside just north of Hoggie, immediately behind Greenhill, halfway down the Mid Skeith brae and half-way between Swailend and Carrothead. Little or no physical evidence of any of these remains.

Gelignite house at Craibstone, mid 1990s.

Craibstone was a major industrial concern with, in the 1930s, ten or twelve full-time employees and up to thirty seasonal ones. For much of its existence it was operated by the inter-linked Shepherd and Simpson families. It operated for around 300 years, and its product was used for mortar, plaster, whitewash and fertilizer. The main product was quicklime or slaked lime, sold in the C20th in 1cwt bags. The stone is of the Sandend Group of the dalriadan limestone series which is a high calcium non-hydraulic lime which contains significant calcite (pure calcium carbonate). Initially it was quarried using wooden wedges, and then by explosives, firstly black powder then gelignite.

The quarry comprised a large quarry hole, one earth dam and one stone dam, crushers, a gelignite house which was also used as a blast shelter, an overshot wheel and gearing, three kilns, a lade and tail race, a grinder and silo shed and a hydrator. All three kilns were bank kilns, the first two being built between 1870 and 1902, and the third, larger one, around 1920. Initially peat from

Aultmore was used, but once the railway arrived in the 1880s the limeworks changed to coal. Coal was also brought in on occasion in 600-ton boatloads through Cullen harbour. The quarry's own lorry collected the coal from Tochieneal Station and dumped it on the public road opposite Craibstone Cottages from where it was barrowed down a no-longer-existent track to the quarry. Initially the lorry was horse-drawn, and the additional arm of the crossroads at Craibstone Farm had been built by the quarry to make it easier for the horses to pull the loads of lime up onto the main road. By the 1930s the quarry lorry was a Foden, RSX117, which also delivered slaked lime locally.

Access to the quarry was by a track across a ford from the old main road at Three Burns Meeting, near the foot of the Upper Skeith track. The wheel sat on cast iron bearings, which were stolen in 2012, and was probably around 15' in diameter. There was a set of wheels between the wheel shaft and the off take shaft to speed up the drive to the crusher, at a ratio of probably 3:1 or 5:1, and in all probability there was also an air compressor driven by the wheel. An accident in which the air compressor failed probably hastened the closure of the Limeworks. In the accident the load was taken off the wheel which speeded up and burst apart. After this a much more expensive mobile power unit had to be used.

The lime used was so pure that Mr Shepherd, the proprietor around 1900, demonstrated this to prospective customers by mixing some in a bucket, using it to whitewash a wall and then showing that there was no residue left in the bucket. In 1933 James Simpson was paying rent of 6/- per kiln full of lime burned in the small kilns and £1 per kiln full in the large one. When the kilns were fired by peat, sufferers from asthma and croup came from far and near to inhale the fumes which were thought to cure the illnesses.

Burnside Cottage, beside Backies Croft, halfway between the quarry and Backies Farm, was part of the lease. In 1858 this group comprised four small buildings including a shop which persisted well into the C20th and served local farms as well as workers at the Limeworks.

The Craibstone Limeworks closed down during World War II, allegedly, though not convincingly, because the glow from the kilns might have been seen by enemy aircraft. The final lease terminated in 1947, by which time the Limeworks was again operational, and the lease was extended into the 1950s, when it finally ceased operation. Much of the information above is taken from a major survey of Craibstone Limeworks which was undertaken in the 1990s.

Limestone was not the only mineral quarried. For many years coarse "slates"

Slate quarry waste near Slatehaugh in Sheilmuir.

were obtained from quarries which lay on the banks of the Darbreich Burn. These existed between Briggs and the Easter Darbreich track, on the steep slope between the burn and the public road, from where 500 slates were used to reroof the tollbooth in Cullen in 1719. There were also quarries between Burnside of Aultmore and the burn. However the most extensive of the quarries lay in Shielmuir, near the crofts of Slatehaugh and Slateheuch, where spoil heaps can still be seen immediately to the north of the public road.

The "slate" was of very poor quality and quarrying ceased when better quality slate from Ballachulish and later Wales became available through the expansion of the railway system.

A number of sand quarries existed in the area, for example at Cultain, and many gravel pits were opened for the purpose of road surfacing. When the turnpike road was being built in the early C19th, quarries for road metal were opened at Windyhills, Clochmacreich, Upper Tillybreedless, Nether

Tillybreedless, Ramore and Mosside. Contractors were paid to fill and level them when the road was completed. The 1867 map shows gravel pits above Clochmacreich, immediately south of the burn at Langlanburn, adjacent to the steading at Upper Blairock, beside the public road just west of the Upper Blairock track, on the opposite side of the main road at Clune, on either side of the road going from Todholes to Lornachburn near Todholes, and on the opposite side of the public road at Aultmore Lodge. Of these, the one beside the public road near Upper Blairock can still be seen clearly.

Immediately north of the parish boundary, on the east side of the Deskford Burn, Towie Mill had been in operation since 1668. Further upstream Milton Mills was in operation before 1745, and was, in the early C20th, operated by the McLean family. It now houses a motor-engineering business run by Duncan McLean. The mill had two dams, one of which was filled by a long lade from the Deskford burn and the other, higher one, from the Ha' Burn. Milton Mills ceased to exist as a mill in the 1950s.

The other major mill in the parish was Berryhillock Mill, which was in operation before 1800, and was operated for many years by the Cruikshank family, one of whom was also Inspector of the Poor. In the mid C19th, in addition to milling oats, it also had a barley mill attached. Like Milton Mills it also had two dams, a large one opposite Woodend Smiddy and a smaller one immediately above the mill. The mill had a wind vane in the figure of a horse on top of its pagoda-like louvred roof. There was also a crane to move the heavy millstones,

The range of buildings built as a bleachworks at Bleachfield in 1750, viewed across the site of the former bleaching grounds, canals and drying field.

initially of Pennan sandstone then of French burr, into position. Berryhillock Mill closed in 1965.

The industry which brought greatest prosperity to Deskford, albeit for a relatively short time, was the Bleachfield and Lintmill. In 1724 Lord Deskford commissioned an Irish Quaker called John Christie to lay down a new bleachfield near the Deskford Burn. It began operation in 1752, and at its peak around 1790 employed eighteen weavers. The site included 4½ acres of bleaching grounds, canals and housing, and a 5½ acre drying field. Buildings included a rubbing mill, boilers and bucking and sour basins, all powered by a horizontal water wheel. A dam on the Deskford Burn, just below Inaltrie, drove a wheel to power the mill machinery, and water was also fed along canals to wash the cloth to remove the alkalis and acids used in bleaching. However complaints were received that the lime and pigeon dung used for bleaching damaged the cloth. If drought caused the Deskford Burn to provide insufficient water, provision was made for the machinery to be powered by horses.

The mill dam was in existence and the water wheel visible into the C20th. Two exit ditches from it could still be seen, one passing down the east side and round the back of the mill buildings and the other along the front of them. The associated lint mill existed close to the village named after it, in the grounds of the first two modern houses in Ellyside. At this point the burn flows under the road in two channels, the southern one of which has been artificially cut, and which was used to power either an undershot wheel or a horizontal one.

At its busiest, 1,500 pieces of cloth and 1,700 spindles of thread, each of 1,400 yards length were produced annually, and every family in Deskford contributed. In 1795 the Minister of Cullen stated that the earnings of the considerable number of women employed had been "of great advantage to themselves, and beneficial to the public". Women who became too old to work as household or farm servants could earn 4d or 6d per day from spinning, which was enough to support themselves. Weekly earnings from yarn spinning in the 1780s ranged from 1/8d to 2/- at a time when crofts rented for as little as 20/- per year. Many young and old people found employment of some sort related to the Bleachfield, and as a result, the second half of the C18th was a very prosperous time in this area, as evidenced by the people's "comfortable mode of living and their dress".

However by 1790 the industry was already in decline because of cheap imports from Ireland and greater use of cotton. By 1836, when the industry ceased, spinners were only making ½d to 2d per day. The bleaching ground and drying field were ploughed back in as farmland and operated as a croft named The Field, and the buildings became a woollen and carding mill, operated in the 1880s by William Grant. This had ceased to operate by 1900. Recently the buildings have been renovated and are a private residence and holiday cottage.

To the north of Deskford, just outside the parish, Tochieneal Brick and Tileworks was established in 1837 by Mr Wilson, the Seafield Estate Factor, on the site of what had been Smithstown Farm. In 1840 it was one of only ten in Scotland. Clay was brought in from the adjoining beds by shelt-powered light bogey railway, and the works were powered by a horizontal steam engine. The main items produced were field drains of diameters 2", 4", 6" and 9", which were used extensively in Deskford, improving the yield on many farms. In addition there were also produced, in smaller quantities, roof tiles, bricks and flowerpots. At its peak there was a workforce of about 30, but the Tileworks closed down shortly after World War II. In 1832 the same Mr Wilson had also established a distillery at Tochieneal, a few buildings of which can still be seen, but after a disagreement with the Seafield family he transferred the distillery to Inchgower near Buckie in the 1870s. This event is commemorated in a bothy ballad entitled "Tochieneal".

Of all of the crafts which were carried out over the past millennium by farmers, crofters, cottars and their families, spinning was the most common, carried out by every family and producing a wide range of materials from webs of plaid to hair cloth from horses' hair for malt bags to fine cloth for mutches and cambric napkins. Shirting, sheeting, diapers and gravecloth were also produced. Spinning wheels were still to be found in most houses in the 1890s, but by this time most of them were unused. Over the centuries the wheel had evolved from the "muckle wheel" to the "little wheel", the latter driven via a crank by the foot. There was always at least one wheelwright in Deskford making these wheels.

Cloth spun at home was initially also woven at home on vertical looms, however this task was gradually taken over by specialist local weavers, after which a local tailor would come to each house and make items for the household. Most dyed items were in a variety of shades of brown, however woad produced indigo, crottle lichen russet, heather grey/green, blaeberry purple, bedstraw red and gorse or weld (dyer's rocket) yellow. In addition to spinning, women also knitted stockings and sold them to merchants from as far away as Aberdeen. Men produced lathe-turned wooden bowls, ladles and troughs, and also did some leatherwork and a very limited amount of iron work. During quiet times in the farming year there would be production of furniture, tools, ropes etc.

During the C19th, in parallel with the rapid advances in farming, there was also a major increase in the number of specialist trades carried out in the parish, in addition to the many cottars who hired their labour to Seafield Estate as masons, thatchers, builders, carters, quarriers and dykers etc. In 1799 Deskford had 18 weavers, 8 shoemakers, 4 tailors, 3 masons and 2 each of blacksmiths, wrights (carpenters), wheelwrights, cartwrights and ploughwrights. During the 1830s a lot of alder was cut down and made into herring barrel staves.

The 1841 census revealed 6 wrights, 6 tailors, 11 shoemakers, 1 slater, 5 millers, 4 masons, 1 millwright, 2 carpenters, 1 gardener, 1 midwife, 3 blacksmiths and 1 woollen manufacturer. In addition, in the 1851 census there were 1 seamstress, 1 cattle driver and 1 dressmaker. By 1861 there were also 1 stocking weaver, 1 cartwright, several spinners and weavers and 1 baker. In 1880 a business directory listed 3 blacksmiths in Deskford, James Brander, William Duncan and Robert Sanderson, 2 carpenters, joiners and wrights, Alexander McHattie and John Reid, and 2 millers, Robert and William Steven. By 1901, diversification had also produced 1 hind, 1 builder, 1 contractor, 1 lime quarryman, 1 traction engine driver, 1 former marine engineer and 1 salmon fisher.

Throughout the C20th a large number of, mostly small, enterprises have operated in Deskford. Certainly the largest was Versatile Windows, a double-glazing and conservatory business started in 1975 by two joiners, Colin Miller and Bill Paterson, which grew rapidly till it had around 70 employees and a turnover of millions. It had premises in the old Parish Hall, part of the old school, and Swailend, all in Deskford, and also in Keith. The office and show house were in Deskford, and it had had customers as far away as Edinburgh. It was the only company north of Perth to make thermally-clad aluminium frames. Unfortunately the firm collapsed in the 1990s.

Another major business in Deskford is the plant hire, farm contracting, snow-clearing and earth-moving business run since the early 1970s by Ian Currie from Greenhill. He also owned and operated until fairly recently the Lythe Old Folks Home and operated a large quarry near Buckie, and has more recently diversified into property lets and ownership of a garage in Keith.

Ian Currie, local Deskford entrepreneur.

Mr Bruce of Ardicow and Kirktown operated 10 JCBs from around 1958. In 1930 the two meal mills employed a total of 4 men. Cottartown Smiddy also employed 4 men and Woodend Smiddy 3. Alec Craib was a blacksmith and fabricator at Muir of Squaredoch from just after World War II till around 1972, after which he ran it as a coal depot and sawmill with his son, Willie until the 1990s. Alistair Buie had a joiner's business in the West Manse steadings around 1960 but died young, and Stuart Donald operated a joiner's business from Barone around 1980.

Banff and Buchan Nurseries operated from the Clune before moving to a site between Lintmill and Cullen. Since then it has ceased operation but an offshoot still operates as Moray Landscapes, with a depot between Bleachfield and Leitchestown. In the 1950s there had been an agricultural engineer and two joiners in Deskford, one of the latter being Johnnie Gordon, who operated from Caroline Cottage, Berryhillock and also operated as an undertaker. The Dutch Bulb Garden at Cottartown had a brief existence as a visitor attraction in the 1990s, and blind Keek McKay made and sold clothes pegs from his house in the Muckle Hoose in the 1960s.

In addition to the enterprises run by the Currie family and Moray Landscapes, a small but increasing number of commercial enterprises now exists in Deskford.

Duncan McLean in his workshop at Milton Mills

For many years Duncan McLean has run a highly regarded motor engineering business at Milton Mills.

At Braeside, Neville Wood runs Pickwick Cars, offering higher end imported motor vehicles for sale at competitive prices.

More recently the Deskford Galleries Tearoom and associated antique, art and craft shop at Cottertown, run by Meryl Ives, has established a widespread clientele, as has the South Lissens Pottery at Ardoch, run by David and Lynn McGregor, which in addition to its shop on site has sold its products to a major upmarket Edinburgh department store and has fully equipped a large new hotel near Munich.

Neville Wood at his Pickwick Cars business at Braeside.

Lynn and David McGregor of South Lissens Pottery at Ardoch and Meryl Ives at her Deskford Galleries at Cottartown.

The most recent enterprise in Deskford is Poseidon Navigation Services, with 12 employees, run by Tom Gunn from Maritime House at Carestown. The company provides admiralty charts and publications, a chart outfit management service, nautical books, stationery, navigational instruments and compass adjusting.

From all of the enterprises above it would have been surprising if native ingenuity had not produced some inventions. One of these was a well-regarded cattle crush crate designed by Alec Craib at Muir of Squaredoch. Another inventor, from the late C19th, was William Gordon of Broadrashes, who invented and patented both a land-tilling machine and a type-setting machine.

Tom Gunn and staff in Poseidon Navigation Services, Maritime House, Carestown.

RELIGION

RELIGIOUS ESTABLISHMENT

From the very earliest times of human settlement in Deskford the people would have had a framework of beliefs and rituals which guided their lives. Different pagan beliefs persisted for several thousand years before Christianity was introduced during Pictish times. The change from pagan to Christian beliefs did not happen suddenly or consistently. Many pagan beliefs continued to exist alongside Christian ones and many were incorporated into the Christian framework of belief.

There was a great struggle for dominance. For example, horse meat was widely eaten until the C7th, but the horse was the symbol of a powerful pagan religion, so in order to undermine that religion Christian clerics claimed that horsemeat was unclean, and that by association, the pagan religion was also unclean. People stopped eating horsemeat.

Christianity came to Banffshire either through St Columba, or, more likely, through one of St Ninian's missionaries from Whithorn. Often churches were built on old pagan Pictish sites. Monastic Christianity was tribally based, with a teind going to the church of one-tenth of the tribe's produce plus the first born child and the first-born beast. In return the Church provided, for members of the tribe, baptism, communion and requiem for the soul.

In the mid C8th, ascetics, monks and secular clergy were brought more under canonical rule. Abbacies and monasteries fell into the hands of laymen who employed others to carry out the ecclesiastical functions. Many Church offices became hereditary, but in the C9th King Giric freed the Celtic Church from the control of mormaers and toisechs. Earlier that century St Mauire had claimed that there still existed a "wood folk" who believed in the old superstitions and spoke a separate language. The teinds given to the Church by the tribe ensured a priest was appointed to every church to offer mass and to baptise and pray for the dead. Wells and springs which had been centres of pre-Christian activity, probably including St John's Well in Deskford and St Mary's Well in Ordiquhill, were adopted for Christian use.

In the C11th the church lacked organisation and there were irregularities in the ordination of priests. The structure of the church gradually decayed. A form of polygamy was accepted and it was very easy for husbands to divorce their wives, both of these probably being hangovers from pre-Christian society. These weaknesses, together with the influence of Queen Margaret, after she married King Malcolm in 1069, brought an end to the Celtic Church, which had a poorly educated clergy, and in which sacrilege and blasphemy were common, as was the use of church and churchyard for inappropriate purposes.

The main changes around this time included the establishment of a system of parishes for the first time. Confession was to be made to priests, not laymen, and Scots were instructed to abstain from vices, to preserve chastity and modesty, to do works of mercy, to go often to church, to confess sins frequently to priests, not to abstain from communion, not to work on a Sunday and not to marry a close relation. In the C12th King David I formalised the system of teinds.

Soon after the establishment of a system of parishes in 1130, Fordyce was elevated to this status, together with its pendicles or dependent chapels at Cullen, Deskford and Ordiquhill, which at that time was known as Tullywhull. Parish boundaries often paralleled land ownership ones. In 1256 the endowment and income of the Church of Fordyce and its chapels, including Deskford, were appropriated, together with the endowment and income of Logie Mar, to the Dean and Chapter of the Cathedral at Aberdeen. In exchange the Dean and Chapter had to appoint and support a vicar pensioner at Fordyce and curates in each of the chapels. The Loutin' Cross on Fordyce Hill was used for blessings when the Bishop of Aberdeen came to collect his revenues.

Authority was given by King Alexander III in 1272 for the appointment of a vicar to the Church at Fordyce, and in 1352 a charter confirmed Fordyce as a common church belonging to the Cathedral of Aberdeen. As early as 1236,

Cullen had petitioned to become a separate parish, but this did not happen for several hundred years. Fordyce, including Deskford, originally lay within the Deanery of Buchan, but when this was split Deskford became part of the Deanery of Boyne, which after the reformation formed the basis for the Presbytery of Fordyce. This could suggest that the centre of the Deanery may have been at Fordyce. The fact that the three original Deaneries replicated the land holdings of the Earls of Mar, Garioch and Buchan emphasises how important Boyne was in the North East, becoming as it did the fourth Deanery.

The 1256 Chapel of Deskford was almost certainly wooden. No evidence of it exists, but it is probable that it was at the same site as Old St John's in Kirktown. In the C12th and C13th there was little spirituality in local churches. Marriage could only be solemnised by a priest and often took place some time after the couple started cohabiting, providing an interesting parallel with today. The marriage might not be solemnised at all if the woman did not prove her fertility. At burials, distribution of alms for the soul of the deceased often led to drunken riots. The priest's priority was tending his acre of land.

After 1256 the next reference to a church or chapel in Deskford is in 1541, when Alexander Ogilvie of that Ilk was patron. However it is almost certain that a dependant chapel of the Church of Fordyce existed throughout that period, a time in which much criticism developed of the way in which the church operated. In the early C14th there was a recruitment crisis for clergy, and this was made worse at the time of the Black Death in 1349 when a higher proportion of clergy died than amongst the general population. This was due to the clergy's role in helping the sick. As a result there were many appointments of unskilled and illiterate priests in the second half of the C14th.

Lesser clergy, such as the curates appointed to Deskford, had long been impoverished, and did not earn enough to allow them to be on the same level socially as the more prosperous tenants, as was supposed to happen. All of this caused neglect of baptism, communion and confession. Church authorities permitted deathbed confession to anyone, even to a woman, in the absence of a priest. In the C14th there was much immorality and corruption, with priests carrying weapons, dancing, breaching chastity, wrestling, having bidie-ins and celebrating extra masses solely for financial gain.

Weekly mass was attended by most if not all of the local community. Baptism was universal and communion took place once a year, at Easter. Holy Days were holidays for all, absolution was given before death and confession made at least annually. From 1215 it had been declared that secular society, not just clergy, could get into heaven, and this increased the levels of piety and religious observance shown by many. The important feast days were the Nativity of the Virgin Mary on September 8th, Easter, Christmas and Corpus Christi. Because of the system of dowries and marriage contracts, many people did not marry, and just cohabited, though there was a problem when, if priests married, their offspring might seek to inherit church land. This was one of the main reasons for the introduction of celibacy, though, even in the C16th, deans were often bribed to ignore the existence of priests' concubines.

Parish priests around 1540 were often desperately poor and ill educated. They were not respected, were considered sexually immoral, covetous of their neighbours' goods but indifferent to their wellbeing. Excessive demands for mortuary dues from people who could not afford them was a source of friction between priests and parishioners and was expressed as "Na penny, na paternoster".

Within Deskford there was reputed to have been a small convent attached to St John's which in later times was used as an almshouse for indigent and elderly women, and is shown on the Cordiner drawing of 1788. The Reformation when it came in 1560 caused enormous change. It got rid of confession, the communion wafer, Latin, purgatory and prayers to the Virgin Mary and the saints. The interiors of churches, including Deskford, were stripped of any decoration, and simplified. People no longer knelt for communion, but instead sat round ordinary domestic tables and used ordinary bread and wine.

The history of the Church in Deskford for some years before and after the Reformation is complicated. On several occasions it was either conjoined to or separated from one, two or three other local parishes. The first of these occasions was in 1543 when the Chapel of Deskford was erected into a parish church by William, Bishop of Aberdeen. This occurred because the combined Fordyce and Deskford Parish Church in Fordyce was too far away for many who lived in Deskford. There were too many people in the combined parish for one pastor and there were difficulties caused by inclement weather.

The official charter states "The said Bishop, with consent of his chapter, and sixty days notice having been given to all parties having interest, by public edict, erects the chapel in the barony of Deskford into a Parish Church, with all the privileges and immunities belonging by right or custom thereto, with belltower and bells, baptismal font, cemetery, and right of sepulture and ministering and bestowing all other sacraments of the Church on the parishioners within the bounds of the barony of Deskford, to be called in all time coming the parish Church of St John of Deskford, the said Alexander Ogilvie having rebuilt the chapel in honour of Almighty God, his mother the Virgin Mary, and in memory of the most blessed John the Baptist, and having adorned it within and without with ornaments and priestly vestments, and procured its dedication and consecration into a Church by the hands of the priest (Pontificis), presented by the Dean and Chapter, who provide for his sustenance out of the tiend of the Church of Deskford, a yearly stipend of £8 Scots. Alexander Ogilvie of that Ilk having granted a garden and manse suitable thereto in perpetual alms. To all which, also by notarial instrument, Sir John Robertson, perpetual vicar of the Church of Fordyce, for himself and his successors, gave his consent. Dated at the Chapter House (Canonian) of Aberdeen. 14th October 1543".

This indicates that, though there would have been a wooden church in 1256, a stone one had subsequently been built, probably at a fairly early date as it had been rebuilt twice, once about 1460 and again about 1540. It certainly predated the building of the Tower of Deskford. It was also at this time that Alexander Ogilvie of that Ilk and his wife built the wonderful sacrament house which later only escaped zealous desecration because it had been covered by the new plain wood panelling on the inside of the Church.

In 1569 Boyndie and Banff Churches were separated from Fordyce but Deskford and Ordiquhill remained attached. In 1590 Cullen with Deskford was detached from Fordyce. In 1594 all three, together with Ordiquhill, were once more conjoined. In 1601 Cullen and Deskford were disjoined from Fordyce and

Deskford became a separate parish in 1627. It rejoined Fordyce again in 1650 but disjoined in 1654.

The Reformation was not welcomed particularly enthusiastically in the North East, and an Episcopalian structure would have been preferred to a Presbyterian one by most locals. The Presbyterian orthodoxy eventually had to be enforced from outside by force of law. There was little ill feeling in 1560 when the Reformation replaced Catholicism with Protestantism. Existing Catholic clergy were left in possession of two-thirds of their income for life. The new Church of Scotland involved itself in education, poor relief and social obligation in every parish. It was expected that everyone would attend church and "searchers" were sent out to persuade malingerers to attend. All non-attendance was punished. In the C16th and C17th the church exercised strong discipline over the population but was by and large respected by them.

An example of this discipline occurred when, in 1716, Rev Murray of Deskford was appointed to go to Fordyce and chastise the members of the Church there, as they were not sticking to orthodox worship. For example they indulged in "the singing of the doxologie after the last psalm, which was not agreeable to the practices of the Established Church, and could not be tolerated". It seems that the congregation at Fordyce were strongly inclined towards Episcopalian modes of worship, and sometimes even Roman Catholic ones.

The earliest Deskford Kirk Session minutes still in existence date to 1684, though Dr Cramond, in the late C19th, quotes extensively from earlier minutes which must have been in existence at that time. From 1720 they are written in a modern script which replaces the clerk's hand used until then. In 1840 there were in existence Registers of Births and Marriages continuously back till 1669. Sadly none of these seem to have survived.

There were a number of occasions on which Kirk Session Minutes were lost or destroyed. From 1731 to 1734 there are no minutes because of the carelessness of the Session Clerk, who had only left "a few confused scraps which nobody could connect".

In November 1741 it was recorded that "it happened that the neglect, omission and carelessness of Mr (scored out), late Schoolmaster and Session Clerk, that the minutes for a whole year and upwards are lost and perfectly extinct". The Minister stated "if a man is dignified with an office which should be conducted with care and trust, he ought to lay down rules strictly to observe what it is he is to do for the present time and to lay down a method of acting in his profession with regularity, steadiness and attention. Every moment should be employed and taken up in doing something. A man should not refer anything of importance to another time, and that only to do something which may be more agreeable to him at that time, but turn out otherwise when too late. If he has two things on hand to execute at one time, let the most important thing, and what affects his employment and Business of Life, let this be the first effort to perform, and then, if necessary let him execute the other. Everyman should say with Solomon, that wise Prince, that a slothful man is a disgrace to his friends, but are in Horace very beautifully described. This has happened through the neglect of Mr Alexander Philp, late Schoolmaster and Session Clerk in this place that the Minutes, from November 5th 1741 to August 15th 1742 are lost".

The minutes from the 16th of September 1774 to the 6th of November 1774 "have been, by some heedless neglect, mislaid, they being wrote on a bye piece of paper while the Session Book was at Portsoy with Mr Johnston, late Schoolmaster". On another occasion they were eaten by mice.

The importance of religious belief can be exemplified by the actions of the Society for the Propagation of Christian Knowledge in 1755. They sent out a questionnaire to be completed by every Minister in Scotland. In Deskford Rev Morison replied that the Earl of Findlater was patron and sole heritor, and that there were about 750 parishioners over 7 or 8 years of age. There were no papists in the parish except for one old man who sometimes came to church, and no Episcopal Dissenters except one family and another old woman.

During the almost 300 years between the Reformation and the Disruption, attitudes and beliefs alternated between the extremes of strict Calvinist orthodoxy and much more liberal ones. The expectations which the congregation had of the Minister also varied significantly.

In the C18th all families in a particular district of the parish would be summoned on a particular day to be examined individually in the shorter catechism, the psalms or the paraphrases. Many young people, having learned them both at home and at school, could recite all the paraphrases plus over 50 psalms and many hymns.

Sunday services were very long. They started with slow singing led by the precentor, followed by a prayer, then a half hour explanation by the Minister of some aspect of Calvinist theology. There would then be a lecture on a particular 20 or 30 verses of the Bible, a sermon of up to an hour and a second prayer. In summer there were often two services without a break between them. Before the service members of the congregation would socialise in the graveyard, walking about or sitting on stones or inspecting them, and after the service the Kirk Officer would announce any sales to be held in the parish or in adjoining ones.

For attending church women wore a tightly-fitting cap, over the front of which was tied a bright, broad ribbon which passed above the ear and round the back of the head. Over this was placed another cap of muslin with a border of lace. According to wealth and social standing they wore hooded scarlet cloaks to the ankle or plaids. Men wore blue bonnets, short blue serge coats, knee breeches, ribbed stockings and brogues with buckles.

Preparation for the Sacrament of the Lord's Supper (communion) which only happened once every two or three years, was a long and complex process. For months all young people underwent instruction. The Thursday before communion was observed as a Sunday and there were also services on the Saturday during which all work stopped. Each member of the congregation who had proved their religious knowledge and understanding was given a metal communion token about the size of a 20p piece, which gave admission to the Sacrament. A Fast Day was held during the week before Communion.

The day itself began with public worship at around 09:30. After this came a long address which excluded from church everyone who was not eligible. Tokens were taken in and a collection made for the poor, followed by a lecture relevant to the Lord's Supper. Tables covered in linen lay end to end along the entire length of the Church and held the bread and wine which all communicants took. There would be another talk encouraging perseverance in the Good Way. Communicants would leave the table and others take their place, and throughout the entire service worshippers went out and in the Church. Once everyone had received communion the Minister gave another long address (the congregation were getting their money's worth), and the service ended with praise and prayer.

By now it was lunchtime and everyone went to friends' houses or bought bread and ale nearby. After this a second service was held which did not finish till evening. Communion was usually held in the summer and on the Monday immediately following it there was another service, during which no work was done. This was followed by a party in the manse for all the other Ministers who had assisted, and their wives, at which strong drink was taken to excess. This was called "Muckle Munanday". In 1726 there was no Communion in Deskford because the Minister considered that there were too few parishioners who qualified, but he hoped to have sufficient numbers in a year or two.

In 1701 tokens were distributed on Wednesday July 23rd and Sunday 27th was a day of fast and humiliation. At the preparatory service on Saturday August 2nd tokens were issued to those who didn't already have them. August 3rd was Communion and August 10th a day of thanksgiving after having received the Sacrament. In 1703 there was the first occasion on which the thanksgiving service was held on a weekday, a Monday.

In 1744 the elders who comprised the session, in the sort of gesture of relaxed compassion not often associated with the Calvinist Kirk, outvoted the Minister by granting a communion token to Ann Duncan, as they thought "she was exposed to less sin living separately from her husband than when living with him". The Session also outvoted the Minister in 1786 when they agreed to admit to communion "certain persons found guilty by a court of the Justices of the Peace of cutting down and carrying off greenwood". It is perhaps not too cynical to recollect that the Minister depended on the patronage of the Earl of Findlater to remain in post, and that the Earl owned the said greenwood.

On June 30th 1728 the Minister announced that, with divine assistance, he intended to administer the sacrament of the Lord's Supper once that summer and would soon start examining those who wished to partake. The elders wished communion to take place before harvest and the Minister agreed to try to do so. On July 20th the Session agreed that it would take place on the third Sabbath in August, the 18th. On July 30th the Session decided that it did not wish to use the old tokens and agreed to get 200 new ones made, which they decided should be "pretty big". The old Communion Cloth was coarse and worn, and Session wished the Minister to provide a new one, finer than the old. Locks were to be fitted to the Church doors, and anything else thought necessary done. All this was to be paid for from the Poor's money till the Earl of Findlater could be spoken to about reimbursing the Session.

Thursday August 15th was to be observed as a Day of Humiliation before the Lord's Supper. The Session agreed to only collect at the door on the Lord's Day, and within the church on the other days. Some elders were deputed to serve at the tables, and others to wait on the elements, and a grave and decent carriage was recommended to all. The people were to meet on the Saturday, being the Day of Preparation before Communion, between 10:00 and 11:00, and to wait after that service to receive tokens.

The procedure in 1738 was typical. On May 13th it was intimated that Communion would be held the following week. John Reid, James Cameron and James Mury were ordered to take the collections at the two church doors. John Grant and William Murray were to wait on the Sacramental Elements and the tables were ordered to be set and the floor cleared of stools and seats which might cause obstruction.

On March 28th 1756 the Minister intimated that the Sacrament of the Lord's Supper was to be held on April 18th and that all belonging to the Church on this side of the Deskford Burn should attend the Church on Thursday for a diet of examination so that those who were successful could be given their tokens. Those on the other side of the Burn could meet on Friday for the same purpose.

The Sacrament of Communion is central to the Kirk, but has undergone many changes over the years. In 1629 Communion was suspended because of the murder in the parish of James Lawrence, "till the people should be better fitted for the same". By 1726 no Communion had been held for several years. In the mid C19th, before the Lord's Supper it was the habit for the elders to scrutinise the Communion Roll and purge from it any individuals whom they considered unworthy of taking communion. In 1916 it was agreed to hold a Communion Service at 16:00 for those who could not attend the forenoon service. In 1933 it was decided to hold three Communion services per year instead of the two held until then.

In the mid C18th Church membership was almost universal and attendance levels were very high, except for those who were too young, too old, too infirm or "toun keepers". Everyone went early and met in the kirkyard to socialise, gossip, smoke, take snuff and talk about local markets. The young flirted or played. After the service, in the kirkyard, proclamations were made about roups, bargains, lost property etc.

Around 1750 services were announced by the ringing of the first bell. On the second bell the people entered the Church and were led in a psalm by the precentor. On the third bell the Minister entered. The order of the service was a prayer, followed by a lecture from a passage from Scripture, commented on verse by verse by the Minister. Then came another prayer, the sermon, a third prayer, a psalm and the benediction. The congregation remained bare headed till the Minister began his lecture, when they put on their bonnets. The same order of service was repeated in the afternoon service, except that there was no lecture.

When a psalm was sung, each line was read out before it was sung, originally for the benefit of those who could not read. Prayers were dramatic performances, full of pious fervour, tears, shouts, rapture, pathos and joy, often spoken by the Minister in a whining voice in broad Scots. Perhaps a parallel could be drawn with some born-again pastors in the southern states of the USA today. It was, however, a sin for the Minister to prepare a prayer in advance, the words having to be uttered according to how the Minister was moved by the Spirit. If a Minister stumbled or paused it was considered a sign of Divine displeasure. Prayers were often vulgar, fanatical or foolish. The themes of teaching were mainly original innocence, the fall, under the gospel of grace and the Eternal State. These tended to be shoehorned into any passage from the Bible.

Major changes in religious belief and practice took place at the same time as agricultural improvements. Towards the end of the C18th sermons became milder and Ministers more measured, less puritanical and more convivial, and there was greater tolerance. Many parishioners did not like it. Moderates took over within the Church and preaching became dreary. Attendances dropped, there was less fear, less imposition and the rigidity of Sabbath observance lessened.

However all this changed again in the early C19th when there was a revival in zeal and earnestness and a sterner tone. By 1820 there could be no bathing, swimming, games, travelling (except to church), shaving or letter writing on the Sabbath. If work had to be done then no tools could be used. For example potatoes could only be lifted by scraping them from the ground using one's fingers. This stern and earnest attitude continued throughout the C19th. In the late 1830s an association was formed in Deskford for promoting the spread of the Gospel, Church extension, the circulation of the Bible and Indian and Colonial Missions. They also intended to extend the Sunday school library, to procure bibles for poor people in the parish and to pay part of the school fees of the children of poor people in the parish.

Throughout the C18th and C19th many days of thanksgiving were observed in Deskford at the behest of Presbytery, Synod, General Assembly, Government or King. For example, on 23rd April 1746 thanksgiving was given for the glorious victory over the rebels at Culloden, where large numbers of the enemy were slain and a complete victory obtained. Soon afterwards this was reinforced when the Synod of Aberdeen intimated a joint Day of Thanksgiving for the good weather over the winter, but particularly to "offer up our joint and hearty prayers to the Almighty for the glorious victory gained by His Royal Highness the Duke of Cumberland over the rebels at Colodden upon the 16th inst. Where numbers of the rebel army were slain and a complete victory obtained by the good conduct and management merely of His Royal Highness and thence an appearance of our deliverance from this wicked and unnatural Rebellion, from the oppression and cruelty of the rebels and the preservation of our valuable laws and liberties, the Duke having come with the King's army to the northern part of Scotland for our relief".

Examples included May 1753 when Synod appointed a Thanksgiving Day to be observed throughout the Province on account of the late favourable harvest, and December 1832 when Presbytery ordained a Day of Public Thanksgiving for the late favourable harvest and preservation from cholera morbus.

Even more common were Fast Days and Days of Humiliation either to apologise when something had gone badly or to plead when a catastrophe was imminent. For example, on December 11th 1720, from the pulpit in Deskford, there was "read and intimat a proclamation for a public Fast to be observed on Friday December 16th against the pestilence in neighbouring countries. All were exhorted to observe the said day". On July 27th 1723 the Presbytery of Fordyce called a Fast throughout their bounds on account of the great drought. On June 27th 1725 an Act of the General Assembly was read out in Church, calling for a day of Fasting and Humiliation on July 18th on account of the persecution of Protestants abroad, and of abounding sin at home. August 7th 1734 was appointed as a day for Fasting and Humiliation for private and public sin.

May 24th 1705 had been a "Day of Humiliation for our sins which had provoked God to give us a bad seed time", and January 25th 1712 was a "Day of Humiliation for imploring God for a weel settled peace in Christendom". August 7th 1735 was a Fast Day throughout the Synod of Aberdeen for public and private sins and on February 1st 1741 the Minister intimated a Fast to be held on the 4th by His Majesty's Order to implore a blessing on his Armies in the War with Spain.

On December 15th 1745 there was read and intimat a proclamation by order of His Majesty, King George, for a day of fasting and Humiliation to be observed "for imploring God's mercy on these lands and praying that the Lord would be pleased to avert the impending judgments of a war threatened by the formidable powers of France and Spain against these Nations, particularly that

He would quell and settle the unnatural rebellion raised in that part of Great Britain called Scotland in favour of the elder son of the Pretender who landed in that Kingdom in the month of August. To beg that God would prevent the shedding of blood, preserve the Protestant interest, secure our valuable liberties and privileges to us and speedily settle all our unhappy divisions, for His glory and in the interests of the Kingdom and the good of the nation in generall".

On December 12th 1776 a Fast Day was appointed by the King's Proclamation to implore God's blessing on the measures to be taken to quell the rebellion raised in the several provinces of North America. June 11th 1783 was a day of Fasting and Humiliation on account of the bad harvest and the great scarcity and dearth of provisions, the poor being in great distress.

Fasts and Thanksgiving days were not observed during Episcopal periods in the Church of Scotland, though in Stornoway, as recently as 20 years ago, a Day of Humiliation was held when the Western Isles Council lost several million pounds to the fraudulent Bank of Credit and Commerce International. Ministers in individual parishes could decide on issues and good causes themselves. For example, in 1648, the Minister in Deskford preached against the late engagement with England, and in 1744 the Minister held prayers in Church on several days "as God appears to be angry with the land", the weather having been extremely bad from September 8th till the end of October.

The Church in Deskford chose to involve itself in the lives of its parishioners in many different ways, some directly relating to the Church, and others bearing little or no relation. Normal practice changed significantly over the years, from generation to generation, much of it unrelated to belief or scripture. In 1728 the Earl of Findlater agreed to provide a fund for communion elements in Deskford and other parishes, despite an allowance for these being part of the Minister's stipend. In 1685 the Minister had required the people to attend a service on Friday December 25th. In 1686 the Minister, in order to ensure that things were done properly, asked the Session Clerk to go to the Minister of Ordiquhill and "get ane copie of the sett for me of prayers to be read before sermon one the Lord's day and prayers to be read at other particular times".

Systems were in place to meet the needs of all members of the congregation. For instance incomers and new members had to request pews. If they were a big family then others might be moved together to share, in order to make room. This sometimes caused upset, but did ensure a precise pew allocation to everyone. The patron, the Earl of Findlater, decided who was to be appointed Minister, but in 1691 the Earl wrote to his son, Sir James Ogilvie of Churchill, complaining "ye have given me no advyse about the plantation (appointment) of the Kirk of Deskfoord, for it is said it must be planted against the 10th of August nixt. I entreat your advyse with the next post".

In 1624 though the parishioners of Deskford had to go to Cullen to worship, many of the elders were from Deskford. These included Walter Ogilvy, Ardauch, Thomas Abercrombie, Skeyth, James Ogilvie, Nether Blairok, George Ogilvie, Cloon, and William Ogilvie, Leitchestounne. This concentration of local control in the hands of relatives of the dominant local families of Ogilvie and Abercrombie was common throughout Scotland. In 1643 all parishioners in Deskford signed the Solemn League and Covenant. In 1644 Presbytery made proposals to attach parts of Fordyce parish to Deskford, Ordiquhill and Cullen, and in 1648 it instructed each Minister to ensure that there was a school in every parish. In 1649 there were two services every Sunday in Deskford, except in winter, and weekly meetings were held for catechising.

Some aspects of church life in Deskford were perhaps unexpectedly democratic with elders being elected annually, and throughout its existence Deskford was always a generous parish to those in need, both from outwith and within the parish. There was often great want, and there were many vagrants, especially after a series of poor harvests in the area. For example in 1649, in Cullen, the beadle was paid 15/- and later 6/- to bury "poor objects" who had died of starvation.

The Church also took seriously its responsibility to ensure that at all levels of society its members behaved appropriately. In 1721 elders in Deskford were exhorted to faithfulness in their station and it was earnestly recommended to them to check how well the Lord's Day was observed by parishioners. In 1722 elders were quizzed about the conduct of church members in their districts and were themselves exhorted to faithfulness and exemplary conduct.

However in 1722 some Ministers had their knuckles rapped by Synod for using the Poor's money to buy Communion elements.

In 1628 elders had to investigate parishioners in their respective districts about pilgrimages to idolatrous places (often old pagan sites adopted by the pre-reformation church). The elders reported that there had been no idolatrous pilgrimages by Deskford members, but this probably involved the turning of a blind eye since a good number of locals were known to go to St Mary's Well, Ordiquhill, amongst others.

The whip was cracked in 1703 when it was announced that anyone who failed to attend church on three successive Sundays would be called before session to repent and be fined. In 1756 conduct relating to weddings came under scrutiny, with both parties to a marriage contract being required to attend upon the Session Clerk on the Friday, otherwise their banns would not be called on the Sunday. Any couple who, after their marriage ceremony went to one of Deskford's "publick house(s) where ale is sold or money taken on that account" were fined £3 Scots. The General Assembly pronounced against Penny Weddings in 1645, 1701, 1706 and 1719.

On December 20th 1778 the Minister preached and lectured that "the Church of Scotland, being justly concerned at the repeal of the penal laws against Popery in England, and, fearing that the same may be extended to Scotland, some of the Synod have in consequence met and appointed their several members to preach often against Popery and its several dangerous tenets". The Minister accordingly, for a Sunday or two, discoursed fully upon this subject.

Personal disputes were not uncommon. In September 1783, James Wilson, Ardoch, wrote to session on behalf of himself and his wife that though being disappointed by not being allowed to participate in the recent sacrament (communion), for reasons known only to Rev Chalmers, asked that they be allowed to participate in future. The Session, aware of a disagreement between the Minister and James Wilson for some time past, and not knowing any objections to James Wilson's moral character, agreed to recommend them as communicants in any other Christian congregation. Both appeared before

Session and were desirous of being reconciled to live in good neighbourhood in all time coming.

In 1644 the elders of Deskford had been recommended by Presbytery to enquire for witches, charmers, pilgrims to wells and chapels, swearers and scolders. Any who were discovered were to be reported and would be banned from the afternoon service. Masters of families should ensure their servants attended Church and that none of them bought or sold drink. In the late 1600s the Town Clerk of Cullen had been dealt with severely by his own Kirk Session for transacting business at Deskford on the Sabbath.

In the C18th, parishioners about to move away from Deskford frequently requested testimonials of good Christian character from the Minister, who always consulted the Kirk Session about these. They were normally granted on the basis that there was "nothing known against them". However in February 1802 when James McHaty in Squaredoch requested a certificate of his and his family's good moral character, John Smith in neighbouring Mosside objected, claiming that he and several others were deprived of their cow's milk and that Jean Shepherd, spouse to James McHattie, was the person whom he and the others blamed for doing them that injury. Alexander Barnet in Squaredoch claimed that Jean Shepherd had a bad character, and being asked for what, replied "for taking the use of other people's cow's milk". The complaints were that Jean Shepherd was casting spells to make the cows of her neighbours go dry.

Session considered the accusations so absurd and ridiculous, and proceeding either from gross ignorance or malice, that they could not be sustained. The McHattie family had lived in the parish for more than twenty years as neighbours of some of the elders and the Minister, and had always behaved honestly, industriously and usefully. Session agreed to give them a certificate of good character whenever they required. It is quite difficult to believe that as recently as 1802 there was still this belief in witchcraft and spells as an explanation of things going against you.

Practices changed. The mortcloth, which had originally been used to cover the corpses of those who could not afford a coffin, became used to cover the coffin, and was hired out by the Kirk Session. In 1700 the Session paid out 1/6d to buy a new mortcloth but were adequately recompensed by charging 3/- for the use of the handbell to lead funeral processions.

A major recurrent concern was misconduct in the lofts during Sunday services. In 1722 elders complained that there was a great disturbance almost every Lord's Day in the common loft, and proposed that the following Sunday, from the pulpit, the Minister should exhort the congregation there to behave more decently and gravely. Accordingly on April 22nd the Minister admonished "them that sit in the common loft to have a suitable and becoming carriage and deportment during the time of divine service".

In 1769 "to prevent the frequent disorders which happen in the forebreast of the common loft by disorderly young people pressing to get in, the Session select twelve people to give seats to in the forebreast". Action had previously been taken in 1760. "The breast of the old loft being crowded by disorderly people who many times make disturbance in the time of divine worship, the fore seat is therefore to be given to Walter Steinson to be given to whom he should think fit for propagating of Church music". This did not work. However, if at first you don't succeed. By March 1774 "Session took under consideration the disposing of the forebreast seats in the west loft and judging that it might lead to the improvement of church musick to have said seats possessed only by such as could sing. Alexander Duncan offered to take the whole of the forebreast seats and to pay the usual rent, and said Duncan, being skilled in church musick, and promising to train up the youth in that way, the Session resolved to make a trial of this". Misbehaviour was common in all parishes, and in neighbouring Grange parish, action had to be taken to stop those in the loft hitting those below with their staffs and spitting on them.

There was also regular difficulty in ensuring that pew rent was paid. For example, on February 27th 1743 Session noted that "some tacksmen in the new loft are backward in paying" and decided that "The Minister would intimate next Lord's Day that if they were not more punctual in paying they will be turned out of the said loft and the tacks disposed of to others that will pay better".

Throughout its existence after the Reformation the Church in Deskford, in common with other places, was concerned about the presence of adherents of other denominations. It was contentedly recorded in 1667 that there were no Quakers in the parish. In 1792 only two adults in the parish did not belong to the Kirk. They were Roman Catholics. By 1836 there were six individuals who did not belong to the established Church and in 1950 there were two families who belonged to the Episcopal Church and two to the Roman Catholic Church.

The Church continued to evolve during the C19th, with the Disruption of 1843 being the main event. However both before and after this there were a number of interesting developments in both attitude and procedure. Much of the change was toward a less judgmental church. The 1834 declaration by the General Assembly that sinners should no longer have to stand before the congregation, and the 1841 declaration that fines should no longer be imposed for fornication took several decades to be fully implemented in Deskford, but implemented they finally were. Despite this, in 1883, James Wilson sen, Little Knows, felt duty bound to resign as an elder when his daughter, Joan became pregnant outwith wedlock. Other traditions continued to hold sway. As late as 1879 Christmas was celebrated on January 6th, according to the old calendar. In 1885 a Church Defence Committee was established to watch over and protect the interests of the Established Church in the face of the development of various sects and revivalists. The number of communicants was stable at 300 - 400.

In 1836 a letter was read out in Church from Dr McGill on the present state of the Jews and the prospects in regard to their conversion to Christianity, calling for the prayers of the people on their behalf. Every year money was donated to the Mission to the Jews. As early as 1841 a meeting in Church was addressed by Mr Reid, Portsoy on the subject of total abstinence from intoxicating liquors.

Regular pastoral activities continued. In 1841 the Rev Innes announced that he would shortly visit families at Backies, Clochmacreich, Tillybreedless and Langlanburn. Flexibility was shown on August 8th of that year when the reading and the exposition were omitted in order to shorten the service because many of the people were in a wet and uncomfortable state in consequence of heavy rain on their way to church. In 1840 seven diets of catechising during the year had been attended by 322 persons.

The richer members of the congregation began to have private baptisms and marriages and thought it worthwhile to pay the fine this attracted, in order to be fashionable. This practice lasted until the middle of the C20th. Only the poor continued to have them in church. Previously funerals and burials had no religious element. They were civil activities and no religious service was permitted. The bellman summoned all to a funeral. Absence was considered a discourtesy to the dead, an insult to the living and a gross neglect of Christian duty. When the new, central, section of the graveyard was opened in 1886, the first person to be buried there was Mrs Taylor, Cultain.

In 1872, at the opening of New St John's, a circular was issued by Mr Bryson of Seafield Estate stating that parishioners (tenants) paying rental of £5 and upwards would have priority in occupying their allocated pews, but that this was not a legal right. At the first service in New St John's these members should come early to occupy their pews. Those not having had pews allocated should wait outside till they were shown which pews they could occupy. By the end of the C19th Deskford was considered to be "The Model Parish", and was widely admired.

It cannot be emphasised enough how significant were the events leading up to the Disruption in 1843 and the emergence of the Free Church at that time. There had been much concern and dissent in the period leading up to the event, focussing largely on whether the landowners should have the right to determine and appoint new Ministers, or whether that power should lie with the members of the Church. In Deskford the Earl of Seafield does not seem to have been too concerned.

At the Disruption Rev George Innes, then aged 66, and all the elders except one, James Mitchell, Knows, left the established Church and set up a Free Church congregation, worshipping first in a barn at Mains of Skeith, and thereafter in a new Church one mile west of the parish Church. There was a partial break up of the Free Church congregation after Rev Innes died in 1852, with some rejoining the established Church. Some had only joined the Free

Church in the first place out of respect for Rev Innes. Rev James Mackintosh, who was born in Ordiquhill, became Minister of the parish church. The Free Church was opened in 1844 and the manse, which is still occupied as a private house, was built in 1845. The Free Church was renovated in 1900 and the manse was enlarged on several occasions during the C19th.

In the mid 1850s Free Church Sunday Schools were established at Alexander Wright, Saughs, James Lorimer, Kirktown, John Reid, Squaredoch, Alexander Reid, Berryhillock and James Gordon, Broadrashes. Teachers were appointed, and in addition fortnightly meetings were established in each district for Christian Fellowship.

In April 1859 the Free Church Session enquired into the state of religion in the congregation, and remedies were suggested against the prevalent uncleanness (fornication), lying, profane swearing and Sabbath breaking. They also considered that there was a general absence of family discipline, which led to many of these evils. There was a discussion and report on revivalist activities. Three elders, John Watt, John Lawrence and Alexander Reid resigned over matters of faith. John Watt was later erased from the Communion Roll because of his connection with a revivalist group in Banff, where he had been publicly baptised. The Sabbath School in his house was terminated.

In 1862 an application was received for the establishment of an Association of Total Abstinence under the aegis of the Free Church. It was rejected. However in July 1866 an elder, James Lorimer, was suspended for public drunkenness. He was reinstated in July 1867, though no mention is made about whether the Sabbath School continued in his house. It is unlikely. In 1870 he resigned once more as an elder because of repeated intemperance.

In 1888 there was enthusiasm, and a good attendance at a meeting called to set up a Christian Union or Association, and in 1893 the Free Church congregation agreed to the permanent use of an organ in Church services. Each of the six districts was allocated to a personable young lady member to request contributions for a Sustenation Fund which would allow the appointment of a new Minister to such a small congregation, after Rev Ker resigned. In 1886 it was agreed that the congregation should sit during prayers and stand during hymns.

There had always been good relations between the Established Church of Scotland and the Free Church in Deskford, and members of the respective congregations often attended services in the other Church. In 1886 the Free Church agreed to change Fast days before Communion from Fridays to Thursdays to be in line with St John's, after a request from Rev Mackintosh. In 1901 St John's offered the use of their Church for Free Church services while the Free Church was undergoing repairs. This offer was accepted with thanks. For several months during World War I, whilst Rev Park of St John's was caring for an Aberdeen parish whose Minister was chaplain to a regiment in the trenches, Rev Morrison of the Free Church preached in both Deskford Churches.

The Disruption had not happened suddenly in 1843 and there had been considerable soul searching in the years leading up to it. In 1840 there had been several public meetings for prayer "in reference to the present very critical and alarming position of the Church". Nevertheless ordinary business continued, with seven diets of catechising attended by 322 persons. On February 28th 1841 the Minister read to the congregation an address from the elders and parishioners of Marnoch. He exhorted them "to sympathy with that much oppressed people in being driven, by the intrusion of Mr Edwards, from the church of their fathers, and to assist them in providing a church, and religious ministrations by which that may be edified". On May 19th 1841 there was a meeting for prayer in the church "for imploring the Divine blessing to the General Assembly to meet under peculiar circumstances of such momentous trial and interest and importance".

By January 26th 1842 the church in Kirktown was full to hear addresses about the state of the church. A majority signed the resolution that they would only stay in the Established Church if its principles changed. On December 28th that year, the Minister, Rev Innes and John Watt, Alexander Wilson, John Reid, Alexander Smith, Alexander Russel and George Murray, elders, signed a declaration that they would form a new church which they felt would better represent the true nature of the Church of Scotland than that recently imposed by the Court of Session and the House of Lords.

On June 4th 1843 Rev Gardiner of Rathven preached and declared the Church and parish vacant by the demission of Rev George Innes. On June 21st Rev Innes handed over three books of records, 1684 – 1807, two Communion plates, four Communion cups, one Communion table and cloth and a bag with Communion tokens to a meeting chaired by Rev George Henderson, Cullen. A receipt was provided. In order to constitute a Kirk Session in St John's, Rev Grant, Ordiquhill, and Rev Henderson, Cullen, met with James Mitchell, the only elder not to have left the Established Church, together with Mr G Wright, Session Clerk. A second elder who had retired was willing to resume his duties.

The first service of the Free Church was held in the Barn of Skeith on June 4th 1843. A Sunday school was established and on June 26th a Kirk Session was constituted. There were 126 communicants. The new Free Church demonstrated great energy. Diets of catechising were offered to the congregation and were carried out at farms such as Oathillock and Nether Blairock. Because of the split the Church of Scotland lost control of poor relief, education and public morals, and Parochial Boards were established. Later in the C19th in Deskford, Church of Scotland numbers increased and Free Church numbers declined, though this was partly because of the Free Church Minister, Rev Ker who was not universally popular.

By and large, at the time of the Disruption, farm servants and crofters came out and joined the Free Church, while wealthier tenants and other better-off individuals stayed with St John's. Perhaps these wealthier tenants felt they might have more to lose in terms of their relationship with the Earl of Seafield, though he had readily provided a piece of ground for the new Free Church.

The commitment of Rev George Innes in abandoning a comfortable manse and a generous stipend, at the age of 66, for a very uncertain future, with no guarantee of house, stipend, church or congregation can only be admired. His principles shine through and it is a tribute to him personally that the new Free Church in Deskford was so successful, even though numbers fell after his death in 1851. In contrast, the Minister of Fordyce, also a Rev Innes, spoke strongly before the Disruption in favour of coming out when he said that the man occupying the pulpit in Fordyce after him and the Disruption would be a wolf in sheep's clothing. In the event he did not come out.

From 1851 to 1931 there were three other Free Church Ministers, two of whom, vastly contrasting individuals, the Revs Ker and Morrison, occupied most of that period. Rev Ker was a member of a wealthy Greenock shipbuilding and sugar-importing family and had significant private means. He had strong views and in 1883 he produced a report on Religion and Morals in which he made his views clear. He was unhappy about the revivalist movements and sects, and stated that "The religious excitements and enthusiasms encouraged by well-meant artificial effort on the part of zealous men lowered the tone of spiritual religion. Falsehood, fraud and evil speaking have too often been counted venial offences against morality, condoned by religious zeal". In Deskford he bemoaned an abandonment of Church connection by many in the district, and a lapsing of Free Church members, an open exodus.

The Free Church Presbytery had concerns about the state of matters in Deskford, including the fact that Rev Ker resided in Aberdeen. He had been largely self-financing and felt that he had the support of the congregation. However it had been split since 1863, and a number had left. On June 17th 1883 Presbytery rebuked the session for certain items in its report on Religion and Morals, and stated that it was really Rev Ker's report and not one written by session. The remaining members of the congregation, the session and the deacons' court supported Rev Ker strongly and feared that should he leave, the Deskford congregation would be merged with another. However agreement was reached that Rev Ker would resign and the congregation would be given permission to call a new Minister, and that they would contribute to the Sustentation Fund at the rate of £60 per annum plus £60 from the deacons. After this things settled down.

Rev Morrison was a very different character, being a very gentle and humble man. He donated money for an annual prize in Deskford School in memory of his son, Jim, who had died in childhood. He was popular and respected by both Free Church and St John's congregations and served as Minister in the former for over forty years until the union of the two. In the early decades of the

C20th both Churches continued to operate separately, but having good relations with each other, and with members of both often attending services and social events in the other church.

Around 1900 in Deskford almost all families went to church, with children attending both Sunday school and church. Almost everyone walked to and from services. The only accepted non-attender was the toun keeper on each farm, and he often went to the evening service instead. If someone missed Church it was quite common for the Minister to visit them on the Monday to see what was wrong with them. Many families took a Sunday afternoon walk, often to the churchyard. In St John's the front seats in the gallery were occupied by farm servants and shooting tenants and their servants.

St John's Church Women's Guild 90th Birthday party, 1985. (All L to R) Front – Betty Guthrie, Rev John T Guthrie, Minnie Angus, Rachel Cruickshank, Mary Currie. Middle – Ina Barclay (Pres), Jane Robertson, (Pres of Presbytery Council), Dorothy Stewart (Treas), Kathleen Christie, Nanny Forsyth. Back – Margaret Strathdee, Eleanor Cruickshank, Ethel Ewen, Nina Cameron, Ann McLaren, Jean Taylor (Sec), Nettie Weakley, Nellie McDonald.

In 1910 the Woman's Guild of St John's presented the congregation with two solid silver communion plates to replace the pewter ones in use since 1796. They also presented a new communion table. In 1925 a major change took place. Under the Church of Scotland (Property and Endowment) Act it was confirmed that the church, manse, outbuildings, offices, ground and garden policies and fittings belonged to the heritors of the parish. This transferred ownership but also responsibility for upkeep from the Earls of Seafield to the congregation. In 1928 each family was asked to contribute 2/- before May 28th when the property would pass into their hands.

The Church of Scotland and the Free Church united nationally in 1929, and the Deskford congregations did so in 1932. In the period leading up to this union there was a gradual integration with, for example, marriages in which bride and groom were one from each of the churches being conducted by both Ministers. In 1930 though separate Easter services were held, the respective choirs took part in both.

There were still however separate occasions. In 1930 the Free Church Sale of Work raised £63 while the St John's Woman's Guild sale of Work raised £57. Both were attended by members of both churches. Stalls included work, woollen, dairy, toffee, soap and perfumes, flowers and fruit, art and fancy goods, with both having teas, and St John's also having a fish pond, shooting and ice cream.

The separate Sunday schools held separate picnics at St John's manse and the west manse. Separate remembrance services were held in the two Churches on November 16th, and the Free Church still ran its Welfare-of-Youth class in which ten pupils had achievements recorded. Mr Alexander Fraser, Rottenhillock, was presented with a clock, Bible and silver flower vase for having completed 35 years as a teacher in the United Free Church Sabbath School. The last baptism in the Free Church was that of William John Chalmers on July 5th 1931.

On union in 1931 following the retiral of both Ministers, Rev Park after 41 years service and Rev Morrison with 43, there was a slight problem when the sole nominee for the united charge, Rev R G Buchanan Miller from Aberdeen, withdrew in January 1932, however the new sole nominee, Rev William R Brown of St Modan's Falkirk was unanimously elected. He was originally from Newmill and was ordained on May 6th 1932. The congregation of the Established Church felt strongly that the united church should be called St John's and this was agreed. After the union a monthly service was held in the old Free Church and Sunday Schools were held in both Churches until 1940.The union seemed to give an injection of energy and enthusiasm. A branch of the Young Worshippers' League started in 1933 and 39 individuals received prizes for regular attendance. In 1934 160 people, including 20 from Deskford, attended the summer meeting of the Western Banffshire Branch of the Scottish Sunday School Union in Deskford, an event which took place annually in the parish for many years. In 1936 Mr James Wilson, Parklea, Fordyce, presented to Deskford Church an individual communion set, in loving memory of his father, mother and wife. That same year, in a practice more democratic than the present one, the congregation elected elders and the Kirk Session only endorsed their choice. In 1939 the Young Worshippers' League visited the

Tash Robertson with horse decorated and cart spruced up for the 1926 Free Church Sunday School Picnic.

Pictures in Keith.

In the period after World War II, in line with the population of Deskford and the number of working farms, membership of and consequently viability of Deskford Church declined. However it still had life and energy, particularly in the 1950s and 1960s. In both 1948 and 1949 one service each year, in July, was held in the roofless Old St John's, and in 1958 the Moderator of the General Assembly visited the parish. However the roll declined from 300 in 1958 to 264 in 1960 to 228 in 1966.

In 1956 the membership of Deskford Church had been 301. There was a Sunday school with 57 children and 7 teachers, a branch of the Woman's Guild and a youth club. For ecclesiastical purposes the Shielburn part of Rathven parish was associated with Deskford Church. There were two families in the parish who belonged to the Episcopal Church and two to the Roman Catholic Church. The Rev Hamilton, writing around 1950, was of the opinion that farm servants avoided organised religion, that vows given on marriage were often not adhered to and that there was a general indifference towards religion. He also felt that the general world malaise was the fault of Stalin and Hitler.

With the decline in membership, Deskford Church became a linked charge with Cullen in 1967 under Rev J T Guthrie. On his death, they became a joint charge under Rev Alexander McPherson in 1987. Though attempts to revive the fortunes of the Church in Deskford were made, including the resumption of a Sunday school in 1993, the inevitable end was in view.

The last service was held in New St John's on November 14th 2004. The building had needed £3,500 for repairs. Wreaths were laid by Cllr Ron Shepherd, Community Councillor Ian McLean and Mr Jim Muiry (93), originally from Berryhillock, who had not missed a service since 1947. The last service was conducted by Rev Melvyn Wood and the occasion was a very sad one. Now, in 2016, fortnightly services are held in the Jubilee Hall by Rev Douglas Stevenson.

MINISTERS, SESSION CLERKS AND KIRK OFFICERS

Little is known of the pre-Reformation clergy in Deskford. For the majority of that time they were curates appointed by and paid by the Dean and Chapter of the Cathedral in Aberdeen which had gathered to itself the revenues from the Church in Fordyce and its associated chapels, including Deskford. The only name known from pre-Reformation times is Alexander Fordyce in 1472, but it is unknown whether he was the priest or vicar of Fordyce Church or a curate based in the chapel at Cullen.

In the years after the Reformation there were problems obtaining Ministers for every parish, and until the early C17th sometimes there was a Minister solely for Deskford, sometimes for Deskford shared with Cullen and sometimes for Deskford shared with Cullen, Fordyce and Ordiquhill.

The first Minister whose identity is known was William Lawtie, 1563 to 1568. He was followed by Gilbert Gardyne who was Minister of all four parishes from 1568 to 1589, and again from 1594 to 1599. He "seldom went to the pulpit without his sword for fear of papists" He was appointed Moderator of the General Assembly of the Church of Scotland in 1571 so was presumably held in considerable respect and esteem by his colleagues. Between 1590 and 1594 Alexander Hay was Minister of Deskford and Cullen. In this period of scarcity of Ministers the role of reader was important and a number were appointed to assist. In Deskford the first of these was John Thain or Thom between 1567 and 1574, at a stipend of 20 merks plus the Kirklands. He was succeeded by John Pilmuir from 1576 to 1578, Alexander Forsyith from 1578 to 1580 and David Henryson from 1580 to 1589. Though the supply of Ministers improved in the early C17th, George Andersone still had the post of reader in 1644.

Gilbert Gardyne was succeeded as Minister by George Douglas and Patrick Darg in turn. Patrick Darg in particular had been well respected and in 1626 was appointed Moderator of the Presbytery of Fordyce. In 1627 he was succeeded by his son, Walter Darg and this began thirty years of upset, embarrassment and problems for Deskford parish. In 1644 Walter Darg was deposed by the Synod for "gross prevarications", despite all the elders giving him a good testimony in all matters. He was deposed as Minister in 1650, but refused to go gracefully. In October 1651 the Session emphasised to the two heritors, Lord Findlater and Abercromby of Skeith that a vacancy had now existed for some considerable time, and urged them to fill it by February 1652.

Nothing had happened by December 1652 and the elders and parishioners made supplication to Presbytery that they should be provided with a Minister, and by April 1653 Presbytery instructed Mr James Chalmer to speak to Lord Findlater about the matter. A letter was also written by Mr Andrew Cant to Lord Findlater on behalf of Presbytery. Over the following year pressure increased, till eventually, in June 1654 Mr Walter Ogilvie was appointed. However he died, aged 30, in 1658.

Early in 1652 Walter Darg had been "silenced" by the Synod of Aberdeen which prohibited the people from hearing him preach. They appointed another local Minister to preach and make this intimation, but he had to do so in the churchyard, Rev Darg refusing to come out of the pulpit to allow the other Minister in. Eventually he was excommunicated for baptising whilst prohibited from doing so, but this was annulled in 1664. In 1666 and 1667 he was in trouble for marrying people irregularly in Rathven where he was living in very poor circumstances. By 1681 he was so poor that he received assistance from the Kirk Session of Cramond, near Edinburgh.

Andrew Henderson was appointed Minister in 1659, having been schoolmaster in Rathven, then Cullen. In 1661 he was sent by Presbytery to the tolbooth in Banff to converse with the Laird of Bog who was under sentence of excommunication for fornication for the fifth time, on this occasion in the tollbooth with a woman put there for murdering her own child. In 1664 he was appointed to consider the case of Andrew Herd, who had been excommunicated for "slaughter". Henderson was presbytery clerk from 1673 to 1679. He was succeeded by Alexander Gellie, 1680 to 1684, and then by James Henderson in 1684. Henderson was deprived of his position as Minister of Deskford by the Privy Council in 1689 for refusing to pray for William and Mary and presumably supporting King James II and VII, however he continued to preach in Deskford until 1694.

In 1698 William Murray, who had been a preaching deacon in Deskford under the Episcopacy, was appointed Minister and served until 1719. In 1693 a letter had been written by Rev George Meldrum in Aberdeen to Sir James Ogilvie requesting that his nephew, Mr David Meldrum, should be appointed in place John Murray, who was " not well liked by the Ministers in Moray", and who "as a prelaticall deacon baptizeth and marryeth, which office we do not allow". Nothing happened. In 1694 James Ogilvie wrote to his father, the Earl of Findlater, by hand from Edinburgh, urging that the bearer, Mr Leslie, be settled as Minister of Deskford. His views were stated to be orthodox, unlike those of Mr Murray whose views were unlikely to be accepted by many Ministers. Despite all this, Mr Murray was ordained.

Alexander Philp was Minister from 1720 to 1730. In 1726 he reported that he did not have a legal glebe and requested that it be valued, increased in size and made to adjoin the manse. For his stipend the Earl of Findlater paid 1 chalder of meal and 100 merks money, and Abercrombie of Skeith paid £3:18/- Scots in lieu of 11 chalders of meal. The tenants in the parish, except those in the lands of Skeith, who paid nothing, gave about £100 Scots, called teind silver, and other small tithes were also valued at about £100 Scots. The total was just over 500 merks, but the tenants' share was not well paid. Seeing that this was was too small, Presbytery applied to the Earl of Findlater for an increase, to which he agreed. Rev Philp transferred to Boyndie in 1730 because it was bigger and had two Jacobite prelatical meeting-houses which needed someone strong to stand up against. Deskford had none.

Walter Morison succeeded Mr Philp in 1731 and remained Minister of Deskford till 1781. In 1725 he had been appointed itinerant preacher to Bellie and Rathven where, when attempting to enter the pulpit, he was attacked by a mob of papists and prevented from doing so. In all he was a Minister for 65 years, 49 of them in Deskford where he was very well liked and respected. His beliefs were orthodox but he was no puritan, had no fanaticism, nor any hatred of Episcopalians or Catholics. In fact he supported and protected a Catholic family who were accused of being in league with the devil because their cattle, alone in Deskford, survived a deadly epidemic. He also gently countered the more extreme and inventive antiquarian beliefs of Rev Lawtie of

Fordyce. On his death aged 88 Rev Morison left the several hundred pounds he had saved for the support of his granddaughter who was an imbecile, that she might live out her years in comfort.

In 1739 the Earl of Findlater agreed to convert the vicarage tithes into a yearly sum of £262:14:3d Scots. He also paid, as part of the stipend, a chalder of meal and 140 merks. The stipend also included £104:16/- Scots of teind silver plus £21:3:4d as the annual rent of Sharp's Mortification, which latter amount he bound himself and his successors to pay yearly. He also paid £20 Scots to Rev Morison for communion elements of bread and wine. Rev Morison negotiated a conversion to money of previous elements of his stipend such as one lamb in every ten born, one fleece of every ten shorn, 10d for every calf born and 16d for every ewe's milk. Every lamb was valued at 16d and every cow's milk at 10d. He did not demand the tithe of linen yarn due to him.

Rev Morison was succeeded by Rev Walter Chalmers who was in post almost as long, for 48 years from 1780 to 1828. He was a very able individual who wrote the Deskford entry in the First Statistical Account and who published a pamphlet entitled "The Prevalent Disregard to Religion and Virtue, the Ruin of Individuals and of Nations" in Edinburgh in 1794. He also supported tenants against aspects of their tenancy agreements which he considered unfair or onerous.

Rev Chalmers was in turn succeeded in 1829 by Rev George Innes who had been Minister in Cullen, but obviously thought Deskford a better place. He wrote the Deskford entry in the New Statistical Account, but is best remembered for resigning his post in 1843 to found the Deskford congregation of the Free Church, an act of pure principle which saw him giving up a good stipend and a comfortable manse at the age of 66 for a very uncertain future. The respect in which he was held was largely responsible for all but one of the elders and many of the congregation leaving to join the Free Church.

In 1843, after the Disruption, Rev James Mackintosh, a native of Ordiquhill, was appointed to St John's Church, which he served for 47 years, retiring in 1890. The new manse was built in 1873 to accommodate his very large family, many of whom were successful in their chosen careers, particularly so Professor Sir Ashley Mackintosh who in 1902 unveiled stained glass windows in New St John's in memory of his parents. In 1893 a Complimentary Dinner was held for Rev Mackintosh in the Seafield Hotel, Cullen, by the Presbytery of Fordyce. In 1895 he was awarded an Honorary Doctorate by the University of Aberdeen.

Rev James Mackintosh.

In 1890 Rev Park was appointed from amongst eighty applicants, of whom six were invited to preach, before the congregation of 198 voted for their new Minister, using a form of proportional representation under which the candidate with fewest votes in each round dropped out. Had the election been run on a first past the post system he would not have been appointed as he was a distant second to Rev Lamb in every round of voting till the last one. James Wilson, in his autobiography, gives his views on the qualities and disadvantages of each of the candidates who preached. Rev Park was Minister for 41 years, from 1890 to 1931 when St John's and the Free Church united. He had been responsible for getting an organ for the church and the Public Hall for the community. When he retired in 1931 he was paid £25 for items in the manse which belonged to him. Both he and Rev Morrison of the Free Church retired to allow a new appointment to the united charge.

Similar tragedies attended the lives of both Rev Mackintosh and Rev Park. Rev Mackintosh's wife fell out of her top floor bedroom window in the manse and died and Rev Park's wife also fell to her death, from the cliffs near Portknockie. Both were originally considered to have been suicide, Mrs Mackintosh having been depressed and Mrs Park being rumoured to have a forlorn attraction to another Minister. However in both cases, within days, they were recorded as being accidents. The truth will never be known, but as accidents, there was no difficulty about the women being buried in consecrated ground.

Rev George Park.

Rev James Morrison, Free Church.

There were only four Ministers of the Free Church in Deskford. Rev Innes, who has already been mentioned, was followed in 1851 by Rev W T Ker who had private means and who, though popular with some of his congregation, alienated others. He gradually neglected his parish work and eventually wished to have his main residence in Aberdeen while continuing to be Minister in Deskford. There was doubt about whether the congregation could support a new Minister, but, with Presbytery involved, an agreement was reached that a new appointment would be made if Rev Ker resigned. This took place in 1883 with Rev Alexander Walker being appointed to succeed him in 1884. He was only in post for three years and when he left he offered to sell to the Church nine grates, one kitchen range, one dresser and a number of window rollers all for £5.

Replacing Rev Walker, Rev James Morrison took up post in 1888 and remained Free Church Minister till 1931 and union with St John's. He was a popular, decent and modest individual who kept peacocks. In 1906 he participated in a six-month exchange with Rev John Scott MacDonald of Brisbane, Queensland.

Rev William Brown.

The first Minister after the union was Rev William Brown who was well liked in the parish and visited members widely, by bicycle. On one such visit to Inaltrie in 1945 in bad weather, he collapsed and only lived another week. He held two services each Sunday so that farm workers who "kept toun" could go to the evening one. He was succeeded from 1945 to 1952 by Rev William Hamilton whose ministry saw the numbers of Woman's Guild members rapidly and significantly increasing , a fact often attributed to the Minister's film star good looks. He in turn was succeeded by Rev Alfred J Armour till, in 1967, Deskford became a linked charge with Cullen under Rev J T Guthrie who was very widely respected. When he died in 1986 the two congregations were united, firstly under Rev Alexander J Macpherson from 1987 to 1997, then Rev Melvyn Wood from 1997 to 2004. On his resignation the first female Minister of Cullen and Deskford Parish Church, Rev Wilma Johnston, was appointed. When she resigned in 2008 the parish was put under an Interim Minister in order to resolve some significant issues which had emerged. Since 2010 the Minister has been Rev Douglas Stevenson, and the Church is in good heart.

One aspect of the Minister's life which often caused concern was the stipend and this was often linked to concern about the glebe, even though, in the late C16th, King James VI had settled Scots Ministers' minimum stipends of £360 Scots (£30 sterling), much more than their equivalents in England who might only get £5 a year. In 1675 the Deskford stipend was "500 merks with a glebe sowing 5½ bolls, with foggag, fewell, fail and divot but no grasse".

Rev Douglas Stevenson.

Ministers would store the meal part of the stipend in the manse girnal and sell it as money was required.

In the C18th Ministers were very poor and got little sympathy from either parishioners or heritors. In 1781 the glebe was excambed to make it more coherent. It became two parts, on either side of the old main road. In 1790 the stipend was £44:15:3d sterling plus 24 bolls, one firlot of

Deskford Church 2015. A typical congregation.

barley and the same of meal at 8/- the boll. By 1792 the stipend was £63 in all, including a glebe of about 4 acres. By 1842 the stipend was £193: 12:10d plus the glebe which was worth £8, plus 14 chalders, half meal and half barley, plus £1:15:3d from the Sharp mortification of 1675 plus £8:6:8d for communion elements. In 1871 the stipend was set at 50 bolls, 3 firlots, 2pecks of meal, 30 bolls, 1 firlot, 4 pecks of bere and £241:0:8d for both stipend and communion elements. In 1880 the stipend was £193:12:10d plus £74:16:1d of unappropriated teinds, and by the 1890s had become solely money, £329.

In 1941 the salaries were, Minister £360, organist £18, Church Officer £12, organ blower £2:5/- and Session Clerk £2:2/-. In 1956 the Minister's stipend had risen to £600 and by 1965 the minimum stipend was £925. In 1959 the organist, Church Officer and organ blower's salaries were raised to £27, £26 and £5 respectively, after no change for many years.

Well into the C20th the Minister was a very important individual in Deskford. He was personal confidante, legal adviser, umpire in quarrels and general support and guide in time of trouble. He had a school to superintend, was often asked to write wills and was a counsellor. He visited every family in the parish over a period of time, accompanied by the appropriate district elder. There was competition to have the good fortune of having a baby son the first to be baptised by a new Minister, but to be the first married by him was considered to be unlucky. Despite all this Deskford was a very desirable charge, having an above average stipend and an excellent manse.

In addition to the Minister, other roles were important in the operation of the kirk, Session Clerk, Kirk Officer and later organist and organ blower. In 1906 St John's still had a precentor, Andrew Reid, Burnheads, but by 1918 this post had disappeared. The roles of the elder and the Kirk Session were vital, and in 1885 the Free Church created four elders' districts under John Lawrence, Alexander Reid, Alexander Mackay and James Hay, but also appointed five deacons to cover six districts. William Milton covered two, and the other four, James Russell, Alexander Taylor, John Grant and James McKenzie, one each.

Elders fulfilled a very important role in terms of law keeping, finance, charity and support of parishioners and ensuring their righteousness. In the C17th many elders were illiterate. In 1628 there was a visitation by Presbytery at which elders and deacons present were "James Ogilvy of Blairok, Andrew Lauty of Innaitry, Walter Ogilvie of Cairstoun, Patrick Stewart of Clochmacrich, Mr James Ogilvie of Skeith, Johne Ogilvie in Berryhillock, James Fordyce in Knowis, Viliam Brobner in Over Skeith, Johne Shipherd in Crabstoune, Walter Brobner in Deskfoord". Absent were James, Lord Deskfoord who was in London, Thomas Abercromby in Skeith and Johne Innes of Auchluncart.

In March 1743 the Minister reported that, for the purpose of having some more persons of good standing added to the number of elders, he had spoken to James Smith in Mosside, James Keir in Broadrashes and David Grant in Ramoir who he judged would accept the offer of being elders in the parish. He proposed the edict be intimated asking for any objections. This was agreed by Session who also suggested that since there was no elder in the head of the parish, that Alexander Barker in Tillybreadless should be added to the number. In May 1759 James Murray, younger, in Ardicow, William Gray in Inaltrey and Alexander Taylor in Kirktown were invited to become elders. Two accepted but William Gray wanted time to consider.

In May 1845, since all but one elder had moved to the Free Church, new elders were elected in St John's. There were 20 candidates, and the number of votes for each ranged from 20 down to 1. It was agreed to appoint the top eight, but only five accepted, James Wilson, William Longmore, John Whyntie, William Stephen and John Bagrie, though four more from the list of candidates were appointed in June. Several of those appointed at this time were to remain elders for a very long time, perhaps because they were younger than was usual when appointed, because of the difficulties in getting suitable candidates following the Disruption.

Elders in 1930 were James Duncan, Cottartown, Charles Cooper, Knows, Alexander Ross, Kirktown, John Longmore, Cottartown, James Craib, Cottartown, John Gordon, Berryhillock and William C Stevenson, Careston. New elders were appointed in 1936. They were JA Beveridge, the Schoolhouse, John Cooper, Knows, John Meldrum, Wester Blairock and William Simpson, Woodend. In 1998 for the first time, three women were ordained as elders to

Cullen and Deskford Kirk Session. They were Ann Morrison, Nether Blairock, Wendy Bennett and Isobel Patterson.

Over the years a number of different methods were used to decide on new elders. Sometimes they were nominated by the Minister and endorsed by the Kirk Session. At other times they were proposed by members of the congregation and selected from these nominations by the Kirk Session and at yet other times they were nominated by the Kirk Session and voted for by the congregation.

From the time of the Reformation the Session Clerk held a pivotal position within the church. He took the minutes of Kirk Session meetings and was responsible for much of the administration connected with the kirk. As such it was essential that he could read and write and accordingly it became the custom that the position was offered to the schoolmaster. This was the case in Deskford with each new schoolmaster until the middle of the C20th. In addition, and dependent upon circumstances at the time, the individual might also be precentor and/or treasurer. As in all such occupations, some were assiduous and competent and others less so. Some took comprehensive minutes and other much briefer ones, though they tended to be longer at the beginning of an individual's term in office. On several occasions minutes were lost, for example when the Session Clerk was too indolent to write them up, or when mice ate them when they lay in a cupboard in the schoolhouse. The former incident, in 1741, led to the Minister, Rev Morison, normally a pleasant and gentle man having a long rant about the "neglect, omission and carelessness" of Alexander Philp, the Session Clerk. He remarked that "a slothful man is a disgrace to his friends".

In the early C18th things were complicated. In 1724, John Dugal, treasurer, died, leaving his wife very poor. He was not replaced permanently until 1726. In the meantime, in 1725, James Sinclair, Session Clerk and precentor, demitted office because of old age and infirmity and asked the Session to give him something yearly to help him subsist, to which it agreed. The new schoolmaster, William Gordon, was made Session Clerk and precentor on a trial basis, receiving as his salary the dues for baptisms, marriages and testificats, together with two-thirds of the fines for fornication. He was made permanent in 1726 but requested an annual salary instead of these dues and penalties. The Kirk Session agreed and gave him £8 Scots and also gave £8 to the previous Session Clerk, James Sinclair, for the previous year and because of his circumstances. Also in 1726 John Davidsion, elder, became treasurer.

In 1727 the Kirk Session reversed their decision and declared that the Session Clerk's and Kirk Officer's fees should be paid out of penalties, the Clerk to receive 16 merks (£10:13:4d Scots) and the Kirk Officer £4 Scots. The Officer agreed to this but Mr Gordon, the Session Clerk, did not, and resigned. The Minister had to take minutes of session meetings until the end of 1728 when Mr Gordon left to become schoolmaster at Cairnie and was replaced as schoolmaster by Alexander Geddes who agreed to become Session Clerk at a salary of 16 merks. When he left in 1724 it was discovered that, due to his neglect, the minutes for two and a half years had not been written up. In 1734 the Session gave £6:13:4d to Mr Harie Spence for his Session Clerk duties in the absence of Mr Alexander Geddes.

In 1737 Thomas Riddoch, Session Clerk, had served for four years and was granted £1 sterling (£12 Scots) for each. This was complicated by the fact that he had received payments for loft rental and penalties, so the exact balance due to him for the four years was £12:0:6d Scots which was paid. In May 1743 Alexander Philp had died and the Earl of Findlater had appointed Thomas Ogilvie, son of a deceased merchant in Cullen, as schoolmaster. He also became Session Clerk. However in 1747 he left to become a Writer (lawyer) in Edinburgh and was replaced respectively by Alexander Paterson, James Robertson, son of Alexander Robertson in Skeith in 1748, Colin Morison in 1751 and William Stevenson in 1754.

After this things settled down with schoolmasters automatically becoming Session Clerks, for example James Brander in 1858, followed by James Smith and in 1909 by John Scott, whose salary was two guineas per annum plus all proclamation fees. He was given the Post Office Savings Book which was in credit to the sum of £28:9:10d, plus a number of Kirk Session records, Volumes 1, 2, 3 and 4 of Session minutes which went from 1684 to 1909, the Register of Proclamation Banns 1879 to 1909, the Account Book 1896 to 1908, the Session Book 1731 to 1783 and Account of All Monies Belonging to the Poor, the

Register of Cases of Discipline 1903, the Book of Payments for Proclamations etc and List of Poor of the Parish 1807 to 1855 and the Baptismal Roll 1855 to 1909. Present and previous Communion Rolls were left with the Minister. The location of many of these is now unknown.

In 1930 the first non-schoolmaster to become Session Clerk, Robert Cruikshank, was appointed, still at a salary of £2. He was tenant of Little Mosside and was still Session Clerk in 1950. He had been gassed in World War I and his speech was affected.

The post of Kirk Officer was one which could encompass a variety of tasks, including some or all of beadle, gravedigger, bell ringer and keeper of the graveyard. It was not always possible to find a suitable person for the post, and there were frequent disagreements about pay.

In 1726, on the death of the Kirk Officer, Alexander Wood, a meeting of the great and the good was held to decide whether to employ as his successor the man recommended by Wood, his servant Walter Milton, a grave and sober young man. It was agreed to appoint him at a salary of 8d sterling for each grave that he dug, except for graves within the church, for which he would be paid more, and graves for the Poor, for which he would not be paid. For marriages he would be paid 12d sterling where the woman being married was from within the parish. His pay for baptisms was 4/- Scots as was his pay for charging each delinquent. In addition he was to receive one third of all fines plus 18d Scots out of the collection every Lord's Day, except when there was a public collection. Walter Milton accepted the post on these terms.

In 1735 Alexander Bainzie was Kirk Officer and the Session was not happy with him. He continued to cohabit with Jean Stables, despite having been frequently instructed not to, even though they were contracted to marry. She was of very poor character. For example she frequently threw her children from a previous marriage out so that they had to sleep in the open or in outhouses, unless neighbours showed pity and took them in. Alexander Bainzie was suspended until the session saw he could "restrain that woman". In the meantime the Minister was to employ a substitute. In December 1737 it was discovered that the Kirk Officer had not received the price of a pair of shoes at the previous communion, as was the custom. It was agreed to give him 1/- sterling for this purpose.

By 1879 John Lorimer, beadle, gravedigger and bell ringer was often to be found drunk. When he died in 1885 the balance of his salary was paid to his representatives. George Joss of Kirktown was to be paid 1/- per week for carrying out the duties of beadle till a new Kirk Officer could be appointed. Mr Bryson, on behalf of the Dowager Countess of Seafield, as heretrix, agreed with whoever the Kirk Session wished to appoint, and Alexander Morrison, Kirktown was appointed at a salary of £2:5/-, exclusive of the 15/- given by the Dowager Countess.

The Free Church was not able to pay its officials as much as did St John's. In 1884 they agreed to pay the beadle and precentor £2 annually and the Session Clerk £1. In 1885 the Free Church beadle was James Russell. In 1888 the Free Church precentor resigned and steps were taken to appoint a replacement at a salary of £6. Alexander Morrison was appointed but soon resigned. There was a continuing difficulty in getting and keeping precentors.

World War I was responsible for a significant upward pressure on salaries. On August 10th 1919, James Fordyce, Church Officer at St John's, offered his resignation, but would stay on as keeper of the cemetery. The Session offered to increase his salary from £5 to £7:10/-, which he accepted. At the same time Miss Reid, the organist, had her salary increased to £18 and Master John Jamieson, the organ blower, had his increased to £2:5/-. In May 1922 Mr Fordyce, Church Officer for 17 years, resigned. James Watson, Kirktown, was appointed in his place at a salary of £8, payable in two halves, at Whitsunday and at Martinmas. He resigned in 1935 and was replaced by Alexander Masson, Berryhillock, from amongst five applicants.

CHURCH MEMBERSHIP

Membership of the churches in Deskford has fluctuated in line with the local population, however the reduction in membership during the C20th was much steeper than the decline in the population. Membership of whichever church was the national one was almost universal until the mid C19th when people felt freer to join any of a number of denominations or sects, and by the end of the century increasing numbers felt free to give up their church connection.

The highest recorded roll of St. John's over the past 200 years was 357 in the 1860s which was also the time of the highest population recorded in the parish, 1060. The number 357 does not however fully reflect weekly attendance which also included young family members who had not yet joined formally. At this time the Free Church also had a healthy membership, which at its peak around 1850 numbered between 150 and 200, but this had gradually declined to 101 in 1901 and to 68 by the time of union in 1932. Comparisons between the sizes of membership of the two churches are made difficult because the Free Church was more active in purging its communion roll before each communion service than was St John's.

St John's roll had fallen to just 135 immediately after the Disruption in 1843 but rapidly recovered from the 1850s on. In 1878 it was 336, in 1925 301 and by 1932 it was still 280. The union was responsible for a slight increase in the combined membership of the united church whose roll numbered 350. From this point it fell continuously. In 1941 many of the members lived outwith the parish, and by 1946 the roll had fallen to 306. The Sunday school was however very active. In 1933 there were 70 children and five teachers, in 1946 there were 69 children and even by 1960 there were still 55 children. In 1961 there were 13 boys and 27 girls in Sunday school and bible class, taught by three women and two men, including the Minister. The women were Miss Currie, Greenhill, Miss McKenzie, Wester Darbreich and Miss Armour, the manse.

Decline in membership during the second half of the C20th was very steep as the population of the parish fell to an all-time low of 158 in 1991. Elderly members who died were not replaced by younger ones, and in 2004 New St John's Church was closed with services being taken fortnightly in the Jubilee Hall. Membership remained fairly steady at a low level in the C21st, with most remaining members being over 60 years of age and average attendance being between 10 and 15.

CHURCH BUILDINGS

Church buildings have existed at one time or another at five different sites in Deskford though information about two of the pre-Reformation ones is very sketchy. Old St John's in Kirktown is probably the oldest site, though the present unroofed building was a much-altered version of the 1543 church which was itself a rebuilt structure based on significantly older stone church. Even this was probably not the oldest building on the site, on which a chapel, probably wooden or built of turf, is recorded in 1256. The more commodious New St John's replaced Old St John's in 1871. It lies by the side of the turnpike road on what was the farm of Knappycausey. The ruins of the Free Church lie a mile west of the Community Hall, beside the road to Sheilmuir and Buckie. It operated as a Church from 1844 up to World War II.

The pre- Reformation Chapel of Our Lady of Pity lay in Chapel Haugh, between the old road just south of Berryhillock and the Deskford Burn, just north of the

Site of Our Lady of Pity in Chapel Haugh.

Mains of Skeith track. It may have been connected with the Castle of Skeith in the early days of that building. The church buildings were no longer standing in 1732 when it was recalled that "Our Lady of Pity stood here". The tenant of the ground in the mid C19th, Mr Thomson, removed stonework and also found human remains when laying field drains. Remains in the Chapel Haugh were remembered in 1866 by Mr McWillie senior, and even in the 1880s distinct traces could still be seen, when the cultivated ground where the chapel site had been was of a lighter colour than that of the surrounding site. For many years a wooden panel supposed to have come from Our Lady of Pity was held by the Catholic Church in Aberdeen.

The 1st edition 25" to the mile OS map of 1866 shows a chapel site on top of Chapel Hillock, between Backies and Clochmacreich. A C19th tenant stated that he had dug up foundation stones and Mr McWillie remembered distinct traces of a building. There are also repeated references in C16th land transactions to "Clochmacreich, including the Ladyland". This latter would refer to land attached to a chapel dedicated to the Virgin Mary. It did not survive the Reformation.

Old St John's is referred to as a chapel in 1541 and as a church in 1545. It was at this time that it was rebuilt, probably to support the case for Deskford becoming a parish in its own right. The nationally important sacrament house was built in 1551. The walls of the Church contain a number of stones of red sandstone which may have been part of the fabric of the earlier stone church. The earliest part of the present structure may date to 1437, though there was certainly a chapel recorded in Deskford in the time of Robert the Bruce in the early C14th. The Church is about 20' wide and about the time of the Reformation was extended to 60' long. Two pewter cups from the 1660s, 4" high and 3¼" in diameter had the letters MAH (Maister Andrew Henderson), Minister from 1659 to 1679 on one side and D for Deskford on the other. They were ornamented with vine branches and grapes.

At one time or another lofts existed on each of the four sides in Old St John's. The first of these started as the laird's loft, in timber, at the east end, reached by an external stair and a doorway which can still be seen, high in the east gable. This was built around the time the church was renovated in 1628, at which time the Session wished to discuss with Lord Deskford the lack of a bell. In 1739 the laird's loft became known as the old loft or common loft and was used by members of the congregation. It comprised twelve pews, the rental of which went into the Poor's Box. By 1751, when it was inspected, it was found that some of the pillars supporting it were failing. They were to be repaired as soon as possible out of public money. By 1760 it was "crowded by disorderly people who often cause disturbance in time of service".

The new loft or west loft was built in 1734, which confusingly made it five years older than the new name for the laird's loft, the old loft. The costs of the new loft were:-

ITEM	£	s	d
From Glasssaugh 30 dales (deals)	3	0	0
To nails from Berryhillock		12	0
Workmanship, nails and glew	27	19	4
Wages to wrights	2	8	0
Making test holes	1	11	0
Building the stair and slapping for the door	7	4	0
Alex Bainzie for leading sand		4	0
John Minster, wages		2	0
Sowering lime and sand		6	0
To dale and spar from Fochabers	47	13	6
To lime from Mr William Spence, 8 bolls	1	12	0
To carriage		4	0
To lime from Walter Wright, 10 bolls	2	4	0
To carriage		4	0
Windows in the new loft	2	13	8
Robert Davidson for helping at the work		4	0
To boards from the Minister at 5/- each	1	0	0
To the lock bands and gudgeons to the loft doo	1	11	0
To James Reid for lime		12	0
Total (£ Scots)	116	4	6

In 1786 the small loft on the south side, the "faulters loft" was ordered to be taken down as it was in danger of falling down, and in 1787, 39 seats in the new or west loft were let for 1d to 4d each, and 12 in the East Loft for 3d each. The west loft was also accessed by an external stair and a doorway in the gable, which can also still be seen. The pew rent was paid twice a year, at Whitsunday and Martinmas. A small north gallery was erected between 1837 and 1839, which meant that when the building closed for worship in 1871 there were three galleries, on the east, west and north sides, with the pulpit on the south. Headroom in the east and west lofts was only 6'6". The walls of the Church were entirely panelled in wood, which saved the hidden sacrament house from destruction. The Church had no ceiling but was open to the roof.

As described by Historic Scotland the church has a blocked window on the south wall of the sanctuary which has a splayed segmental rear arch defined by a thick roll on its interior arris. Also in the south wall were two partially recessed water stoups with ogee-arched heads. After the Reformation two plain lintelled doors were formed in the south wall and another in the north. In earlier times it was recorded that there was an inscription on the alter piece on the north wall which read "Thou art my bone and my flesh". Unfortunately some of the carved and inscribed stonework was damaged and hidden when the lofts and galleries were built. When the church was abandoned in 1872 it was unroofed but the wallheads were sealed with cement to protect them. The original plaster was still in evidence on the walls in 1890. The interior floor level was also heightened at this time by about 3 or 4 feet. It had contained pews dated 1627 and 1630. There are two aumbries near the position of the alter and a broken piscina.

It is likely that originally, before the Reformation, any pews would have faced east, with later ones also facing west after the Reformation when the focus moved to the pulpit in the centre of the south wall. There may have been pumphrels or box pews along the north wall which would have allowed the sides to be folded away and laid flat to form a continuous long table for communion. In addition to the main building of the church there was also a small nunnery attached to the east end, which, until the end of the C18th, served as an asylum for several old women, supported by the Earl of Seafield.

When Old St John's was abandoned it was planned to remove the sacrament house to New St John's, but this did not happen, solely due to oversight. It had been damaged when the laird's loft was built and may have been replaced higher up the wall when the ground level was raised. It is 2.45m high and 1.06m wide and comprises three registers enclosed by a vine scroll border, flanked by rectangular pilasters, supported on scalloped corbels with their pinnacles missing.

The upper register contains two angels supporting a monstrance. In the middle register is the aumbry itself, enclosed by a vine scroll. Above it are two scrolls bearing the inscription "OS. MEVM. ES. ET. CARA. MEA" (You are my bone and my flesh). Below the aumbry is written "Ego sum panis vivus qui de cello descendi quis manducaverit ex hoc pane vivet in aeternum" (I am the living bread, who came down from heaven. If anyone eats this bread he will live for ever). In the lower register are two shields, the first of which contains the arms of Ogilvie of Deskford and Findlater with the motto "TOVT JOUR" (always), flanked by the initials A.O. Tout Jour is part of an Ogilvie motto. "Tout Jour Fidele". The shorter version was used by some branches of the family. The other contains the same arms impaled with those of Gordon, with the motto "LAVS DEO" (Praise God), for Ogilvie's second wife, Elizabeth Gordon. Her arms

The sacrament house of 1551 in Old St John's Church.

have been vandalised, perhaps by Alexander Ogilvy's son. Below these is the inscription "THIS. PTN. LOVEBLE. VARK. OF. SACRAMENT. HOVS. MAID. TO. YE. HONOR + LOVIG. OF. GOD. BE. ANE. NOBLEMAN. ALEXANDER. OGILVY. OF. YAT. ILK. + ELIZABET. GORDON. HIS. SPOUSS. THE. ZEIR. OF. GOD. 1551".The sacrament house is of national importance, being very rare in having this inscription in Scots. It is also superior to the similar one in the Auld Kirk in Cullen, which was also erected by Alexander Ogilvie and Elizabeth Gordon.

Throughout its existence Old St John's has experienced repeated reconstruction and repair. In addition to what has already been mentioned, by 1676 it was felt that the fabric of the kirk and churchyard dykes were in good condition and kept so by the fines of fornicators and other delinquents. In 1686 John Shepherd promised lime for pointing to pay part of his fine. By 1698 Mr John Murray was appointed to speak to the Earl of Findlater about repairing the church and manse and providing utensils for the church. Much of the roof of the church was uncovered and at risk of falling in. The manse was ruinous and uninhabitable. In 1737 the stool of repentance was repaired at a cost of 18/- Scots, and in 1739 both the kirk and the school were said to be in good condition and had good slated roofs with slates probably from Sheilburn or Darbreich. In 1740 4/- was paid to mend the lock of one of the Church doors and in 1743 1/- was paid to the smith for the key to the new loft door. In 1763 John Smith was paid 6/- for cleaning the condies at the side of the church to carry water. In 1781 a bell was provided which had the inscription "Deskford 1781. And. Lowson. Old Abd".

In 1790 the Minister reported that the west loft was now repaired and the two front seats had been replaced by the Earl of Findlater for the singers. Session requested the Minister to employ Peter Lyon in Cullen to build two additional seats, and if there was demand for more, to build another two, which would fill the loft. In 1797 Rev Chalmers wrote to John Wilson, Factor, "I expected that some repairs to the Church of Deskford would have taken place before this time. It has lately been discovered that the beam of the east loft has come from the wall and that it is altogether unsafe for the people to let in it without an instant repair". He also requested that communion cups and cloths be supplied and that the communion table, given to the schoolhouse since there was no furniture there, should be replaced.

Repairs to the church also took place in May 1841, which prevented a diet of catechism taking place. The Tower of Deskford, which had been unoccupied since the end of the C16th was demolished in the late 1830s to prevent it collapsing on and destroying the church. The stone from it was used to rebuild the nearby bridge over the Deskford Burn. In 1884, after the church had been abandoned, a drain was built to remove the water of St John's Well which appeared to issue from beneath the church.

In 1840 Rev Innes felt that the church was conveniently situated for the parish. It was in good repair, but did not have a ceiling, being open to the roof. However it was rather small for the parish and it was suggested that a third, central, gallery would help. It had accommodation for 357 people but required accommodation for over 400. All pews were free except in one of the galleries, occupied by the Kirk Session, which had been built by the Earl of Seafield. Pew rents in this gallery were not expensive, being 3d at the back and 6d at the front. There were regular complaints to Presbytery during the C19th about the old church being too small and dark. In 1869 a petition was sent saying the church was ruinous and insufficient, and it was agreed to build a new one.

After much discussion the Ministry of Public Building and Works took responsibility for maintaining the sacrament house around 1930 and in 1938 it estimated that a plate glass ventilated cover to replace the wooden frame which was causing the stonework to decay would cost £120. For two years in the late 1940s an annual service was held in the unroofed Old St John's. The church and churchyard are A Listed.

One of the most contentious and persistent issues was over seating. After the Reformation, each worshipper who wished to sit in church had to bring his or her own three legged stool or "creepie". The Kirk Session rented out stances for them and later charged individuals to build fixed seats, and also charged rents for them. Disputes were common.

In 1721 John Gordon, Crabstoun, was permitted to erect a new seat "where he presently sat, for the accommodation of himself and his family". In 1748 there was a dispute between Janet Davidson in Over Skeith and William Reid in Faichiehill "anent a seat in the church formerly possessed by the said Janet Davidson's husband and John Skinner in Faichiehill, both deceast". Session decided that Janet Davidson should possess the whole seat and William Reid should possess the seat belonging to Walter Robertson, now in Cullen.

In 1751, since "there is a great backwardness and deficiency in payment of such as posses the new loft" it was decided to sell off the six rows of pews at the following rates. Every single person's seat in the breast or foreseat would cost 2 merks. Each person's seat in the second pews would cost 2/- sterling, and in the third pews 1/6d sterling. Seats in the fourth pews were to cost 1/4d and in the two back pews 1/3d.

In 1769 Mr Russel's seat was inconvenient. Andrew Littlejohn was to remove to another part of the church, which he did not agree to, so discussion was suspended. There was not enough room in the church so it was agreed that the front pew in the common loft would be rented, which would also prevent disorderly behaviour and a breach of the Lord's Day by some young people. In 1776 William Milne put up a seat at his own expense near the pulpit, by allowance of the session.

In 1777, John Lawrence, merchant in Kirktown, complained to the Session that as he had a seat in the foremost deck of the east loft, he was often hindered from taking possession because Alexander Donald brought several persons and filled up his seat. The Session called Donald and remonstrated with him against such behaviour and desired him, for the future, only to take in persons to fill his own seats, or they threatened to prosecute him at the Baillie Court. In 1778 James Black, Nether Blairock, was ordered to take possession of an armchair in the Church which formerly belonged to his ancestors. In 1780 John Smith, Broomhaugh, was desirous of having the property of his seat in the church registered in the session book. This was done. "It is hereby declared that the fourth seat from the west gable on the north side of the church is the property of the said John Smith, he having bought the same from Alexander Geddes, late proprietor".

There were many memorials, carved stones and gravestones within the church and the churchyard. Some which are now lost were recorded by Cramond and others, and a number within the Church were relocated to what had been window openings. Some may have been covered when the floor level was raised by four feet in the late C19th, in order to bring it up to the same level as the churchyard. Though now no stone or inscription can be seen, there is a tradition, backed up old written sources, that Mary Bethune (Beaton), one of "The Queen's Four Maries", who married Ogilvie of Boyne, was buried in Deskford Church or churchyard sometime after 1606.

Within the Church at the end of the C19th there was a roughly carved figure, perhaps of a Highland soldier. In the middle of the north wall an inscription read "MRI VALTRUS OGILVY VERBI DIVINI MINISTER PIVS NUNC INTER COELITES BEAT QVI FATIS CESSIT XV KAL FEB ANO ON 1658" (Mr Walter Ogilvie, a pius Minister of the divine word, now among the blessed inhabitants of heaven, who yielded to the fates on the 15th day before the Kalends of February, [ie Jan 17th], the year of our lord 1658). Ministers were well represented. An inscription to one on a flat slab inside and near the south door read "H RIS PROBAE MS. A GUETE SIMSON MRI ANDREAE HENDERSONI, ECCLESIAE DESKFORDENSIS MINISTRI CONJUGIS DILECTAE QUAE PER DECENIUM MARITO NUPTA SEPTEM LIBERAS ENIXA QUOR TRES HIC PARITER SEPULTI SUNT QUAE PLACIDE AC PIE MORTI SUCCVBVIT XVI KAL SEP AO AET XXXIV AER CHR MDCLXIII". (In this tomb are laid the ashes of a virtuous woman, Mrs Agnes Simson, the beloved wife of Mr Andrew Henderson, Minister of the Church of Deskford, who, married to her husband for ten years, and having borne seven children, of whom three are buried here alongside her, who peacefully and piously yielded to death on the 16th day before the Kalends of September, [ie 16th August], and 34 years of age, 1663 of the Christian era). Another states "Here lies in the hope of a blessed resurrection John Mure, Minister of the gospell at Deskfoord who departed this life March 1st 1719. Also Iean Ord his spouse who departed the   17   . As also James Murray their son who departed the Meay the 5, 1717" The Henderson and Murray slabs had formed part of the paving within the Church. On the door sill was a verse, JohnVI, verse 51, from the vulgate.

Within the graveyard there was a gravestone which said "HIC JACET JOHANNES ANDERSON, ABERDONIENSIS (Here lies John Anderson, an Aberdonian) – WHO BUILT THIS CHURCHYARD DYKE AT HIS OWN EXPENSE". The oldest gravestone seen in the churchyard in 1890 was bevelled on two sides and was initialled and dated "TD:MC 1668" There had been a stone built into the old west dyke of the graveyard, demolished to make way for the 1886 extension, which was inscribed " AD 1743. Here lys the corps of Iohn Dowgall and Elspet Skinner. Io Dowgall who died in the year 1723 and his wife Elspet Skinner who died 1746. This stone is erected by Alexr and Ianet Dowgalls".

A table stone existed, "Sacred to the memory of James Frazer, sometime smith at Ardoch who died Nov 9th 1788, aged 76 years. He was an honest man, friendly, benevolent and open hearted, and a strict observer of every religious duty. Isobel Gerry, his spouse, died Nov 8th 1789 aged 73. She was a dutiful wife, an affectionate parent and a friend to all in distress. This stone is erected by their son, James Fraser, smith in Banff". Another table stone was inscribed "This stone is erected by George Wright, Carrothead, in memory of his spouse, Ann Andrew who died 29 Aug 1791 aged 30, was married 1774 (aged 14?) has left 5 sons and 4 daughters.

> O Annie dear the grave has twin'd
> Thy loving heart and mine
> But I hope we'll meet in heaven above
> No more to part again".

Most of these old stones were lost when the churchyard was "improved"and tidied, including the removal of old stones to which no current resident of Deskford had any connection. There is no record of exactly when this occurred, but it may have been in connection with the extension to the graveyard in 1926, but is more likely to have taken place sometime between 1890 and 1910. Rather strangely no mention of this action is to be found in session minutes. Several interesting stones do however remain.

On the north wall of the churchyard is a stone to another Minister, Rev George Innes. It is inscribed "The Rev George Innes, born at Huntly 7 July 1777; ordained Minister of Cullen 1 Dec 1808, transferred to Deskford 7 Aug 1829:

and since the Disruption Minister of the Free Church here, died 1 Oct 1852 aged 75 years. His wife, Jane Milne died 7 March 1836 in her 45th year. Beside the remains of his beloved mother lies all that was mortal of her dear son, the Rev George Innes, Minister of Seafield Church and afterwards of the Free Church, Canonbie, who died 24 Nov 1847 in his 29th year and 5th of his ministry, having been subjected to much hardship in consequence of the refusal of a piece of ground on which to build a house, in which he and his congregation might assemble in comfort to worship Him to whom the earth and the fullness thereof belongs".

In an enclosure, still in existence, adjoining and outside the east gable of the church is a grave inscribed "Sacred to the memory of Mrs Sarabella Morison, daughter of the Rev Walter Morison, 49 years Minister at Deskford: married first to the Rev Henry Gordon, Minister at Ardersier by whom she had five children and 2dly to the Rev Walter Chalmers, present Minister at Deskford. Pius in heart and benevolent in mind, in person graceful, and in manners affable, a dutiful daughter, an indulgent parent and a tenderly affectionate wife; a warm and judicious friend. She died 3 January 1811 aged 76".

She is one of Deskford's forgotten heroines, giving much help and support to individuals and families who were in danger of becoming outcasts in the community. These included an alcoholic schoolmaster and a Gaelic-speaking Roman Catholic family who were thought to be in league with the Devil, and responsible for the death of everyone else's cattle.

Over the years there was a repeated struggle to repair the kirkyard dykes. In 1628 the dyke had been well begun but the elders were exhorted by presbytery to complete it. In 1721 Session, "understanding that the Minister had bought 5 bolls of lime for repairing some of the kirkyard dykes, recommended to him to agree with a mason to repair such places as were fallen and proposed that the heritors, the Earl of Findlater, Abercrombie of Skeith and Lawtie of Inaltry should be spoke to anent reimbursing of what the Session shall expend in this way". In 1724 the money which had been used to repair the churchyard dykes and to stock the bell had come from the Poor's money, in total £7:3:8d Scots. The Earl of Findlater, now sole heritor, was to be approached to reimburse this. Also in the C18th John Anderson, a sailor who had made some money, left some in his will to his brother, a local farmer, to rebuild the walls of the churchyard. In 1739 the churchyard dykes were again ruinous.

In 1744 the Minister agreed to speak to the Earl of Findlater anent repairing the kirkyard dykes, but in 1745 Session discovered that this was the responsibility of the parishioners. They agreed to get the work done but would nevertheless ask the Earl to pay. The people from the Crookie (Creichy) Burn to the end of the parish on the north side of the burn were to clear the kirkyard and rid it of stones. The people in Berryhillock and Burnheads were to cart and

Old St John's Church with Cotton Hill in the background and no trees in the Orchard. The date must be 1886 or 1887 since only the original bottom section of the graveyard is in use, though the new middle section has been laid out. The unusual cast iron gravestone towards the left of the photograph is still there.

lead the flags for making the condie. Those from the Ward (Waird) Burn to the head of the parish on the west side of the burn were to lead the sand and pinnings. Those from Clochmacreich to Skeith on the east side of the burn were to lead the lime and those from Skeith to the end of the parish on the east side of the burn were to lead the stones.

In 1749 Alexander Barker had been to buy timber for the churchyard doors but had not yet made them. It was agreed that if he did not do so within 14 days he should return the money. In 1764 £4:4/- was spent on making a causeway (paved path) to the kirkyard out of the penalties for penny weddings.

Within the churchyard was an ash tree, known as St John's Tree, believed to be one of the largest in Britain. It had a circumference a yard above ground level of 27'. A violent storm around 1800 tore away its largest limbs and destroyed its beauty. Its size was attributed to its being watered by the adjacent St John's Well. The tree had entirely disappeared by 1873, and the well by 1884.

Until 1885 the kirkyard of Old St John's comprised only the bottom one third of the present graveyard, the portion nearest the Church. In 1885 there was an agreement between the Parochial Board and the Kirk Session to extend the churchyard into what is now the middle section, but which at that time was occupied by a number of cottages and gardens.

This was dependant on consent being obtained from the Earl of Seafield, and from lessees and occupants within 100 yards of the proposed extension. This was duly obtained. An alternative proposal that the graveyard be extended into the orchard was abandoned and it was decided that it was preferable to extend 40' westwards to the garden dyke of Mr Smith, schoolmaster.

The old west wall of the original graveyard was demolished to allow the extension and the headstones which lay against and near it had to be lifted and moved. Around this time or shortly afterwards the graveyard was "improved". Many of the other headstones were also lifted. The tidying of the graveyard saw only the headstones of those who still had living descendants in the parish being put back, and these not always in their original position. Some of those lifted and not replaced lie in a neat pile outside the east gable, beside the grave of Mrs Sarabella Morison.

In the graveyard there still remain one example of a cast iron headstone, dated 1871, and commemorating Mrs Jane Edward or Russell from Miltown of Deskford, and one example of a glass bell jar containing white doves, dated

1897 and commemorating Alexander Murray of Berryhillock and his wife Margaret Milton (she may have been the wise woman known as Lucky Murray who was called upon to attend births and serious illnesses). Both are examples of types of grave markers which were fashionable for a short period. Originally all of those buried in the old graveyard would have been buried with their feet to the east and their head to the west, so that on the second coming of Christ they would see Him rising in the east and they would be resurrected themselves. Headstones were placed at the head end of the grave, to the west of the body.

Mr Bryson, Factor, on behalf of Lady Seafield, agreed to sell the land which was wanted, 18 poles, 19 yards in extent for £10, to include the solum of the Old Church. The Parochial Board was to be responsible for all expenses of the transfer, for the building of a new stone and lime wall and to maintain the walls of the Old Church in their existing state. The Parochial Board did not agree to maintain the Old Church and voted 4:3 in favour of a suggestion that the price should be determined by the valuation of arbiters, rather than accepting Mr Bryson's proposed price. However one week later they reversed this decision and agreed to pay the £10.

Mr. McWilliam, land surveyor, Broomhills, Fordyce, produced plans for

Deskford graveyard today with Old St John's and the Muckle Hoose to the rear.

trenching and levelling the new churchyard and an advert was placed in the *Banffshire Journal* for mason work. Messrs Morgan and Co, Fife Keith were appointed to do this at a cost of £43:7/-. William McLean, Berryhillock, was appointed to do the trenching and levelling at a cost of £17:10/-. Regulations for the use of the new churchyard were decided upon.

Less than forty years later, in 1924, the clerk of the Parish Council was instructed to approach Mr Lawson, Factor, about the proposal to extend the Churchyard once more, this time into the final, top section of the present graveyard, nearest the public road. Lady Seafield's Trustees agreed to this in December 1925 so long as the Parish Council also bought the Muckle Hoose, because of the adverse effect the graveyard extension would have on it and on the leases of ground for the gardens of cottages which would lose theirs. The Parish Council did not wish to buy the Muckle Hoose, but the Trustees would not agree to the sale of the land for the graveyard extension without this. The sale was finally agreed when the Trustees reduced the price for the Muckle Hoose to £100. For many years afterwards it was split into single room apartments for let to poor families. Cllr Ron Shepherd lived in one of these in his childhood. Stones for the new dyke came from Mains of Skeith and Hoggie.

New St John's Church, opened in 1872.

The estimated cost of the new churchyard was £450, which included layout, paths, walls, new gardens, fees and expenses and changing the position of the old entrance gate and path. This had originally been a road down the middle of the land used for the extension, but was now moved to its present position at the southern end of the new part of the graveyard. The Parish Council decided to apply for a loan of £600 from the Public Works Loan Board, but did not go ahead with this when the cheapest tender for the work, from Mr John Longmore, Springwells Croft, Bauds, came in at £159. It was accepted.

Six pages of close written rules for the new churchyard were introduced. Charges for burials were; children under 7, 4/-; children between 7 and 14, 6/-; persons above 14, 10/-; paupers, 5/-; mortcloth if required, 5/-. In pre-Reformation times there was almost certainly also a burial ground beside the Chapel of Our Lady of Pity at Skeith, as bones were dug up at this site in the 1840s. There may also have been burials on Chapel Hill.

New St John's Church, which replaced Old St John's in 1871 was designed by

The interior of New St John's Church.

John Miller, Architect and Clerk of Works at Cullen House. It was a cruciform gothic church, oriented to the east, with the entrance in the west gable. It was built of harled rubble, some of which came from Meikle Knows, with tooled and polished ashlar dressings and margins. There was a slightly advanced and pinnacled centre bay in the west gable, with the central entrance under a pointed headed Y tracery light and with double leaf plank doors with ornate cast iron hinges. It had a large two light window above with flanking, smaller, pointed headed lights, all under hood moulds. There was an apex bellcote.

It had five bay flanks including shallow transepts with large traceried windows in the north transept incorporating a decorative R for Reidhaven and cross. There were narrow hood mould pointed headed windows elsewhere with lattice pane glazing, with coloured margins and an apex cross finial. It had a slate roof and the gallery was to the west. Just before it opened two old women, observing the new church with its datestone AD1871, were puzzling on what the letters might mean until one of them had an idea. "Oh yes, they'll be for Alexander Desson the slater".

The foundation stone was laid, after completion of the Church, by Viscount Reidhaven, in the presence of the Earl and Countess of Seafield on March 13th 1872. The bell in the bellcote was reused from Old St John's and remains part of the property of the building, now a private house, due to an oversight in the contract of sale drawn up by the Church of Scotland in 2004. The War memorial stands within the Church grounds beside the public road. Two beautiful stained glass windows were installed in 1902 in memory of Rev Dr James Mackintosh (1809-1902) and his wife Elsey Fraser (1828-1889). The dedication service was attended by the Dowager Countess of Seafield, and the windows were unveiled by Mr McConnachie, Ardoch and Mr Wood, Cottarclump.

There was fairly continuous repair, maintenance and upgrade of the building. In 1891 Rev Park got agreement for a door to be fitted to prevent draughts in the gallery and for a goblet to be purchased for communion. In 1893 it was decided that the woodwork should be varnished, walls painted and windows repaired. Lady Seafield agreed to give £20 if the congregation would pay the rest. This was agreed and the total cost came to £53:10/-. In the event Lady Seafield gave £25. During the work services were held in the school. In 1912 the Trustees of the late Lady Seafield handed over to the Kirk Session of Deskford Parish Church the silver and ivory trowel presented to her son Viscount Reidhaven when he laid the foundation stone. It was returned to the Earl of Seafield when the building ceased being used as a church in 2004.

In 1923 thanks were given to the heritor for arranging for painting of the doors, windows and wood and ironwork of the church and the iron gates and railings in front of the War Memorial. The work was carried out by Mr Fleming, Keith.

One of the main issues considered was Church music, with a precentor still being appointed and paid into the C20th. Despite this, in 1886, subscriptions were raised to purchase a harmonium for the church. A new American organ was bought on trial for £25, and Miss Mackintosh, the Minister's daughter, was to be the organist. It helped the singing but it was agreed to raise a further £5 to purchase a stronger one. Under Rev Park, in 1904, a pipe organ was installed at a cost of £200, £100 of which was contributed by the Carnegie Trust and £100 by the congregation. It was built by Lawton's and had two manual and nine sp. The pulpit was built into the organ casing.

Heating was an ongoing concern, and the first system was installed in 1888, just 16 years after the building opened. In 1946 a new heating system was installed in the Church by JTL Parkinson, Aberdeen at a cost of £315:13/-. In 1948 it was working well and two new radiators were added. In 1967 a modern heating system was installed. A new boiler house with two electric boilers linked to the existing pipework was built. It was thermostatically controlled and had a time switch to use off-peak rates.

In 1951 Mrs Craib of Bankcroft gave money in memory of her husband, for cushions for the pews, but the Minister and Kirk Session persuaded her to use it instead for three communion chairs, for the Minister and two officiating elders, and an oak screen for the organ console, with a red velvet or velour curtain. That year a baptismal font was purchased for the first time as more and more children were being baptised in church rather than at home, reverting to an older practice.

In 1952 another baptismal font was purchased in memory of Rev Brown, communion chairs and screen in memory of Mr Craib, a lectern in memory of Mr and Mrs G Wright, Upper Skeith, and two brass vases for the communion table. The pulpit and choir were reconstructed with plans by David Waugh,

Deskford Free Church, opened in 1844, known as the West Church after the union in 1932.

architect of Hughes and Waugh, Glasgow. The contractor was Mr Smith, Portsoy, painter Mr McGregor, Cullen, electrician Mr Davidson, Cullen, with linoleum from Mr Greig, Keith.

In 1957 special gifts were solicited to pay for the connection of the church, manse and Glebe Cottage to the public water supply, and repairs to harling and slates. £117:9:6d was raised towards the cost of £150. Youth club members dug the trenches and laid pipes for the water supply, demonstrating a somewhat different attitude towards health and safety than would be likely to be found today. When New St John's finally closed as a church, it was offered for sale in 2005 at offers over £50,000. There were eight expressions of interest and it was bought for conversion into a house by Mr and Mrs J Robertson.

The Free Church congregation broke away from the Established Church in 1843 and met initially in a barn at Mains of Skeith. On September 9th that year the Earl of Seafield granted a site for the erection of a Free Church in the parish. When this was opened in 1844 it was described as a "dreary barn-like structure". It had seating for 200 in straight rows of deal pews, all of which were free. Material for the building was carted there by members.

Free Church manse with Church behind, late C19th.

Alterations and improvements to the church, manse and other buildings took place at various times, and an organ built by Hewitt and Co was installed with eleven stops and three couples. In the 1880s the pulpit and pews were painted by Mr Masson, Cullen at a cost of £6:10/-, Mr Wood's cottage was refloored in cement, the water pipes in the manse were repaired and the outside doors and windows were put in proper repair for £1:10/-. Subscriptions covered the entire cost of £45 for the extraordinary repairs to church and manse. In 1908 a new kitchen range and hot water system was installed in the manse and in 1909 the drawing room was papered and painted. That same year new windows were installed in the church.

After the union of 1932 the West Church, manse, hall and cottages were all intended to be sold as dwelling houses, though some were never used for this purpose, and the only one currently used as a house is the manse, occupied by Mr and Mrs P Mason.

The 1786 manse to the left with the 1873 manse behind, from the public road.

Over the centuries, various manses used by the Ministers of St John's, in common with many others throughout Scotland were wholly inadequate, and sometimes ruinous. At best they were thatched, with low doors, earthen floors and semi glazed windows. They had one bedroom plus low sleeping accommodation in the roofspace, and were usually rat infested.

In 1628 the Minister of Deskford had possession of his glebe, but not his manse, and was therefore not resident in the parish. The Kirk Session pressed Lord Deskford to ensure that the Minister gained possession of the manse. In 1654 the manse was valued at 250 merks but was ruinous, and various things were decayed in all of its buildings. Manses were short lived, particularly after the Act of 1663 which limited the budget for building or repairing one to £1,000 Scots (£83 sterling). By 1673 the Minister did not have a manse, and, though there was one by 1698 it was ruinous and uninhabitable.

In 1720 the manse was valued at £236 Scots and the three heritors, the Earl of Findlater, Abercrombie of Skeith and Lawtie of Inaltry agreed to build a new one. When it was completed in 1732 the Earl had bought out the other two heritors and was sole heritor in Deskford. The new manse was valued at £629 Scots but Rev Philp was also paid £173 for repairs he had had carried out.

In 1780 the Earl of Findlater agreed to consolidate the glebe into a single unit instead of the existing several detached pieces. By 1786 the old manse in the kirkyard was ruinous and a new one was built, which still exists today, beside the road into Kirktown from the south. The ruinous old one in the kirkyard became the school and schoolhouse. The new manse consisted of four rooms in the body of the house, together with garrets etc. The offices consisted of a brewhouse, kitchen and stable etc. Presbytery was of the view that "the noble heritor has bestowed not only sufficient but ample accommodation".

The Earl had been generous in allowing the Minister to plan what he wished, but the quality of building work was shoddy and by 1790 the building was not

The 1873 manse.

wind or watertight. The Minister, Rev Chalmers, had to apply to the Earl for repairs, a request which was not met with enthusiasm. The Minister felt that an overseer should have been appointed or payment not made until the house had been satisfactorily occupied for a year.

The manse which had been built in 1786 was thoroughly repaired and extended around 1835, and in 1840 Rev Innes considered it to be "an extremely commodious and good house". However by 1871 Rev Mackintosh petitioned Presbytery for a new manse as the old one was "unhealthy and incommodious, and the offices unsuitable and ruinous". He considered that the manse was repairable but not the offices. Presbytery recommended that a new manse be built on a different site and the old one converted into offices.

Lord Seafield agreed to this and on November 13th 1873, just two years after new St John's was built, the new manse was completed, inspected and found to be highly satisfactory. Presbytery accorded thanks to the Earl of Seafield. The new manse lay at the end of a short drive which followed the route of the old Keith to Cullen main road and was immediately to the south of the manse it was replacing.

In 1946 electricity was brought to the manse, and in 1956 the bathroom was gutted, refitted and decorated, ready for the public water supply which arrived that year. When Deskford became a linked charge in 1967 there was no requirement for a manse so two or three years later both it and its predecessor as a manse were sold by the Church of Scotland as private houses which they remain today.

EDUCATION

In the early C17th it is estimated that in the North East only one man in five could sign his name, and that fewer women could do so. However literacy had improved significantly between 1550 and 1650. At this later date children started school between 5 and 7, though those from the poorest families left as young as 8. School opened six days a week, and took place during all the hours of daylight. There were no official holidays but most children were kept off to help with the harvest. The use of the tawse was first recorded in 1639, while in dame and adventure schools the saugh waan (willow wand) was used.

Deskford had a school from the C17th with, on average, 1 schoolmaster and 60 pupils. By 1800 there were also dame schools in Berryhillock and Kirktown, and adventure and Sunday schools in remoter parts of the parish. Almost everyone could read and write by 1750. In the 1790s fees in the parochial school were 1/6d per quarter for reading and writing and 2/- per quarter for Latin and arithmetic. Many pupils attended only in the winter when there was little farm work to be done. The Kirk Session supervised the Schoolmaster closely to ensure the orthodoxy of what was taught.

In the late C18th the Schoolmaster's annual salary in Deskford was £12 plus grass for a cow. In addition he had fees, though many poorer families could not afford to pay these. In 1767 the Kirk Session agreed to give £4 for the education of the poor children of the parish, to be taught at 10d per quarter. In 1786 they nominated James King and William Chalmers to be taught at the school gratis "until Whitsunday upon condition that they give due attendance and be serviceable to the Schoolmaster".

The Kirk supported education in a number of ways. In 1837 it spent £2:16:2d on supplies of Sabbath school books, £1:9:6d on fees for 16 children, 3/6d on school books for 3 children educated gratis at the parish school, and gave £5 to Mr Webster, the Synod's Treasurer, for children's education.

During the C19th there was improved literacy and much improved education for girls. In the mid century the various schools in Deskford were well attended, with some children walking four or five miles to get there, throughout the year. Sometimes older children were kept at home in summer for herding or weeding or other farm work, but during the winter there was full attendance, and sometimes a parent or two joined the class. Several pupils, some from very poor families, and some very young, won bursaries to Aberdeen University, where they studied all winter and came home to help on the farm in the summer.

In the late C18th the Deskford parish school and Schoolmaster's house occupied a single cottage at the south end of what is now the central section of the graveyard. The schoolroom was low, with a floor of beaten clay, which was dusty in summer and sticky in winter. There was a row of desks round the walls and a chimney without a grate. There was no ventilation and each scholar brought a peat each day for the fire. The room was very overcrowded and there was a wide age range of scholars. Punishment was by a leather belt known as the "tag", with six narrow thongs, knotted if the leather was new. If the offence was very serious then the punishment would be on the bare backside in front of the whole class.

The school was inspected annually by representatives of Presbytery. This was prepared for by strict drilling and rigid rote learning, with often a particular pupil prepared for a particular question. This could however prove disastrous if, as did happen in Deskford, the nominated pupil was absent during the inspection and the rote learned answers went out of sequence. Presbytery representatives

The 1876 school, rebuilt in 1900, and with later extensions, now the Deskford Community Hall.

were usually the Minister, the Factor and some elders. The names of able pupils were noted as were any problems with the fabric of the building, which were passed on to the Earl of Seafield as heritor.

The new combined parish school, with accommodation for 162 pupils, was opened in 1876, having cost £1,182 to build. It was completely rebuilt in 1899 after a fire, and was extended in 1939, by which time it was known as Deskford Junior Secondary School. The extensions included a new school hall and a classroom for primary pupils. In 1949 a new building was built for science and technical subjects, which necessitated the electricity supply being extended as far as the school. This building is now the Jubilee Hall.

The Science and Technical building, now the Jubilee Hall.

In 1851, in the North East, 65% of teachers were male, but by 1911, 70% were female, because women were cheaper, willing and plentiful. In the late C19th, the average male teacher's salary was £130 per annum and that of a female teacher £67. The 1872 Act had made education compulsory up to the age of 13, and in 1891 it was made free for all children between the ages of 5 and 14. At the end of World War II the leaving age was raised to 15, and in the early 1970s to 16. Girls got the belt far less often than boys and usually more gently. For most girls getting it was a humiliation, but for many boys it was a badge of pride. When Orchard Cottage ceased to be the library, it was used as the schoolhouse for a time.

An inspector's report of 1887 stated that in 1842 10% of the then population of Deskford had attended school. The comparable figures for Cullen and Fordyce were 16% and 12%. By 1887 the Deskford figure was 16%. This shrewd report stated that, in Deskford, between 1842 and 1885, the roll had risen from 40 to 110. It criticised however the absence of a school library.

In the late C18th and early C19th, success in the Aberdeen University Bursary Competition was seen as a great honour for the individual, but also for his family and for the community. Older brothers and sisters would often contribute small amounts from their earnings to help the able brother to go.

He would take with him a small trunk containing books and clothes, and a small box with butter, eggs, smoked haddock or cheese. A sack of oatmeal and one of potatoes would follow by carrier. He would rent a small room in Old Aberdeen if attending King's College or Aberdeen if attending Marischal College, and give his food to his landlady to prepare for him. A box might be sent every fortnight with clean linen and underclothes, butter, eggs, smoked haddock and perhaps a fowl and a piece or two of mutton or beef, plus suet and oatmeal puddings. The tale of students subsisting for a full term on cold porridge cut from a drawer is gross exaggeration.

In the early C20th in Deskford school as in all others, girls and boys were strictly segregated, having to enter and exit using different doors, and being banned from going together into the adjacent belt of trees. When going on to more advanced schooling it was normal to go to Fordyce Academy, which was four or five miles away on poor roads which were not tarred until the 1950s. Most pupils cycled and took sandwiches with them, having their midday dinner followed immediately by their tea when they returned home in the late afternoon or early evening.

The alternative to Fordyce was Buckie, cycling to Tochieneal Station then catching the train. During World War I passenger trains did not stop at Tochieneal, so these pupils had to cycle to Cullen. There were fewer trains and the timetable was different, so pupils had to catch the 7:00am train from Cullen. The return train did not get back to Cullen till 7:00pm, but the Rector at Buckie High School allowed train pupils to wait in his study in front of a roaring fire. Initially bicycle lights were very poor paraffin ones but these were superseded by the much better acetylene ones.

At Deskford in the early 1900s, a group of pupils truanted and went to the fugie (fugitive) block by the burnside. However the whipper-in routed them out and drove them back to the school where they each got six of the best from the Dominie.

In 1900 the five members of the School Board, immediately after the school had been rebuilt, were James Campbell, Old Cullen, Factor, James Clark, Mid Skeith, Alexander Duncan, Kirktown, Rev J Morrison, Free Church and Rev G Park, Established Church. They had all been reappointed unopposed. School Logs from this time onwards have survived and show the changes and improvements which took place during the C20th, and also the constantly increasing bureaucracy.

Contrary to established folk belief, there were many days in the early C20th when Deskford School was closed due to inclement weather. Registers were cancelled if fewer than one third of pupils had attended, and if this happened too often, the school opened during the summer holiday to make up lost time. Pupils frequently took unauthorised days off to attend fairs in Rathven, Cullen or Keith.

Fast days were regularly observed by the school during the week before communion and there were many full day and early closures. Attendance was variable and suffered on the days of fairs and markets and because of the requirements of farming. There were also many absences because of weather. Christmas Day was sometimes a holiday while Shrove Tuesday was a holiday until 1934. It was known as Brose Day and two suggestions are made about the possible meaning of this name. The first is that it comes from St Ambrose but the two dates for his saint's day are not at that time of year. The second is that it refers to the final feast before the self imposed hunger of Lent.

Around this time there was a rapid turnover in lady assistant teachers, the main reasons for this being transfer, often to be nearer home, and resignation on marriage, which was compulsory. One example of this was when Miss Longmore, Cottartown, lady teacher, resigned on marrying Mr Beveridge, the Headmaster. In addition to teachers there were also monitors, for example Nellie McKenzie, appointed on August 2nd 1904, and pupil teachers such as Miss Williamina McCombie, aged 17, appointed on October 4th 1904. In 1907 a senior girl was helping in the infants because of teacher shortages.

Deskford School pupils, (roll approximately 100), around 1910.

In 1909 the Secondary Section of Deskford School opened, with times being 9:30 – 12:30 and 1:30 – 3:30, in order to allow the teaching of Latin and science. Parents requested secondary education for William Rumbles, George Benzies, James Wilson, George Morrison, John Topp, John Black, Janet Cruikshank, Eleanor Longmore, Catherine Watson, Agnes Clark and Maggie Rumbles. The Inspectors stated that equipment for practical instruction in subjects such as woodwork, cookery, laundry work and household management should be provided, and at the same time water should be provided for the Practical Room and the Cloakrooms.

In one of the early signs of bureaucracy the headmaster had to claim grants on Form 17A. These totalled £141:2:5d, with pupils under 7 years of age attracting 18/- each, those between 7 and 10 years of age 21/6d each and those over 10 years of age 23/9d each. That same year Form 8M was sent to the Inspectorate and Forms 62A, 62B, 60, 61 and 96 to the Clerk. In July 1909 the Education Department recognised Deskford as a Sub Intermediate School, so long as adequate arrangements were made to teach science, and so long as the teaching of the Intermediate Certificate pupils did not interfere with courses for boys and girls who did not intend to stay on at school beyond 14.

There were occasional difficulties in getting replacement teachers. For example, in May 1914 Miss Murdoch was off on a Tuesday, Wednesday and Thursday as her mother was very Ill, and the headmaster had to attend a funeral on that Thursday, so Rev Park took charge of the school for the day. In 1921 it proved impossible to get replacement teachers, so senior girls were used in the infant and middle classes. In 1922, T Macauley Smith, a retired teacher, was on duty as temporary Head Teacher. In August and September 1923, a local man, John Jamieson MA, Blackhillock, undertook teaching practice in Deskford School in preparation for the Graduate Course at Teacher Training College. In 1930, another local, Miss Eliza Meldrum, Wester Blairock, a student at Aberdeen Teacher Training College undertook three weeks continuous teaching practice. She continued duties as a temporary additional teacher on April 18th 1932.

In parallel with the increasing bureaucracy, the Headmaster gradually lost some power and autonomy. By the early 1920s he had to refer much to the Director of Education for a decision. This official visited the school occasionally. In 1924 the Headmaster could only recommend to the Director the appointment of an Attendance Officer for "whipping in laggards".

Progress was however being made. 1926 saw the first appointment of a lady teacher with a degree when Miss Cruikshank MA started work in the middle room. The first visiting music teacher, Mr Roger, made his first visit to Deskford in 1928. By 1938 there were visiting teachers in domestic science, Miss Roy, and in music, Miss Esplin. There was also a visiting benchwork instructor, Mr GK Ironside. By the late 1930s Deskford School had a headmaster plus three lady teachers and visiting teachers in art, singing, woodwork, cookery and physical training. The school was by this stage graded officially as a four-teacher school. In 1929 discussions had taken place about responsibility for retarded children.

One of the more unusual incidents took place in 1918 when Edwin Morrison was sent home as he said he had been told at home not to take any punishment for playing truant the previous day. This stance took a great deal of bravery in the culture of the time.

Evening classes proliferated. In 1933 there were such classes in English, arithmetic, dressmaking and needlework. Before that, in 1931, Miss Dunn of the College of Agriculture had conducted a class on farming subjects on Wednesday evenings over the winter. Evening poultry classes were held in 1938.

The balance of the School Fund was £2 in January 1930 and £3 in December 1930. In 1935 the house in Kirktown occupied by the female teachers, which belonged to Banffshire Education Committee was sold by auction in Cullen Town Hall to Mrs Morrison, Clunehill, for £138.

The earliest recorded continuation classes, in dairying and poultry management, taught by Miss Findlay, and in English and arithmetic, taught by Mr Craigmyle, were held in September 1920. By 1937 there were continuation classes in English, arithmetic, dressmaking, cooking and first aid and nursing. The last one had a roll of 31.

In 1936 a room in the school was granted for the Agricultural Unemployment Scheme on four dates and that same year, the Education Committee considered renting the Public Hall as an extra classroom. During World War II the use of the school hall was granted to B Company, 1st Banffshire Battalion, Home Guard, for indoor training.

In 1922 Mr Ross was authorised to engage a man to clean out the Deskford School privvies (dry toilet pits), at a charge not exceeding £3:10/- per annum. This started a forty-year period of incidents and disagreements regarding toilets and cleaners. In 1929 the cellar had a capacity of 8 tons of coal. The Deskford School trial of the Dusmo system of cleaning had been so successful that all other schools were to adopt it. Deskford School was to use Elsanol for its Elsan closets.

In 1932 Mr Beveridge requested an increase in salary from £4 to £6 per annum for the person who would now empty out the toilet cubicles to the pit fortnightly instead of monthly. The cleaning out of the pit would remain annual. Inspectors had required more effective cleaning than at present. The

Committee refused this increase and emphasised that Elsanol should be used in the closets.

However Mr Beveridge had discussed the situation with the Director of Education in Banff, Mr Kennedy, who agreed with him and suggested that the Area Committee reconsider their decision. They did so but only agreed to fortnightly cleaning out of toilet cubicles in the summer months, with Mr Watson to receive an additional £1 per annum for this. In 1937 Mr Geddes had replaced Mr Watson and was paid £6.

In March 1939, after comments by the Inspectorate, Mr Currie reported that the Deskford members of the Cullen Area School Management Committee had met Mr Geddes who had the contract for cleaning the toilets, and asked him if he was prepared to clean the offices (outside toilets) oftener than at present. He agreed to clean the closets, seats and urinal weekly with remuneration increased from £6 to £9 per annum. This was agreed by the Council, but a reminder was given that Mr Geddes was not to be regarded as an employee but as a contractor.

In April 1942 Miss Thom, the cleaner, died suddenly. Miss Jessie Bell Inglis was appointed by Mr Beveridge on a temporary basis. He said that there would be great difficulty getting anyone else. However, since Miss Inglis was between 20 and 30 years old, her particulars had to be given to Cullen Labour Exchange, who phoned to say that she could be appointed as there were no other applicants, though this did not mean that she could not be called up. She was appointed at £32 plus £7 War Bonus per annum.

By May she had been informed by the Ministry of Labour that her part-time work did not constitute a sufficient reason for deferment, and that she should now proceed to undertake work of national importance. Mrs Gordon, Ardoch Cottages, was appointed in her place, but over the next eighteen months she and several subsequent cleaners resigned.

In September 1943 Mr Beveridge reported that Miss Geddes, a domestic servant in Edinburgh, might be persuaded to come home and look after her mother, and could be appointed cleaner. However, by October, due to the difficulty in getting a cleaner, Miss Evelyn Mellis, who was 14, c/o Mrs Merson, Ordens, had been appointed at £32 plus £7. There was a query as to whether it was acceptable for a 14-year-old girl to attend to the heating boiler. It was felt that it was acceptable as it was a low pressure boiler, but the Clerk would make enquiries.

In November she was granted exemption from school, but she was not giving satisfaction in her cleaning duties and was dismissed. Mrs Clark, Kirktown, took her place at £32 plus £10 War Bonus. A few weeks later Mrs Clark said she could not continue because it was such a small salary and such a large amount of work. She was then dismissed because the school was in such a filthy condition and no fires were being lit. She was replaced by Mrs Robertson, Faichyhill, who resigned four months later, in April 1945. The job was then advertised in the *Banffshire Journal*.

Mr McKenzie, Stripeside, was appointed cleaner on April 1st and resigned on May 15th. Mrs Lobban, Kirktown, was then appointed at a salary of £32 plus £24:10/- War Bonus, but resigned on July 4th. No successor could be found and it was agreed to advertise the post again. Miss Lily Martin, Ardoch, was appointed from September 3rd. She resigned on June 15th 1946 and Mr Alexander Masson, Berryhillock was appointed at a salary of £58:10/-. As late as August 1962, Mrs Simpson the cleaner had an accident when the wood she was putting in the furnace hit her in the face and broke her spectacles, which resulted in her getting glass in one eye.

School Class around 1970. (L to R). Colin Taylor, Sheila Bowie, Alison Beattie, Frances Stewart, George Bruce, Gail McAllister, Charlie Thomson, Brenda Geddes, James McHattie, Linda Stewart, Alison Strathdee.

At the start of World War II pupils got an extra week's summer holiday, after which the new classroom and hall were occupied and used. The War caused significant new problems. There was a major turnover in staff, with many being called up, and, in 1940 pupils attended in either the morning or the afternoon, so large was the roll with the addition of the evacuees from Portobello. Some of the problems however were not new. On January 24th 1945 there was a burst pipe in the new building, which put all the central heating out of action, so all pupils were accommodated in the old building. Two days later the heating was still very poor with the highest temperature recorded being 5 degrees Celsius. Paraffin heaters were borrowed from the Public Hall, but did not help much.

After the War there were many more innovations. Mr Macdonald, the Youth Employment Officer, visited the school for the first time on March 8th 1951. In

Primary 1 – 3 class 1960/1961. (all L to R). Back – Lorna Christie, Ian Bowie, Catherine Bowie, Jim Milton, Unknown, Forbes Mitchell, Alan Espie, Ian Davidson, Jimmy Thomson, Norman Christie, David Currie, Billy Reid, Hamish Stewart. Front – Unknown, Gladys Milton, Anne Duncan, Jean Milton, Unknown, Margaret Milton, Elizabeth Milton, Elaine Smith, Unknown, Audrey Smith.

1950 biros were used for the first time, but were considered less legible than pen and ink. In 1952 Miss Hay went to Vancouver as part of an exchange with Mr Odin S Sostad. In October 1955 Mr Beveridge retired and was succeeded by Mr Espie. Pupils returned to using ink instead of biros. In December 1955 there was a visit from Mr Harriet, Children's Welfare Officer, Corporation of Glasgow, to discuss a boarded-out girl. He promised cooperation.

In March 1956 the school commenced a house system, with the pupils choosing house names and electing House Captains. The houses and their Captains were Cunningham, James Duncan, Fleming, Ann Finnie, Hillary, Isobel Thomson and Livingstone, Sandy Milton. In June 1956 Hillary House Captain, Isobel Thomson, was presented with the Inter-House Shield, the first time this was awarded.

In May 1956 there was a discussion with Mr Brannan and Mr Barber from Lanarkshire about the possible use of Deskford School as a summer camp. As a

Secondary class 1950s. (All L – R). Back – Unknown, Unknown, Brian Smith, Tony Morrison, Roddy Dawson, George Smith, Charlie Bennett.
Middle – Elsie Duncan, Dorothy Hay, Dorothy Morrison, Isobel Milne, Margaret McKenzie, Kathleen Simpson, Ethel Ewen, J Duncan, Ettie Mitchell.
Front – Raymond Murray, Ernie Rumbles, Hazel Reid, Lorna Christie, Catherine Ewen, Lewis McConnachie, Stewart McLean.

result, between June 30th and July 14th 1956 the school was occupied by Lanarkshire Holiday Camp. It was reported that there was slight damage to desks, blackboards and a piano.

On November 17th 1960 there was a visit from an Education Committee delegation plus the Director of Education and an Assistant Director to discuss the future of the secondary department. There was an acceptance that it was too small to survive. On January 25th 1961 a letter was issued to all parents intimating the transfer of secondary pupils to Cullen Secondary School on February 6th. Ten days' notice does not seem very long.

On February 3rd, William Espie ceased to be Head Teacher and 21 pupils transferred to Cullen. On February 6th Deskford became a Primary School with a roll of 55. Mrs Innes took the Infants, Mrs Cattenach the Juniors and Mr McKay, the Acting Head Teacher, the Senior Primary. There were now only two visiting teachers and there was concern that some of the primary pupils would opt to attend Cullen Primary School. This did not happen and Deskford Primary School survived for another 10 years. However, during that 10 years much equipment was transferred from Deskford to other schools.

SCHOOLS

An Act of Parliament of 1496 had stated that the eldest sons of the great landowners should go to school to learn "perfyte Latyne" and then to university. However in the second half of the C16th half the parishes in Aberdeenshire had no schools. In 1633 there was no school in Deskford, but there was one at Ordens. The next school recorded in the parish was in 1644 when an English school existed in Deskford, but without any maintenance. In 1687 the Minister "declaired that ther was not a Grammar School in the parioch, but on(e) James Sinklar, who is of good life, taught English and precented in the Church".

A momentum towards improvement in education developed in Deskford in the C18th. In 1725 the Earl of Findlater promised to have a schoolhouse built, and in the years before 1750, though the kirkyard dykes were ruinous, the Kirk and school were in good repair, with a "good sclate roof" on each.

In 1749 the Kirk Session gave a premium to the scholars in the Stocking School. This was a school established by the Earl of Findlater, teaching them gratis to weave stockings, "being a thing that tends very much to the promotion of industry in the countries where it is practised". On October 8th that year the Minister ordered the elders in their several quarters to advise the common people to put their sons to this school.

In 1775 the schoolhouse in Kirktown, at the south end of what is now the middle section of the graveyard, was a miserable cottage, a but and ben, with one end for the use of the Dominie and the other for the scholars. The Dominie's room served as his kitchen, parlour and hall; his dormitory being an opening in the wall with a folding door. The only difference between the schoolhouse and a poor peasant's habitation was that the school was slated. There was no playground so the pupils played in the graveyard, the walls of which were dilapidated.

In 1786 the school and schoolhouse were transferred to the building nearby that up to that time had been the manse, which itself had transferred to the earlier of the two old manses which today lie beside the southern entrance road to Kirktown. The new school building was only a slight improvement on the old. Teaching continued in this new school building and then the house now known as Dominie from 1786 till 1875 when the new school, which is now the Community Centre, was built. The old school continued as the Schoolmaster's house until the early 1920s when the new schoolhouse on the main road was built by the Education Authority.

In 1790 there were usually about 30 scholars in summer and more in winter. There was also a dame school in Berryhillock. In 1801 there was a parochial school which had 12 scholars who were taught the usual branches of education. There was also a private school where the reading of English and the catechism were taught by a woman. By 1820 the same two schools in the parish continued, the dame school now taught by two respectable sisters. In this school little boys as well as little girls were taught to read, and the girls were also taught to knit and sew. The average number of pupils at the dame school was about 28, and the fees were, for reading alone, 2/- per quarter and for reading, sewing and knitting 2/6d. The parochial school accommodations were stated to be very liberal and excellent.

Besides these two schools there were, in the remoter parts of the parish, little schools taught by aged women, partly out of a love of the job, and partly to eke out a precarious living. In these schools, smaller children in their neighbourhood, around 6 or 10 in each, attended and learned to read the Shorter Catechism, the Psalms and the New Testament.

In 1842 all the parish schools in the Presbytery of Fordyce, except Rathven, were satisfactory. All dame school and adventure school buildings were wretched. Brodiesord had an earthen floor, dirty walls, no playground, was ill-lighted and had no blackboard or maps.

The building in which a dame school had existed in Kirktown since the 1830s was absorbed into the central section of the graveyard in 1886, though it had been closed for a few years by then. In the 1830s the dame school in Berryhillock was taught by Jean Sim. A different dame school was built in Kirktown around 1860, taught by Miss Martin. It had the school at one end and her living accommodation at the other. From the 1870s, when it closed as a school, till the 1920s, it was used as accommodation for female Assistant Teachers. It is now a private house called "The Old Schoolhouse".

A school and schoolhouse were built beside the Free Church and opened under Mr John McHattie in 1847. A female school which had existed there since 1844 was soon absorbed into it. The parochial school in 1837 had 59 pupils and in 1842 it had 40. The Kirktown dame school in 1837 had 34 pupils. The Schoolmaster at the parochial school had a salary of £32.

Several of Mr Brander's pupils in the 1860s went on to become headmasters themselves. Sandy McKay, Oathillock, became Rector of Rothesay Academy, Alexander Murray, Berryhillock, Headmaster of Birnie School, Adam Longmore, Cottartown, Headmaster of Auchterless and William Christie, Berryleys, Headmaster of Skene.

A revolution took place in 1875 when the new Parish School was opened, the building which in a rebuilt form is still in use as the Community Centre today. At that time all other schools ceased to exist under the new legislation. The new school was burned down in 1899, almost certainly as a result of arson, though nobody was ever charged. It was completely rebuilt in seven months, during which time classes were conducted in the Church.

The new school of 1899 had three classrooms, with capacities of 56, 53 and 53 pupils respectively. The dimensions of the classrooms were 26'2" by 21'4", 22'8" by 21'4" and 21'8" by 21'6", all with a ceiling height of 15'3". By 1909 it was reported that there was a draft in the Headmaster's room. It was considered that the roof ventilation should have been automatic to prevent teachers interfering with it, and that something needed doing to improve the opening of the windows.

By 1925 the school had a Headmaster plus three qualified lady teachers and approximately 150 pupils. There was also a new brick built Headmaster's house about 200m away, and a new annexe for staff accommodation was begun on August 30th 1926.

Through the middle of the C20th the school continued in good heart, with the inclusion of evacuee children from Portobello boosting its numbers during World War II. It acquired a secondary department which was well equipped and had three-phase electricity installed in the early 1950s, which allowed the use of equipment such as power lathes. However times were changing and the secondary department closed in 1961, with the pupils transferring to Cullen Secondary School. The end was close and Deskford Primary School closed in 1970, with the pupils transferring to the brand-new primary school in Cullen.

Locals in Deskford were against the closure of the school, but this fact was flatly contradicted by an inspector. The decision had already been taken by those in authority and any consultation was a sham. A letter was sent by Mr Purves, Director of Education for Banffshire County Council, on April 3rd 1970 to the Scottish Education Department, requesting permission to close Deskford Primary School. The SED requested certain information and Mr Purves replied stating:-

1. The roll was 55 and if anything would decrease slightly.
2. It was a two teacher school which was only moderately effective. The Head Teacher did not have wide experience of teaching in a Primary

School and was lacking in imaginative ideas. The Assistant Teacher was about to be married and was anxious to move to Aberdeen.

3. It was proposed that P1 – P6 would move to Cullen with P7 going to Keith, to avoid a double switch in a short period of time.
4. Special transport would be provided and no pupil would have to walk further than before.
5. The buildings were in a deplorable condition with temporary toilets.
6. There would be no difficulty in replacing the Assistant teacher if Deskford was to stay open.
7. Closure would save the Authority £1,250 per annum.
8. Deskford was only 4 miles from Cullen. The school was as integral to the community as was normal in rural situations.
9. Parents accepted closure and transfer completely.

Her Majesty's Inspector, Miss MB McNeill, had recommended from 1961 that Deskford should be assimilated into Cullen. She agreed with Mr Purves and claimed that "The battle of Deskford was fought and won years ago when the secondary department was discontinued. The parents now accept the proposition that the large school (at Cullen) offers opportunities for the children hitherto denied them. This (closure) should therefore be approved". The SED approved closure and Mr Purves informed everyone

Presentation of a shield, to be competed for at the Flower Show, by the School Reunion committee as thanks for help provided. Mrs Shand (organiser), Mrs Jaffray (former teacher), Ken Fordyce (committee member), Ian Currie (President, Flower Show Committee), Fraser Duncan (Treasurer).

that the actual day of closure would be July 2nd 1970.

It is difficult to escape the conclusion that the Director, the Inspectorate and the SED had made up their minds in advance, exchanged letters to give a gloss of respectability to the process, but were determined to ignore the views of the parents, or misrepresent them. A similar attempt to close a school today, made so casually, would not be successful, but 50 years ago there was still possibly a feeling of powerlessness by local people in the face of the "authorities".

SCHOOLMASTERS

In 1721 Deskford could not provide a legal salary to its schoolmaster, and in 1724 Rev Philip declared that he had neither schoolmaster, Session Clerk, schoolhouse nor (schoolmaster's) salary; that he had on several occasions represented the want of these to the Earl of Findlater, sole heritor of the parish, but that nothing as yet was done. Presbytery resolved to make application to the Earl.

In October of that year the Kirk Session met with the Earl of Findlater and the gentlemen of the parish. The Earl said that, being informed by the Minister and others that the parish was at a considerable loss for want of a schoolmaster, he did now resolve that a schoolmaster be settled, have a legal salary and a sufficient schoolhouse. James Sinclair, who had been schoolmaster, was now, through old age and infirmity, rendered incapable of the work. The Earl promised to build a schoolhouse and chamber for the Master, and when this was done, to call a young man, sufficiently qualified. The Minister said that there was a great need for a speedy settlement, and His Lordship assured them that the schoolhouse and chamber would be built by the following summer.

In November 1725 William Gordon had been appointed, at 100 merks salary, by the Earl of Findlater to be schoolmaster. The Kirk Session agreed to make him precentor and Session Clerk, on paid trial till Whit Sunday next, and also agreed to allow him the dues for baptisms, marriages and testificats, together with two-thirds of the fines levied for sexual transgressions. In those days, schoolmasters' tenures were often brief, as the job was very poorly paid, even with the additional earnings as precentor and Session Clerk. When William Lorimer from Dytach was appointed in 1737, the Earl of Findlater had given the Kirk Session the authority to make the appointment. In 1743, Thomas Ogilvie, son of a deceased merchant in Cullen, was appointed. In 1747 he became a lawyer in Edinburgh and was replaced by Alexander Paterson, Assistant Teacher at Fordyce Grammar School.

In the late C18th schoolmasters were paid the same as ploughmen, and had very poor accommodation and food. Things were only a little better by 1830. The schoolmaster's salary in 1792 was £2:18/- paid by the heritor, plus meal to the value of £4 paid by the tenants, plus fees for about 30 scholars. There were cockfights every year on Fastern's E'en. Each boy paid the schoolmaster 12d for the privilege of entering a cock. The schoolmaster's salary had risen to £34:4:4d a year plus £12 in fees by 1842. There was also about £25 from the Dick Bequest. In 1880 it was £52:10/- plus £16 in fees plus the Dick Bequest money.

Despite there not having been a school continuously in Deskford, several schoolmasters' names have been recorded. The first of these was John Thayne in 1574. George Lesley was in post in 1654 and William Gardiner in 1655. George Lesley, "haveing produced testimonials from Fyfe and Mortlighe (Mortlach) quhair he had served befor, of his gud carriage and conversatione, was licentiate to teach ane Inglishe school and to be Precentor at the Kirk of Deskford". In 1687 James Sinklar's whole income was probably 40 pecks of meal plus £2 or £3 money annually, being a peck of meal from every chalder produced in the parish. He also received £8 as Session Clerk plus fees for baptisms and weddings. William Gordon was schoolmaster in 1725 and Alexander Geddes in 1728, following Alexander Gordon. Alexander Geddes earned 16 merks as Session Clerk.

A full list of schoolmasters is available from the start of Rev Morison's ministry.

Alexander Geddes
Thomas Riddoch 1731, son of George Ruddoch, Blairock
William Lorimer 1737
Alexander Philp 1738
Thomas Ogilvie 1743
Alexander Paterson 1747
James Robertson 1748, son of Alexander Robertson, Skeith
Colin Morison 1751
William Stevenson 1754
Robert Alves 1764, went on to be Rector of Banff Academy.
Andrew Johnston 1767
Abercromby Gordon 1773, went on to be Minister in Banff.
Alexander Riddoch 1780
James Clapperton died 1786
James Russel 1786
Walter Reid 1806
George Wright 1806
FW Grant 1845
James Allan 1850
Lewis Grant 1856
James Brander 1858
William Smith 1868
AW Farquhar 1908 (temporary)
John Scott 1909
AD Craigmyle 1920
Robert Watson 1925
John A Beveridge 1926
William Espie 1955
George Addison 1962
George Campbell 1969

In the 1760s one schoolmaster was Robert Alves MA who, besides being an excellent classical scholar, was a mathematician and "unhappily for himself as well as his pupils, a poet". He had published a small book of verses, was a scholar, but neglected his school. He was not good at imparting his knowledge to his pupils, was too indulgent and "spared the rod when he would have been better using it".

He gave the Minister, Rev Morison's, grandsons, who lived at the manse with their widowed mother, private tuition, and did their work for them before their grandfather checked it. He became lazier and lazier and went about with holes in his stockings and his elbows out of his jacket. However Sarabella Morison, the Minister's daughter and one of Deskford's most impressive individuals, whose headstone is situated beyond the east gable of the Old Church, decided to save him, starting with mending his jacket.

He moped and pined and strayed about the meadows spouting his verses, whilst being derided by his pupils. He was shy and reserved but developed a taste for alcohol, and soon became totally unfit to carry out his duties and would have been dismissed but for Sarabella. She flattered his poetry, persuaded him to give up alcohol altogether and to attend to his duties.

He published a second book of poetry, helped by a donation of £20 from the Duchess of Gordon, to whom it was dedicated. He sold a few hundred copies which allowed him to buy a badly needed new suit of clothes. He focussed only on his poetry and would have forgotten to eat if it had not been for an old woman in the village whom he allowed to clean his house and make him porridge.

He completed a third volume and sent it to his publisher in Edinburgh, who replied that two-thirds of his previous volumes were unsold and that he owed them £11:17/-. He was devastated and went back on the drink. Complaints were also coming in about him on a regular basis to the Minister that "the Dominie paid no attention to his school and that the pastor's interference was required".

When summoned, he appeared before the Minister drunk, so the lecture was put off till the next day. The following day his cleaner reported that he had a "sair heid" and was incapable of getting out of bed. When this was investigated it was found that he did have a genuine high fever, and his strongest critic, the farmer from Kirktown, dropped everything and went to Cullen to get the doctor, who, when he arrived, announced that the Schoolmaster was in extreme danger. However his strong constitution brought him through the crisis, which would have killed 19 out of 20 alcoholics.

His long recuperation allowed him to reflect; he gave up the drink, and a year later was appointed Rector of Banff Academy. For his first day in this new post Sarabella bought him a decent stock of linen and a suit of good clothes. He made a good impression and remained Rector for many years.

Mr Brander, the Headmaster from 1858 to 1868, came originally from Ordiquhill, and by 1861 was earning £52:10/- plus fees of 2/- per quarter for reading, 2/6d for writing, 3/- for arithmetic, grammar and geography and 5/- for Latin. Mr Brander probably endowed the Brander Prize for Dux, but was well known for his excessive use of the belt, and also more informal physical punishment. He left to become a Minister in Lanarkshire. He was replaced in 1868 by Mr Smith who came from New Spynie. There were 10 applicants for the job, amongst which were ones from Wiltshire, Lumsden, Aberdeen, Banff, Keith, Fraserburgh, Cairnie, Daviot and Kintore.

Senior Class with JAB. (All L to R). Back – Mr Beveridge, G Gray, Alf Bowie, Willie Fordyce, F Mitchell, Ian Davidson, D Brooks, Kenneth Fordyce. Middle – N Geddes, Isa McConnachie, B Stewart, C Smith, C Allardyce, M Cowie, E Smith.   Front – M Milton. Edith Coull, J McLean

Mr Smith was universally known as the Dominie, the last known by all as such, and saw out the remainder of the century and beyond. Dominie Smith was a leading light in the Deskford Horticultural Society. He was presented in 1888 with a gold watch, and in 1908 with other gifts by former pupils both locally and in Glasgow, as a mark of their esteem. He was Dominie for 40 years, and was very popular, though in his later years in post was believed to have become a bit lazy and to have too great a liking for whisky.

Mr Scott succeeded Mr Smith in 1909. He became secretary of the Horticultural Society and as Headmaster was ahead of his time. He began to serve coffee, milk and cocoa to pupils, and persuaded local farmers to donate potatoes and vegetables so that he could provide a bowl of soup each day to every pupil for ½d per week and for less if there were several children in the family. It was tattie soup on Mondays, Wednesdays and Fridays, with different kinds on Tuesdays and Thursdays.

Alexander Craigmyle, who had tenure from 1920 till 1925, helped restart the Mutual Improvement Association, and was followed briefly by Robert Watson. From 1926 to 1955, the next Headmaster was JA Beveridge, known to all as JAB.

He also was ahead of his time, and was very popular with the pupils as he was fairly easy-going, even sometimes reading his newspaper while the pupils worked. In 1938 he broadcast an account of the Mutual Improvement Association from the new BBC Wireless Station in Glasgow, to great excitement in the parish.

Sheila Stewart, Mr Espie, Isobel Simpson.

He was also very keen on drama and produced and directed the very successful Deskford Amateur Dramatic Society productions for many years. After JA Beveridge's near 30 years in post, in the last 15 years of Deskford School's existence, there were three headteachers, William Espie, George Addison and George Campbell.

For many years in the first half of the C20th Miss McIver, a kind and gentle Highland lady, taught the infants. Her classroom had a large fireguard in front of the coal fire, on which gloves, coats and hats were hung to dry. The first Assistant Teacher in the new school in 1875 had been Miss Mutch.

In October 1940 the staff consisted of John A Beveridge MA, Headmaster, Marjorie H Forsyth, Edith McBean and Isabella McHattie, Teachers, plus two Edinburgh teachers, Margaret E Drysdale and Neil Buchanan MA who accompanied the evacuees. In 1948 it comprised JA Beveridge, Miss Lena McLaren, Mrs A Robertson, Miss Mary Gregor, Miss Jessie Reid MA, Miss Elsie Roy domestic subjects, Mr WD Henderson technical and Mr Douglas Summers, art, some of whom were visiting teachers.

The Free Church Schools ran for a relatively short period from 1844 till 1875, but were well supported. The first to open was a girls' school which ran briefly between 1844 and 1847, and was taught by Miss Wilkie, who until then had taught in the girls' school in Kirktown. The first Headteacher of the Free Church School when it opened in 1847 was John McHattie, a native of Deskford, who had been born at Clunehill Croft. His successors did not stay for long and were, in order, Mr Forbes, James Wright, James Walker, James Meikleham and lastly John Mitchell, who saw it through to closure in 1875. From that year all pupils in Deskford were taught in the new Parish School.

Teachers of dame schools and adventure schools were usually unqualified, and came from a variety of backgrounds. Their methods were extremely ineffective on the whole, and they often taught into their 70s. Within the Presbytery of Fordyce, including Deskford, in 1842, their number included failed saddlers, clerks, shopkeepers and labourers.

Not all of the headteachers of the parochial school in Deskford were as pure as the driven snow. In 1785 James Clapperton left the country in an abrupt manner while managing to avoid "any legal confession of guilt", and in 1806 Walter Reid resigned as schoolmaster and was dismissed as Session Clerk for "immorality".

CURRICULUM

The newly established Church of Scotland in 1560 published the Book of Discipline, which stated that each parish should have its own school in which reading, writing, arithmetic and, if possible, Latin and a little Greek should be taught.

In the C17th the Parochial School in Deskford taught reading, writing, English grammar and, when required, Latin. The Schoolmaster's salary was £32 Scots plus annual fees for each pupil of 10/-, or £1 if Latin was included. The curriculum centred on godliness, good behaviour and reading and writing. The Bible was the only reading text. In 1675 the Synod of Aberdeen made only three demands of a schoolmaster, that he made the bairns learn the catechism, that he taught them prayers for morning and for evening and for saying grace and that he "chastise them for cursing, swearing, lying, speaking profanitie, for disobedience to parents, and what vices that appears in them".

In 1775, Latin, English, writing, arithmetic, book keeping, geography and the first four books of Euclid were taught. A peripatetic fiddler, Mr Douglas, came to Deskford twice a year to teach the boys how to dance reels and bow properly. He charged half a crown (2/6d) for 12 lessons.

In 1842 schools in the Presbytery of Fordyce, including Deskford Parish School, taught reading, writing, arithmetic, English grammar, geography, history and Latin. Reading was done in a monotonous, drawling manner, with no pauses, emphasis or expression. There was no writing practice from dictation, and the books used were unsuitable. Both the Old and New

Testaments were used as ordinary class books and also for teaching reading, parsing and correcting grammatical errors. English grammar was seldom taught and there were no maps and few globes. There was no attempt to get pupils of different ages or abilities to do different work. In one day in 1842, in the combined schools of Deskford, Cullen, Rathven, Ordiquhill and Banff, the total number of pupils present was 324, of whom 4 studied algebra, 9 mathematics, 36 Latin, 129 arithmetic, 133 English grammar (perhaps they knew the Inspectors were coming), 237 writing and 0 French or Greek.

In Deskford School in 1899, mental arithmetic was taught, but some pupils were not capable of it. The geography of Europe and North America was taught and in history the pupils were up to the end of the American War. On July 7th revisals in geography were done but the pupils had forgotten much about England. However on July 27th it was noted that mental arithmetic was improving.

The pupils were examined by the Minister on scripture knowledge in August 1901, and in July 1902 they had a better understanding of interest rates and of measuring floors and walls for carpeting. In January 1908 the senior class began Julius Caesar, and seemed, after a little explanation, to enter into the spirit of the play.

In 1909 the Inspector recommended clay modelling for the infants. That year, when Mr Scott took over from Mr Smith, the school received practical equipment for boys and cookery, laundry work and household management equipment for girls. In 1910 there was singing and recitation instead of woodwork and sewing in the afternoons in December because it was too dark.

In November 1911 it was now a rule of the school "that no sewing work be prepared during the time that should be devoted to other subjects, and that no sewing material be out except during the sewing lesson". The Lady Assistants, for they were the culprits, were each given a copy of this rule. In the Inspection on June 14th 1912, the subjects covered were arithmetic, composition, dictation, poetry and geography. In June 1915, because of the danger of the unsafe roof after a fire, classes in cookery, woodwork and science were suspended, and in November there was no lesson in laundry because the hot water circulation was disrupted.

In 1909 the school had become a sub-intermediate one, presenting pupils for their intermediate certificates. Practical subjects were at this point added to the curriculum, and a new wing built for these. This was partially destroyed by fire in 1915.

In 1927 Miss Dunn commenced a course in poultry keeping for senior girls. In 1928 there were more continuation classes (night school) in English and arithmetic, but provision was very poor compared with other schools. Ordiquhill additionally offered book keeping, cookery and needlework, Bogmuchals beekeeping and Cornhill horticulture. By 1937 Deskford was much better, offering English, arithmetic, dressmaking, cookery and first aid/nursing. This last class had 31 students.

In 1934 there were evening lectures on gardening by Mr Ames of the College of Agriculture, and in 1957 a woodwork evening class was begun under Mr Henderson, with 11 students. In 1959 Miss Nicol from the North of Scotland College of Agriculture arranged poultry lectures.

In 1938 the school syllabus included reading, composition, parsing, analysis, singing, sewing, arithmetic, geography, grammar, mental arithmetic, Latin, history, science, nature knowledge, drill, writing in copy books, scripture knowledge and dictation. In 1969 there was an afternoon closure to allow the staff to attend a lecture at Buckie on the implications of the change to decimal currency and metric measurement.

INSPECTIONS

Particularly in the early part of the C20th these were frequent, and it was important to receive a favourable report. In 1899 Inspectors reported that the school had a few dullards. However in the circumstances of having had to use the Church, "It says much for the determination and zeal of the staff that the efficiency of the school has been so well maintained". Comment was made however that there was no drill, and there were other problems such as the school having to be closed on May 3rd, because that was the day for cleaning the Church. The Friday of Cullen Mart and the following Monday were both given as holidays instead of the two days generally given after an Inspection.

In 1900 the Inspection Report praised the school's academic standards and well-equipped, well lighted, airy new building. In 1901 the general tone of the school and its academic standards were both judged excellent. In 1902 it was the same, except for attendance, which must be improved. This was done.

In 1905 the Report stated that the standard was reasonable, but that the infants' reading was monotonous and artificial. The middle room was satisfactory and the highest class very sound, but overall several suggestions for improvements were made. 1906 produced a very good HMI Report, which suggested however that some new desks were required for the infants, some new books for the library and more frequent promotion between classes.

In 1907 HMI McCombie was expecting more than rote learning. He commented that "pupils should be stimulated to attempt difficulties" and that "with one or two exceptions pupils seem to refuse to think", that "confidence and effort should be cultivated from the beginning", that "the pupils are totally ignorant of the subject matter of their songs" and that "in geography mere lists of names should be dropped". This was near the end of the 40 years service by Dominie Smith, and may reflect him being more comfortable with the, by then outdated methodology of the 1860s, when he had begun his career.

That year, for the first time, the visit of James Morrison, a member of the School Board, to examine the registers, was recorded. In 1910 the HMI reported that he was very impressed by the "gratifying advance" made by the senior class, but that the desks were still inconvenient, and that there was still no scheme of cleansing and disinfecting, as he had required.

In March 1911 HMI Morrison reported that the middle and upper school were excellent and the infants, in the main, satisfactory. However reference books, terrestrial globes, a practical room blackboard and a new PE syllabus should be obtained. Almost all desks were obsolete and should be replaced gradually by modern dual desks of suitable sizes. At the end of July he enquired as to whether these recommendations had been carried out. This had still not been done by May 1913, and the School Board was required to state their intentions to the Education Department in Edinburgh at an early date.

Changes had taken place by the 1930s. An HMI Report in October 1927 stated that the infants were very good, the middle class excellent and the seniors reasonable, but gave several recommendations. The new staffroom was praised but the tidiness of the Headmaster's room was criticised. In 1929 the Report said that both the infants and the middle room were very good, while the seniors were mixed, being "imperfectly acquainted with idiom and punctuation in written composition" and "showing considerable inaccuracy in arithmetic".

The 1930 Report repeated the criticism of the state of tidiness of the Headmaster's room, and also of the practical room, and stated that it was "desirable that the apparatus used in the teaching of science should be kept free from dust".

By 1931 the Headmaster's room was "efficient and a most noticeable improvement", however "the offices (toilets) are of the objectionable pit type, and there was an objectionable odour in their vicinity". They should be improved and there should be a thermometer in every room. This report was considered highly favourable and the Clerk to the School Management Committee: District No 2 (Cullen, Fordyce, Deskford and Ordiquhill) of the Education Authority of the County of Banff was to write to JA Beveridge with congratulations.

By 1932 HMI Reports were much more detailed and specific, with recommendations. In 1935 the school was reported as satisfactory, except the senior class, which was unsatisfactory. JAB was a popular headmaster, but not all the HMI Reports were positive. In April 1939 the report stated that in needlework and cookery "the teaching is limited in its scope and not closely related to home conditions and prices. Quantities and the question of home diet have been neglected". An additional cupboard should be supplied.

When HMI Logan visited on October 21st 1941 he found that the school was closed for a local holiday. The 1945 Report stated that the annexe had been unavailable during the War. The main building would require improvement when conditions permitted. The cookery store had become unserviceable. Attendance and therefore classwork had been considerably affected by the potato harvest and snowstorms. However the staff and pupils worked in happy cooperation. The primary section was good, and the secondary section mixed, but it had been affected by the War. There was a lack of science equipment, no visiting teacher of technical and no specialist visiting teacher of PE. The range was out of operation (a new stove was fitted on October 16th) and the practical room had a neglected appearance. Staff had made commendable efforts in the circumstances.

In August 1948 HMI reported that a practical room, a dining room and a kitchen were soon to be added to the building. He hoped that, when possible, modernisation of the heating, lighting, water and sanitation in the main building, and the playground surface, would take place. The school was in good heart and very harmonious. The Report was good, very detailed and much longer than those previously made. The HMI Report on August 29th 1954 was positive about standards, ethos and building improvements. There were however some recommendations for improvements in the secondary section.

ROLL, ATTENDANCE AND HOLIDAYS

The school roll at Deskford throughout the C20th was always healthy and sometimes proved too large for the accommodation available, not only when the Portobello evacuees were on the roll.

Because the school logs for the time before 1900 were lost in the fire, we do not have a figure for the roll then, however average attendance in October 1899 was 128. By 1903 the roll was 65, 32 of whom were boys, and by 1905 it had risen to 75. By August 1908 it had fallen to 53, but in May 1909 it was 86, and by August 1916 it was 120. In July 1921 the roll was 107 and school opening times were 9:00 – 1:00 and 2:00 – 4:15, with French being taught daily between 4:15 and 5:00. In January 1925 four pupils were admitted from Shielburn, and the roll stood at 111, but by April 1925 it was down to 92. This fell further by January 1930 to 79, but by August 1932 was up to 98, and by April 1935 to 112. Much of this fluctuation was caused by the mobile nature of the dominant agricultural employment in which, farm servants moved every 6 months. The high point for the roll was in March 1940 when, including the evacuees, it reached 155.

In January 1945 the roll was 108, but by December it had fallen to 92, though once more it rose to 102 in January 1948, and to 104 in August 1954. It fell slightly during the 1950s but by April 1960 was still 90. In December 1960 two pupils joined from Shielburn School when it closed. With the closure of the secondary department at Deskford the roll fell, but throughout the 1960s ranged between 40 and 67. In 1970, when the decision to close Deskford Primary School was taken, the roll was 55.

Throughout the C20th attendance was affected by a number of different factors, weather and farming having perhaps the greatest effect. In the late C19th, common reasons for absence included helping with the harvest, sowing, turnips, hay, hoeing, peats, moss-cutting, driving peats, rolling, weeds, potato planting, potato-lifting, carrying seed and steam threshing mills. Girls were commonly kept off if needed to help their mothers, or if their mother was away from home.

On the Wednesday of Keith Cattle Show in August 1890, attendance at school was poor. On May 18th 1900 only 40 pupils attended as it was Cullen Market Day. In May 1901 attendance was similarly poor for Cullen Market, and on November 28th that year attendance was low because it was term day. On July 25th 1902 it was noted that attendance had been good the previous week, except on the Friday, which was Rathven Market.

On July 7th 1905 the Headmaster reported that attendance that week had not been satisfactory owing to turnip hoeing and carting of peats. In October 1905 steam mills working in the parish was the reason for poor attendance; in November potato lifting was the reason and in April 1906 it was potato planting.

Term days always caused much absence, as was the case on June 1st 1906 when there were many flittings. In 1908 this was further exacerbated because there were several roups in the area. In January 1909 a steam threshing machine was at Berryhillock and 4 or 5 of the older boys were absent, assisting. On the 25th of that month, 4 boys asked and were granted leave to go home as they were required by their parents. They were Lawrence Ogg, George Farquhar, George Benzie and Charles Duncan. However in the May of the following year there was disapproval of George Garvock who was employed illegally, driving cattle.

In May 1916 Robert Fraser and George Taylor were granted unconditional exemptions, Jessie Ingram till the end of the summer holiday, James Milton, James McKay and William Milne till November 26th, and Herbert Reid, conditional on him attending an evening class. In April 1917, Robert Topp, James McKay, William Rumbles, Jessie Ingram and Lizzie Duthie were all granted exemptions, and in the August one boy was granted exemption for the benefit of a shooting tenant. As late as 1947, attendance was down to 50% at some points in the year because of exemptions.

Severe weather often played havoc with attendance. School was closed between March 21st and March 24th 1899 because of a snowstorm. There was also a snowstorm on Good Friday and few pupils came to school. On January 3rd 1900 the rain was very heavy and only 36 pupils turned up. They were sent home. On February 5th only 75 out of a roll of 135 were present, because of snow. They were sent home. On February 12th the roads were blocked with snow and no pupils turned up, nor did the woman who lit the fires. A few pupils attended on the 13th but there was more snow on the 16th, 20th, and 21st with roads blocked by drifting. On a Friday morning at the start of July there was poor attendance because of heavy rain.

On July 25th 1901 there fell the first rain after a period of excessive heat. Few pupils attended. On December 18th there was heavy snow and an attendance of less than 33%. The register was taken and the pupils sent home. On July 6th 1903 there was rain and wind and only 66% of the pupils attended. On November 27th few pupils attended owing to snowstorms and on August 5th 1904 there were few at school because of heavy rain.

On March 9th 1906 the roads were blocked by snowdrifts and few pupils turned up, those who did being dank and drooping. A half day was given. On January 15th 1909 there was a poor attendance because of threatening weather, with those present being sent home at lunchtime.

On January 11th 1918, only one pupil, Willie Rumbles, turned up. The Headteacher read the story of Sir Walter Scott's early life with him and then sent him home at 10:15. By the 18th the frost had burst the pipes and prevented the use of the range, which was still out of use on February 1st. A major snowstorm in early March meant attendance of under 50% all week. By the end of the week men were still cutting through the snowdrifts at the Cullen end of the parish to try to reopen the roads. On January 28th 1927 the school was closed because of gales.

On January 25th 1945 only 53 pupils out of 108 attended. The roads were snow-bound but passable, and in many cases lack of adequate footwear was the problem. On the 30th there had been fresh snow overnight and the roads were again blocked. Miss McBean phoned to say she could get no further than Lintmill, so would report to Cullen School. On February 5th, Mr Henry, the benchwork instructor, got to school for the first time. In mid April the school opened on a Saturday to make up for attendance lost during the storm. By the 1950s there were fewer closures because of the weather.

Holidays were given and school closures made for a wide variety of reasons, many of which appear obscure and strange to us nowadays. In 1890 a holiday was given for the Flower Show and another on the day after the examination in scripture knowledge. In June 1900 a holiday was given to celebrate the surrender of Pretoria during the Boer War, and, on the day after her death, a holiday was taken to mourn the death of Queen Victoria.

April 12th 1901 was a holiday because the Headmaster had to deliver the completed census papers to the Sheriff in Banff, and July 29th was a local Deskford holiday when, perversely, 23 pupils attended. They were sent home. In June 1902 a week-long holiday was announced for the Coronation of King Edward VIIth. A half-day holiday was given on October 21st because the Headmaster had to meet with the Inspector of Poor and the Registrar of Births. In July of that year pupils had been given a week-long holiday because the Headmaster had influenza. In July 1906 a holiday was granted to mark the marriage of the Chairman of the School Board, Dr Campbell.

In 1910 the school was granted a week's Spring Holiday for the first time. This has now evolved into the annual two week Easter Holiday. In May 1910 the 20th was observed as a day of mourning for Mr Pate (Peter) King. In March 1911, on two successive Fridays, the school was dismissed at 3:00 to allow the concert party into the school. In June of that year a week-long holiday was granted to celebrate the Coronation of King George Vth.

On February 16th 1912 the school was dismissed at 2:00 to allow preparations to be made for a dance that evening, and on March 1st it was dismissed at 1:10 to allow preparations to be made for a social evening. In June, the assistant teachers, to allow them to attend an ambulance class, dismissed their classes at 3:30. In 1913 the summer holidays lasted from July 12th to August 31st, earlier than in previous years, and by now there was also an annual Christmas Holiday. On Thursday July 22nd 1915 there was a holiday to allow a sale of work to take place, and on Friday 23rd another holiday was given for Rathven Mart.

In February 1918, in order to make up 400 attendances for the year (200 days) the Tuesday and Wednesday of the week ending March 9th 1917, which had been cancelled, were reclaimed, and the summary amended accordingly. On September 6th Rev Morison announced that the autumn holiday would begin that morning because of the illness of Mr Scott and Miss Murdoch. In February 1922 there was a holiday to celebrate the wedding of Princess Mary, and on April 26th 1923, one to celebrate the marriage of the Duke of York. On August 23rd that year there was no school because of the Horticultural Society Show. In October 1924 pupils got an extra half-day holiday because the school was needed for an election.

In April 1926, the Fast Day before Communion was not observed generally in the parish, so the school did not close, as it had done previously. Some modernisation and rationalisation took place in 1929 when local holidays in Cullen, Deskford and Fordyce were standardised. In May 1937 three days holiday were given to mark the Coronation of King George VIth. At the end of World War II holidays were given to mark VE Day, and in November 1947 there was a holiday to celebrate Princess Elizabeth's wedding. In 1948, in February, there was 100% attendance, so school was dismissed at 3:00 on the Friday. On April 26th the same year there was a holiday to mark the Silver Wedding of the King and Queen. Finally, and somewhat strangely to Scottish eyes, though I'm sure the pupils did not object, there was a holiday to mark the signing of the Magna Carta.

In 1927, Banffshire had the best attendance figures in Scotland, at 92.28%. Equivalent figures in the first decade of the C21st were around 95%. However, despite these high attendance figures there were always individual cases to be dealt with. In October 1910 the continued absence of Mary A Spence and Nellie Smart was reported to the School Board, and in June 1914 it was discovered that an unnamed girl had been allowed to leave when she should still have been attending, because her parents had given a false date of birth. When they refused to produce her birth certificate she was placed back on the roll. On May 30th 1921 there was poor attendance because of the presence of a menagerie in Cullen. In

October of that year a report on the attendance of Ella Smith, Poolside, was forwarded to the Clerk of the School Management Committee.

On January 21st 1925, Henry Lewis, a boy from a travelling show company, was enrolled, but he left on the 26th. In 1928 the irregular attendance of Ella and Ian Bowie, Briggs, was reported to the Clerk. In 1964 there was excitement when two pupils from Southern Rhodesia enrolled.

PROVISION

In November 1911 hot dinners began but ceased for a while in January 1920 as a result of the school cleaner having met with an accident. These dinners cost ½d per pupil with every third member of a family free. Seventy pupils benefited from the generosity of parents and friends. All vegetables were donated, so the only costs were for bones, lentils, barley and a cook. Rabbits were also donated. The School Board donated coal and the use of the cookery room. £1:15/- was donated which almost paid for the cost of bowls and spoons. The entire scheme was self-financing, with teachers acting as a management committee and helping in serving. The children, especially those who lived too far from the school to go home at lunchtime, greatly benefited, and attendance improved, which caused the financial grant to the school to be increased. From ½d in 1911, the cost of school meals had risen to 1/6d in 1968, a 36 times increase. In the 1930s cocoa was provided at lunchtime during winter, served in chipped enamel bowls. Pupils had to bring their own lunch piece.

In 1931 Dr Frank Innes Mackintosh left a legacy of £100 to Deskford School for prizes. Rev and Mrs Morrison established a prize fund in memory of Jim, their youngest child, who died in childhood. Every year the pupils voted for the two most helpful pupils in the school, one boy and one girl, and they were awarded the Jim Morrison Prize. By including the pupils in deciding who got the prize they were far ahead of their time. For a time pupils in Shielburn were given bicycles by the Council to allow them to get to Deskford School. In 1939 the Christmas tree in the school had 150 presents under it, rather than the usual 100, because of the absorption into the community of the Portobello evacuees, which was genuine and warmhearted.

By the 1950s there were great changes. In October 1955 there was a visit from Mr Hurst, the music supervisor, to discuss the use of wireless and gramophone. In 1957 visits to the school by officials include the Clerk of Works, Assistant County Librarian, Mr Harper, Youth Employment Officer, Miss Glennie, Domestic Science and Meals Supervisor, Mrs Connell and the Milk Officer re foreign bodies in the school milk, the supply of which was briefly suspended in 1958. Perhaps the most powerful and influential people to visit the school were Sir William Muiry, Secretary of the Scotch Education Department, Mr J Gunn, Chief HMI and two other HMIs, which took place in 1953.

Poverty had been an ongoing concern over the centuries. Just after World War I Mrs McPherson, Bleachfield, was awarded one coat and one pair of shoes for each of her children, Mona and Sheila, and an attempt was to be made to recover the cost from their father. In December 1921, the Morison Educational Fund, held by the Inspector of the Poor, Mr Cruikshank, reported that £5:4:3d had been spent in the previous year. On December 19th 1922 the Headmaster received £2:7:7d income from the Fund for the year. In September 1939 John Packman, Craibstone Cottages, was provided with clothing for his stepson, George Dalgarno, viz 1 suit, 2 pairs of stockings, 2 shirts, 2 pairs of pants, 2 vests, 1 jersey, 1 pair of boots and 1 pair of sandals.

REQUISITIONS

Over the years, the number and range of supplies and services for Deskford School increased significantly right up until the final ten years of its existence, when many items were removed and given to other schools. This must have been a melancholy process for those involved with Deskford School.

There was a feeling of celebration in 1899 when drill requisites were delivered. Unfortunately however, the hoops were not considered suitable. On November 28th 1901 the piano was tuned, a regular occurrence, and in November 1903 two drawing boards were delivered, just one week before an Inspection by the Inspector of drawing; perhaps a coincidence. In 1917 it was felt to be worth recording that Miss Taylor had been provided with two dozen pencils for her class.

In 1930, during the summer holiday, the whole school was distempered and varnished, the latrines were lime washed and the chimneys swept. The delivery of coal was meticulously recorded. For example, on September 23rd 1936, 2 tons 9 cwt of coal was delivered, and even with wartime shortages, on February 27th 1942, 2 tons of Scotch coal arrived, while in February 1944 2 tons of Scotch coal and 2 tons of anthracite were delivered. However in March 1945 five bags of coal had to be borrowed from the Church.

As soon as World War II came to an end there appears to have been a major effort to improve the supplies, equipment and condition of the school. In May 1945 a new battery for the projector was received from the Education Committee, and in 1949 the new science and technical building was officially opened. In August 1951 a new kitchen for the School Meals Service was built, and school meals, brought from Buckie, started in December. In April 1952 the new water closets were in operation, the first time Deskford pupils had anything other than dry latrines. A telephone for the school was installed in 1954.

In both January and February 1955 snow caused the latrines to freeze, and prevented the delivery of school milk and school dinners, but the staff arrived, having walked halfway from Cullen over blocked roads. In February 1955 new blackboards were installed. In October of the same year there was a visit from Mr Christie who promised to arrange for the installation of shelving to accommodate an adult library in Room 3. This was completed by June 1956, and was to comprise both Juvenile and Adult sections of the County Library.

Mr Addison, plumber, repaired the schoolhouse cistern, and Mr Fraser, mason, repaired harling on the school wall for the second time. In November, Mr Runcie, slater, spent three days clearing rones and downpipes and suggested that in future this be done annually. A new wireless receiver arrived which allowed the use of BBC Schools' Broadcasts.

Amongst the items received in 1956 were six pairs of spiked running shoes, an electric hot cupboard for the canteen, records for music and a new lathe. On June 1st a British Railways lorry delivered 19 assorted packages from Arnold's, the educational supplier. On the 4th they delivered a set of netball stands and on the 6th two more packages from Arnold's. Still in 1956, a 1926 Singer car engine was delivered from Mr Chalmers, Fordyce, for use in the technical department. Also that year there were delivered two drums of rural gas, an electric bandsaw, a Singer Sewing Machine, and a forge and brazing hearth.

In February 1957 workmen began erecting a new staffroom, store, and an extension to the hall building, and the Clerk of Works visited to discuss the supply of hot water for the new pupil wash-basins. In March the Director of Education, the County Architect, Provost Bain and Rev Armour agreed that the County would discuss acquiring part of the glebe as a school playing field.

Still in 1957, on June 13th, one vaulting buck and two boxes of science supplies were delivered. In autumn an electric wash boiler for domestic science and an anvil and heavy stones for the forge were delivered. The exterior of the hall building, including the extension and the doors of the horsa building were painted and a gate was erected in the playground. In November a typewriter was delivered from Messrs Webster, Aberdeen.

In April 1958 a new roller blackboard was delivered and fitted. In May an ML8A woodworking lathe and accessories were delivered and a tape recorder was purchased. In February 1959 there was discussion about the possibility of forming school playing fields from part of Kirktown Farm, and in March two gym benches were delivered from Lumley's by British

Railways. In May 12 violins were received and issued, though No 11 was slightly damaged. Some were shared. In September one dozen stacking chairs for needlework arrived and in October a power drill was installed.

In May 1960 cycle shelters were completed and put into use. In September a new Ellams duplicator arrived and in October the hall floor was sanded and sealed, and wire mesh fitted to the inside of the windows. In January 1961, just as the secondary school closed, new roof lights were installed in the school hall. In February strong winds brought down two chimneys, which in turn brought down slates. The other two chimneys were removed and the roof sealed. In May the Floor Polish Company representative left floor polish and the Cresco Paper Towel Company representative left paper towels and dispensers.

In October 1961 there were discussions about converting the Horsa building or the domestic room into a kitchen and canteen. In December it was noted that mice were eating their way through the emergency rations. Three bags of crisps were gone. In October 1962 the Director of Education visited to discuss converting the technical building to a canteen and kitchen, but in November it was decided that the Horsa building would be used instead, and the domestic room used for cloakrooms and toilets. New power points were installed in the hall but there were no heaters. Two convector heaters were installed in March 1963. Over the Easter Holidays in 1963 42 new chairs and 19 new desks were delivered.

In November there were still more discussions about the proposed playing field. In January 1964 gas heaters for the hall arrived and in March a 23" TV was installed in the General Purpose room. In August the exterior of the hall was redecorated. In June 1965 the piano in the hall was tuned and new castors were fitted. The piano in the old infant room was condemned. In October the playing field was fenced and an entrance formed.

In October 1966 the boiler was inspected and the typewriter mechanic cleaned the typewriter. In November the fire extinguishers were checked, and in November 1967 three cartons of paper towels were delivered. In December the fire extinguishers were again checked. Practically all of them were unserviceable. In November 1968 material for a fibreglass course was delivered, and in May 1969 new girls' lavatories were being erected and they came into use in August. In November the GPO separated the telephone link between the school and the schoolhouse. The school now had its own direct line, Cullen 245.

In March 1970 the Parents' Committee decided that, in light of the expected closure of the school, they would buy 70 Bibles with commemorative labels for presentation to each child, members of staff received a New English Bible each from Mrs Guthrie. Rev Guthrie conducted the closing service.

Despite a frenzy of repairs and provision of new equipment during the 1950s and 1960s, this was paralleled by an almost catastrophic failure to maintain the utilities, which caused major disruption over the same two decades. In March 1956 there were major problems with the boiler and with a flood, which meant that lunches had to be taken in two sittings in the infant room.

On January 19th 1960 all pupil lavatories were frozen. No milk or meals arrived so emergency rations had to be used. Roads were blocked and teachers and 8 pupils from Bleachfield, who were the last to leave, had to turn back. Everyone spent the night in the schoolhouse, the pupils in beds and the adults round the fire. The fathers of the stranded pupils got through the following day on tractors, but the staff were still stranded. On the 20th 5 pupils out of 83 attended and they were sent home. The road was eventually cleared by the big plough from Keith.

On February 11th there was again snow. Two fathers arrived before lunch to take their children home, and Mr Smith, Braidbog, drove 7 children who lived west of the school home. On February 16th school meals were cancelled so pupils were issued with cocoa and the school was closed at 1:00. On the 17th teachers could only get as far as the Clune and the Headmaster instructed them by phone to go back.

On May 29th 1961 there was trouble with the water supply, two constantly running cisterns, and the headmaster felt that the outside toilets were in such a poor state that they should be condemned. On June 5th there was trouble with the water supply again, attributed to an electric pump at Kirktown, though it was also thought that there might be a leak somewhere. Then it was decided that the problem was caused entirely by faulty school latrine cisterns. On December 7th 1961 the outside latrines were again frozen, and the minibus got stuck in the snow at Burnsford. On January 3rd 1962 it got stuck at Briggs.

Between January 10th and 18th 1963, burst pipes brought down the domestic science room and hall ceiling, and on the 25th only the staff toilets were working. On February 15th infra red lamps were installed in the toilets as an anti freeze precaution. On March 4th pupil toilets were working for the first time since Christmas.

There were many discussions and promises about the heating, water, toilets, harling, canteen and kitchen, but little was done and what was done was not always successful. For example, on December 13th 1963 a bulk storage water heater was installed. This overloaded the circuit and blew a main fuse. The heater had to be disconnected and replaced by an electric boiler.

On April 24th 1964 the drains from the lavatories were choked. However, to look on the positive side, they were no longer being called latrines. In October 1965 repairs were made to the toilets as there was no hope of any alterations or improvements being made. On January 5th 1966 there was a burst pipe in the toilet, and on the 21st, and on the 10th and 11th of February the toilets were again frozen. On November 10th 1967 there was rain coming through the roof of the north cloakroom.

In January 1968 the pupil lavatories were again frozen so pupils were allowed to use the two staff ones. By the 21st the cold water supply to the hall and the cookery room were also frozen. Only one lavatory, that in the ladies' staff room, was working. Between January and March the outside lavatories were continuously frozen. In 1969 the toilets were frozen between January 6th and 9th, and again on February 3rd. On the 10th all water was frozen except in the staffroom toilet. By the 11th only the outside toilets were still frozen. The canteen, cloakroom and hall toilets were all OK. However, on the 17th, once again, all toilets except the staffroom ones were frozen. Water for washing dishes had to be carried from the boys' cloakroom. On the 18th pipes burst in the canteen. On the 21st the toilets were still frozen. On the 26th a plumber arrived to fix the burst. On March 3rd the toilets were still frozen, but were OK by the 6th. They froze again on the 10th.

On January 6th 1970 the pipes were frozen as were the boys' toilets. It is not difficult to conceive of what a negative effect the above litany must have had on morale in the school. One has to wonder if there was an element of deliberately allowing conditions to become so abysmal that there would be little opposition when closure was announced. Morale could only have been further adversely affected by the constant loss of equipment after the secondary section closed.

The first loss was on September 4th 1959 when five science stools were taken to Banff Academy. In February 1961 English text books and all serviceable domestic science equipment and science equipment were transferred to Cullen. On September 5th that year canteen equipment was sent to Keith for a camp. Earlier in the year the buck and a 6-foot bench were removed to Portsoy and a fire blanket to Findochty.

On November 30th 1962 two PE benches and science benches were removed to Keith Grammar School, and in February 1964 the gas cooker and a container of rural gas were transferred to Ordiquhill Secondary School. In December the metal lathe was transferred to Keith Grammar School, and in October 1965 the power drill was removed to Portsoy. On September 9th 1966 two technical benches were removed to Portknockie, and in January 1968 surplus anthracite was removed to the Education Offices. In March spare wood in the technical room was collected by Aberchirder School and in November surplus tools were removed from the technical building.

On July 1st 1970 canteen equipment was removed to the new school in Cullen. Mr K McBride, Head Teacher at Cullen, wasting no time, informed the last Deskford Head Teacher that he had permission from the Director of Education to take away the TV, the school football strip, the jumping stands and a paper dispenser, which he promptly did. On the 2nd he returned and removed a variety of books.

The drip, drip effect of regularly losing equipment and of having to endure frequent frozen pipes could not have done much for the self esteem of Deskford School in the 1950s and 1960s, and would suggest incompetence on a massive scale or a deliberate plan to run down and finally close an effective and happy rural school, Deskford Primary School.

ACTIVITIES

Over the centuries a wide range of different activities took place in association with the different schools which existed in Deskford at different times. On Shrove Tuesday, or Brose Day, in the 1770s, cock fighting took place in the Parochial School in the middle of Kirktown. The school benches were formed into an arena. Each boy brought a few cocks, up to a maximum of four. If cocks were not killed in a fight but ran away, they were immediately decapitated and given to the schoolmaster for the pot. Cocks which ran away were called fugies (fugitives).

The owner of the winning cock was crowned "King" for the day, with a crown made from the tail feathers of the losing birds, and carried round Kirktown on the shoulders of his schoolmates, who sang a song in Latin, in praise of cocks. A fete and feast for all pupils was provided at the manse, the meal consisting of barley broth made with four of the dead cocks, a leg of mutton and curds, cream and pancakes. An event as elaborate as this was however the exception, and until the late C19th there was little in the way of one of a kind activities for the pupils. Throughout the C20th however there was a rapid increase in the number of extra-curricular activities organised for them.

In 1900, when the school was being taught in the Church, a Punch and Judy Show was arranged for the pupils but had to take place on the public road outside as it was considered inappropriate for an event of that nature to take place within the Church. In 1912 there was an excursion for Supplementary Pupils to the top of the Bin, and in 1914 a holiday was granted for the first time for a seaside trip. In both 1917 and 1927 all pupils attended the Cullen House Fete.

May 24th 1922 was Empire Day and the Headmaster addressed the pupils on the duties of future generations to uphold the dignity of the Empire. The whole school sang God Save the King. However it was not possible to give a half-day holiday as requested by the Authority as so many attendances had been lost to medical certificates. On September 13th that year the school did close, as instructed by the Director of Education, for the County Sports, at which Deskford had two entries. In 1926 a concert was held in the new Parish Hall and the following year there was a concert followed by a dance.

At the end of June 1928, on the last day of session, there was a school picnic on Cullen Links between 1:00 and 7:00, to which pupils were transported by bus and by car. In 1930 the school concert was the operetta The Pearl Fishermen. This was followed by a dance to Younie's Band, Keith, at which £25 was raised. At the Christmas parties in 1930 there was a tree provided by Seafield Estate, and a present for each pupil and their younger siblings not yet at school, from Santa. There were games, singing and dancing, with fruit and sweets given to each child on departure.

The school concert of 1931 was outstanding, probably because of the energy, expertise and enthusiasm of JA Beveridge, Headmaster, who was producer and director for the local amateur dramatic society. Music for the dance which followed was provided by Ross's Band, Buckie. On May 29th that year the school was closed as 47 pupils were attending the Buckie Music Festival. On November 11th, following a two-minute silence, the first recorded poppy collection in the school raised £5:0:6d.

In 1932 the Headmaster addressed the pupils on the Disarmament Conference in Geneva. That same month, February, he warned pupils against the wanton destruction of wild birds' nests and eggs. In May that year pupils were taken to the Induction Service for the new Minister, Rev Brown, who was the first Minister of the united Churches. In September, Sir Walter Scott Centenary celebrations were held. The Headmaster gave a lecture and then a half-day holiday to the pupils. One wonders which of the two elements they enjoyed more. At the Christmas parties that year Santa gave each teacher the present of a new tawse. This may have been a joke.

On Jubilee Day, May 6th 1935, pupils were taken to the Pictures at Buckie by bus and then brought back for tea in the hall. Each was presented with a Jubilee Mug. In 1936 the picnic went further afield, to Whitehills. That year a whist drive was held for school funds. However, in 1940, because of World War II, the picnic was held on a field at Ardoch Farm. In 1941 parents were not present at the prizegiving, and there was a film shown rather than the usual concert.

Following World War II the social whirl got back into gear. At Christmas 1945 there were films, tea and buns, and by April 1948 the concert

1950s school play. (L to R) Patsy Fetch, Hazel Reid, Kathleen Simpson, Ethel Ewen, Dorothy Morrison, Isobel Currie.

reappeared with a performance of the operetta "Peach Blossom". However that year the picnic, which had been intended to be held at Sandend, had to be cancelled because of the weather. The Christmas party in 1948 was more elaborate, with films, games, tea and a bag of buns and a bag of sweets for each pupil. In November 1949 there was a puppet show and in 1950 there were two performances of the operetta "The Magic Ruby", and the picnic was held at Sandend.

1960s school play. L to R Ettie Mitchell, Margaret McKenzie, Kathleen Simpson, Isobel Milne, Isobel Currie.

In 1952, on the funeral of King George VI, there was a two-minute silence at 2:00pm and Rev Hamilton took a half hour service in Church. On Coronation Day that year there was a general picnic in the parish. Each pupil and pre-school child was given a propelling pencil, a mug and a handkerchief. In December 1955 there were three separate Christmas parties, for junior primary, senior primary and secondary pupils, and for the first time, 29 pupils, 10 parents and 2 teachers went to the pantomime in Aberdeen.

In 1955 the picnic went to Banff Links and, for the first time, P1 and P2 pupils presented a nativity play. In March 1956 the senior boys painted the playground for netball and other games. In May that year there was a puppet show which was also attended by pupils from Shielburn School. Empire Day was still being celebrated. There was a service in the school hall and £1:18:7½d was collected for the Forces Help Society and Lord Roberts Workshops. The picnic was ranging further afield and in 1956 went to Lossiemouth's Stotfield Beach for sports and a picnic, and returned at 7:00pm.

In March 1957 there was a bulb show in aid of school funds. It also had a cake and candy stall, a pound stall, teas and competitions and raised £54. In September the science club held its inaugural meeting. School shows were still a highlight of the year.

On June 19th 1958, P7 and secondary pupils, together with Miss Hay, Miss Cowie and the Headmaster went on an educational excursion, paid for by the Education Committee of Banffshire County Council. Between 8:00am and 6:00pm they visited Herd and McKenzie's shipyard in Buckie, Laidlaw's Mills in Keith, Parkmore Limestone Quarry in Dufftown and Balvenie Castle, with lunch in Keith School Meals Centre. In 1958 PC Stevens inspected bicycles and one was found to be slightly faulty. Raymond Murray was instructed to attend to it.

In 1959 there were talks by Mr Grieve on fire prevention, on nursing as a career and on the Navy by a recruiting officer. Empire Day had now become Commonwealth Day, but there was still a half-holiday to celebrate it. 1959 was a busy year. In May a team of boys took part in a 7-a-side football tournament in Keith and a team of girls took part in a 7-a-side netball tournament. Both performed creditably. Deskford School hosted a rehearsal for a dancing display at Buckie Area School Sports, and entertained 100 girls and teachers to tea. That same month, June, there was a holiday on the occasion of the last visit by the Royal Highland Show to Aberdeen. 29 pupils and all staff attended the show. At lunchtime on September 2nd pupils were allowed to see a partial eclipse of the sun, but there is no record of what, if any, health and safety precautions were taken. In October the secondary pupils' badminton club met for the first time.

In 1960 there was a holiday for Princess Margaret's wedding, Mr McKenzie, Portsoy, took school photos, Mr Bill McInnes, a young farmer from Australia, gave a slide show and there was a concert by pupils in aid of Church funds which raised £30:2:3d. In June it was so cold that the school sports and picnic was replaced by a bus tour to Banff, Huntly, Rothiemay and Grange, and back to school for tea. In November, 13 violin pupils, accompanied by Mr Merson, attended a concert in Elgin by the Boyd Neil String Orchestra.

In 1961 senior pupils presented a pantomime, "Alice in Wonderland" in the parish hall and then to patients in Ladysbridge Hospital. In March there was a party for the badminton club and for the seniors who were now at Cullen. That same month the bulb show and sale of work raised £60. The school sports and picnic went to Fraserburgh Beach, with 120 present. The parents' committee held a beetle drive and whist drive, and Mr Espie, a former Headmaster, came back for a visit, accompanying a Nigerian visitor, Mr Michael Ibowe.

In 1963 there were two films and a talk from Lt Col Callander of the SSPCA, and the school sports were held in Cooper Park, Elgin. In October 1964 there was great excitement when a reporter and photographer from the P&J visited the school. In 1966 the school sports and picnic were held at Banff Links with 160 pupils, parents and teachers present. In December two films, on Ghana and Brazil respectively, were shown by a representative of Cadbury's Limited.

Cycling Proficiency tests were held in 1968, which was another busy year. In April the boys' football team took part in a 7-a-side tournament in Buckie and in September pupils went to Portsoy Secondary School to see the play, "The Key". In December 12 children went to "Singing Together" in Keith Grammar School. It was a very successful evening.

SUCCESSES

From the early 1900s Deskford School recorded with pride its pupils' academic achievements. After World War II they also participated in competitive events such as music festivals and sports competitions. Sometimes Deskford pupils won, and sometimes they did not, but they always gave it their best shot.

In March 1900 notice was received that Lizzie Reid, M Murdoch, Lizzie Benzie, Alister Smith, Frank McConnachie and George Smith had passed their Merit Certificate, and that all those presented in stage 1 Latin had passed. In March 1913 two boys attended Leaving Certificate exams in Cullen Higher Grade School in English and maths. In April 1914 examinations for the Leaving Certificate were held as usual in the cookery room, except on the Friday, when pupils sat the French exam in the senior room. However in March 1918 the Intermediate Certificate exams were held in the Church vestry, because of the impossibility of having a fire in the cookery room.

In June 1928 all 11 candidates in the Qualifying class passed, and two scholars sat and were awarded university bursaries. In June 1930 the Director of Education himself examined the Qualifying class, when 11 out of 14 passed. That year the Dux was Jessie B Inglis and the Proxime Accessit was Ethel M Raffan.

However it was not only in academic matters that Deskford pupils wished to do well. In 1928, from a roll of 108, Deskford School closed for a day and entered four choirs in the Buckie Music Festival. The juniors came 1st in their section, the entry in the rural schools' section came 2nd equal, the seniors obtained a 1st class certificate and the infants a 2nd class certificate. The year before, at the first holding of the festival, of the two choirs entered by Deskford School, the juniors came 2nd equal, but the seniors were poorest in their class. Entry to music festivals continued until the 1960s. In 1961 the senior primary percussion band performed at the festival and were excellent.

Sports competitions were also entered. In 1928 four Deskford pupils each won three prizes at the Keith Sports, but the high spot for Deskford for sports competition was the 1950s and 1960s. In 1951 Deskford School won the EIS Cup at the inter school sports for schools with fewer than 100 pupils

In 1956 four relay teams competed in invitation events at Fordyce Academy Sports, against Fordyce and Portsoy. Unfortunately Deskford only achieved one 2nd place. However that same year Deskford won the rural school championship at the Buckie Area School Sports, which they repeated in 1957, 1958 and 1959. In 1958 the only solo success was Sheila Taylor, who came 1st in the girls' high jump. In 1959 Ian G Smith, P7, was a star, and Isobel Simpson, S3, won the girls' high jump. Deskford School seemed to specialise in the girls' high jump, for in 1960 it was again won, this time by Ethel Ewen, who cleared 4'2". There were further overall victories for Deskford School in 1961 and 1966.

There was also competition in other sports. For example on March 21st 1960 the secondary badminton club hosted a match against Botriphnie secondary badminton club and won 5-3.

MILITARY, POLITICS, LAND OWNERSHIP AND ARISTOCRACY

WAR: C1st AD – 1900

The North east in the first millennium AD was a power centre of Pictish tribes, a large part of whose focus was on war. The carnyx was used by similar tribes across Europe, as shown on a decorative panel on the Gundestrop cauldron from Denmark. Picts who lived in Deskford may have been part of the victorious army which defeated the Angles at Nechtansmere in Angus in 685, and may have helped when the Pictish forts at Burghead, Portknockie and Cullykhan were successful in repulsing the Vikings. This conflict continued with the merged Pictish/Scots nation as when King Indulf reputedly defeated Eric of the Bloody Axe at the Battle of the Bauds near Cullen in 951. Vikings were also defeated at Gamrie in 1004, Banff Links the same year and Mortlach in 1010.

Though no Pictish documents remain except king lists, and though Edward I removed much historical Scottish documentation to England in 1296, which was never seen again, there is much which can be learned from Irish, Welsh, Northumbrian and other English and Norse annals and sagas, together with remaining fragmentary and secondary Scottish sources.

For much of the 1st millennium AD Picts controlled most of Scotland except the South West, Argyll and Lorne and the eastern borders. Around 750 they defeated the Scots and became over- kings of the whole country. This was a short-lived success however, and in the early C9th the Scots in the form of the Cenél nGabráin conquered east central Scotland and in the form of the Cenél Loairn conquered eastern Scotland north of the Mounth. Later the two Cenéls fought each other for over-kingship (Duncan v Macbeth), and the leader of each was seen as a king in his own right. The last claimant from amongst the Cenél Loairn was a three year old McWilliam girl who was put to death in Forfar in 1230 by having her head struck against the market cross and her brains dashed out. During this period of conflict the Earl of Buchan took the side of the victorious southern dynasty against the people of Moray and was appointed justiciar across the entire North East. This gave him control over the lordship of Deskford and of the Thanage of Boyne.

By our standards the fighting between Pict, Scot, Norse and Northumbrian and amongst each was vicious. Claimants for kingship were many, with it being common for nephew to succeed uncle, brother to replace brother and different dynastic strands to compete against each other. It was considered normal during this competition for over-kingship for losers to be drowned, beheaded or burned to death. If the victor was magnanimous the defeated claimant might only have his eyes put out or be castrated to prevent any continuation of his line as competition for kingship. It was only during feudal times from about 1100AD onwards that a tradition of son succeeding father emerged, and even then there was a powerful faction opposed to this which coalesced around the rulers of Ross and Moray. This group was however unsuccessful in the civil war which ensued.

King Malcolm twice led military expeditions through this area, the second in 1078, and Alexander 1st also attempted to put locals in their place by pursuing them into their North East heartlands in 1116 and 1130. Thereafter the feudal system was increasingly firmly embedded.

Until 1600 landowners had additional responsibilities to lead war bands and protect their people. The Black Death in 1350 brought about the existence of paid soldiers for the first time and becoming a well-paid mercenary, first for England and later for several large continental armies, was very attractive to many young Scots. In the mid C17th, one in every eight Scotsmen of military age was a mercenary soldier somewhere in Europe. It is beyond belief that this did not include some young men from Deskford.

In 1643 War Committees were set up across Scotland. Every Minister, including the Deskford incumbent, had to provide one soldier, fully clad and equipped with weapons. Farm servants were forbidden to leave their place of employment in case they tried to avoid military service. The Minister had to prepare and submit a complete roll of able-bodied men, fit to bear arms, from the age of 16 to 60 so that, if required, one out of every four of these could be chosen for battle. All of this was to support Presbyterianism and the Solemn League and Covenant.

In 1674, James Philp was ordered to stand barefoot and in sackcloth at the door of the Kirk in Deskford, between the second and third bells, because of fornication, but at the next meeting of Presbytery the Minister reported that he had been taken away to the wars as a soldier for France. He had been committed to prison by the Earl of Findlater but had escaped and was fugitive.

On June 14th 1689, an order was read out by the Minister from Sir Thomas Livingstone, Colonel of the Old Regiment of Dragoons, whereby all heritors in the parishes of Fordyce and Deskford should deliver four score (80) horses and sacks at Gordon Castle on the 17th, for carrying provisions for their Majesties' Army.

Thanksgiving was offered in Deskford Church in 1746 for the "glorious victory gained by His Royal Highness the Duke of Cumberland over the rebels at Colodden upon the 16th inst, where numbers of the rebel army were slain and complete victory obtained". This area certainly favoured the Government side, and in 1750 the inhabitants of Inaltry, Ardicow, Nether Blairock, Cluinhill, Leitcheston, Nether Cluin and Over Cluin lent fourteen plaids to the soldiers who were garrisoning Cullen. In 1751 three men from Deskford were "imprest" into the Navy. There is a gravestone in Banff to Sergeant John Wright, born in Deskford in 1778, who served for 23 years in the Royal Artillery. He was an elder in the parish of Banff and died in 1851.

In 1798, the local Volunteers, raised against the threat from Napoleon, were split into two battalions, of which the first had nine companies, five in Banff and one each in Cullen, Macduff, Grange and Portsoy. Presumably Deskford volunteers joined the Cullen, Grange or Portsoy companies. In 1803 the newly reconstituted Volunteers had seven companies in Banff and one each in Boyndie, Cullen, Grange, Marnoch, Portsoy and Rothiemay, all part of the 1st Battalion.

In the late C18th and early C19th, membership of the Militia was drawn by lot. In 1797 the list of Deskford men liable to be balloted under the Militia Act comprised Andrew Hilton, servant at Clune, John Anderson, servant at Nether Blairock, Walter Reid, servant at Ardoch, John Wilson, student at Ardoch, John Howie, farmer at Faichyhill, James Longmore, servant at Kirktown, Charles Reid, servant at Kirktown, James McHattie, farmer's son at Squaredoch, Alexander Chalmers, servant at Tillybreadless, Alexander Reid, tailor at Hollanbush, Alexander Laurence, servant at Croftgloy and Alexander Shepherd, servant at Inaltrie. Those whose names were drawn, but who did not want to join up, could pay a substitute to take their place. This cost between £5 and £40.

Those who joined had to spend a month in spring and six weeks in autumn on exercises. In 1813, a Deskford woman, Christian Marquis, wife of George Marquis, a private in the Aberdeenshire Army, was paid 13/- for 13 weeks via the Kirk Session by Alexander Young, Collector of Cess, as part of the scheme of payments to families of men serving in the Reserve. Not long after this Lieutenant Riddoch, a veteran of Waterloo, returned to live in Kirktown. Throughout the remainder of the century there would no doubt have been Deskford representation in the British Army throughout the Empire and in conflicts such as the Crimean War.

The Deskford Parish Council, in May 1900, recorded its thankfulness on the glorious news of the Relief of Mafeking, and its admiration for the valour and heroism of Col. Baden Powell and his little band of brave men. Volunteer young ladies made a collection from Deskford and Badenhannen for the Transvaal War Fund to be sent to the Soldiers and Sailors Families' Association, East Scottish Branch.

WORLD WAR I

World War I was undoubtedly the greatest military conflict the world had ever seen, though strangely neither Kirk Session minutes nor School Log mentions it except obliquely. In early October 1914 a recruiting meeting was held in

Deskford School with Rev Park presiding. The platform party included the Countess of Seafield, Mr MLF Davidson, Cullen, Major Grant, Banff, Mr Sharp, Cullen, Col. George, recruiting officer and Pipe Major Fraser, Banff. Several ladies were also present.

The National Anthem was sung. Rev Park gave a vigorous speech and pressed the young men present to join the colours. Major Grant gave a rousing speech which seemed to take the young lads present quite by storm. Mr. Sharp and Mr. Davidson spoke and encouraged the young lads to join right away and keep their King and Country safe.

Quartermaster Fraser took names and seven joined. Charles Rumbles, Muir of Squaredoch, and William Quinn, tailor, Berryhillock joined the Flying Corps and William Milligan, James Garvock, Backies, John Lawrence, farrier, Hillhead, George Raffan, Combs Croft, and William Harper, also Combs Croft, joined the Army. By some strange quirk of irony the six of those above who are mentioned in Deskford's Roll of Honour all survived the entire war whilst many who joined later were either killed or wounded. For some reason William Milligan is not mentioned in the Roll of honour. Several more went to Keith and joined. From a population of less than 700, Deskford at this time had between twenty and thirty serving the colours. These numbers increased substantially first through volunteers to Kitchener's Army and finally through conscription. The evening following the Deskford meeting Col George addressed a similar meeting at Sheilburn School.

Most local servicemen (30) joined the Gordon Highlanders, with several each in the Black Watch (7), Seaforth Highlanders (6), and HLI (4). Individual servicemen joined a further 43 different units including, inexplicably, the Somerset Light Infantry, the Fife and Forfar Yeomanry, the 6th Cheshires and the Dorsets. Many of the 43 units which were joined by Deskford men were Canadian, Australian or New Zealand ones, and modern warfare was also represented by the Motor Tractor Transport, Machine Gun Companies and the 4th Canadian Railway Troops. In all 92 households in Deskford are known to have been represented in the armed forces by the householder, his son or his stepson. The true number is greater than this since for various reasons not all those who are known to have fought are mentioned in the Deskford Roll of Honour.

Some families were particularly badly affected. Several had two or three sons serving and did not know, when the telegram arrived at the door, which son had been killed until they opened the telegram. The McGregors of Kirktown had one son badly wounded and one killed. Mrs Stewart of Cultain had twelve children. She had moved there a few years before the War from Portsoy after her two oldest sons had been washed off rocks and drowned. Three of her other sons fought in World War I, two being invalided out with serious wounds and the third being killed. When Jimmy Stewart's father George, later tenant in Braehead, was invalided out, having had most of one buttock shot away, he was given a badge to wear to prove he had done his duty and to prevent anyone presenting him with a white feather.

Other than death and bereavement and the fear which the War brought to every family, there was only limited impact on local life. Many horses, particularly the best ones, were commandeered for army service. In 1915 the Free Church held a sale of work to provide soldiers' comforts. Local ladies collected sphagnum moss on Cotton Hill and elsewhere for use in bandaging casualties from the trenches. In January 1916 Miss Murdoch, one of the schoolteachers, was off duty from 11:30 on the Thursday till the end of the week on receipt of notice of her brother's death in action. In 1917 a War Savings Association was formed in connection with the school. The first collection was made on April 23rd and Monday mornings before the school opened were to be the time for collections.

In 1918 the headmaster had leave of absence from May 14th to 24th to attend a Military School of Instruction. The same year Rev Park asked for leave for five months to replace the Minister of Holburn Church Aberdeen who was at the Front, and also to act as chaplain to the Gordon Highlanders in Aberdeen. Rev Morrison of the Free Church had offered to take the services in St. John's as well as in his own church. Leave was granted.

The Parish Council called a public meeting in early 1919 to discuss steps to be taken to commemorate men belonging to the parish who had fallen during the war. When a decision had been taken, the Minister arranged the taking down of the church gates to allow the construction of the war memorial, over which the two churches cooperated, with Rev Morrison chairman and Rev Park secretary of a committee established for the purpose.

The war memorial was unveiled in 1921 by Sir Ashley Mackintosh, son of the previous Minister, and commemorated the 17 dead from World War I. It was unveiled by Robert Cruickshank, Session Clerk, who had lost a son. It is situated in front of New St John's Church and is a column type in Kemnay granite, about 10' tall and inscribed "To the Glory of God and in honoured and loving memory of the men of this parish who made the supreme sacrifice in the Great War 1914-1919". In 1946 there were added the names of the 7 men who died in World War II under the inscription "Also to those who gave their lives in the World War 1939-1945". The memorial was carved by Messrs J Robertson and Son, Hardgate, Aberdeen and cost £256:13:7d. The present occupants of New St John's, which is now a private residence, Mr and Mrs Robertson, have erected a flagpole and flag and installed granite kerbing. They paint the railings, and keep the flower bed tidy. In 2008 a grant of £2,172 was received from the War Memorial Trust to tar the adjacent lay-by for parking.

WORLD WAR II

The Second World War differed in many ways from the First. There were fewer fatalities. There was a greater variety of support from the local community, and attitudes were perhaps more realistic about the potential horrors.

Amongst the support from the community, in 1940, £7:18:3d was raised for an appeal on behalf of Church of Scotland Army Huts. In January 1941 a Red Cross work party was busy making comforts for the troops. The ex-servicemen of Deskford arranged entertainments, the profit from which went to buy materials. At this early stage of the war 22 local men were on active service, one was a POW and one was reported missing. The POW, William Garden of the Gordon Highlanders, had been adopted by a local ex-serviceman, Mr Raffan, Comb's Croft. He and his wife were also informed that Marshall

Simpson, who had been boarded out with them, was missing, presumed a POW. Fifteen months later it was confirmed that he was dead.

Early in the War the Women's Guild sent a parcel to each local serviceman. The contents were worth 4/- and in addition there was a pair of socks. Those serving overseas got a little extra. For Christmas 1940 the Deskford Ex-Servicemen's Association agreed to send a parcel to all 21 local serving young men, each to contain a helmet, scarf, gloves, socks, currant loaf and chocolate. The Poppy Day appeal raised £6:17:2d, which was the biggest sum for fifteen years.

Several local men were members of the Territorial Army and were the first to be called up. They were stationed in the Longmore Hall, Keith, while waiting

Deskford Home Guard, around 1941/42. Photograph submitted by Mrs I. Milton, of Ellon, whose father, John McConnachie, is standing second left in the third row. Also, Mr J.A. Beveridge, who was headmaster of Deskford School, is sitting fourth from the left in the front row.

for a posting. Several members of the militia, including Ian McLean, Milton Mills, were posted to India. There were 40 members in Deskford Home Guard in 1941/42, including a Langlanburn Unit. In June 1942 the Headmaster of Deskford School attended a Home Guard Parade on the afternoon of the 30th and in October the same year he had three days off on Home Guard duties.

Research by Alison Smith has illustrated the role of the Deskford Auxilliary Unit whose task was to go underground in the event of an invasion and conduct guerrilla warfare against the occupiers and any collaborators. This Deskford

"Secret Army", comprised Sgt Bill Smith, Braidbog and Privates Willie Currie, Greens of Blairock, George Currie, Greens of Blairock, Ian Bowie, Briggs of Darbreich, Stewart Milne, Clune, Tommy Rumbles, Kirktown, Willie Pirie, Bogside and Peter Smith, Darbreich. They held weekend camps at Blairmore House, Glass, the local HQ, and also held joint exercises with neighbouring units.

Members of the "Secret Army" were trained in silent killing, booby traps, and night-time manoeuvres. The Deskford Unit's underground bunker was dug into the west bank of the Broxy Burn between Braidbog and Davie's Castle, but has now completely collapsed. Weapons, ammunition and provisions were stockpiled there. There was complete secrecy and even wives and parents did not know that their husbands and sons were members of an organisation which no one else knew existed. Many of the members went to their graves decades later without having said anything. Written records were forbidden. There were other units in Banffshire at Grange, Clochan, Portsoy, Banff, Marnoch and Rothiemay.

Some members of the Women's Land Army worked for Seafield Estate and "Lumberjills" of the Timber Corps worked on Lurg Hill and Greenhill, and were billeted at Greenhill Farm and Oathillock Farm in temporary huts. One of the regular events of the War in Deskford was practice artillery firing across the Howe o' Deskart, from the hills in the east to those in the west and vice versa.

On August 28th 1939 Deskford School was closed for the evacuation and on September 18th it reopened with 42 evacuees from Portobello in Edinburgh enrolled. They were accompanied by two teachers from Portobello High School, Miss Margaret Drysdale and Miss Margaret Craig, who taught in Deskford School. The two teachers and 12 of the pupils from Portobello were billeted in Aultmore Lodge and the rest of the evacuees throughout the parish.

Cycle sheds at the school were turned into an air raid shelter. Building started on December 13th 1940 and was completed on December 20th. They were ready for occupation on March 11th 1941. In 1940 the reopening of the school after the summer holiday was postponed from August 20th till October 1st until all the windows in the classrooms could be protected by wire netting as a precaution against air raids.

Amongst the unusual occurrences was the occasion when teenagers from the area surrounding Deskford visited by bicycle the site of the Wellington Bomber crash at Greens of Blairock, took smashed Perspex home and fashioned it into rings and other types of jewelry.

POWER AND DECISION MAKING IN ANCIENT TIMES

Politics, which is probably now at a low point in terms of widespread respect, is also probably the most convenient and fair way of organising any society's decision-making. Without politics we would be likely to suffer anarchy or dictatorship and there would be few protections for ordinary people.

As early as the C8th there were tax collectors and a sophisticated system of administration throughout Pictish areas. Power and politics were based on a tribal system within which there was no automatic succession and leadership was exercised only with the approval of the tribe. Taxation was a levy on the tribe. This system was replaced when feudalism was introduced under David 1st, and then amended when Sheriffs replaced Earls as tax collectors under Alexander 3rd.

Feudalism concentrated power in the King's hands, and those nobles and thanes who owed allegiance to him exercised this power in their local areas. Under feudalism slavery was abolished and then, about 1400, Scotland became the first country in Europe to abolish serfdom. Nevertheless power was concentrated in the hands of a very few individuals and the ordinary person had very little influence. Even the development of Trades Guilds in towns only extended a few closely defined powers to a very small number of people. In rural areas power became increasingly concentrated in the hands of the landowner or lord.

In areas such as Deskford the important day-to-day decisions were taken by overseers and then by Birlaymen and Birlay Courts which resolved disputes and disagreements about local activities. Birlaymen were respected local "elders", but almost nothing of the precise activities of the Birlay Courts is known as no written records were kept.

BARONY AND BURGH OF REGALITY

Deskford became part of the Barony of Ogilvie when this was erected in 1517, and later, between 1698 and 1747, was the administrative centre of the Regality of Ogilvie. Regalities had greater powers than Baronies. As a Burgh of Regality, Deskford was only a "parchment Burgh" and, although it had days laid down for markets and for fairs, these never fully developed in reality. The establishment of the Barony and then the Regality gave enormous and unquestioned power to the landowner, styled in turn Ogilvie of that Ilk, Earl of Findlater, and finally Earl of Seafield.

The Regality of Ogilvie was established in 1698 when King William made a Ratification in favour of James Ogilvie, Viscount Seafield. He conveyed to Sir James Ogilvie of that Ilk the Barony of Ogilvie comprising the lands of Findlater, Cullen, Deskford, Redhythe, Raggal, Finauchtie, Upstrath, Fordyce, Kempcairn, Milton of Breadhaugh and Scotston. Kirktown of Deskford was ordained the principal burgh of the Regality, with accompanying rights for the burgesses. There was to be a weekly Wednesday market and fairs were to be held on the second Thursday in April, the last Thursday in June and the second Thursday in October.

James, now Viscount Seafield, did not have his former rights and infestments such as the Balliary of Strathisla and the Constabulary of Cullen prejudiced by the establishment of the Regality of Ogilvie in Deskford. He did however have to pay the King £160 Scots at Whitsunday and at Martinmas for the Barony of Ogilvie, £1,000 Scots on the occasion of the marriage of his heir, 5 merks Scots at Whitsunday and Martinmas, with double on the entry of the heir, for Clochmacreich and Tillybreedless.

The Regality comprised "The Town and Kirklands of Deskford, manor place, Tower, Fortalice and Yards thereof. The Town and lands of Over Blerock. The

Town and lands of Fauchyhill. The Town and lands of Swallowhillock. The Town and lands of Knows. The Milltown of Deskford with the mills of the same, Millands, multures, Thirlage and Knaveship, Sucken and Sequells thereof and that part of Clune, John Thom's land and all whole the Town and lands of Clockmacreech. The Town and Lands of Over Skeith. The Town and Lands of Middle Skeith, The Lands of Wairds, commonly called My Lord's Wairds. The Town and Lands of Craibstoun. The Town and Lands of Croftgloy. The Lands of Aires of Squaredoch. The Town and Lands of Ramore. The Town and Lands of Ordins. The Town and Lands of Oathillock. The Town and Lands of Airdicow. The Town and lands of Nether Blairock. The Town and Lands of Airdoch. The Town and Lands of Cultain as also that part and portion of the Lands of Cultain called Little Cultain as the samen is Meiches and Marches from the rest of the Lands of Cultain and has been possessed by Colonel James Abercrombie of Glassah and his predecessors and their Tenants with Teinds and pertinents thereof. The Town and lands of Cairstoun. The Town and lands of Inaltry. The Town and lands of Coattain. The Town and lands of Meikle and Little Knows. The Town and lands of Nether Clune. The Town and Lands of Clunehill. The Town and Lands of Smithstown. The Town and Lands of Leitchestown. Together with the hail lands of Skeith and all other lands pertaining and belonging to the said Barony of Ogilvie as well not named as named with all and whole the other Houses, biggings, Yards, Orchards, Tofts, crofts, Mosses, Muires, Meadows, Fishings, Commonties, Common Pasturages, Outsetts, Insetts, Annexis, Conexis, Dependances, Parks, Wairds, Tenants, Tenandries and service of free Tenants, parts and pendicles. Signed Jo. Maule". Almost all of the farms mentioned remain today either as farms or as occupied private houses.

It also included "The Constablelands of Cullen, called Pittenbringands with the advocation, Donation and right of Patronage as well Parsonage as Vicarage of the Kirk of Fordyce, as also the Kirks of Deskfoord, Cullen and Ordiquhill and the Chaplaincies of Cullen and Deskford." It also outlined the details of possessions in other parts of the Regality, including Cullen and Findlater.

The Regality of Ogilvie was abolished together with all other Heritable Jurisdictions in 1747 in order to prevent the proprietors using their great powers to challenge the government. Memories of the Jacobite campaign were still raw, although ironically the Earl of Seafield had been a staunch government supporter. Unfortunately, though the Court Books of the Regality were in the custody of Cullen Town Council in 1900, they are no longer in existence and all that we know of them is from secondary, and often fragmentary, sources.

OTHER POLITICAL STRUCTURES

Other forms of political organisation also existed. In 1617 James Ogilvie of Blerock and John Ogilvie of Over Blerock were both members of Cullen Town Council where John was a Baillie. In 1689 Walter Ogilvie of Ardoch was admitted as a burgess of Cullen and in 1711 James Abercrombie, second son of Alexander Abercrombie of Skeeth was admitted as one of the three burgesses of Cullen, at a time when there was no provost. Very few individuals in those days were entitled to vote, the qualification for which was possession of one ploughgate. Banff had been a Sheriffdom by 1286 and Ogilvie of Deskford was Sheriff about 1455. In 1587 there were only seven JPs in Banffshire, but by 1663 there were twenty three.

Commissioners of Supply were established in 1667. The qualification to become one was the ownership of land to the value of at least £100 per annum. They were responsible for education, roads, bridges, the upkeep of justice and prisons. There were no Deskford Commissioners of Supply in 1670, 1685 or 1689, but Abercrombie of Skeith was appointed in 1690, and his son, Alexander Abercrombie of Skeith became a Commissioner of Supply in 1702. Lord Deskford chaired the Commissioners of Supply for some considerable time until the early C18th.

Road Overseers for the County were appointed in 1722, and for Deskford, John Gordon of Drumwhindle was appointed. Many local farmers were liable for the Horse Tax in 1797/98 but the only person in Deskford liable for the Clock and Watch Tax of the same date was Rev Chalmers. In 1667 the Poll Tax for Gentlemen and their families was £6 per annum, for Tenants it was £4, and for

Tradesmen, Cottars and Servants it was 20/-, all Scots. In 1697 only three persons in Deskford were behind in paying their Poll Tax. John Lawrence, pyper, in Milntoun, was due 18/-, Janet Hay in Nether Clune was due 6/- and Margaret Cameron in Little Knows was also due 6/- . This was in stark contrast to Fordyce where many individuals were in arrears.

From 1727 till 1835, in addition to the Earl of Findlater, Skeith and Craibstoun were also valued separately in the Cess Books. Assessments were paid on the term dates, four times a year. In 1727 Craibstoun was valued at £150 and paid £4:14:4d per quarter, Skeith was valued at £180 and paid £5:13:2d and the Earl of Findlater was valued at £1,250 and paid £39:5:6d. It is possible that Craibstoun had been sold by the Earl around 1690, though his son purchased both Skeith and Inaltry in the 1720s.

In 1875 there were no JPs from Deskford, but by 1880 George Duncan, Kirktown had been appointed. There was also no Deskford representation on the County Licensing Committee, the Commission of Supply, the Constabulary Committee, the Prison Visiting Committee, Banffshire Local Authority, the Lunacy Board, the Road Trustees, the Local Authority under Contagious Diseases: Animals Act, the United Banffshire Agricultural Society, the Central Banffshire Agricultural Society, the Banffshire Analytical Association, the Banffshire Horticultural Society or the Banffshire Branch of the Educational Institute of Scotland. It seems that then, as now, Deskford folk were not great joiners of organisations.

In the 1880s there was strong encouragement from crofters and small farmers locally for legislation to prevent engrossment (large farms absorbing small ones), and rack-renting. This did not happen, though larger farmers in Deskford were happy with the legislation which ensured that landlords would have to compensate tenants for improvements they made. The Deskford branch of the Mutual Improvement Association frequently debated these issues. It was strongly opposed to engrossment and felt that small farms were better for the country than large ones.

In 1885 election meetings were held in Deskford by both Mr Darling, the Conservative candidate, and Mr Duff, the Liberal candidate for Banffshire. Both meetings were well attended, particularly the Liberal one. There were speeches, questions and heckling. The polling booth for Deskford voters was in Portsoy, and there was a large Deskford turnout in spite of the very poor weather. The total Electoral Roll was 7,018 and there were 5,748 votes cast in total, an 82% turnout. Mr Duff got 3,740 votes and Mr. Darling 2,008.

Throughout the past few centuries a number of locals paid a price for choosing the wrong side in political, military and religious disputes. The Earl of Seafield was a very strong supporter of the government side during the Jacobite Rebellion, and on their retreat towards Culloden, the Jacobites caused great damage to Cullen House. James Abercromby of Skeith, however, supported the Jacobites and appeared in Lord Rosebery's "List of Rebels". As a captain he had assisted in collecting revenue for the Rebels and gave them intelligence about government forces and their state of arms. He was probably pardoned under the Act of Indemnity of 1747 and may have returned to Skeith. Alexander Gordon of Pattenbringan was also a rebel.

In earlier times Walter Ogilvie of Carestounne had been a strong supporter of the rebellion of 1647 "against the work of the Reformation". He was obliged to recant publicly. In 1651 George Abercrombie of Skeith, younger, similarly "humblie supplicated to be received to repentence ....for his ingagement to the lait unlawfull Ingagement to England". In 1715 Lord Deskford was imprisoned as suspected of having Jacobite leanings, unlike his son some 30 years later.

After 1720, heritors ran parish affairs as patrons, as payers of stipends, as supporters of the fabric of the church, manse and school and as the main source of funds for the schoolmaster's salary and for poor relief. Landlords had great influence over church and social matters through Baron and Regality Courts, control over JPs and power as Commissioners of Supply. When Regalities were abolished by the Act of 1747, Baillies lost significant wealth from bribery, blackmail and extortion.

From 1750, paralleling the rest of the country, political and social activity was controlled by the local lord, in Deskford's case the Earl of Findlater, and by the Kirk Session. However, by the mid C19th the system was not coping with rapid advances in society and the economy. This was exacerbated by the Disruption in 1843, which meant that no longer did a parish come under the control of a single church. This was in particular a complication for the provision of poor relief. As a result Parochial Boards were set up in each parish in 1845.

PAROCHIAL BOARD

The first meeting of the Deskford Parochial Board took place on September 9th 1845. Present were Rev James Mackintosh, who was elected chairman, John Wilson, Factor and the Earl of Seafield's representative, James Mitchell, John Whyntie, William Longmore, William Stephen and James Wilson, all elders. Francis William Grant, the schoolmaster, was appointed Inspector of the Poor at a salary of £8 a year. A committee was set up to make a roll of the poor persons claiming and entitled to relief from the parish, and the amount to be given to each.

A meeting was held on December 19th 1845 to consider claims. They also considered traditional practice with regard to occasional relief and agreed to give Ann Russel in Aultmore £1, Ann Milton in Aultmore £1, Alexander Murray in Aultmore £1 and Isobel Smith in Kirktown half a peck of meal and 6d weekly till her case could be further considered. Keith Parochial Board asked for money to support John Smith, now in Keith, but formerly from Todholes in Deskford. To avoid a lawsuit it was agreed to go to arbitration by Mr Dunlop, Advocate in Edinburgh, but Deskford did accept a claim on behalf of John Smith's daughter. A claim was laid by John Merson, Langlanburn, on behalf of George Reid, 9 years of age, son of Jane Merson, a pauper in the parish, and of John Reid Merson, deceased. It was agreed to allow John Merson one shilling a week for the maintenance of the child.

On February 5th 1846 the Board considered those parts of the Act which directed provision to be made for medicines and medical attendance for the Poor. It was decided that none of the Poor required medical aid, but that the Inspector, if he thought fit, could employ either Mr Hugh Sharp, Surgeon in Cullen or Mr John Munro, to give necessary attendance.

The Parochial Board in Keith declined to submit the claim for John Smith to Mr Dunlop in Edinburgh and instead proposed to submit it to Mr Thorburn, Solicitor, in Keith. The Deskford Board agreed to Mr Thorburn as arbiter.

On June 23rd 1846 it was decided to allow James Stewart one shilling weekly and Jane Smith, his wife, the same, in respect that although James Stewart had a small croft of land and was able to earn a little by carting fuel, and was moreover aided by some of his sons, it was not the opinion of the meeting that, with all these aids he was able, without Parochial Relief, to support himself and his wife. William Benzie, on the other hand, was refused relief because he was an able-bodied labourer, in possession of a croft and a horse, and able to support himself and the other members of his family.

It was decided to change arrangements for medical aid in order to be like other parishes. An annual retainer would be, in the first instance, offered to Dr Sharp, failing that, Dr Munro and failing that Dr Greig, Portsoy. The numbers of paupers had increased to 52.

A meeting on November 24th 1846 considered the failure of the potato crop and the consequent high price of meal. For almost all paupers on the Roll it would be necessary to increase the allowances to the extent of half a peck of meal weekly during the months of December, February and March, but not in January which was the month in which the quarterly allocation was made in Moray. The Inspector was authorised to purchase the necessary meal from Mr Stephen who had agreed to supply it at the current price. This indicates that although the potato famine was not as severe as in parts of Ireland and in the western Highlands, it did cause problems for the poor of Deskford.

The application for an allowance for the illegitimate child Alexander Forbes, residing with his pauper father, was refused because his mother, a farm servant, could contribute at least £1 per annum. James Stewart in Aultmore was reduced from 1/- to 6d per week because his brother offered to make him an allowance. Mr Thorburn, solicitor, Keith, had written re the farm servant William Smith's illegitimate child by Barbara Black. The Inspector had been directed to recover aliment from Smith. The Board agreed to Smith's suggestion that he pay all but £1:3:6d, which he was unable to pay.

On February 2nd 1847 the Treasurer reported that funds were only £22 and that this would soon be expended. The meeting agreed to put in place an Assessment to raise further funds and that £170 per year would be necessary to support all the poor of the parish, with £142 needed that year, half on April 17th and half on July 31st. Half the sum required would come from the owners of property and half from the tenants and other occupants of all the Lands and Heritages within the parish, places of public worship to be excepted. Mr Grant, Schoolmaster, was appointed Assessor to make up a roll of all the Lands and Heritages within the parish and their annual value. This was to be issued to the Board by March 9th to allow parties to give in appeals by March 23rd. Mr Grant was to be paid £2 for constructing the roll plus £3 as Collector of Assessment. If he found any difficulties he was authorised to use the help of Mr Reid, Berryhillock, and pay him out of his salary. He could also take advice on valuation from Mr Peterkin, Nether Blairock and Mr Murray, Mosside, hoping that this would be accepted by all. Funds raised were to be lodged with the Commercial Bank of Scotland, Keith. There were many appeals against assessment, a significant number of which were successful.

There were many applications for support for illegitimate children. The Board made detailed examinations of the individual circumstances in each case before reaching a decision. On August 18th 1847 the Earl of Seafield indicated his intention of discontinuing the six bolls of Charity Meal formerly given to the parish by him about this time of year. The Board agreed that they would have to make good this shortfall.

On November 11th 1847 the Board authorised the Inspector to pay 15/- "to clean Margaret Clark's house and person, both at present in a filthy state". The board also resolved to charge the husband and family of Ann Burgess, the lunatic pauper, £8 annually among them, being one third of the annual expense. John Burgess, her husband, agreed to pay £2 and to inform his three unmarried sons that they should each pay a similar sum.

The application from Elspet Lawrence, Berryhillock, for an increase was refused because the income she made from selling bread, together with her current allowance, was deemed sufficient. The account from William Reid, wright, for a coffin for Barbara Black was agreed, but Mr Reid was to be instructed not to make any more coffins without instruction from the Inspector. William Smith, Burns (between Burnsford and Upper Blairock), whom Dr Sharp had considered a dangerous maniac, could not be found. The Board agreed to find someone to supervise him and keep him at work. He was put under George Anderson, Leitchestown at £2 per quarter.

On July 2nd 1850 a number of appeals was heard. John Reid, Squaredoch, appealed against being assessed for a room which is now unoccupied (shades of the current bedroom tax debate) and also a room in which his mother lived. Sustained. George Barclay, Craibstone, appealed on the grounds of being too highly assessed. Dismissed. George Redford appealed on the grounds of his living in his mother's house, she being unable to pay. Sustained. Janet Wood appealed on the grounds of being unable to pay. Dismissed. Alexander Currie appealed on the grounds of being unable to pay. Sustained. William Smith the dangerous maniac was now better so there was no need for supervision.

By August 1850 the Poor Roll was down to 27. The Board refused to send Jane Merson to a Lunatic Asylum as proper procedures had not been followed. Isobel Lawrence requested a person to attend her. It was agreed that she would live with her daughter in Cullen who would be paid 6d per week. The Inspector was instructed to procure blankets for the needy and shoes for Margaret Clark.

In 1851 there was an appeal from Bell Black or Benzies as her husband was in jail. It was agreed to pay her 5/- per week till he was liberated. John Burgess was not paying his wife, Ann her due support. He was warned that unless he paid the arrears, legal steps would be taken. Elizabeth Sutherland in Squaredoch received 1/- per week, it being known that she also received ½ peck of Bede Meal in the week. Isobel Lawrence in Berryhillock was to get 3/- per week for fuel. The other half of the new Poors House at Muir of Squaredoch had been allocated.

In 1852 Betty Smith's child was struck off the Roll as, firstly, Smith had taken no steps to establish the paternity, and secondly she should be able to support it herself, for, though she was nursing a second illegitimate child she was paid for so doing. The majority of claims by young women with illegitimate children were accepted. It was agreed to pay Elsie Smith for herself and her illegitimate child, but the Board also directed the Inspector to prosecute Lewis Cameron, the acknowledged father, on the grounds of his refusing and neglecting to maintain the said child, being able to do so.

By 1853, in a bout of apparent political correctness, the Board stopped referring to "Imbecile Paupers" and started calling them "Fatuous Paupers". Such individuals probably suffered from a range of conditions, including learning difficulties, Down's syndrome and Alzheimer's, while others would have mental health issues such as bi-polar disorder, schizophrenia and depression.

In August of that year Jane Merson had left her residence and could not be found anywhere, despite several days of searching by the woman who was in charge of her. The constables had been given notice to look out for her. The meeting of the Board agreed to wait to see if the police obtained any clue as to her whereabouts. If not they instructed the Inspector to advertise for her in the local papers. On September 23rd it was stated that she had been brought back from Banchory. The Board agreed to pay £4:4/-, including 6/- wages and 1/6d reward to the man who brought her back. It was also agreed to pay the accounts for advertising. It was deemed necessary to change Jane Merson's residence, and Messrs Stephen and Mitchell and the Inspector were instructed to look for a more suitable place of abode for her.

It was agreed to pay Rathven 5/- a week for Isobel Black and her six children whilst her husband, Alexander Benzies was in prison for poaching. Jane Skinner, Milltown, applied to go on the Roll, but this was rejected as she refused to give over her property to the Board, and was in possession of a house which rented at £1:10/- per annum. If she gave over her property to the Board she would be given 1/- per week.

In February 1854 Alexander Munro was granted thatch for his house and a new pair of shoes. That same year the Board was instructed to establish a Register of Births, Deaths and Marriages. Jessie Riddoch was informed that unless she gave back the blanket given to her late mother in law, steps would be taken for its recovery. Janet Morrison or Walker, a travelling woman, had failed on the road on April 17th. The Inspector had been obliged to provide accommodation for her. She was now keeping a little better, but was as yet unable to leave the parish. The Board agreed to let her stay with Barbara Gracie, even though it was unlikely that they would recover the costs from any other parish.

In 1856 James Morrison, Clunehill left £50 to the Board in his will, the interest on which was to be used in educating poor people in the parish of Deskford. It was called "Morrison's Educational Fund". The £50 became £45 after legacy duty of 10% was paid. In February Margaret Gray's house fell down. There was a dispute with Forglen about who was responsible for her. James Howie, pauper lunatic, was to be accommodated in Garngad House Asylum in Glasgow at 10/6d per week plus 1/- for clothing.

In 1858 the Board agreed to give one bottle of wine to Ann Desson plus 3/6d monthly for attendance on her. Alexander Geddes' daughter Ann was in his house nursing her illegitimate child but was disagreeable to his family. It was agreed that she would look for a person to nurse her child whilst she went into service to assist in supporting it. The father, who she claimed to be George Pollard, railway labourer, at that time with Mr Dean, contractor, Monymusk, was to be found. In October payment was refused of an invoice from Mr Bidie, merchant, Backies, for items provided to Alexander Howie, pauper, because the Board had not instructed or agreed to this.

In 1859 the Inspector was instructed to inspect pauper bedclothes and to furnish blankets to those requiring them. The population of the parish was at its highest ever and there was a shortage of accommodation. Ann Milton, Faichyhill, and Margaret Lawrence, Swailend, were occupying houses which were in a dangerous state and so ruinous as to render them not worth the expense of substantial repairs. Temporary repairs were agreed and plans for a new cottage to join onto the east gable of the Poors House were to be obtained.

At the end of 1860, John McBeath, Inspector of the Poor in Fordyce, was appointed also as Inspector of the Poor in Deskford. There were major concerns about his competence and honesty. He resigned as Inspector in January 1865 and was dismissed as Collector of Poor Rates and Assessor. In

1861 the Inspector was instructed to sell immediately all effects belonging to the deceased pauper, Isobel Lawrence, excepting the bedclothes and body clothes. Several paupers were to be given barrels of coal since they had been given insufficient peat. Three blankets were issued. Thatch was to be repaired in Janet Reid's and Ann Milton's houses. In 1866 three ladies were allowed 1/- each for soap to clean the blankets of several paupers.

In January 1868 Jessie Riddoch refused to wash and attend on Ann Milton, Faichyhill unless she was allowed 1/- a week. This was agreed. Jane Smith, lunatic pauper, was to be removed from Aultmore to the Poor Lodging House, Muir of Squaredoch and Georgina Mutch, lunatic pauper, was to be moved from Muir of Squaredoch to Berryhillock under the charge of Mr James Watt.

In January 1872, William Grant, Bleachfield, appealed for relief from assessment on his carding mill machinery. This was refused, but it was recommended that he apply to Mr Russel, Elgin Assessor, to have his name struck from the Valuation Roll. An application was made by James Lorimer for digging the graves of paupers. It was agreed to increase his remuneration from 2/- to 3/- provided he conveyed the handspokes where and when required for a funeral.

In 1873 the Roll was 22. Six were in the Poor's Lodging House. Eight got 1½ or 2 cwt of coal a month. Twenty got cash, ranging from 1/- to 4/6d per week. Two got a free house only. Five were outwith the parish and five were from Aultmore. Imbecile paupers, having earlier become fatuous paupers were now called lunatic paupers.

James Reid, aged 15, in the Poor's Lodging House, was declared incurable by Chalmers Hospital, Banff, without the amputation of his limb. He was allowed 1/6d a week. In May 1875 the Inspector was instructed to look for possible apprenticeships for him as a compositor. The Huntly Express's terms were 2/6d a week, rising by 6d a week each year of a five year apprenticeship. The Banffshire Reporter offered 2/6, rising by 1/- a week. The Inspector was instructed to make arrangements on these terms with the Banffshire Reporter, and to provide the boy with such clothing as may be necessary, vest, trousers, flannel shirt and stockings.

By 1876 James Reid was being apprenticed as a tailor to Mr Will, Cullen, who wrote to the Board saying the boy was not strong, but that he would pay him 2/- a week for six months, then 2/6d a week for six months, then 3/- a week for twelve months, then 4/- a week for twelve months and for the final two years of his apprenticeship such pay as would relieve the Board of any obligation. Later that year the Parochial Board arranged for Dr Sharp to attend at the old Parochial School (in Kirktown) on the first Monday of each month for vaccinating. The fee was 2/6d for each successful vaccination, payable by the parents of the child vaccinated.

In May 1878 Mary Ann Bennett or Geddes would only get aid if she signed over to the Board the whole of her inheritance from her late uncle. In 1879 the Roll was down to 14. The existing four ratepayers on the Parochial Board were reappointed without any contest. In 1880 it was determined that Jessie Smith, 16, had curvature of the spine and therefore would not be able to earn a livelihood. She was allowed 2/- a week, but the previous 1/- a week given to her mother was withdrawn. In 1881, only one of the fourteen on the Roll lived outwith Aultmore, Berryhillock or the Poor's House.

In 1885 the Board agreed to extend the churchyard. There was a proposal to extend down into the Orchard, but it was finally agreed that it was much preferable to extend 40' west to the garden dyke of Mr Smith, Schoolmaster. This is the central section of the present graveyard, and the site of many of the old cottages which had made up Kirktown before this time. The cost of burial spaces in the New Burial Ground was to be from 12/6d to £1 for the first grave space and from 7/6d to 17/6d for each additional one.

In 1890 the Inspector was instructed to lay a cement floor in the house occupied by Joseph Young, and to carry out necessary repairs to the other houses owned by the Board.

PARISH COUNCIL

Parochial Boards were superseded by Parish Councils in 1895. These were wholly elected rather than having several automatic places for Kirk elders. The first meeting of the new Deskford Parish Council was held on April 11th 1895. Much of its work and responsibilities were the same as had been the case for the Parochial Board. For example in May it had been discovered that Ann Ross, a pauper for many years, owned a house in Berryhillock. The Inspector was to seek repayment of the support given to her. Isabella Forbes was to be given a pair of boots for her son. Mrs Raffan was to be allowed two sheets and a bedcover for Isabella Longmore. An application was received from Alexander Morrison for a new lawnmower for the churchyard.

The Council owned six houses at Muir of Squaredoch, occupied by Ann Elder, William Milton, Jane Mackie, Mrs Masson and two by James Farquhar. The house in Berryhillock given to the Council in exchange for aid by Mrs Ross was to be advertised for sale in the Banffshire Journal and on the doors of the Churches. The Inspector was instructed to get, for Widow Thom, two pairs of boots for her boy and girl. He was also to get two suits of clothes for two boys, comprising moleskin trousers and strong serge jackets and vests, ready made, from Alexander Morrison, merchant, Berryhillock.

Banff Lunatic Asylum informed the Council that James Wood could now be quite safely boarded out in a private dwelling. The Council arranged for him to be boarded out with George Bidie, Muttonbrae, Fordyce, for 5/- per week, which was half the cost of the asylum. However he had no clothing so the Inspector was to get him a suit and underclothing, but would write to his sister in Arbroath, enquiring where his former clothing was.

Mrs Ross's house in Berryhillock attracted three bids, of £9, £10 and £10:10/-. It was sold to Mr Stephen, the highest bidder. In May 1896 John Reid resigned as Inspector of the Poor after thirty one years in post, due to failing health. The vacancy was advertised in the Banffshire Journal and the Banffshire Advertiser with an annual salary of £15 for Inspector of the Poor, £4 for Collector of Poor Rates, £3 for Collector of School Rates, £3 for Clerk and Treasurer of the Burial Ground and £2 for Collector of Registration and Vaccination Rates, a total of £27. The Council decided to split the posts and appointed Mr Cruikshank, Berryhillock as Inspector and Mr Alexander Morrison, Berryhillock, as Collector, both on 3-2 votes without any interviews. In each case the defeated candidate was Mr James Wilson Jr, Little Knows (author of the James Wilson Diaries).

At a meeting on July 15th 1896 Council decided that shoes for paupers should be obtained from Mr Gray, Berryhillock, clothes from Mr Ogilvie, Berryhillock and worsted and print from Mr Milton, merchant, Kirktown.

In May 1897 Council deplored the personal conduct of Jane Riddoch but did not see that they could have done differently than to give her aid. The Inspector was instructed to enquire as to the identities of the fathers of her four children and to use every endeavour to obtain from them the outlay for maintenance of these children. It was subsequently reported that Patrick McGruer, labourer, Portsoy, was the father of two of Jane Riddoch's children and that James Cameron, fisherman, Buckie, was the father of a third. Both men were worthless characters and it would be a waste of time to try to recover anything from them.

On January 26th 1901 the Parish Council fulsomely noted that "This being the first meeting of the Council since the death of our Beloved Queen, the Council desires to put on record an expression of their profound regret thereat; their deep sense of the great loss sustained by the Empire through her removal, and their high appreciation of her noble character and untiring dedication to the service of the State. They recognise in her, the best and greatest of British Sovereigns, who, for the long period of sixty three years wielded the Sceptre faithfully and well, conferring inestimable benefits on her people and welding the colonies and mother country into one. They thank Almighty God for her many Queenly gifts of hand and heart and brain; and especially for her graciousness toward the poor and suffering; in whose bodily and spiritual welfare she ever manifested a deep interest. In behalf of the Community which they represent they would offer their condolences to the King and the Royal Family in this the time of their bereavement; The Council also desire to place on record an expression of their loyalty and attachment to the throne in the person of Edward VII; and they humbly pray that the King and his gracious Consort may long be spared in health and happiness to rule this Great Empire; God save the King; Long live the King".

In May 1901 the Inspector was directed to employ Mr Alexander Milton, mason, Kirktown, to execute repairs on several foundations of old tombstones. It may be that this was when the graveyard was "improved", and many old stones and stones with no current Deskford connection were removed. An application by Mrs Stephen, Kirktown, for permission to plant flowers on the graves in which her children were interred was granted.

In 1913 the Council decided that its fire-proof safe was not suitable and enquired where a new one could be got. The Registrar General in Edinburgh refused to give recommendations and suggested that manufacturers' lists be consulted, or local ironmongers. After much correspondence the Parish Council selected a Milners Safes Special at a cost of £8:8/-, giving room for the past sixty years' and a future thirty years' registers. A duplicate key would be provided to the Registrar General to pass to the Sheriff. No Milners Specials were available so a safe was got from Messrs Withers and Co, West Bromwich.

When ex Factor and Parish Council member, James Campbell was knighted at the end of World War I, a letter of congratulations was sent and, in reply, he wrote saying he had always considered Deskford to be the "Model Parish" of the north.

Mr Scott resigned as Registrar in December 1918. He was paid a War Bonus of £3 for extra services rendered. Mr Fordyce resigned as Gravedigger and Caretaker of the Cemetery in January 1919. There were no applications to replace him as Gravedigger so the salary was increased from £10 to £12, upon which he agreed to continue for one year. Robert Cruickshank, who had served in the forces and had been wounded in the Great War was appointed Inspector/ Clerk/ Collector/ Cemetery Clerk at £40 per year. James Ross, Kirktown, was appointed Registrar at £10 per year. He had also served in the Great War. Dr McHardy requested a salary increase and it was agreed to put it up from £12 to £16. George Lobban, Lornachburn was appointed Gravedigger at a salary of £14.

By 1919 Lunatic paupers had become Mentally Defective Paupers. One of them, Lizzie Thom, was removed from the care of her aunt in Grange because of poor treatment, and placed with Mrs Jamieson, Berryhillock, instead, at 7/- a week.

Also in 1919 it was reported that the present Registrar seemed to be doing satisfactory work, however in 1920 ink of an inferior quality was being used and, in 1921 a new Registrar was appointed at a salary of £10. In 1931 the Registrar spelt "McKonachie" wrongly and in 1936 entries had been faint but the Registrar had treated himself to a new bottle of ink and current entries were much clearer. In 1946 spellings of "Willma" and "Francis" for a girl were queried, but the Registrar said that the parents concerned had requested these spellings. In 1952 the Registrar was doing excellent work but this did not prevent the Deskford District being merged with Cullen in 1958.

In 1929 the Parish Council applied for exemption from paying income tax. Income tax staff were uncertain about whether or not the application was legitimate, but, after consideration, agreed. One of the complex issues was whether rents from the Muckle Hoose could be applied only to poor relief. The Parish Council had become owners of the Muckle Hoose at Martinmas 1927 at a cost of £400, as a condition of being sold additional land for the graveyard, bringing it to its present size.

Deskford Parish Council came to an end in May 1930. A vote of thanks was given by Mr Ross, Kirktown, to Mr Morrison, who had been a member for 27 years, and Chairman since 1919. Mr Morrison thanked Mr Cruickshank for the great interest he had taken in the poor of the parish, and great satisfaction for his work was formally minuted.

OTHER POLITICAL ACTIVITIES AND ORGANISATIONS

Other political activities, bureaucracies and organisations also existed. The first meeting of the School Management Committee, District No 2, of the Education Authority of the County of Banff (Cullen, Deskford, Fordyce and Cornhill) was held on July 13th 1919. Representing Deskford were Mr Alexander Ross, appointed by the Parish Council, Rev James Morrison, appointed by the School Board and two co-opted parents, Mr John Gordon, joiner, Berryhillock and Mrs

Maggie Kitchen, Clune. The committee dealt with exemptions, repairs, piano tuning, cleaning supplies, attendance including prosecution, janitors and cleaners, recommendations re salaries, temporary teacher appointments, holidays, lets and enrolments. In 1938 the Chairman expressed relief that World War II had been averted.

In 1924 the Ministry of Public Works, when considering taking responsibility for the maintenance of Old St John's Church stated that the population of Deskford was around 750 and that there were more than 100 tourists annually. Currently the graveyard was locked and they had to apply to the gravedigger for keys. They decided not to take guardianship of the whole building, only the Sacrament House and a small portion of the wall. They intended to approach the gravedigger to become the paid custodian. The Parish Council agreed to hand over custodianship. Seafield Estate wished the Ministry to take over the entire building but they refused and Seafield Estate declined their offer to take over only a portion.

The Ministry wanted Seafield Estate to preserve and protect the aumbry, but the Estate said it was the responsibility of Banffshire County Council, as successors to the Parish Council. There was considerable argument and Rev WR Brown also chipped in with his tuppence worth. Finally the Ministry took responsibility for the whole building in July 1930 with everyone's agreement.

In 1935 there was an 80% turnout in local elections, helped by the use of cars. William Currie, Greenhill, was elected to the County Council, and later that same year George McConnachie, Ardoch, was elected to the District Council. William Currie was a Councillor for many years and was awarded the MBE in 1970 for services to local government.

The Unionist Association held a whist drive in Deskford in December 1937, and in the late 1930s there was a meeting of the Farmers' Union at which all farmers were encouraged to join.

LAND OWNERSHIP

We know quite a lot about C16th and C17th land transactions in Deskford, thanks to Graeme Wilson of Moray Heritage Centre, who, in the mid 1970s when Cullen Town Council was abolished, intervened to save some of the records of John Duncansone, Notary Public in Cullen at that time, from being thrown into a skip. Graeme thinks he saved about a quarter of these documents, which makes it agonising to think of the many others which were lost at this time. He then spent several years transLating and transcribing the ones he had saved. In the C16th all legal agreements had to be recorded and witnessed in a Notary Public's Protocol Book.

We also still have records of a few earlier transactions. In all of these records spelling, punctuation and capitalisation are all random and inconsistent. It is also interesting to note that oxgates, oxgangs and bovates, terms which are synonymous with each other are all used indiscriminately for land measurement in Deskford.

In 1408 there was a charter in favour of John Haya (Hay), confirming the gift by John Mantullen de Netherdale of the lands of Pattenbringand and the office of the Constabulary of Cullen. In 1470 there was a precept of sasine by George, Lord Gordon, to Walter Ogilvie of that Ilk, of the lands of Bogmuchals. In 1498 there was a lease by the Abbot and Convent of Arbroath to Sir James Ogilvie of Deskford, knight, of the greater tithes of the churches of Banff and Inverboyndie. In 1511 Alexander Ogilvie obtained a charter for incorporating the lands of Deskford, Findlater and Keithmore into a barony called Ogilvie.

There were early records of Ardoch and Skeith in 1325 and there were writs of Inaltrie and Cottown in 1481. In the C16th there were records of Easter Skeith (1521), Ardiecow (1531), Inaltry (1541), Knows (1545), Clochmacreich (1562), Leitchestown (1586), Oathillock (1587), Upper Blairock (1587), Squaredoch (1588) and Clunehill (1588).

In 1531/32 the King confirmed a charter of Alexander Ogilvie of that Ilk by which he sold to Mr Alexander Ogilvie in Glashaugh the lands of Ordecowy (Ardicow), Cultene, Ovir Echinaltry (Upper Inaltrie) and Neutown (perhaps Lurgbrae) in Deskford in the barony of Ogilvie.

In 1537 lands in Strathisla and Deskford were granted by the Abbot and Convent of Kinloss to Alexander Ogilvie of Windyhills if Ogilvie paid them a certain sum of money. In June that year there was a contract between The Abbot and Alexander Ogilvie for setting the marches of the Debatable Lands. In 1567 there was a charter by Walter, Commendator of Kinloss to Sir James Ogilvie of Deskford of the Lands of Clochmacreich.

In 1541 there was an instrument in favour of Alexander Ogilvie of that Ilk and Elizabeth Gordon his spouse over the lands and barony of Deskford, with the tower fortalice, mills, multures, fishings, tenants, tenantries and services of free tenantry, the advocation and donation of the chaplaincies of the chapel of Deskford. They were also infested with certain lands at the old castle of Echinaltry, "called the old castle thereof". Also in 1541 they intimated to John Urquhart that he should compeer to the parish church of Fordice to receive 80 merks as redemption of "the lands of myordingis (Ordens), lying in the barony of Deskford".

1542 seems to have been a very busy year. Alexander Ogilvie in Reidhythe purchased the lands of Nether Skeith which lay between the Keil (Kil) Burn and the Stotfauld Burn and George Abercromby purchased the lands of Echinaltry from Alexander Ogilvie of Deskford. Alexander Ogilvie and Elizabeth Gordon his spouse also gave instrument in favour of George Abercrombie over the lands of netherechinaltery (Nether Inaltrie). That same year Alexander Ogilvie of that Ilk paid 520 merks to Alexander Ogilvie of Glashaucht for redemption of "the lands of ordecow, cultanne, vnerechinaltery (Nether Inaltrie) and knowis". John Ogilvie of Dun retained right of access. Still in 1542 there was an instrument in favour of John Duff of Muldaivatt and Elizabeth Abercromby, spouse of the said Duff by Alexander Ogilvie of that Ilk and Elizabeth Gordoun over "the lands of myordingis".

In 1543 by Memorandum, there was a grant of sasine by "Alexander Abercrombie of Nethir Skeycht, Baile in that part to Robert Reid, archdeacon, bishop and abbot of monastery of Kynloss, to Alexander Ogilvie of that Ilk and Elizabeth Gordoun over the lands of clauchnacreycht (Clochmacreich) called our laddis landis (Our Lady's Lands), lying within the barony and Regality of Strathila".

In 1544 there was a grant of sasine by James Scott, mayor general of the sheriffdom of Banff to Alexander Ord of that Ilk over the "lands of ordekow, cultane and verechinaltry". That same year Queen Mary invested Sir Alexander Ogilvie of that Ilk in the lands of Ardicow, Cultaine, Under Thinaltry and Knowis.

In 1545 there was a Charter of Alienation by Sir Alexander Ogilvie of that Ilk to John Gordon of the lands of Clochmacreich commonly called Ladyland. The same year the Queen confirmed to Alexander Ogilvie of that Ilk and Elizabeth Gordon his spouse, the lands of Ordecow, Cultene, Over Inveraltry, Knowis, Castelfeild and the office of Constable of Cullen.

In 1563 Queen Mary invested Sir James Ogilvie in the lands of Clochmacreich in the barony of Deskford, fallen into her Majesty's hands by the forfeiture of John Gordon. In 1566 there was an agreement that John Gordon got Auchindoun and Keithmore while James Ogilvie got all the rest, bringing to an end the dispute over inheritance and ownership of Deskford. When Queen Mary reached full age in 1567 she also presented James Ogilvie inheritable tenant to the Abbot of Kinloss, superior of the lands of Clochmacreich and also the lands of Tochynell.

In 1564 the Lords of Secret Council ordained James Ogilvie of that Ilk to deliver to Margaret Gordon, relict (widow) of the deceased George Abercrombie of Pitmedden, and Alexander Abercrombie her son infestments of the lands of Echinaltre and Cottoun, "conform to the auld takand (tack) of them". In 1586 James Ogilvie gave charter to Thomas Ord of various lands including Greenhill.

1586 saw George Duff, Burgess of Cullen and Alexander Syme (Sim), junior, in name of Marjorie Mawer, spouse of said George having a charter of alienation of the town of Nether Skeyth. It also saw a sasine to John Abercrombie of Skeyth of two crofts in Cullen from Duff in Boigs. That same year Alexander Davidson of Dallachy and Janet Abercromby, his spouse, granted the lands of Leitchestoun to William Abercrombie of Over Skeith.

1587 was one of the busiest years in the C16th. There was a sasine for George Ogilvie of Cullane and Janet Abercrummy over the lands of Leitchestoun. There was a precept of sasine for Sir Walter Ogilvie of Findlater over the lands of Skordiacht (Squaredoch), and also a resignation of land at Squaredoch by George Coull in Pettinbringend in favour of John Goodbrand and a precept of sasine for Sir Walter Ogilvie over lands at Upper Blairock. There was also recorded the renunciation of the "tak and rowme" of Ley by Thomas Graye younger, in favour of Alexander Abercrummy, "his maister", and the removal by John Brebner in Ester Blerake from "tak and rowme" in favour of James Ogilvie of Blerake.

1587 also saw the resignation by Agnes Brebner, relict of John Gudbrand in Aittishillock (Oathillock), with the consent of James Gudbrand and John Gudbrand, sons of the said Brebner, in favour of Janet Chalmeris, relict of Thomas Gudbrand, and James Wordan, future spouse of the said Chalmeris, over "tak and rowme of Aithillock, for the quhilkis (which) the sad (said) Janet and James sall teill (entail) ane aikir of land zerlle (yearly) to the said Agnes". An instrument was passed in favour of "Alexander Fraisser, procurator for Thomas Fraisser and Elizabeth Forboiss, spouse of the said Thomas Fraisser of Knokke over precept of sasine by Walter Dunne of Rettie, baile in that part to Sir Walter Ogilvie of Fynlater, knight, of the lands of Smychtstonne (Smithstoun), enaltre and cottone of enaltre, aithillock, kyrktonne in Daiskford, Skordiaycht fru the hill and Ower Blaraycht".

Still in 1587 there was an instrument in favour of Walter Ogilvie in Ardaycht (Ardoch) on behalf of James Ogilvie of Blaraycht over receipt by Gilbert Barclay in Swalbog (Swailend), husband of Margaret Ord, of 300 merks as redemption of "four oxengang of land in Burnlivned". There was also an instrument in favour of David Gardner in Kyrktonne, procurator for Robert Innes of that Ilk, over requisition to Christian Gordonne, relict of George Abercrummy in Over Skeycht, and William Abercrummy, son to the said Gordonne, to receive 600 merks as redemption of "the myll and myllands of Crummy (Abercrombie)".

In 1588 there was a sasine to William Ogilvie of Over Blairok and Clunehill. Harry Gordon and Katherine Clark removed from "aucht (eight) oxengang of land of overblerrack" and there was a discharge by Henry Leycht to William Vat (Watt) in Garreaucht of obligations concerning "the lade of Lie (Ley)". That same year there was also an assignation by Thomas Graye, younger, to Andrew

Haye for "the maistrefull spoilationne and away tekking of his tak and rowme", and a warning by Sir Walter Ogilvie of Findlater over redemption of lands in Clune Hill. There was also a renunciation by Walter Ogilvie and Janet Ord of the half lands of Ardaycht.

Still in 1588 there was a grant of sasine by Alexander Haye to John Abercrummy of Skeycht over "ane croift of land called thaynis (Thain's) croift land lyand within the freedom of Cullane". There was another instrument in favour of John Abercrummy over receipt by John Gordonne of Corrydowne of 300 merks as redemption of "part of the landis of nether skeycht called burnheddis (Burnheads), sumtyme occupiet be William Ewin, Johnne Cruikshank, James Gyb, John Stenson (Stevenson) and George Brebner, lyand within the barony of Deiskford".

1589 saw the grant of sasine to James Ord over "three acres of the lands of Skordeaycht" and another grant of sasine to the same person over "the half part of the lands of Ardaycht". There was a grant by William Ogilvie of Over Blairraycht, baile in that part to Sir Walter Ogilvie of Fynlater to James Ord over "the half part of the lands of ardaycht and to moss le (Ley) and to three acres of the lands of skordeaycht". In 1589 William Ewin was in Berryhillock (a farm), a Robertson was in Skeycht, Charles Geddes was in Daiskford and Matthew Steward was in Ordenis.

In 1590 there was a grant of sasine to James Ogilvie of the "half tonne (town) of Ardaycht". He also obtained a grant of sasine to James Ogilvie of "three acres of the land of Skordeaycht". It is not known if this is the same three acres granted to James Ord the previous year. Still in 1590 there was also a "grant of sasine to George Ogilvie in Cullen and Janet Abercrummy of the lands of Nether Clune". There was an instrument in favour of Andrew Tynet over renunciation by James Ogilvie, son of George Ogilvie in Cullen, of right to the "towns and landis of Lechistonne".

There was a grant of sasine by George Gordonne in Faichehill, baile in that part to Sir Walter Ogilvie of Fynlater, knight, to Walter Ogilvie, portioner of Ardaycht over "nynne aikiris of land in the Skordiaicht, thre of them occupiit be the vater Ogilvie, thre by Manis Cobane and vther thre be Katerine Smycht and

Alexander Abercrummy hir spouse". Mr John Duff of Maldauid and Margaret Gordonne his spouse received 600 merks from Sir Walter Ogilvie of Fynlater, knight, as a redemption of the lands of Owir Pettinbringand. There was also a grant of sasine by John Hempseid, baile of Cullane, baile in that part to Sir Walter Ogilvie of Fynlater, knight, to James Ogilvie, sone of George Ogilvie in Cullane and William Abercrummy, procurator for Marjorie Winfre, spouse of the said James Ogilvie over "landis of Owir pettinbringand".

In 1591 there was an instrument of sasine for John Abircrummy over the land occupied by William Fordice at Knowes. In 1592 there was a renunciation of land at Middle Skeith by William Ord in favour of Sir William Ogilvie of Findlater. Later that year there was an instrument in favour of John Abercrummy of Skeycht over grant of sasine by William Abircrummy in Over Skeycht, baile in that part to Sir Walter Ogilvie of Fynlater, knight, to "a piece of land lying between the lands of knowis and aithillock on the east side of the lands of daiskford occupied by James Braibner and Andrew Gray and also to the lands of knowis now occupied by William Fordice". There was also renunciation by William Ord, son of the deceased Thomas Ord, younger, in Middilskeycht with consent of Mr Thomas Gordonne in Merraik and Thomas Ord in Revalter, curators to the said William Ord in favour of Sir Walter Ogilvie of Fynlater, knight, of the lands of Middil Skeycht following payment of 800 merks as redemption of the same lands.

In 1593 there was the removal of Alexander Abercrummy and Hector Abercrummy from "the est part landis of Arddecow". In 1594 there was a grant of sasine to Alexander Forsycht of Vindehills (Windyhills) and Katherine Reid over "eight oxgangs of the lands of Crabstonne, now occupiit by Andrew Brabner".

Things did not quieten down in the C17th. In 1605 there was a contract between Sir Walter Ogilvie of Findlater and Mr Patrick Duff, setting the marches between the Barony of Deskford and Darbreich. In 1601 James Ogilvie was in Cairstoun and John Ogilvie was in Miltoun, in 1612 Andrew Lawtie was in Inaltrie, in 1613 John Wallace was in Tocheneill and in 1615 James Ogilvie was in Blerock. In 1625 there was a charter to James, Master of Deskford and Lady Elizabeth Leslie, his spouse, of half of the Mains of Fyndlater and the

House of Deskford upon their marriage settlement, upon the resignation of Walter, Lord Deskford.

In 1623 Thomas Abercrombie of Neither Skeith was served heir to his deceased father, John Abercromby of Nether Skeith. The said John had inherited these lands from William Abercromby, rector, who held them in 1586, at which time George Duff presented a charter of alienation of the lands of Over Skeith in favour of William Abercromby.

In 1624 Lord Deskford disponed the lands of Leitchestoun, Clune, Smithstown and Dytach to Robert Leslie of Findrassie for £5,000 Scots. In 1627 the Prebendary lands of Mary Magdalene, St John the Baptist, St Andrew and Holy Cross were mortified to the Minister in Deskford. In 1628 there was recorded the alienation by John Logie, Rector of Rathven, of Farskane to Walter Ogilvie of Ardoch and James Ogilvie of Nether Blerack. In turn, in 1629, James Ogilvie, with the consent of Walter Ogilvie, alienated his share to Henry Gordon of Auchanassie.

On March 23rd 1636 a decree of mails and duties was recorded in favour of James Shephard, son of the umquhile James Shephard in Crabston against John Shephard there, of half the lands of Crabston and croft called Shephard's Croft in the Barony of Deskford. There was a contract of wadset between the Earl of Findlater and Mr John Abercromby of Glassa, of Little Cultain by which it went to Abercromby.

In 1652 there was a disposition by Thomas Abercromby of Skeith to James Ogilvie of part of the lands of Skeith including Hogmanseat (Hoggie), Broadrashes and Burnheads, and in 1669 there was a disposition by William Ogilvie in Newtown of part of the lands of Skeith, Hogmanseat and Broadrashes to Walter Ogilvie, Overlochan.

In 1671 there was a sasine in favour of Sir Alexander Abercrombie of Birkenbog of the Mains of Skeith, Hogmanseat, Berryhillock, Clochmacreich, Ramore, Broadrashes and Burnhead, proceding upon a charter by James, Earl of Findlater. That same year Jean Abercrombie, spouse to John Gordon, younger, of Thornebauk, renounced her liferent right of the lands of Overskeith,

Crabstoune, Over and Neither Tillabreedles, in favour of the Earl of Findlater. In 1681 signature of the lands of Over Skeith was granted to Alexander Hay.

As the C17th drew towards its close there were still many land transactions taking place. In 1682 there was a sasine by George Abercrombie of four oxgates of land of Little Skeith, proceeding upon a disposition by Marrion and Janet Abercromby. Also in 1682 there was a mutual contract of tailzie between George Abercrombie of Skeith and Alexander Abercrombie of Berryhillock whereby the said George Abercrombie disponed to the said Alexander Abercrombie and his heirs male, which failing, to Alexander Abercromby, second son of Sir Alexander Abercromby of Birkenbog, the lands of Skeith, Mains, Little Skeith and the wadset rights therein in the parish of Deskford, and on the other part the said Alexander Abercrombie of Berryhillock disponed to George Abercromby of Skeith and his heirs male, which failing, to the said Alexander Abercromby, second son of Sir Alexander Abercromby of Birkenbog, the lands of Berryhillock and mill thereof and sums for which they are wadset.

In 1684 Sir George Abercromby of Skeith resigned the lands of Nether Skeith, mill thereof, Broadrashes, Berryhillock, mill thereof, Burnhead, Carrothead, Harder called new and old wards of Broadrashes, the four oxgates of land in Little Skeith in favour of himself and to his heirs male, and assignees whatsoever, which failing to any of the daughters or heirs female of the nearest male heir, marrying a second or third cousin of the family of Birkenbog or Glassaugh. Also in 1684 there was a Precept of Clare Constat of James, Earl of Findlater to Alexander Abercromby of the lands of Nether Skeith, later dated 1701, for infesting him in the said lands as heir to George Abercromby of Skeith, uncle to Walter Abercromby of Berryhillock who was father to the said Alexander in whose favour the precept was granted. Narrating that the said lands of Wards had been wadset by the deceast James, Earl of Findlater to the said George Abercromby for 1,000 merks by contract dated 1681. And that the said four oxgate of land at Little Skeith had also been wadset by the said deceast James, Earl of Findlater for 1,600 merks for the said George Abercromby, all of which were contained in a charter dated 1684 by the said James, Earl of Findlater to the said George Abercromby upon his own resignation and the said four oxgate of land at Little Skeith were disponed by

Alexander Hay of Arnbath with consent of the said deceast James, Earl of Findlater to the said George Abercromby under back bond by him of even date with the disposition. There was a Tack of Teinds of the said lands by his son the Earl to the said Alexander Abercromby in 1717.

In 1689 James, Earl of Findlater, with the consent of his oldest son, Walter, Lord Deskford, sold to his second son, Mr James Ogilvie, for £11,230 Scots, Kirktown of Deskford, Overblairock, Fechiehill, Swallowhillock, Mill of Deskford plus some properties in Fordyce plus Clochmacreich, Over and Nether Tillibredlies, Over Skeith, Middle Skeith, Little Skeith, Craibston, Croftgloy, Squaredoch, Ramoir, Ordens, Ardicow, Cultain, Nether Blairock, Inaltry and patronage of Deskford. This did not leave the Earl a great deal of land in Deskford, but he had been deeply in debt to a range of individuals and this might have helped him pay this off. He had only redeemed the lands of Mid Skeith from George Shephard, for 2,200merks, in 1686. In 1689 reference is made to "Mr Patrick Ogilvie of Pittinbringand". It is believed that two inscribed stones on top of Castle Hill in Cullen may have been removed from his house.

In 1697 there was a retour of George Innes, heir of James Innes of Oathillock, his father, in the annual rental of £40 from four bovates of land of Oathillock and in 1698 there was a retour of Alexander Hay of Ardinbath, heir of Alexander Hay of Ardinbath, his father, in Overskeith and Bognagath, also in Little Skeith and in eighteen acres of Squaredoch, with the privilege of taking limestones from Kerstoun (Careston). In 1699 the 1st Earl of Seafield purchased Bogmuchals from Braco.

This was sign of an enormous turnaround in the fortunes of the Earls of Findlater, from poverty and indebtedness to great wealth. Soon the great number of financial, and particularly land transactions seen in the C16th and C17th were a thing of the past. The Earl of Findlater was able to buy out Abercrombie of Skeith and Lawtie of Inaltrie in the 1720s and consolidate all of Deskford in his possession either by paying off loans secured on parts of the parish or even acquiring new land.

There were however still occasional transactions. In 1736 there was a contract of marches between the Earl of Findlater and Sir Robert Abercrombie of

Birkenbog, setting their marches from the Burn of Cullen between Tochieneal and Towie and Leitchestoun. In 1738 there was a Decreet Arbital between the Earl of Findlater and Andrew Hay of Rannas, determining the marches between Deskford and Darbreich. In1745 there was agreement between Sir Robert Abercrombie and Alexander Grant, factor for Lord Findlater, setting the march between Sir Robert's lands of Towie and Lord Findlater's lands of Tochieneal and Smithstown.

An extract of mutual obligation was signed in 1750 between the Earl of Findlater and William, Lord Braco and William the Master of Braco of the one and other parts settling the marches betwixt the Lands of Deskford, Windyhills and Goukstone belonging to Lord Findlater and the land in the parishes of Grange and Keith belonging to Lord Braco from the High Road that leads from Keith to the Kirk of Deskford, to the three burn meetings where the march with the Lordship of Enzie began. That year there was also a contract of marches betwixt the Duke of Gordon and the Earl of Findlater setting the marches betwixt the Lordship of Enzie and Deskford.

In 1748 there had been a disposition of the lands of Nether Skeith, Hogmanseat, Berryhillock and miln thereof, Burnheads, Carrothead, Broom and lands of Raemoir with the tiends and pertinents by Alexander Abercrombie, elder, and George Abercrombie, younger, of Skeith in favour of James, Earl of Findlater, containing proxy of resignation ad remanentiam with an assignation to the Writers of Evidents which are said to have been herewith delivered in general, without referring to any inventory, and, an obligation that in case any of the writes should fall into their hands they should make the samen forthcoming to the Earl. This was dated 1721, the year of the sale.

In 1764 General Abercrombie wrote to the Earl of Findlater requesting some moss for his feus in Fordyce. In 1765 there was a contract of marches betwixt the Earl of Findlater and John Innes of Edingeith setting the marches betwixt them along the top of Lurg Hill. In 1766 there was a contract of marches betwixt the Earls of Findlater and Fife, settling the marches betwixt their respective lands in the Lurghill.

In 1783 there was a charter in favour of Thomas Ogilvie of Logie including the town and lands of Craibstoun, over and neither Tullybredlies and seventeen and a half acres of the lands of Squaredoch and the tiend sheaves of the said land with houses and biggings, mosses, pasturages and pertinents belonging thereto in the Lordship and parish of Deskford, confirming the charter of 1781. This was later redeemed to the Earl. Also towns and lands of Windyhills, Saughtertown alias Netherseat of Aichries and Newlands or Nearlands, now commonly called Lurgbrae. Also the tiends, pasturage and vicarage of the lands of Pittenbringands, Bruntons, Smithstown, Upstrath, Castelfields and Claypots in the parish of Rathven.

LORDSHIP AND ARISTOCRACY

The social structure of the Bronze and Iron Age tribes who occupied Deskford would have included tribal chiefs, but we know nothing of them, and in any case their role would not have been one we would recognise, since they were war leaders or leaders of kinship groups unlike in the residual elements of the feudal system to which we are accustomed today.

There were, under the Picts, Mormaers of both Buchan and Moray. Deskford however lies in the border lands between them, though it is likely that it came under the sway of Buchan, whose first recorded King was Bede the Pict in the C6th. In the early C12th many of the mormaers became earls and many of the toisechs became thanes, accepting allegiance to the King under a feudal system. One such was the Mormaer of Buchan, who became the Earl of Buchan. For some considerable time in the C12th and C13th Deskford was controlled by the Comyn Earls of Buchan as Justiciars for the entire North East, having backed the winning side in the civil wars. This was the reason given in 1382 by King Robert II, when he gave Deskford to the Wolf of Badenoch through his wife, Lady Euphemia Ross's descent from these Comyns.

In earlier times thanes had power over lands not belonging to feudal lords. In the North East, tribal territories not directly under the control of one of the Earls of Buchan, Moray, Mar, Garioch or Fife were ruled by thanes who were high status land managers for the king. Their role changed in the C14th when they became hereditary landowners. The valley of Deskford was part of the Thanage of Boyne. Its boundary with the Thanage of Enzie, according to several sources, ran from the mouth of the Cullen Burn over the top of Bin Hill and across Aultmore. Blaeu's map however, puts the boundary slightly to the west of the burn. Cullen was also in the Thanage of Boyne and was originally known as Cullen of Boyne, in order to avoid confusion with Cullen of Buchan, near Macduff. The part of present day Deskford which lies on Aultmore, and areas such as Bogmuchals, lay in the Forest of Boyne. It is likely that when, in 1056, Malcolm Canmore passed through Banffshire with an army to put the local population in its place and confiscate its land, he redistributed it on a feudal basis, perhaps as early as this, to the Earl of Buchan.

In Laurence Nowell's map of Scotland of between 1561 and 1566 Boyne is shown in as large script as Murray, Ross or Sutherland. There is no mention of Buchan. Similarly Mercator's 1595 map of Scotland, based on the Nicolae map of 1583, shows Moravia and Buquhania in only slightly larger script than Ainzie (Enzie) or Boena (Boyne). Boyne was a very important place.

Banffshire only became an identifiable entity when created a sheriffdom. This postdated the establishment of thanages of which there were seven known in Banffshire, Enzie, Netherdole (Netherdale), Aberchirder, Conveth (Inverkeithney), Glendowachie(Macduff), Mumbre(Montblairy) and Boyne, which was by far the largest. It was at this time, in the C12th that Ha' Hillock was built and would have operated as a hunting lodge for the Thane or the fortified house of one of his feudal supporters. A wooden hall surrounded by a wooden stockade would have lain on top of the motte which remains today. Between 1249 and 1285 Alexander III obtained rental of 66/8d from the lands of Fynletter, 26/8d from the lands of Castelfelde and 40/- from the lands of Petynbruyan (Pattenbringan).

In the time of Robert the Bruce the Thanage of Boyne was held briefly by Randolph, Earl of Moray after Bruce destroyed the Comyn Earl of Buchan and his supporters. From the Earls of Moray it passed to the Edmonstone family, the first of these recorded being Sir John de Edmonstone, an incomer from the south. From them it passed to the Ogilvies when, in 1484, Walter Ogilvie, the second son of the first Ogilvie of Findlater, married Margaret Edmonstone.

In 1325 King Robert granted a charter to Sir Christian de Forbes, knight. (translated from the Latin) "Robert, King of Scots by the grace of God, to all good men in our whole land, greetings. Know you that we have given, granted, and by this our present charter confirmed to our beloved Christian Forbes, knight, for his homage and service, the third part of the davoch of Ardoch and the third part of the davoch of Skeeth with what pertains to them in the barony of Deskford, to have and hold by the said Christian and his heirs of us and our heirs in feu and inheritance ..... to render for it the service thence owed and customary in Scotland. In witness of which matter we have ordered that our seal be affixed to the present charter. With witnesses Bernard, Abbot of Arbroath, our Chancellor, Thomas Randolph, Earl of Moray and Lord of Annandale and of Man, our nephew, Hugh, Earl of Ross, Walter Seneschal of Scotland, James Lord Douglas, and Alexander Fraser, our chamberlain of Scotland, from the knights. At Scone, on the 27th day of the month of March, and of our reign the twentieth"

He granted another one third of each to Christian del Ard around the same date. At an early date in the C12th or C13th Alexander de Ard had been Earl of Caithness, which title he sold and alienated to the Sinclairs. The de Ard and Sinclair families were inter-related with each other. This raises the liklihood that the Del Ard of Ardoch and Skeeth was connected to the Sinclairs of Deskford and Findlater. The de Ard surname persisted for several centuries in Deskford as Ord.

The earliest Findlater on record is Galfridius de Fynlater who was hereditary Sheriff of Banff in 1342. In 1356 a vassel who farmed the land on behalf of the King took his name from the land and became John Fynletter of that Ilk. However when Galfridius' daughter married Richard Sinclair, a younger son of the Sinclairs of Roslyn in 1366, she resigned the lands into the hands of King David II, who immediately regranted them to "Ricardo de Sancto Claro and his wife, Joanna de Fynletyr". In 1381 King Robert II granted the Grieveship of Cullen to his Shield Bearer, Richard of St Clair. The Sinclair family had been in favour with the monarchy since the Battle of Bannockburn when one of their number was presented by Robert the Bruce with the latter's own sword, for gallantry.

In 1370 King Robert II had given a charter, now lost, to Ade Buthergask and his spouse, of the barony of Deskford, Ardacha and Skeythis. This confirmed a charter of 1329. However, in 1382 King Robert II changed this and granted to "our son Alexander, the Seneschal, Earl of Buchan (the Wolf of Badenoch) and to Euphemia Lady Ross, his wife, the lands of Deskford which belonged hereditarily to Lady Ross, in virtue of her descent from the Comyns".

There was trouble however in 1391 when Richard's son, Johannes de Sancto Claro de Deskford and Ricardus de Fynletter were put to the horn (outlawed), probably as a result of their involvement in the burning by the Wolf of Badenoch of Elgin and the Cathedral there. Johannes de Sancto Claro died at the King's horn. Briefly the Barony of Deskford, the principal messuage of which was the Castle of Inaltry, was placed in the hands of John, Earl of Moray. This arrangement did not remain in place for long and in 1406 the lands of Deskford were returned to the son of Sir John Sinclair (Johannes de Sancto Claro), Ingram, who in turn was succeeded by his son, John who then died at the battle of Harlaw in 1411.

This John's daughter and heiress Margaret married, in 1437, Sir Walter Ogilvie of Auchleven, second son of Sir Walter Ogilvie of Lintrathen, High Treasurer of Scotland. In this way the the lands of Deskford and Findlater passed by marriage into the ownership of the Ogilvie family which was descended from the Earls of Angus. They had two sons, the elder of whom became Sir James Ogilvie of Deskford and Findlater, and the younger of whom, Sir Walter Ogilvie, married Margaret Edmonstone and became Thane of Boyne. In 1566, a successor, Alexander Ogilvie of Boyne, married Mary Bethune (Beaton), one of "the Queen's Four Maries". Both were still alive in 1606 and were both subsequently buried in Deskford Church. Deskford, Findlater and Boyne were the oldest Ogilvie possessions in Banffshire, though many others followed.

The Tower of Deskford was first occupied by either Sir Ingram Sinclair or Sir John Sinclair around 1400. In 1420 a grandson of the Sir John who died at Harlaw, also Sir John, had been Lord of Deskford, but his son Alexander renounced in 1435 in favour of Margaret, his aunt, thus allowing her to bring wealthy estates to her marriage.

In 1471 Sir James Ogilvie of Deskford was Provost of Banff and in the succeeding decade acquired several pieces of land. In 1472 Alexander Fordyce, chaplain of Cullen, disponed his lands to Sir James Ogilvie of Deskford. In 1479 the Baillies and Town Council of Cullen granted a bond of manrent to James Ogilvie of Deskford and in 1481 John Hay, Constable of Cullen, disponed the Constabulary, which included the land of Pattenbringan, to him. This was confirmed by James III. In 1482 a charter was granted by the Baillies of Cullen to Sir James Ogilvie of Deskford of the lands of Findochty, Smithstown and Seafield. At this time the Ogilvie family must have been wealthy as, when Sir James' daughter Margaret married the Laird of Grant her tocher (dowry) was 300 merks.

Not all was plain sailing however. In 1493 John Duff of Darbruche (Darbreich) raised an action against Sir James Ogilvie for wrongful occupation and manuring of his lands of "Findochty feild". In 1497/98 the King confirmed a charter of George, Earl of Huntly, Lord of Badenoch and Forrester of Aynye (Enzie) and Boyne by which, for a certain sum of money, he sold and alienated to James Ogilvie of Deskford, knight, and his heirs, the lands of Darchailye, Langmure and Tulinach within the Forests of Boyne and Aynye. Reddendo a penny in the name of white farm.

There was an inscription in Fordyce cemetery which translated as "Here rest two honourable men, James Ogilvy of Deskford and James Ogilvy his son and heir presumptive. The former died 13th Feb 1509 and the latter 1st Feb 1505. Pray for their souls".

In 1516, John Ogilvie, son of James Ogilvie of Deskford, and Principal of Civil Law at Aberdeen, as Envoy to France in 1514, brought two ships laden with wine, artillery and military stores, a gift from Queen Anne to the King of Scots. In 1541 the King confirmed to "Alexander Ogilvie de eodem and Elizabeth Gordon his spouse", among other lands, "the land and barony of Desfurde with the tower and fortalice thereof and the patronage of the Chapel of Desfurd".

This is referred to in the will of James Ogilvie of Findlater, dated 1565, where he recalled that he was the victim of a conspiracy to defraud him of his inheritance in favour of the Gordon son of his father's second wife. He only recovered his estates a few years before he died through the good offices of Mary Queen of Scots. The reason for his father having disinherited him was that he was alleged to have importuned his stepmother, his father's second wife, Elizabeth Gordon, to have sex with him, and that he locked his father in a dark house, kept him awake and tried to drive him mad. Nobody knows if this was true or was Gordon propaganda. Once he was reinstated by Mary Queen of Scots however it is suggested by John Rennie that he was responsible for defacing and erasing Elizabeth Gordon's initials from the carving on the sacrament house in Deskford Church. This vandalism can still be seen clearly.

His grandson, Walter Ogilvie, who was recognised by Alexander Ogilvie of Boyne as his chief, was the first Lord Ogilvie of Deskford and father of the 1st Earl of Findlater. By the end of the C16th the Ogilvies were one of the most powerful families in the North East. Sir Walter Ogilvie was created 1st Lord Ogilvie of Deskford and Findlater in 1616 and his son, James, became the 1st Earl of Findlater in 1638. In 1625 Sir Walter had given a charter to his son James, then Master of Deskford, and his wife, Lady Elizabeth Leslie of half the Mains of Findlater and the House (Tower) of Deskford.

James, the 1st Earl of Findlater, had no male heir, although twice married, so procured a new grant of his honours patent which allowed his son in law, Sir Patrick Ogilvie of Inchmartine, who had married the Earl's daughter and heiress, Elizabeth, to succeed him.

Though the Ogilvies were very wealthy at the end of the C16th, one hundred years later the 3rd Earl, in the 1680s, had several legal judgments against him for non payment of debts. These included £12,127:13:4d to John Lorimer, merchant in Dundee, £1,595 to John Man, Bailie of Dundee, 1,276 merks to James Brown, Advocate, £1,496:13:4d to John Cunningham, Auchenharvie, £11,584:13:4d to David Halyburton, Pitcur, £5,889:19:10d to Isobel Fetchie, £1,266:13:4d to Sir James Ogilvie (his second son and successor) and £4,306:13:4d to Rev James Gordon, Minister in Rothiemay. The Earl sold off most of Deskford to his second son, a wealthy Edinburgh lawyer and politician, in order to repay some of his debts. Following his elder brother's death, this second son in due course became the 4th Earl of Findlater, having already, in 1701, been created 1st Earl of Seafield in his own right.

The 4th Earl paid off all his father's debts and amassed a fortune. He was a lawyer with "a soft tongue", who held various important positions including Chancellor of Scotland. He was considered greedy, was known by his nickname of "the hyena", and obtained for himself a pension of £3,000 per annum, an enormous sum in those days. He had much to do with bringing about the Union of the Parliaments in 1707. To him is attributed the quote about "an end

Aultmore Lodge, Deskford Estate's main shooting lodge, which was located less than half a mile uphill from Craibstone farm.

to ane old sang". He was one of the "parcel o' rogues in a Nation" who were bribed by the English Government to ensure they voted for the Union. He was very successful in everything he did, for example in purchasing small estates to establish the unified Deskford Estate, but was also very unpopular.

In the List of Claimants under the Act for Abolishing Heritable Jurisdictions in Scotland, 1747, James, 5th Earl of Findlater and 2nd Earl of Seafield was awarded compensation of £5,500 sterling, including £1085:19:4d for the

Regality of Ogilvie, Constabulary of Cullen and Balliary of Strathisla. This was less than he had claimed, even though, when making his claim, he stated that if the sums he suggested were low compared with other claimants, he should not be paid only what he claimed, and less than others.

The 6th Earl of Findlater and 3rd Earl of Seafield was one of Scotland's leading agricultural improvers who was responsible for the major changes to agricultural practice in Deskford in the mid C18th. He also planted large acreages of trees in the years after 1750. He is believed to have been subject to occasional fits of madness throughout his life, and that when he felt one coming on he would ask his Factor, Alexander Grant, to lock him in a tower room till he recovered, before letting him out. On one such occasion in 1766 it is alleged that he was released before he had recovered, chased the Factor up the pink staircase and stabbed him to death. Some years earlier, in 1738, suspicions were voiced when he had been the only other person present when John George, 5th Lord Banff drowned at the Black Rocks off what is now Cullen Golf Course, in calm conditions. On 03/11/1770 the Earl is believed to have taken his own life by slashing his wrists. The Aberdeen Journal spoke only about "the melancholy reports of his death".

He was succeeded by his son, the 7th Earl of Findlater and 4th Earl of Seafield who returned from the continent soon after his father died, accompanied by a very recent wife and a pastry cook. The Earl was gay, the marriage was one of convenience and the wife very soon fled back to the continent. During his brief stay at Cullen House he held open house on Wednesdays and his table was plentiful, though few of his guests had any idea what the elaborate and sophisticated dishes which they ate were. They were disguised and quite French. He introduced strange new fashions such as serving potatoes and vegetables with the meat. His butler served at table wearing white gloves, and after the meal guests were expected to wash their fingers and mouths. The Earl was considered pompous, proud and very refined in his manners.

Young gentlemen were invited to stay with the Earl at Cullen House but usually declined, "for various reasons". On one occasion the Earl held a lavish dance and included many poor commoners in the invitations, which displeased some members of the local gentry who left in the huff. Soon afterwards the Earl was accused of "certain unnatural transgressions", and pursued by a blackmailer, he fled into exile at Dresden.

During the several decades he lived there, never returning to Banffshire, he became one of the foremost residents. He offered to finance Dresden City Council to build the tower of the Church of the Three Kings. His primary interest was in the Loschwitzer vineyards and he eventually owned five of the eight. He arranged for the master builder Giese from Gotha to build him a

The 7th Earl of Findlater's magnificent palace on Bredemannschen Mountain.

magnificent palace on Bredemannschen Mountain. This was considered to be the most beautiful family palace in the Dresden region. After the Earl's death it was turned into a luxury hotel called "Findlater's" where many famous people, including Wagner were guests. It was demolished in the mid C19th during Prince Albrecht of Prussia's programme of improvements and the site today is occupied by Castle Albrechtsberg.

The Earl is buried in the graveyard of Loschwitzer Church, Dresden and much later, on their deaths, two brothers called Fischer were buried in the same grave beside him. On his death the Earl had left his entire property and estate, worth £65,000, to his secretary and constant companion, Johann Georg Fischer and upon their relationship becoming public, Fischer was divorced by his wife, a notably principled action since he was now a very rich man. The Earl's family back in Scotland contested his will but lost in court, which left his successor as Earl of Seafield much poorer than would have been hoped.

The death of the 7th Earl without issue meant that the title of Earl of Findlater was extinguished. He was succeeded as 5th Earl of Seafield in 1811 by Sir Lewis Alexander Grant who added the name Ogilvie to the end of his name. He was feeble-minded and unable to look after his affairs so the estate was managed by his brother who succeeded him within a few years, when, despite being young and in good health, he died suddenly and unexpectedly. His brother, the 6th Earl of Seafield, changed the surname from Grant-Ogilvie to Ogilvie-Grant. He was MP for Elgin Burghs and later Inverness Burghs. After succeeding he sat in the House of Lords till his death in 1853. He was Lord Lieutenant of Inverness-shire from 1809 to 1853.

Throughout the remainder of the C19th the Seafield fortunes improved and when John Charles, the 7th Earl died at the age of 65 in 1881 he had been responsible for extensive improvements throughout his estates and had planted more than 60 million trees. When he died in 1881 his hearse left Cullen accompanied by two thousand people on its journey through Deskford to Keith station en route to Grantown on Spey. Unfortunately the 8th Earl, Ian Charles died in 1884, aged only 32, to be succeeded as 9th Earl by his uncle, the fourth son of the 6th Earl. He had been a lieutenant colonel in the army and MP for Elginshire and Nairnshire. The 10th Earl, son of the 9th Earl, only survived a few months after succeeding in 1888. He was succeeded by his son, the 11th Earl.

In October 1911 Deskford Parish Council recorded "their deep sense of loss on the death of Caroline, Dowager Countess of Seafield, in whom the poor had always a generous and warm benefactress and whose policy it was to promote the happiness and welfare of her people. They recognised that in her they had a most liberal proprietrix who took a keen and enlightened interest in all that pertained to the moral and social wellbeing of her tenantry and whose generosity had done so much within recent years to increase the prosperity of the inhabitants of the parish".

The 11th Earl died of the wounds he received in the trenches in 1915 and was succeeded by his daughter, Nina Caroline Studley-Herbert, 12th Countess of Seafield. She was reputed to lead an expensive lifestyle and rumours abound. One is that she lost the quarry on the north face of the Hill of Maud on a hand of cards. Another is that she ordered the clay tiles on all steading roofs on the estates to be replaced by 8x4 asbestos sheets, because she was Romantically involved with the son of the largest American manufacturer of 8x4 asbestos sheets. On her death in 1969 she was succeeded by her son, the 13th and current Earl of Seafield. Cullen House was sold in the 1970s and when he and the countess are in the area they reside in Old Cullen, the former factor's house. They have two sons.

Deskford is unusual in that in the Valuation Roll of the parishes of Banffshire in 1690, it is shown as having only two heritors, Sir James Ogilvie, £1,400, and George Abercrombie of Skeith, £180. Rathven had 25 heritors, Fordyce had 15 and Grange had 19. In the Pasch Roll of 1717, Lord Deskford appeared for the "thayndom of Boynd".

The Abercrombies of Skeith were an old established family in Deskford when Abercrombie of Skeith, known as Old Tullibody, died on June 26th 1699 with his son, Alexander Abercrombie, who had married the daughter of Duff of Braco, in close attendance. Indeed his son's behaviour was the subject of a critical letter written by James Baird of Banff shortly before Old Tullibody died. He wrote as follows.

"Braco's son in law, Alexander Abercrombie was with old Tullibody, keeping physitians from the old man who is dyeing a verie miserable death. I went there upon Saturday last and was sorie to find him in such a lamentable condition. His left leg is swelled as big as a post, and it, with his foote and all, is all as black as pitch, and all putrified to that degree that, if a knife were put in his leg from the on side to the other, he would not at all find it, neither in leg or in foote, and it has a very nautious smell. His other leg is beginning the same way, and a few days will carry him off. When I sayed that I thought it ane odd thing that the gentleman had an opulent fortune (without any debt at all) of 7000 merks a yeare, it was the strangest thing in the world that he was allowed to dye lyke a dog and to rott above the ground without so much as ane physitians being called to sie him and that I thought it would be honourable, both for the dyeing man and his apparand unwourthie successor to call a consultaone of good men together, if they should do no more than looke upon him and say he was dyeing, all the ansre that I got was that I was impertinent and took too much on me, and truely we pairted at the wrong hand. All that he takes cair of is to sitt by him from 5 in the morning till 12 at night to sie that non come near him, and I truely believe: if the old laird does not die soon the young man will die of melancholy".

The above gives an interesting account of Deskford's second most important family, indeed one which rivalled the Ogilvies for land and wealth throughout the C16th and C17th. Alexander Abercrombie later sold Skeith to the Earl of Findlater in 1721, about which time the Lawtie family also sold Inaltry, making Findlater the sole heritor in Deskford. Largely as a result of this, in 1836, it was reported that there was no common land in Deskford, though Fordyce had 1,500 acres in 1842 and Rathven had, on the Common of Aultmore, 2,874 acres of hill and moor and 730 acres of moss.

In the 1950s all farms and crofts in Deskford belonged to Seafield Estate. In 1953 tillage was 2,306 acres, temporary grass 1,625 acres, permanent grass 226 acres and rough grazings 416 acres. There were 73 holdings of over one acre in size. Langlanburn (including, later, Clochmacreich land) was sold around 1968, and other farms such as Nethertown, Lurgbrae, Marchbank, Myreside, Wester and Over Windyhills, Craibstone and Backies more recently.

It would be easy, viewed through the prism of today's values and attitudes, to see the behaviour of some members of Deskford's most important families as being less than commendable. That would be a mistake. Each lived in a different era which had different belief systems and in which life was conducted under different standards and conventions. The history of every family in the area would be likely to throw up similar examples and personalities but only the most prominent families are likely to have had them recorded. There should be no embarrassment in the behaviour of any ancestor but pride in the achievements of many.

Times change as do attitudes. What was thought of as acceptable behaviour in the past is often seen nowadays as worthy only of criticism, and vice versa. Any intent we might have to characterise behaviour from the past in this way is surely only indicative of our own arrogance and judgmentalism.

LAW AND ORDER

In Pictish times and in earlier Iron Age and Bronze Age societies, law was a fairly arbitrary concept, based on the power of local and regional leaders. Fairness and equality are relatively recent ideas in relation to the law. In tribal times law usually meant power which benefited the tribe, or the leader and his friends. This was mitigated by the methods under which new leaders emerged, neither a matrilinear succession nor one of primogeniture, but one in which the new leader was whichever member of the ruling family gained the support and approval of the tribe. A present parallel might be an elective dictatorship. The arrival of Christianity diluted the power of the tribal leaders, as it formed an alternative power base.

Probably the first documented law which affected Deskford and the North East was the Law of the Innocents, written by St Columba's biographer, Adomnan, in 697, and which was accepted by both Pictish and Scottish rulers. Under it women were not to be killed by men in any circumstances. It also listed fines and punishments for injury to women. In addition it outlined offences involving industrial injury, dangerous workmanship, dying in a quagmire and injuries from tame beasts. Other offences included injuries from raiding parties, slanderous allegations and kin aiding and abetting a crime. The law also protected non-combatants during warfare.

The next codification of law of which we know was the Law of the Brets and Scots of the early C12th, under which there were five grades of men, King, Mormaer or Earl, Thane or Toisech, Octhigem and Serf. Previous to this there had also been slaves, the accumulation of whom was the main reason for warfare in Pictish times. Octhigem literally means young lad, but was used to describe a free man.

Under this law there were penalties for killing, including honour price which was paid to victims or their families. For example, the guilty party would have to pay 1,000 cattle for killing the King, 150 for killing the King's son or an Earl,

100 for killing an Earl's son or a Thane, 66 for killing a Thane's son, 44 for killing an Octhigem and 16 for killing a Rusticus (serf). Payments for a female victim were two-thirds that of her husband, but were paid to her birth family, not her husband.

In 1197 Earls, Barons and Thanes were required to swear an oath that they would not receive or help thieves, manslayers, murderers or robbers. Instead, if they encountered them amongst their own men or someone else's, they should bring them to justice. They were also banned from accepting bribes to influence their administration of justice.

In the C13th Lords had the right of gallows and ordeal pit. This raises the possible use of Pum's Pot on the northern boundary of Deskford for this purpose. These rights probably evolved from the rights of Thanes in earlier times. Small tenants were responsible for their men and would be responsible for paying their fines, even for minor offences.

In early mediaeval times many aspects of the law were in the hands of the church. It was accepted widely that most of society should be controlled by the church and the landowner. Offences included quarrels with blows or words, slander, lack of charity to the Poor, lack of Sabbath observance, Sunday drinking and sex outwith marriage. Drunkenness was acceptable on weekdays and wifebeating was seen as normal discipline. The Church gave sanctuary to killers guilty of "suddenty", but not those guilty of "forethocht felony".

By 1398 the Chronicler of Moray stated that there was no law in Scotland. "He who was stronger oppressed him who was weaker, and the whole country was a den of thieves. Murders, herschip, fire-raising and other offences went unpunished". However being "put to the horn", was used from the C13th to the C19th. Local offenders were denounced as guilty of serious crimes by three blasts on the horn at the Mercat Cross at Banff. As late as the mid C19th an attempted rapist from Kirktown was put to the horn in this way.

Around 1400 Scotland became the first country in Europe to abandon serfdom. Before this a serf could only gain his freedom by staying unchallenged for a year and a day in a Royal Burgh such as Cullen. Within Deskford, Law Hillock stood near the present public road on the opposite side to Inaltrie. It was a conical artificial mound and was believed to be an ancient site where justice was enacted. It was taken down and the site ploughed in the early C19th by the then tenant and the stones used to build steadings. The tenant who did this had first attempted to use the stones of Inaltry Castle, but they could not be separated. The present tenant, Jimmy Stewart, says that he had long wondered what caused a patch of very sandy soil at the location of the former Law Hillock.

Landowners in areas such as Deskford controlled the population through Baron Courts, by which means they had largely unchallenged power, and could try a wide range of crimes. Under these were Birlay or Birlaw Courts comprising respected and representative tenants plus the landowner's representative. These were responsible for keeping the peace, resolving arguments between tenants in multiple tenancies and deciding when communal activities such as ploughing and harvesting would begin. They also dealt with the maintenance of feal dykes, damage caused by straying cattle and boundary disputes. The activities and decisions of Birlay Courts were not recorded in writing and there are no records from the Baron Court in Deskford, though these will have existed at one time. Both types of court would have been very important in the lives of the people of Deskford.

The church was also important in maintaining the law. In 1681 Thomas Legg of Deskford and Alexander Howie of Grange gave "great scandal" in Deskford by getting drunk on the Lord's Day and beating and wounding a parishioner in Deskford with drawn swords. Legg was ordered to appear before the Kirk Session.

A major development in the administration of law took place in 1698 with the establishment of Deskford as a Burgh of Regality, the centre and administrative headquarters of the Regality of Ogilvie. This form of legal administration gave almost absolute power to local aristocrats, in this case the Earl of Findlater, until their abolition in 1747. Two Head Courts were held annually, at Michaelmas and Pasch (Easter). Although Deskford was the administrative centre of the Regality of Ogilvie, its prison was in Cullen.

It was the establishment of the Regality of Ogilvie which led to the building of the gallows on Gallows Knowe. This lay on a slight eminence just within the Parish of Deskford, beside the old main road from Cullen to Keith. It is written that when the gallows were being erected, an old cadger on his way past with his ass from Cullen to his home in Keith was grabbed and strung up to test its effectiveness. It proved very effective and on dark and stormy nights for hundreds of years the forlorn cries of his ass could still be heard in the woods on Clune Hill.

This area was notorious. It was also believed that the cries of murdered children could be heard amongst the ruins of nearby Pattenbringan. In the C19th three would-be poachers saw the ghost of a lady in white on top of a feal dyke there. They threw away their guns and ran home at full speed in a panic. There was also thought to have been another murder nearby and fishwives on their way from Cullen to Deskford refused to pass the spot.

It is likely, from ancient accounts and current observation that there are one or more graves on the Gallows Knowe. In the early C19th a body was discovered there at a depth of eighteen inches. No coffin had been used. The bones were gathered together and placed in a small enclosure of rough stones, covered in earth and with a small cairn placed on top. The stones which had held the gibbet were restored in situ, and an old wooden roller placed perpendicularly to mark the spot. Nobody in Deskford at that time had been aware that a body had lain there. In the late C19th an examination found two flat circular stones, about two feet in diameter, surrounded by half a dozen longitudinal stones, fixed perpendicularly in the ground to support the gibbet which had consisted of a single tree, believed to have been the only beech on Clune Hill.

Regality Courts were usually held at the Tower of Deskford, though on some occasions at Ardoch and other locations in the parish. For much of its 50 year existence Walter Ogilvie, Ardoch, was Baillie, Robert Blinshell, Cullen, was Clerk and Walter Buie was Fiscall. Amongst the Court Officers was William Taylor, Squaredoch. In March 1703, Marjorie Gairden of Newmill was cited before the Justices of the Peace for carrying seven ells of cloth from Deskford to Grange on the Sabbath, and in 1709 James Dovern from Deskford was ordained to compear in the public place of repentance in Grange for removing cattle from Grange on the Sabbath.

Courts, which were never meant to be impartial, were held frequently and quickly after a crime had been committed. For example, in 1722, the Court was convened eighteen times, during which there were 37 actions for money or goods, 6 for breach of the peace, 28 for not having corn milled at the estate mill at Milltown, 9 for non payment of cess (local tax), 16 for non- attendance at the Pasch Head Court, 15 for non-attendance at the Michaelmas Head Court, 2 for not appearing as witnesses, four for kindling mosses, 1 for damaging a road, 3 for damaging neighbours' characters, 3 for stealing and 3 for cutting green wood. In addition there were cases of contempt of court and sheepstealing.

By 1745 twenty-one courts were held in the year, but actions for cutting wood or harming mosses were by now rare, and cases of small debts and non-delivery of goods were more common. In almost all cases the accused were found guilty and given heavy fines, though scourging and use of the pit and gallows were no longer used as punishments.

Masters were fined £4 for paying their servants in "bounty and bere" instead of in money. Nobody was allowed to remain out of service if able to work, and any tenant reporting such a case was rewarded by being allocated that person to work for him as if he were a serf. Sometimes searches were made of farms for illegally cut wood, used for making creel rungs, door heads, door cheeks and ploughheads. Tenants often adulterated corn being paid as rent by mixing it with bere, pease and other grain, which made it unsalable in the south of Scotland. Those guilty of breach of the peace were usually women. By 1747 tenants were trying to refuse to accept the jurisdiction of the Court of Regality, but its decisions were still being enforced.

In June 1746 the king pardoned the lower classes who had fought on the Jacobite side, including a few from Deskford, so long as they laid down their arms, signed an obligation to be at His Majesty's pleasure, and assisted in bringing in others and giving information about where any arms were hidden. With the abolition of the Regality jurisdictions in 1747, Justices of the Peace became much more important, dealing with wage disputes, weights and measures, suppressing riots, helping administer prisons and almshouses, supervising roads and bridges and the application of the Poor Law. They worked in conjunction with the Commissioners of Supply, an early type of local government, but comprising only landed gentry.

In the C17th and early C18th there were also harsh laws which protected the kirk. The death penalty still existed theoretically for blasphemy, stealing vessels or utensils from a church, assault on a Minister, and for children over 16 cursing their parents. It was rarely if ever applied for these offences. However the heavy penalties for breaking the Sabbath through hard labour, selling drink, hiring servants, cursing and swearing and drunkenness were applied. Penalties for breaking the law in the C17th still included the jougs, the pillory, lug gristle being torn away, flogging, head-shaving and banishment. All of these were used locally though the system in Scotland was less severe than that in England.

The second half of the C18th and the C19th were almost crime-free in Deskford, apart from drunkenness and immorality. By the end of the C18th the cutting off of ears, public flogging of women, banishment, fines for Sabbath breaking, cursing and imprecations had been abolished. Well into the C19th however the death penalty could still be used for robbery, arson, theft and hamesucken (housebreaking). At the start of the century it was still theoretically possible to be hanged for being in disguise on a public road, cutting down young trees, shooting rabbits, stealing anything worth 5/- or more or begging without a pass from a magistrate.

In the late C19th Deskford was considered to be one of the most law-abiding places in Scotland, and though there was a fair bit of petty crime between the wars, by the 1950s there was again very little crime, except breaches of driving and lighting regulations. Despite a few cases of theft by housebreaking in the second decade of the C21st, by and large Deskford is still a law-abiding place.

There were certainly many more individual cases of lawbreaking recorded in the C16th, C17th and early C18th. As early as 1391 Johannes de Sancto Claro de Deskford and Ricardus de Fynletter were put to the horn, probably for helping the Wolf of Badenoch burn down Elgin Cathedral.

In the C16th, civil law was used widely for a number of private transactions. In 1521/22 the King confirmed a charter of Alexander Ogilvie of that Ilk, by which he granted to Elizabeth Craufurde, for the wrong done by him to her, and for the support of herself and her offspring for life, the lands of Easter Skeith in the Barony of Deskford or Ogilvie. It is not recorded what wrong he did her. There were also criminal law issues. In 1562, Sir John Gordon of Deskford, "the hopeful Laird of Findlater, Erle Huntley's gallant son", was under a charge of assailing and mutiLating the Lord Ogilvie in a street skirmish in Edinburgh. In 1588 there was assigned to David Nicoll in Tullebradless in favour of John Forsycht in Vindehills of "gudis and gere quhilk appertenit to him be the deceis of athir his fader or moder".

In 1593 there was a renunciation by William Leslie in Blarrack in favour of Katherine Leslie, sister of the said Leslie, of 10 merks "left hymme be his umquhill moder, Eosabel Ogilvie". Also that year, Katherine Leslie, daughter of the deceased Isobel Ogilvie in Myltonne, in favour of William Leslie, brother of the said Leslie, of £40, "restand in the handis of James Ogilvie of Blerake and to ane cow in the handis of Walter Ogilvie in Ardaycht and to ane withir cow in the handis of Johnne (Purss???).

In 1594 there was an instrument in favour of George Anderson in Cottone of Enaltre over requisition to George Haye in Smychtstonne to collect "corne sold by the said Andersonne", and a separate confirmation by George Haye in Smychtstonne of his readiness to collect corne from George Andersonne in Cottoune of Enaltre.

Civil law transactions continued into the C17th. in 1604 there was a tack of the teinds of the parishes of Fordyce, Cullen and Deskford by Mr Patrick Darg, Minister, to James Ogilvie, son of Sir Walter Ogilvie for thirty eight years from "lambas". In 1610 Harper's Croft in Cullen was mortified by William Ogilvie in Over Blairock to two Bedemen. After William Ogilvie died, ownership was challenged successfully by the Knights Templar of St John and the Earl of Melrose. The mortification was nullified, but this was later overtaken.

In 1614 John Ogilvie of Over Blairock took action of removing against five persons, and later that year John Ogilvie of Glassaugh, Walter Ogilvie of Ardoch and John Ogilvie of Over Blairock each agreed by law to build a house "by March next, 25 feet long, twa haus hight, and to be scleitit". The same year, criminal law was also being observed. "William Macky, scourger, halds out this bounds (Cullen) and the paroche of Deskford all stranger beggaris".

Earlier, in 1601, there was a payment of 400 merks by Thomas Lawtie, son of Mr William Lawtie, Burgess of Cullane, to James Ogilvie of Cairston following "reckless bluid drawing and mitilitationne (mutilation) of twa of his fingeris be the said Thomas". This was followed by a letter of slains by James Ogilvie of Cairstoun and three of his brothers in favour of Thomas Lawtie giving forgiveness following payment of 400 merks, "for the negligent and rakles mutilation of twa of my fingeris, rakleslie done be the said Thomas to me in redding of and pley".

In a notorious case in 1646, the Laird of Glassaugh went to the house of Patrick Gelly in Fordyce and his brother in law. He was accompanied by his brother and two servants, all armed and with "fire and kindled peats, of plain purpose, to burn the complainer's house and hail family". Gelly had complained that the Laird refused to pay off a debt to him. They "bodden with their weapons, by way of hamesucken maist presumtuoslie and cruellie put violent hands on the person of the said Patrick Gelly, took him captive and took him to the Cleanhill of Deskfuird", in order to frighten him. This was a particularly lawless time, but Gelly, after having been taken to Enzie, escaped and managed to bring his case before the Sheriff.

In 1653, John Scrimgeour of Kirktown raised letters of horning against Patrick, Lord Deskford for non-payment of 500 merks etc. In 1669 "Helen Gray, spous to Thomas Ewin was unlawed in £10 money for beating and blooding of Thomas French in Deskfuird". In 1678 Jhone Thayne, Clunehill, had to pay Jhone Thayne in Goukstone 16 merks for having cut corne belonging to him. In 1698 there was a case against a Deskford man for having taken limestone from Kerstoun. Also in the late C17th, the Banff Dean of Guild reported that William Thomson in Deskford and 19 others had been arrested for forestalling at the

Summeruiftis Fair. This meant making bargains to buy or sell before the Fair began.

Around the end of the C17th, with the establishment of the Regality of Ogilvie, serious cases were heard. In 1697 George Syme, prisoner in Cullen, and John Ritchisone, Mains of Bracco, were accused of stealing "from the kiln barn of Inaltrie, ane load of oats and two panfuls of sowens". They were found guilty and sentenced to death.

In 1699 James Gray of Durn was hanged on Gallows Knowe, Clunehill, the first execution recorded there. He and his brother George had stolen a cow from Peter Abernethy, tenant in Durn, to be revenged on him for taking over their father's tenancy of that farm. James and George Gray had killed the cow in the farm of their uncle, John Gray at Tilliebriedless. All three had eaten the blood of the cow.

James Gray was also accused of stealing corn from another tenant's farm. George Gray escaped before the brothers were brought to justice. Both James and John Gray had previously been indicted for "common and nottorieous theift", and it was proven that James "was commomly bruted for a loose man and common thief before". He was "lykwayes of evill fame and reputation off befoir".

Witnesses were John Reid, Ramoire, Jon Grant, grieve to Crabstoun, Robert Hiltoun, Broom, and Andrew Longmuir, Ramore of Skeith. Amongst those summoned as jurors were Alexander Abercrombie, Berryhillock, Walter Ogilvie, Airdock, James Ord, Miltoun of Deskford, Jon Simpson, Cloackmacreigh, Alexander Dason, Over Tilliebreidless, James Simpson, Over Skeith, James Grant Ramoir, William Beidie, Ordains, Jon Johnston, Crabstoun, James Dow, Skeith, James Stronach, Squaredock, Jon Dougall ther, Walter Dougall, Cnappicassa, Geo Shiphart in Fachihill, Geo Taylor in Kirktoun, Jon Kempt in Knows, Tho Reid, Cairnstoun, Geo Smith Squaredoch, Walter Brember, Milntoun, John Stitchells, Over Clune, Walter Reid, Leitchistoun, Jon Aven, Pittenbringand and Walter Brember, Over Pittenbringand, together with others from within the Regality but outwith the parish.

Sheriff Nicolas Dunbar of Durn presided (could he be unbiased, owning the estate from which the beast was stolen?). He was the judge who, one year later, in 1700, would sentence the legendary freebooter, James McPherson to be hanged in Banff. In passing sentence he stated "the Shereff heirby decerns and adjudges you, the said James Gray, to be takin upon Fryday nixt, the sevinteint day of this instant moneth, above, sett downe from the prison of Cullen wher you now remaine to the Clune Hill thereof and gibbit standing thereon, betwixt the hours of two and four o'clock in the afternoon, and thereupon hang'd up by the neck by the hand of the common executioner till ye be dead. As also decerns and adjudges you, the said John Gray, the said day and place to be whipt about the said gibbit and your ear nailed thereto by the said executioner, and to be banished from the shyre in all tyme comein heirafter for ever under the pain of immediate death if he shall happein to be again found or apprehended therein without any furder sentence to be pronounced against you for that effect, and ordains your haill moveables to be exhest and inbrought and this for doome".

The hangman who hanged James Gray was George Cobban who lost his job immediately after this, after being arraigned for the theft of a wedder and other petty crimes. He was banished from Cullen on pain of death if he returned, and was replaced in 1700 by George Milne, a thief from Keith, who was given the option of taking the job or being hanged for stealing a peck of grain. He took the job.

Crimes recorded in the early years of the C18th were numerous but on the whole less serious. For example, two servants coming home from Rathven market were each fined £10 Scots for breach of the peace. This equated to two month's pay or the price of a horse.

In 1718, at the Regality Court, 51 individuals out of 58 charged from Deskford were each fined £4 Scots per boll for going past Milton Mill to get their corn ground, on the complaint of James Peterkin, the miller. In 1724, 81 persons were similarly found guilty. In January 1719, 23 individuals were fined £10 Scots each for cutting, peeling and destroying the green wood belonging to the Earl of Findlater. Another 49 appeared, pled innocence, and got off. The accused came from Clune, Oathillock, Kintywairds, Kirktown, Over Skeith and Ordens amongst other places.

In 1721 the tenant in Leitcheston was fined £15 Scots, being a third offence, for cutting green wood for a head to his plough. The same year a riot and breach of the peace was committed by three married women who were fined 5/- each.

In 1722 George Peterkin was fined £50 Scots for leading and stealing Alexander Anderson's peats and clods from the Moss of Aultmore. In addition he had to lead 8 cart-loads of clods to Alexander Anderson or pay sixpence for each undelivered load. Also in 1722 all the tenants in Deskford were ordered by the Baillie to repair the garden dykes. This referred to the dykes between the Orchard and the kirkyard which were ruinous and had been removed. That same year two married women were fined £3 Scots each for scolding and reflecting on each others' good names. This was obviously not as serious as the offence caused by a married woman in Squaredoch and her neighbour who were each fined £6 Scots for "scolding and beating and blooding" each other.

In 1723 Janet Davidson was accused of taking James Wright by the leg, putting him in the burn and dragging him through the water, because he used abusive language to her. Each was fined £3 Scots. In 1725 Robert Gerrie in Ardoch accused two married women, Marjory Davidson and Margaret Abernethy, of having defamed his wife's character by accusing her of witchcraft. In 1726 the Earl of Findlater sued John Stitchell for 110 merks, being 22 years bygone feu duty of Clochmacreich.

In the Court of Regality at Deskford in the 1720s there were actions for non-repayment of loans, for failing to keep a feeing agreement and for selling a plough which was ineffective. Other offences were varied. For example some young persons, for their amusement, rang the church bell, without consideration for others who might think it was a funeral. There were actions on intestate deaths, wills and succession, weights and measures, libel and inventories of goods. There were accusations of beating, blooding, abusing and assault by putting two thumbs in an opponent's mouth and tearing it.

There was a petition from Alexander Barker, Tillibreidless, against John Marquess in Craibstone to return a gavelock he was meant to be mending. There was a counter claim that it was owned by Marquess and that Barker had only borrowed it. No one knew who had broken it. The court found against Marquess, who was made to pay £6 in recompense.

In 1732, Walter Ogilvie of Airdoch was Bailzie, John Lorimer was Clerk and James Forsyth Procurator Fiscal. In a court held in the house of James Stables, Kirktown, on April 13th 1732 it was announced that Deskford tenants would no longer be permitted to cast for peats on parts of Old More (Aultmore), which were more convenient for tenants in Findlater, Pattenbringan and Cullen etc. Deskford tenants were to move to other mosses, mainly on the east side of the valley. Over and Nether Tillybreidless were to move to the moss on Windyhills, and then, in succession, moving north from there, were to be accommodated the tenants of Craibstown, Ramore, Berryhillock, Squaredoch, Kirktown, Airdoch, Faichyhill, Over and Nether Blairock, Clunehill, Clune, Milltown, Inaltry and Leitchestown. If there were any disputes the advice of the Factor and Moss Grieves were to be followed. All tenants had to be of assistance to those being moved, and the tenants of Clochmacreich, Bognagight, Over Skeith and Mid Skeith were to cast their fewel on the Lurg Hill. At a court held in the dwelling house of John Grant, Ramore, on April 20th 1732, John Marquies, Craibston was appointed Moss Grieve in Windyhills and Alexander Cameron, Darbreich, Moss Grieve in Old More. Both appeared and took their oaths of fidelity.

The verdicts of the Court of Regality were not always accepted. In 1723 Alexander Abercromby of Skeith appealed against a successful action by a ploughwright and in 1725 two youths appealed against having been fined £10 Scots each by the Bailie for having had a common tulzie (fight). There is no record of whether or not these appeals were successful. In 1735 James Reid, Over Skeith, was fined £15 Scots by the Bailie and had to compeer before the Kirk Session for slander, having called Robert Wood, Bognageith, James Fyntie, Over Skeith, and Wm Spence, Backies, knaves and other opprobrious names, and also for riot and breach of the peace.

As the century progressed Deskford became more peaceful and its people less lawless, though there were still issues to be addressed, even after the Court of Regality had been abolished. In 1772 George Steven, Burnheads, submitted a petition to the Earl to ban young lads going to the moss and to the peat from taking their dogs with them and allowing them to run free as he had had several sheep killed. In the 1780s several neighbours complained about George Cock and his wife in Aultmore for their treatment of their neighbours' and their own cattle. They were accused of cursing and swearing and threatening to kill their neighbours and burn their houses, and of having said that they would do God good service by putting to death "plenty of Presbyterian Heretics", who should not be allowed to be among "such honest people as Papists such as ourselves". There was a counter petition by George Cock, criticising his neighbours and asking for an increase in the acreage of his lease. This was followed by a letter from several Aultmore tenants saying that Cock was of good character and should keep his tenancy.

The C19th was increasingly law abiding though there were some major offences. In 1839, Margaret Lawrence, a farm servant at Ardoch was found guilty of murdering her newborn child, in a ditch near Ardicow. The case was not straightforward and was dealt with by the authorities with some compassion. She was imprisoned in Banff for 6 months.

Six years earlier, Charles McHardy, a lawyer residing in Kirktown, was accused that on May 17th 1833, in the High Glen Road, "he did wickedly and feloniously attack and assault Isobel Archibald, servant to John Reid in Darbreich, with intent to ravish her, did seize hold of her and did forcibly throw her down upon the ground, did raise her petticoats and get above her and did unbutton his breeches and did attempt to have carnal knowledge of her person, forcibly and against her will." He absconded and fled. The witnesses were Isobel Archibald, John Smith, gamekeeper to the Earl of Seafield, Barnyards of Cullen House, and Jean Reid, sister of, and residing with, John Reid at Darbreich.

Isobel Archibald had been returning from Cullen market at eight or nine o'clock in the evening and was followed by a man who accompanied her till they came to a lone place called the Glen of Cullen. He addressed her in immodest and obscene terms, then attacked and assaulted her in the most violent manner.

She resisted but was overpowered, thrown to the ground and he attempted to commit rape. She was rescued by John Smith, who had been in the wood laying snares for foxes and who ran to the spot on hearing her cries. She was sixteen.

She had been detained at Cullen Post Office, so had no neighbours to go home with. McHardy told her the High Glen Road would be quicker and accompanied her to show her the way. During the attempted rape he had said "if she came into the wood a maiden, she should not go out of it so". She kept her legs close but he forced them asunder. She continued to cry out desperately till Smith pulled him off. McHardy ran away while Smith helped her up and saw her home to Darbreich. She was very distressed.

McHardy spoke with a Highland accent and said he came from Kirkmichael, but in truth he lived with his wife in Kirktown. He had been married twice and had family with both wives. On February 8th 1833, Archibald Young, Procurator Fiscal, obtained a warrant for McHardy's arrest and was informed that he was hiding up country and working as a lawyer at Boat o' Brig. He instructed an active and intelligent officer at Keith to proceed immediately to apprehend McHardy, but he was not to be found. He was never seen again and it was suggested that he had left the country. He was tried in absentia at the High Court in Edinburgh, found guilty and put to the horn.

Another major crime took place in January 1899. At seven o'clock in the morning the cleaner opened the school door to be met with dense smoke billowing out. She raised the alarm but the draught from the door set the whole building ablaze, and the entire interior was gutted. It had been built in 1875 of stone and lime, with seating for 200 pupils. The walls remained standing, but had been damaged by heat and were later demolished. It had been insured for £800, but the cost of the damage exceeded this. It was very suspicious because the Church had been broken into the same night, a stained glass window broken and 4/- stolen from the Mission Box. There had also been an attempted housebreaking at the manse. None of the crimes was ever solved.

The second half of the C19th was exceptionally law abiding, with fewer than one crime a year in Deskford, despite the population being at its highest ever. The occasional crime included one in 1890, when at Banff Sheriff Court, Daniel McLennan, contractor, Fordyce, was found guilty of having been in search of game in the Cotton Hill Plantation. He was fined 10/- plus £2:10/- expenses, or 7 days imprisonment.

In January 1915, George Williams, a pedlar residing at Little Skeith, was fined 10/- or 5 days imprisonment by Hon Sheriff Substitute Colville at Banff Sheriff Court. He was an American from New Orleans and, since the United States was at that time neutral, he should have registered as an alien, but had failed to do so. The fact that his father was Welsh was not considered an excuse.

In the years between the two World Wars, and during World War II, there was a significant level of crime in Deskford, much of which was minor in nature. This seems to have diminished significantly after World War II, and is still at a very low level. The following examples relate to the 1930s and early 1940s.

In 1935, John Gordon, joiner, Berryhillock, was fined 10/- for failing to set the brake on his car correctly, so that it ran away down Seafield Street, Cullen, and crashed into a parked car. In August of that year a police check was established on the main road opposite Mosside. Donald Spence, farm servant, Ellyside, was fined £1:5/- for riding his bike without lights. James Wilson, Mains of Birkenbog, was fined £1:7:6d for the same offence plus trying to evade capture by the police.

Also in 1935, W Nicol, farm servant, Ardoch, was fined £5 or twenty days imprisonment for breaking into farm servants' quarters in Kirktown and stealing £5 from R Henderson, farm servant. Nicol's bicycle had been seen nearby, and despite at first denying it, he later admitted theft. He had hidden the £5 note in a field at Ardoch where it was found by the police. Sheriff More said it was a rotten thing to do. In 1936 Seafield Estate wrote to all tenants pointing out the recent judgment in the Court of Session that march fences were the property of the estate, and could not be removed by outgoing tenants. In 1937, George Marr, farm servant, Mid Skeith, was fined £1 or ten day's imprisonment for assault and giving a false address.

In 1938, William McKandie, Netherton, Grange, was fined 10/- for stealing a coat from John Burns, Cullen (perhaps the John Burns on the Deskford War Memorial) at the New Year Dance in Deskford. Burns had given it to him outside so that he could try to get in without paying, pretending he had already been in. Burns was later ejected for making a nuisance. The following morning McKandie woke up with the coat, panicked, and hid the coat in the roof of the loft above the stable. Later that year, Robert Davidson, trapper, Aultmore, was fined 10/- or five days in prison for careless and reckless cycling, when he collided with a car driven by Alexander Ewen, Kirktown, at the Ha'Hillock junction. Davidson was thrown over the bonnet of the car head first and through the windscreen.

Also in 1938, D G Currie, Wester Darbreich, was fined £3:5/- for riding a motor cycle without a licence, Edith Smith, farm servant Upper Braeside, was found guilty of stealing two bicycles in Huntly and was considered for borstal, John Forsyth, farm servant, Squaredoch, was fined 5/- for carrying James Martin, farm servant, Clune on his bicycle, George Ewen, farm servant, Bogrotten, was fined £1:5/- or fourteen days in prison for theft and reset of an electric lamp for a bicycle.

In 1939 John Forsyth, farm servant, Squaredoch, was once again in trouble. This time he was fined 2/6d for breaking the telephone in the telephone box at Lintmill. James Whyte, labourer, Muir of Squaredoch, was fined £1 for assault and breach of the peace against Jessie Inglis, housekeeper, Muir of Squaredoch. Maggie McHattie and Francis Grant, both Bleachfield, were found guilty of stealing ten larch trees worth £1. They were reported by local farmers who feared they would be blamed. Still in 1939, John Mulgrue, farm servant, Whiteknowes, got off with a warning for riding a bicycle while drunk.

In 1940 James Ross, farmer, Kirktown, was fined 10/- for parking his car in the Square, Cullen without lights where it was struck by a bus. George Scott, senior, Upper Blairock, was fined £1 for driving a car without a license. The licence had expired on 31/12/1939 and he had driven on 01/01/1940. In 1941 William Milton, farm servant, Duffushillock, was fined 10/- for stealing an air washer filler cap from a tractor at Greenmoss, Shielburn, because he had lost an identical one from his own tractor. That year there were two more serious offences. John Sutherland, farm servant, Mosside, was jailed for two months for theft of two rings and two watches. He had previously been birched and sent to Approved School and Borstal. A 14-year-old girl from Keith stole £4 from a house in Deskford. In 1942 Robert Reid, Craibstone Cottages, was fined 10/- for assaulting John Packman, also Craibstone Cottages.

During the later 1940s, Mr Bruce, a local farmer, was sentenced to six months in prison for setting fire to an enemy's garage. Around this time five window panes in the school were broken by a boy called Fulton from Kirktown on the day he was leaving the area with his parents. Because he had left the district no action was taken by the police, but the Clerk was to ascertain the father's new address and demand payment for the damage done. In 1945 Seafield Estate banned the collection of gulls' eggs on Lurg Hill and threatened prosecution if the ban was ignored.

Around 1950, in Berryhillock, some boys strung the Cullen policeman's bicycle half way up a telegraph pole. None was apprehended, but the name Dodo Stewart was suggested recently in connection with the prank. The 1950s was also the time of the legendary adventures of two loons from Deskford, involved in stealing the fishing boat "Girl Pat" and sailing it across the Atlantic.

Despite the fact that most of the crime in Deskford, particularly in the last 200 years or so has been of a relatively minor nature, it should not be forgotten that, in the more lawless times previous to this, there were two murders in the C17th and a man was shot dead at a wedding celebration in the C18th.

THE CHURCH AND THE LAW

The Church, particularly after the Reformation, had shared with landowners' power and responsibility for administration of the law. Between 1563 and 1617 Acts were passed making adultery, fornication, Sabbath breaking and drunkenness all illegal. Indeed between 1563 and 1581 those guilty of serious adultery could be put to death.

The main focus of the Church was on sex offences and it largely ignored greed, pride, untruthfulness, self-righteousness and hypocrisy. However it did take action against idle slander, blasphemy, swearing, murder, manslaughter, assault, perjury and the observation of Christmas. It was also strongly opposed to avarice, oppression of the poor, excess, riotous cheer, banqueting, immoderate dancing, whoredom, pagan bonfires, pilgrimages, carol singing, plays, failing to work on Christmas day, excessive drinking, card-playing, gluttony, gorgeous and vain apparel, filthy and bawdy speeches and merrymaking at weddings and burials. Gradually, over the succeeding centuries this initial puritanical attitude was relaxed as indeed was, even more gradually, the power of the Church.

Deskford, as elsewhere, from the C15th, punished able-bodied vagrant poor for their idleness, but from 1535, before the Reformation, it was responsible for its own helpless or impotent poor, victims of age, disease or disability. In 1519 an Act had been passed that sturdy beggars should be arrested and scourged.

The Kirk in Deskford was very strongly opposed to Penny Weddings. In 1724, the Kirk Session was particularly outraged by one such Penny Wedding at which William Mill, Ardoch, was shot and wounded so badly that physicians despaired for his life. The Minister drew up an Act, got the agreement of the Baillie of the Regality of Ogilvie and intimated it a week after the shooting, by which time William Mill was dead. The Session wanted Penny Weddings suppressed and the disorder which frequently accompanied them prevented.

They banned all individuals from holding their weddings in Alehouses or Taverns unless the woman to be married was the daughter or servant of the Alehouse keeper. They also banned "all buying or selling of meat or drinking of ale or other liquor, all piping, violing, promiscuous dancing, excessive drinking, swearing, quarrelling, fighting or such like abuses". Anyone in the parish found guilty would be liable to church censure and fines, and this was endorsed both by the Presbytery of Fordyce and the Baillie of the Regality of Ogilvie. Persons in whose houses such weddings were held were fined £10 Scots and those getting married would forfeit their pledges (guarantees) to the church which would be used by the session to help the Poor.

Also in 1724 some elders reported that the Sabbath was much profaned by people wandering through the fields in crowds. In 1727 the session, believing that "the Lord's day is much profaned by drinking in alehouses after sermon, and even till very late on Sabbath night", decided to prosecute both alehouse keepers and their customers. In 1728 Session was concerned about the drying of clothes and the carrying of peat and water on the Sabbath. The Minister therefore intimated that no such things should be done.

The level of lawbreaking varied. For example, in 1628 the only common offences were swearing and blasphemy. It was decided to try those accused of such offences as fornicators. Community responsibility was emphasised, for example in 1699, when the Minister instructed everyone to bury the corpse of any poor person who died near their house. Failure to do so meant a fine of 20/-. Punishment was taken seriously, and in 1713 the Kirk Officer was instructed to buy 5 ells of harn cloth, and have a tailor make it up as sackcloth to be worn by defaulters during Sunday services. Behaviour in church was often poor. For example, in Grange there was fighting, spitting from the loft on those below (also hitting them with staves), shouting and scolding, all during the Sabbath service.

In 1743 Session declared that if those who had not paid for their seats in the new loft did not do so they would be prosecuted before the Baillie of Regality. The Kirk Officer should also keep the key and only let in those who were fully paid. In 1744 it was reported that "frightful oaths" had been uttered, and the officer was ordered to cite the individuals accused.

In the C17th and C18th the Kirk Session took themselves very seriously as indeed did all the residents within the parish. They operated as the effective civil and criminal law within the parish, except where they had to call upon the Baillie or, later, the Justices of the Peace to enforce their verdicts. They were much exercised over scandalous drinking, noise, behaviour, comments and slander. There were many accusations of petty and vicious slander, always by women, with evidence and counter evidence being recorded in great detail, and often both protagonists being found equally guilty.

In 1760 it was reported that the front seats in the old loft were crowded by "disorderly people who many times made disturbance in the time of Divine worship". The Minister and elders ordered these seats to be given to Walter Stevenson so that he could give them to those he thought fit, in order to improve the quality of singing during services. In 1775 Session was once more becoming concerned by the number of Penny Weddings taking place, those involved being in the main, very poor, and in need of much catechising.

Punishments for many offences were clearly set down. For example the sentence for simple fornication was three appearances in Church, standing at the pillar beside the pulpit, dressed in sackcloth. For a relapse, or second offence it was six appearances, for adultery 26 appearances, and for incest one year, all in addition to the appropriate fines. Soldiers, vagrants and landowners were exempt from church discipline.

As late as 1821, the Kirk Session, considering "the gross profanation of the Lord's day in this place", thought it fit that intimation should be made the following Sabbath day from the pulpit that whoever were found guilty of profaning the Lord's day by walking in crowds throughout the fields or frequenting alehouses should be required to confess their crime and accept punishment. However, by the middle of the C19th not everyone summoned and interrogated gave session the respect, fear or obedience it thought its due. The session's view of law had also widened. For example, in 1839 it sent a petition to the Lords of Treasury, signed by 135 people, against the running of stagecoaches to carry the mail on the Lord's Day, and in 1842 the Minister preached against the threatened operation of the Glasgow and Edinburgh railway on the Lord's Day.

By the early C20th the nature of the Kirk's legal concerns were similar to those today. In 1927 the Church of Scotland General Trustees and the Minister of Deskford took legal action against the Heritor, Seafield Trustees, claiming that the Church, manse and offices, which were the responsibility of the Heritor, were not in a reasonable state of tenantable repair and requested a sum of money in lieu of repairs by the Heritor. The architect for Seafield Trustees approached Rev Park, offering to do the necessary repairs, but Rev Park asked for his proposals in writing and refused to accept any repairs except as in Statute Law.

The General Trustees of the Church of Scotland pressed the Seafield Trustees who then said they were going to go ahead and do the repairs in any case, and went as far as to have materials delivered. The General Trustees pointed out that they had to agree to them before any repairs could be made. Nevertheless the Seafield Trustees started repairs, despite the law requiring agreement. The General Trustees asked the Court to order all materials removed, at which point the Seafield Trustees felt that the General Trustees were playing silly games. The claim by the General Trustees was advertised in the *Banffshire Journal* and they obtained an Interim Interdict against the Seafield Trustees, who then appealed.

The Church obtained detailed inspection reports, after which the Seafield Trustees offered £300 plus judicial expenses. The General Trustees said they would accept £642 plus £40 for grates, hot water piping and a wash-hand-basin. AHL McKinnon, architect, Aberdeen, was asked by the Sheriff to inspect the properties and compare the two proposed sums. Eventually both sides agreed to a sum of £463:11:6d. Thus did ownership of and responsibility for the upkeep of church buildings move from the Heritor to the congregation.

INDIVIDUALS

The Kirk Session Minutes consistently mention individuals punished, their offences and the punishment given. The vast majority referred to various forms of sexual activity and these are discussed elsewhere in this book, but the remainder, some of which are outlined below, comprise a disparate collection. Overall the C17th and C18th seem to have been far more lawless than the C19th and C20th. In these earlier times the church was often responsible for dealing with crime whereas in the later centuries the civil policing system took over.

In the C17th there were two murders in Deskford. In May 1653 Thomas Herd, Deskford, violently murdered Walter Chalmer, also Deskford, "on the Sabbath day at night". He was excommunicated on the following Sabbath, but no record of any other action taken exists. In 1663 he offered his repentance and was ordered to satisfy church discipline. In 1664 he appeared barefoot and in sackcloth before Presbytery, requesting absolution. He was ordered to appear before the Synod in Aberdeen.

In 1668 James Lawrence was murdered in Deskford by George and John Chalmers, who then disappeared from their own houses and fled the parish. All Ministers in the diocese intimated from their pulpits that no one should give refuge to either of the Chalmers. In Deskford itself the Minister abandoned his plans to hold communion till the people deserved it, and also intimated that anyone suspected of being an accessory would not receive communion.

There were two cases of attempted rape or "attempting to force the girl's modesty", in 1744 and 1833. In the earlier of the two the Session seemed more upset by the noise made by the accused, during the time of the Sunday service, than in the poor girl's plight.

A relatively common offence was drinking or being drunk on the Sabbath. In 1728 George Peterkin was charged with causing great offence by being overtaken with drink on the Sabbath, in his own house at Nether Blairock, a little before the ringing of the the third bell as the people were coming to church. He was interrogated and confessed that he had been drinking in James Bremner's house in the Backies, and had stayed there till after sunrise on the Lord's Day. He had been in the company of James Bremner, James Dason in Upper Tillybreedless, Alexander Barker and John Marquis in Nether Tillybreedless, and William Symon, drinking and playing cards.

Since he admitted the offence he was only rebuked, admonished and fined £3 Scots. He promised not to repeat the offence and was dismissed. When the Minister investigated the others they all said that they had stopped drinking and playing cards before midnight and had gone home. Bremner said he could not get rid of Peterkin who slept most of the night after the others had left. They were all rebuked and admonished.

In 1738, James Cameron, who was an elder and serial sneak, informed session that he had heard that some individuals had gathered two Sundays before, in the Alehouse of Walter Syme in Berryhillock, where they had stayed for a considerable time, drinking and carrying out other activities which made much noise and caused great offence. Cameron, together with another elder, John Grant, were asked to investigate and reported that several individuals might be prepared to confess that they had stayed up the entire evening and night of the Lord's Day, but that it would be difficult to prove that they had done anything else of a scandalous nature such as "playing on the fiddle".

The Kirk Session summoned all of those named, Peter Robertson in Ordens, James Keir in Skeith and Walter Syme in Berryhillock and his wife. They also wrote to the Minister of Fordyce, citing John Robertson, servant of the Laird of Glassaugh, who had also been present. John Robertson admitted being there in the evening and drinking four or five bottles of ale, then going to go home, but the night being dark, he returned to Walter Syme's where he stayed till daybreak. He denied that there was any dancing or playing on the fiddle, and all the accused agreed. "In consideration that they had been idly and scandalously employed in drinking on the Sabbath day and spending the whole Sabbath night in that manner, the Session agreed to severely rebuke them".

In September 1762 the Minister had been met, late one Sunday afternoon, in Kirktown, by James Smith, Kirktown, who was bleeding from the head, and who said that John Stables, heckler in Cullen, had struck him on the head with tongs. Noticing that Smith was drunk, the Minister rebuked him, judging that this was a scandal on the Lord's Day.

Two weeks later Stables, when questioned, said he had done it in self-defence after he had told Smith to stop swearing as it was the Sabbath, and that he would not swear if he was in Church, where he should be. Smith had lifted the tongs and attempted to strike him. After interrogating witnesses, Session found Stables not guilty and Smith, not for the first time, guilty of drinking upon the Sabbath day. Ten years previously Smith had caused offence on the Sabbath by cursing, swearing and drunkenness and by throwing a woman violently in the street, in the sight of the Minister, who was exhorting him to behave and trying to dissuade him from his unacceptable behaviour. Smith did not cooperate with the Church, and had to be brought before the Civil Court, where he was fined.

There were many other breaches of the Sabbath. For instance in 1685 Isobel Wans was summoned for spinning on the Sabbath day. She denied it but two witnesses said that they saw the rock in her bosom and the spindle in her hand. Her husband, Alexander Young, was also charged with selling and carrying skulls (small baskets) on the Sabbath. They were ordered to stand at the pillar in the church, and if they did not, the Justice of the Peace would be informed and would deal with them. Also that year three Sabbath breakers were summoned for breaking down the alehousekeeper Walter Milton's door because he would not sell them drink. In the late 1600s the Town Clerk of Cullen was dealt with severely by his Kirk Session for transacting business at Deskford on the Sabbath.

In August 1737 Walter Sinclair, Little Blairock, confessed himself guilty of breach of the Sabbath. He had to stand before the congregation for one Sabbath and was fined 20/- Scots as a penalty. The following month he was absolved after paying in £4 for the Poor. In 1739 Walter Sinclair in Nether Blairock craved that the session would alleviate their former sentence against him in regard that he had yoked his horse on the Sabbath day, not deliberately but merely out of forgetfulness, promising to be more circumspect in the future. This was not agreed by Session as the noise he had made had disturbed some of his neighbours.

In January 1745 George Strachan was interrogated as to his guilt of threshing on the Sabbath. He admitted the offence but claimed the usual excuse, that it was only forgetfulness. He was given a public rebuke and fined 20/-. His wife was rebuked for having borrowed several things on the Sabbath.

One of the regular offences was that involving slander, calumny or false accusation and cursing. Casting spells and scolding were also common. In 1724 Andrew Moir, Nether Blairock, complained that James McAndie and his wife, Margaret Cook, were wishing imprecations and curses to him and his family in the presence of several witnesses, namely Thomas Ogilvie in Cottartown of Airdoch, John Milton and Anne Shepherd, servants to George Peterkin in

Nether Blairock. Andrew Moir asked the Minister to lay this before session, as he was unable to do so through sickness and infirmity. The Minister asked the officer to summon James McAndie and Margaret Cook, but only James McAndie appeared, and he denied that he had ever wished any curse or imprecation on Andrew Moir or his family. Session ordered him to compear at their next meeting and summoned Margaret Cook to do so as well.

One week later both James McAndie and Margaret Cook denied the charges and asked that the witnesses be called and examined. The officer was ordered to do this and when the witnesses appeared they were "solemnly sworn, purged of malice and were separately interrogat". All said they had heard Margaret Cook curse bitterly and with imprecations to Andrew Moir and his family, but did not hear James McAndie do any such thing. James McAndie was then gravely admonished to deal with his wife and stop her carrying out such practices, and to make her attend session when summoned. The Minister was also to meet with her and deal with her conscience. Several months later the Minister reported to Session that he continued to deal with Margaret Cook and that he had some hopes of bringing her to a sense of her sin.

On August 7th 1726 it was reported by some elders that Margaret Strachan and Elspet Imlach in Oathillock had given offence to the neighbourhood by scolding one another and by cursing on the previous Lord's Day. James Davidson, elder, was appointed to make enquiry into this and to report. He did so one week later to the effect that the allegations were groundless. On April 9th 1727 Janet Donald in Cottartown of Ardoch complained that Janet Ogilvie, also there, had called her a thief and a witch. The argument was over the ownership of a sheep. The Session found Janet Ogilvie guilty and ordered that she had to stand before the congregation and also that she had to pay £3 Scots to Session for Poor Relief.

In 1713 Helen Beidie was ordered to stand at the pillar in the kirk for cursing and imprecating Alexander Wood, and praying that he, his house, his wife and all that he had would be burned with fire, as had happened to Lord Banff. In July 1738 John Reid informed session that he heard Alexander Bainzie, Kirk Officer, and his wife give great offence by their frequent cursing, swearing and beating one another. Elders were appointed to look into this. Witnesses were

Alexander Stables and his wife, Jean Taylor, Alexander Barnet, Elizabeth Watt, William Raich and Margaret Innes.

In February 1747, Angus Cormack, servant in the Cross of Ardoch, complained to session that Janet Forbes in Ardoch had imprecated him by taking the Lord's name in vain, praying that God might give him an evil quarter (three months), and that it might begin on Monday next. She also prayed that he might never go off the earth till as many should wonder at him as ever wondered at one going to the gallows. As witnesses he named John Forbes in Cross of Ardoch, George McWilliam there and John Machatie, tailor in the head of the town of Cullen.

The Session considered it extremely serious and had her summoned, though it was pointed out that she was living in George Wright's house in Ramoir, where she had brought forth a child in fornication. It therefore recommended that the Minister and two elders should take the trouble to go to that house and take her judicial confession.

Throughout 1747 Janet Forbes still refused to attend before the Session so they declared her "contumacious to discipline" and referred her to the Baillie of the Regality of Ogilvie, earnestly entreating that he may "interpose his authority in causing her to give obedience to discipline and causing her to pay the penalty according to the law and justice, to be forthcoming for the Poor of the parish". It further appointed Mr Ogilvie, the Kirk Treasurer, to wait upon the Baillie for the outcome of his action.

In 1751 the Session found for John Symon in Tillybridles and against James Raich in Crabston for "calumnicating" him and taking away his good name by claiming John Symon stole his timber. In August 1756 Janet Morrison, spouse to John Donald in Skeith, complained that her character had been injured by a slanderous aspersion made by Margaret Ogilvie, spouse to Alexander Reid in Berryhillock and Barbara Reid their daughter, that she had taken the milk from Margaret Ogilvie's cow (casting spells to make the cow go dry). Barbara Reid had gone to milk the cow and could only "draw her paps". They were found guilty of injuring Janet Morrison's character and instructed to appear next

Lord's Day before the congregation to be rebuked. Margaret Ogilvie was also fined £3 Scots plus half a crown (2/6d) for the poor of the parish.

In April 1760 William Donald, son to John Donald in Swilend, made a complaint that William Wright in Ramore had, the previous March, calumniated William Donald by calling him a thief and stealer of gold and money out of the said William Wright's night chest, and that he would prove the said William Donald to be guilty. Wright denied that he had said this, and several witnesses agreed with him. John Donald said that William Wright had obtained an order to search John Donald's house and only John Donald's house from Tochieneal as Justice of the Peace and Lord Findlater's Baron Baillie. Nothing was found and William Wright was rebuked in front of the session.

In July Alexander Andrew in Carrothead complained about Jannet Clerk, daughter to James Clerk in Ramore for abusing and giving unseemly language by calling his wife a thief and a whore, within the bounds of Alexander Andrew's farm. He also accused her brother, also James Clerk, of attempting to beat John Milton, Andrew's servant, who only escaped by putting the cattle he was in charge of into a field. Clerk met Andrew and cursed him, swore and dammed him to fight, which Andrew did not because it was the Sabbath.

The Session considered it "of a heinous nature of scandal and offence, very unsuitable to the Christian profession, and injurious to the complainer's character". The officer was instructed to summon both Clerks as witnesses. Two weeks later Jannet Clerk admitted her guilt with repentance, and, since she was very young, Session only rebuked her and placed her on caution. James Clerk pled guilty and was to be both publicly rebuked before the congregation, and privately rebuked and required to pay a crown (5/-) to the Poor.

The Kirk was very powerful and almost the entire population of Deskford were members. The Session's judgement was viewed with fear in most cases and eagerly complied with. In 1660, James Cruikshank, Deskford, who had been excommunicated, humbly supplicated the Presbytery to admit him to public repentance, and release him from the fearful sentence of excommunication. In 1667 James Ogilvie was absolved after he "in ane most humble manner did confess all his guiltiness, specially his contumacie", and promised to be a new man. In 1713 the officer was ordered to go to Janet Muet and desire her to repentance the following Sabbath, otherwise he would cause her to be put in the tollbooth of Cullen. She appeared and was repentant.

However, despite the power the Church held, not everyone accepted their judgment. In 1674 the Minister reported James Philp, alleged adulterer, to the Justices of the Peace to try him as he was a Catholic. He had been held prisoner in Cullen but had escaped and was now a soldier in France. In 1715 Agnes Young was banished from the parish, but did not go. Skeith, her master, or Lord Findlater were asked to compel her. In February 1717 John More told the Session that neither Minister, Baile or Justice of the Peace could make him stand at the pillar of repentance, even if they offered to hack off his head. On July 20th 1718 he appeared in the public place of repentance.

Even Lord Deskford felt the power of the church. In February 1650 he appeared in Fordyce Church and publicly acknowledged his grief before the congregation. He declared himself "willing to give all satisfaction, as he should be enjoyned that it was very grievous to him that he had given offence to the Kirk of Christ for being accessory, as he had been, to that unlawful Engagement, and desiring that the Presbytery would represent his willingness to give satisfaction, and his humble desire to be received to the Communion of the Kirk".

Though many of the cases and issues with which Deskford Kirk Session dealt can be put into one of a number of obvious categories, others cannot. The kirk dealt with a very wide range of situations. In 1709 three elders were appointed to attend the Justices of the Peace Court in Cullen to report on idlers and those who disobey church discipline within the parish. Two penny weddings were held in 1761 and two in 1762. In each case the parties forfeited £3 Scots, and in 1764 James White also forfeited his £3 pledge for the same reason.

In 1743 all those who had not paid for their seats in the new loft in the kirk were to be prosecuted before the Baillie of Regality and refused entry to the new loft till they paid. In 1786 the Kirk Session overruled the Minister and determined that several kirk members who had been found guilty by a court of

Justices of the Peace of having cut down and carried off greenwood belonging to the Earl of Findlater should be allowed to take communion. Perhaps the Minister felt he had to take the Earl's side as the Earl paid a large part of his stipend and had the power of patronage in deciding who should be Minister.

In 1774 the Minister was unsure whether Anne Duncan, living in Upper Skeith, should be allowed to take communion, as she had moved away from her husband and lived separately from him. The Session advised that she should be allowed to take Communion since "by living separately from her husband she was exposed to less sin than when living with him, being they could never agree".

In 1765 Anne Keir in Smithyhillock reported to the Minister that her son, Andrew Shepherd in Bogs of Ordens, had the previous Sunday been hit by a stone thrown by James Duffus, a farm servant in Ordens. The Minister considered it a scandal since it had taken place on the Lord's Day and instructed the officer to summon James Duffus. He did not appear, but his father did, apologising for his son and saying that the stone had been thrown accidentally and not deliberately. Session did not accept this and ordered the son to appear in person, which he did a week later, saying that if he had seen Andrew Shepherd he would not have thrown the stone. Andrew Shepherd agreed that it had not been done intentionally, and both were dismissed under caution.

In 1796 there was a complaint by James Longmore and Janet Wright in Ramore against William Morrison from Grange for defacing an inscription on a gravestone in the graveyard at Deskford which bore the name Allardyce, and inscribing on the stone the name of his daughter who was buried under it. At this time the Deskford graveyard was only one-third the size it is today, and somewhat congested.

William Morrison handed in a letter from his brother-in-law, Thomas Allardyce in the parish of Alvah, stating that his ancestors had lived in Deskford, that some of them were interred under the stone in question, and that he, as their representative, had authorised William Morrison to bury his daughter there and inscribe her name on the stone, since she was his, Thomas Allardyce's niece. Session did not consider themselves competent to judge the case, and suggested that the opposing parties should compromise in the matter.

Involvement in law continued into the C20th. In 1917 there was a dispute between Mr Russel and the Free Church Deacons' Court over arrangements in regard to a rented house. Mr Macnaughton, solicitor, Buckie, was consulted. Mr Russel was given statutory notice to quit the house at Whitsunday 1917, but refused, determined to "defend his rights". The Deacons' Court let the house to Miss Clark, Backies, and reiterated to Mr Russel that he should quit. Mr Macnaughton suggested that they should apply to the Sheriff for a Warrant of Eviction, at which point Mr Russel left and Miss Clark got entry. The coal house, mantlepiece, window, press etc were valued at £1:19:6d which was paid to Mr Russel. He refused to accept this and they were revalued, including the range, at £5:1:6d, which he accepted.

FINANCE AND ECONOMY

To those struggling with personal finances today it is probably of little comfort to be told that in past times there were often greater financial difficulties for individuals at all levels of society.

Scotland was always a poor country and only established its own currency in the C12th. Prior to that even Pictish silver jewellery was made from melted down English and Frisian coins, or in even earlier times from Roman hack silver. In the C12th the economy was still a subsistence one, and barter was widely used. Though Scotland shared in the general European economic growth of the C13th, it also shared in the European recession leading up to 1400. For example Banff was a significant trading port, but not a single trading ship visited it for several years before 1389.

When Scotland established its own currency it was used across the country. Two bodles equalled one plack while three bodles equalled one bawbee and two bawbees equalled one shilling. As an example of our relative poverty, a bodle was worth one sixth of an English halfpenny. One merk was worth 160 sterlings (silver pennies) in the C13th and was also worth two thirds of £1 Scots. In mediaeval times £1 Scots had been equal to £1 sterling, but over the years it gradually became more and more devalued, till by the C18th £1 sterling was worth £12 Scots. Another example of this devaluation is the increase in the number of pennies produced from 1 lb of silver. In 1393 this was 353, but by 1483 it was 1680. In 1314 a cow was worth 160 sterlings and an ox 80.

Between 1500 and 1700 one third of the crop in areas like Deskford went for rent, one third for seed corn and one third for food, which meant that teinds (tithes) to the Church and thirlage to the mill had to be found from the animals which each farmer also kept. In addition to this, unpaid labour had to be given to the landowner. From a relatively early time in Deskford income could be augmented by obtaining licences to quarry limestone on Lurg Hill (from about 1600), to quarry "slate" from Darbreich, Burn of Aultmore or Shielmuir, and to cast peats from Aultmore. In 1719 Cullen Town Council paid £2:6:8d for 1000 slates from Darbreich.

In the C13th there had been large increases in rents, but after 1350, recession due to the Black Death caused rents to fall. Tenants did well with falling rents at the same time as they were getting higher prices. However by the late C16th there was much unemployment and vagrancy. Prices for grain and clothing and also rents were virtually unchanged between 1640 and 1740, but after that there were steep increases. Rents rose steadily, but then doubled between 1783 and 1793, and doubled again between 1794 and 1815. Despite this, new capitalist improving farmers profited from rapidly increasing prices and from the labour surplus caused by landless former crofters and cottars and by veterans returning from the Napoleonic Wars. This was a relatively new phenomenon.

WAGES

In 1790 Rev Chalmers stated that in Deskford wages "had increased, were increasing, and in the opinion of the farmer ought to be diminished". A capable ploughman was paid between £6 and £7 per year and an inferior farm servant £5, while a female servant got about £2:2/-. Rev Chalmers did not approve of how all this money was spent. "These gains are not now, as formerly, laid up for future support and provision, but generally expended upon dress, the desire of which has gained great prevalence within these few years". The lower levels of society at this time in Deskford were relatively well off because of earnings connected with the Bleachfield.

Day wages were 1/- per day without victuals for carting peats and 10d for a man and 6d for a woman per day, with victuals for harvest work. Day rates were 6d per day for a labourer, 1/2d for a mason, 8d for a common wright and 6d for a tailor, all with victuals. Between 1748 and 1798 a ploughman's wage had increased seven times, and it more than doubled between 1794 and 1810.

Farm servants' earnings did not rise significantly during the C19th and many were relatively worse off at the end of the century than their grandfathers would have been at the start of it. In 1886 Willie McWillie hired servants at the Hallow Fair, Fordyce, for six months, for both Backies and Langlanburn. For Backies he hired Alex Smith, foreman at £11:10/-, Wm Legg, second horseman at £9 and Mr Forsyth, cattleman, at £9:10/-. For Langlanburn he hired James Taylor, foreman, at £11, Mr Duncan, second horseman, at £10:10/- and Joseph Mason, loon, at £4:10/-. By 1935 farm workers were paid £1 per week plus perquisites of tatties, meal, milk and a cottage. In 1935 the Rural Workers' Society had paid sick benefits to 51 male claimants (£224) and 23 female claimants (£62), in Banffshire. After World War II farm workers were on an hourly wage plus overtime.

PRICES

Between 1760 and 1790 prices increased significantly, that for a hen from 4d to 6d or 8d, beef and mutton from 2½d to 3½d per pound and haddock from 2d per dozen to 8d or 1/- per dozen. Butter was 6d to 8d per lb of 24oz and cheese was 4/- or 5/- per stone. In 1794 produce would be sold at one or more of the weekly markets at Banff, Cullen, Portsoy, Keith or Fochabers.

The war with France greatly increased meal prices, from 8/6d per boll in 1758 to £1:1/- per boll in 1795. Prices for other farm produce also increased between 1748 and 1798; a draught ox from £1:13:4d to £20; 20 sheep from £4 to £12; 1lb of beef or mutton from 2d to 6d; a dozen eggs from 1d to 5d; a pair of geese from 2/- to 5/6d; a pair of turkeys from 3/- to 7/- and 14 haddocks from 1½d to 1/6d. A bottle of claret, not consumed widely in Deskford, increased from 1/- to 6/-

In 1860 Scottish wages were 60% of English ones, by 1910 it was 90% and by 1980 they were equal. Now Scottish average wages are slightly higher than English ones. In 1885 farmers obtained the lowest prices ever known for both barley and beef, because of competition from the USA, Argentina, Australia and New Zealand. Many local farmers faced extreme difficulties. As a result many landlords in the North East gave rent reductions, in the case of Seafield Estate 10% against the more common 15% to 25% by other large estates.

By 1850 eggs cost 5d or 6d per dozen and butter 8d or 9d per lb. In Deskford a good-sized fowl cost 7d or 8d, and although beef and mutton were not cheap a large price reduction could be obtained by buying some when a farmer "killed himself". Farmers could sometimes do well when selling prize cattle. In July 1899 Mr W Stewart, Nether Blairock, sold the Aberdeen Angus bull Prism of Preston to Mr Ralston, for Lord Strathmore's herd for 100 guineas (£105).

Such good fortune was not always the case as can be seen from the advert in the Aberdeen Journal of 03/07/1786, which states:-" NOTICE. To the Creditors of Andrew Johnston, late in Inaltrie, and Roup of his Subjects. The said Andrew Johnston, having lately deserted his possession of Inaltrie, and gone abroad, has returned a trust deed and deposition to certain trustees therein named, making over the whole of his subjects for the behoof of his creditors. The whole creditors of the said Andrew Johnston are hereby required to meet, at the house of Andrew Ogilvie, vintner in Cullen, upon Monday the 10th of July curt. By ten of the clock in the forenoon of the said day, when the said trust deed will be laid before them. It will be proper that the creditors bring with them their respective grounds of debt, that the extent of the whole debt standing against Mr Johnston may be known. There is to be exposed to sale by public roup at Inaltrie, in the parish of Deskford, near Cullen, upon Thursday the 13th day of July curt. The whole STOCKING of the said farm of Inaltrie, consisting of five large sized work horses, a mare and foal, one one year old and one two year old colts, four cows and calves and nine young cattle of different ages, with variety of labouring utensils. The whole HOUSEHOLD FURNITURE; consisting of beds, tables, chairs, bed and table linen and Feather Beds will be exposed to sale at the same time".Much later, in 1932, Robert Henderson, Oathillock, was sequestered with total debt of £475:14:3d. The amount recovered was £100, of which legal fees took £83:16:10d, leaving only £17:3:2d for creditors.

Being in debt was common for all classes of society over the centuries, but circumstances could change rapidly. For example in the late C17th the Earl of Findlater owed £400 to the Deskford Kirk Session as well as many thousands to other creditors. Twenty years later his son, by a variety of means, had turned things completely round and was buying up the debts of the Lawties of Tochieneal, which allowed him to force the buyout of the ownership of Inaltrie from the Lawties. At this time it was very common to buy up the debts of third parties.

Most landowners' wealth was in kind in the C15th and C16th, but the Ogilvies did possess money which allowed them to build the Tower of Deskford. In the early C18th there were no banks locally so Kirk Sessions, including that of Deskford, lent money as bonds to parishioners and others in time of difficulty, at moderate rates of interest.

Financial transactions involving Deskford residents are recorded as early as the C16th, and occurred very frequently. They were of a variety of different types. For example, in 1587 there was an obligation by Archibald Gillanne in Cullenne to pay duties on bere received from Walter Ogilvie in Ardaycht. That same year there was a requisition by John Innes of Edingeycht to William Abercrummy of Overskeycht to pay victual due to the said Innes. In the Executry Accounts of Alexander Innes of Pethnik in 1630 there is included "100 merks to Thomas Abercromby of Skeith, being the balance of 200 merks due as tocher (dowry) of Grizel Innes". In 1688 there was a deposition by Sir James Abercromby of Birkenbog to George Abercromby of Skeith of an apprysing of said lands, of Nether Skeith, mill thereof, Broadrashes, Berryhillock, mill thereof, Burnhead, Carrothead, Harder (near Lower Broadrashes), called new and old wards of Broadrashes, the four oxgates of land in Little Skeith, which apprysing may properly be found among the wadsets or debts.

From 1800, with the rapid development of the capitalist style of improved farming, financial transactions became increasingly sophisticated. The Cullen Savings Bank was established in 1816, and the 464 depositors included tenants and crofters from Deskford. No depositor could deposit more than £20. In 1840 the Kirk in Deskford collected £2 annually for each of Aberdeen Infirmary and a Pauper Lunatic Fund. Annual collections for the poor of the parish totalled £20, and there was also £10:12:2d interest on money left or donated by individuals. Lime of a "very superior fineness and strength" was being sold from Craibstone. By the 1880s farmers were getting regular visits from insurance agents. In 1888 a Berryhillock merchant held a roup before emigrating to the USA. At this time a paraffin stove cost 3/- and a good man's suit of black coat and vest, and striped trousers cost £2:17/-. In 1887 the Women's Jubilee Collection, to celebrate the Golden Jubilee of Queen Victoria, raised £3:1:8d in 229 separate donations of between 1d and 1/-

The Deskford Mutual Improvement Society (Association) existed intermittently through the C19th when it held lectures and debates on the great issues of the day. It kept detailed accounts. In 1856/57 income was £27:4:11d, mainly from soirees and from attendance at lectures. Expenditure was £24:6:2d on books, ledgers, tea, sugar, bread and candles, a bookcase, corn and straw, boiling water, erecting a platform, lecturers' expenses and printing of a catalogue and of soiree tickets.

In 1883 income came from entry money, fees for non-attendance and subscriptions for social evenings. Expenditure was on printing, fire and light, cleaning the School Board Room, tea, sugar, bread, ginger ale, postage and stationery, making tea, advertising meetings in the Banffshire Journal and arranging the school. In 1887 expenditure included additionally 1/- for advertising at the Church door, 4½d for blackening for the grate, 6d for a lampglass, 3/6d for an indiarubber stamp for the library, 10/- for hire of the piano, 6/- for the hire of singers and 8d for a gallon of paraffin.

Into the C20th financial activity became much more varied. In 1930 the poppy collection raised £4:19/-, whilst by 1935 it only raised £2:18:10d. By 1940 it was up to £5 and from 1945 to 1952 was always above £8. By 1958 it had fallen to £6:8/-

In December 1933 a house-to-house collection for Aberdeen Infirmary and the Chalmers Hospital, Banff raised £12. On 02/10/1935, Mr Charles Cruikshank, Cottartown, purchased "Broomlea", Cullen for £1,080, and in 1938 George Sutherland, retiring from Bloomfield, bought Kinbate House, Kirktown, the former Schoolmasters' house. In 1940 a collection for the SSPCA raised £2:12:7d and in December of that year the hospitals' collection raised £18:4:9d

In 1920 the school charged 10/- for the hire of the piano for a concert and £1 for a concert and dance. A savings machine was purchased for the school at a cost of £7:16/-. In 1960 the Deskford Public Hall Committee applied to the Carnegie United Kingdom Trust for a grant to cover the cost of 80 stacking chairs @ £160, a Rayburn No1 Cooker @ £50 and a portable electric fan heater @ £12. The grant application was successful. In 1940 the school cleaners' salaries were increased from £26 to £32 per annum, because, with the arrival of the Portobello evacuees, six rooms were always used and were required to be cleaned. The difference was to be reclaimed from Edinburgh as that was where the refugees were from.

LOCAL GOVERNMENT FINANCE

The "Deskford Trust" for the poor of the parish, administered by Moray Council and paid over to the Minister of Deskford for distribution, was only terminated in 2013. The total funds in 2011/2012 were £106 and the interest available for distribution was £9.

Local government assumed a far greater importance during the C19th, and of course it had to be paid for. In 1901 the Parish Council raised £209 from owners of properties and the same from occupiers. This was raised through the Poor Rate @7d in the £, the Education rate @5d in the £ and the Registration rate @¼d in the £. It also received from the government a rate grant of £100. County Assessments also had to be raised. In 1879/1880 the Police Rate was 1¼d in the £, the Roll of Voters Rate ¼d in the £, the Cattle Diseases Rate ½d in the £. In addition to these the Roads and Bridges Rate was 6d in the £ and the Turnpike Road Debt Rate was ¾d in the £, but was paid by proprietors only.

Throughout the C16th, C17th, C18th and C19th and into the C20th money was raised to pay for the Poor, first by the Kirk, then, after 1845, by the Parochial Board, and after 1894, by the Parish Council. What had started as a very simple system gradually became more complex and more sophisticated. In November 1898 the Parish Council passed for payment the following:-

Alexander Taylor, Moss Grieve,	£1:16:6d
Alexander Morrison, for clothing,	£3:15:1d
Mr Seivwright, for stationery,	15/1d
William Ogilvie, tailor, for clothing,	£1:17:8d
William Gray, shoemaker,	£2:19:8d
Robert Cruikshank, for casting peat,	£1:16:9d
Mr Reid, for rent of Widow Thom's house,	£1:5/-
Mr Sim, Cullen,	5/-

All of this was distributed to the Poor as follows. Many of the recipients lived outwith Deskford, but were its responsibility as they had been born here.

Widow Fraser, Grange,	2 chemises
Jessie Russell, Rathven,	6yds flannel, 1 petticoat
Alex Russell, Rathven,	6yds flannel, 1 pair of drawers
Ann H Duncan, Huntly,	3 yds flannelette, 3 cuts worsted, 3 pinafores, and cloth for a dress and a cap
Robert Wood, Milltown,	2 shirts, 2 pairs of drawers
Hellen Munro, Greens,	1 pair of carpet shoes
Isabella Longmore,	2 aprons, 2 flannels, 1 pair Stockings
William Jamieson, Tod's Cottage,	1 pair drawers, braces, 1 pair Leather slippers, 1 shirt, and 6 cuts worsted

On 21/07/1904 expenditure and income for the current year were estimated.

<u>Expenditure</u>

Poor in the Parish	£66:6/-
Poor out of the parish	£80
Clothing, boots etc,	£14:5/-
Rents and Fuel	£18:10:9d
Lunatics boarded in Asylum	£80:1/-
Lunatics boarded in private dwellings	£27:2/-
Inspector's salary	£15

Collector's salary	£9
Printing, postage, advertising and interest	£5:14/-
Preparation of Auditor's fee	£3:13/-
Medical Officer's salary	£15:3/-
Cost of Poor from other parishes	£55
TOTAL	£389:16;9d

Income

Grant in respect of Pauper Lunatics	£42:9:4d
Grant in Respect of Medical Relief	£4:16/-
Grant in respect of Rates	£7:8:9d
Repayment by relatives	£4
Repayment by other Parishes	£55
Mortifications etc	£1:19:10d
TOTAL	£115:13:11d

The difference between income and expenditure had to be made up from the Poor Rate paid by local residents and landlords. In the early C20th the Parish Council was more professional in its approach and planned and organised its finances meticulously, whilst retaining Deskford's long-lasting reputation for dealing sympathetically and caringly with those in need.

In 1916 there was a request from the County Clerk urging Deskford Parish Council to set up a War Savings Association. This was rejected because many farm servants had already invested their money in Exchequer Bonds, and few in the area were paid weekly or monthly. However they requested leaflets to be sent to every farm, and, if there was interest, an Association would be formed.

Estimated expenditure by the Parish Council in 1923;-

Aliment for Ordinary Poor	£100
Additional Aliment for Ordinary Poor	£15
Medical Charges	£20
Mental Defectives (half cost)	£12
Lunatic Poor (half cost)	£80
Removals, Certificates of Lunacy etc	£5
Inspector's Dept	£25

Collector's Dept		£20
Auditor's fee and Audit expenses		£6
Law charges		£5
Bank Interest		£1
Other Parish Poor		£39
	TOTAL	£328

Grants for 1923:-

Lunatic Poor		£18:17:3d
Mental Defectives		£13:19:2d
Medical Relief		£2:11:7d
Relief of Rates		£6:13:4d
Mortifications		£3:12:11d
Rents		£4:15/-
Repayments by other Parishes		£39
	TOTAL	£89:1:3d

Therefore £238:18:9d had to be made up from the Rates, which were paid by property owners at 8d in the £ and by occupiers at 9½d in the £.

From owners		£123:17:4d
From occupiers		£66:1:6d
Agricultural Rates Grant		£53:13:10d
	TOTAL	£243:18:10d

In January 1925 Alexander Findlay, tailor, Kirktown was paid £7:4:10d for clothing for Paupers and in March that year James A Muiry was paid £1:10/- for the hire of a car to Gartly. John Gordon, carpenter, was paid £1:4:6d for repairs to Muir of Squaredoch and George Findlay, chemist, Cullen, was paid 2/3d for medicines.

There were a number of different issues to be addressed. In 1887, Alexander Morrison, Kirktown, was appointed Sexton by the Parochial Board. He would be paid £3 per year plus fees for grave digging, however the Board would supply a grass mower. Strangely, paupers were often assessed to pay the Poor Rate, but usually won on appeal.

Deskford had very high illegitimacy rates and in 1903 the Superintendant stated that "In the long experience of the Board it has proved to be detrimental to grant any but Indoor Relief to women with illegitimate children. When Indoor Relief has been strictly adhered to, applications from this class have ceased and in many parishes it is claimed that illegitimacy has been greatly reduced". In 1903 the Poor Roll included 18 Ordinary Poor and 6 Lunatic Poor. Half of the 18 lived outwith the parish.

By 1929 the Parish Council was having difficulty finding tenants for the Poors Houses at Muir of Squaredoch, but one was rented to Mr Peter Christie, Engine Driver, at £1:10/- per year. In 1930 another was rented to Mr Peter Flaws, labourer, also at £1:10/- per year. By this stage the Parish Council was very near its end, with its responsibilities for finance about to be transferred to Banffshire County Council and central government. Though this had obvious advantages in terms of equity across the country, it also broke the rule of individual parishes having responsibility for all who lived in them, and also further reduced the feeling of community identity.

CHURCH AND FINANCE

In today's circumstances it is difficult to comprehend how important and significant were the Church's finances in the past. The breadth of responsibilities undertaken and the sums involved were enormous, though as time progressed from the C18th through to the C19th the focus changed from local and regional concerns to national and international ones.

In 1630 the charge for burial within the kirkyard in Deskford was 10 merks for those over 7 years old, 40/- Scots for those between 4 and 7 and 20/- for "bairnes" under 4. In 1675 Robert Sharp, Sheriff Clerk of Bamfe, and brother of the murdered Archbishop Sharp of St Andrews, married the heiress of Ordens, and in 1676 he mortified to the Minister of Deskford and his successors 500 merks to help with their maintenance. That same year Thomas Ogilvie of Ardoch left money to buy a "great Bible" for the use of the Church and a "basin of tin" to serve at Communion. In 1678 Alexander Abercrombie of

Berriehillock, "now possessor of Ardoch" had taken over a bond or loan of 100 merks from Robert Ogilvie who had died. In 1685 Jhon Lawrence, smith, was paid 50/- for making 500 Communion tokens. In 1701 James Simpson was given a bond of £100, which he would have to pay back immediately if he was found in any "scandalous place". In 1709 32/- was collected for about 60 persons who had had their houses destroyed by fire in the Cowgate in Edinburgh.

Perhaps a more detailed look at the Church finances from the year 1720 would be informative. On June 13th 1720 the Session Clerk and Treasurer opened the wooden box in which coinage, loan agreements and other financial documents were kept, and the contents were inspected. They found that £18:9/- Scots had been collected since August 10th 1719, which when added to the £51:2/- in the box made £69:11/-. Since then there had been paid £14:4:2d to the Poor, £6 each to the Session Clerk and Kirk Officer and £40 had been loaned to John Dougall, which totalled £66:6:2d, leaving £3:5:10d which was put back in the box.

They then inspected the bills and bonds lying in the box which were:-

No.	DESCRIPTION	DATE	£	s	d
1	A bill from William Ord, merchant in Craighead	21/10/1718	200 merks		
2	A bond to Walter and Alexander Taylor	21/12/1709	33	6	8
3	A bond to John Reid in Raemoir	30/06/1707	7	10	0
4	A bond to Alexander Abercrombie of Skeith	31/07/1718	53	6	8
5	A bond to William Tailor in Crabstoun, of which all but 2 merks had now been repaid	13/08/1705	25 merks		
6	A bond to Alexander Anderson, Milntown of Noth	15/12/1707	33	6	8
7	A bond to Alexander Anderson, Milntown of Noth	17/12/1709	133	6	8

In addition the Minister acquainted the Session that there was a bond granted by James, Lord Deskford to Rev Murray, late Minister, and his successors in office, for 635 merks, 500 merks of which comprised Sharp's Mortification. The bond was dated November 11th 1717 at Cullen House, and he had now in his possession repayment from Mrs Murray. (This was the mirror image of the situation in 1680 when the then Earl of Findlater took a bond for £400 Scots from the Deskford Kirk Session). The Minister also informed the Session that he had spoken to the Earl of Findlater about the two bonds granted by the deceased Alexander Anderson of Crabstoun, and that the Earl was willing to give his own bond in their place.

In January and May 1721 the Session made a number of occasional disbursements :-

No.	DESCRIPTION	£	s	d
1	To a wright for a bar to the Kirk door		1	9
2	To a smith for work about the Kirk		6	0
3	For 5 bolls of lime to repair part of the kirkyard dyke	1	0	0
4	To John Man		4	0
5	To James Ogilvie, mason, as part of his wages for repairing the kirkyard	1	10	0
6	For charges in obtaining decreet (a legal decision) against Wm Ord in Craighead, who owed the Session 200 merks	3	13	0
7	To Margaret Grant		4	0
8	To Walter (Gatling??)	6	9	0
9	For the bridge at Annachy		18	0
10	To Henderson, a sup. (supplicant)		6	0
11	A sup.		6	0
	TOTAL:	13	10	10

On February 26th 1721 it was intimated that a collection would be held for some Inverness men held in slavery by Barbary pirates. On March 26th £4:13:10d was collected. The Session was then informed that the Inverness men had been set free without any ransom having been paid, so decided to keep the money.

On August 6th 1721 Alexander Abercrombie late of Skeith, had paid back to the Minister the £60 he owed to the Kirk, perhaps from the money he made from selling Skeith to the Earl of Findlater. On May 20th 1721 it was announced that a collection would be taken the following week towards building a Church in the parish of Durness. £3 was duly collected but the Session felt this was too little so added £2 to it. In January 1723 the Minister received from Lord Deskford £70:12:6d as proportionally their share as creditors of William Ord in Craighead. Session empowered the Minister to do the same with any others who owed them money.

In February 1723 the following financial transactions were recorded:-

1. Paid to James Reid, for making a coffin for a poor man, 12/-
2. Received for use of the mortcloth, £1:10/-
3. Received for the sale of a tree in the kirkyard to George Smith, £1:16/-
4. Paid for ropes for interring corpses, 6/-

And in 1724:-
1. Paid for mending the back leg of the bell, 4/-
2. Paid for iron, wood and workmanship for stocking the bell, and to the Officer for attendance, £6:14:8d
3. Paid for 9 clasps for the Kirk gate, 9/-

In 1726 there was a dispute. Alexander Wood, the previous Kirk Officer, had bought a hand bell at his own expense which he hired out for 3/- at funerals. It was considered unreasonable that any private person should be allowed any benefit arising out of the hiring out of a hand bell, which "rather ought to be a publick good and redound to the benefit of the Poor". Wood had not left the bell to the Kirk Session on his death, as had been expected, so they decided to buy a new one to be hired out for the benefit of the Poor. The Minister would approach Wood's executors to see if they would sell him the bell, and if not he was authorised to buy a new one quickly.

On January 9th 1726 William Taylor and Janet Shepherd in Squaredoch repaid the principal owed by them to Session and begged exemption from the interest. Session accepted 2 merks from Taylor and £10 Scots from Shepherd and agreed to forego the interest because of their poverty. In March 1726 there was a collection on behalf of some distressed Protestants in Heidelberg, and in July the same year £2:10/- was collected for building a bridge "upon the River Dee at Ballader". In November the Kirk lent Lord Deskford £200.

In March 1727 a collection was taken for two fishermen's wives in Broadhythe of Findochtie, and their children, in straitened circumstances. £4 was collected, £2 to be given to each by the Minister when they called for it. In June £2:14/- was collected for Banff harbour, and in December collections were held for two men in different parishes whose houses had burned down. In 1731 the Kirk in Deskford was owed £200 Scots by the new Earl of Findlater and also £200 by the recently deceased one. In June 1734 £20 each was given as loans to Walter Sinclair in Little Blairock, and to William Murray in Mousehillock, both payable with interest in one year's time. In August £1:12/- was paid to James Reid for a coffin for Margaret Bruce, a poor woman.

A similar pattern continued throughout the rest of the century. For example in 1735 Session gave:-

1. To a poor man, 1d
2. For 5 ells of harden to be sackcloth, 10/8d
3. For the hand bell from a collection, 17/10d
4. To Alexander Bainzie, Kirk Officer, a full year's fee, £4
5. To paint the new loft, £2

On August 1st 1737 the Minister and Session again inspected what was in the box. There was £35:4/- Scots in good money, and the Minister declared that he had given out two loans, one of £88:16/-, and the other a guinea, both bearing interest. Robert Garioch in Ardoch owed £20 from Whitsunday last and Walter Sinclair in Little Blairock owed £20 plus £3 interest, due at June 1st last. James Reid in Croftgloy's loan of £6 plus 1/- interest was due to be repaid the previous year. The Earl of Findlater owed the Session £400, but had paid the interest.

The total of all money due to the Session plus what was in the box came to £586:4/- Scots. In addition there was a penalty due by Mr Gordon of Crabstoun for a relapse in fornication and a penalty for Elizabeth Spence. There were also loans due for repayment by John, Bedeman in Cullen, and by Walter Bremner, Berryhillock, but seeing both were desperately poor, the Session agreed not to seek repayment, but instead to cancel them. The box also contained bad money in both silver and copper with a face value of £21:5/-. Much of the copper was in the form of bodles, a small coin worth one sixth of a penny. Session agreed to sell off all the bad money in the box, 3lb 7oz of silver and 7lb

8oz of copper, and accepted a price of 8/- a pound for the silver and 5/- a pound for the copper.

In 1738 Session's transactions included:-
1. For a glass window for the schoolhouse, 16/-
2. For the schooling of Mr Walker's daughter, one quarter, 8/-
3. Collected for seat rent in the new loft, £6:4:6d

In 1739 the Poor money included:-
1. Loans to the Earl of Findlater and his father, £400
2. Accounted for by the Minister £101:8/-
3. Loan to Walter Sinclair in Blairock, £20
4. Loan to Robert Garioch in Ardoch, £20
5. Joint loan to John Gordon and John Ruddach, merchants, £20
6. Loan to James Reid in Croftgloy, £6
7. Loan to Mrs Abercromby in Skeith, £12:12/-
8. Loan to James Murray in Tillybreadless, £4:16/-
9. Money in the box, £68:3:10d

In 1741 Session paid:-
1. To Walter Robertson in Ordens for making a coffin to a poor stranger woman, £1:4:6d
2. To George Sinclair in Burns for making a coffin to Walter Imla's son, £1:10/-

In 1744 a collection to help build a place of public worship in Portsoy raised £2:11:2d, and in 1746 five trees in the kirkyard were sold by public roup. The tree nearest the school was bought by Walter Reid in Squaredoch for 14/-, the one next to that by Walter Syme, alehouse keeper in Berryhillock for 13/-, the third and fourth by the Minister of Ordiquhill for £3 and the final one by George Wright in Burnheads for £1:7:6d.

Money began to be collected for purposes such as Aberdeen infirmary and the Pauper Lunatic Fund, but most was still for purposes within the parish. In 1750 17/- was given to scholars within the Stocking School established by the Earl of Findlater, and which trained locals in a skill which was relatively well paid. In

1755 the Minister had loaned 300 merks of the Poor's money to the Laird of Buckie at 15 merks interest, about which the Session was "weel pleased". In 1757 3/- was received for the use of the hand bell at George Ogilvie's funeral. In 1758 £1:10/- was paid to William Murray for nails and workmanship in repairing the old loft and in 1759 £2:8/- was paid for a coffin for a poor woman who had died at Leitchestown.

In 1765 Session received interest of £50 Scots on the Earl of Findlater's loan which now stood at £1,000. They also received £12:12/- as Mr Russel and his wife's penalty for their irregular marriage and antenuptial fornication.

In 1776 seat rents for the new or west loft were 4d each for William Murray, Alexander Copland, Andrew Reid, William Simpson, John Hay, Alexander Milne, George Reid, Donald McBain, Alexander Barnet, William Milltown, William Lawrence, James Reid, another William Lawrence and William Grant. George Milne alone paid only 2d.

In 1777 the Session paid:-
1. To mending the school door, 2/-
2. To a poor man in Glenlivet, 10/-
3. To John Smith, sick, for 12 days attendance by a woman, £3
4. To a Minister's daughter, in poverty, £1:10/-
5. To the Kirk Officer's shoes, £1:16/-
6. To William Duncan for teaching Church music, £3

Throughout most of the C17th and C18th, weekly collections averaged less than £1 Scots, but towards the end of the C18th there was some lack of clarity as the £ sterling gradually replaced the £ Scots. Sometimes one currency was used, sometimes the other and sometimes a mix. To add to the confusion merks (£ ⅔ Scots) were also still used.

In the second half of the C19th Church finances settled into a pattern which remained recognisable, with minor amendments, throughout the C20th. For example in 1859 Deskford Church donated £2 to the Educational Scheme, £2 to the India Mission, £1:14/- to the Home Mission, £1:10/- to the Colonial

Mission, £1:10/- to the Jewish Mission, £1:0:5d to the Endowment Scheme, 10/- to combat Popery and 10/- to finance. By 1881 money was additionally being donated to support Small Livings (Ministers who had a very small stipend), Patronage Compensation and the Aged Ministers' Fund. By 1910 the pattern was very similar, though the amounts had increased by on average 60%. Donations were also given to the Highlands and Islands Scheme, Christian Life and Work, Church Interests and Social Work. That year St John's had £15 in the bank, £12:4:5d in hand, £29 from weekly collections and £1:9:10d from bank interest, totalling £58:12:3d. Expenditure was £32:3:1d, leaving £26:9:2d to be carried forward.

In 1915 a special collection was made to provide a Christmas present for soldiers at the Front and at home. The two Churches in Deskford cooperated on this. By 1930 donations were being made to the same good causes as had been the case the previous century, plus additionally to Christian Instruction of Youth, Reformed Churches, The Temperance Committee and Psalmody and Hymns. The Organist's salary was £18, the Church Officer's £9 and the Organ Blower's £2:5/-. Assembly, Synod and Presbytery expenses were £5:2:4d, and £5:13:6½d was spent on such items as tuning the organ, 55 prizes, coal, light and insurance etc.

Finances were broken down in detail in 1932:-

Income
1. Rent on West Church houses, £12
2. Grazing on the glebe, £13:13:10d
3. Ordinary collections, £55:1:8d
4. Special collections, £35:11:11d

Expenditure
1. Church Schemes (mentioned above), £40
2. Salaries, £46:7/-
3. Insurance, £5:14:6d
4. Fire and Light, £3:7:6d
5. Presbytery and Assembly expenses, £5:6/-
6. Printing and Postage, £4:7:11d

7. Taxes and Assessments, £14:5:5/-
8. Communion elements, £2:18/-
9. Repairs, £2;12/-
10. Tuning the organ, £1:6:3d

In a plea which was repeated throughout the 1930s the Minister stated that more money was required and that regular giving was needed instead of the current haphazard system, as the Church had regular commitments such as wages and repairs. In January 1943 the system of Free Will Offerings began, using weekly envelopes which encouraged members to give money each week, whether or not they attended Church. In 1940 the increase in Sunday School collections was attributed to the evacuees from Portobello.

Money was often given to the Church for different charitable purposes, but was not always safe. In 1896 Mr Proctor's £50 had been lodged with the Oriental Bank which went into liquidation. Only £21:17:6d had been recovered, which was deposited in the North of Scotland Bank, (later the Clydesdale), in Cullen. In February 1929 £300 was received from the executors of the late George Duncan, elder, Old Schoolhouse, Kirktown, to be invested and known as the "George Duncan Trust". The interest was to be used for any purpose the Kirk Session resolved, but only for such purposes as were within the jurisdiction and for the best interests of the Church and congregation. He additionally left £100, the interest from which was to be used to help any deserving parent in the education of their children. Andrew Milton, a retired policeman in the USA, donated £500 to the parish in memory of his father and mother who had lived in Berryhillock. It was invested in 2½% consols, yielding an annual income of £22:9/- for all time.

In 1955 the Church administered the following :-

1. A Coal Fund for the Poor from which 12 recipients were given money in lieu of coal.
2. The George Duncan Fund of 1928, the interest to be used to repair Church buildings.

3. The George Duncan Fund for the promotion of education amongst young people
4. A Fund from ex-servicemen of World War II for the care and repair of the War Memorial.
5. A sum from the ex-servicemen to the Trustees of the Public Hall, to be used to build a room in the Hall when alterations were next made.

Throughout its history the Free Church was less well off than St John's. Even in the first flush of enthusiasm when it had just come into existence, in 1846, annual income and expenditure was £30. There was £200 in the Manse Building Fund, of which £182 had been spent. The School Building Fund contained £12, but £45 had already been spent, a true victory of faith over reality.

Throughout the C20th Women's Guild sales of work were one of the most significant income streams. Before Union of the Churches, each held its own sale, a month apart, in the summer, and each raised between £50 and £80. After the Union, the combined Sale in 1933 only raised £87, but by 1947 this had risen to £132. Part of the money raised in this sale was used to donate £20 to the Organ Repair Fund, £9:7:6d for the West Church organ and £3;14:6d for Church window blinds.

Income from the sale included a donation from Mrs Wilkie of 10/-, £11:13/- from the Work Stall, £7:11:4d from the Toffee Stall, £2:7:6d from the Soap Stall, 10/10d from Quotations, 15/6d from Dips, £1:7:6d from the Pound Stall, £7:4/- from the Variety Stall, £1 for the Turkey, £3:2:1d from the Tea Stall, £8:5:4½d from the Dairy Stall, £1:19:2d from the Flower Stall, £1:2:6d for Ice Cream, 8/6½d for Flowers, 17/- from the Shooting and 12/3d from the Dance.

In 1934 they spent £1:2:6d on crockery, and in 1937, for the first time, they had hoop-la and roll-a-penny. During World War II the sale was replaced by collections, but after the War it began again, and in 1951 raised £101:17:10d.

THE KIRK AND THE POOR

A significant part of the role of the Church was to provide for the Poor. At the time of the Reformation this was codified in the "First Book of Discipline" 1560/61, when each parish was instructed to "provide for the poor within itself". This provision was to be for "the widow and the fatherless, the aged, impotent or lamed who neither can nor may travail for their sustenance". The parishes were however not to help "stubborn and idle beggars who, running from place to place, make a craft of their begging". The "stout or strong beggar be either compelled to work or returned to his native parish". The Act Anent the Poor, 1574, permitted the levy of an assessment for the poor, to be administered by the Kirk Session.

Poor relief worked better in the countryside where elders knew each individual intimately. Deskford seems to have been a parish in which the kirk members took their responsibility to look after the Poor seriously. Even then what was given to the Poor was very limited, enough to barely eke out a miserable existence. There was a widely held view that it was a personal disgrace to accept Poor Relief, and most people tried their utmost to avoid it. This was a view which persisted late into the C20th. From the 1720s the Kirk Session and landowners had equal responsibility for Poor Relief and from 1847 the new Parochial Boards took over responsibility. This continued to comprise the Minister, the Factor and several elders, but in addition had several elected members. The Parochial Board had a legal right to tax and assess local people in order to provide Poor Relief. Parish Councils took over responsibility in 1894 and were wholly elected.

In the C17th and C18th there were many famines which put pressure on the Kirk Session and its ability to cope. In 1751 the Sheriff of Banff instructed every parish to account for their Poor's money and make a list of the Poor. Deskford Session, together with Alexander Grant, Factor to the Earl of Findlater, sole heritor in Deskford, met and made their list, and at the same time made an order restraining "idle vagabonds".

The number of Poor requiring assistance in 1751 was 6. Collections over the year raised £18:4/- and income from mortifications and other financial transactions raised £25:6/-, but from this total of £43:10/- there had to be deducted, amongst other expenses, the Session Clerk's and Kirk Officer's salaries, being £16 in total.

The Roll comprised:-
1. Margaret Herd in Clinhill, 4/- per quarter
2. Margaret Innes in Oathillock, 3/- per quarter
3. Christian Guthrie in Berryhillock, 3/- per quarter
4. Janet Shirer in Berryhillock, 3/- per quarter
5. Isobel Faitch in Langlanburn, 3/- per quarter
6. Peter Machattie in Clochmacreich, 2/- per quarter

In addition several other poor householders in the parish, but not on the Roll were given help twice a year or even more often. In total the Kirk Session paid £27:6/- Scots, the Earl of Findlater £13:13/- and his tenants £13:13/-, all annually, and the Schoolmaster, Colin Morrison, made the payments. In order to receive Poor Relief, the individual had to agree that, on their death, ownership of all their possessions would pass to the Kirk Session who would roup (auction) them. Whatever money was raised, after paying funeral expenses, went to the Poor Fund.

In 1783 there was a national enquiry about lack of food, how much money each parish had, what had been done to relieve hardship and what still required to be done. Deskford was less badly affected than some parishes and had already taken action. It partly supplied 54 adults together with their 59 children weekly. However there were also another 40 adults with 64 children who were greatly in need of assistance but which the Session was unable to provide. Session asked the Minister to use Mr Wilson's donation to buy 6 bolls of white pease meal. One month later the Minister reported that he had received 6 bolls from the Sheriff. This was part of Deskford's share of 48 bolls of meal from the 1350 bolls provided for Banffshire by the Barons of the Exchequer. As the Session only had funds to buy 8 bolls, private individuals were encouraged to buy the rest and sell it on at cost. The Minister had it collected from Portsoy and lodged it in the Miln of Deskford. He had also paid £14:8/- to Mr Wilson at Cullen House for 12 bolls of pease @ £1:4/- per boll, which yielded 17 bolls 3 firlots of meal for which, being sold at 8d per peck he had received £9:9:4d. Mr Wilson had also said that the Session could have some (oat) meal, and the Minister was appointed by Session to purchase 6 bolls to be sold weekly. Mr Wilson, Ardoch, lent £200 sterling to the Session to buy victual.

This was just the most challenging of many similar years. In 1700 the Session, "considering the scarcity of victual and the dearth", agreed not to wait till the appointed day to distribute money to the Poor, because it was needed immediately. In 1735 £3 was sent to Synod in Aberdeen for the relief of individual persons within the bounds, but half was returned for distribution in the parish.

In 1740 the Session, considering the scarcity and dearth of victual, made larger distributions and bought 60 bolls of victual @£9 Scots a boll and sold it in small amounts at the school for no profit. In addition they distributed most of a bag of doits (very small denomination coins) which they held, worth in total £22. In March 1741 things were so bad that Session decided to buy 50 or 60 bolls of victual and sell it in small amounts to poor people. It was thought that 3 bolls a week would come close to satisfying demand. The Minister would attempt to buy locally.

By the end of April he reported that he had agreed to buy 24 bolls of mixed meal @£7:10/- Scots the boll and 20 bolls of good oatmeal @£9 Scots the boll, and proposed that the mixed meal be sold at 10 merks a boll and the oatmeal at £8:8/- a boll. It was hoped that the Earl of Findlater would indemnify the Session against their losses. The Kirk Officer was to inform the people of the parish to attend at the school the following Saturday with ready money, when they would be supplied.

At the end of May they found that more victual than expected was required. The Minister informed them that he could obtain oatmeal @£9 a boll or unshelled bere meal @£8. Session appointed one of the elders, John Reid, to go and buy 30 or 32 bolls of oatmeal. It was also agreed that the Poor would receive both their Lammas and Martinmas allocations at Lammas, with nothing at Martinmas because the immediate need was so great. In 1757 the Minister bought 30 bolls of meal @£9:6/- Scots per boll as the Poor could not find any to buy, and sold it to them @£8:16/- per boll, a loss.

In 1796 there was a great scarcity of meal. The Session purchased 16 bolls @ 16/- sterling the boll. In 1801 13 bolls of meal were sold @£2 sterling the boll by the Minister, significantly below the normal price. As late as 1847, 65 bolls of meal and £26 were collected in the parish of Deskford for the most necessitous of the labouring classes, owing to the dearth of provisions. This was the time of the Potato Famine which, though Deskford did not suffer as much as many places, still caused scarcity here and an increase in the numbers of the Poor.

In 1790 there were 32 people on the Poor Roll which was considered a large number, caused in part by the attractiveness of Deskford to poor people across the North East because of its great supply of peat mosses. The Kirk had the interest on loans totalling £1000 Scots, weekly collections amounting to about £8 sterling a year and 6 bolls of meal annually were given by the heritor, the Earl of Findlater. There were few or no beggars.

In June 1793 Session discovered that the relatives of some of those who had died whilst on the Poor Roll, had claimed assistance towards their funerals, when they themselves had sufficient funds for this purpose. Session decided to give no such assistance in future unless the effects belonging to the deceased were given to it on behalf of the Poor of the parish. By 1840 there were on average 37 people receiving Poor Relief, each getting on average 16/- sterling per year, according to their circumstances. Church collections totalled about £20 sterling per year and interest on the poor Fund was £10:12:2d.

In cases of extreme emergency there were house-to-house collections for meal or money. There was only one local travelling beggar, but she was lame and did not go far. There were however many beggars from elsewhere whom the Minister felt should be discouraged so that they stayed in their home area where they would be known and therefore less likely to thrive by imposture or idleness. By and large locals were reluctant to accept Poor Relief unless it was really needed, but unfortunately there were too many cases where it was really needed. In addition to the 6 bolls of meal given annually by the Earl of

Seafield as heritor, he also gave up to half a peck of meal a week to a number of poor and aged individuals.

In 1930, 18 lbs of tea, 9 stones of sugar and 4 tons 5cwt of best English household coal were distributed on Christmas day and were much appreciated. Session ordered a second distribution of coal in early March. In 1931, 16 households each got 1lb of tea, 7lbs of sugar and two consignments of coal, all of which came from the Milton Fund. In the 1950s there was a "Coal Fund" for the poor, with just over a dozen beneficiaries who, because of rationing, received money instead of coal.

In earlier times, though much of the money and meal for the Poor was obtained from collections, individuals also contributed in a number of ways, and the Poor Fund was also used to give short-term loans, though at lower interest rates than present day payday loan companies. For example in 1676, Robert Ogilvie, son of Thomas Ogilvie of Ardoch, gave 100 merks for the use of the Poor, and in 1726 there were mortifications to the Poor of 100 merks by Robert Ogilvie of Ardoch, 100 merks by Robert Ogilvie in Blerock and 200 merks by Mr Anderson in Crabstoun. In 1738 Session agreed to lend £12 Scots out of the Poor's money to John Gordon, chapman, in Mid Skeith till Whitsunday. In 1755, Andrew Reid, late in Bognageith, left £20 to the Poor of the parish, and in 1762 James Cameron, sometime in Oathillock, bequeathed his effects to the Poor of the parish. £10 was raised at the roup.

In 1829 Rev Walter Chalmers left a legacy of £20, reduced to £18 by Legacy Duty, for the poor of the parish. In 1837, 1838 and 1839 respectively Col Grant gave £5, £10 and £10 to the Poor and in 1841 the Earl of Seafield gave a donation of £10 to the Minister for the Poor of the parish. He also donated, for the same purpose, a fine of £1 which had been paid for game trespass.

In 1885 the existing mortifications for the poor were:-
1. Mr Murray, Demerara, £50
2. Mr and Mrs Littlejohn, Tillybreadless, £10
3. Rev Chalmers, £18
4. Mr James Morrison, Nether Blairock, £45

In 1891 Mr Proctor, late farmer in Ardoch, left £50, the interest on which was to be given to poor people not in receipt of Poor Relief. In 1928, Andrew Milton, retired Chief Constable, 145 Hunter St, Fall River, Massachussets, USA, sent a cheque for £500 via his niece, Mrs Murdoch, Berryhillock, to be invested and the interest disbursed amongst the deserving poor as coal or provisions. It was to be called the "Berryhillock William and Annie Milton Fund" in memory of his father and mother and a happy childhood spent in the parish. The money was invested in 2½% Consols via the Post Office Savings bank.

The names of individuals in receipt of assistance, whether on the Poor Roll or by way of occasional disbursements, were usually given. For example in 1720 those on the Roll were given the following disbursements, all in £ Scots :-

1. Elizabeth Coull, 16/-
2. Janet Shepherd, £1:10/-
3. Isobel Davidson, £1
4. Janet Milton, 16/-
5. Agnes Davidson, 15/-
6. Walter Anderson 14/-

In 1721 the following payments were made:-
1. Janet Imlach in Mid Skeith, 10/-
2. Janet Bain in Ardoch, 12/-
3. Isabel Fetch in Knows, 5/-
4. Archibald Sluie in Blerock, 12/-
5. Robert Copland, 6/8d

In 1722 the following payments were made:-
1. Robert Copland 6/-
2. William Larie, 4/-
3. Katharin Baillie, 2/-
4. To a poor man, 1/-
5. John Wilson, £1
6. Agnes Davidson, 5/-
7. To two supplicants, 10/-

In October 1722:-
1. Robert Copland, 6/-
2. Mrs McKay, 10/6d
3. Elspet Machatie, 12/-
4. To a poor man, 1/-
5. Robert Copland, 3/-
6. John Wilson in Crabstoun, £4:5/-
7. To several supplicants, £1:18:6d
8. To the Irish Bursar, £1
9. To two supplicants, 9/-
10. To the erection in Durness (building a Church), £5

In 1734:-
1. Robert Copland, 16/-
2. Isabel Davidson, £1
3. George Piper, 12/-
4. Pat Gordon, 10/-
5. William Cobban, 10/-
6. Margaret Lawrence, 6/-
7. Agnes Crookeshank, 6/-
8. Janet Brodie, 10/-
9. Janet Stuart, 17/-
10. Margaret (??), 12/-
11. Agnes Mitchell, 12/-
12. John and Huiey Daier, 16/-
13. Robert Davidson, 10/-
14. James Anderson's children, 6/-
15. (Church) door beggars, 4/-
16. Two orphans in the parish, 12/-

On 4th November 1764, after compting with William Stevenson, late Schoolmaster here, and his heirs and executors, in the period from 16/12/63 till 04/11/64, there was found to be in the possession of William Stevenson, the sum of £20:4:3d Scots, which was delivered up to the Minister and given out as follows:-

1. To Andrew Stables in Squaredoch, 18/-
2. To George Piper in Kirktown, £1:4/-
3. To Alexander Smith in Todholls, £1
4. To George Milton in Todholls, £1
5. To James Ewen in Milntown, 18/-
6. To a travelling supplicant, 4/-
7. To the chest (coffin) of Peter Murray's daughter, deceased, £2:8/-
8. To John Nicol's mother, Little Skeith, 14/3d
9. To Helen Reid in Broadrashes, £1:4/-
10. To Anne Abercromby in Craibston, in sickness, £2:8/-
11. To Andrew Lawrence in Cotton, 18/-
12. To Anne Dougall on the weekly roll and in December, £1
13. To Anne Abercromby's funeral, in Craibston, £3
14. To Janet Taas, on the weekly roll for December, 16/-
15. To William Donal in Kirktown, in his distress, £3
16. To Elspet Stables, on the weekly roll for December, £1
17. To a supplicant 2/-
18. To Thomas Lawrence's family, Oathillock, 18/-
19. To Margaret McHatty, on the weekly roll for December, 16/-
20. To Anne Dougall in Squaredoch, on the roll, £1
21. To James Keir in Croftgloy, his relict (widow), 16/-
22. To Janet Gray in Berryhillock, 18/-

In addition to regular disbursements there were also occasional ones. For example in 1721 money was given to Walter Anderson, blind, to two shipwrekt seamen, to (??) Gordon, dumb, shoes to Walter Anderson, lame, to Mary Row, an idiot, to a beggar, to Elspet Coull in Raemoir and to Isabel Davidson in Clun.

Between 1764 and 1775, amongst others, the following are examples of relief given on an occasional basis:-

1. To a woman with dropsy and to Janet Marquis in Tillybreadless, 14/-
2. To Mr Shaw at Inveresk, much recommended as a sufferer of fire, £1:4/-
3. To Mr Graham, a sufferer by fire on the borders of England, 18/-

4. To widows and children whose husbands and fathers had been lost at Shore of Buckie, £8:8/-
5. To a poor widow woman in Keith, 12/3d
6. To a mortcloth for W Pirie's funeral, 6/-
7. To Janet Innes in distress and to a poor stranger in distress, £1:4/-
8. To Alexander Howie's wife's chest (coffin), she being dead, £3
9. To Isobel Guidbrand and to a poor sailor, 14/-
10. To a poor woman in Boharm and to Lady Home's daughter, 18/-
11. To a poor gentlewoman from Grange, going to London to be cured by the King's touch, £3
12. To Janet Murray, to help her put up a house, 12/-
13. To fishers' widows in Cullen, £10:7:4d

In addition to people in Deskford in need, money was paid to supplicants from outwith the area. For instance, in 1723 donations were given to individuals from Dyke, Alves, Golspie, Liberton (Edinburgh), Elgin, Aberdeen, Caithness and Alloway, and to Mr Fraser, shipwrecked. In 1735 12/- was given to a traveller soldjer to help him bury his child that dyed in this parish, and 13/- to Christian Fendy, a converted Turk.

In 1745 the money for the Poor was exhausted, but some more was borrowed against a loan which had been given to Mr Barnet, Ardoch, and in October 1746 the Minister reported that a number of indigent people had applied for money to buy winter clothes. Session agreed to give Margaret Davidson in Berryhillock £2:8/-, Isobel Faitch in Tillybreedless £2:8/-, and John Wilson in Tack of Craibston 12/-. As late as 1837, £15 sterling was collected for certain poor families in the parish who had typhus.

The numbers of Poor receiving relief and the amounts given varied significantly, often depending on the weather and consequent quality and quantity of the harvest. For example:-

1. In 1684, 14 people received sums of between 40d and 24/- annually, totalling £7:18:4d
2. In 1709, 9 people received a total of £13 Scots
3. In 1743, 24 Poor received £21:1:6d per quarter

4. In 1750 5 people received 2 haddishes of meal or 6d each, weekly
5. In 1755, 4 people received 10d, 5d, 5d and 3d weekly
6. In 1792, 32 people were given relief
7. In 1836, 37 people were each given 16/- per quarter
8. In 1883, 15 people received £200 in total

In addition to general and occasional disbursements, special collections on specific Sundays were made for individuals or families with particular needs. In July 1720 Session agreed a special collection the following Lord's day for Alexander Sluie in this parish, whose wife was labouring under a decay and therefore not able to nurse her child and who had also some other small children to maintain. £6:13:4d was collected. In August 1722 John Wilson in Crabstoun petitioned Session for a day's collection for the relief of his indigent and distressed family. £4:5/- was collected.

In June 1723 George Innes in Ordeins represented to Session his indigent condition, craving some supply for his relief and family. £3:9:6d was collected. In October the same year a collection was taken for John Cruikshank in Upper Blairock, considering his trouble and straitened circumstances. £5:1:10d was collected. In March 1726 William Imlach had died and his children were in necessitous circumstances. Session agreed to pay James Mill, the tenant of Mid Skeith, the rent of the ½-acre croft which William Imlach's children sub-rented from him. In October that year, a collection for Robert Bartlet in Leitchestoun, for his indigent family, raised £5:15/-.

In April 1727 collections were taken for Jean Reid in Raemoir, aged and starving, and for Janet Herd, a widow with some children in Crabstoun. On February 9th 1729 it was reported to Session that a poor stranger woman called Isobel Stewart had died that morning at Janet Steenson's house in Cleanhill, and had left behind there a child of about 2 years of age. They agreed to provide grave cloths and coffin to be made out of the old Communion tablecloth and table. They would ask Presbytery for assistance and would keep the woman's clothes for the child's use. Isobel Ritchie was awarded £4 per quarter for looking after the child.

In June 1734 Janet Bain in Squaredoch made application to be considered an indigent person, but this was not agreed until the Minister got a testimonial about her good character from her previous Minister. In January 1735 a collection was equally divided between John Gordon in Over Skeith and John Piper in Skeith, both in deep distress. In March the same year £1:10/- was given back to William Murray in Kirktown, which was part of his penalty (fine for fornication), considering his mean circumstances. In April 1736 Session agreed to pay the funeral expenses of a poor man who died in the parish, 4 merks for coffin and £1:8/- for gravecloths.

In January 1738 Janet Mackie had died so poor as not to be able to afford funeral expenses, and her friends appealed for help. Session agreed to a public collection next Lord's day, when £2:10:8d was raised. The coffin, made by Walter Hilton, cost £2:8/- and the linen from Andrew Longmore cost £1. In July that year 2/- was given to a poor woman in the convulsive fits. In November 1739 £6 Scots was paid to Walter Sym, Berryhillock, who was an Alehouse keeper, for his expenses and care of Agnes Cruikshank, a poor woman on the Roll, in her sickness and for her interment.

In July 1741 £4:3:4d was collected for the widows and orphans of the fishermen who were lost at Sandend and Whitehills. In December 1743 £3:3/- was collected for the widow of Murdoch McKenzie in Little Skeith. In March 1745 £3:17:2d was collected for Isobel Faitch who was blind and therefore could not provide for herself. In August 1747 Walter Hilton pleaded with Session to pay him for the coffin he had made for Isobel Henry who had died in George Wright's house in Ramoir. They agreed to pay £2:8/- but would try to claim it back from her friends in the Kirk Session in Grange where she was born.

In August 1749 Elspet McLon, who was on the Poor's Roll died. Her effects were inventoried and rouped by James Robertson, Schoolmaster, and the money raised was used to pay for her funeral, to pay Jane Ewen for having looked after her for several months and to pay any small debts she had. In April 1755 the day's collection of £6:6/- was given to the widows in Cullen whose husbands were lost at sea.

In July 1764 James Anderson's effects were rouped for the Poor. £14:5/- was raised, of which £8:10/- was paid for all the funeral expenses, and £5:15/- was placed in the hands of the Kirk Treasurer. In 1765 Isobel Laing, wife of Peter Mathieson in Faichiehill, had applied to the Minister for a recommendation to be received into the Infirmary in Aberdeen for the cure of one of her hands which was in a very bad way. Session agreed and also said that if she died in the Infirmary they would pay for her funeral.

In 1766 and 1767 there was a fashion for Session paying to replace poor men's only cow or horse. In August 1766 Alexander Taylor, smith in Squaredoch, lost his cow. 20/- sterling was collected to allow him to buy another. In March 1767 Alexander Smith, Todholes had £1 sterling collected for him to allow him to buy a replacement for his horse, on which he depended. He could not afford to do so himself as he had a poor and numerous family. In August 1767, 14/- sterling was collected for Peter Matheson for having lost his horse.

In January 1779 the elders advised the Minister that a collection should be made for James Smith, elder, in Kirktown, he being in great poverty and sickness, and having a hired woman to attend to him at 5d per day. A week later £10:10/- was raised for Smith and his wife and was delivered to his son, also James Smith, in Mosside, to be used as needed. In August 1783, Session, considering the distressed situation of James Milton's family, and particularly him having a child 5 months old, the mother having died, agreed 6d a week to Margaret Reid, Ramore for caring for the child. A collection two weeks later raised in addition £1:2:6d for his family.

PEOPLE

POPULATION

The population of Deskford has varied significantly over the years from a high of 1,031 in 1861 to a low of 158 in 1991. In 2001 it was 180 and in 2011 it stood at 198. Many of the factors which have had an impact on local population numbers were national or international while some were purely local. In general Deskford has been affected by the same influences as other parishes in the area and more widely across the North East.

There was a huge population explosion across Scotland in the C12th and C13th, and by 1300 numbers had reached almost 1 million. In comparison, today's Scottish population is more than 5 million. After the first outbreak of plague in 1349, the population, which was largely agricultural, and spread evenly across the country, fell by around 30%. This decline was made worse by poor weather and wars with England. During the C14th and C15th the population continued to fall, but in the C16th it started to increase once more. However in the C17th it stopped increasing.

Particularly because of crop failure in the 1690s the population fell by 7% as people died of starvation. By 1750 the Scottish population was at an all time high of around 1¼ million. Between 1750 and 1850 there was a significant increase in the national population, but in Deskford, because of changes in agricultural practice, the population increase was not so steep, with some of those who would have constituted the increase moving away to industrial towns and cities.

Between 1750 and 1800 the Deskford population had actually fallen from over 900 to just 600, before recovering to 900 by 1850. Despite these figures Deskford suffered less of a decline than many other North East parishes because many of those evicted and made landless were able to obtain crofts on Aultmore, taking in new land from moss and moor.

In the early C18th 90% of the Scottish population lived in the countryside, and by 1830 this figure was still 70%. Despite the Deskford population recovering to 900 by 1850, this figure would have been higher had it not been for the large number of deaths amongst those in their teens, twenties and thirties, which significantly reduced life expectancy.

In Deskford in 1790 there were 145 children under 8, 171 children above 8, 68 male servants, 44 female servants, 18 weavers, 8 shoemakers, 4 tailors, 2 wrights, 2 cart and ploughwrights, 2 wheelwrights, 3 masons and 2 blacksmiths. The population increased in the C19th to its peak of 1,031 in 1861 despite the increasing mechanisation of agriculture. Between 1830 and 1890 this is calculated to have displaced one man's labour for each 34 acres of crops. By 1901 only 14% of the Scottish population was employed in agriculture, by 1951 it was 10% and now it is under 2%.

The census continued to be carried out by local headmasters till 1921. By 1925, when the population in Deskford was below 600, Mr Park, the established church Minister, commented that "with a fast decreasing population, and the young manhood and womanhood of the country nearly all flocking to the towns or emigrating, it is difficult to keep up our (the Church's) numbers. Perhaps the lowest point has not yet been reached". He was correct. By 1971, after the closure and amalgamation of many crofts and farms and the abandonment of their houses, the population of Deskford was down to 269. However the population at that time still had an identifiable local identity. Almost none had been born outwith the North East. By 1950 one child in Deskford had a Polish father, but all the German and Polish soldiers had returned home.

Though there has been a 20% increase in the population of Deskford since 1991, this has been largely made up from incomers from the rest of Scotland and the UK, and some from even further afield. This has brought in an energy and enthusiasm, and, today, in 2014, a majority of, for example, Community Association members are from this group.

SURNAMES

Many of the old surnames had very specific meanings. Findlater comes from the Gaelic for white slope, and Ogilvie is either Ogle's town or yew tree hill. Thain, of which there were some in Deskford in or before the C16th comes from Thane, and Dempster comes from the Doomster, the official charged with reading out the sentences in the Court of Regality.

The spelling of surnames was not established until the second half of the C18th. Below are some of the surnames present in Deskford in the past, together with their present spellings.

> Bainzie = Benzie
> Brebner = Bremner
> Cair or Care = Kerr
> Cuie = Cowie
> Dason = Dawson
> De Ard = Ord
> Dowgall = Dougall
> Faitch = Featch
> Huie = Howie (possibly Albigensian heretics forced out of France around 1200)
> Muet = Mowat
> Raich = Rioch
> Rainnie = Rennie
> Shirer = Shearer
> Steinson = Stevenson
> Taas = Tawse
> Vat = Watt

LANGUAGE

The language in daily use by the people living in Deskford has changed a number of times. Though it has been the Scots dialect known as Doric for several hundred years, this has changed within itself over the centuries, and someone born in 1950 and using the local Doric dialect would struggle to understand someone born in 1750 and using the local dialect of that time. In recent years the dialects and accents used by the people of Deskford have become much more diverse, because a significant proportion of the current population is not native to the North East. We have probably seen the end of a universal local language.

In the Iron Age, Celtic languages were spoken across Britain, including in the North East, though these had supplanted earlier languages. The Iron Age language in this area evolved into Pictish, a P-Celtic language similar to Welsh, which was used by the C3rd. In the period between the C6th and the C8th, the Picts needed interpreters when communicating with the Scots who spoke Gaelic, a Q-Celtic language, or with the Angles.

By the C9th, Gaelic, a language similar to Irish Gaelic, was gaining ground, partly through the spread of Christianity, and then through the emergence of the united kingdom of Alba. It became the majority language about 900, though this area was bilingual in Pictish and Gaelic. Pictish died out in the late C10th. The two languages were mutually unintelligible, though Pictish words were frequently adopted into Gaelic.

In 1100 Gaelic was the universal language across the entire country, but already by the C12th the Scots variant of English was beginning to become established in some areas. In the North East, Gaelic declined and Scots was increasingly adopted between 1150 and 1400, with Scots being used first in the coastal areas. This trend was encouraged with the defeat of the Comyn Earl of Buchan by Robert the Bruce, and the replacement of native landowners by Scots-speaking incomers. Despite this the status of the two languages was confused. In the C15th and C16th Gaelic speakers were seen as savages and had fun poked at them. However as a counter to this, scholars at Aberdeen Grammar School in 1550 were permitted to converse with each other in the classical languages of Latin, Hebrew, Greek and Gaelic, but not in the Scots language which was thought too common.

There was still some Gaelic spoken in Deskford in the C14th, however by 1400 the area was totally Scots speaking, though we today would not understand anyone speaking the Scots of that time. At this time Grange was still partly Gaelic speaking and Keith wholly so. Even as late as 1800 there was still some Gaelic spoken in the more remote parts of Keith parish. Nationally, one of the most important factors in the spread of Scots was the introduction of the printing press. The demise of Gaelic in this area was also helped by the fact that Banffshire Gaelic was always idiosyncratic and demonstrated differences from more mainstream Gaelic.

By 1400 all sections of society here, including the aristocracy, spoke a very broad Scots which over the years evolved into Doric. However just as Gaelic had borrowed words from Pictish, so Scots borrowed words from Gaelic. The clyack, the last sheaf to be harvested, comes from the Gaelic word for old woman, "cailleach". Deskford placenames also record the changing language of the area. Pattenbringan is the only one which unarguably has a Pictish derivation, but many of the oldest farms have names of Gaelic derivation, some of which may have been borrowed and translated from Pictish. Following these, many farms have Scots dialect names, though the crofts established in the C19th tend to have diluted Doric or standard English names.

Doric has a number of features common across the North East. For example "wh" is pronounced as "f", though even this was a carry over from Gaelic. There were however differences between the Banffshire and Moray dialects. For example, what in Moray would be a "fricht" was a "fleg" in Banffshire and what were "laces" in Moray were "pints" in Banffshire.

In lower Banffshire, including Deskford, the double e pronunciation was standard, with stone being pronounced "steen", moon "meen" and boots "beets". The farms of Cleanhill in Drybridge and Clunehill in Deskford are the same name, with Clunehill in Deskford having been pronounced "Cleenhill" in the past. By comparison, in mid Banffshire, around Keith, stone was pronounced "stehn" and bone "behn". Both "steen" and "stehn" differ from the more common Scots "stane".

In both Deskford and the fishing villages "th" was pronounced "dd", as in "mudder", "fadder" and "widder" for weather. Sometimes the "th" was shortened and hardened to "t", as in "fort" for fourth and "fift" for fifth. The w was often pronounced v, as in "vrang" for wrong. The "wh" was pronounced "f", as in "fite", "fahr", "fit" and "fahn". There was often a broad "aa" as in "aall", "baall", "caall" and "faall". In addition pole became "poll", rope became "ropp" and road "rodd". Made became "med" and fade "fed".

Other examples of local pronunciation include school becoming "squeel", master becoming "maister", hot becoming "hait", sore becoming "sehr", want becoming "wint", ran becoming "rin", whins becoming "funs" whistle becoming "fussel" and speak becoming "spyke". Even with prominent placenames there were distinct local pronunciations. For example, as late as the C19th, Cullen was often pronounced "Coolan" or "Kulyan".

The use of the diminutive was common, such as man becoming mannie, horse horsie and in extreme cases even the quadruple diminutive such as "little wee horsikie" (horse, horsie, horsikie, wee horsikie, little wee horsikie). Several diminutive devices were used in the same expression. It was also common for expressions such as "bit", "piece" and "puckle" to be used to enhance the diminutive. Also common was the augmentative. A "trail" (dirty woman), became a "trailach" and a "dorle" (piece of bread and cheese) became a "dorlach". Verbs were also conjugated in the Doric. For example, to jump: loup, lap, luppen, to cry: greet, grat, grutten and to go: geh, geed, gane.

INDIVIDUALS

Over the centuries Deskford has seen a significant number of people who stand out from the crowd for a variety of reasons. For example the second Minister after the Reformation, Gilbert Gardyne, became Moderator of the General Assembly of the Church of Scotland. Slightly later, Mary Beaton, one of Mary Queen of Scots' Four Maries, who had married Alexander Ogilvie of Boyne, was buried in Deskford Church, some time after 1606.

Mr Robert Sharp, brother of the famous Archbishop Sharp, married the heiress of Ordens and, in 1675, made a mortification of 500 merks, which generated £1:15:3⅓d per annum towards the Minister's stipend. He was Sheriff Clerk of Banffshire.

One of the very few people locally who supported the Jacobites was James Abercromby, Skeith, who held the rank of Captain. He assisted in collecting the Revenue for the Rebels, and passed intelligence to them about Government forces. He was accused of lurking. He probably laid down his arms under the Act of Indemnity of 1747, and may have returned to his farm. The daughter of Mr Morison the Minister, when married to her first husband, and living in Alves, was presented with a silver medal by the Duke of Cumberland for the hospitality she had shown him.

On their respective tours of Scotland in the late C18th, both Thomas Pennant and Dr Johnson passed through Deskford, though the latter kept the blinds on his carriage drawn, so saw nothing of the parish.

A bede man called Geordie Raeburn visited Deskford every year from 1764 to 1785. He was an ex-soldier who was over 6 feet tall, over 70 years of age and attended Church regularly. He wore the blue gown, badge and bonnet of the bede men, and was a minstrel, ballad seller and seller of "auld writings" and story books. He carried three packs, one over his left shoulder for his meal, a leather one over his right shoulder holding his "orra sark, hose and shoon, his drinking horn, sneeshin mill and other such gear". The third and largest was a knapsack of goatskin on his back, and held by a strap across his shoulders, which was crammed with his pamphlets and books. He recited ancient ballads from memory and also played the fiddle. When he was given accommodation for the night, he would entertain by playing, to allow those present to dance. He lived mainly on porridge and brose and a glass of ale, and slept in farm barns. He claimed allegiance to the Hanoverians but had probably been a Jacobite, and sang the songs of both sides. He travelled from Brechin to Speyside and had some money saved in an Aberdeen bank, of which he said that "there would be aneuch fund in his kist to bury him".

Another former soldier was Captain Steinson, raised in Deskford where his father was a small farmer. He rose through the ranks and retired on full pay around 1810. He had served widely, including in the American War of Independence. He did not like Americans, whom he considered dishonourable as they shot at the enemy from hiding. Indeed Captain Steinson had been shot in the leg by an American who was hiding up a tree. Around this time a man named John Low lived in a cottage beside Bleachfield and watched over it with a loaded gun at his side in case anyone tried to damage it or cause him trouble.

In the late C18th the Rev James Lawtie of Fordyce was considered a learned man and a renowned antiquary. However much of what he believed was rooted in his imagination and enthusiasm rather than in fact. He believed that Deskford had been a Roman Station, that the name Deskford meant Decius' Fort and that a Roman road led down to the bridge at Kirktown. Rev Morison of Deskford, however, remembered this road being built to improve an old road which had been impassable in winter. Rev Lawtie believed that a particular ditch was evidence of a Roman camp. Rev Morison remembered it having been dug as a field drainage ditch to drain part of the glebe. Rev Lawtie believed that everything old was either Roman or Viking and had persuaded the great Lord Monboddo of some of his beliefs. He was laughed at behind his back by locals who knew that what he thought were tumuli were actually fairy hillocks.

Recent academic writing has cast some doubt on the idea of the "lad o' pairts" rising from rural poverty through intelligence, commitment and the university to success and wealth in life. However several examples from Deskford in the late C18th and early C19th lend support to the idea.

James Gray, who attended school in Deskford in the 1770s, later became editor and proprietor of the *Morning Chronicle* in London. When his father died, his mother could not afford to continue running their farm, so retired to a small croft, half a mile from the manse. Gray had won 1st prize and £5 per annum in the Aberdeen University Bursary Competition, and this enabled him to go to university and gain a degree.

Another Deskford loon of the same period earned between £2,000 and £3.000 a year, an absolute fortune, from a West Indian plantation. Another, a poor cottar's son, eventually took ownership of a large firm of conveyancers in London. He was known to all in Deskford as "Carroty Sandy", and his mother ran the only alehouse in the parish. Yet another, a pauper orphan, worked his way to a degree with the help of a bursary. He became a Church of England Curate, in charge of a parish in Bedfordshire where he had a living of £600 a year. In order to add to this already comfortable income he also acted as the village schoolmaster. Another Deskford orphan ran away to sea, was press-ganged and worked his way up to the rank of Admiral.

Robert Alves, born in 1745, and one time schoolmaster in Deskford, who narrowly avoided getting the sack for being constantly drunk, was one of Scotland's minor poets of the time. He wrote two books of poetry and one of prose. He later became Rector of Banff Academy. The mother of George Chalmers who wrote "Caledonia", was a native of Deskford. In the C19th, Surgeon General George Bidie CIE was born at Backies, and Professor Sir Ashley Mackintosh, a son of the Deskford manse, had been 1st Bursar at Aberdeen University in 1884.

Auld Willie Black, fiddler, originally from Broadrashes, died at the age of 97 in February 1867. He was reputed to have been a member of Niel Gow's string band. When John Reid, Squaredoch, died, aged 87 in January 1887 it was believed that in his younger days he had been the strongest man in Deskford. In 1900 Miss Jessie Ann Reid, daughter of Mr Reid, Swailend, was appointed Post Mistress of Cullen.

Robert Cruikshank was born in 1834 and had managed Earl's Mill in Keith from around 1860. In 1869 he took over the vacant and almost ruinous Berryhillock Mill. A new kiln was built in 1879 and a second pair of millstones added. He additionally became tenant of the old glebe lands in 1888 and was known to be generous to the community. His family produced Inspectors of the Poor and Registrars for many years.

A Deskford quine, Dr Alice Ker, daughter of Rev Ker, Minister of Deskford Free Church, was one of the first women in Britain to graduate and qualify as a doctor. She was a noted suffragette, and was imprisoned for breaking windows in Selfridge's store in London.

The C20th also produced its share of memorable individuals. In the early years of the century, Mr Wilson, cottager at Milltown, had been a schoolteacher in South Africa. He was an ardent communist and atheist. One day when at Inaltrie to buy milk, he was bitten by one of their notoriously bad tempered dogs. He said nothing, but the next time he was there the dog approached him and he threw pepper in its face, after which he had no trouble from it.

In 1928 Hugh Shearer, Ardoch Cottages, applied to emigrate to Canada. He was 28, a Presbyterian, and was employed as a horseman. His nationality was "Scotch" and he had been married for four months. He had £19 saved and this would rise to £30.

In 1921, James Maitland, Raemore, made an attempt to become the Scottish Champion Heavy Athlete. He did serious training for the 56lb hammer, the 16lb hammer and putting the shot, and was also talented at the high leap and long jump. He was six feet three inches tall, raw, of a commanding appearance, but still somewhat clumsy. "Rob Roy" from Buckie, who had been fee'd at Raemore 14 years previously, wrote a poem about him.

> "Good morning Jeems, my stalwart chiel,
> I'm unco gled tae ken ye're weel.
> My blessings on yer honoured name,
> Likewise tae a' the folks at hame".

Alexander Taylor, the former farmer at Little Skeith, died in Little Skeith Cottage in August 1910. Whilst in Little Skeith he had also built houses and drained land. He had acted as Moss Grieve on the Aultmore Mosses for the Countess of Seafield and had attended 66 consecutive Peter Fairs at Rathven.

John Scott the Schoolmaster was also Registrar till 1918. He was succeeded as Reistrar by James Ross, farmer, till 1942. When inspected in 1937 the report stated "Entries are as usual both well written and free from error. He is a middle aged farmer, hard working and intelligent, and has been persuaded to appoint his wife, Alice Ross, as Assistant Registrar". In 1957 Robert Cruikshank was thinking of resigning as Registrar because of ill health. The Local Authority had already decided to merge the Cullen and Deskford districts, and in 1958 James Ogilvie, who was already Registrar in Cullen, took over Deskford as well.

The Curries of Greenhill are a well-known local family. William Currie was a County Councillor as a Liberal, and was also active in other local committees and organisations. He was awarded the MBE for services to Local Government in 1970. His brother, Sir George Currie, retired in 1963 as Principal of the University of Western Australia.

Some people lived to great ages. Jimmy Watt, who had been a joiner in Berryhillock, died at Grange at the age of 103 in 1989. He had lived in Canada for some time and had retired in 1955. Other people were very conscientious. Ethel Raffan from Comb's Croft married Bobby Combe who at one time became a gravedigger. Every week she got the local paper early and told him what graves he would have to open that week.

Carestown Lodge was purchased around 1990 by Count Calvi, the brother of Roberto Calvi, the banker found hanged under Westminster Bridge during the Banco Ambrosiano scandal. There were many stories and rumours surrounding him; that he always carried a loaded gun with him in Deskford, of Mafia connections, of bodyguards and of busloads of young ladies of a certain type from Aberdeen attending his parties.

Around the same time Rora Pagliera bought Carestown. She developed the gardens with ponds, shelter belts, a 65 metre laburnum walk, a maze, much willow, beech and rowan planting and an organic vegetable garden, all surrounding a courtyard centrepiece which was built by demolishing the old steading and employing a busload of construction workers from Elgin every day for almost a year. She opened the garden to the public every second year. It was bought by Tom and Sheree Gunn who have continued to develop the garden and enhance its impressive nature. It now opens annually.

This section has outlined a few of the more interesting characters who have illuminated the Deskford scene over the years. Many more could have been included, but not all are as well known. Some evidence is plaintive, including a flat stone of "Darbreich Slate", which for many years was used by Geordie Smith as a drain cover at Easter Darbreich, and which is inscribed "Within the compass of this little spot concentrate lies the ultimatum final of all the terrestrial acquisitions of ANDREW WILSON some time in Rashiehill: and those of his descendand (s) who lies or by fate's decree". The continuation of the inscription has been broken off and is missing.

During the 1930s the Rev William Brown was considered to be a very nice man, JA Beveridge the Schoolmaster was well liked and easy going. Farmers such as Bill Johnston, Todholes, took in individuals from Ladysbridge Asylum and looked after them well. Not all however was sweetness and light. The daughter of Mr Muiry the shopkeeper became deaf after a fight with the daughter of Dovey Legge, the cobbler. Beel Johnston, Todholes married a Miss Reid but he also had a housekeeper named Moggach to whom he was very close. When Johnston and his new wife married she went to Todholes with him but only stayed one night before returning to her previous home for good. Sandy Clarke of Mid Skeith had a reputation for pouncing on unsuspecting young women on dark nights.

SOCIAL CLASS

Social class distinctions were sometimes considered important in the history of Deskford and at other times were not. In the 1920s they were. At a dance in the newly completed Public Hall, a local farm servant was teased by his friends who dared him to go up and ask a farmer's daughter whom he greatly admired for a dance. He finally plucked up the courage to do so and was rewarded for his impertinence with a slap. Farm servants kept crowded to the far end of the hall while farmers and their families occupied a greater space at the end nearest the band. Not all dances were however as ugly. In 1930 Mr and Mrs

Murray, Little Skeith, won the fancy dress competition at a dance run by the Badminton Club, dressed as a Persian Prince and Princess.

Attitudes towards social class have changed significantly over the years, and each generation has probably been comfortable with the etiquette of their own time. This probably applies even to the 1st millennium AD when slaves were widely held. There were several classes of nativi or unfree who were considered similarly to beasts for their value. They could be bought and sold, but were usually included in the price when land changed hands. Most slaves were spoils of battle but were then sold on to different end users. Slaves and their owners were the same race as each other, and the practice existed at all levels of society. The average free peasant had eight cows, two horses and three slaves. Slavery however died out by the middle of the C12th.

Serfdom however persisted until the end of the C14th. Partly because of the effects of the Black Death, Scotland became the first country in Europe to abandon the practice, except for coal miners and salt panners, who remained serfs till 1802. Serfs could also be bought and sold and were tied to an estate and to labour for the landowner. Under serfdom, a serf's wife and children were his lord's property, and the serf had to ask permission and pay a "merchet" if his daughter wished to marry outwith his village, to compensate the lord for the loss of her labour and for her future children which he would otherwise have owned. The concept of the freed man was common. They became the poorer elements of society but valued their freedom. Thirlage to estate mills was a practice which survived in Deskford as in other areas till the C19th and was a survival from serfdom.

There were three grades of peasant, in descending order. Firstly there were bonders, paying food rent and only having to undertake seasonal work such as ploughing and harvesting. Secondly there were hurd (hired) men, who gave general service to the landowner or tenant. Thirdly there were gresmen (grassmen) who had only a pastoral holding and paid rents in hay. It was very difficult for unfree nativi or nyefs to escape their servitude. They belonged to their lord and could not move without his permission. Throughout the C12th there were many fugitives who roamed the countryside. Small-scale nativi were sometimes cleared from their holdings to permit ploughing, as part of the move from small fields, cultivated by hand, to the rig and furrow system.

In the Middle Ages, when a peasant died, his lord was entitled to take his best cow before the peasant's son was permitted to take over his father's rigs. If the peasant had only three cows the lord could take his most valuable possession instead, a brass pot or a woollen cloak for example. By the C14th and C15th there was a greater distinction between rich husbandmen and poor peasants, as the population decreased. In the C16th the tenantry and the upper grades of the peasantry were free in law and also in spirit. They were "much more elegant than those in France", though rough and dirty. Scotland largely escaped the class wars of England and much of Europe in the C14th, C15th and C16th. There were however many vagrants, especially after crop failure. Sorners (strong sturdy beggars) and Egyptians (gypsies) were feared for extorting money or food.

This class system persisted, though in a significantly evolved manner, in places like Deskford until the second half of the C18th. It comprised tenants, sub tenants, crofters and cottars, all of whom cooperated to achieve an effective society based on subsistence agriculture. Though there were different classes in society this did not produce the hard class boundaries which followed in the C19th with the change to a capitalist system of agriculture. By and large status did not dictate esteem. However in the mid C18th visitors to the area considered the peasantry to be "poverty stricken, with pinched faces, wrinkled features, tattered dress, foul skin and fouler habits".

The *Gentlemen's Magazine* in 1776 stated that "you would not take them at first to be of the human species, and in their lives they differ very little from the brutes. They would rather suffer poverty than work. Their faces are coloured with smoke, their eyes are shrunk and their hair is long and almost covers their faces". By 1760 rural areas still displayed great poverty, but gradually, as agricultural improvements accelerated, there developed a class system in which farm servants no longer ate or slept with the farmer's family. By the end of the C18th the people of Deskford were considered in general to be honest, industrious and sober. There was only one alehouse in the parish and it was not well frequented. In consequence of their sobriety and good conduct they had large families and were long lived.

In the C19th tenant farmers and farm servants became distinctly different classes in a capitalist system of agriculture. This was fully established by 1830. In the 1840s many cottages were pulled down to prevent them being allocated to paupers under the new Poor Law. At this time the middle class comprised only those in the professions. In 1850 in Deskford, only the two Ministers, the schoolmaster and the vet were given their titles, everyone else was known by their Christian and surnames. In 1842 Grange had "long been infested with cairds, tinkers and sturdy beggars". It is unlikely that Deskford was much different. During the early C19th some farmhouses kept a special teapot for regular vagrant visitors, who were allowed to sleep in the barn. Well-known vagrants included Peter Fraser, of whom many stories were told, some of them true.

By the late C19th cottars and their families had a much lower status in society than had been the case a hundred years previously, and many were very poor. However they usually kept a vegetable garden and had a cow, pigs or poultry. They could get a licence to hunt hares and rabbits, but not pheasants or partridges. One of the few occupations which had a lower status was that of molecatcher. The agricultural class system persisted till the middle of the C20th, after which it declined with increased mechanisation and a much reduced population. During the 1930s there were two tramps who visited Deskford regularly, Happy Harry and Meg Pam. Most farmers were happy to allow them to sleep in barns.

Deference largely disappeared, and in the second half of the C20th there developed a much more egalitarian and meritocratic society. It has been argued that we are now however entering a period in which social mobility is reducing and in which a much harder and more rigid class system is re-emerging, a situation reinforced by those who currently have power or wealth.

Until recent times many of the residents of Deskford were the descendants of families which had lived here for hundreds of years. Very few now are, but there are still one or two who can be identified as having ancestors in Deskford hundreds of years ago and who would have experienced class systems much different to those which we know today.

HEALTH AND ILLNESS

In the C14th the average man in the North east was 5'7½" (169cm) tall and the average woman 5'2½" (157cm), though the rural poor were shorter. Only one third of women survived beyond child-bearing age. Middle age was the mid 30s, and to be 45 was to be old. Men lived longer than women because of the risks of childbearing, the opposite of today. One third of the population died from the Black Death in 1350, spread evenly across the country.

There were many diseases which resulted in death in the period before 1500. There were outbreaks of plague in 1349/50, 1361/62, 1379, 1392, 1401-03, 1430-32, 1439 and 1455. Leprosy was frequently diagnosed, but was probably a range of skin infections, which the clergy attributed to sin, fornication, adultery, avarice, usury, perjury or bearing false witness. The last cases of leprosy were recorded in Scotland in 1798.

Smallpox was universal and had a high mortality rate of 10% across the country but higher than this in the countryside. From these early times right up to the C18th the ague (malaria) was very common, and very debilitating among the rural poor. Levels of smallpox, malaria and rheumatism fell in rural areas when widespread drainage was introduced. Before 1500 there were high death rates amongst the young from respiratory ailments and from gastro-enteritis. Tuberculosis, cholera, amoebic dysentery, spina bifida, arthritis, gingivitis and caries were all common and there were also the debilitating and nauseating effects of ringworm and parasitic worms. Syphilis made its appearance in the C15th and became increasingly common. By around 1800 it was endemic and was known to be sexually transmitted. It was known as grandgore or glengore. Many sufferers were killed by the mercury which was thought to be a cure.

Even though the climate deteriorated after 1300 there was no vitamin C or vitamin D deficiency, which could have caused scurvy or rickets, because there were adequate amounts of fruit, vegetables and dairy products in the diet. There was however widespread iron deficiency due to prolonged breast feeding and a high fish content in the diet.

In the 1690s crop failure caused destitution, starvation and death. Sometimes whole families, or all of several families on one multiple tenancy farm died. Across the North East 25% of the population died from starvation. The dead lay by the roadside and some people, too weak to walk, crawled to the kirkyard to try to ensure themselves a Christian burial. In 1699 an intimation from the Commissioners of Supply was read from the pulpit in Deskford as elsewhere, to all persons "to bury the corps of the poor timeously under failzie (fine) of 20/- to those persons adjacent to where they dye".

In the C19th overall life expectancy was relatively low because of the high number of deaths in the teens, twenties and thirties. By 1900 there was still a great deal of early death, though some individuals survived into their 80s and 90s. Despite the introduction of vaccination by the mid C19th, cholera and typhoid were still a problem and measles, whooping cough and scarlet fever could be fatal. People with lengthy terminal illnesses often suffered great pain while confined to their beds. In Deskford one very large family lost every son and daughter to consumption as they reached their 20s. In 1890 there was a widespread influenza outbreak during which hardly a house in Deskford escaped and there were several deaths. There were other major outbreaks locally and also worldwide in 1918 and 1937 and there were two major outbreaks of scarlet fever in the 1930s.

Before the introduction of the NHS in 1947, most people could not afford to go to the doctor unless their condition was very serious. From 1900 the school log gives some indication of the health concerns in Deskford. In January 1900 influenza was present in almost every home in Deskford and the school closed for three days because the Headmaster was also ill with it. In February 1901 there was heavy absence because of German measles, in December 1903 there was a lot of whooping cough in the parish and in January 1904 the school was closed because of it. That same year the school was also closed because of measles, which Miss Grant also caught.

In July 1909 whooping cough was reported in two families in Backies, the Garvocks and the Reids. This was reported to Dr Ledingham, Banff, who, after visiting these and other victims, said that all but the boy Stuart could return to school at the end of the month. Influenza was widespread in December 1909 and scarlet fever in January 1911 and again in that July. In March 1912 more than a quarter of the infants were off with whooping cough, which continued until April, by which time mumps was also a problem. Measles was present in four houses in March 1913 and then spread more widely. On November 8th 1918, Dr Ledingham ordered closure of the school for three weeks because of the influenza epidemic, which continued into December.

In February 1922 the school was closed for one week because of verminous children and an influenza epidemic which both the Headmaster and Miss Wilson fell victim to. In March 1923 there was an outbreak of infectious jaundice and in May that year fifteen pupils from five different families were absent with measles. The school was closed between October 15th and November 5th because of whooping cough.

On April 19th 1923 one girl was sent home to be cleaned because her head was in a dirty condition. On May 23rd another was sent home to be cleaned as she was in a verminous condition and would not be readmitted to school until she had been thoroughly cleaned. On June 14th a third was sent home to have her head cleaned as she was in a verminous condition.

On September 13th 1923 Mr Robert Forbes, Old Schoolhouse, Kirktown, wrote to the Headmaster intimating that he would not allow his children to attend Deskford School till it was ascertained by the proper authority whether or not any of the pupils were in a verminous condition. That day the headmaster, together with Miss Raffan and Miss Wilson sent fifteen pupils home to be cleaned of vermin and not allowed to return until clean. For some reason, perhaps because of their having longer hair, all were girls.

On September 20th the School Nurse examined various suspected cases of body vermin. As a result the Headmaster wrote to Mr Forbes, Old Schoolhouse, and ordered him to return his children to school, which he did. On October 10th Mr Forbes again complained of body lice in his boys. The complaint was forwarded to the Medical Officer and Dr Ledingham visited the school and ordered it to be closed from October 16th till November 2nd. That same year whooping cough affected four Wilsons from The Field, two McLeans from Milton and three Simpsons from Milton.

On April 30th 1924 the family of Cruikshank, Little Mosside was excluded for diphtheria. In February 1925, Dr Ledingham excluded Mary and Elsie Duncan, Kirktown on account of severe infectious skin disease. In March 3 children from another family were excluded for impetigo. On April 20th a letter was sent home to parents of children with dirty heads. On the 24th Dr Ledingham and Nurse Reid visited the school by request and examined the heads of all scholars present (roll 92). Nine parents were warned of their children's dirty heads.

On June 1st 1926 Dr Ledingham ordered the school to be closed from that day till the summer holiday because of scarlet fever. The prizegiving was postponed until August. On November 11th a pupil was sent home because of ringworm. On December 1st 1927, in response to a parental complaint, Nurse Reid examined every pupil present (roll 98), but could find no evidence of itch or scab. There was a chickenpox outbreak in October 1928 and on November 16th 1931 Dr McHardy and Nurse Leggat excluded nine pupils for a week with whooping cough. In November 1935 the MOH closed the school for two weeks because of scarlet fever. It did not reopen till January 14th 1936. On March 23rd 1936 the school was closed till after the Easter holidays because of measles.

Scabies was a persistent problem in the 1940s, and on December 23rd 1952 38 pupils were absent with measles. In October 1954 the school was closed for two weeks because of an outbreak of poliomyelitis. In February 1956 attendance was poor because of influenza and jaundice and in June 1961 there was an epidemic of chickenpox in the infant room.

MEDICAL PROVISION

Medical provision was very limited indeed until Victorian times. In 1723 there was so much sickness in Deskford that the Minister had to give up three or more days each week in visiting the sick. In July 1766 Isobel Laing, wife of Peter Mathieson, Faichyhill applied to the Minister to be received into Aberdeen Infirmary for the cure of one of her hands which had been for some time past in a very bad way. The Kirk Session asked the Minister to make the recommendation, and agreed that if she died in the Infirmary they would pay for the funeral. At this time broken bones were often set by the blacksmith, and during the 1740 crop failure, the Session planned ahead and bought coffins in advance.

In the 1840s there was no hospital in the parish, but local people, because they took an annual collection for Aberdeen Infirmary, were entitled to admission there if required, though this was not common. There was also an annual collection for a pauper lunatic fund to allow admission, where necessary, to the Lunatic Asylum in Aberdeen, this being before the one at Ladysbridge was built.

In 1848 the Parochial Board appointed Hugh Sharp, Surgeon, Cullen, doctor for the Poor of Deskford at a salary of £10 per annum. The Board also received an allocation to Deskford Parish from the Parliamentary Grant in Aid of Medical Relief to the Poor in Scotland. On April 17th the Inspector laid before the Parochial Board a report from Dr Sharp stating that he considered William Smith, Burns, to be a dangerous maniac and requesting the Board to put him under proper control.

In 1858 the Parochial Board approved vaccination arrangements for paupers. That year a letter was also received from the General Board for Lunacy in Scotland regarding lunatic and fatuous persons chargeable to the parish. There was also a letter from the Medical Superintendant of the Lunatic Asylum in Aberdeen saying that Alexander Howie, Pauper Lunatic, was not expected to recover ultimately, but that he might soon be able to be transferred to the Poor House.

On June 25th 1866 the Parochial Board gave consideration to the Nuisances Removal (Scotland) Act in connection with the appearance of malignant asiatic cholera in the UK. A sub-committee was formed to supervise the removal of nuisances from the parish.

In the late C19th various ladies helped out at births in Deskford, Mrs Seivwright from Portsoy, Mrs Gray, and Mrs Murray (Lucky Murray) from Berryhillock. In 1901 there was an official criticism of the Parish Council for including all vaccinated people in the Medical Officer's salary when this should just have covered the vaccinated Poor. In 1916 Helen Howie, a pensioner on the Poor Roll was given three pints of whisky and 4/1d for medicine between mid October and mid December.

Regular Medical Inspections were taking place in the school before World War I. In September 1912 the Medical Officer of Health for Banffshire recommended spraying all woodwork and floors with Cyllin, which was done. In October the Sanitary Inspector ordered disinfection of the school because of scarlet fever. By 1921 there were regular visits to the school by Mr Dunlop the dentist. On May 23rd that year John Clarke of Hoggie was ordered by Dr McHardy to live in the open air as much as possible, and not to attend school for an indefinite period.

In 1923 Mr Yorstan the School Dentist examined the teeth of pupils aged 6, 7, 12 and 13, and two weeks later spent several days operating. The School Medical Officer, Dr Grant, examined all pupils aged 9 and 12. From that year there was also kept by the Registrar a record of all vaccinations. Glasses were provided for three pupils, Helen Forsyth, Hellen Ettles and Edith Smith.

On October 26th 1932 Dr Walker examined four pupils for deafness, two mentally and two physically. Together with the Nurse he also examined boarded-out children and those under observation. The Health Inspection on September 16th 1938 revealed two cases of ringworm, 1 case of scarlet fever and 1 case of diphtheria. Ringworm had become more prevalent but was well attended to. There was 1 case of scabies in March 1939, and several pupils were excluded by the Nurse for itch and impetigo on November 25th 1940.

Diphtheria immunisation was carried out on May 22nd 1941 and three pupils were excluded for scabies on October 2nd 1941, with four more on the 11th. Diphtheria immunisation took place on May 6th 1943 and in the summer term there were several cases of scabies, mumps and scarlet fever. Several pupils were sent home with dirty heads.

On November 6th 1949 Mr Lang the optician fitted spectacles which had been prescribed eighteen months previously. There was no explanation for the delay. In 1956 pupils were given the BCG vaccination and also the new polio one. Boarded-out children were still being inspected, for instance the 10 seen by Dr Deas on June 8th. By the 1950s visits were taking place by the speech therapist, Miss Cochrane, and in June 1963 Mrs Boyne, the audiometrician tested the Primary 1s. One pupil was absent, one uncooperative and the rest normal. By 1966 visits by the school psychologist were also taking place.

The establishment of the NHS brought great benefits to many. In the 1950s Deskford was served by doctors from Cullen, Buckie and Keith, and by a district nurse who lived in Portknockie. It certainly was a marked advance from the day around 1941 when Tommy Davidson, then aged 9, and his brother both had their tonsils removed by the local doctor on the kitchen table in their house at Aultmore.

In the days before organised healthcare and the scientific approach of Victorian times, local people held a number of beliefs which they felt explained aspects of health and illness. In the C18th and earlier some people were believed to have the power of "casting ill", of causing a slow, lingering death. However it was also possible to rid oneself of a disease by transferring it to another creature such as a cat. This was related to the older belief of demonic possession. To drink cold water was dangerous when one had an acute illness. Boils would only appear on those who were exceptionally healthy. Hops, which were only used after about 1800, were thought to cause gravel, and tea caused rheumatism.

It was believed that pre-menstrual conception resulted in a male child and post-menstrual conception in a female child. A woman who menstruated during lactation would never suckle a male child. A woman who slept on her left side after intercourse would have a girl while if she slept on her right side she would have a boy and a child conceived amongst green grass or in the greenwood would be male. Any longing for particular food during pregnancy would transfer to the child and a pregnant woman must not be caused distress or have any of her wishes denied or the child would be born lacking one of its senses.

Crossing one's arms in the presence of a woman in labour caused the labour to be long and difficult. All door locks should be unlocked in a house in which a woman was in labour, and no pregnant woman should be allowed to enter the room. If the umbilical cord was tied carelessly and bled then the child would be a bed wetter.

There were very many traditional cures, some general but some specific to particular ailments. Some individuals had the power or gift of being able to cure any disease and some families were known to be able to cure particular diseases, illnesses or injuries. Charms and incantations were often used as were herbal remedies. A tablespoon of the liquor in which a mouse had been boiled was used to cure enuresis. Sulphur, sewn into a garter and worn, was used for cramp. Black slugs brewed in a teapot produced an oil which was used for rheumatism, and the oil of slugs and snails was also used for pulmonary complaints. Red silk was worn round the wrist as a cure for rheumatism and red worsted round a child's wrist kept witches away. Leeches were widely used.

Washing one's penis in one's own urine was a cure for venereal diseases, and impotence could be cured by smearing the gall of a wild boar on one's penis.

Turning a baby upside down and shaking it prevented colic. Warts could be transferred to snails by rubbing them with one. A hare's skin was applied to the chest for asthma. Whooping cough could be transferred to a dog by feeding it a hair of the sufferer between slices of bread and butter. Other cures for rheumatism were drinking skate bree, or turpentine mixed with sugar, or by carrying a potato or the left fore foot of a hare in one's pocket. Skate bree was also used as an aphrodisiac, and sterile women could conceive by having intercourse on the ground, out of doors. Several well-known abortifactants were also used.

To cure consumption the sufferer should pass through a circular wreath of woodbine. Broom blossom could induce sleep. Rickets could be cured by having the child bathed by a blacksmith, and having all his tools passed over it. Lumbago, rheumatism and sprains could be cured by anyone who had been born feet first, or by using skate bree as a lotion. Epilepsy could be cured by drawing blood from an arm or finger, or by wearing a shirt in which someone had died, before it had been washed, or by burning all the clothes the epileptic was wearing.

Whooping cough and jaundice could be cured by drinking a decoction of sheep excrement, by eating with a horn spoon taken from a live animal, or by drinking asses' milk. Eye disease could be cured by having someone else lick a frog's eye and then the diseased eye. Nettle rashes were rubbed with docken leaves and ringworm with silver. Toothache could be cured by going to a churchyard and pulling a tooth from a skull, or by lifting a stone from a stream or a ford. Warts could be cured by licking them every morning or by rubbing them with dust from below a stone where four roads met. Henbane induced sleep and, in large quantities, narcosis. Deadly nightshade was a muscle relaxant and opium poppy a sedative. Posset was a mixture of ale and honey used to treat a cold.

When a woman had just given birth she had to sup a strong ale gruel, boiled with great care to prevent it catching alight. Different ales were used medicinally. For pulmonary problems, including consumption, horehound, pennyroyal and sage, with liquorice and honeysuckle to sweeten it, were used. For scorbutic complaints there was water trefoil. For jaundice there was barberry bark and for dropsy, juniper berries. The gudewife would keep a store of these kebbacks, a similar word to that for cheese, beside the fireplace. These were medicinal herbs for use in winter.

In the C15th anaesthetics were used for operations such as amputation. They were often a mix of poisons including black henbane, opium poppy and henbane. During the same period ergot fungus and juniper berries were used to induce contractions in childbirth and for abortion.

The syrup of figs and other laxatives known to children born in the 1950s and 1960s were perhaps a hangover from the days of an oat based diet of brose, porridge and sowens, which often did induce a need for such products.

Not all actions, attitudes and beliefs in distant times accord with our attitudes today, though some are uncannily close. The present day argument about euthanasia has echoes of the times in which old people who were suffering badly were sometimes smothered. This was also done to babies who had been born deformed.

DIET

In Iron Age, Pictish and mediaeval times people who lived in Deskford had a mixed diet consisting of meat, poultry, fish, cereals, berries and nuts. Horse meat was eaten until the C7th when this was discouraged by the Church because of its association with pagan horse worship. There was often great hunger in the spring, when wild tubers, leaves and roots were eaten. Butter was stored in bogs to keep it fresh. The mixed diet gradually changed to a cereal-based one in which the standard bread was a flat, unleavened bannock of beremeal, peasemeal or oatmeal, cooked on a flat stone on an open fire.

After the Black Death in 1350, with a significantly reduced population, the diet improved and oats, mutton, beef, dairy produce, fish and ale were all consumed. The full range was oatmeal for porridge and oatcakes, bere (ancient type of barley) for broth and ale, milk, butter, cheese, beef, mutton, chicken, rabbit, pigeon, fish and fruit. Kale, peas and beans were also eaten. Ranulph Higden, an English monk, said that the Scots "fedde more with flesche, fisches, white meat and with fruits". All of this, together with seasonal cherries, apples, brambles, raspberries and hazelnuts was eaten by the ordinary people.

In 1435 it was reported that "even the common people eat flesh and fish to repletion". The proportion of livestock farming had increased after the population decrease from death caused by the plague, as this required less labour. Prices fell and there was often a glut of meat at Martinmas in November as beasts were killed to avoid the cost of fodder over the winter. Salt beef became common and milk, eggs, butter and cheese were plentiful, but not considered essential. Vegetables such as cabbage and onions were considered a luxury. Despite this relative plenty, crop failure was still difficult to deal with.

During the C13th braziers for cooking were replaced by stone hearths. All cooking vessels were ceramic till the C15th, when iron ones were introduced. The most commonly used mediaeval pottery in this area was redware, though some higher status white gritty ware may have been imported from the south of Scotland. The quality of pottery available had been transformed in the C12th with the introduction of new technology by Normans and by monks.

In the C16th there was a collapse in living standards. Meat was largely eliminated from the diet, dairy produce reduced and oatmeal began to dominate. Almost in contradiction, flour "baikes" and scones were introduced and ale was considered as a food. After 1600 oatmeal took the place of beremeal except among the poorest, and it was only now that it came to be seen as the mainstay of the Scottish diet. Peasemeal and beanmeal bread were used occasionally, particularly at times of scarcity, however wheat bread was never used because there were no ovens or yeast available. All "breid" was flatbread, baked on a stone or girdle.

In the C18th ale was drunk as soon as it was brewed, almost before it was cold. Whisky only made an appearance in the C15th and even at the end of the C17th was often made from oats. There was a basic whisky and a superior, thrice distilled type. In the early C18th fermented whey was also drunk, having been kept in barrels for a year. Milk quickly went sour and it was believed that the consistency of butter depended on the numbers of hairs put in it while it was churned. The best cheese was considered to come from ewes' milk rather than cows' milk, though it was the opposite for butter. In fact, butter made from ewe's milk was considered almost inedible and was used largely for greasing farm machinery.

Farmers' families and servants ate together and sat together at the fire in the evenings. Each man had his own horn spoon which he kept on his person, and used to sup brose, porridge, sowens and kail. Knives and forks only appeared gradually towards the end of the C18th. Before this time, most farms had little in the way of earthenware crockery or metal cutlery. There were wooden bowls and plates, and a few pewter ones, and wooden or horn spoons were used. Any cooked meat, a rarity, was eaten with the fingers. If meal ran out before the harvest, sometimes green corn was cut, though this produced a very inferior food.

Food improved between 1750 and 1800. The kailyard, in addition to cabbage, onions and kale, also now had carrots, turnips, potatoes and other vegetables, together with currants and gooseberries. A ploughman might have meat twice a week. Whisky took over from ale because of the excise duty on the latter, but the language of brewing was transferred to the making of tea. From the late C18th tobacco was chewed, smoked or used as snuff.

In the 1770s and 1780s wages accelerated much more quickly than prices, allowing cottars to afford potatoes, tea, and some sugar and meat. There was a reduction in consumption of warm cow's blood mixed with milk, of peasemeal and of beremeal. Before 1800 sowens, made from prone (oat husks) was widely eaten for breakfast or midday dinner, but had largely disappeared by 1900, though drinking sowens lasted longer. Sowens was always cooked in brass pans rather than iron ones. The evening meal was often kale or cabbage boiled with oatmeal. On Sundays barley broth with some meat might be eaten. Tea was introduced just before 1800, and there was much criticism of it because it had to be bought rather than being produced on the farm. However it gradually replaced ale and drinking sowens, though the mother of the farmer at Auchip in Fordyce around 1850 had only tasted tea for the first time at her wedding in the early C19th.

In the North East in 1830 there was more kail and less potato in the diet with very little meat and no tea for the poor. Even by 1840 in Deskford the diet comprised people's homegrown oatmeal, kail and potatoes together with other produce from their kailyards. By this time no ale was brewed because of the heavy duty on malt. Only during the C19th, with the introduction of cheap beet sugar, were jams, jellies, sponges and biscuits produced widely for the first time.

In Deskford in 1850 the peat fire was used for roasting potatoes in the warm ashes, and for keeping small pans and the teapot warm. At harvest time a cask of beer was purchased, mixed with half its bulk of water, and treacle or honey added together with a little ginger and a little barm. It was then all allowed to ferment again. Out in the field it was served with a little oatmeal in the bottom of a mug.

Oatcakes were known as "breid", and wheat bread, which had now been introduced, was bought from a baker and known as "loaf". To make an oatcake the oatmeal was mixed with water, rolled out to about ½ inch thick, slipped on to the girdle over the peat fire, turned and cut in four. As an occasional treat cream was spread over it. Fish was brought round by fishwives from the coastal villages in creels supported by a broad band round the shoulders or forehead. Fish caught overnight was brought round in the forenoon. People grew their own potatoes and vegetables. Gull's eggs and chicks were taken illegally from Lurg Hill and Aultmore.

Gradually throughout the late C19th and C20th the diet of the people of Deskford became more varied, with an increasing range of foodstuffs becoming available for purchase, however oatmeal remained the staple well into the C20th. During World War II, rationing did not have an enormous effect locally, particularly on farms, and in the mid C20th both brown trout and sea trout were caught in the Deskford Burn as far upstream as Kirktown. In 2013 only one farm in Deskford, Burnheads, still grew a park o' corn (oats) every year, and that largely through nostalgia, however by 2015, because of European Union regulations against monoculture, several felt obliged to replace one of their fields of barley with a park o' corn. The Deskford inhabitants of 100 years age would fail to comprehend today's diet.

Throughout much of its history Deskford was affected by intermittent famine. These go back as far as recorded history in the North East. There was famine and pestilence in 1154 and famine in 1256. In 1259 there was a great famine across Scotland with a boll of meal costing as much as 48 sterlings (small silver coins). Between 1315 and 1318 many people died of famine, or were driven to eat the flesh of unclean animals such as horses, cats and dogs and, according to some sources, children. Cannibalism was certainly recorded in Perth in the 1330s. Most of the famines between 1550 and 1660 were because population increase was greater than the increase in food production. The worst famines during this period were in the 1570s, 1590s, 1630s, 1640s and 1690s. The worst famine year of all was in 1623. The years between 1694 and 1699 were known as "King William's dear years". Haar, extremely wet summers, early frosts and storms meant that the corn hardly ripened. Harvests often did not take place till December or even into January. Humans, sheep and oxen died in great numbers and people were reduced to eating nettles, dockens, grass and snails.

There were stories of bodies lying at the roadside with grass in their mouths, and of people, too weak to walk, crawling to kirkyards to ensure a Christian burial. One quarter of the population of the North East died from starvation during these five years. Deskford suffered, but escaped the worst.

1715 was a famine year. Banffshire JPs banned hoarding and the export of corn, the price of which was not to exceed £9 Scots the boll. 1740 was also a famine year. There was an intense spring frost and the Deskford burn froze. This was followed by a cold, wet summer in which the crops failed. 1742 was a terrible year of food shortage. The harvest was very late and the worst ever. On October 5th a snowstorm lasted for two weeks. Unripe crops were left in the field, and what was cut was inedible. In 1743 some people got frostbite from trying to cut unharvested crop in February. Flour and peasemeal were imported from England. 1765, 1766 and 1767 were famine years. 1782 promised a heavy crop but a frost in August ruined the corn. 1783 was an "ill year" and 1795 bitterly cold. Free meal was distributed.

After the mid C18th, though there were still many years in which there were poor harvests, the numbers dying from starvation were much fewer because the authorities were better able to cope. In Deskford the Earl of Findlater and the Kirk Session provided some meal at subsidised prices, and the Commissioners of Supply imported meal into ports such as Portsoy. The final emergency was the potato famine of 1847. In Deskford the recently established Parochial Board had to deal with this. The effects here were not as severe as in some areas because potatoes were not the main fod crop. For some however there was a serious impact and the numbers on the Poor Roll increased significantly.

CLOTHING

In mediaeval times wool, linen, fur and leather were the main materials used for clothes. For the better off, twills were hard wearing and wind and water proof, and fulled and felted cloths were also used. Most dyes were only for the wealthy, with the exception of drab colours produced locally from weld, heather and onion. Styles of clothes remained unchanged and there was no concept of fashion.

From the C14th new styles and fabrics emerged. Woollen cloth of varied quality was worn by the poorer people. The knitting of bonnets and stockings was introduced from Spain in the C15th, and an Act of Parliament in 1429 forbade farmers from wearing ragged garments. In 1430 another Act was passed stating how people should dress according to their rank and class, and in 1471 yet another Act stated that only minstrels, heralds, knights and the wealthy were permitted to wear gowns of silk. This did not have a great deal of relevance in Deskford.

In the C16th and C17th plaid was worn by working and lower middle class men and by women of all classes except the very wealthy. A foreign visitor recorded

"From the middle of the thigh to the foot they have no covering for the leg, clothing themselves with a mantle instead of an upper garment and a shirt". The plaid was up to 5 metres long and was worn as an outer garment. By the late C17th and early C18th peasant men wore plaid and trousers while women wore linen skirts with a plaid. Men had shoes but women and children did not. However, for the first time, within the general population there was a wish to appear as well dressed as possible. Clothes were home-produced from flax and wool, except for the farmer's bonnet and his wife's velvet hood. Cloth was spun on the farm, woven by local weavers and made up by local tailors. The quality of cottage-produced cloth was poor.

By the mid to late C18th people had some clothes made up for them by local tailors, though undergarments were still made by women at home, often of linen spun from their own flax. Women made their own dresses, and for many poor people shoes were only worn on Sundays. Towns such as Cullen and Keith had been able to provide some ready-made clothes since mediaeval times, but these were mainly for wealthier individuals. Most Deskford people could not afford to buy such linen under garments, stockings, caps and shoes, but second-hand clothing was sold widely.

In the early C18th men wore "scourin" or "hodden gray" at home and knee breeches, hose and blue coats with home-made wooden buttons. In 1750 Ministers wore black only on Sundays and the rest of the week they wore a blue suit. Only the laird and the Minister wore a hat rather than a bonnet. Unmarried girls wore "snoods". Women wore coarse home-made drugget, a matted wool mix, with a short petticoat. On Sundays they went to Church wearing a coarse linen head-covering and a tartan or red plaid covering their shoulders and head. Women only wore shoes on Sunday, and they found them uncomfortable so often walked barefoot to Church before putting their shoes on.

Men wore rough clothes, often in rags. Hose was pieces of reused plaiding sewn together. Coats were of coarse woollen cloth or harn, which was similar to sacking. These clothes were changed only two or three times a year. They wore shoes only on Sundays or on holidays or when there was frost or snow on the ground. On special days, holidays or for burials, for courting and on the Sabbath they wore a homespun suit of friezed cloth, often decked with ribbons and bows. Larger farmers' dress was little better, but they did wear black bonnets to distinguish them from farm servants who wore blue ones.

By around 1790 agricultural improvement and greater prosperity had brought massive change. Even labourers wore a short doublet and linen trousers. Plaiding had been abandoned and most people were well clothed. Linen shirts replaced woollen ones, though old people said that this caused more rheumatism and colds. Sunday attire for a farmer would include a coat of blue cloth, velvet vest, corduroy breeches, white cotton stockings, calf-skin shoes, black silk shoulder knots, a shirt with ruffles at the breast, a white muslin cravat, a hat worth eight or ten shillings and a watch on a fob. Forty years previously only the laird and the Minister would have had a watch. The plainest farmer now dressed in English broadcloth and wore a hat. Young women wore cotton dresses, and on Sundays were well shod, wore good cotton dresses, a duffle cloak and a bonnet. The wealthier farmers' wives had gowns of silk.

In the C19th, as well as flax, wool was also spun, in different qualities. By this time the Bleachfield was a woollen mill. The coarsest were greys for common use, at 2/6d the ell, and plaiding at 10d the ell. Finer wool "double blues" were produced for men's best suits and winceys and plaids for women's best clothes. Wincey was a popular cloth which combined a linen warp with a woollen weft. Breeches were now of corduroy, if it could be afforded.

Early in the 19th century women wore a petticoat and a jerkin, and, if married, a mutch, which was a triangle of muslin or linen tied below the chin. All married women also wore a "front", an arrangement of brown or dark hair over their own. Higher-class women wore in addition, a curtch, which was a folded piece of muslin or linen in front of the mutch, down the side of the head and also tied under the chin. They also wore a cloak with a buckle. Quines wore no headgear but had their hair in the latest style and wore white and blue striped petticoats plus red plaids, even sometimes of satin or velvet.

By 1850 red cloaks were no longer worn in Deskford, but the mutch was still worn by a few old women. When one of these was widowed she put a black ribbon on her mutch, passing over the crown and round the nape of the neck. In the late C19th no schoolchildren in Deskford wore shoes, not from poverty, but simply because they felt that their feet no more needed covering than their hands. Women going to Cullen took off their shoes and stockings to walk there and then sat down at the side of the road to put them on before entering the town. Apart from summer, in the 1890s, boys wore tackety boots and girls wore leather ankle boots. No doubt when future historians analyse the C20th, shell suits, Bermuda shorts and mini-skirts will merit comment.

HOUSES

There were at one time four grand houses in Deskford, Inaltry Castle, The Tower of Deskford, the Castle of Skeith and the mansion of Ardoch. Of these, remnants of the first two still survive together with one or two decorative stones and a tread from a stone circular staircase at Skeith. The precise location for Ardoch is unknown, but the occupants of what was the C19th farmhouse are intrigued by a massive stone wall built in to it.

The earliest of these grand houses, the Castle of Inaltry, was probably built in the C13th, and was already known as "the auld castle" in 1541. When the Barony of Deskford was first established its principal messuage was the Old Castle of Inaltrie. By 1840 it still had a deep circular hole, about the diameter of an ordinary draw well, enclosed by a wall of masonry which rose to a considerable height. The hole was filled in by rubbish about this time and a vault to which a stair had led had been covered over by a tenant's kailyard. It is highly likely that significantly more masonry than the fragment now visible remains buried. For a time there was a suggestion that it might have been a religious establishment, because a crucifix was found there in 1780 and an enthusiastic antiquarian of the C18th suggested that the name Inaltry includes "altar". This ignores the fact that Inaltry is a Gaelic placename which means hill pasture, which is supported by its persistent local pronunciation of "Nyattery".

In the early 1720s the Earl of Findlater purchased Inaltrie from the Lawtie family, thus reducing the number of heritors in Deskford from three to two.

The Tower of Deskford is probably very late C14th or very early C15th, with improvements made in 1560, and is attributed to the Sinclair family of Findlater and Deskford. It formed a courtyard on the north side of Old St John's Church, with the entrance to the courtyard facing north. With the continuing rise in the fortunes of the Ogilvie family, the Tower became the most important castle in the parish. The associated orchard, which retained some fruit trees well into the C19th, was probably planted around the early C16th when such possessions became fashionable among wealthier landowners.

The existing Muckle Hoose, by far the oldest dwelling in Deskford, and probably early C17th with some even earlier work incorporated, is believed to have been the western, accommodation range of the courtyard. The Tower occupied the south range, and it is believed that the great hall was the eastern range with the northern range comprising domestic features such as stables and kitchen, though this northern range was still occupied as a house in the C19th. In 1790 the Tower comprised four storeys above a barrel-vaulted entrance chamber, with a garret storey on top, taking it to a height of 70 feet. It was around this time it was drawn by Cordiner for inclusion in his "Remarkable Ruins of North Britain", published in 1788.

The Muckle Hoose is a west-facing five bay house with four window fenestration and an off centre door in the penultimate bay from the south. This is now enclosed by a modern stair tower which projects from the front. The building has small windows with chamfered margins which are harled over. It has irregular rear fenestration and ridge stacks and a slate roof. It was sympathetically renovated by recent owners, Judith and Tom Johnson.

The Tower had a steeply pitched roof with crow stepped gables and angle turrets at the fourth floor. It had a doorway on the north under a portico with extensive decoration. Occupation ceased by the end of the C16th when Cullen House opened, and it remained unoccupied thereafter, even though it had been described as a "commodious mansion house" after the improvements of

1560. In the early C19th two large parts of the Tower collapsed, just missing an adjacent cottage. The rest was examined and found to be in a dangerous condition so, in the 1830s, what was left was pulled down to prevent the possibility that it might collapse onto the Church.

The Muckle Hoose from within the ground floor of the tower.

In the 1920s Seafield Estate insisted on Deskford Parish Council purchasing the Muckle Hoose as part of the agreement under which it sold the Council the land to make the top part of the present graveyard. For some time thereafter it was used by the Parish Council to house poorer families in one-room apartments, one of which was occupied by the family of a child called Ron Shepherd, currently a Councillor on Moray Council.

No evidence survives about when the Castle of Skeith was built, though it may have been C15th or C16th, but the landowners and main occupants were the Abercrombie family, a cadet branch of the Abercrombies of Birkenbog. In 1724 the Castle was bought by the Earl of Findlater from the Abercrombies, thus reducing the number of heritors in the parish from two to one. By 1790 the Castle was ruinous, though by 1840 it was still a striking feature to passers by on the new turnpike road. By 1871 only a small fragment remained, forming part of the north end of the front garden of Mains of Skeith.

The Castle of Skeith was considered to have a delightful situation, on an eminence above the burn, and having a glimpse of the sea and an extensive view of the Deskford valley. Like the Tower of Deskford, the Castle of Skeith also had an orchard in the haugh land between it and the Burn of Deskford. Now all that remains are two skewput stones, a slab dated 1687 and some dressed lintels, all built into the facade of the late C19th farmhouse, together with a single stone tread from a circular stair, recovered when the stone steading was demolished a few years ago.

Skewput stone from the old Castle of Skeith, now built into the facade of the present late C19th Mains of Skeith farmhouse.

In 1724 William Ogilvie wrote that "About one myle from the Church, to the north east is a dwelling house, call'd Airdoch, belonging to a vassel to the Earle of Findlater, of the name Ogilvie". This may well refer to the mansion of Ardoch which is recorded, but of which the exact location is unknown. Nor is there any other record of its existence.

There are a number of other houses worth noting. Within Kirktown there are the two manses of respectively 1786 and 1873 together with Dominie, though none of the three is now in good condition. Dominie is a west facing, two storey, three bay harled house of about 1827 which is "B" Listed. Also in Kirktown is the cottage which was originally a dame school, then became the house which was used for accommodation by the lady teachers at Deskford School. Between Kirktown and Berryhillock is the brick built Schoolmaster's House of 1924, and in Berryhillock several of the cottages are "B" Listed. The Muckle Hoose and the Bleachfield are probably the only houses still standing which were built before 1800, but there are a few early C19th farmhouses such as those at Leitchestown and Langlanburn, at opposite ends of the parish. There is however a large number of substantial late C19th and very early C20th farmhouses, often replacing a farmhouse which was part of the steading and which in turn became the chaumer for farm servants. In many cases the steadings are now derelict or unused. Some ornamental stones were reputedly taken from the House of Pattenbringan, just outside the parish, when it was demolished, and placed on the top of Castle Hill in Cullen. Several modern houses have recently been built within the parish.

The villages of Kirktown and Berryhillock may have begun as Cottartouns for the Tower of Deskford and the Castle of Skeith respectively. There had certainly been Cottartouns linked to the Castle of Inaltry and the mansion of Ardoch, the latter of which still exists as a farm name. The only other village in the parish was at Milltown. In all of these the cottages were very small, usually two rooms and a closet, earth floored, turf or clay and bool walled and thatched. By the late C19th cement floors were beginning to become common in kitchens and corrugated iron roofs were often preferred to thatch, sometimes being fitted over the thatch, which was retained as insulation. In the 1950s several cottages in Berryhillock still had corrugated iron roofs.

The row of council houses in Berryhillock is post World War II. They replaced a row of derelict cottages sold to the Council by Johnny McLean, Duncan McLean's great uncle, for £14. The small size of most old cottages is illustrated by the fact that both Keills and its neighbour in Kirktown started as two semi-detached cottages. Most of the houses in Berryhillock and Kirktown were once owned by Seafield Estate.

The Poors Houses for Deskford were at Muir of Squaredoch and were only finally demolished and replaced by two new houses in 2012. The Poors Houses were shown in a map of 1858. By 1866 they comprised four dwellings, each with a separate entrance, and in 1871 there were two families in each of the two Poors Houses. The houses were clay built and were only allocated to persons of good character. Inhabitants had their own furniture, did their own cooking and treated the houses as their own. The houses were often fully occupied and additional accommodation had to be found by the Parochial Board. For example in January 1868 it was necessary to find accommodation for Catherine Fordyce or Raffan, then residing in Banff. In addition to the Poors Houses, individuals were often boarded out with some of the poorer families, usually in Berryhillock or the Aultmore Crofts, for whom this provided useful additional income.

In 1901 it was agreed to repair the roofs of the Poor's Houses. Mr John Gordon, carpenter was paid £9:15/-, and Mr Andrew Mitchell, slater, Cullen £30:7/-. At the same time the drains were also repaired. Thirty drains cost 3/1d and Mr McLean, labourer, was paid 7/6d. All of the costs were borne by the Parish Council, which also inspected the four Poors Houses in 1910, finding that three were in good condition and one in fair condition.

By far the largest percentage of the population of Deskford until 1950 was occupied in agriculture, and therefore farmhouses and cottar houses were by far the most common type of accommodation. By today's standards these were often unimaginably basic. Going back a thousand years, cottar hooses might have been tepee-like tents which gradually gave way in the following centuries to round turf built, single-room cottages, which were built in a day and only lasted for four or five years, before being consigned to the midden to help fertilize the fields.

They were often schelis (shielings) made of thick turf (faill) for the walls and thin turf (dovett) for the roof. Until around 500AD most huts or cottages were round, and then gradually, over the years, became rounded oblongs. These cottages housed entire families in a single room, which by the C17th was about 10 feet in diameter and five feet high. There were no beds or chairs, with people sitting and sleeping on the floor. Indeed on entering it was the practice to sit down on the floor immediately, otherwise the thick smoke, which had no chimney to escape through, would make breathing difficult.

By the early C18th cottar hooses were slightly larger, being about 12 feet square, built of turf and stone and thatched with bog sprotts or broom. There was often no wood in the turf roof. When this dried out it was replaced and the old turf used as fuel. On eviction the whole hut or cottage was put into the dung heap. It had a single unglazed window and still no chimney, just a hole in the roof. It might have by now a fully enclosed box bed, a kist, two stools, a cooking pot and wooden bowls and horn spoons. In Pennant's Tour of Scotland 1769, he states that peasants' houses in the Shire of Banff were decent, however in Moray they were very miserable. During the C18th some single room stone cottages, about 13 feet by 9 feet were built for superior farm servants. They had a corner hearth.

Cottar Touns had existed in the C16th, at Inaltry and at Ardoch as well as probably at Kirktown and Berryhillock. The one at Inaltry had disappeared by 1800 and that at Ardoch by 1900, having been replaced by a single farm which is still named Cottartown. During the early C19th farm workers' cottages were about sixteen or eighteen feet square and seven or eight feet high.

During the late C18th backing stones (brace steens) were introduced for the farmhouse fire which was in the centre of the house, and gradually, into the C19th these stones were extended to form two rooms. The next change was for the fire to be moved to a position against the kitchen gable and, from about 1770, hingin' lums were introduced. In the good room chimneys were built into the thickness of the gable and coal fires were introduced. However in the kitchen it was still an open-hearth peat fire. These were only replaced by chimneys within the gable not long before 1900.

From the C13th and C14th cruck framed longhouses had been developed as the standard farmhouse. These were still common well into the C19th. By 1400 they were between 25' and 65' long and between 3m and 6m deep, with turf walls and thatched or turf roofs supported by crucks. They housed people at one end and animals at the other, and had a single entrance for both and a central fire. The wooden crucks were the most valuable part of the house since they were load bearing, while the turf walls were not. Before this, farms had comprised a collection of small buildings including a dwelling, an ox stall, a hog sty, a sheep pen and a calf house, all surrounded by an earth rampart called a rath. Raemore means big rath. Longhouses were thatched with turf, heather, reeds or sprotts, and in the C16th and C17th the outgoing tenant took his couples and rafters with him, the new tenant having to build a new house.

After 1750 it became common to have three rooms, and for the house to be unconnected to the byre. In the kitchen was the spence, the length of the kitchen and six feet wide. This was where the quines slept. The house was only ten feet from back to front, and the four-foot high stone wall behind the fire, the "gresche", might be the only stone within the house. It had small stone niches at either end, the "lugs o' the gresche". The gudewife's spinning gear was stored in one, and fir candles in the other. On the gudeman's side of the fire, the fixed seat between the gresche and the wall was called the "deece" or "dyce". It could seat two. There would also be a table, chairs, a dresser for pots and crockery, and two wooden stoups for water.

The other room or aumry had a large cupboard for crockery, and a totally enclosed wooden box bed with checked linen curtain at the entrance. At the bottom of the cupboard or "press" was a black pig, (a large black bottle for whisky), and on the top shelf was an upside-down punch bowl and ladle. In older times there had been an ale jug and wooden caup. The punch bowl went out of use before 1850. On the other side of the kitchen was the "chaumer" where the loons slept, and where also could be found the meal girnal, spinning wheels and accoutrements, hesps o' yarn and webs o' claith. In this room there might be a twelve or sixteen inch square window.

Mid and late C18th pre-improvement farmhouses were still supported by couples but had stone and turf or stone and clay walls, with both inside and outside plastered with clay and whitewashed with local Craibstone lime. With materials prepared in advance, and with the help of neighbours, the house could be built in a day.

The couples had two legs, two arms (hoos) and two braces, the lower one the beuk and the upper one the croon piece. Couples were bound together by a beam laid along the top (the reef tree). Across the hoos, and at right angles to them, were laid three or four "pans" on each side of the roof. On these, and parallel to the couples, were placed pieces of trees or bog fir (kaibers) split by an axe. Such a roof was known as a pan and kaiber. Over this was placed the divots, and then finally the entire roof was covered by a thatch of heather, broom or sprotts.

In front of the single door lay the midden which took kitchen waste plus farm sewage, both human and animal, called "the green brees". Close to the door was the peat neuk, a favourite roost for hens. Inside, the main room was the kitchen, which had an earthen floor and no ceiling, just the soot-blackened roof couples, between which were boards on which cheese (kebback) was stored. From other couples hung onions and herbs plus a bunch or two of the pith from rushes which were used as wicks in the oil lamp (eely dolly). There might also be dried cod or ling and bog fir for making fir candles.

The crook dangled over the open fire from the rantle tree as the swey had not yet been introduced. There was a niche (bole) on either side of the fire which might hold tobacco and pipes and a knife (can'le gullie) for cutting bog fir candles. The bole at the other end held the salt bucket, which was kept by the fire to keep the salt dry. On the side wall was hung the bench which held plates, bowls and spoons and under this was the dresser with a row of wooden basins (caps) and cogs. Under the dresser were the pots, pans, pails and milking cogs. By the other wall was a settle and a folding down table, fixed to the wall.

Opposite the fire would be a box bed and perhaps a cupboard which together formed the partition with the other room(s). On top of the box bed were stored tools and other possessions which were only required occasionally. The kitchen had a single, small, four-pane window, of which sometimes only the top two panes were glazed. In one corner, at the foundation, was the dog hole which allowed the dog to come and go as it pleased, and in another corner, under the eaves, was another hole to let the hens in and out with the door closed. A jawhole in the wall was used for emptying water out of the kitchen.

A corridor (trance) led to the good room at the but end (but ein) of the house. This might contain a few chairs, a table, an eight-day clock, a chest of drawers, a mirror, a wooden bed (bun breest) and a cupboard or two with panelled doors. The floor was earthen, but there was a wooden ceiling and a window. Another door opened from the middle of the trance into a small bedroom.

Back in the kitchen there would be likely to be two pots on the hearth, the bait pot with turnips and shillicks for the farm horse, and the lit-pot which was covered with a slab of stone. This contained dye, usually blue, for dying wool, and which smelled strongly of ammonia. Fir candles were between one and three feet long and were fitted in a candle holder called the poor man (peer man) which was often a rounded stone with a hole in the middle which held a piece of wood with an iron clasp at the top from which hung the candle, with the flame toward the door.

The eely dolly comprised two iron shells, the outer of which was attached to the wall and the inner of which held the oil, from haddock, cod and ling livers, and the wick. There was a knob with notches to regulate the supply of oil. Rush wicks (rathin wicks) were replaced by cotton thread wicks at a later date, and when the lamp was dirty it was cleaned by burning.

The gudeman and his wife each sat at one corner of the fire, the man to the left as you faced it. Family and servants sat between them. Women knitted and made and mended while men did odd jobs such as cleaning candles, making wooden harrow tines and sewing brogues. Children did homework for school.

The size and value of a house was measured by the number of crucks used in its construction. Houses were between 14 and 16 feet deep, and crucks were between 6 and 9 feet apart. Cottar hooses had one or two crucks, farmhouses more. When new houses were required the landowner supplied the timber which was very valuable, and the tenant supplied all other materials, cartage and building costs. In an attempt to ensure that there was sufficient timber for crucks, all tenants were required to grow trees round the perimeter of the farmyard. The only iron used was for the nails to make the door.

Clay and dab and clay and bool construction were both used in the late C18th for agricultural buildings of all sorts. They were built with large foundation stones for the crucks to stand on (a dry pair o' shoes), and overhanging thatch (a dry hat). Clay and dab was a mixture of clay, straw and small pebbles, while bool and clay was round boulders set in clay, with a hearting of small stones and clay. Both were usually lime-washed annually. Walls of 7 feet in height had to be 22 inches wide while higher walls had to be wider. Only two or three feet of height were built each day, then three or four days were left before the next course was built. Houses of this type were cheap, reasonably durable and warm. Farmers' daughters and female servants slept in the kitchen, whilst sons and male servants slept in the low space in the roof, accessed by a ladder. This type of house was known as a stair hoose, but if there was no sleeping space in the roof, sons and male servants slept above the stables or in the "chaumer".

There were rituals associated with the building of new houses. When the foundation was laid, known as the founding point (funin' pint), the workers were given whisky or ale with bread and cheese. If this was not done, happiness and health would not be present in the house. In the evening after the house was built, there was a celebration and feast known as the hoose heatin' or fire kinlin.

Longhouses had been universal, and, as was often the case in agriculture, there was much resistance to change, such as the provision of separate doors for cattle. However change was inevitable, and the period of agricultural improvement accelerated many of these changes. In 1820 the Tower of Deskford, the Kirk, the manse and the Schoolhouse were the only buildings in the parish to be slated, every other one being thatched. By the end of the century every farmhouse was slated with many steadings being tiled with clay tiles from Tochieneal. In the villages, by the later C19th, corrugated iron had replaced thatch in many cottages.

Masonry and lime mortar was used increasingly to build houses, and as time went on, even humble ones. The arrival of the railway made the use of corrugated iron and Ballachulish and Welsh slate much cheaper and more convenient. Concrete sills and lintels were cast on site. Some new farmhouses were built as early as 1830, but in the period between 1880 and 1910 the majority of farms in Deskford were totally rebuilt with new steadings and a detached farmhouse, with garden.

When Mid Skeith was rebuilt in 1880 it had an indoor lavatory, a bathroom and water on tap. In this it was exceptional, and for many small farms and crofts indoor flush toilets were only acquired in the 1950s or 1960s. Each farm had a well, but these could be some distance from the farmhouse; however gradually improvements were made, such as surface piping of water from the well instead of carrying it in buckets, and the use of rotary pumps in kitchens to draw the water

In these new houses, built at the end of the C19th, suspended wooden floors were introduced, instead of earthen ones, and there was much varnished woodwork. The Seafield Estate specification for the new farmhouse at Inaltrie, built in 1880, incorporated very detailed measurements, often to the half inch, and instructions about where stone, concrete, brick, hollow brick, Caithness slabs, wood and cement were to be used. The level of the internal floors was to be not less than two foot six inches above the external ground surface. The walls were to be harled, but even when covered in this way were to be constructed of the very best hammer dressed rubble masonry. Concrete lintels, soles and rybets round doors, windows chimneys and corners were to be cast on site. Tochieneal bricks were specified. Ground floor partition walls were to be of hollow brick, with nine inch by five inch wooden blocks every eighteen inches on which to attach the skirting.

In 1882 the rent of Knows was £45. With a new lease it was agreed to build a new house and tile the roof of the old one, now to be part of the steading, all of which was also to be tiled. In 1913 Seafield Estate invited tenders from masons, carpenters, plumbers, slaters and plasterers for a new farmhouse at Oathillock.

Though farmhouses improved continuously from the early 1800s, the same could not be said for farm servants' cottages. In 1870 many of these were still built of undressed stone and were only 5 feet high, with one door, two windows, gables of turf and an earthen floor lower than the level of the ground outside. By the 1920s, a farm cottage would contain a dresser, a chest of drawers, a table and chairs and a bed with a chaff-filled mattress, perhaps with mice in it. It would also have a zinc bath, two enamel basins, one kist for clothing and one for bedlinen, box beds, an armchair and a poker and tongs for the fire.

Eventually the poor quality of housing for farm labourers was addressed after World War II, when in 1947 four Cruden houses were built by Banffshire County Council at Bleachfield. Expectations had increased. In the 1930s farm kitchens still had flagstone floors, a range burning peat and a cast iron kettle on a swey. There were still some clay built, earth-floored, thatched cottages with hingin' lums. The 1951 census enquired about whether houses had piped water, a cooking stove, a kitchen sink, a WC and a fixed bath. By 2001 it was enquiring about central heating.

Over the last 200 years many changes have been made, some just following fashion. Wall heads in many farmhouses were raised by two or three feet to allow suspended wooden floors to be put in. By 1830 prosperous farmers had bought mahogany tables, four-poster beds, fenders, feather mattresses and mirrors. In some farmhouses separate stairs for servants were installed. In the mid C20th almost all farm steadings in Deskford had the clay tiles stripped from their roofs and 8 feet by 4 feet asbestos panels fitted in their place.

Local Authorities did not always look after houses which they owned to a standard which was acceptable. In 1921 the Parish Council finally agreed to make repairs to the Lady Teachers' house in Kirktown, to remove the box bed, to paper and paint the bedroom and to distemper the lobby and kitchen. In 1936 an ingress of water to the Schoolhouse continued to be a problem, a temporary repair having been unsuccessful. It was referred to the Education Committee of Banffshire County Council for permanent repairs. They in turn referred the matter to the Property and Works Committee.

During the second half of the C20th many farmhouses were demolished, though a public meeting around 1981 was strongly of the view that abandoned farmhouses should be renovated and used as Council houses. This never transpired. For example, Blackhillock, a good farmhouse was abandoned in 1962/63 and demolished in 1985. Another good farmhouse, Upper Broadrashes, was abandoned in the late 1960s and demolished in the late 1980s, having had its slates taken and reused on the Cullen Tollhouse in 1971. Other farmhouses demolished in the late 1980s included Duffushillock, Poolside, Braehead and Rottenhillock. Lornachburn was not demolished till the early 1990s. The impressive Aultmore Lodge was last occupied in 1962 by forestry workers. Trees were planted round it in 1963. It was demolished in 1993 and the trees harvested in 2013. There had been scores of small cottages which were also demolished. Examples include Mary Anne where the Bloomfield to Cottar Clump road joined the present public road, Tod's Cottage near Braehead and Little Skeith Cottage, where a row of beech trees on the public road indicate a long forgotten beech hedge. There were many, many more.

Hilary Morrison at her house on the site of the former Poors Houses at Muir of Squaredoch.

In 1831 there were 189 houses in Deskford, and by 1950 there were 110. The number reached an all time low in 1991, but in recent years there have been several examples of derelict old farmhouses or steadings having been renovated, for example Ardoch, Kintywaird and Little Skeith. New St John's Church has been converted into a private house and new houses have been or are being built, for example at Bossy Hillock, Muir of Squaredoch and Oathillock, at the latter two locations by local builder, Daryl Skinner.

The number of houses in Deskford which are occupied is increasing, though in itself this can cause confusion. Upper Squaredoch was renamed Hillview and in the 1980s a new house called Muir of Squaredoch was built on the site of what had been Little Squaredoch. In 2012 two new houses were built on the site of the Poors Houses at Muir of Squaredoch and these are called Nos 1 and 2 Muir of Squaredoch. In 2015 the mill at Oathillock was converted into a new house.

Conversion of the mill at Oathillock into a new house.

ACCIDENTS

Deskford has witnessed a great number of accidents over the years, some minor, some amusing, but many serious and even fatal. Thankfully the number of accidents recorded in the area seems to have fallen even more steeply than the population. There were many road accidents in the 1930s and the 1940s, perhaps because roads were poorer and cars less safe. A selection of these accidents is outlined below.

In April 1933 there was a crash on the hump-backed bridge over the Burn Of Aultmore, near Keith, involving a car and a motor cycle. Mr Ernest Boyd, farm servant, Deskford, was taken to the Turner Memorial Hospital, Keith, with serious head injuries. His pillion passenger, Miss Johnstone, Horsebog, Grange, suffered bruising and the car driver, Mr Hume, Keith was uninjured. The motorbike was smashed and the car badly damaged. In May that year Mr Muiry, Berryhillock was the car driver who collided with a motor cycle at Cullen Toll Bar. Mr Muiry was uninjured, but the motor cyclist, Mr Bert Taylor, Buckie, had two broken legs.

In April 1936, Robert Barber, 21, farm servant, Mid Skeith, cycling downhill from the farm towards the main road, came off his bike and was thrown violently onto the road, striking his head. He died in Chalmers Memorial Hospital, Banff, without regaining consciousness.

In 1937 the steering of the car owned by James Chalmers, Bogside, locked and he crashed into a telegraph pole at the Reid Gate between Lintmill and Clune. He was not seriously injured, though this corner was notorious for accidents. In 1941 George Martin, Nether Blairock, cycling past the Reid gate hit a tree lying across the road. Some years later Muiry's taxi crashed into a tree here, and as late as 1982, George Bruce was killed here.

Also in 1937 there a crash between a lorry and a horse and trap on the Deskford to Cullen road. Both ladies in the trap were shocked and bruised, and the horse was caught further along the road. Still in 1937 a cattle float owned by William Jamieson, Drybridge, burnt out when passing Braidbog. Mr Jamieson managed to jump clear with his clothes alight. The lorry ran on into a ditch where it burned out. In January 1938 the steering snapped on a lorry owned by George Raffan, Rottenhillock, driven by James A Muiry and it went into a field through a fence, above Squaredoch. In June of that year there was a crash between a cyclist, Robert Davidson, trapper, Aultmore and a car driven by Alexander Ewen, Kirktown, at the Ha' Hillock junction. The cyclist was thrown over his handlebars and through the windscreen of the car. In September 1942, local roadman, Alexander Coull, Kirktown fell of his bike near Kirktown Bridge and injured his head.

Perhaps more surprisingly Deskford has also witnessed a number of aeroplane accidents. Before World War II there was a forced landing on Mosside when a plane ran out of fuel. School pupils who ran over to see it during their morning break, and were thus late in returning to school were all belted. Many air accidents occurred during the War. Two planes crashed in mid air over "Deskford Hill" and one crash landed at Greens of Blairock. In both cases all crew were killed. Greens of Blairock also saw drama when in 1942 or 1943 a Wellington Bomber was seen crossing Deskford from east to west with smoke pouring from it, and gradually getting lower and lower. It finally crash-landed on Greens of Blairock but all seven crew members survived. During 1943 there was a plane crash on Hill of Maud during a snowstorm. Eight crew members were killed.

On August 27th 1978, just before 2:00 in the afternoon, a Jaguar jet from RAF Lossiemouth, on a training sortie, crashed just below Oathillock, killing both crewmen, Flight Lt Christopher Everett and Flight Lt John Rigby, instructor and trainee. Wreckage was widely strewn across adjacent fields. There had been previous complaints about low flying by Mrs Gittings, Oathillock. The RAF arrived and brusquely ordered away Cullen Police, who had been the first officials on the scene. The road down to Kirktown was closed, even to local farmers including Jimmy Stewart, Knows. The RAF suppressed the story, and a full-page 1 article in the local newspaper gave virtually no information. Two RAF squaddies on guard duty however, did tell locals that the controls on this type of plane were well known as being very imprecise. At the site of the crash the RAF installed vertical searchlights to prevent aerial photographs being taken, and a press helicopter was chased away. Wreckage was dug up and removed for two or three days.

There were also many household accidents. In April 1934 16 month old Helen McKay, Berryhillock died of scalding after falling into a bath of very hot water on the floor. She was an only child. In January 1938 Forbes Howie, Kintywaird, died of gunshot wounds to the head in his farm kitchen. Not long after World War II, an orphan from Berryhillock, staying with the Taylors, drowned in the smaller Berryhillock Mill dam. Mr Robertson attempted a rescue but was unsuccessful.

Agricultural accidents were very common. On Saturday October 21st 1899, Alexander Keir, 64, farm servant at Little Skeith in the employ of Mr Taylor there, fell off a loaded cart in the cornyard whilst working with Mr Taylor. He said he was not hurt but had lost the "fusion" of his legs, so was carried to the farmhouse. He died the following Wednesday and Dr McHattie, Cullen, said the spinal column was fractured and death was due to compression of the spinal cord. Keir was of a pleasant, quiet disposition, but had broken his shoulder a year earlier at Knows. Witnesses said that he was usually careful but that morning had been a little stupid and forgetful of his work.

James Wilson of Little Knows was struck by lightning in the early 1880s but survived. However in July 1934, 34 year-old Robert McHattie was killed by lightening at Inaltrie, and his brother James, the tenant, was rendered unconscious. They had been hoeing neeps about a quarter of a mile uphill from the steading towards Cotton hill. He was struck on the right side of his head and both boots were blown off. Death was instantaneous and his body was taken to his home at Bleachfield. His niece, Margaret Smith, still lives at Inaltry.

Also in the mid 1930s the threshing mill belonging to Mr Christie, Smithfield, Bogmuchals, was threshing oats at Bellcroft, occupied by James Taylor. Mrs Chalmers, Bogside, the wife of the roadman, and mother of the last child baptised in the Free Church, was assisting and allowed her foot to get into the drum of the mill. Dr Paterson, Buckie was called and ordered her removed to Chalmers Hospital, Banff, where part of her foot was amputated. In 1935 there was a fire in the stackyard of William Pirie, Bogside. Eleven small stacks were destroyed, but the wind direction saved the steading. The clean land crop had been built separately and was not destroyed. Also in 1935 there was a fire in the stackyard of Alexander Davidson, Braeside. Six stacks of hay were destroyed and one pig had to be put down. No water was available to fight the fire.

In 1941 Robert Mitchell, Croftgloy, was seriously injured when his binder broke and threw him against his tractor mudguard. Worse happened in 1967. There was a Fatal Accident Enquiry when George (Geddes) Rumbles, 52, farmer, Mosside, was crushed under his tractor when it capsized down a steep bank. Many locals believed the tractor stalled when he missed a gear. He died from crush injuries to his chest. In the 1970s the loon Morrison from Keith was at Craibstone where he worked, cutting down a tree. It split and fell, hitting him on the head. Around 1953 a hill fire started in the Enzie and burned all summer towards Deskford. It proved useful in setting off unexploded ordnance on the wartime firing range. At Braehead fire arched over the steading and caught on the downside. During the winter, fire even came up through the snow.

Deskford also experienced industrial accidents. In August 1941 the workshop of John Gordon, carpenter, Berryhillock, was destroyed by fire. The alarm was raised by Miss Reid, postmistress and help from his neighbours prevented the fire spreading to his house. Cullen Fire Brigade attended and extinguished the fire. All his machinery and tools were destroyed, together with some wood and three tons of coal. He was not insured, and died a month later, aged 66. In the mid 1990s Mr Bass, a worker at Versatile Windows was killed at the industrial unit beside the Community Hall.

There were many minor accidents at the school which were recorded in the log. In June 1915 a fire in the shelter shed burned through a portion of the roof of the cookery room on a Saturday morning, making the roof unsafe. In November 1938 there was an accident to a pupil's hand at lunchtime, getting caught in the handmill on an adjoining farm. Mr Ironside took him to the doctor and then ran him home. In November 1945 Alexander Taylor jumped the wall outside the school and cut his hand on glass. He was taken to the Cullen chemist where his hand was bandaged and then home, where his parents were told to get medical attention. In April 1946 Frank Shearer cut his finger at handwork. He then fainted and cut his head. After First Aid treatment he was taken home by Mr Henderson.

A similar range of accidents continues through the 1950s. In November 1955, Jim Leslie, P4, fell and cut his leg badly. It was dressed and he was then sent in the school car to Dr Thomson in Cullen where he got three stitches. The car then took him home. In June 1956 Joan Duncan, P4, cut her knee, was taken to Dr Scott in Cullen where it was stitched and then she was taken home. In October 1957 Mrs Simpson the cleaner cut her hand while chopping kindling. It was dressed then stitched by Dr Thomson in Cullen in the evening.

As the school moved toward closure there were still accidents. In June 1969 Sheila Bruce went to the toilet. As she was closing the door, someone at the other end of the school opened a door, the draft causing the toilet door to slam shut, severing the point of one of her fingers. Mother was contacted and Sheila was taken to hospital. Finally, in June 1970, on return from the school picnic at Whitehills, Graham Barclay ran out from behind a bus into the path of a car. He was taken to hospital for examination after attendance on the spot by Dr Thomson, Cullen. He had bruising only and was allowed home.

STRANGE AND UNUSUAL

In any attempt to write the history of a small area like Deskford one is likely to chance upon a number of tales and incidents which cannot simply be fitted into a single category. These are the strange and sometimes bemusing events outlined here.

In the late C18th the wife of a local farmer, Alexander McHattie, "gave birth to a child with a wooden leg". This was recorded in the Kirk Session minutes and subsequently someone else had written that presumably the father was a Chelsea Pensioner "with a wooden haugh". This had later been scored out by a third person who presumably felt it too frivolous for inclusion in the Session minutes.

On March 10th 1887 Deskford was visited by James Sparke from Kirkcaldy, the "original wheelbarrow man". He was strictly 'tea total' and was journeying from John o' Groats to raise money for an artificial limb to replace his right arm which had been taken off by a chaff-cutting machine. He was well received and put up by Mr Cruikshank, Berryhillock Mills, while Mrs Captain Thomas raised 12/4d for him.

One of the strangest stories is of the "Girl Pat". It was a 75 feet Grimsby trawler, GY176 which was stolen, and in 1936 sailed across the Atlantic. It was skippered by Dod Osborne and included in its crew his brother, Jim. They had been brought up by foster parents in Kirktown and had attended Deskford School. Its cook was Howard Stephen who had been fostered by Miss Kate Donald, Berryhillock, and who had also attended Deskford School, then worked for Mr Morrison, Ordens.

The route taken was from Grimsby via Dover, the English Channel and the Bay of Biscay to Corcubion in Spain where it stayed for 14 days. From there it went to Tenerife then down the coast of Africa to Dakar from where it was navigated across the Atlantic with the help of a 6d school atlas. The entire crew was arrested in Georgetown, British Guiana. Dod and Jim Osborne were sentenced to 18 months and 12 months hard labour respectively. Dod later became a Lieutenant Commander in the Royal Navy in World War II and died in 1957 in France. The "Girl Pat" was brought back to Britain and exhibited for money. It became a minesweeper in World War II and then worked for the Port of London Authority, and was reputed to have become a ferry in the Greek island of Rhodes in the 1970s. Howard Stephen, on his release, put on a grand firework display at Berryhillock, paid for with money he got from the *"News of the World"* for his story about the "Girl Pat".

For a small community, nature has been bountiful to Deskford. In addition to the poaching for the usual game, there were trout to be taken from the Deskford Burn, and gulls' eggs, a local delicacy from Lurg Hill and Aultmore. In addition to the limestone, peat and slate there have even been small amounts of gold found in one of the tributary burns by John and Pam Robertson.

There is no record of whether any Deskford residents were members of the Hellfire Club which was established in Portsoy in the early C19th, and which undertook communion in Satan's name. Probably not. The people of Deskford became excited about other things. One of these was on November 22nd 1938 when JA Beveridge, the Deskford Headmaster, was interviewed in the BBC wireless studio in Glasgow, from where an item on the local area was broadcast.

Much later, in 1994, there was much excitement when a Dutch Bulb Garden was opened at Cottartown of Ardoch by Arnaud Kwint. It opened from mid March till the end of May, was open seven days a week and drew visitors from far and wide. Unfortunately its closure was announced in October 1995 because of cold, wet springs and a lack of interest from bus tour operators. A two and a half month season was also not long enough to sustain the enterprise.

Between the Wars, Deskford folk knew the miller at Berryhillock well, an ex-Londoner called Stanley Baldwin, who joined in many local activities. The coincidence of him having the same name as the Prime Minister was just accepted. However, when driving home from Aberdeen with friends he was stopped by the police in Inverurie and asked his name. He replied truthfully, but the Inverurie Constabulary were outraged that he was trying to take the mickey, and it took him a great deal of persuasion before they allowed him to continue on his journey home to Deskford, rather than putting him up in a cell.

CELEBRATIONS

For many years Deskford shared the same calendar of celebrations as the rest of the country. Fastern Eve (Shrove Tuesday or Bannocky Day) was a day of entertainment, fun and special bannocks. There was pancake cooking on Pasch Sunday (Easter), and cock fighting at Candlemas. Holidays were taken at Hallowe'en, Hogmanay and Handsel Monday (the first Monday of the year).

By the 1880s farms still held a dance on the taking of clyack. This evolved into a Harvest Home Dance between the two World Wars, held in a farm loft after the corn and potatoes were in.

The biggest celebration of the year was at Christmas, but held at Aul' E'el (Old Yule), on the 6th of January. In the mid C19th, New Christmas and New Year were both celebrated, but when New Christmas finally replaced Old Christmas, the fun went out of it, and New Year took over as the main winter celebration, till the second half of the C20th when Christmas reasserted itself. In the C18th and early C19th on Aul' E'el there was much "daftrey". The gudeman and his wife kept the toun and welcomed gangers and comers. There was a special dinner and tales and stories were told. After the meal the loons went visiting and the quines stayed to welcome visiting loons. The quines and sometimes older women sang songs, but never the older men. The culture of the Christmas celebration passed down from generation to generation, but many old customs were lost with agricultural improvement and formal education in the C19th.

There were other special celebrations too. The annual Deskford Pic-Nic in the late C19th, held in the Orchard, often attracted a crowd of over 500 people. For Queen Victoria's Golden Jubilee in 1887 bonfires were lit on the hills, cannons were fired and all the Poor got 2/-. Similarly there were coronation celebrations on May 12th 1937. There was a picnic in a field at Squaredoch with swings, children's and adults' races, teas and a presentation to each child of sweets, fruit, a pencil and 1/-. A football match was held between the single and married men which the single men won 4-0, and in the evening there was a dance with tea at midnight. Deskford even had its own Monday holiday from the late C19th, on the third Monday in July. This was advertised in the local papers until very recently, and may be the date of an annual fair associated with Deskford being erected a Burgh of Regality

Certainly the high point of home-made entertainment was in the C18th when quarter days, fairs, markets and sacraments were used as excuses. There was much drink at christenings, more at funerals and even more at weddings. Penny Weddings were extremely rowdy, with guests no longer contributing 1d each, but instead giving meal, a fowl or ale. The Kirk fulminated against promiscuous dancing but locals continued to thoroughly enjoy their "promisky" dances, which were often vigorous and wild. Ballads were sung which could be sweet and loving, shrewd and humorous or utterly gross, coarse and earthy and filled with innuendo. Robert Burns bowdlerised many, and the original rude, coarse versions are lost. This pattern continued with the bothy ballads of the C19th, which were often crude and explicit. Many people nowadays prefer a Romanticised and well-mannered version of history rather than reality that was. Complaints about the excesses of "the young people of today" have existed throughout history.

SOCIAL ACTIVITIES

Society in the North has always indulged in a variety of social activities. In the late C14th the end of harvest and Holy Days were observed as days of rest. In some cases things went too far, and in the C13th the Diocese of Aberdeen banned wrestling and other sports in churches and churchyards. In the C15th peasants played football, golf and dice, though they were encouraged to focus on archery. The Robin Hood story was very popular amongst poorer people. Prostitution was common at all levels of society, and prostitutes were an accepted social group. Indeed even King James IV had entries in his household accounts of payments to "Janet bare ars".

In the centuries before 1800 social activities tended to be informal. Much of what took place did so round the kitchen fire and within the family, and might involve story telling, ballad singing and playing of cards or dambrod (draughts). Drinking, even to excess, was widely accepted, as was the use of tobacco for chewing or smoking or as snuff. Major occasions such as weddings and funerals were an opportunity for great celebrations, and often excessive enjoyment.

Dancing masters, who travelled from place to place, were employed in the late C18th to teach locals the steps of all the fashionable dances. At funerals mourners met at the deceased's home for cakes, bread, cheese, ale, snuff and tobacco. After the burial they returned for a larger feast called the "dredgy", which comes from the word "dirge". Behaviour often became riotous and scandalous. The Minister took no part in the funeral or burial, and need not be present, though he usually attended as a mark of respect.

Things changed significantly during the C19th, as improvements in agriculture were introduced, education improved and prosperity arrived for some people. In Victorian times a "can do" attitude developed which extended to organised social activities. In the 1840s the Sunday School Library was the only one in the parish, but was also used by family and friends of Sunday school members. The Scottish Christian Herald was widely read.

One of the most impressive organisations was the Deskford Mutual Improvement Society, later Mutual Improvement Association, which existed intermittently throughout the second half of the C19th and was one of the earliest of its kind in Scotland. It first met in 1856 and finally ceased in 1952. One of its relaunches was in 1886, when at the first AGM it established a library for the parish. The MIS had thirteen laws, six by-laws and four laws regarding the library. Its object was to "promote the intelectual (sic. Probably not a deliberate spelling mistake) improvement of its members". Lectures and debates were held as well as soirees and other social events. All sectarian questions were excluded and no smoking or profane swearing was allowed.

Amongst the papers presented were those on "Books", "The Facilities for Self Improvement Offered by the Present Age", "Moral Opinion", "Labour and

Rest", "Phrenology", "Artificial Light" and "The Evils of Pride". A debate on "Whether is the Spendthrift or the Miser most useful to Society?" saw the spendthrift winning by three votes. One on "Whether is the Cow or the Ewe Most Useful to Scotland?" was won by the ewe. One on "Whether Do We Derive Most Enjoyment from the Eye or the Ear?" was won by the eye and one on "Whether It is Best for Scotland to be Divided into Large or Small Farms?" was won by small farms by three votes.

Meetings were held in the School Board Room in Kirktown. On social occasions, with 60 being the normal attendance, tea was served at 8:00, followed by a debate and then a dance. Some debates had surprising results. When "Is the Pulpit or the Press the Most Instructive Agent?" was debated, the press won. Some debates were very close. Indeed there was a tie when the votes were counted on "Is the Flirt or the Gossip the Worst Member of Society?" Other results included support for the contention that strikes were beneficial to the working class and that the eight-hour working day should be enacted into law.

Meetings were changed from Fridays to Tuesdays because of a clash with a singing class. A 1d fine was levied for absence or latecoming, and in 1887, by a unanimous vote, ladies were allowed to become members. At a social meeting in 1890 cakes and jam were ordered from Urquhart the baker in Cullen, and lemonade from Robert Cruikshank, Berryhillock. Isabella Milton was paid for providing tea and sugar and for making the tea. The MIS was dissolved in 1890 though the library continued and opened on the second and fourth Tuesdays of each month from 7:00 to 7:30.

The MIA was re-established in 1923 and amongst the talks were "Germany as I Saw It 40 Years Ago" by Rev Morrison, "Socialism" by Rev Park, "Past V Present in Rural Life" by Mr Longmore, "Scottish Humour" by Mr Watson, "On Being Methodical" by Rev Souter, Cullen, "Country Life 100 Years Ago" by Mr GK Drimmie, Dufftown and "Hillclimbing in Scotland" by Mr Robertson, Crossroads School. Lady members were also allowed to give talks, but it would appear, only about their holidays. Examples included "A Motor Cycle Tour Through Perth, Argyll, Inverness and Moray" by Miss Raffan, "A Holiday in Austria" by

Miss Morrison, "A Cruise on the Neutralia to Norway, Denmark, Holland and France" by Miss Forbes, Cullen and "A Holiday in Kent" by Miss Cruikshank.

There were also debates such as on "Is Sport Overdone?" (yes 12-7), "Are We Really Progressing Socially and Morally Today?" (yes 18-11), "Married V Single Life: Which is Best?" (single 17-16), "Should Women Be in Parliament?" (yes 23-20), "Is Women's Place in the Home or in a Profession?" (home 40-22) and "Should Scotland Have Its Own Parliament?" (yes: majority not recorded).

In 1923 the annual subscription was 1/-. Musical Evenings, Burns Nights, Ladies Nights, Hat Nights, Whist Competitions and Whistling Competitions were also held, and there was an annual picnic, depending on rail and bus costs, to Banff, Forres or Inverness. The President was Mr AD Craigmyle, Vice President Mr Stanley Baldwin and Secretary and Treasurer Mr W Currie.

In 1930 the County Library took over most of the books and served Deskford from a mobile library. The books remaining were sold or given to the two Churches, the money raised being split between the School Fund and the Public Hall.

The MIA closed during World War II and restarted again in 1946 with membership 3/- or 6d a night for non-members. The Secretary was to write to the Food Office to try to get biscuits and sugar for teas as these were still rationed. Braddies were to be ordered and each member was to bring a few cakes. Post War there were more concert parties, eg from Findochty, Newmill and Buckie, than serious talks. In 1949 three German ex-POWs, now agricultural workers, sang German songs and earlier that year there had been a bus outing to Strathpeffer, via Inverness, Beauly and Dingwall, for 60 members and guests. By 1952 membership was still high but it proved impossible to appoint a Secretary or Treasurer, and the Mutual Improvement Association finally ceased to exist in 1953, going out with a whimper.

The library had been a much-appreciated facility. In 1899, when it was almost entirely destroyed in the school fire, a few young ladies went round the parish and raised £33. In addition 100 books were donated, mainly by gentlemen in neighbouring towns, and by April the sum raised had increased to £50. In 1907,

Mr James Coats, jun., Paisley, presented to the school a handsome library of 170 books to suit all classes of scholar, and also a large bookcase.

In 1879 James Wilson and William McWillie had been joint librarians, as part of a committee which re-established the library. Money raised by entertainments, amounting to £4 net, was to be used to buy books. At this stage, the library, which had originally been in tailor Reid's in Berryhillock, but which had moved to the School Board Room in Kirktown, where Orchard Cottage is now, had 152 books. New books purchased included 25 volumes of the Waverley novels of Sir Walter Scott, plus 8 books by George MacDonald. All books were covered in 1880 to protect them, and a catalogue was printed and some books rebound.

In the 1880s Deskford had a library, a Mutual Improvement Society and a Vale of Deskford Temperance Society. Social life included agricultural shows, ploughing matches, picnics, soirees, concerts, Burns nights, dances, visiting friends, lectures and debates. The Temperance Society was begun in March 1887 with 32 members. The President was Rev A Walker of the Free Church, Secretary was Mr Mitchell and Treasurer Mr Hay. The membership was expected to rise. At the end of June 75 members and friends had a Saturday outing to Findlater Castle, in 6 carts and 2 phaetons. The weather was not great. Tea was had immediately on arrival at 3:30 and this was followed by dancing and games, Messrs Steven supplying the music. Findochty Good Templars, who were at Sunnyside, were challenged to a tug-o-war, but the outcome was uncertain. Tea was taken at 7:00.

The annual Pic-Nic was held on July 9th 1879 with Rev Mackintosh giving the ground and Mr Smith, Schoolmaster, as chairman. There were stewards and stewardesses for serving and dancing was held from mid afternoon to the music of several fiddlers, after which tea was served, followed by more dancing and games. The event was rather spoiled by rain. One week later the Bogmuchals Pic-Nic was held, and the Fordyce Pic-Nic was also well attended by Deskford folk.

The Temperance Society held a Pic-Nic at the Orchard on a Wednesday afternoon in August 1889. There was a procession of children, followed by "tripping the light fantastic toe". Tea was taken at 5:00 followed by games and sports. After 3 years in existence the Society now had 70 members.

Deskford Women's Guild, one of the oldest in Scotland, was established in 1895 and held a 90th anniversary lunch in 1985 in the Seafield Arms, Cullen, at which Mrs Rachel Cruikshank, 92, cut a special cake. A Draughts Club was started in 1902 but did not last very long.

A meeting was held in the School Board Room in May 1886 about the future of the annual Pic-Nic. After considering what new features this should have, it was decided to form a Horticultural Society to encourage an improved taste in flowers and increased attention to the cultivation of fruit and vegetables in the district. The Society still exists today. At the first Show there were 400 entries and 600 visitors. It was followed by a dance at Carestown. Initially entries were only accepted from within Deskford, but this was soon widened out to the surrounding area. A Committee was elected and a secretary and treasurer appointed. Rules and regulations were drawn up and a yearly subscription of 2/- for ordinary members and 3/- for hon. members was agreed. A flower show was to be held about August in connection with the Pic-Nic, and the School Board granted the use of the Public School for the purpose.

The Pic-Nic and games were held each summer in the Orchard and were famous for miles around, attracting attendances of well over 500. The Church had a sale of work in August which was well attended by holidaymakers from Cullen. The Sunday school picnic was held at the manse, where there were games, tea and cookies with gooseberry jelly and fresh gooseberries to take home. There were many concerts, dances and whist drives and a special picnic was held for Queen Victoria's Diamond Jubilee at which every child received a medal and an enamel mug with a Pict of the Queen on it.

At this period there were also random events. For example in February 1879 there was a lecture from Mr Anderson, Boyndie, on "Travels in Italy". There was a concert by four comic singers from Cullen, and a choir, a magic lantern show, songs and readings, and a lecture on "The Orkney Islands". In March 1880, a "Negro Entertainment" was given in the school by some young men from Cullen. Many Deskford people attended the Highland Society Show in

Aberdeen in 1885. The early train, boarded at Cornhill station, required 24 carriages and 2 engines.

There were also many uplifting talks and lectures. For example, on October 20th 1885, Mr Benzie, a blind lecturer from Banff, talked about "Different Systems of Writing for the Blind" and also on "Matrimony", in which he stated that a young man should make sure that the young woman who was to be his wife was a religious person, healthy, good tempered, cleanly and thrifty etc. At a MIA debate only one person voted in favour of farm servants having a weekly half day, perhaps because most of those voting were the farmers who employed farm servants.

In 1886 the School Board gave the MIA permission to hold a social evening in the school on March 19th, but there was to be no dancing. At the end of May 60 people went on an excursion to Gordon Castle. The first Burns Supper in Deskford was held in 1889.

Soirees were usually held by one organisation or another in aid of funds. A small sum was paid at the door which included admission and a paper bag of buns and scones, plus an orange or a handful of raisins. Those attending brought their own mugs and sat in rows drinking weak tea and eating the contents of their bags. There were speeches, readings or unaccompanied

Deskford ladies on an outing around 1900.

songs. Soirees were always held when the moon was nearly full to help people see on their way home. In 1886 the annual Shooting Match and the annual New Year Ball were held at Raemore.

The first Flower Show attracted over 400 entries and was held in the school with a picnic in the playground. Classes included flowers, fruit, vegetables, dairy produce, honey and scholastic and industrial work. It was open from 1:00 to 3:00 and then there was dancing till 9:00. The total attendance was between 500 and 600 and the total income £30, which gave a profit of £10 to carry forward to the following year.

In August 1910 there was held the 25th annual Flower Show, by this time recognised as one of the best in the North of Scotland. Thirty feet of additional staging had been acquired but there was still difficulty in displaying all the entries. Mr Morton, Cullen House, and Mr Petrie, Gordon Castle took 4½ hours to judge the pot plants, cut flowers and fruit and vegetables. Single, double, variegated and zonale geraniums attracted attention as did calceolarias, petunias and fuschias.

Kathleen Rennie, Winnie Miller, Eileen Miller and Cathy Davidson, all dressed up for the Flower Show centenary in 1999.

Mr W Duncan, Woodend Cottage won for double geraniums, Mr James Lorimer, Kirktown for single and variegated geraniums, dark calceolarias and mignonette, Mr James Maitland, Raemore for hydrangea, pelargonium, greenhouse and window plants and myrtle, Mr James Murdoch for yellow calceolaria and pot of lobelia, Mr William Gray, Berryhillock for zonale geranium, Mrs Shepherd, Craibstone for begonia and Mr John Stephen, Berryhillock for petunia. Best in section was Mr Maitland's hydrangea. There were many other sections. Cut flower classes included godetia, bridal robe chrysanthemum, gladiolus, perfection chrysanthemum, clarkia, French marigold, sweet william, foxglove, antirrhinums, lysimachia vulgaris, alonsoa, shirley poppy, lebanthus, sweet pea, stocks, alyssum, asters, candytuft, roses and kaulfussia, double dahlias, cactus dahlias, pompom dahlias, quilled asters, phloxes, geranium trusses, penstemmon spikes, pansies, peony asters, gladioli spikes, violas, and African marigolds. In vegetables there were classes for leeks, potatoes, kale, cabbages, peas, cauliflower, lettuce, beans, greens, parsley,

Flower Show committee and judges, 1996.(all L to R). Back – R Cruickshank, W Taylor (VP), T Davidson, J Stewart. Middle – B McLaren, J Rennie, G Stewart, K Rennie, S Christie (VP), A Currie, E Stewart, A Simpson, H Milne, D Hall, J Mitchell, W Miller, J Stewart, I Currie, G Stewart, G Duncan, G Farquhar, F Duncan, M Jesson, L Hall (Sec), C Davidson. Front – (Judges) D Blanch, W Ingram, C Henderson, R Gardiner, D Runcie, K Ingram, K Turner, D Fowler

carrots, white and yellow turnips, shallots, parsnips, red beet, rhubarb and onions.

There were also sections for heather honey, clover honey and extracted honey as well as sweet butter, salt butter, sweet milk, skimmed milk cheese and picking cheese. In addition to these there were 100 additional prizes for industrial and scholastic work and baking. In the afternoon there were air-gun competitions and dancing. It was widely believed that anyone who was a good gardener and won prizes at the Flower Show could not be a very good farmer.

At the 90th Annual Flower Show in 1989 entries were down to 900 from the previous year's 1200 because early growth had caused many items to be past their best. The Centenary Show in 1999 was opened by Robbie Shepherd while James McPherson, the Lord Lieutenant, forwarded the Queen's congratulations. There was a special cake and several new prizes but few Deskford winners.

On Saturday July 20th 1902 the Annual Pic-Nic and Games was held in the Orchard with 500 people sitting down for tea at 4:30. There had been dancing on a dancing board from 1:30 including prize dancing. Music was provided by Mr Gray, Knows, on the violin and Mr George Smith, Upper Blairock on the bagpipes. MC was Mr Alexander Johnston, Todholes, assisted by Mr John McLean, blacksmith. Mr Currie, Burnside, was judge.

Quoits was won by McCulloch, Fordyce, Heavy Stone by Clayton, Light Stone by McCulloch, Heavy and Light Weights and heavy and Light Hammer all by Clayton, Long Leap by Smart, Fordyce with 17'3", Hop Step and Leap by McDonald with 37'6", High Leap by Geddes, Vaulting by McCulloch, Highland Fling by Miss Guthrie, Huntly, Sword Dance by Miss Grant, Huntly, and Highland Reel and Schottische by Miss Guthrie. The Special Highland Schottische was won by Jeannie Cruikshank, Berryhillock, who won 2/6d. Second was Maggie Duncan, Cottartown, who won 2/- and third was Mary Ann Mason, Knowiemuir, who won 1/6d. The Picnic and Games did not take place during World War I, but was revived in 1919 when Jim Maitland, farmer at Raemore, won the medal for most points in the heavy events.

Ploughing matches were very popular at the end of the C19th and the early years of the C20th. The ploughing match held on February 3rd 1887 at Oathillock, tenanted by Mr McKay was very successful. 29 ploughs took part which was the best turn out in living memory. Mr John Clark, Hoggie, aged 75, came 5th and took the greatest number of prizes. For ploughing, 1st place and a silver medal went to George Taylor, Little Skeith, with John Morrison, Clunehill 2nd and Alexander Duncan, Kirktown 3rd. 1st to 13th places all came from Deskford. In grooming, 1st place and a silver medal went to George McCombie, Leitchestown, with Walter Keir, Nether Blairock 2nd and John Morrison, Clunehill 3rd. 1st to 8th places all came from Deskford.

There were other prizes for the straightest furrow, neatest ends, best feering, best-matched pair, best going pair, neatest yoked horses, best ploughed ridge and best work in a small field. In addition, and rather oddly, there were prizes for the ploughman with the largest family, the one who was most recently married, the one who had most daughters, the one who had been longest with their current employers, the youngest and the oldest.

At the ploughing match at Greystone, hosted by Mr Lobban, on February 21st 1889, James McKenzie, Barone came 1st and David Wood, Cottarclump 2nd. A Trades Ploughing match, for anyone whose job did not include ploughing, was held at Milltown, hosted by Mr Stephen, on February 27th 1890. There were 13 entries and though none was accustomed to ploughing, the quality was good. In ploughing lea, W Bremner, blacksmith came 1st, Alexander Milton, merchant 2nd and Robert Horne, blacksmith 3rd. In addition to these, masons, shoemakers and carpenters also competed. In ploughing stubble John Leitch, carpenter came 1st, and there were many other prizes. At the annual ploughing match at Bellcroft, John Grant tenant, in February 1894, 1st place and a silver medal, donated by Mr Angler, watchmaker, Buckie, went to Frank Rumbles, with William Wood 2nd.

Hoeing matches also took place. On February 3rd 1887 there was a hoeing match at Braeside, Mr Inglis tenant, at which there were more than 50 contestants. There were men's and boys' prizes as well as novelty prizes, with Percy Reid winning the prize for the best-looking hoer. On July 28th 1898 there was a hoeing match at Bellcroft, Mr Grant tenant, at which there were 30 competitors. 1st place went to Niven, Mosside, 2nd place to Christie, Ardoch and 3rd place to Wood, Cottarclump. Given a creditable mention in 12th and 13th place respectively were Miss Raffan and Miss Lobban.

Unusually, and in order to give Mr Grant, Bellcroft a "friendly yoking", (perhaps a reference to marriage), a number of ladies undertook a ploughing match, "something never before recorded in Scottish history, nor as a probable outcome of the new woman". On the whole the quality was good, and in several cases would have done credit to men. In 1st place was Miss Lizzie Smith, Little Darbreich, 2nd was her sister, Maggie and 3rd was Miss KA Raffan, Combs Croft, who was also given the accolade of being the strongest competitor.

In the early years of the C20th, most children hung up stockings for New Year's Day, and Mr Shepherd of Craibstone acted as Santa at the school. Such lighthearted attitudes were not however universal. For example in 1900, when the school having been burnt down, classes were held in the Church, a visiting Punch and Judy show had to perform out on the public road, because the Dominie did not consider it suitable for such a show to be performed in the Church.

Amusement took a different tack when, well into the C20th, beaters, mainly from local farming families, were allowed a rough shoot for hare, and sometimes for roe deer. There were many white mountain hares on Aultmore and also brown hares. In 1910 a Hogmanay dance was held in the barn at Berryhillock Mill. There were 50 couples present and the music was by Messrs Gray and Sudding. On the Monday an air-gun shooting competition was held at the blacksmith's shop, Berryhillock, with a special prize of a young pig. At socials in the early C20th tea was served from brightly polished brass kettles, and there was great competition amongst the ladies to see whose kettle would be most highly polished.

In 1913 the Draughts Club was still going strong, and in January of that year medals and prizes were awarded. Amongst the adults 1st place and a medal were won by William Taylor, Raemore, 2nd place went to William Quinn, Berryhillock, 3rd place to James Murdoch, Kirktown, 4th place to Bob Taylor, Swailend, 5th place to James Maitland, Raemore and 6th place to John Duncan,

Cottartown. Amongst the juveniles, 1st place and a medal went to Milton Cruikshank, Berryhillock, who was only 12 and the youngest person in the club. 2nd place went to John Topp, Berryhillock, and 3rd place to Charles Taylor, Swailend.

World War I meant that many clubs and organisations suspended their activities, some never to resume. Fundraising events and activities were however undertaken. For example, on January 1st 1917 a concert on behalf of Lord Roberts' Memorial Fund raised £8:9/-, and in February 1918 a concert run by the Horticultural Society raised £9:1/- for the Prisoners of War Fund. In March there was a collection of waste paper, and a collection by the Women's Guild raised £5:3:1d for Aberdeen Infirmary and Banff Hospital. On New Year's Day 1920 a collection for Lord Roberts' Workshops, Inverness Branch, for the

A school class outside the entrance to the Public Hall.

training of disabled soldiers and sailors raised £13:10/-.

Not all was sweetness and light however. In November 1919, Mr JA Muiry, Secretary, Deskford Horticultural Society, refused to return the key to the school. He was informed that unless he handed it over the Society would no longer be permitted to use the school, nor would any other organisation with which Mr Muiry was associated in an official capacity. It had not yet been handed over on January 22nd 1920, so it was agreed that new locks would be fitted.

Following World War I, in Deskford, as in the rest of the country, there was a desire for fun and an explosion in organised social activities. In 1923 a real need was met in Deskford when a Public Hall, built of wood on a stone foundation, was erected by public subscription on a site adjacent to the school, where the recycling receptacles now are. It was administered by the Minister, the Schoolmaster, the County Councillor, the District Councillor and two parishioners, elected every three years by public vote. The balance of the Forces' Welcome Home Fund was handed over for improvements and later Rev Park left a sum in his will for the upkeep of the fabric.

The Public Hall, where the recycling facility now is.

The Hall was opened on November 16th 1923, had cost £690 to build and was free of debt. A cake and candy sale was held which raised £33. An evening concert by a party from Buckie made £16, and was followed by a dance to

Morrison's Orchestra, Portgordon. There were donations to the Hall of £100 from the Women's Guild and £50 worth of manufactured timber from the Seafield Trustees. An extension to the hall was opened in November 1932 which cost £160 towards which there was £80 in hand and fundraising was still required for the other £80. However a free gift sale in December raised £45. The extension gave better kitchen facilities and a larger room for the ladies.

In 1960 the Public Hall applied for and received a grant from the Carnegie United Kingdom Trust for the purchase of chairs, a cooker and a heater. The money required was £222, of which they had £30 in hand, would raise £44, and asked for a grant of £148. The main hall was 140 square yards and there was a caretaker's room, cloakrooms and a vestibule at one end. At the other end was a small hall, kitchen and toilet, and there was also an outside toilet.

It had electric light and heating, a solid fuel cooker, an electric urn, trestle tables, heavy wooden forms, a piano and a stage. It could accommodate badminton and carpet bowls and was used by the Women's Guild, Youth Club, Farmers' Union, Horticultural Society, Sunday school, Football Club dances and Deskford Secondary School, and was in use three nights a week. £160 was required for 80 stacking chairs, £50 for a Rayburn No 1 cooker and £12 for a portable electric fan heater. The grant was agreed. When Deskford School closed, the school building took over as the Community Hall, with the old Public Hall being used for a variety of purposes including as an industrial unit for Versatile Windows. It was demolished in the 1990s and the site is now used for recycling bins.

The great increase in organised social activity after World War I, much of which used the Public Hall, can be seen from the selection noted below. At the start of March 1921 the Deskford Amateur Dramatic Society performed Miss Argo's Scottish comedy, "The Makkin' o' John", to crowded and appreciative audiences. The play was about the influence of a city girl on a slow, silly country lad. Babs was played by Miss Milne and John by George Wood. A very enjoyable dance was held after the Friday performance. They also performed in Cullen Town Hall on behalf of the Cullen Reading and Recreation Rooms Committee, when the hall was filled to overflowing and the play received a very positive crit. The star was Jinse the kitchen maid, played by Miss Taylor, and also attracting positive comment were Jean, played by Miss Raffan, the Old Man, played by John Milne and the Tinker Wife, played by Miss Wilson. In May 1923 the Buckie Oratorio Society gave a performance of the Messiah in Deskford Church which was full and at which £18 was collected.

The 1930s were even more active. Deskford Dramatic Society performed "A Ravelled Yarn" in Cullen Town Hall on May 9th 1930 in aid of the funds for the erection of a golf pavilion in Cullen. That same year the Mutual Improvement Association ran a Fancy Dress Dance on June 20th to the Twilight Dance Orchestra from Portsoy. It was the first of its kind in Deskford and there were several prizes, but, surprise, surprise, more women than men dressed up. First prize was won by Mr and Mrs Murray, Little Skeith dressed as a Persian prince and princess. Evening cookery classes were held over the winter of 1929/1930 in the school by the Infant Teacher, Miss McIver. In November 1930 the Badminton Club held another Fancy Dress Dance to Younie's Orchestra, Keith. There were teas, and the dancing carried on into the wee sma' hoors. It was repeated the following year. 1930 finished with a Hogmanay Dance to Ross's Band from Buckie, organised by local young men.

During 1931 there were several whist drives in aid of the Hall Extension Fund. On February 27th, Deskford Amateur Dramatic Society performed "Kirsty's Surprise", a Doric Comedy in 3 Acts, directed by JA Beveridge, who was the main strength of the Society. It was their third consecutive year of performing and they were improving. That year they joined the Scottish Community Drama Association (SCDA). In December the newly reformed Quoiting Club held a Hogmanay Dance to McQueen's Band from Buckie. On January 1st 1932 a shooting competition was held, with profits going to the Hall Extension Fund.

By this time all dances had a Master of Ceremonies and amongst the bands not otherwise mentioned, the following played at dances in Deskford, Beattie's Band from Aberchirder, Thomson's Orchestra from Tarrycroys, Robertson's Band from Newmill, The Moonlight Band from Deskford, Stewart's Orchestra from Keith, Geddes' Orchestra from Tynet and the Nightingales Band from Portsoy.

The Horticultural Society Social on January 22nd 1932 made £50 and two days later the Buckie Oratorio and Operatic Society held a sacred concert in Deskford Church. That year the Dramatic Society performed "Uncle Audie" at the King Memorial Hall, Grange, on February 5th for the Ploughing and Hoeing Association, and also one week later in Deskford. They won the SCDA Festival in Cullen in March, beating two other clubs including Cullen. In March some ladies organised a Leap Year Dance on behalf of the Hall Extension Fund, and in April, also on behalf of the fund, Portknockie Amateur Dramatic Society performed "Mill o' Tifty's Annie".

In 1933 the Sunday School Picnic took place on September 9th, and a week later the Horticultural Society organised a Harvest Home Dance. Earlier the P&J had printed a photograph of Rev Brown with a freak potato at the Horticultural Society Show. Evening classes in English, Arithmetic, Dressmaking and Needlework were held in Deskford over the winter of 1933/34. However because Hogmanay 1933 fell on a Sunday there was no public celebration. Instead a dance was held on Monday January 1st 1934.

In 1934 200 people attended the Horticultural Society Social and 120 the MIA talk on "Schoolroom Humour". The Dramatic Society was going from strength to strength. It performed "Kye Amang the Corn" to a large audience, including many from outwith the area, who had come because of the excellent reputation of the Society. It performed the same play two weeks later at Rathven WRI Hall. In the SCDA 1 Act Festival the Deskford B Team won against eight other teams with "In the Darkness", to go forward to the Divisional final in Inverurie. Moultrie Kelsall was the adjudicator. A term dance was organised on May 25th by the local farm servants. The Women's Guild Sale of Work that year raised £55:10/-.

The Horticultural Society Show in 1934 was larger than ever, with more competitions and more prizes. Produce was widened out from horticulture and the sports included heavy and light events, hammer, 28lb weight, long jump, hop step and leap, 100 yards cycle race, single ladies race and married ladies race, all followed by a dance.

In 1935 in the SCDA 1 Act Festival in Cullen, Deskford A team won the first night against Cullen B, Portknockie A and Portsoy B with "The Door on the Chain". The Deskford B team won the second night against Portknockie B and Cullen A with "Salmon Poachers". Deskford B went through to the semi-final at Inverurie. A harvest home dance was held in Shielburn School. At the Jubilee celebrations on May 6th 1935 all schoolchildren received a Jubilee mug. The older ones then went to the cinema in Buckie and the younger ones had a party in the hall. There was a dance in the evening. At the end of the year the Dramatic Society performed the 3 Act play, "Apron Strings" to a full house including visiting parties from Bracoden and Enzie.

In 1936 the Flower Show introduced new prizes for heaviest apple, heaviest carrot, tinted eggs, brown eggs, white eggs, trussed fowl for boiling, best darn on stockings, best plough reins made from binder twine and best hearthrug made from old wool. A whist drive, held on behalf of Aberdeen Infirmary with James Currie, Clune, as MC had more than 120 present.

In 1937 between 30 and 40 people attended First Aid classes held by Dr Wood, Cullen. There were over 300 at the Flower Show dance and, later in the year there was a concert by Strathlene Glee Party. The Women's Guild bus tour went to Keith, Dufftown, Aberlour, Craigellachie for lunch, Rothes, Elgin for shopping after tea at the Oakwood, Fochabers and Cullen. That year they had a Garden Fete instead of a Sale of Work and raised £57. On April 2nd 1938 there was a concert in the Parish Hall by Aberdeen Railway Male Voice Choir for funds to buy a new piano for the Hall. In 1939 the Dramatic Society performed at Forglen, Hilton and Buckie.

There were changes during World War II though the Badminton Club continued, defeating Fordyce 10-6 on January 18th 1940. The Horticultural Society also continued. The new ex-servicemen's organisation held dances and whist drives to provide support for men on active service. Wool was bought for socks and in 1939 20 pairs were handed in. Balaclavas were also knitted. The Young Worshippers league went on a visit to the Pictures in Keith. In 1940/41 the ex-servicemen's winter season of whist drives and dances had raised £60. Parcels were made up which included 46 pairs of socks, 14 pairs of gloves and 12 balaclavas. The Woman's Guild decided to have a door-to-door collection instead of a sale of work and raised £40. The ex-servicemen's dance on June 21st 1940 had raised £16. A dance was organised by young men working with the timber on Lurg Hill, with profits to the Comfort Fund.

By the end of 1941 the ex-servicemen had raised £160 of which they had spent £140. In October 1942 the Home Guard organised a whist drive and a dance, and in December of that year the Langlanburn unit of the Home Guard held a dance. Later that month the Red Cross Work party held a whist drive and dance.

In the 1950s Deskford had a Church, School and Public Hall, all close to each other. The Church Youth Club had 20 members and met on Mondays and Wednesdays for badminton and on Sunday evening for viewing filmstrips of general interest. The Women's Guild had been in existence for 60 years and had 39 members. It met monthly throughout the winter and held an annual sale of work.

Only recently defunct was the local branch of the Mutual Improvement Association, one of the oldest in Scotland. The Dramatic Society, which had been very active and successful before World War II, had been reconstituted. Occasional concerts were given by schoolchildren, and there were visits from neighbouring dramatic societies.

Deskford Horticultural Society held its 57th Show in 1956. A football club had been formed in 1949 and played on various farmers' fields, often at Ardoch. There was a branch of the National Farmers' Union, and 12 young people were members of the Lower Banffshire Young Farmers' Club. The Deskford

Maud Simpson, who had been in the Land Army during WWII, in fancy dress as a fireman.

branch of the Red Cross had reconvened.

Entertainment and dances were still frequently held in the parish, and fancy dress still amused. Several men went as spectators to football matches on Saturday afternoons, and parties went to cinemas in local towns in the evenings. There was a branch of the County Library in the School. Daily newspapers were widely read as were farmers' weekly magazines and popular picture weeklies. Almost every house had a wireless and seven had television. Newspapers and magazines were often exchanged.

Since the 1950s a declining population has meant difficulties for existing organisations in retaining viability or for new ones wishing to start. There have been several attempts to begin youth clubs and Sunday Schools, but these have foundered after initial enthusiasm.

SWRI 10th Birthday Party 1978. (All L to R) Front – Kathleen Christie, Mary Brown (Sec), Mabel Gauld, Jean Taylor, Gladys Duncan, Winnie Miller, Catherine Fletcher. In front of banister – Nett Weakley, Chrissie Addison, Nancy Whitelaw, Marion Yule, Barbara Courage. From top of stairs downwards – Annie Smith, Nan Casey, Margaret Strathdee, Nelly Macdonald, Doris Hall, Gladys Smith, Nina Cameron, Nan Hay, Nannie Fordyce, Mary Stewart, Dorothy Stewart (Treas), Minnie Angus, Jean Stewart, Ann Furness, Jane Milton, Jane Morrison, Cathy Davidson, Effie Stewart.

The Horticultural Society continues to be healthy but much of the membership comes from outwith Deskford. The same applies to both the badminton and indoor bowling clubs which meet in the Community Centre and are run by The Community Association which has also over the years ensured that the Community Centre in the old school is regularly upgraded to meet the needs of the present day. It also addresses matters related to the community of Deskford and issues a newsletter twice a year.

One organisation which has bucked the trend is the Deskford SWRI which restarted on December 2nd 1969 with 52 members and is still going strong. On December 27th 1994 it held a 25th anniversary party in the Community Centre. A cake was cut by the first President, Effie Stewart, Barone, and founder member, Nett Weakley, Easter Darbreich. Other members of the original committee included Elsie Bruce, Kirktown, Vice President and Dorothy Stewart, Meikle Knows, Treasurer. In 1994 Doreen Blanche was President, Ann McLaren Vice President, Mabel Gauld Secretary and Ann Morrison Treasurer. In 2015 it still meets regularly.

In 1994 the Youth Club was reformed with 20 members. There was a fund-raising daffodil tea. George Smith, Redmoss Croft, was President, Valerie Lyon,

Youth Club members on top of the Bin.

Lintmill, was Secretary and Linda Burgess, Lintmill, was Treasurer. The Youth Club was for 14-18 year olds, and in 1996 went on holiday to Dounans, Aberfoyle.

In June 1998 the Community Association elected a new committee with Sandy Christie, Chair, Bruce Mclaren, Vice Chair, Bill Jesson, Treasurer and Debbie Bell, Minute Secretary. Other Committee members were Mary Jesson, John Meneer, Jack Mitchell, George Milton, Jackie Smith, Joyce Smith, Jimmy Stewart, Knows, Jimmy Stewart, Barone, Willie Taylor and Adrian Bell. Business included heating in the kitchen, a fence round the football pitch, possible purchase of the old hall, participation in the Best Kept Village competition and holding a tombola and a harvest home dance.

In 2000 an internet computer for community use was installed at the Community Centre, and that same year a public meeting agreed plans for the renovation of the hall, increasing the number of rooms, upgrading facilities, adding an extension, upgrading toilets with disabled access. It would be a two-year project and fundraising would be required. In 2001 the Community Association was awarded £72,000 by the Community Fund, £12,000 from the Scottish Land Fund and £5,000 from Awards for All. In addition £4,500 had been raised from a disco, competitions, a mini lottery, an auction and a sponsored walk. The money was used to make the planned refurbishment and for upgrading to both the Community Hall and the Jubilee Hall.

SPORT

The type and variety of sport in which Deskford people participated was very limited until the C19th, and the high point for sporting participation was probably the early and mid C20th.

In Victorian times the New Year's Day Foxhunt was a great occasion, using part- bred greyhounds. In some years there were as many dogs killed as foxes, and those foxes which were killed were mainly dug. This event was changed and reduced by tree planting. Tenants hunted deer until this was prohibited, and also hares. Much crop was ruined until an 1878 Act gave tenants the right to protect ground crops from game. In late Victorian and Edwardian times there were many ploughing and hoeing matches.

When the Pic-Nic, held in the Orchard, became such a massive event it included a wide range of athletics competitions with prizes, and these were eagerly competed for. Over time these became associated with the Flower Show.

In the early C20th there were flourishing rifle and quoits clubs, the latter playing in the field opposite the Community Hall and next to New St John's Church. Ian Mclean, Milton Mills, who died in early 2011 at the age of 91, was possibly the last survivor of the quoiters. The club had been established in 1898 with Rev Park President, Mr Smith, Schoolmaster, Vice President, and Mr Cruikshank, Inspector of the Poor, Secretary and Treasurer. Play took place every Friday evening and in that first year, in the club championship, 1st place and silver medal went to A Masson, roadman, with 2nd place to W Gray, shoemaker.

Football was also popular in the early C20th. In May 1912 there was a crunch match between the Deskford Buffaloes and the Lintmill Swifts, played on a field at Croftgloy. Such was the interest in the match that the bicycles were parked three deep round the pitch. The Deskford Buffaloes took the lead through Quinn, to great cheers, but unfortunately the Lintmill Swifts ran out deserved winners 6-4. Later the Deskford football team usually played on one field or another at Ardoch, depending on crop rotation, though they had played for a time before World War II, before they were in the league, in the Orchard. It was suggested that at that time the main qualification for a place in the Deskford Football Team was an ability to fight.

Jackie Smith captained the Deskford Football Team in the early 1950s, during which time they won the Lower Banffshire Football league two or three times, as well as other trophies. Mr Muiry from Lintmill, whose father had a shop at Berryhillock, was the trainer. Players included John Reid, a joiner from Berryhillock, Jackie Smith, a horseman then tractorman at Greens of Blairock, Jimmy Paterson, a farmworker, Ian Morrison, the goalkeeper, who worked with his father at Clunehill, Trux, a German POW, Frank Burgess, an Insurance Agent from Slatehaugh, Shielmuir, Ian Davidson, the son of the farmer at Ardoch, and then the farmer himself, Jack Reid who had a garage in Cornhill, Sigi Irowski, another German POW, Charlie Geddes, Lower Squaredoch, who was an excellent all round sportsman, Jimmy Ingram, a dairyman from

Deskford Football Team around 1950. Back – J Muiry, J Watt, J Smith, J Patterson, I Morrison, Trux, F Burgess. Front – I Davidson, J Reid, Geeks, C Geddes, J Ingram.

Woodside, Portknockie, and several from nearer Elgin. The two German POWs played for two years before going home. Sigi, who many years later visited Jackie Smith whilst on holiday, was a centre forward and had worked with Jimmy Currie at Clune. Trux worked at Croftgib near Crossroads School.

In 1921 James Maitland, Raemore, was a renowned heavy athlete who won the cup for the best heavy athlete at Keith Highland Games. The Curries from Greens of Blairock were also well known heavy athletes.

Badminton became very popular between the two wars and competitive matches were held. In 1937 Deskford played Fordyce home and away and won

15-1 and 14-2. That year they also beat Cullen 11-5. In 1938 Deskford lost 10-6 away to Portknockie, but later beat them 13-3 at home. In 1939 there was a close match between the Deskford Badminton Club and the Deskford Church Badminton Club which ended 8-8. For several years the Badminton Club organised an annual dance in the Parish Hall.

Though there was very briefly, in 1982, a wrestling club, nowadays the only sports which are played in Deskford on an organised basis are carpet bowls and badminton, both in the Community Centre.

WEDDINGS

Around the year 800, the law which governed marriage was pre-Christian and allowed concubines, polygamy and divorce. Marriage to close relatives was banned in the C12th in order to prevent customs which survived from polygamy. In order to get married, a woman had to bring a tocher (dowry) of land or goods, a practice which lasted into the C20th with the idea of "the bottom drawer". Around 800AD there was a high fertility rate but also a high mortality rate. This meant that there were many children but fewer teenagers. Girls were ready for marriage at the age of 13 or 14 and boys were legally competent at the same age.

Before the Reformation, because of the requirement for dowries and wedding contracts, many couples did not marry but just cohabited. Marrying into a social class above one's own was, at all levels of society, a way to advancement. Women retained their maiden name, and marriage was more of a civil contract rather than a religious ceremony. By the C16th and C17th marriage tended to take place between people in their late 20s. Sex had become much more confined to marriage, and because of the high mortality levels, many individuals were married more than once and there were very many step families. In the C17th it was unusual for any Deskford native to marry outside the parish.

Handfasting was common until the C17th and was only made illegal in 1939. It gave rise to the phrase "tying the knot". Handfasting ceremonies took place on quarter days, often at Lammas, and were formalised by the joining of hands over running water, and the declaration of intentions. These trial marriages lasted for a year and a day, and if successful were often subsequently formalised through marriage by the Minister. If the couple decided not to continue the relationship, the woman was considered pure and unsullied, and the man was responsible for the upbringing of any child which had resulted.

In the C18th, when weddings took place, the wedding dress was bought by the groom and the bride retained it as her "good dress" thereafter. Wedding dresses were brightly coloured, but never green, because that colour was associated with the fairies. Nor were they black, because of that colour's association with mourning, though black became fashionable in the C19th before white became the standard colour in the early C20th. Until the C17th wedding rings were worn on the right hand.

In the C18th, before the banns were read, a pledge had to be paid, which became forfeit if a Penny Wedding took place. The General Assembly of the Church of Scotland had pronounced against Penny Weddings in 1645, 1701, 1706 and 1719. In the C18th, when a woman married, she immediately span the winding sheet for her funeral. These were taken out and aired once a year, and treated with great reverence till the day she died.

Men married later in the C18th because farms were small and could not support their family in addition to their parents' family. They often married women considerably younger than themselves, which in turn led to young widows, who often did not give up the tenancy of the farm. Therefore their sons could not, and did not marry, and the family became extinct.

In the 1860s around 90% of brides in inland Lower Banffshire were pregnant on the day of their marriage. The average age for marriage was 28 for the man and 25 for the woman. Women were considered to be "lowered" if they married a social inferior, but men were not. In the late C19th weddings were usually held at the bride's house in the afternoon, and were often held on Christmas day. At one wedding at Little Knows in the 1880s, 32 guests sat down to dinner in the parlour. This comprised Albert soup, beef, gigot of mutton, two turkeys, rabbit pie, boiled and roast fowls, plum pudding, apple tart, prunes, custard, jellies, creams, wines, oranges, apples, grapes, figs, nuts and raisins. On his wedding day in the 1880s, James Wilson, as was common, worked in the morning, in his case whitewashing houses on the farm. The wedding was at 4:00 in the bride's house at Kirktown Farm. In the mid 1800s men were criticised for marrying very young, and without asking the consent of their parents.

In the 1920s few brides married in white unless they were the daughters of wealthy tenants. The first furniture was often purchased at a roup. The bridegroom was "blackened" with boot polish, black lead, treacle and soot. After the wedding ceremony there would be tea for a few close friends. The location of the wedding night was kept secret because of the possibility of pranks being played by friends, for example with the bedding. The newly wed couple would often cycle to their honeymoon, which, for poorer couples, might be two or three nights with friends in a neighbouring parish. A couple were not considered properly married until they had been to Church on the Sunday after their wedding, to be "Kirkit".

In the C17th and C18th Penny Weddings were common amongst poorer folk. In earlier days each guest brought a penny to help pay for the occasion, but in later times guests provided food and drink. Penny Weddings were often riotous occasions, with much drinking and "promisky" dancing. The Church disliked them strongly and individuals who held one forfeited their pledge of £3 Scots to the Church. In Deskford, in the C18th, a guest at one was accidentally shot dead, the gun having been fired in celebration.

The Church did not like them because it felt they led to immorality, but they were an effective way for poorer people to celebrate the occasion. Male guests also contributed by helping to pay the fiddlers for the dancing. Such weddings often lasted several days and any profit made on food or drink which was sold was given to the newly married couple to give them a good start in life.

The formal marriage usually took place at the manse, the first person to be met by the bride and her family en route to it being given a glass of whisky. After the ceremony there was much pipe music and guns and pistols being fired. The new wife was welcomed to her new house as the gudewife. At the wedding dinner much was eaten and drunk, and immediately after this the Shamit Reel was danced outside the house. It was named thus as it would remove the new wife's shame. There was then more food including salt haddock and wastles (cakes made of half flour and half oatmeal)

Dances were often interrupted as anyone could shout "kissing time" and had to be enthusiastically obeyed. At midnight the bride was put to bed by her bridesmaid and the groom was informed. There was a rush to witness the "bedding" and the "throwing the stocking". The groom stripped to his shirt and drawers and got into bed. The bride took off her final stocking and threw it over the heads of the guests present in the bedroom. Whoever caught it received good luck. The bedroom was then cleared, the bride and groom wished a good night and the door locked. Dancing continued amongst the guests until the following morning and around 9:00 the bride and groom's bedroom was unlocked and the groom given whisky.

CHURCH INVOLVEMENT IN EVERYDAY LIFE

Until the middle of the C20th the Church in Deskford was a major, and sometimes dominant, element in the lives of the people in many different ways. One of these was the sets of belief which underpinned their faith. In 1597, in common with the rest of the country, there was a great panic about witchcraft, and the lower slopes of the Bin were notorious for covens.In 1644 it was recommended that elders enquire in their districts about the presence of "witches, charmers, pilgrims to wells and chapels, swearers and scolders". In 1628 however when the Deskford elders had been required to discover which idolatrous places there were pilgrimages to, and how many parishioners were involved, they declared, perhaps truthfully, that there were none.

In 1721 elders were urged to encourage the "suppression of and bearing down on sin, and the promoting of piety and holiness in their districts". Even in 1776 the Minister warned the people of Deskford against the superstitions and heathenish practices he had observed in the parish such as the lighting of Beltane fires and other customs to which the more ignorant locals were still attached.

The pre-Reformation Church had emphasised the miraculous healing power of saints but the post-Reformation Church saught to eradicate this. It had great problems with persistent popular beliefs and practices relating to healing, believing them to be idolatrous. There were pilgrimages by people in Deskford, in addition to those to St John's Well, to Tarlair, Jenny's Well at Portknockie and St Mary's Well at Auldtown, Ordiquhill, which were all considered to have great powers. Wells dedicated to St John were considered effective in curing eye problems.

As late as 1802, John Smith, in Mosside, objected to the Kirk Session giving a certificate of good moral character to James McHattie and his wife, Jean Shepherd in Squaredoch. He accused Jean Shepherd of "stealing his cow's milk", ie using witchcraft and casting spells to make his cow go dry. Rev Chalmers told him the accusations were ridiculous and absurd.

There was great competition to have a baby son the first child baptised by a new Minister as this brought good luck. However to be the first to be married by him was unlucky. During the act of baptism no water must enter the child's eyes, or it would see ghosts throughout its life. If the child did not cry when the water touched it, its life would be short, so sometimes it was nipped to make it cry. In the 1880s newly married local couples were still "Kirkit" when they attended their first normal service after the wedding. For example this happened to Peter Rumbles, Tochieneal, and Lizzie Gray, Hoggie, in February 1881. There were many religious revivals, with a major one in Cullen and Portsoy in 1921-1923.

There was repeated preaching against popery in all parishes within the Synod of Aberdeen, including Deskford. In 1748 the Minister preached from 1st

Timothy, Chapter 4, which he believed described Roman Catholics and their faith.

4.vi. Now the spirit speaks expressly, that in the latter times some shall depart from the faith, giving heed to seducing spirits and the doctrines of devils.

vii. Speaking lies, in hypocrisy, having their conscience seared with a hot iron.

viii. Forbidding to marry and commanding to abstain from meats, which God hath created to be received with thanksgiving of them which believe and know the truth..............

5.vii. But refuse profane and old wives' fables and exercise thyself rather unto Godliness.

xiv. Neglect not the gift that is in thee, which was given by prophecy, with the laying on of hands by the Presbytery.

In the mid C19th there was a strong feeling, led by Rev George Innes, in favour of Sunday Observance. In 1839 a petition was sent to the government against stagecoaches which carried the mails running on Sundays. In January 1842 Rev Innes preached against the threatened opening of the Edinburgh and Glasgow Railway on the Sabbath, and in May of that year, as part of the continuing outrage against this, a petition was signed and sent off. In 1850 Session authorised the Minister, Rev Mackintosh, to forward a petition, signed by him, in the name of the Session, to parliament, against the continuation of Sunday labour in the Post Office.

Prohibition and abstinence were major issues which attracted much support in Deskford in the late C19th. The first mention is of an address on the subject of total abstinence by Mr Reid, Portsoy, in 1841. This did not win majority support, but, when the subject was debated 40 years later, the majority of the Church membership was in favour.

The waning of Church influence in the C20th can be demonstrated by Rev Hamilton, writing around 1950, who complained that though almost every family had a Church connection, attendance was poor and falling, except for Communion and special occasions. He criticised the widespread disregard of solemn vows and said there was a need for a return to reverence for the truth and a fulfilling of solemn obligations. He also felt that many parents should show a better example in matters of religious belief and practice, as this would be a stabilizing influence and great help to their children. He placed much of the blame for the situation on the influence of Stalin and Hitler.

The quality of Kirk Session minutes varied greatly from one Session Clerk to the next, in neatness, detail and content, and sometimes there were unexpected problems. In May 1751 the Session Clerk reported that he had left the minutes about discipline as usual in a shelf in the school closet, but that mice or rats had destroyed a good part of them from November 1750, so that they could not be filled up in the Register. The Minister, finding that there were some scraps of these minutes which could be read, offered, when he had time and opportunity, to resurrect them.

At different times particular events were recorded, some major and some minor. For example, in 1658, the vacant stipend of the parish was taken to help pay for repairs to King's College, Aberdeen. With some melancholy it was recorded that the final baptism in the Free Kirk was that of William John Chalmers, son of James Chalmers, roadman, Bogside, and his wife, Isabella Pirie. The baptism took place on July 5th 1931.

The Church had always been a focus for social life, but the form this took becomes much more recognisable to us in the C19th and C20th. For example, on February 21st 1889 a Free Church Soiree was held, with talks, singing and a choir, while at St John's, over 400 people attended a Congregational Soiree on February 25th 1891. In 1933 it was recorded that the choir was going very well, but needed more tenors and contraltos. The Women's Guild was very active and raised much money.

More marriages took place during World War II than had done before it and most were now happening in Church rather than at home. In 1956 the Church set up a youth club in the Parish Hall on Mondays and Wednesdays, with an annual subscription of 10/-. It closed however in 1960 due to lack of numbers.

That year however the Young Worshippers League continued and the choir was re-established. Tickets for the Church Social cost 2/6d.

It is sometimes difficult for us now to fully comprehend the detail and importance of day-to-day Church business. For example in 1907, the precentor, Mr Reid, was interviewed about playing the organ. He resigned shortly thereafter, both as Choirmaster and Organist. The posts were advertised in the Banffshire Journal and the Aberdeen Journal at a salary of £15. Three candidates performed on separate Sundays and then the congregation voted. Votes cast were 73 for Miss Stevenson, 53 for Mr Harper and 6 for Miss Hendry. Miss Stevenson was appointed, but resigned soon thereafter because she had been appointed to a similar post at Boharm, which was nearer her Dufftown home. It was then decided to offer the post of organist to Miss Reid, Berryhillock, without advertising it, at a salary of £10.

In 1911 it was decided to dispense with the services of Mr Taylor, Choirmaster, and to offer to increase the salary of the Organist, Miss Reid, by £4 if she agreed to take leadership of the choir in addition to her other duties. She agreed. At the same time the Church Officer's salary was increased to £5 per annum in order to provide a more frequent cleaning of the Church. In May 1916 John Jamieson was appointed Organ Blower in place of Henry Dalgarno, who had resigned.

SOCIETY

POVERTY

Throughout the centuries a recurring theme in Deskford, as in most of the other communities in the North East, has been poverty. This manifested itself in a number of different ways and was often related to the quality and especially quantity of the harvest. The further back in history we go the more serious the consequences, and, like all areas in the North East, there were years in which people died from starvation. If the harvest failed in the pre-1100 subsistence society, then small farmers were in deep trouble, having nothing to barter with.

Between 1550 and 1600 the country was overrun by a large number of vagrants, thieves and beggars. The kirk took on the role of poor relief and Justices of the Peace were established to deal with vagrancy. The Poor Law of 1574 laid down that only "cruikit folk, seik impotent folk and waik folk" were permitted to beg. Those who were not permitted to do so included jugglers, wandering minstrels, palmists, "taill tellaris" and " vagaboundis Scollaris". In 1623, when the crop failed, many poor peasants abandoned their farms and crofts and wandered the countryside begging in order to try to prevent starvation. So great was this threat that a temporary Poor Rate was established.

Around this time there was a great deal of emigration, with up to a quarter of all young men volunteering for service as mercenaries in foreign armies as far away as Turkey, Russia and Spain, as well as those in northern Europe and Scandinavia. Many did very well for themselves, but many, many more were killed.

In the early C18th English visitors considered Scottish peasants to be very poor, clad in rags, their skin brown with dirt, their horses very small, their cows emaciated and stunted, their houses miserable hovels of turf and clay and the land they tilled surrounded by nettles and thistles. By the end of the century great advances had been made.

In the Statistical Account of 1790, 4.9% of the population of Deskford was officially poor, the fourth highest level in all of the parishes in Aberdeenshire and Banffshire. By the time of the New Statistical Account of 1843 Deskford was second top with a figure of 4.47%. In both years Cullen was the parish with the highest level of poverty, 6.59% in 1790 and 5.57% in 1843.

Throughout the C19th, with the development of improvements in agriculture there was a big reduction in levels of absolute poverty, however the gap between the well off and the poor in the parish grew. Towards the end of the century the introduction of the bicycle proved a great liberator to individuals trying to improve their situation.

By 1900 the General Inspector, after an inspection, stated that "the paupers in Deskford seem to be well cared for". Deskford did indeed have a good reputation for the way in which it looked after its poor in many different ways. For example in 1901 £1:16/- each was paid to Miss Mullen, Berryhillock and Mrs Farquhar, Craibstone, for washing and keeping clean the house of an elderly and incapacitated couple, the Gibbs. There was however some irony in the fact that in 1905, on the day before she died, the Parish Council agreed to let Mrs Chapman, Mid Skeith, have the use of one of the Poor's Houses at Muir of Squaredoch.

The Parish Council was careful with its finances. In 1905 James Wood, pauper lunatic, was to be boarded with William Benzie, Barone, after removal from the Asylum with the agreement of the Superintendant there. This new arrangement would be much cheaper at 5/6d a week than the 8/2d a week the Asylum cost. Being careful did not however mean being miserly. For example the Inspector purchased half a dozen books for the use of pauper lunatics in private dwellings.

An example of the aid given to the Poor in one year, 1845, by the Parochial Board is shown below:-

AGE	No.	NAME	£	s	d	ANNUAL MEAL BOLLS	FIRLOTS	PECKS
52	01	James Reid	3	18	0	0	0	2
66	02	Elspet Buie	3	18	0	0	0	3
30	03	Elspet Gray	3	0	0	0	0	2
61	04	John Raffan	2	12	0	-	-	-
82	05	Janet Milne	2	12	0	1	2	2
75	06	Elspet Longmuir	1	10	0	1	2	2
73	07	Jane Bremner	2	12	0	0	1	0
33	08	Mgt. Clark jun	3	18	0	0	0	3
73	09	Mary Taylor	2	12	0	0	1	1
60	10	Mary Strachan	2	12	0	0	0	3
64	11	Mgt Clark sen	2	12	0	0	0	3
63	12	Mgt Lawrence	3	18	0	-	-	-
76	13	Ann Ewen	3	0	0	0	1	0
73	14	Elspet Milton	2	12	0	0	0	3
48	15	Mgt Skinner	1	12	0	1	2	2
65	16	Mgt Donald	2	12	0	0	0	2
22	17	Elizabeth Elder	2	12	0	-	-	-
39	18	Jane Merson	7	10	0	1	2	2
73	19	George Reid	3	18	0	1	2	2
55	20	Isobel Shepherd	2	0	0	0	1	0
92	21	Helen Fraser	5	4	0	0	1	0
60	22	Janet Munro	2	12	0	0	0	3
65	23	Janet Russel	2	0	0	0	0	2
89	24	Isobel Cumming	5	4	0	0	1	1
69	25	Elspeth Lawrence	2	12	0	0	0	3
66	26	Isobel Lawrence	2	12	0	0	0	3
63	27	Catherine Kemp	5	4	0	-	-	-
82	28	John Anton	2	12	0	-	-	-
40	29	Mary Black	3	18	0	(for illegitimate child)		
34	30	Jane Keith	3	0	0	-	-	-
86	31	Mgt Taylor	2	0	0	1	2	2
73	32	James Fraser	1	6	0	-	-	-
8	33	Robert Raffan	1	6	0	-	-	-

Fifty years later, in 1898, the Parish Council agreed that 6cwt of coal would be given in two instalments during the winter to each of:-

Robert Wood	Milltown
Helen Munro	Blairock
Jane Thomson	Berryhillock
Ann Tough	Berryhillock
Widow Thom	Berryhillock
Isabella Forbes	Poor's Houses
Jane Riddoch	Poor's Houses
Ann Watson	Poor's Houses
Alexander Duncan	Berryhillock

Still in 1898 the Poor Roll listed the following recipients of relief:-

ORDINARY POOR:

AGE	NAME	LOCATION	PER WEEK £	s	d
86	Ann Ross or Currie	Glasgow		3	6
35	Jessie Smith	Keith		3	0
44	Jane Riddoch	Fordyce		1	0
40	Widow Milton	Fordyce		3	6
59	Jessie Russell	Rathven		4	6
55	Alexander Russell	Rathven		3	6
9	Ann H Duncan	Huntly		2	6
74	Widow Fraser	Grange		3	0
12	Charles Raffan	Keith		2	0
10	Maggie Raffan	Cromdale		2	6
58	William Duff	Squaredoch		2	0
86	Ann Milton or Tough	Berryhillock		4	6
47	Isabella Forbes	Muir of Squaredoch (free house during summer)			
39	Widow Thom	Berryhillock		4	6
61	Robert Wood	Milltown		3	6
59	Jane Thomson	Berryhillock		2	6
66	Hellen Munro	Greens of Blairock		2	0
58	John Wright	Edinburgh		5	0
67	Jane Riddoch	Muir of Squaredoch (free house during summer)			
-	Ann Watson	Muir of Squaredoch (free house during summer)			

LUNATIC POOR:

AGE	NAME	LOCATION	PER WEEK £	s	d
52	James Wright	Asylum		7	0
25	Ann Wright	Asylum		7	0
38	James Wood	Asylum		7	0
55	William Jamieson	Tod's Cottage		3	6
60	Isabell Longmore	Comb's Cottage		5	6

In 1906 the inspector reported that he had been able to get Barbara Gracie or Wood removed from her old house at Blackhillock to one of the Parish Council's houses at Muir of Squaredoch. He also had a letter from the Countess of Seafield accepting the Parish Council's renunciation of the house and yard at Blackhillock.

In 1907 it was agreed to give five loads of peat to each of seven paupers. That year also Ann Ross or Currie died in Glasgow aged 95, having received poor relief from Deskford for several years. In 1909 Mr Brander, Kirktown complained to the Parish Council about the filthy habits of George Ritchie, pauper. In 1910 it was presumably the same George Ritchie who was to get the new Old Age Pension of 5/- a week. As a result he would cease to be a pauper for which he was currently getting 3/- a week. The money would therefore also cease. Several others from among the 17 paupers who were currently receiving 2/6d, 3/- or 4/- poor relief per week would also lose this and cease to be paupers when they got the Old Age Pension.

Also in 1910 Miss Murdock, teacher, Fyvie, donated £7 towards the upkeep of her sister Jessie who had been at Ladysbridge Asylum for several years. Still in 1910 the Medical Officer wrote that Widow Wood, 87, Muir of Squaredoch, was living in very insanitary conditions and recommended help to clean both her and her house. This was agreed. She was moved to Comb's Croft where Mrs Raffan was very kind to her, for which she was paid 10/- per week.

In 1911 Widow Wood, Milltown, applied for money to re-thatch her house which was in a bad state of repair. It was agreed to give her £1. A letter had also been received from Mr Gordon, carpenter, requesting an increase in what he was paid to make coffins for paupers. It was agreed that he would be paid £1:8/- each in order that they might have a decent appearance. For this each would also have a nameplate and a shroud, to be supplied by Mr Gordon.

In 1914 it was agreed to put a new grate in Mr Rumbles' house at Muir of Squaredoch, at a price of no more than 10/-. By 1915 there were 6 Ordinary Paupers, 2 of whom lived outwith the parish, 1 Mentally Defective and 6 in the Asylum. In 1916 Isabella McKinnon died in Banff District Asylum. Her aunt wished her to be interred in Grange, and the Parish Council paid for a motor to convey her remains there at a cost of £2:2:9d. Mr Gordon made a coffin for £4:14:4d. The grave cost 6/- and the certificate of death 3/1d. However her life had been insured by the British Legal and United Provident Assurance Company, so the Parish Council got £4:9/- back from them.

In 1917 Lizzie Thom, Grange was given 3cwt of coal, 3 yards of grey flannel, 3 yards of print, 3 yards of cotton, 2½ yards of wincey, ½ yard of lining, 3 yards of braid, 1 pair of divided skirts and 1 pair of boots, size 8. Also in 1917, in consequence of the large number of men drawn from the parish to join the forces, it would be extremely difficult to find a competent successor to Mr Cruikshank, Inspector of the Poor. It was decided, subject to the approval of the Local Government Board, to appoint his daughter, Miss Isabella Cruikshank, Interim Inspector of the Poor and Collector of Rates. She had assisted her father for several years, but would however refer to a specially formed committee in all cases of difficulty. She would be allowed to sign cheques, but a decision on her salary was deferred.

In 1925 Maggie Bell Duncan applied for Relief on behalf of her 4-month old illegitimate child. The parish of Keith admitted liability and asked that she be removed to the Poor House in Stonehaven. She refused. Also that year Widow Rumbles was not entitled to a widow's pension as she had no children under 14, so she was added to the Roll. In December 1926 it was decided to remove all the teeth of James Inglis, a 36-year old mental defective, and replace them with artificial ones.

In 1927 Innes Smith, who lodged with Mrs Ettles, Blackhillock, had been ill for several weeks, and she wished him removed. A suitable alternative home was found for him with Mrs Ingram, Stripeside. In 1930 the Inspector's salary was increased to £30 per annum and that of the Secretary to the Burial Ground to £10. In 1929 the doctor recommended that Mrs Inglis, Berryhillock, who was 75, should be looked after. The Inspector was unable to find a suitable home in the parish to have her, therefore, in consultation with the Medical Officer she was removed to the Morayshire Combination Poorhouse in Elgin. Six weeks later she was removed from the Poorhouse and boarded with Mrs Taylor, Berryhillock. In April 1930 Mrs Inglis, now much improved, successfully requested that her name be removed from the Roll of the Poor.

In 1930 2½ cwt of coal was given to each of the widows Stephen, Thom and Rumbles and also to George Williams. On May 15th 1930 the Parish Council ceased to exist, and responsibility for the Poor passed to the County Council and the government.

SEX, MARRIAGE AND CHILDBIRTH

If poverty was an enduring theme of society in Deskford over the centuries, so also were the beliefs and practices surrounding marriage and childbearing. In 1690 a local farmer's wife had triplets, all of whom survived, which was considered extremely unusual in those days. Much earlier, about 800 the law of marriage had permitted concubines, polygamy and divorce, and established the precursor to handfasting or trial marriage. In the C14th the eldest male child was dominant within the family. Family sizes were smaller, partly because breast-feeding was prolonged until the child was two or three years old, which reduced both the woman's fertility and the birth rate.

In the middle ages women were considered to have a much greater sexual appetite than men, however by Victorian times this belief had been completely reversed. In Scotland, unlike in England, subsequent marriage legitimised a child born out of wedlock. The only problem was if the father did not acknowledge the child. Monogamy was not seen as important whilst courting, and would have been difficult to enforce with so many teenagers working in farms away from their families. Previous sexual activity by a woman was not seen as an impediment to marriage. Indeed women were often married in church surrounded by their illegitimate children. The new husband often saw this as a good thing, as a guarantee of the woman's fertility and as a supply of free labour.

The vast majority of mothers of illegitimate children were farm or domestic servants, and the majority of fathers were farm servants. Reasons suggested for high levels of illegitimacy included poor moral training of the young, uniformity of food and poor supervision by masters of their servants' moral conduct. There was an element of heredity with many parents of illegitimate children having been illegitimate themselves. There was no real family life for the farm servant.

Throughout the past four or five hundred years there have been several periods in which there was a strongly puritanical society, and during the C18th there was a reduction in adultery, fornication and illegitimacy. These periods however, constituted the minority of the last 500 years.

Around 1850 the high number of illegitimate births was condemned. In the second half of the C19th Banffshire had the highest illegitimacy rates in Scotland. Within the Banffshire figures, those for Cullen and for other coastal villages were very low whilst that for Deskford was very high. Until this time it was normal for women to retain their maiden name when married.

Illegitimacy in the 1850s was much higher than it was a hundred years later in what was seen as an era of loose morals during the rock and roll years. In 1850 the illegitimacy rate in Banffshire was 16.6%, with almost all illegitimate births being amongst the farming community and almost none in the fishing villages. Young farm workers wanted proof of their girls' fertility before they married them, because a large family was useful or even necessary to help with the work demanded of them.

Attitudes within the Church softened throughout the C19th. By 1841 it had decided that there would be no more fines imposed for fornication, just rebuke, admonition, repentance and a swift readmittance to membership. At this time many of the cases of fornication which the kirk had to deal with were ones of antenuptial fornication. There were however still local scandals. In 1886 Alexander Brander, shoemaker, Berryhillock ran away, leaving a wife and a great deal of debt.

Up to the start of World War II babies were born at home and the mother was kept in bed for a week afterwards. Usually a local woman came in to help with the birth, either paid for, or as a friend of the family. For a long period, stretching well into the post-war period, many local families took in boarded out children, who often came from areas such as Glasgow, as a result of incompetent or even abusive parenting or because they had been orphaned. Some families took in large numbers. For example in 1947 there were 5 boarded out children at Slatehaugh in Sheilburn.

A scandal occurred in 1928 when there was a mix-up at the Registrar's. The birth of the illegitimate child of Isabella Henderson Grant, a widow, in July 1925, fifteen months after her husband had died, had not been recorded on the correct form. Because of this, and because the mother had reverted to her maiden name of Mitchell, by which the child was now known, paternity had still not been officially acknowledged in 1928.

One of the saddest sequences had happened in 1839. Margaret Lawrence secreted the body of her dead child on the hill road past Ardicow. It was brought back to her parents' house by her mother, Margaret Duncan and Jean Skinner, the mother's friend, and deposited in the session house of the churchyard at Fordyce in the presence of the Minister and some elders. Jean Skinner stated that she and Margaret Duncan had found the child's body on the Hill of Summerstown between Deskford and Fordyce, near a march stone, and in a hole left where some turves or sods had been dug, and the baby covered by these.

Margaret Lawrence had been a servant in the household of James Black, farmer in Ardoch, and his family for two years, and had recently had the appearance of being with child. She denied this and said it was an obstruction of the bowel. She had risen from the bed she shared with Margaret Ingram, another servant, and gone away between 1:00 and 2:00 in the morning, telling

Margaret Ingram that she would be back before the time of milking the cows that morning, and that she was going to her father's at Baronsmill in Fordyce.

James Black sent a servant to Baronsmill first thing that morning where he found Margaret Lawrence, her father and her mother, the latter saying that Lawrence had been delivered of a child on the hill but had not brought it to her father's house. Another servant, Alexander Moggach, who had now left Mr Black's employ, was thought to be the father of the child. Margaret Lawrence's mother and her married sister had both suspected that she was pregnant, but when asked she had replied that she "didna ken".

When she had arrived at Baronsmill she had gone into a room at the other end of the house, but her mother followed her and found her in a deplorable state, her clothes being all wet, it having been a rainy morning. She was tearing off her clothes and her mother hoped she was not "going to cry" (go into labour), and her reply was that she had "cried" already. When her mother asked her where the bairn was, she replied that it was on the Hill of Summerstown and that it was dead and had been stillborn. She said she had carried it a short distance but could not carry it further, and described where she had left it. She had put two small feals or divots over it and did not know whether it was a male or female child. She also said that the father was Alexander Moggach.

The mother sent for the midwife, Mary Christie, who came in the afternoon and removed the afterbirth. Lawrence said she had tried to walk from Ardoch to Baronsmill, some five or six miles, to be delivered. Her mother sent her sister to look for the child, but she could not find it, so her mother then went herself to look for it. En route she met a friend, Jean Skinner, who went with her and together they found it. They brought it back, called the Minister and several elders, and placed it in the session house. Lawrence was questioned by the authorities in her mother's house as she was not in a fit state to be taken to the jail in Banff.

The body had been found in the Slack of Standingman, on the boundary between Deskford and Fordyce parishes in 15 inches of water. Various officials visited the spot and accurate measurements were taken, detailed forensics for the time carried out and a map drawn. The doctor's opinion was that the child had died from smothering and haemorrhage from the umbilical cord. The body weighed 6¾ lbs and was 22 inches long, and had probably smothered by its face lying against the ground under the body of its mother, who may have become insensible and fallen on the child by accident. The Procurator Fiscal stated that the child had been breathing. Mixed soil was found in its mouth and aesophagus. Death was caused by suffocation or drowning.

Margaret Lawrence was arrested and held in the Tolbooth in Banff, charged with child murder, found guilty and sentenced to six months in prison. After her release nothing more is known about her. Alexander Moggach appeared before Deskford Kirk Session several years later to be disciplined for fornication, but, because of the circumstances, was treated with understanding and leniency. The incident highlights many of the attitudes and beliefs of society at that time and, though the events were distressing, the way in which everyone involved dealt with them demonstrated great understanding and decency.

ENTERTAINMENT

Entertainment available to most people changed significantly over the generations. In mediaeval times work was everything and there was no concept of leisure, except on Holy Days. The working day lasted throughout daylight hours and even very young children worked. The main pastimes were gossip and story telling. By the C17th or C18th almost every house had a bible which was read regularly. Packmen sold cheap books which were coarse, gross and vulgar, but often reflected society accurately. The kirk drove these books out of sight but not out of use.

From the C17th whisky became more popular and was used on all social occasions, funerals, weddings, christenings, paydays, fairs and markets. There was a tolerant attitude to drunkenness, except on the Sabbath.

With the introduction of agricultural improvement much superstition disappeared, and there was a great modernisation of society throughout the C19th. No longer did young women carry their spinning wheels to a friend's house to spin and chat with four of five friends. Gradually visits from chapmen, and tailors working in the good room disappeared. Young men no longer played games such as "drawing the sweer tree", "tod and the lam's", "the glaiks", "the dams" and "dambrod". The singing of rude and bawdy ballads, some satirising locals such as a mean farmer or a courting couple, faded from use, as did the telling of supernatural stories or much-distorted tales of history and heroes.

One aberration was the establishment, in the early C19th, in Portsoy, of a Hellfire Club, which took communion in Satan's name, but it did not survive very long. More widespread was the reading of the Banffshire Journal, and the organisation of a wide variety of groups and organisations, such as the Mutual Improvement Society and different temperance organisations. Churches held social events such as picnics, as well as starting organisations such as the Sunday school and the Women's Guild. In the later C19th tenants of medium and larger farms all had pianos, and at least one daughter who could play. Men played fiddles and melodions, and these were often used to provide music for dances.

Into the C20th radios became widely used in the 1930s, and almost every house had one by the 1950s when televisions were also starting to make their appearance. Buses, cars and bicycles allowed people to travel more widely, and the commercial entertainment available in the towns proved to be very attractive. However within Deskford the number of sports and social clubs and organisations also increased dramatically.

ETIQUETTE

A detailed picture of society's attitudes and beliefs can be augmented by an understanding of its etiquette. In the C18th and C19th accepted standards and attitudes were strictly observed and rigorously enforced. One example of this was Sabbath observance. Fuel, food and water were obtained and, where possible, prepared on the Saturday, as was fodder and water for the beasts. Where possible all work was done on the Saturday or deferred till the Monday.

Drawing water, carrying peat from the peat stack, walking (except to Church), shaving, whistling, laughing, carrying a parcel, begging and reading (except the bible) were all banned.

Cattle were pumpheled (put to the byre) before the hour of the church service, and midday milking was delayed. Sunday was holy and the hours of the Sunday service even holier. In the C18th however, if the gudeman had a que, it was the loon's job every Sabbath morning to comb back all his master's hair, gather it in a single plait at the back, and tie it tightly with a tape till it formed a pigtail. With the oldest men this could reach the waist. All men were however cleanshaven.

In the C18th, when courting, this had to be done openly, or the young man could be "douped", by which four people each took an arm or a leg and battered him against a wall, dyke or tree. He had to accept his girl being kidnapped by his friends at weddings, markets, meal and ales etc. However once it was accepted that a courting couple were serious about each other, she was considered a "bun's sheaf and laid by".

Drunkenness and swearing were common in all sections of society, though the kirk did not approve. Women did all the housework, and men and boys did not even brush their own boots. When walking to church, the man always walked a few paces ahead of his wife. Before toilet paper was invented, people used torn up old newspapers and before even that moss was widely used.

If common people bumped into the gentry they had to doff their cap or bonnet, and well into the C20th children were expected to salute if they saw the gentry passing. If this was not done there might even be a visit to the door from the police to enquire why. Young men remained loons till they married or leased their own farm or croft while young women remained quines till they married, upon which they became the gudewife of their husband's farm or croft.

In the mid C19th all adults in Deskford were known by their Christian name and surname, and married women retained their maiden name. The only people who were given a title were the two Ministers, the schoolmaster and the Veterinary Surgeon, though Mr Lorimer, the latter, was often just referred to as the farrier. The tenant of a large farm was called by the name of his place but there were not many of these in Deskford.

One example of the retention of the maiden name was when, in the mid C19th, George Taylor's wife was always known as Betty Black, and when she died it was the initials BB which were engraved on the wood of her coffin, brass plates not yet having been introduced. Instead of dying people were said to have "worn awa" or "won awa". There were always a number of feeble-minded individuals or "naitrels" (naturals) and they were well treated. One of these, Sandy Howie, when asked what use the sun had, replied "for makin' rainbows", and on another occasion, when offered a large copper 1d coin or a small silver 6d coin said "I'll nae be greedy, I'll jist tak the wee ane".

In the later C19th people became very aware of fashion, and, for example, took to fitting new tiles to parlour fireplaces, hanging wallpaper and buying iron beds. Curtains and floor coverings were updated, and people began to send Christmas cards, though for some reason this habit fell away between the Wars. There were also fashions in the collective name for the feeble-minded poor or those with mental health issues, changing for a few years around 1850 from Lunatic Poor to Fatuous Poor to Imbecile Poor. In the early C20th it became common for the Minister, when cycling round the parish, to drop in on parishioners for a cup of tea, on which occasion the good room would be used.

Despite the enormous changes which did take place through the ages, change was usually opposed and the old ways of doing things clung to tenaciously. This altered in Victorian times which were seen as scientific and rational, and during which change was seen as good, and as evidence of progress. Summing up what society is really like and what it stands for is difficult, but aspects may be highlighted by the following, fairly random, examples of attitudes and behaviour over the years. There is no common theme.

In the C14th and C15th kinship was the main form of obligation in local society, with identifiable common ancestors being valued. Only the male line was important. Kinship became equated with surname with, for example, many Ogilvies and Abercrombies being spread round Deskford, in leases of larger farms and occupancy of official positions. This facilitated genuine cooperation between landowner and tenants.

In the C18th Deskford was a more charitable parish than many, and church collections per capita were higher than most. At this time poor maimed beggars were sometimes wheeled from parish to parish in barrows, and were generally well treated. At the same time every man possessed firearms, often single-bore flintlocks which had a four-foot-long barrel and a $7/8^{th}$ inch bore. These often misfired.

In the mid C19th an untrustworthy person might be described as being "as leein' as a newspaper", so not much change there. In the 1880s Willie McWillie was given £2:10/- by Mrs Wright, Upper Skeith, as thanks for helping her settle her deceased husband's affairs. With it he bought a suit from Mr Mitchell, tailor, Berryhillock. Around this time farmers in Deskford were becoming very concerned about the rise in vegetarianism. One real advance in the second half of the C19th was that railways had made possible travel to visit friends and family at great distance, and also the purchase of goods from anywhere in the country for rapid delivery.

There were however problems attached to a hard adherence to traditional attitudes and values. In 1880, James Wilson Jr, Little Knows, was a highly moral, but also highly judgmental individual. He was tee-total and spent much of his honeymoon in Aberlour inspecting farms and attending and passing comment on church services there. His sister Joan became pregnant whilst unmarried, and because of this he never again spoke to her, even though she still kept house for his father and himself. He refused to attend her marriage to the father of her child and felt it inappropriate for them to have a large party. He ploughed instead. He did however attend her funeral when she died relatively young in 1890. His father had resigned as an elder when she became pregnant.

By this stage in communities such as Deskford there were large families, a strong sense of community, a great deal of self-help and a sense that the individual should try to be all they could be. There developed a large and successful Deskford diaspora.

Within Deskford, at the start of the C20th there were still disputes and disagreements. In 1906 Alexander Morrison resigned as sexton after 20 years in post, due to poor health. James Fordyce, Muir of Squaredoch, was appointed in his place. In 1907 he demanded an increase in salary from £3 to £5 per annum, was offered £4, but rejected this. The Parish Council agreed to pay him the £5 till they could properly consider the matter of the gravedigger's salary. In 1915 his salary was increased to £7. In 1923 the Public Hall was built of wood on a stone foundation and was run by six trustees.

In the mid C20th Deskford was a very peaceable place. There was no pub and a policeman had to come from Cullen if required. However there were two local farmers who were JPs. Perhaps being so peaceful was a contributory reason for the large number of boarded-out children and the evacuees from Portobello who were welcomed in many houses in the parish, the former particularly in some of the poorer ones in Muir of Squaredoch, and in Berryhillock. The Johnstons from Todholes took in females from Ladysbridge Asylum, one in the house and one in the byre. The Poor's Houses at Muir of Squaredoch were occupied by two or three couples up till World War II.

Before the Reformation in 1560 there was great permissiveness and immorality, so many people embraced the new strict morality which became the norm. By 1750 the people were still however considered poor, ignorant, slothful and enemies of planting, enclosing or any other improvements. They were unclean and did not look after their sheep, cattle or roads.

By 1840 the moral nature of the people had improved, and drunkenness was much less common. The Sabbath was treated more reverentially and it was felt that the introduction of Sunday school and Sunday school books had helped. Previously cards were commonly played in the evening by all classes, but this was now very rare.

By the 1930s parents were not so strict with their children. They were more free and easy, and many did not insist on attendance at church. Football coupons were regarded as harmless. Before World War II most Deskford people still married within Deskford, but after the War this changed.

In 1950 the Minister felt that the people were essentially hard working, progressive in their outlook towards agriculture and new methods, tolerant in judgment and kindly and hospitable by nature. They responded to good leadership (presumably the Minister's), although they were somewhat conservative in outlook generally. In the parish there was a fine nucleus of forward-looking men who had the highest interests of the community at heart, and their leadership was the best hope for the future.

CHURCH AND SEX

Fornication was the issue which received by far the greatest coverage in Deskford Kirk Session minutes, though there were also instances of adultery and incest. Extraordinary lengths were gone to in an attempt to establish the truth and to punish wrongdoers. If proven they had to stand at the pillar beside the Church door as the congregation arrived, and then stand beside the pulpit, dressed in sackcloth, during the service. In addition they were fined. In the C18th, throughout Banffshire, including Deskford, fines were, for fornication £4 Scots, for a second offence £8 and for further offences similar incremental rises. The fine for adultery ranged from £20 to £40. These fines were eagerly collected since they formed the greater part of money distributed to the Poor of the parish.

Over the centuries from the first references in the Kirk Session minutes of the mid C17th till the last case in the early C20th, there was a gradual, though not consistent, softening of the session's attitude, though they did remain, throughout the entire period, the court which addressed cases of alleged sexual impropriety. The language used also changed, for example from fornication to uncleanness and then back again. Some cases were simple, straightforward and almost routine, but others were very complex, with contradictory evidence, denial and counter-claim. Indeed reading them today, some seem to be direct precursors of our more lurid TV soap operas.

There is evidence that the Kirk was managing to limit sexual activity to within marriage in the C17th, but this success certainly did not continue throughout the C18th and C19th. Latterly offenders were treated with greater compassion and understanding. For example in 1891 no action was taken when Helen Topp, Faichyhill, aged 15, gave birth. She later married the child's father, and in 1894 was absolved of antenuptial fornication, and became a member of the Church. However it remained a source of great shame and humiliation to many families which considered themselves good, decent and moral kirk adherents when one of them transgressed.

Over the years there were a number of occasions on which individuals refused to pay their fines. Between 1623 and 1806 the Deskford Session referred to Presbytery 25 cases of relapse (second or subsequent offence) in fornication and 21 of adultery which they felt unable to deal with. At some points Session seemed to be faced with epidemics of fornication. At no point was there any attempt to compel those guilty of fornication to marry each other, though this did often happen.

Circumstances changed over the years. Agricultural improvement led, particularly in the C19th, to a system in which farm servants moved, often some distance, every six months, and this meant that they were often no longer in the parish when accused of having got a servant quine pregnant. By this time letters admitting guilt were often accepted instead of a personal appearance being required. Also by the second half of the C19th antenuptial fornication, taking place in the lead up to marriage was the most common offence. Indeed Synod recommended that those guilty of antenuptial fornication should no longer have their names entered in session records.

In the C18th Deskford session was very strict, and reluctant to absolve adulterers and fornicators, and was on several occasions overruled by Presbytery. As late as the end of the C18th young women's breasts were being examined by female experts for evidence of milk, where an accusation was made of someone having given birth. If a baby was found abandoned all young women in the parish might be so examined.

Men were sometimes treated more leniently than women, but in the later C19th only the man's address was entered in session records. In the C18th it was standard practice for an offender to have to stand at the pillar in sackcloth for three consecutive weeks before being absolved, though in extreme cases this could last for over a year. The Minister's views on whether or not repentance was genuine were important in deciding how many appearances were to be made.

The last reference to any sexual offence in St John's Church was in 1905 and in the Free Church in 1913. It is however not certain that adultery and fornication ceased at this time. The final offence, recorded in 1913, was an open local scandal in which William Stewart, Greens of Blairock, elder in the Free Church, confessed to adultery with Margaret Bella Davidson, Burnheads. He had confessed before the scandal became public, and was deposed from eldership, but not, as would have happened in earlier times, stripped of his church membership. There is no record in St John's Session minutes of any action taken against Mrs Davidson.

The earliest reports on action against sexual impropriety are from the C17th, from secondary sources reporting on now lost session minutes. In 1661 the Minister of Deskford was sent by Presbytery to speak to Thomas Stewart, Laird of Bog, who was under threat of excommunication for having "fallen in fornication for the fyfth time, and this time in the Tolbooth of Banff with a woman put there for murthering a chyld". In 1660 James Cruikshank was excommunicated for adultery. He "humbly supplicated Presbytery to be admitted to public repentance and released from the fearful sentence of excommunication". In 1671 Helen Steinson, who had been found guilty of fornication, was made to stand before the congregation every week for fifteen months, repenting her sin.

A snapshot of the period of the early 1720s shows a large number of cases. On June 12th 1720 Christine Rattery, Cottartown of Ardoch, was detected to be with child. The officer was ordered to cite her to appear before session on the next Lord's Day. On June 19th she stated that she was with child to William Reid, Cairstoun, who admitted this on July 3rd and was "sharply rebuked for his sin, exhorted to repentance and appointed to begin his public appearances next Lord's Day for removing the scandal". He was also to meet in private with the Minister, who would have to be persuaded that the repentance was genuine before he could be absolved. They did not deal with Christine Rattery till she produced testimonials from the different places where she previously lived. William Reid began his appearances before the congregation on July 10th. On October 23rd he appeared before the congregation for the third time, was rebuked, exhorted to repentance and, confessing his sorrow for his sin, was absolved from the scandal. This was fairly standard practice, however, the following year, on June 4th 1721, Jean Mackenzie appeared before the congregation for the 16th time, and on June 21st she appeared "in sacco" for the 20th time.

On August 14th it was discovered that Margaret Machatie, Raemoir, was with child. Although she was now living some distance away she was cited to appear before session. On October 16th she confessed to being with child to Alexander Hilton, Raemoir. This being a relapse (second offence) she had to meet with the Minister frequently so he could convert her and deal with her conscience. Alexander Hilton was summoned. On January 29th 1721 the Minister informed session that Margaret Machatie had not yet appeared in Church to satisfy for her relapse in fornication, because he found her very ignorant.

On August 27th 1721 Isobel Nicol, wife of John Murray, gave birth in the seventh month of their marriage and admitted antenuptial fornication. They both appeared on October 18th and denied it, but she confessed she "had been quietly with Alexander Grant, Tochieneal before she was married and that he was the father".

On February 2nd 1722 Peter Young and Janet Smith, Squaredoch, admitted antenuptial fornication together, however this became more complicated when it emerged that he was already under church censure for uncleanness in another congregation, so he was referred to Presbytery. On March 8th 1724 Elspet Stables, Milntown, and William Donald, Cairstown were accused of fornication and of her being pregnant by him. They were cited but did not appear. Eventually they did so on August 19th when both denied their guilt. However they were gravely exhorted to confess as the "scandal was flagrant", and on the 26th they did so. On May 10th 1724 it was discovered that Margaret Raffan was with child to Adam Lobban who lived in Rathven. The Deskford Minister would contact the Rathven Minister about the matter.

On February 4th 1728 Christine Rattery was once again in trouble. She appeared as a quadruple fornicator, lastly with James Barnet, and was still not relieved of her appearances, showing "gross ignorance and obdurateness". On March 10th she compeared in sacco (sackcloth), desiring to be absolved from her scandal. She was referred to Presbytery, which she attended on March 24th, but they referred the matter back to session to deal with. She was finally absolved on May 5th.

On April 18th 1734 Elizabeth Mill, late servant to James Keir in Croftgloy was summoned to compear, accused of being with child. Mary Bowes, Kirktown, was also alleged to be pregnant and the Minister would speak to her to see if this was true. Andrew Reid, servant to John Grant in Ramore, was summoned to satisfy his guilt with Jean Johnstone. In 1737 Jean Cuie was excommunicated for incest and adultery, though the former may have meant, for example, fornication with her brother-in-law.

On October 30th 1737 session found that James Hay, a young man from outwith the parish, frequently resided with Mary McKenzie in Squaredoch, "and none in the home with them but young children". Their conduct gave offence and they were cited to appear before session to answer for it. On November 7th they confessed to cohabiting together for some time. This was considered scandalous and they were ordered to stop "having any further correspondence together".

On September 7th 1738 Janet Gray confessed to being in child in fornication to George Gaul. The child had been begot the previous April and since then Janet Gray had received communion, which made her offence even more serious. She was ordered to compear three Sabbaths in the ordinary place of appearance for her fornication, and a fourth Sabbath, in the body of the Kirk, in sackcloth. In 1740 £3 Scots was given back to Peter Robertson out of his fine for fornication as he was marrying the woman concerned. Also that year Jean Ewan confessed and said that the father of her child was John Strachan, son of William Strachan in Inaltry. He was told that as he admitted guilt with the woman he would be considered the father of her child, even though he suspected her of also having been guilty with someone else. He agreed to this.

In 1742 Jane Brebner repeatedly named Mr Peterkin, now a lawyer in Edinburgh, as the father of her child. The Minister wrote to him demanding that he come back to Deskford to answer the accusation. He replied that he could not possibly do so, so session referred it to Presbytery. On October 7th 1743 John Grant in Broom refused to accept punishment for antenuptial fornication as he said it was no sin and he had done no evil. Session was outraged at him perverting the words of the Apostle Paul, and referred him to Presbytery.

On April 29th 1744 it was reported that Janet Smith in Cottartown of Ardoch received strangers and vagabonds, especially one poor man who, for the most part, resided with her. The Minister would speak with her. On September 14th 1746 Jean Imlach confessed to being with child to George Geddes "sometime servant in this parish, and engaged in the late wicked rebellion". That same year Janet Forbes had failed to compear on three occasions. Witnesses said she was guilty of fornication and she was referred to the Civil Magistrate, the first occasion on which this was done.

In 1747 Andrew Longmuir Jun was informed that he was under no pressure to deny his guilt since Isobel Henry and the child she had brought forth were both dead. Presbytery would be consulted before session took any action. That same year Janet Forbes was referred to the Baillie of the Regality of Ogilvie as she had repeatedly refused to appear before Session to answer the accusation of fornication. However May 6th 1753 was an occasion for celebration, for on that day it was reported to session that, for a second time in a row, nothing scandalous or irregular had happened since the last meeting.

On May 2nd 1756 Janet Henderson, Kirktown, admitted being with child in fornication to William Downie, Berryhillock. He denied this. Janet Henderson said that the guilt might be a small thing to Downie, but that it could ruin her. William Downie said that there had been talk of her scandalous behaviour with some members of the Military at the Peter Fair in Rathven, which fitted well with the time of her giving birth. She denied this and claimed that the child had been conceived at a drinking session in the house of John Ord and his wife in Kirktown. However witnesses reported that they had neither seen nor heard anything that was scandalous in the behaviour of either on that occasion. On

December 12th Janet Henderson admitted that her evidence had all been false, and begged the pardon of William Downie. She stated that the father of the child was James Morison, a married man to whom she had had another child before his marriage. She was sharply rebuked.

On March 22nd 1761 Janet Reid in Squaredoch was said to be with child. William Garioch in Ardoch acknowledged himself to be the father, and because this was his second offence was fined £8 Scots. However, as he was a papist he pleaded exemption and was referred to Presbytery.

On October 16th 1763 James Reid acknowledged himself to be the father of Isobel Adam's child, born in fornication, but asked to be absolved immediately as he was contracted to go to Antigua, and had no time to stay in this country. Session considered his intentions good and agreed to absolve him on payment of a fine of 15/- sterling.

On August 20th 1768 Elspet Reid refused to compear for alleged pregnancy and the Kirk Officer reported that when he went to summon her she had threatened to beat him. She had also abused the Minister and elders in very unsuitable language. She was deprived of church privileges, but finally admitted guilt and named the father, who promptly denied this. She named several witnesses who had seen them together in indecent postures in a hollow near Berryhillock, at the burnside above the village and in a little house at Squaredoch. The witnesses confirmed this.

On November 19th 1775, Anne Wier, an unmarried papist in Berryhillock was accused of being with child. She confessed and said that James King was the father. On April 6th 1777 Elspet Reid and Matthew Manbie admitted to having a third child in fornication. On January 4th William Wat in Clunehill paid his son's penalty for fornication of £12 Scots. On July 13th 1777 Margaret Gray, wife to Alexander Andrew in Carrothead, confessed to adultery with Alexander Robertson, late of Berryhillock, and now a carpenter in Cullen, and to being with child to him. Session considered this to be an extraordinary affair. However she then denied her confession and was clearly "disordered in her mind".

On October 10th 1785 a letter was received from William Reid, formerly in Faichyhill, now in Demerary, acknowledging himself to be the father of Margaret Wright's child. On November 27th that same year Janet Munro in Broadrashes admitted being with child to William Bruce, merchant in Cullen. Guilt had been committed in his shop in Cullen so it fell under the discipline of the Session in Cullen. Session was also informed that Janet Smith, an insane woman, had brought forth a child. She was summoned and gave the name of James Wright as the father, but he denied it.

On April 15th 1794 it was reported in the parish that Elizabeth Black, a widow in Greenhill, was with child. She completely denied that she was or ever had been with child since the death of her husband, and that the report was made with malice and ill will against her. Further procedures were delayed until time proved or disproved the accusations against her. On October 20th there was a report that she had given birth to a child in Fordyce. She was summoned to Session where two elders from Fordyce were also in attendance. She was exhorted to honesty but denied the accusation. A midwife from Cullen was of the opinion that she had not given milk in the past six months.

In 1803 the Sheriff Substitute of Banffshire ordered AL (full name not revealed) to pay Session £100 Scots for a trelapse in fornication, the penalty being that affixed to the offence by the laws of the land. This was much more than if he had paid Session the fine they had originally imposed, but he had refused to pay this.

In 1834 Elizabeth Strachan compeared before Session craving absolution. She professed repentance, paid her penalty, was suitably addressed and absolved, and her child was baptised. The father acknowledged paternity but was now in Canada. On October 31st 1841 three women were delated as being with child, Elspet Gray, Margaret Clark and Barbara Russell.

In early 1846 Jean Moggach, a member of the Free Church, claimed that the father of her child was John MacWillie, a member of St John's. The Free Church Minister, Rev Innes, communicated the situation to his St John's counterpart, Rev Mackintosh, who replied that John MacWillie confessed but had a strong desire to marry her. Rev Mackintosh had already established that such a marriage was not expressly forbidden by church law and was not considered unlawful in civil law.

On May 4th 1851 Robert Gray and Jane Riddoch confessed to antenuptial fornication. They had various portions of Holy Scripture pointed out for their prayerful consideration. In 1853 James Packman and Isabella Johnston confessed to fornication but he, as a Roman Catholic, declined to put himself under the discipline of the Free Church. On May 3rd that year she applied for the baptism of the child, but this was refused as the father of the child was RC and could not possibly take the baptismal vows, and she could not take them as she was not bringing up the child. Eventually the baptism was carried out with her father taking the vows.

In August 1858 Elspeth Wilson compeared, admitted she was with child, and stated that about April 1st, a man who had seen her in the shop of James Allan, merchant in Macduff, had followed her between Macduff and Banff and raped her. He was wearing a sailor's uniform. She was exhorted again and again to tell the truth but stuck to her story.

From the 1850s onwards references to sexual impropriety become more perfunctory. On November 7th 1858 Jamesina Wood was with child to John Inglis in Berryhillock. Both were to compear. On December 5th Mary McQueen was pregnant with the claimed father being James Morrison, now living in Marnoch. Both were to compear. On January 2nd 1859 Jean Metcalfe produced a letter from Alexander Young, Old Rayne, admitting he was the father of her child, and had paid aliment up to this date. This was satisfactory to Session and she was admonished and absolved.

In the 1860s there was very widespread fornication, but most instances were now dealt with in a low-key way, with the civil law being far more often involved. The most common offence was antenuptial fornication, with the guilty parties being admonished and absolved immediately. On June 3rd 1867 Alexander Russell denied being the father of Jane Jamieson's baby. The case was eventually dismissed as Session could not find out the truth. She was rebuked, admonished and restored to Church privileges. On December 7th 1879 the same Jane Jamieson produced a letter from Messrs Coutts and

Morison, Solicitors, Banff, stating that decree had been pronounced in the Sheriff Court at Banff against the father of her child, John Henderson. She was absolved. On January 4th 1880 George Taylor, farm servant at Cultain, admitted adultery, was admonished by the Minister and directed to his own church, the United Presbyterian, for further discipline.

Throughout the period in which church discipline was very important and central to the life of the population of Deskford, but particularly during the C18th, some investigations became very complex, long-lasting and fraught, as individuals sought to avoid the loss of their good character.

For example on November 15th 1725, Janet Bain, Cottartown, was accused of cohabiting with a stranger, David McLaughlan. Both were summoned, and Janet Bain denied any uncleanness with him, saying that he was often at her house but had only stayed overnight twice, when her son was also there. Both were cited, as were the witnesses, James Barnet, John Stables, Andrew Miltown and Alexander Barnet. John Stables, an unmarried man of 28, said that he saw them alone and in her house, and that after eating and drinking they had gone to the end of the house where the bed was, but he could not say whether they had gone to bed together, even though he looked through some holes in her door and house. He could not write, but touched the pen. James Barnet could not attend but sent a letter saying he had seen them in bed together, but could not say if they were doing anything as he was some distance away. Janet Bain and David McLaughlan failed to turn up.

Another very complex case involved Walter Hilton, Ramoir and Jean Machatie. In October 1726 she had recently come to Deskford from Kildrummie. They were cohabiting together as man and wife, but session demanded to know if they were really married as they claimed, and if so, by whom. They answered that they had been married by Rev Robertson, late Minister in Strathdon. When asked, they could produce no documentation, but said they would do so by the next Lord's Day. Session knew that Machatie was already under censure in Kildrummie for adultery, and agreed to place the matter before Presbytery for advice, and in the meantime prohibit them from cohabiting with one another till they produced marriage documentation.

They were sharply rebuked for their disorderly procedure in going to a deposed Minister to be married without proclamation of banns. On November 6th Presbytery informed the Minister that Walter Hilton and Jean Machatie had been married in a clandestine manner, if at all, and that he should communicate with the Presbytery of Alford before doing anything. When asked if she was married, Machatie said that she thought so, having been married by a certain Dunbar, keeper of an alehouse in Newmiln in the parish of Auchindoir, before named witnesses. She declared that Alexander Lumsden in Birkenbrewl went to Rev Robertson, a deposed Minister in Strathdon, to marry them, but that he refused and Dunbar did so instead. He desired them to join hands and made them swear by their Maker that they should be true to one another during life, and then declared them married before God and the witnesses, but that they should not tell anyone.

Walter Hilton, when interrogated, denied he was married but consented to accept Janet Machatie as his wife, on condition that the Laird of Cushnie gave him 200 merks plus some nolts (cattle) and sheep, and a tenancy on his land in case he was turned out of his own in Deskford, or met with any trouble for marrying her. They were rebuked for their actions and also for "disingenuity".

The Presbytery of Alford replied that Janet Machatie had had a child there. She then confessed that the Laird of Cushnie, a married man, was the father. The child had been taken from her by those trying to arrange her marriage but she had tried to get it back. She had previously alleged that the father was John Hay in the parish of Bellie, because she was advised to do so by some women present at the birth, because they knew that Hay had an affection for her, and that since he lived at a distance, this was a good way to conceal the true father of the child.

She said that she knew nothing of the letter alleged to have been written by Hay, in which he admitted the child was his, but said she thought the letter was a forgery. William Gib and Charles Grant had been sent by the Laird of Cushnie or some of his friends to speak to Hay, who later claimed that he had written a letter denying that the child was his. When asked why she had lied to the session of Kildrummie and the Presbytery of Alford, she said that she was overawed by some of the persons in that district, and afraid of bodily harm being done to her, and her brother-in-law, Alexander Troupe, his wife and her sister. She felt in less danger in Deskford telling the truth.

Asked why the Deskford Kirk Session should believe that the Laird of Cushnie was the father she said that Rev William Brown, chaplain to Leith Hall and brother-in-law to the Laird of Cushnie, had baptised the child in the house of James Shaw, the ground officer, and that he could tell who the father was, having been asked by the Laird of Cushnie to baptise the child. Only Shaw, his wife, Rev Brown and Janet Machatie were present and Brown instructed them not to tell anyone who had baptised it. He would rather give away 500 merks than this was known. She had also told the Laird of Cushnie, in front of the said Shaw and his wife, and Alexander Troupe and his wife that he was the father and he accepted that this was the case in their presence.

She was ordered to attend Alford Presbytery to give satisfaction and her confession and declaration was to be sent to them in addition to information about the alleged marriage to Walter Hilton, who would now be treated by Deskford as a single fornicator, and also be required to attend the Presbytery of Alford. On October 1st 1727 Janet Machatie asked the Deskford Session if she might appear without sackcloth. They refused because of the great scandal she had given. If she did not appear she would be put into the hands of the civil magistrates. She was finally absolved on November 19th 1727, but still had to satisfy the Presbytery of Alford. After this they both disappear from the records of Deskford parish.

Another convoluted case took place between 1744 and 1746. Jean Howie was the servant of Alexander Smith in Hoggie in 1744 and part of 1745 when they had "conversed together in too intimate a manner". She subsequently married Alexander Fowler on June 20th 1745, and gave birth to a child on February 13th 1746. Fowler thought the child was not his and complained to the Kirk Session. The woman, "teased and harassed by her husband" gave up Smith as the father. When she and Smith were called before Session she felt obliged to stick to her story. He admitted fornication, but denied the child was his.

Fowler, having proved his wife a whore, took civil action before the Baillie of the Regality of Ogilvie against Smith, for aliment. The Baillie remitted the matter to the Kirk Session who decided that since she had been consistent in her evidence, while he had not, Smith should be considered the father of the child. The Baillie, without taking any evidence himself, or allowing Smith to see the Kirk Session report, which he should have done, determined that Smith should pay aliment for the time since the birth and also in the future.

Smith appealed to the Lord Justice Clerk who ordered that memorials (legal arguments) should be given in by both parties. Smith's memorial was written by a lawyer, and claimed: 1. That the law states that if it is possible that the husband could have been the father, then he is considered as such, even if adultery can be proven against the wife. Birth had been 248 days after marriage, whilst the most learned physicians stated that a child might survive even if born only 180 days after conception. 2. The only evidence of intimacy at a relevant date was her statement, and the dates she gave may have meant that the child was overdue. 3. The decision of the Baillie was inept and void because he had taken no evidence and was based solely on the report of the Kirk Session, which was so trifling and inconclusive that no judge could proceed on its basis. 4. The Kirk Session had not been even-handed in their treatment of Howie and Smith and had based their decision on a presumption which they held to be fact. They insisted that Smith was guilty because he had not produced evidence that any other man was guilty of fornication with Howie, but the Lord Justice Clerk stated that it was not Smith's responsibility to produce this. 5. There was no ground for a presumption of guilt, far less proof.

Following this Smith was successful in his appeal and was not held to be guilty or responsible for paying aliment. However the final act in a long-drawn-out dispute which saw many in a poor light, took place on December 21st 1746 when Smith at last confessed his guilt.

Yet another soap opera unfolded in May 1744. Jean Lawrence declared that, as she was attending and taking care of a cow of her master's which had recently calved on the hill, Alexander Huie met her, though she could not say where he was going. He "wrastled" with her and she felt that he intended to "force her modesty", but she resisted and he gave up and went away. She was "gravely recommended" by Session.

Alexander Huie at first denied the charge, but on being pressed, confessed that as his mother had neither straw nor pasture for her cow, he went with it to the hill in order to feed it there. He accidentally met Jean Lawrence, but only put his hands round her neck, and did not "wrastle" with her or have any bad intentions.

Session decided that since the incident had been very noisy, and took place during the church service on the Sabbath, from which Alexander Huie had absented himself, that the Minister should rebuke him sharply before session, order him to appear before the congregation to be censured for the scandal, especially breach of the Sabbath, and also exhort him to behave well in the future.

Alexander Huie then complained that he had been hurt and bruised by a rabble of people, gathered together to punish him for the matter, and that some of the mob pronounced bloody oaths and imprecations, especially Robert Gerrie and Alexander Barnet, both in Cottartown of Ardoch. He named several witnesses. Session decided to investigate, and call the alleged persons to account. Two elders, James Smith and John Reid, were to speak to all involved.

Both Alexander Barnet and Robert Gerrie said that although they could not remember, they may have uttered oaths. Witnesses said that Barnet had not done so, therefore he was dismissed with an admonition to be careful of his language and behaviour in future. Witnesses however stated that Robert Gerrie had uttered the most frightful oaths, so he was sharply rebuked before session. The Minister would also intimate from the pulpit that all persons should refrain from all tumultuous meetings, and in particular, be careful of cursing, swearing and using any imprecations.

As a final example of the complex situations regarding sexual activity which Deskford Kirk Session had to deal with, in October 1760 the Minister thought it his duty to speak to and question Janet McLachlan, an unmarried woman who was accused of being with child. She strenuously denied this, claiming she had never been with a man. Session decided to wait "to see what Providence might bring forth in the matter". In due course she had a child and was summoned and rebuked by the Minister for her guilt and scandals, and for her prevarications. She was told she should not use any lies or falsehoods with respect to the name of the father of her child.

She named James Reid, son to James Reid in Mid Skeith, but he denied it. Both stuck repeatedly to their stories, so the matter was referred to Presbytery. He was accused of having gone to her bed, himself being naked, and having lain in the bed with her on about December 23rd the previous year. He admitted this, but not, he said to commit guilt with her. She said that on various occasions he had tried to persuade her to commit guilt with him, and that frequently they were in undressed circumstances together. He then said he never intended to commit guilt with her.

Presbytery was told by Janet McLachlan that Elizabeth Grant, Janet Reid, Janet Keir and Margaret Wright had seen them in bed together. James Reid said that he had evidence that she had behaved similarly with John Ord in Clochmacreich. Presbytery remitted the matter back to session and detailed evidence was then given by the witnesses, of Reid lying on and in her bed with her, at which times there was much activity

John Ord was now in Slains, in Buchan, so could not appear, but James Reid said that George Andrews in Carrothead had also been in bed with Janet McLachlan, and named several witnesses to this. Their evidence was noted in enormous detail over some considerable time, but was very confused, and the matter was not properly resolved.

FOLK BELIEFS AND SUPERSTITIONS

It is difficult today to imagine the extent to which all aspects of life in Deskford were influenced by folk beliefs and superstitions, right up to the end of the C18th and with echoes into the C19th and C20th. It would be easy to laugh at or ridicule many of these beliefs, but first we should perhaps consider how those living in two hundred years time might ridicule the beliefs and superstitions which we today subscribe to.

Many historic folk beliefs were in existence from pagan Celtic times and some were adopted by and integrated into early Christian and then Roman Catholic belief systems. A major interruption occurred in 1560 with the Reformation when the Church of Scotland denounced popular healing beliefs as idolatrous and took action against them. Many of these beliefs however were very persistent and the final blow to them did not occur probably until the rational scientific orthodoxy of the late C19th. Even then remnants and distortions of some of these early folk beliefs were tenacious and can be identified up to the present day.

In 1776 the Deskford Minister, Rev Walter Morison, warned his congregation against the "superstitious and heathenish practices he had observed of lighting Beltane fires and other idolatrous customs which he had observed being carried out by the most ignorant people in the parish". Despite this some Beltane fires were still being lit in the 1830s and perhaps later. In 1802 one local farmer accused another's wife in all seriousness of having cast spells which made his cow go dry.

During the 1770s a man called Machattie, his wife, son and daughter took the lease of the small farm of Broomie Knowe which lay between Mains of Skeith and Berryhillock Mill. They came from Grantown, wore tartan, spoke Gaelic and were Catholics. They had arrived in Deskford with a small cart of household goods, two cows, one calf, two ponies, one donkey and a Highland terrier. Locals viewed them with great suspicion despite them having a certificate of attestation "that the bearer, Donald Machattie, and his family were honest and industrious and of good character".

He was a very hard worker and made a great success of his croft, which probably increased the suspicion. He built his house in fourteen days, though some locals felt he had been helped by the fairies because the fairy hillock was close by (probably between the present B road and the old Berryhillock road, immediately west of the site of the old chapel of Our Lady of Pity). In seven years they made enormous improvements, a larger house, a larger kailyard, an orchard, a kailyard dyke and larger horses.

One year however an epidemic occurred amongst the cattle of Deskford and Donald Machattie's were the only ones not affected. Many locals were convinced that this must be the work of the Devil and that the Machatties must be in league with "Auld Nick". Rumours spread. Elf darts had been found. The situation became very tense.

The young widowed daughter of the Minister, Sarabella Morison, decided to help the Machatties since she had bought their corned mutton and blue vein cheese. The accusers were summoned before the Kirk Session where they were severely criticised by Rev Morison, by now in his 80s. Four culprits confessed that they had said Elspet Anderson, wife of Donald Machattie, was a witch who dealt with the "Evil One" and was responsible for "the death of every head of nowt (cattle), cow, calf, stot and coy that had died in the parish". The Minister, normally a very easy-going man, lost his temper with them and referred them to the Sheriff with a recommendation to prosecute and said that they deserved to be excommunicated from the Church. When the four were summoned they persisted in their accusations and said what they had alleged was true. They were all fined, after which two recanted. Donald Machattie accepted their apologies and suggested that part of their fines be repaid to them which duly happened.

In mediaeval times every inhabitant of Deskford believed in the power of saints, devils, fairies, priests and witches, both for healing and for causing harm. Witches were not persecuted extensively, though there were laws against witchcraft. It would have been seen as just like persecuting a fairy.

After the Reformation a powerful movement against witches developed, worshipping saints was seen as superstition and it became a sin to put out milk for fairies or to give meal to a witch. In Scotland, under Catholicism evil spirits could be placated, but under Calvinism they had to be confronted and defeated. Despite this there were witch-hunts in catholic countries on the continent.

In the North East, witch hunts were not anti-Catholic but were directed mainly against farmers, cottar wives, poor old widows, pipers, tinkers and vagabonds, and never against the wealthy. Good and bad witches were considered equally guilty, both having made a pact with the Devil, though in reality many were just herbalists or healers.

In the C17th and C18th beliefs were many and widespread. Tinkers were known to possess a charm which made any woman follow them and "submit to their embraces". Two sweets held together by sweat would attract any young man targeted by a young woman. A young woman could be identified as having indulged sinfully in sex if her complexion had a blue tinge to it or if she had a prominent blue vein in her lower eyelid. A chamber pot filled with salt was a common wedding present to protect against the evil eye.

The first work a new female servant should be given was to fetch water from the well. Stirring food must be done from left to right. If done the "vrang wye" it could result in an intestinal illness. The right shoe or stocking must be put on before the left, and on wearing new clothes a good luck coin had to be put in a pocket. If sewing or putting a button on clothes was done on the Sabbath, the Devil undid the work at night.

Singing before breakfast brought bad luck. Nothing was loaned on term or quarter days, which coincided with the pagan festivals of Imloc, Beltane, Lammas and Samhain. It was unlucky to report a theft or to accuse anyone of stealing. If you had something stolen then returned it was unlucky to keep it. If horses refused to move they had been arrested by an evil spirit and the wise woman of the parish was called to take the arrestment off.

At Beltane all fires were extinguished and the usual meal cooked over the new Beltane fire. Special oatcakes with small knobs on them were baked and the knobs were broken off and thrown into the fire one by one while saying "This I give to thee; preserve my horses" or "Oh fox spare my lambs".

On May Day a bannock was baked for each member of the family by the gudewife, with egg whipped and spread over it. The gudeman cut and gave a slice of kebback (cheese) to each bannock, all of which had to be eaten by sunset. After eating them they danced sunwise round the fire then went round the edges of their fields with blazing embers and branches to protect the fields from evil. Hallowe'en fires were even more important. All domestic fires were extinguished and relit with an ember of the Hallow Fire on November 11th which was Hallowe'en in the old calendar. These were lit well into the C19th.

Silver guarded against evil and was often given as a gift to a baby on first seeing it, and people often drank out of a vessel with a silver coin in it. Little spectres called tarans, or the souls of unbaptised infants who had died, were often seen flitting amongst the woods and secret places, bewailing in soft voices their sad fate.

St Mary's Well at Auldtown, Ordiquhill, had great powers and people from far and near, including from Deskford, visited it. In the early C17th people who had gone there had to appear before the Kirk Session to be rebuked. It was even condemned by the General Assembly, but any Minister who tried to stop the practice was unpopular and even at some personal risk. St John's Well at Deskford was also considered a healing well, as was the better-known one at Tarlair and also St Fumac's at Botriphnie. When attending any of these wells it was usual to drink some of the water, walk round it three times sunwise and then leave a small offering. Wells dedicated to St John, as with the one in Deskford, were considered effective in curing eye disorders. Jenny's well, on the shore near Portknockie, was also visited, on May 1st, including by people from Deskford, even into the C19th. Pins and other small offerings were left. Jenny's Well was almost certainly a healing well long before it got its present name.

Old women who had the reputation for an "uncanny eye" received presents of food and clothes and had their peats cast for them without having to ask. When passing the cottage of one of these women, men would put their thumb in their palm and cover it with their fingers. This was a post-Reformation relic of the practice of crossing oneself. The Devil was known colloquially as "Auld Nick", "the Gowk" or "Auld Sandy". At the edge of the present wood beside Ley Farm, just over the parish boundary into Fordyce, was a stone with a cavity in it, where mothers took children with whooping cough to obtain a cure. This practice was strongly criticised by the Kirk Session and the Presbytery as being papist, though it probably was a pagan practice which predated Christianity.

Deskford was blamed whenever anything went wrong with Cullen fishermen, who had a saying, "Ye've seen Skeith's cat an' Berryhillock's dog" directed at the individual or individuals who had suffered misfortune.

Many of the old beliefs and superstitions were centred on important stages of life, childbirth, marriage and death. Others focussed on the vital elements of day-to-day life such as those of farming, or the stages of the calendar such as Christmas, Fastern's E'en (Brose Day), Easter (Pasch), Beltane, Lammas and All Hallows E'en. Witches and fairies were taken seriously and various plants and animals had specific powers or could provide omens of future occurrences.

COURTSHIP AND MARRIAGE

There was an immense number of ways in which young men and women could foretell whom they would marry, some of them being carried out as games or entertainments. In the C18th young women could find out the size and figure of their future husband by picking a cabbage blindfold from a field on All Hallow's E'en. A large cabbage meant a large husband, a shapely cabbage a shapely one, and if there was a large clod of earth attached he would be wealthy. It was then placed just inside the door and the first name of the first young man to enter would be the first name of the future husband.

Many alternative methods existed. The first time a young person slept in a strange house, a ring was put on his or her finger, one shoe was placed under the bed, which was then entered backwards. This caused the future husband or wife to be seen in a dream. Alternatively, a young woman wishing to know who her husband would be should read, after supper, Job chapter 17 verse 3, "Who is he that will strike hands with me", wash the supper dishes, go to bed without saying a single word, place the Bible under her pillow with a pin through the verse and she would see her future husband in a dream. Or, the first time a cuckoo was heard in the spring, the hearer should turn round three times on the left heel in the direction against the sun. When he or she looked in the hollow left by the heel a hair the colour of the hair of the future husband or wife would be found. Alternatively, to find if the young man or woman would be true, three stalks of the carl doddie (ribwort) should be pulled when in bloom, stripped of blossom and placed in the left shoe under the pillow. If the young man or woman would become the husband or wife then the three stalks would be in full bloom by morning, or at least be switched by a kind friend. If they were without blossom then the prospective partner would prove untrue.

There are even more. In the evening the young woman had to walk over the ridges of a flax field sowing a handful of flax seed and saying

"Lint seed, lint seed, I saw ye

Lint seed, lint seed I saw ye

Let 'im 'at's tae be my lad

Come aifter me an' pu' me".

On looking over her left shoulder she would see the image of her future husband crossing the field and picking flax. Or she could "fathom a rick". A stack of oats or barley was measured round three times with the arms, against the sun. When going round for the third time the image of the future husband would be seen. Or she could "winnow corn" by going secretly to the barn and pretending to winnow three times. The image of her future husband would walk in one door and out the other. Alternatively she could try "boasting peas". A live peat was taken from the fire, and two peas, representing the lad and the lass were put on it. If the peas burned together they would become man and wife, and the brighter and longer they burned the happier and longer would be the marriage. If one pea fell off there would be no marriage, the fault of whichever of them the pea represented.

The number of children a young woman would have could be determined by her picking a stalk of oats from a stack, with her back to it. The number of grains on it represented the number of children she would have, but if the top grain was missing she would not be a virgin when she married. In order to assist all of this a love potion could be used, made from the ground-up root of the archis.

On Fastern Eve, egg whites broken into a tumbler with a little water in it allowed wise women, such as Mrs Wilson, Knows, in the 1880s, to foretell Romantic attachments. Young men could choose a piece of cake which might contain a ring or a button. A ring meant he would get married but a button meant he would stay single. In the 1860s and 1870s, Mrs Murray, Berryhillock was known as Lucky Murray and her presence at births, marriages and funerals was considered important.

Penny Weddings were riotous occasions, and indeed, at one in Deskford, a local man was shot and killed. Anyone attending a Penny Wedding and not paying their share was called a whistlebinkie, though they could make up for this by singing a song or playing the penny whistle. A pledge of £3 Scots was left with the Kirk by couples before their banns could be called, and they forfeited this if they had a Penny Wedding. The Church was strongly opposed to them.

Marriages were arranged in secret. Sometimes the bride's mother was told, but never the father, till all the arrangements were made. Tuesdays and Thursdays were considered lucky days to get married, or sometimes Saturdays, if the moon was increasing. January and May were considered unlucky months in which to get married, and it was unlucky for two members of the same family to get married in the same year.

The young woman who was about to get married gathered all her "providan", a feather bed, bolster, pillows, blankets and sheets etc. The young man went with the young woman's mother or sister to Cullen or Keith to buy the "bonnie things" and the wedding dress. He also gave dresses to the young woman's mother and sister(s). The bride-to-be bought a chest of drawers or a kist.

All the "providan" was sent to their future home a few days before the wedding, then the place was left unlocked for luck. The bride and her bridesmaids gave out invitations personally and invited two young men to lead her to church. The groom and best man also gave out invitations personally and invited two young women to lead him to church. Only then was the Minister invited, for to do it earlier would have been unlucky.

Each guest gave a gift for the wedding feast, perhaps a chicken, butter or a bottle of whisky. The hen night had a literal meaning and was when the females plucked hens for the wedding feast. Ale was brewed specially, and if it boiled first on the side of the pot nearest those tending it, and if the fermentation was strong, these were good omens for the marriage. The first cake baked for the feast must not be allowed to break as this would have been unlucky.

The day before the Sunday on which the banns were first to be read was called the "beukin' nicht". The groom went to the bride's house where a few friends were present and then went with the bride's father to the Session Clerk to "lay doon the pawns" (pay the £3 pledge) which allowed the banns to be read on three successive Sundays. It was considered very unlucky for the bride to attend Church when her banns were proclaimed. Between the banns being read and the marriage taking place, friends, on meeting the bride or groom, would rub shoulders with them for luck and to catch the infection of marriage. On the evening before the marriage the groom's friends came to his home to give him a robust "feet washing", using scrubbing brushes, soot, boot blackening and other similar items. There was also hospitality, which must not be taken to excess.

A bright, sunny day for the wedding meant good fortune. Everything the bride wore must be new, but if her wedding shoes were too small this foretold many evils. Something must be borrowed, a ring being particularly lucky. If a younger sister got married she had to give any older unmarried sisters a green garter.

The bride's guests arrived early at her home and the groom's at his. There was a special breakfast of oatmeal porridge with milk, sugar, curds and cream. Some years later this became a tea breakfast. There was then often dancing till it was time for Church. Two men, the "sens", were sent from the groom's house to demand the bride. They were met by a volley of firearms and the following exchange took place.

> "Does (bride) bide here?
> Aye. Fit dae ye wint wi' her?
> We wint her for (groom)
> Bit ye winna get her
> Bit we'll tak her
> Will ye come in an' taste a moofu'
> o' a dram an' we'll see aboot it".

Thus the sens got possession of the bride. Both parties, the bride's and the groom's, set out to arrive at the church at the same time. The bride's party had precedence, and she walked at the head of it. She must not look back under any circumstances or bad luck would follow. The groom and his two young maidens led his party. Both parties carried whisky, bread and cheese to be given to the first person they met en route. This "first fit" was particularly lucky if it was a man on horseback or a man with a horse and cart. Both parties were accompanied by pipers and gunfire, and when they left their respective homes, various old shoes, brooms and scrubbing brushes were thrown after them.

On arrival the Kirk Officer led the groom to the "bride sled", the special pew for those about to be married. Then the bride was led to the pew. If she was pregnant the same fate would befall her bridesmaid within the year. Anyone who was a bridesmaid on three separate occasions would never get married herself. After the ceremony the bride kissed the Minister and pinned a favour on his right arm. The groom gave the Kirk Officer his fee of 6d, but a collection was also taken for him.

The joint party left the church led by the bride and her sens, followed by the groom and the bridesmaids and made their way to the groom's home, using the main roads and avoiding any shortcuts, which would have brought bad luck. On nearing the house young men raced to "win the kaill". Whoever won the race would be the next to be married. The bride was welcomed by the groom's mother or next nearest female relation. When she crossed the threshold a sieve containing bread and cheese was held above her head. These were then distributed amongst the guests. In later years this was changed to an oatcake being held over her head and then broken, and even later this became a cake of shortbread.

The bride was then led in to make the fire and sweep the hearth. The crook from the swey was then swung three times round her head in the name of the Father, Son and Holy Ghost and a short prayer was said, "May the Almichty mak this wumman a good wife". She was then led to the meal girnal and her hand pressed as far down as possible to ensure future abundance of food in her household. Beggars would have gathered and would be generously fed and given drink.

There followed the feast. Tables were borrowed from neighbours. Seats were made out of planks laid across any support, and dishes and spoons were borrowed from neighbours and friends. The bride sat at the head of the table and the groom served the guests. The first course was milk broth made of barley. The second course was barley broth made with beef, mutton or fowls, and the third course was eating the meat. This was followed by a variety of puddings with cream. Ale was drunk throughout and after the meal whisky, or a punch made from whisky, sugar and hot water, both of which were used for the toasts. Dancing always started with the Shamit Reel, danced by the bride, groom, best man and bridesmaids. The male dancers paid the fiddler then the same central characters danced again, following which the floor was open for the rest of the evening into the wee sma' 'oors, interspersed with bread, cheese, ale and punch.

After the dancing the bride went into her marriage bed and there was the "beddin' ceremony" at which all her friends crowded into the bedroom and were given bread and cheese. She threw a stocking over her shoulder and whoever caught it would be next to marry. Unfortunately whoever was first to fall asleep would be first to die.

The Kirkin' of the couple was attended by all their friends and relations and the group must enter the church after the service had started. If two different marriages were Kirkit' at the same service, then the second party to leave the Church would not have a successful or happy marriage.

It was very important to start having children very soon after the wedding. To help, a willow branch was placed under the newly married couple's bed, rice was thrown and any knot of any kind nearby was untied. The bride was given a chamber pot filled with salt with a doll inside. If she did not become pregnant within a few months this was considered to be either her fault or that of the fairies, and it caused much gossip. Once a woman became pregnant the sex of the child could be foretold by holding a needle and thread over her bump. If it swung round in a circle the child would be a girl, but if it moved back and forth it would be a boy.

In earlier times trial marriages took place, starting at Lammas and lasting a year and a day. This was called handfasting, and though the practice died out several centuries ago it was only made illegal in 1939. One of the main reasons for handfasting was so that a man could find out if his proposed partner was fertile before formally marrying her. If a child was born but the couple decided not to continue living together after the year and a day, the child was considered legitimate and its upbringing was the responsibility of the father. There was no criticism of the mother and she was still considered pure and clean. It was not uncommon for women to be married surrounded by their children from previous relationships. New husbands welcomed this as it provided additional labour for their farm.

Traditions surrounding marriages are not set in stone and change over the years. Wedding dresses were not used widely until the early C20th, and for the bride to be given away by her father is a relatively recent practice. A ring worn by the bride is a tradition going back to Roman times, but after the Reformation their use was banned, and the practice was only reintroduced slowly. A wedding ring for the husband is a very recent practice.

CHILDBIRTH AND CHILDHOOD

Childbirth was a time of great risk for both mother and child, and great efforts were made to ensure both survived and thrived. In the C16th and earlier perhaps one in every two children born survived to adulthood. No pregnant woman was permitted to be in the same room as one giving birth, and no woman who was suckling her own child could sit on the bed of a woman about to give birth, as this would stop the latter's milk. If it did happen for any reason, the calamity could be averted by secretly passing the child being suckled under the apron of the pregnant woman. When a woman went into labour all the locks in the house were unlocked. If the labour was difficult the first woman to enter the house gave the mother a little water to moisten her mouth, and certain "wise women" might be sought out to perform this service.

On the birth, mother and child were "sained". A fir candle was lit and carried three times round the bed, or if space would not allow, it was whirled three times round their heads. A Bible and some bread and cheese were placed under the new mother's pillow and the blessing "May the Almighty debar all ill from this woman, and be about her and bless her bairn" uttered. The bread and cheese was then given out among all her unmarried friends to place under their pillows and bring favourable dreams.

Careful watch was kept over both mother and child till the mother was Kirkit and the child baptised. When the new mother was Kirkit she and her friends would walk three times round the Church, sunwise. Kirkin' and baptism happened as soon as possible to reduce the risk of either mother or child being stolen by the fairies and taken underground. Deskford's Fairy Hillock was probably the small hillock between the two roads, just south of Woodend Smiddy at the southern end of Berryhillock. New mothers were often taken by fairies who enjoyed their milk. They were only allowed to return home once they were worn out, and then only in exchange for the best mare in milk, which was also, in due course, returned worn out.

When a new child was dressed in clothes for the first time it was turned three times head over heels in its mother's arms, blessed and shaken three times with its head downwards. This kept the fairies away, and was done every time it was dressed. In order to preserve a child from the fairies, a small brooch in the shape of a heart was worn on one of its petticoats, usually behind. Another way to protect mother and child from the fairies was to place the father's trousers over the foot of the bed.

If a newborn child was taken by the fairies, and a deformed changeling left in its place, the test was to place it as close as possible to a roaring fire. If it was a changeling it escaped up the chimney. Another test was to hang it by a hazel branch in a new skull over a fire. If it screamed it was a changeling and was taken to a place where four roads met, a dead body was carried over it and the real child was restored.

When a child was born a feast was held, called the "merry melit", part of which was the "cryin' kebback" (cheese). Everyone present took away pieces of cheese to give to friends. The new mother was not permitted to do any work or visit a neighbour's house until she had been Kirkit, attendance at an ordinary Sunday service. The first occasion on which the new mother went to the well for water she had to do so, not with a bucket but with a thimble.

When a child was born, if it was a boy, it was wrapped in a woman's shirt, and if a girl in a man's. If this was not done the child would never marry. When washing a child the water should never be allowed to touch the palms of its hands or it would remain poor throughout its life, and the water in which a newborn child was washed had to be poured under the house foundations to prevent it coming in contact with fire. This would protect the child from fire throughout its life. If a child urinated freely at birth, this was a sign of good luck, especially for those wet by it.

A child born feet first would have the gift of second sight. If a child spoke before it walked it would become a liar and if suckled after it had been weaned it would become a thief. It would also become a thief if, on the first occasion, its fingernails were cut off by scissors or a knife rather than being bitten off. The first visit of a child to another house brought good luck to that house, particularly if it was carried by its mother. Its mouth should be filled with sugar for good luck and it should be given a gift or "hunger was left in the house". No child was put in a new cradle unless a live cock or hen was put in first, or an old cradle was borrowed and used first.

It was dangerous to speak a new child's name before it was baptised and so at baptism the name was written on a piece of paper and handed to the Minister. In pre-Reformation times, if a child died before baptism its name could not be written in the Book of Life, and therefore it could never enter heaven, so if a child became very ill in the middle of the night, the priest would be summoned to baptise it. In early times unbaptised children could not be buried in the churchyard.

Baptisms were sometimes carried out in private and sometimes in public. The sick-nurse carried the child, handed it to the father who in turn handed it to the Minister and then received it back again. The child would be dressed in white. After a private christening, bread, cheese and whisky were given to the guests, each of whom gave a small money gift to the child. This was passed on to the nurse as her fee. If a boy and a girl were both being baptised during the same church service it was essential that the girl was baptised first, except if they were twins, when the boy should always be done first.

Children in Deskford were baptised with water from St John's Well which emerged apparently from under the Church. The baptism water was kept for eight days, after which it was poured below the house's foundation, or it was drunk, which improved the memory.

DEATH AND BURIAL

Imminent death was announced in many different ways into the C18th or early C19th. Amongst them were three dull, heavy knocks, or the "death drap" which was the continuous sound of water, leaden and hollow, or the noise of something heavy (the coffin) being laid outside the door. Others included the murmer of many voices outside the door, or a pale bluish light, the "deid can'le", moving around the house then along the road to the graveyard, or an apparition of the soon to die person, seen wrapped in winding sheets.

Animals could predict death. For example a white dove hovering above the person about to die, or the crowing of a cock before midnight, or a dog howling at night. Three drops of blood from the nose meant someone in the family was about to die. Not sneezing when ill meant death and sneezing meant recovery. The "fey crap" was another omen. If a farmer had a much better crop than usual it meant he would die. If someone was dying in great pain it might be because their bed or pillow was stuffed with wild fowls' feathers. The person would be taken out of the bed and laid on the floor.

There were many superstitions surrounding death. In Deskford two holes were dug, the "quick grave" and the "deid grave". The ill person was laid between them without being told which was which, and the outcome of the illness depended on which hole the ill person turned to first. The Kirk considered this practice a major sin in the C17th.

A shower of rain meant the soul of the dead person was happy, but a gale meant the dead person had committed some evil deed or had a hidden bad life, or a deal with the Devil. Sometimes, on the night after the funeral, bread and water were left in the room in which the corpse had lain, to permit the soul to be at rest in the next world. This has obvious echoes of Iron and Bronze Age burials when food and drink might be buried with the corpse. Throwing earth on the coffin today may have the same origin. Anyone who looked out on a funeral through a window would soon die themselves, and if a murderer touched a corpse blood flowed from any wounds on the body.

Suicides were not buried in the kirkyard, even into the C19th. Instead they were often buried on the march between two landlords' estates, marked by a cairn or stone at which any passer-by was required to throw a small stone. It was believed that nothing would grow on the grave of a suicide or on the spot where a murder was committed. Later, when suicides were buried in the kirkyard they were buried in a spot where nobody could step over them, for, if a pregnant woman did so, her child would in due course also commit suicide. However possession of a suicide's weapon, such as a knife or a rope, brought prosperity. Stillborn and unbaptised children were buried before sunrise because, if this was not done, their spirits would not be admitted to heaven but would float through space, homeless. Some were buried so their grave could not be stepped over.

In pre-Reformation days alms were given to the poor in exchange for them praying for the dead, and this survived post–Reformation as "deid dole", where food and drink were given to beggars. Also in pre-Reformation times white stockings were provided for the dead, whose soul had to travel over the "Brig o' Dread". The Catholic lykewake continued for 200 years after 1560, but after this date there were no prayers for the dead, since these were unnecessary, as they, being the elect, would automatically go to heaven.

Kirkyards only became properly established and organised at the Reformation, when dykes were built round them. Before this, landowners had been buried within the church, and others somewhere nearby. In 1588 the Kirk banned burials inside churches, so most or all of the memorial stones inside old St John's, both those in the walls and those used as floor slabs, which were covered up by the artificially high floor level, may be memorials, not graves. Deskford Church, like all churches, was at the north end of its churchyard, since most people preferred to be buried to the south of the church.

In early times burials were in an east-west alignment, with the corpse's head to the west so they could greet the Second Coming of Christ, which would be from the east. There is some evidence for this in the Deskford kirkyard, but it is very limited due to late C19th "improvements" and the clearance of many headstones.

Practices associated with funerals have changed considerably over the centuries. In the C16th creditors could arrest a corpse until its debts were paid. Mould from graveyards was commonly used for sorcery. Coffins for ordinary folk were only introduced after the Reformation; before that most folk just had winding sheets. Though some were erected earlier, the use of gravestones only became popular in the C18th. At this time no religious services were held for burials except sometimes a brief prayer at the house of the deceased.

In 1694 an Act of parliament required winding sheets to be made of linen, but this was superseded by another Act of 1705 which required them to be made of woollen cloth, and which also required an elder to be present at the "kistin'" to verify this. Both laws were an attempt to help industries which were in difficulty.

Mourners wore ordinary clothes till the middle of the C19th, and it was only at this time that undertakers first appeared, that spouses first attended each other's funeral and that flowers began being given. One custom which did survive into the second half of the C20th, and even into the present, was the requirement that all men in the community should be present at a funeral. To this day many feel that to be an obligation.

There had been a reluctance to use new graveyards, though this no longer applied when the extensions were made to Deskford kirkyard in 1887 and 1926. Graveyards, gravestones, coffins and mortcloths were viewed in awe, but human bones were objects of dread. This was particularly relevant in Deskford as in other places, when plots and lairs were used repeatedly and in a fairly random fashion. Old rotten coffins were often dug up as were bones, and there were many layers of bodies in the same location. Because of this the old part of Deskford kirkyard was eventually three of four feet higher than the floor level in the Church, something which was only remedied when the Church was abandoned and its floor level was raised by three or four feet. In Deskford there was no open space available for use as the school playground so the kirkyard was used for this purpose.

In the C18th there was a detailed etiquette surrounding death and burial. At the moment of death all doors and windows were thrown open to allow the spirit to depart. The nearest relative had to bend over the dying person in order to receive their last breath. Curtains and blinds were closed and fires put out. Someone went out and informed the bees of the death as these were the "messengers of the gods", a hangover from pagan times. A piece of iron or wood was put in all food to prevent its corruption. All milk in the house was poured out on the ground. All chairs were sprinkled with water as were the clothes of the dead and the clock was stopped and all mirrors covered.

All hens and cats were shut up as, if they jumped over the corpse, the next person to meet them would go blind. Neighbours would not yoke their horse unless there was running water between them and the house in which the body lay. A wright (carpenter) was called who brought his strykin' board on which the corpse was laid after the family had washed and dressed it in a home-made linen shirt and stockings and covered it with a home made linen sheet. Many brides stored their wedding dress to be used as their winding sheet, and she and her husband's wedding linen and stockings were similarly used.

When the eyelids of the corpse did not close themselves, an old penny or halfpenny was laid on them. On the corpse's breast was laid a saucer of salt and to prevent swelling of the bowels a small dish of mould was laid on the abdomen. If this was not done and they started swelling the problem was solved by cutting a small green turf and placing it on the abdomen.

A candle or two were kept burning constantly beside the body. If the candles fell over and set the grave clothes alight, then the corpse, when alive, had possessed more than ordinary powers, had sold his or her soul to the Devil or had been sexually impure. The coffin was made quickly and a day decided for the kistin', which was done by the closest female friends and relatives. At this event there was hospitality and comment about the dead person's qualities and deeds. Other female acquaintances who had not been at the kistin' were then invited to "see the corpse".

The body was watched over day and night. This was the "wyke" or "waukin'" and had its origin in pre-Reformation practice. A few neighbours came to do this each night, and at least one of them had to be awake at all times. They read scripture in a low voice, often Psalm 91, St John chapter 15 or 1st Corinthians chapter 15. Sometimes events were not so solemn, with practical jokes being played. New pipes and tobacco were provided for the occasion, as was whisky, and bread and cheese was served with ale, or in late years tea, about midnight.

For the funeral, the barn was swept out and fitted with seats made of planks. In the middle of the floor was a table covered with a tablecloth, at the head of which was a seat for the Minister. On the table were bread, cheese, whisky, ale and new pipes and tobacco.

Invitations had been delivered personally, and on arrival each mourner was conducted to the barn by the nearest relative of the deceased. People arrived over two or three hours. The Minister, or in his absence an elder, might say a prayer. A toddy was drunk to the deceased, followed by bread and cheese and more drink, following which everyone was invited to "see the corp". Each laid a hand on the breast or brow and made an appropriate remark such as "she's a bonny corp", or "he wis a guid freen tae mony" or "she'll be sair missed". Just before the coffin was closed a corner of the winding sheet and a lock of hair were cut off.

The closed coffin was then taken outside and laid on two chairs whilst the spokes were fitted under it and it was covered by the mortcloth. There were eight spokes for the coffin of a full-sized adult, and the bearers relieved each other frequently. A child's coffin was always covered by a sheet. The first lift of the coffin was taken by the females of the family, at which point the chairs it had rested on had to be overturned. They were righted and washed only when the mourners returned.

As the coffin was lifted all the animals of the farm were driven out to see it. Sometimes the cattle then followed the procession which was of men only, and where it happened, this was seen as an expression of their sorrow and sympathy. The coffin always took the "Kirk road", the route the deceased had taken on his or her way to Church. The Kirk Officer went ahead ringing the hand bell, for which 3/- was charged. Whisky was carried for drinking at each rest stop. Frequently this caused drunkenness and behaviour which was less than perfect. Hats were removed when the coffin was lowered into the grave. Mourners then went home, with only close family and friends returning to the home of the deceased for dinner.

WITCHES AND FAIRIES

There were a number of witches in the areas surrounding Deskford. John Philp was burned at the stake in Banff in 1627 for "charming and washing sick people" at the Lady Well at Ordiquhill. Others in the C17th were accused at

Banff and Keith. In 1655 John Young accused Isobel Ogilvie of Fordyce of witchcraft and in 1671 Margaret Clerk of Cullen was acquitted of witchcraft. There had been witchcraft trials in Aberdeen from 1592, when the Binhill of Cullen covens were mentioned.

Perhaps the best-known local witch was Andro Man, the Rathven warlock who lived at Darbreich, which was technically in Rathven Parish, though it has always been treated as part of Deskford. This place of residence reinforces his self-admitted membership of the notorious Binhill covens, Darbreich lying on the south flank of the Binhill. In 1597 he "was accusit as a manifest and notorious witche and sorcerer, in using and practising dyveris sortis of witchcraft and sorcerie, conforme to his particular dittay (charge sheet) and accusatioun red in judgement; quhilk being denyit be the said Andro, was referrit to the tryall of the assise abovewritten, chosin, sworne and admittit. The hail assise, be the mouth of James Stewart, chancellar, convictis and fyllis the said Andro Man, in nyn or ten poyntis of witchcraft and sorcerie, contenit in his dittay, and as a manifest vitche, be oppin voce and common fame".

After some time in detention he, there's a surprise, admitted all counts. In addition he said he could raise the devil by calling out "Benedicte" and get rid of him by calling out "Maikpeblis". He admitted having had intercourse with the Queen of Elfin, and that when a convention of witches of which he was part raised the devil, "ane blak beist", all of them "kissit the beist arss". He stated that "thair is ane auld agit woman in Fynlatter called Gray, quha is ane waraye gryt weiche", and also claimed that "thair is ane woman in Deskfurd, callit Elspet Graye" who carried out the work of the devil in Deskford.

Where there was any suspicion of witchcraft it was usually of an old woman living alone. Other people in the area tried to stay on good terms with them for fear of the consequences of not doing so. Witches were known to be able to enter or leave a house via the dog hole.

Fairies were very widespread and occupied hillocks and wells. Deskford's Fairy Hillock was probably the small hillock between the main road and the Berryhillock road near the Mains of Skeith track. These "fair folk" or "gueede neighbours" were not considered evil but just mischievous teases. If a house was inadvertently built on top of a fairy dwelling they became very annoyed and made much noise and caused much disruption.

Men and women could be tempted to join the fairies, and, once they had eaten and drunk with them, remained for at least seven years without realising it. On their return they were never happy with reality. Fairies responded well to kindness and favours being done them, and always repaid on time and well, though if any slight or unkindness was done them, they retaliated and took severe revenge. Because of their potential for mischief, drive bands were taken off spinning wheels at night to prevent fairies using them, and similarly meal mills were thrown out of gear. Dust devils were known to be just fairies dancing.

In addition to witches and fairies, ghosts were also very common, in houses, woods, parts of roads, bridges and churchyards. On setting out on a journey one threw a staff end over end as high as possible. If it fell pointing in the direction of the journey then this would be successful. Farm servants sometimes did this when going to a feeing market to decide in which direction their next six month's employment would be.

Dreams often had meanings attributed to them. To dream of a horse meant the arrival of a stranger and to dream of a white horse meant the arrival of a letter. To dream of butter meant good luck but to dream of fire meant bad news and to dream of pigs meant annoyance. To dream of fresh fish foretold the birth of children and to dream of losing a tooth foretold the death of a friend.

FARMING BELIEFS

Farming was rich with beliefs and practices relating to witches, fairies and the Devil and ways of overcoming or at least mitigating their impact. On many farms in the C17th and earlier a small corner of land was left uncultivated for the Devil to use. This was the "Gudeman's Croft", for which alternative names were "Devil's Croft", "Helliman's Rig", and "Clootie Croft". A similar purpose was attached to the raising of neidfire. All existing fires were extinguished and the new or virgin neidfire was lit by rubbing two pieces of wood together. From the new fire embers were taken out into the byre and the cattle made to walk over them to protect them from evil.

These practices probably came down from pre-Christian times and were a way of buying the Devil's non-interference. The Kirk strongly disapproved of the practices, but, together with that of leaving the Fairy Hillock unused, they gradually fell out of use and only vestigial traces survived agricultural improvement. The Gudeman's Croft became cultivated and the Fairy Hillock grazed and what had been belief became myth and then a social event.

Every small farm or croft had a rowan tree planted beside it to ward off the Devil and this practice persisted well into the C20th. Crosses made of rowan twigs were placed above the door of the byre and small pieces sometimes tied to a cow's tail by red thread, which was also effective against the Devil. A saying of that time was

> "Raan tree an' reid threed pits the witches tae their speed"

There were many beliefs attaching to cattle. Newborn calves were never touched by the bare human hand as this could cause paralysis or death to the calf because the human hand was stained with sin. Milkmaids left a bowl of milk for the brownie who was believed to live in the byre, and a coin was placed in the bottom of a milk cog to prevent curdling. Cattle were at risk from the evil eye, and any which died suddenly were considered to have been killed by a "fairy dart". Ill cattle however could be cured by making them drink water which had been poured over a new shilling. Sellers of cattle, on being paid, returned a luckpenny to the buyer.

If a cow did die then the farmer tried to bury it somewhere other than on his own farm, as this would transfer the evil to the other place. One could increase one's own cow's milk yield or reduce that of a neighbour's cow by collecting dew from his fields on the first day of any quarter and using it to rinse one's milk utensils. Several accusations of this nature were made in Deskford, the last being in 1802.

If milk boiled over into the fire it was very unlucky and would reduce the milk yield from that farm's cows unless salt was immediately thrown into the fire. When butter was churned, a crooked sixpence, a cross of rowan wood or a horseshoe was kept beneath the churn, and anyone entering had to help with the churning. Particular individuals whose presence was known to have a bad effect on the quantity or quality of butter produced were kept away.

Witches were the main enemy of the dairy as they could make cows go dry. To prevent this happening at calving, at the moment the cow dropped its calf the latter's mouth was opened and a little of the cow's excrement was put in. The first water a cow was given after calving had to be poured over a shilling. Any unusual behaviour by cattle was attributed to witches.

In 1769, Thomas Pennant, during his tour of Scotland, in which he passed through Deskford, reported that farmers protected their cattle against witchcraft by putting boughs of rowan and honeysuckle in their byres on May 2nd. They hoped to preserve the milk of their cows and protect their wives from miscarriage by tying red threads about them.

The calendar had also to be carefully observed in order to avoid misfortune. Good Friday was unlucky for ploughing. On St John's Eve, June 24th, farmers lit heather torches from a bonfire. To ensure good crops it had to be carried round the field staying alight. Young people jumped through the embers of the bonfire to be blessed. Cattle were made to pass through the smoke of a Beltane fire in order to cleanse them. This practice possibly descended from a pre-Christian ceremony in which bulls were sacrificed. Cattle were usually taken to the bull in the first or third quarters of the moon.

It was favourable for ploughing to begin when the moon was on the wane. There was a ceremony to start the ploughing at which the horse or ox got part of the clyack sheaf from the previous year's harvest to eat. Bread and cheese were given to the ploughman who toasted the farmer and his family. The farmer then also drank a toast of ale or whisky, refilled the glass and poured it over the bridle or plough, saying "God speed the labour". No further work was done that day, instead there was a supper and a dance.

At the start of harvest the reapers drank a toast. The farmer laid his bonnet on the ground, lifted a heuk, faced the sun, cut a small amount of corn, moved it sunwise three times round his head and chanted a blessing on the harvest. A harvester could claim a kiss from any girl bandster who had made a band which broke. The clyack sheaf represented fertility, and part of it might be fed to the first mare which foaled, and part buried beneath the first furrow ploughed in order to transfer fertility. Each farm had a clyack dance (later a meal and ale), when it finished its harvest.

Some of the traditions lasted very late, even into the C20th, such as the taking of clyack. Another tradition, which only developed in the C19th with the employment of specialist horsemen on large improved farms was that of the "Horseman's Word". This involved an almost masonic initiation ritual in which a young horseman gained entry into the fraternity. Being given the word endowed him with supernatural power over horses and women.

ANIMALS AND PLANTS

Many animals and plants were said to possess different qualities and powers. If a mole burrowed near your house it meant you were soon to flit. If it burrowed round your house you were soon to die. If you rubbed a mole in your hands until it died this gave you permanent power to heal a woman's festering breast by rubbing it.

Cats could suck the breath out of a sleeping baby, and a cat dying inside a house meant that an occupant would soon also die. Black cats were unlucky and it was also unlucky for a bride on her way to her wedding to meet a cat. Male cats, when jumping, were thought to emit urine and semen. Because of this, if a male cat jumped over food, women should not eat it in case they became pregnant with kittens.

If a dog approached a person who was ill he or she would recover, and a dog licking a running sore or a wound was a remedy. A dog howling at night meant that someone living nearby would soon die. Dogs never bit idiots and a dog eating grass meant rain.

Roast mouse was a cure for whooping cough. If there were more rats in a house than usual this meant that the people who lived there were soon to flit. The rats had come to "summon" them. If rats left a house then someone living there would either fall down or would die. Hares were not liked because witches turned themselves into hares and then did evil to people. However it was lucky if a hare emerged from the last cut of corn.

Pigs were considered unclean, though their flesh was used. Even into the 1960s pork was always overcooked to make it "safe". There was a mysterious, dreaded beast, the "yird swine", which lived in graveyards, burrowing amongst the dead bodies and eating them.

On a journey, meeting a horse was lucky. A mare about to foal, if kept without water, would paw the ground where an underground spring could be found. When a mare foaled inside a stable, the first time the foal left the stable, it had to do so tail first to prevent it lying down when crossing fords. Sometimes the stable door was taken off its hinges, laid down and the foal pulled over it. The ass was a cure for whooping cough. One should either inhale its breath or pass three times under its belly and then go home through a wood. Sheep were regarded favourably, although black lambs were killed at birth to prevent bad luck. Sleeping amongst sheep and inhaling their breath was a good general cure. Cattle, uniquely, had no part in folklore.

A crow alighting on a house meant death hovering over it, but it was bad luck to destroy a rookery. The pyot (magpie) could be either a good or a bad omen. It was the Devil's bird and to shoot it was bad luck, though one hopping near one's house was good luck. It was unlucky to harm a robin, and the wren was thought to be the robin's wife. Lark's nests should never be raided for eggs. The yellowhammer had a very bad name and was often persecuted.

The cock was a prophet. If it crowed on the threshold then strangers were imminent. If it crowed before midnight then death was imminent. Burying a black cock alive beneath a sufferer's bed was a cure for epilepsy. Hens were not sold at a roup as this was unlucky, and if hens died this meant that cattle would also die soon. A crowing hen meant death so it was killed immediately to protect others. Eggs must not be sold after sunset. Doves were emblems of all that was good. If one flew round a person's head he or she would die soon, but would have eternal happiness. The heart, lungs and liver from a live dove, thrust down the throat of an ox or cow, was a laxative.

If frogs spawned in shallow pools and ditches, then it would be a wet summer, if in deep pools, a dry summer. It was possible to cure red water, a disease in cows, by thrusting a live frog down the animal's throat. Toads were loathed. They were reputed to carry a jewel within their skull. Any man who carried a dried toad tongue on his breast could bend any woman to his will. Bees did not thrive if their keeper was guilty of fornication. Moths were uncanny and dreaded, but spiders were liked and their webs used for healing.

Amongst plants, bluebells were dreaded, were not picked and were called "gowk's (Devil's) thumbs". Gorse, broom or turnip rich in blossom meant there would be a good harvest, but an abundance of wild fruits meant there would be a harsh winter. Dust from a puffball caused blindness.

Many plants and herbs were used as natural remedies, and these practices often pre-dated Christianity. Mustard and garlic were used against the plague and the evil eye respectively. Hemlock in small amounts was used against cholera. St John's wort was used against fever and cough. Sage was used for cuts and bruises and for eyesight. Golden rod and valerian were used for bruises. Beetroot or rhubarb was used for blood disorders. Ivy was used against catarrh. Thyme was used against whooping cough and marigold petals were used against bee stings.

Trees also had their uses. Hazel rods were used by water diviners. Bourtrie (elder) guarded against evil and protected against witches, as did rowan twigs. Oak was venerated, partly because of the magic mistletoe which was dedicated to the Goddess of Love and was placed in the bridal bed. From this has evolved our Christmas practice of kissing under the mistletoe. Trees used to make gallows were usually oak or sycamore, though the one on Clune Hill in Deskford was reputedly a beech. Nowadays we still touch wood for luck.

THE CALENDAR

There were many beliefs and practices which related to the calendar. Mondays and Fridays were unlucky for starting a particular bit of work or for starting school, whereas Tuesdays and Saturdays were lucky. A new moon on a Saturday meant stormy weather was imminent while dusty fields in March meant a good crop. Bad weather at the "Gab o' May" caused great concern. Washing one's face in the dew on the 1st of May prevented a tan or fernietickles (freckles), both of which were to be avoided. If a new moon was seen through a window this meant bad luck whereas if it was seen while holding something this meant good luck. The moon was considered to influence the ripening of corn more than did the sun, and the "mairt", or pig to be killed and salted, must be killed when the moon was on the increase. This was also the time for making rennet.

Or Fastern E'en or Brose Day a beef dinner was compulsory or cattle would not thrive. The brose that day must be made of beef bree. In the evening bannocks were made of beaten egg, oatmeal and milk, and were baked on the girdle in the presence of everyone. A school holiday was given on this day up to the 1930s, and in the past schoolboys in Deskford enjoyed cock fighting. Easter was known as Pasch (Peace) Sunday and eggs were rolled or given to each member of the family for breakfast.

At Beltane, fires were built as witches were about, and rowan branches were placed over byre doors. Fires were kindled by every farmer and cottar, made of old thatch straw, gorse or broom, just after sunset. Embers were carried round the fields and "fire, fire, burn the witches" was chanted. In 1776 Rev Morison preached strongly against these practices in Deskford.

Quarter days were very important. They were pre-Christian but had been adopted by the Church. Samhain was on October 31st, St Bridget or St Bride's Day, which became Candlemas, was on January 31st, Beltane was on May 1st and Lammas was on August 1st. On the first day of each quarter, animals, land, crops, people and houses had to be protected from evil, witches and fairies. Bonfires were lit and lit brands were carried round the field or person to be protected. Thresholds were sprinkled with salt or urine. Dressing up at Hallow

E'en was a disguise to protect against evil spirits, with a bonfire to burn witches. At Beltane, cattle were driven between two fires for "saining", and people jumped across fires for good luck.

There was guising at New Year, but Christmas was more important than New Year until about 1850, despite the Church of Scotland not observing Christmas. In Deskford Old Christmas Day, January 5th, was observed as a holiday until this time, but by 1880 Christmas was not observed by anybody and New Year was the great holiday. Blood had to be shed on Christmas Day so a cock had its throat cut and was cooked for dinner.

In the C18th and early C19th, when Christmas was observed there were three days holiday during which only emergency work was done. All work must be completed before Christmas and any which was started after the holiday had to be completed by New Year.

The Christmas feast included "yeel (yule) fish" which were bought cured and then smoked in the kiln on the farm. "Yeel kebback", (Christmas cheese), was produced specially as was Christmas ale. A variety of bannocks, soor cakes, cream cakes, facet cakes and soft cakes were baked and stored, and it was lucky to keep some for weeks or months. "Yeel sowens" were prepared in every house and young people went from house to house and were given some in each. Small basins and wooden caps or cogs were filled with sowens and into one was placed a ring, into another a button and into a third a sixpence. Whoever got these would become respectively married, single or widowed. Christmas breakfast was the best that could be afforded, milk porridge, creamy milk, butter, fish etc. Dinner, after sunset, had to include meat and the yeel kebback.

There was guising on Christmas Eve, an activity which evolved from the mediaeval plays put on by mummers, and dances were held in barns. Children were warned not to cry on Christmas day. If they did then they would have much to cry about during the following year. Beasts were fed unthreshed corn, and the oldest beast was fed part of the clyack. A fire was lit in the byre on Christmas morning and the byre purified by burning juniper. In the house, the fire burning brightly on Christmas morning meant prosperity. Omens were seen in the Christmas fire.

On New Year's Day groups of young people went round collecting alms (thiggin') for others in difficulty. They went round with a small sack collecting meal and money, and were well entertained everywhere they went. If the sack became full it was left somewhere and a new one started. Later, competitive raffles and shooting matches raised money for those in distress.

On New Year's day children were taught to chant:-

> "Rise up aul' wives and shake yer feathers,
> Dinna think that we are beggars,
> We're jist bairnies oot tae play,
> Get up an' gie's oor Hogmanay"

(The author remembers being taught to chant this on New Year's morning, as a child in West Lothian in the 1950s showing that the practice had continued in existence for several centuries and widely across Scotland)

Adults played dambrod (draughts) and children played "the totum", "nivey neecknack" and "headocks or pintracks" for pins. Adults played for money, and if this was in an alehouse, a proportion of the winnings was taken to buy drink for all. Hosts provided bread and cheese or fish.

OTHER BELIEFS AND PRACTICES

The weather was subject to close observation and displayed different portents. If there was dust on the road in summer, this meant that rain was imminent. Boring a hole in a six-inch long piece of wood, tying twine several feet long through it and whirling it round your head meant thunder would stop and no thunderbolt would strike. This was known as the "thunner spell". If New Year's Day was a gale, it meant it would be a good year for bere, and if it came from the south it meant it would be a fresh, open season and an early harvest.

Men building a house received whisky, ale, bread and cheese. If they did not get this then happiness and health would not be found in that house. When the house was taken possession of there was a feast known as the "hoose heatin'" or "fire kin'lin'".

It was unlucky to move into a clean house. If the outgoing occupant swept the house clean this meant bad luck for the incoming one. The outgoing occupant could also cause bad luck for the incoming one by climbing onto the roof and pulling the swey up and out through the lum rather than through the door, or by tying a straw rope the vrang wye, left to right, and pulling it round the house against the sun. If evil had been left in a house, the new occupant could avoid it by throwing a cat in first. If evil had been left, the cat caught it, sickened and died, but the people were safe.

A baby born feet first would, in later life, be hanged. A strong growth of hair on the chest, arms, legs and hands of a baby was a sign of strength and contentment in later life. When your hair was cut, what was cut off should be burned to stop birds making their nests with it as this would cause you headaches. Having large hands and feet meant great physical strength, and webbed feet meant good luck. The deaf and dumb were held in great awe, and believed to be able to foresee the future. They were consulted on all matters. Those with a mental disability were well treated, and it was believed to be lucky to have such a child.

Boys were obliged to fight if challenged by the "coordie blow", but two boys should never attack a single one. If two boys concluded a bargain they linked the little fingers of their right hands, shook them and said "Ring, ring the pottle bell, gehn ye brak the bargain, ye'll gang tae hell". To break such a bargain was seen as a very serious offence. Lying and informing were seen as beyond the pale and anyone doing so would be ganged up on and taunted.

APPENDICES

1. Sketch map of Little Skeith farm with field names and rotation, c 1960. (Billy Murray)
2. Annotated aerial photograph of Little Skeith farm c 1960.(Billy Murray)
3. Sketch map of pre Turnpike main roads from Keith to Cullen and Portsoy.
4. List of teachers at Deskford School, 1903-1970.(From booklet written by Evelyn E Shirren and M Edith Beveridge, for 1997 reunion).
5. Lists of Ordinary Poor and Lunatic Poor 1898, and payments to them.
6. Resident Voters 1875 and New Resident Voters 1880.
7. Votes cast in Parish Council elections, 1895.
8. Sketch map of Craibstone Limestone Quarry and Limekilns.(after Len Hall)
9. Sketch map of extensions to Deskford churchyard, 1887 and 1926.
10. Transcript of all inscriptions in Deskford Church and churchyard, 1884, (Cramond).
11. Inventory of Deskford Kirk Session Property and Funds, 2004.(Willie Taylor)
12. List of Heads of Families in Communion with the Church, 1834.
13. Cordiner's drawing of the Tower of Deskford, 1788.
14. List of properties in Deskford in the Barony of Ogilvie, 1747.(NAS)
15. Tenancies held in Deskford, 1771.(NAS)
16. Farms and their acreages in the Parish of Deskford, 1866.(NAS)
17. Selected items from a List of Sums Advanced by the Proprietor for Building and Repairing Houses, 1856-1884.(NAS)
18. Sketch of the "twal owsen ploo" (twelve oxen plough) and sketch of positions of individual oxen.
19. A Gamrie Farmer's Money Transactions, 1760-1769.(BFC)
20. Invoice from William Duncan, general merchant, Deskford, to Mr A Wright, Upper Skeith, Nov 28th 1923.
21. Individuals paying Clock Tax and Farm Horse Tax 1797/98.
22. Selected IRS property values 1910.
23. Assessment of Allowances to Wives and Families of Militiamen 1806-1812.
24. List of the Poor in Deskford, 1846.
25. World War I Deskford Roll of Honour.
26. List of World War II Deskford war dead.
27. List of prizewinners at Deskford School. (from booklet written by Evelyn E Shirren and M Edith Beveridge for 1997 Reunion)

28. Population of Deskford 1755-2011.
29. List of post Reformation Ministers and readers in Deskford.
30. Some Deskford farms no longer in existence and those of which no vestige remains.
31. Total acreage of crops and numbers of animals in Banffshire, 1883.
32. Money equivalents and weights and measures.
33. Customs owed by tenants to landlord, 1780.
34. Scots Law word meanings in C15th and C16th land ownership transactions.

APPENDIX 1. SKETCH MAP OF LITTLE SKEITH C. 1960 (BILLY MURRAY)

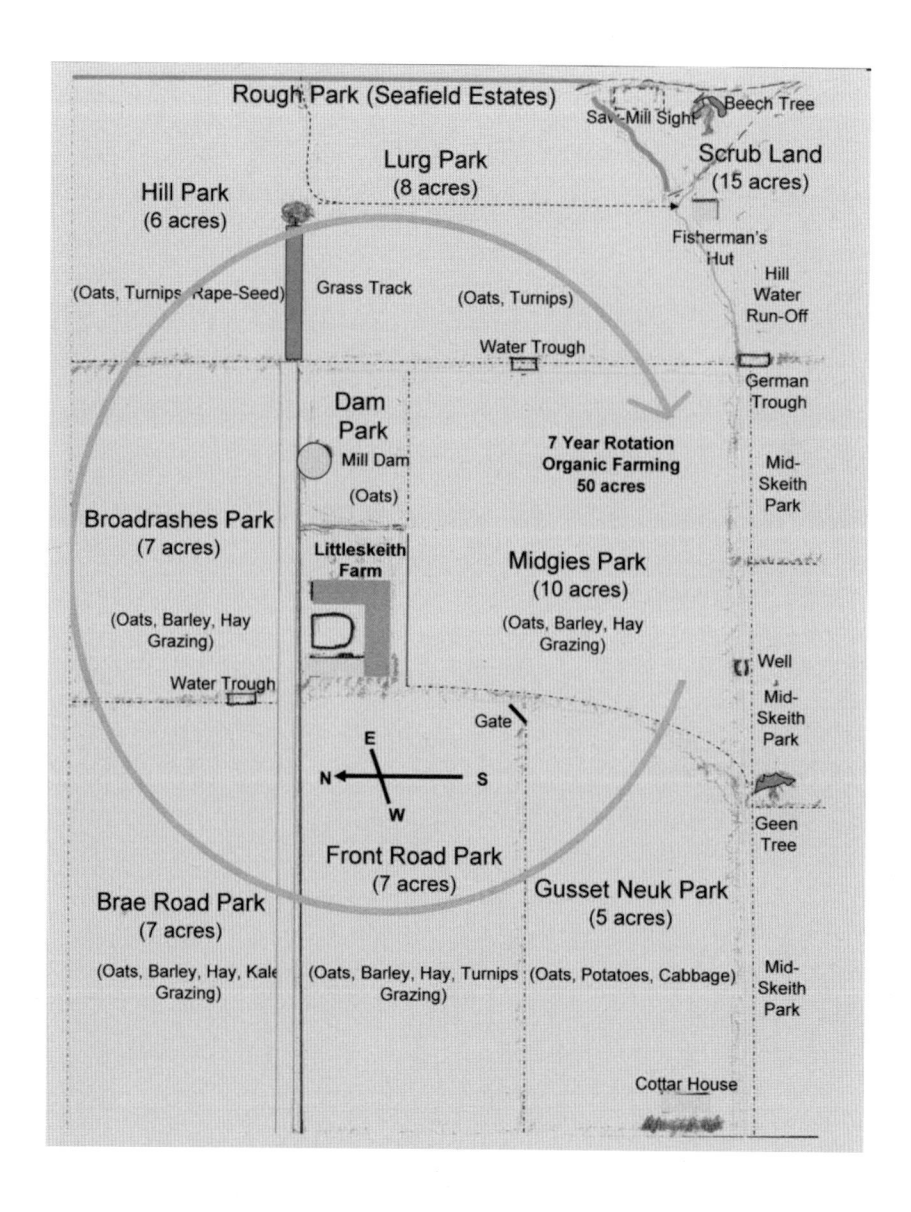

APPENDIX 2. ANNOTATED AERIAL PHOTOGRAPH OF LITTLE SKEITH FARM C. 1960. (BILLY MURRAY)

531

APPENDIX 3. SKETCH MAP OF PRE TURNPIKE MAIN ROADS FROM KEITH TO CULLEN AND PORTSOY.

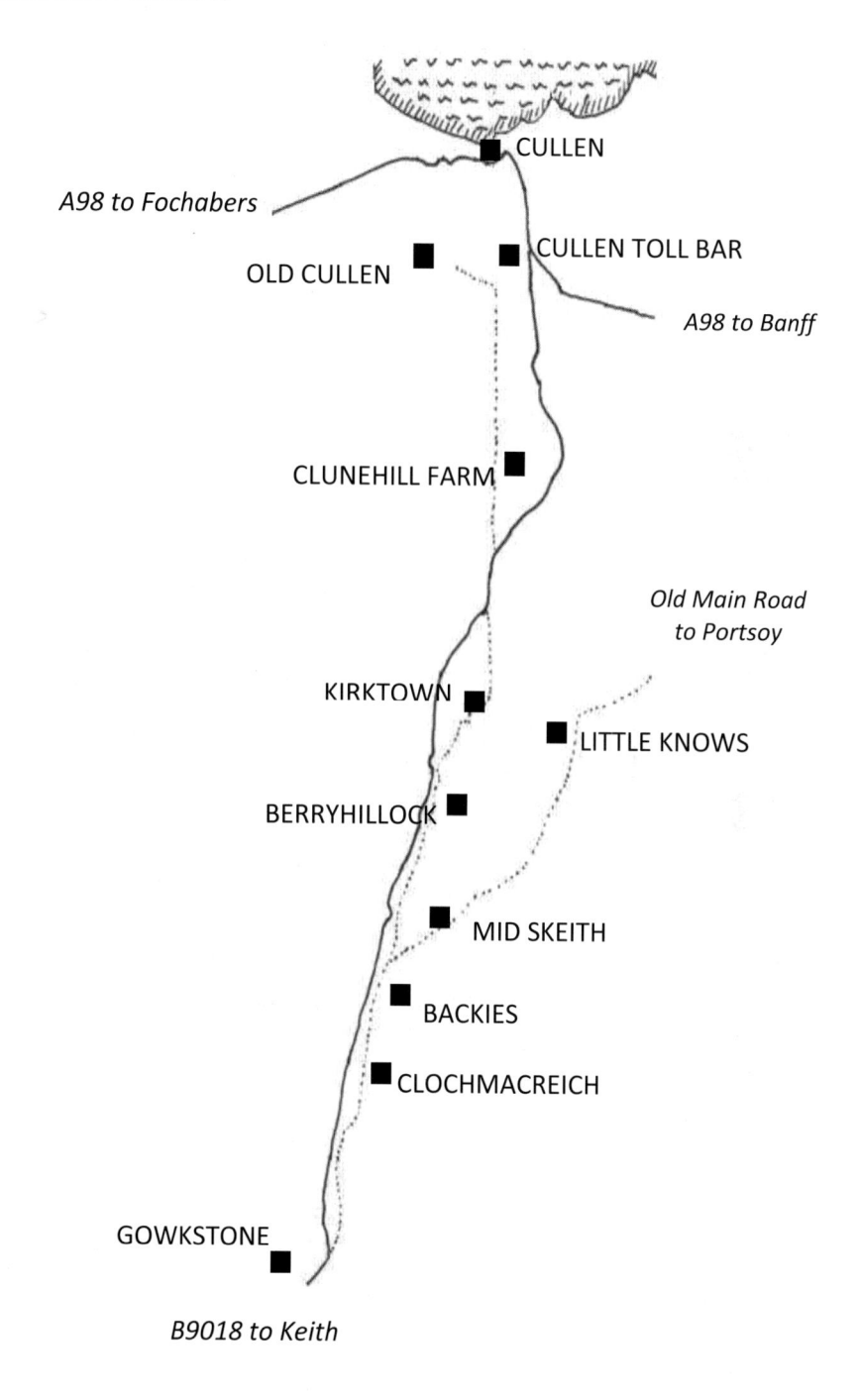

CULLEN

A98 to Fochabers

CULLEN TOLL BAR

OLD CULLEN

A98 to Banff

CLUNEHILL FARM

Old Main Road to Portsoy

KIRKTOWN

LITTLE KNOWS

BERRYHILLOCK

MID SKEITH

BACKIES

CLOCHMACREICH

GOWKSTONE

B9018 to Keith

APPENDIX 4. LIST OF TEACHERS OF DESKFORD SCHOOL (Incomplete)
(EVELYN E SHIRREN AND M EDITH BEVERIDGE)

Name	Started	Left
Miss Chalmers	23/11/03	14/08/05
Miss Williamina McCombie	04/10/04	?
Miss Helen Agnes Grant	03/10/05	15/03/12
Miss Mary Taylor	18/02/07	19/10/17
AW Farquhar (Acting temporary Head)	04/01/08	21/01/09
John Scott	01/02/09	17/09/20
Miss Margaret Murdoch	15/04/12	09/09/19
Miss Charlotte Raffan	16/10/17	19/08/25
Miss Georgina E Wilson	09/09/19	28/06/28
AD Craigmyle	20/09/20	12/12/24
Miss Barbara Milne	25/04/21	09/05/21
Miss Bruce (domestic science)	1922	
Miss Ella Brown	06/01/25	28/02/25
Robert FM Watson	17/02/25	05/03/26
Miss Edith Longmore (Mrs Beveridge)	19/08/25	28/06/28
John A Beveridge	29/03/26	06/10/55
Miss Mina Hendry	21/08/28	01/04/31
Miss Mary McIvor (Mrs Ross)	21/08/28	15/10/36
Miss Georgina Gauld	17/09/28	20/08/29
Miss Murray (domestic science)	1928	
Miss LC Green (relief)	20/08/29	15/11/29
Miss Mary P Smith (temporary)	19/05/30	?
Miss Norah Stuart (Mrs Cruikshank)	14/04/31	21/08/34
Miss Eliza Meldrum (temporary)	18/04/32	?
Miss Simpson (temporary)	15/05/32	?
Miss Helen Cruikshank	21/08/34	23/08/38
Miss Marjory H Forsyth (Mrs Mitchell)	21/08/34	26/08/41
Miss Catherine I Davidson	20/10/36	23/08/38
Miss Edith McBean	23/08/38	14/02/46
Miss Isabella McHattie (Mrs Jaffray)	23/08/38	27/06/47
Miss Margaret Drysdale*	18/09/39	01/09/42
Miss Margaret Craig*	18/09/39	22/01/40
Neil Buchanan*	02/04/40	11/10/40
Michael Small	31/10/40	28/08/41

Name	From	To
Miss Margaret Reid	28/08/41	05/05/42
Mrs Jane Metcalf (Mrs Mathers)	28/08/41	27/08/46
Miss Marjory Thom	11/05/42	16/04/43
Mrs AA Harnden	01/09/42	02/07/43
Miss Elizabeth Dickson (Mrs Currie)	03/08/43	27/06/47
Miss Elsie Innes (Mrs Clark)	30/09/46	27/06/47
Miss Mary Gregor	10/04/47	24/08/54
Miss Elizabeth Murray	19/09/47	?
Miss Lena McLaren (Mrs Henderson)	19/09/47	22/08/50
Miss Anna Robertson (Mrs Rothnie)	19/08/47	03/04/51
Rev Donald Campbell	24/11/48	04/01/49
Miss Ruth Hay (Mrs Summers)	04/01/49	05/12/58
Miss E Grant	22/08/50	10/10/58
Mrs A Legg	03/04/51	29/09/51
Miss Margaret Meldrum	29/09/51	31/10/51
Mrs Janet Cattanach (nee Cruikshank)	31/10/51	12/04/62
Odin S Sostad (Vancouver)	26/08/52	24/04/53
Mrs Edith Beveridge	24/08/54	23/08/55
Mrs Edith Robertson	23/08/55	26/08/58
William C Espie	18/10/55	03/02/61
Mr Thomson (PE)	1956	
Mrs MJ Innes	26/08/58	22/08/67
Bruce Lamont	08/12/58	06/04/59
Miss Georgina McMurray	06/04/59	25/08/59
Miss Allan	?	
Miss JW Mair	25/08/59	?
Alistair P McKay	25/08/59	12/04/62
Mrs Reid	?	?
George M Addison	25/04/62	27/06/69
Miss Cowie	?	24/08/65
Mrs C Farquhar	22/08/67	28/06/68
Miss Irene Sandison	20/08/68	?
George M Campbell	26/08/69	28/06/70

- These teachers accompanied the evacuees from Portobello

APPENDIX 5. LISTS OF ORDINARY AND LUNATIC POOR 1898

Ordinary Poor.	Age	Per Week
Ann Ross or Currie, Glasgow.	86	3/6d
Jessie Smith, Keith.	35	3/-
Jane Riddoch, Fordyce.	44	1/-
Widow Milton, Fordyce.	40	3/6d
Jessie Russell, Rathven.	59	4/6d
Alexander Russell, Rathven.	55	3/6d
Ann H Duncan, Huntly.	9	2/6d
Widow Fraser, Grange.	74	3/-
Chas. Raffan, Keith.	12	2/-
Maggie Raffan, Cromdale.	10	2/6d
William Duff, Squaredoch.	58	2/-
Ann Milton or Tough, Berryhillock.	86	4/6d
Isabella Forbes, Muir of Squaredoch.	47	(free house)
Widow Thom, Berryhillock.	39	(4/6d during summer)
Robert Wood, Milltown.	61	3/6d
Jane Thomson, Berryhillock.	59	2/6d
Hellen Munro, Greens of Blairock.	66	2/-
John Wright, Edinburgh.	58	5/-
Jane Riddoch, Muir of Squaredoch.	67	(1/- during summer)
Ann Watson, Muir of Squaredoch.		(free house)

Lunatic Poor		
James Wright, Asylum.	52	7/-
Ann Wright, Asylum.	25	7/-
James Wood, Asylum.	38	7/-
William Jamieson, Tod's Cottage.	55	3/6d
Isabella Longmore, Comb's Croft.	60	5/6d

APPENDIX 6. RESIDENT VOTERS 1875 AND NEW RESIDENT VOTERS 1880

Resident Voters 1875

J Anderson, Leitchestoun
Jas Clark, Mid Skeith*
John Cowie, Inaltrie*
R Cruikshank, Berryhillock*
George Duncan, Kirktown*
Jas Gordon, Broadrashes*
W Grant, Bleachfield*
Jas Gray, Meikle Knows
Geo Gray, Little Cultain*
Jas Inglis, Aultmore*
James Ingram, Aultmore
Roder Johnston, Aultmore*
Rev W T Ker, Deskford*
James Kitchen, Clunehill*
J Lawrence, Broadrashes*
Adam Longmore, Ardoch*
G Low Jr, Little Skeith
Chas Milne, Burnheads
L A Milne, Raemore
Jas Milne, Mousehillock
John Milton, Aultmore*
John Mitchell, Aultmore
Geo Morrison, Clunehill*
Jas Murray, Ardicow
W McBain, Kentyward Park*

G McHattie, Squaredoch*
Rev J Mackintosh, Deskford*
Alex McKay, Oathillock*
John Mc Willie, Backies
Robert Proctor, Ardoch*
J Reid, Berryhillock
J Reid, Squaredoch*
J Reid, Swellend*
Jas Rumbles, Faichyhill*
Wm Sim, Croftgloy*
J Simpson, Clochmacreich*
Wm Smith, Deskford*
Geo Smith, Upper Blairock*
Jas Smith, Nether Blairock*
John Steinson, Ordens*
W Stephen, Millers Croft*
W Stevenson, Carestone*
John Sutherland, Craibstone*
G Taylor, Meikle Cultain*
J Thomson, Mains of Skeith*
W Thomson, Mains of Skeith
J Wilson, Little Knows*
Alex Wood, Mosside*
Jas Wright, Aultmore*
James Wright, Greenhill*

*= also in 1880

New Resident Voters 1880

Alex Craib, Aultmore
Alex T Garden, Raemore
Walter Gray, Meikle Knows
Jas Lorimer, Kirktown
Jas Milne, Burnsford
John Mitchell, Bogetra
Geo McCombie, Leitchestown
Geo McWillie, Bognagight

John McWillie, Langlanburn
John Shepherd, Craibstone
Geo Sutherland, Aultmore
Alex Taylor, Little Skeith
John Thomson, Carrothead
A Wilson Jr, Aultmore
Geo Wright, Upper Skeith

APPENDIX 7. VOTES IN PARISH COUNCIL ELECTIONS 1895

Elected

J Campbell, Old Cullen	79
A Duncan, Kirktown	72
Rev G M Park,	57
R Cruikshank Jr, Berryhillock	54
W Gordon, Lower Broadrashes	48
F G McConnachie, Ardoch	48
James Lorimer, Kirktown	42

Unsuccessful

J Rumbles, Faichyhill	41
J Clark, Mid Skeith	38
J Fordyce, Squaredoch	37
J Hay, Greens of Blairock	32
Rev J Morrison	29
W McLean, Berryhillock	10

APPENDIX 8. SKETCH MAP OF CRAIBSTONE LIMESTONE QUARRIES AND LIMEKILNS (AFTER LEN HALL)

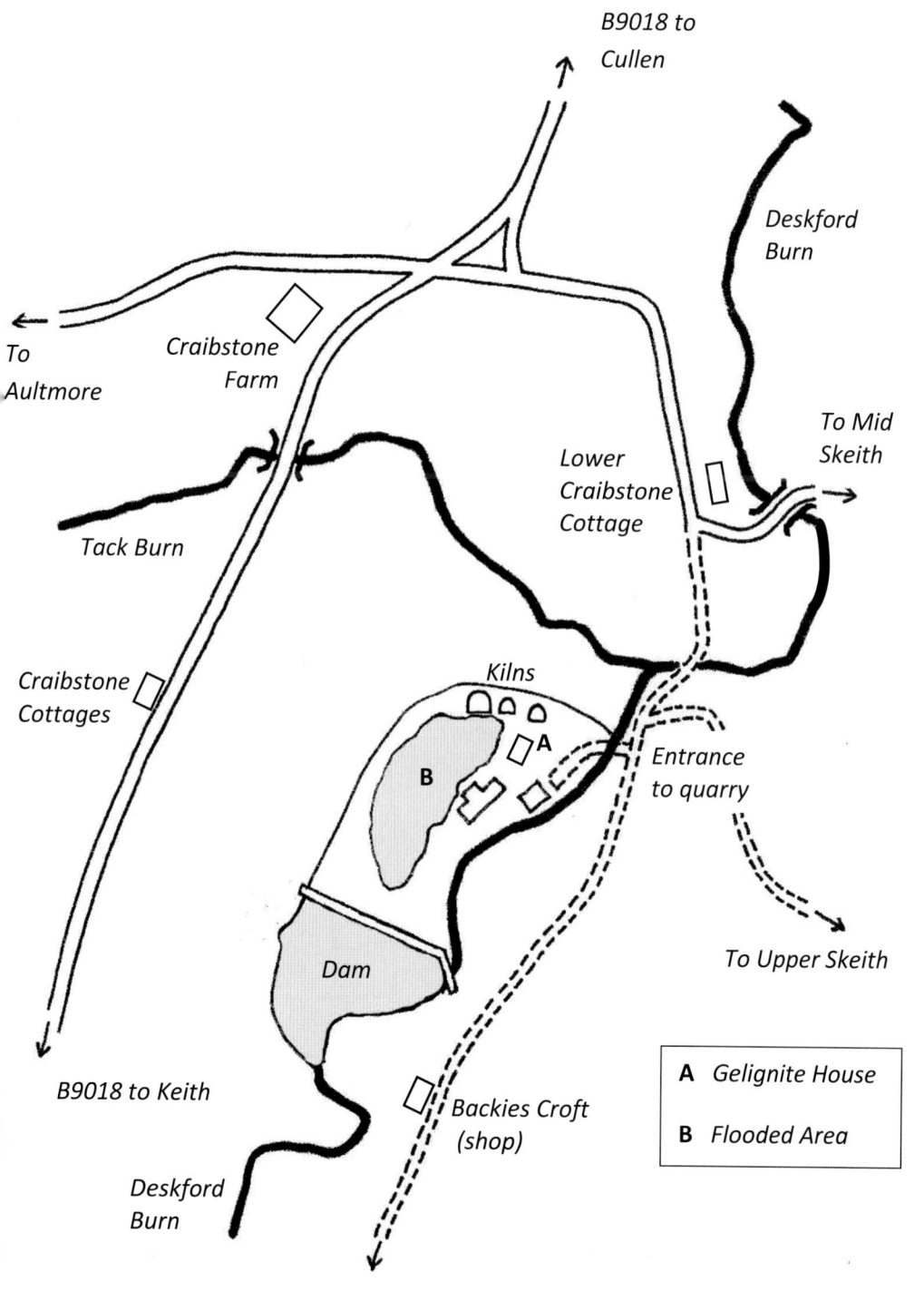

APPENDIX 9. SKETCH MAP OF CHURCHYARD EXTENSIONS 1887 & 1926

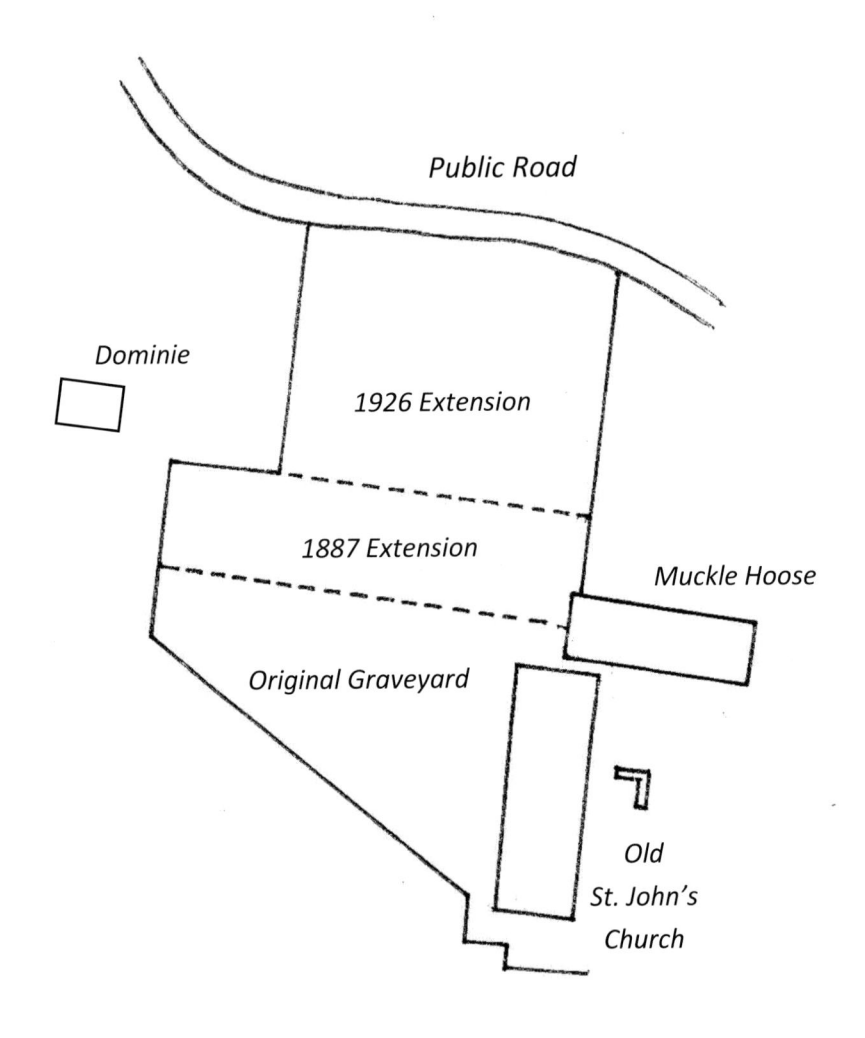

APPENDIX 10. TRANSCRIPTION OF ALL INSCRIPTIONS IN DESKFORD CHURCH AND CHURCHYARD. 1884, (CRAMOND)

1. In memory of Katherine, eldest daughter of the Rev James Mackintosh, Minister of Deskford, who died 18th February 1866, aged 16 years. Luke viii.-52. I Thess. Iv.-4 Here also are interred the remains of three of his children who died in infancy. Mat. Xviii. -14.

2. In memory of the beloved children of Alexander Kitchen and Margaret Shiach, who died at Clune, viz – Elizabeth who died 22nd Nov 1867, aged 7 years, James, died 9th Dec 1867, aged 10 years, Margaret Christina, died 13th Dec 1867, aged 3 years. Lawrence, died 9th April 1878, aged 10 months. John Kitchen, his brother, merchant, Glasgow, died at Clune 7th April 1863, aged 27 years.

3. In memory of Margaret Sherar, wife of Roderick Johnston, farmer, Todholes, Deskford, who died 15th Sept. 1874, aged 77 years; also of the above Roderick Johnston who died 8th April 1876, aged 85 years.

4. Erected in memory of James Smith, farmer, Upper Blairock, who died 12th April 1868, aged 64 years, also his daughter, Margaret, who died 13th Jan 1874, aged 14 years.

5. 1870. In memory of Elspet Shearer, who died at Kirktown of Deskford on the 29th of February 1864, aged 37 years.

6. R.P. Erected by Robert Proctor, farmer, Ardoch, to the memory of his father Robert Proctor, sometime farmer at Lhanbryd, near Elgin, who died at Ardoch on the 25th day of June 1860, aged 78 years, and of his mother, Elizabeth Garden or Proctor, who departed this life the 18th day of December the same year, aged 80 years. Sacred also to the memory of his two brothers, John Proctor, who died at Demerara July 1842, aged 27 years and Alexander Duff Proctor who died at Colombo, Ceylon, August 1845, aged 35 years.

7. Erected by James Lawrence, building contractor, Melbourne, V.A. in memory of his father, William Lawrence, wright, G. Ardoch, who died 7th Oct. 1859, aged 90 years; and of his mother, Helen Wood, died 28th Nov. 1849, aged 77 years; also his brothers, Peter, died 27th Feb 1825, aged 8 years, William, died 3rd March 1826, aged 13 years, George, died 6th June 1845, aged 30 years.

8. This stone is erected by William Moriso(n), taylior in Windiehills, and his wife, Isobel Allardys, in mermory of their daughter, Ann Morison, who died May 1st 1784, aged 22 years.

9. In memory of James Napier, who died 5th Feb. 1855, aged 34 years; also of his family, Elsie and James, who died in infancy; William, who died 10th Jan 1881, aged 25 years.

10. Erected in memory of James Peterkin, who died at Bloomfield 20th January 1868, aged 83 years; and his son, John, who died at Portsoy 11th December 1870, aged 47 years; also Jane Meldrum, his daughter-in-law, who died 18th Novr. 1872, aged 39 years.

11. Sacred to the memory of William Reid, Hollandbush, who died 30th October 1850, aged 50 years. Erected by _____ children, W.A. and Isabella Reid.

12. Erected by James Reid of the Exchequer, Edinburgh, in memory of his parents, James Reid, tenant of Swailend, who died 28th May 1815, aged 57 years, and Janet Clark, who died 26th April 1835, aged 82 years; also of Dugald, his eldest son, who died 16th April 1835, aged 37 years; and his brother, John, farmer, Swailend, who died 30th July 1871, aged 83 years; also his wife, Janet Watt, who died 25th November 1870, aged 80 years; and their son James, who died 10th December 1870, aged 51 years.

13. Sacred to the memory of George Davidson, who died 5th July 1869, aged 66 years; also, of his wife, Ann Reid, who died 25th April 1871, aged 71 years; also, of their son William, who died 12th May 1860, aged 17 years.

14. Sacred to the memory of Isobel Bidie, daughter of William Bidie, merchant, Backies, who died 27th May 1844, aged 4 years. The above William Bidie died at Backies 6th December 1869, aged 76 years. Ann Stewart, his wife, died 28th January 1880, aged 73 years.

A few short years of evil past,
We reach the happy shore
Where death divided friends at last
Shall meet to part no more.

15. Sacred to the memory of John Grant, farmer in Raemore, who died in April 1762, aged 82 years; also in this place ly the bodies of James Grant and Janet Allan, his father and mother, with Jean Bean, his wife,

and John Grant, James Grant and Janet Grant, his children. This stone was erected by David Grant, his son, in grateful remembrance of a kind father, loving husband, and an honest man.

16. A.D. 1743 – here lys the corps of John Dowgall, and Elspet Skinner, and Jo. Dowgall, and Els. Byres, and Jo Dowgall who died the year 1723, and his wife Elspet Skinner who died 1746. This stone is erected by Alexr. And Janet Dowgalls.

17. This stone belongs to me James Shepherd, tenant in Seafield,

> Ah me! I fraile am and dust,
> I yet to the grave descend I must,
> O painted piece of lively clay,
> Man be not proud of thy short day.

18. Erected by Andrew Longmore in memory of his wife, Margaret Bidie, who died at Bauds of Cullen, 6th November 1863, aged 37 years. Also their two daughters, May, died 16th January aged 6 years, Margaret died 28th August aged 2 years, both at Berryhillock in the year 1850.

19. Our conversation is in heaven. In memory of George Longmore, who died 30th May 1872, aged 4 years. Andrew G. Died 26th November 1880, aged 5 weeks.

20. 1867. Erected by William Bremner, farmer, Myreside, Grange, in memory of his beloved father, William Bremner, who died the 4th January 1864, aged 77 years. Also of his son, John Bremner, who died at Myreside February 22nd 1876, aged 42 years.

21. This stone was erected by John Bremner, farmer in Craibstoun, to the memory of his son John, who died October the 14th, 1786, in the 28th year of his age.

22. T.B. ……M.C. 1668.

23. Erected by George Reidford to the memory of his daughter Margaret Reidford, who died 10th January 1857, aged 7 years.

24. Erected by Margaret Loggie in memory of her husband John Donald, who died at Kinchurdie 19th August 1853, aged 59 years.

25. This stone is erected by Alexander McHattie, wright in Cullen, in memory of his wife, Mary Donald, who died 23rd July 1851, aged 39 years; also his father, Alexander McHattie, who died 20th October 1859, aged 85 years; also, his brother, John, Rector, Dalkeith Academy,

died 23rd May 1862, aged 32 years; also his mother, Jane Johnstone, died 2nd February 1884, aged 100 years.

26. Sacred to the memory of James Frazer, sometime smith at Ardoch, who died Nov 9th 1788, age 76 years. He was an honest man, friendly, benevolent, and open hearted, and a strict observer of every religious duty. Isobel Gerrie, his spouse, died Novr. 9th 1789, aged 73 years. She was a dutiful wife, an affectionate parent, and a friend to all in distress. This stone is erected by their son, James, smith in Banff.

27. In memory of Mrs Jane Donald or Russell, who died at Milltown of Deskford, 13th July 1871, aged 53 years. Be thou faithful unto death and I will give thee a crown of life. – Rev ii. 10

28. 1864. Erected in memory of William Ellis, late carpenter, Tochieneal, who died 20th March 1852, aged 41 years; also, his daughter, Jane, who died 21st June 1846, aged 7 years and 11 months, and of his son, Alexander, who died 28th February 1862, aged 18 years.

29. 1874. Erected by Elspet Imlach, in memory of her parents, James Imlach, who died 1847, aged 84; Margaret Lawrence, his wife who died 1842, aged 77; their son, John Imlach, who died 1818, aged 18; their daughter Isobel, who died 1818, aged 21; also Janet, who died 1837, aged 39.

30. In memory of Janet Wright, who died 26th June 1869, aged 73. A faithful servant.: Titus 3. 5.

31. This stone is erected by Margaret Martin in memory of her husband, Geo Ogilvie, late farmer in Burnside, parish of Fordyce, who died July 23 1791, in ye 59 year of his age.

32. This stone is erected by George Wright, Carrothead, in memory of his spouse, Ann Andrew, who died 29 Aug. 1791, aged 39; was married 1771; has left children, 5 sons and 4 daughters.

> O, Annie, dear, the grave has twin'd
> Thy loving heart and mine,
> But I hope we'll meet in heaven above,
> No more to part again.

33. Sacred to the memory of Alex. Baggrie, blacksmith at Ardoch, who died the 6th October 1846, aged 62; also to the memory of his son,

John Baggrie, likewise Blacksmith there, who died the 17th January 1848, aged 34.

34. Erected by William Reid, Edinburgh, in memory of his parents, John Reid, who died at Cullen 7th Feb. 1846, aged 50 years; and Margaret Wood, his wife, who died 7th Jany. 1880, aged 80 years; and 5 of their children who died in infancy.

35. Sacred to the memory of Elizabeth Manson, wife of Alexander Currie, Burnside, Rathven, who died on the 22nd Agust 1872, aged 74 years. Erected by their sons, William, George, Robert and John.

36. Sacred to the memory of James Forbes, late farmer, Raemore, who died 20th December 1850, aged 76 years. Erected by his spouse, Margaret Currie.

37. Erected by Alexander Taylor, Little Skeith, in memory of his son, William, who died 18th May 1859, aged 2 years and 6 months; also James, who died 23rd June 1862, aged 4 months; also, John, who died 8th April 1883, aged 27 years.

38. Erected by James Benzie in memory of his family – James, who died 18th May 1832, aged 14 years; William, died 25th Nov. 1852, aged 25 years.

39. In loving memory of Abercromby Wilson who died at Braehead, Deskford, 29th August 1881, aged 68 years. His wife, Helen Wilson, died 26th Dec. 1874, aged 51 years. Their son, William, died 2nd June 1873, aged 21 years. Their daughter, Margaret, died 19th October 1881. Aged 32 years, and her husband, Alex. Taylor, died 20th October 1880, aged 37 years, and is interred at Forres. Erected by their family.

> A few short years of evil past,
> We reach the happy shore,
> Where death divided friends at last,
> Shall meet to part no more.

40. I.S......I.I. 1779.

41. Erected 1866 by George Hay, Crannoch, Grange, in memory of his beloved mother, Margaret Elder, who died the 24th May 1843, aged about 54 years.

42. G.S. I. B. 1780.

43. Erected by Alexander Black in memory of his spouse, Janet Smith, who died in Cullen 7th March 1863, aged 73 years.

44. Erected by Mary Bremner in memory of her beloved father, James Bremner, Farmer, on Burnend, Grange, who died 10th Augt. 1850, aged 67 years; also her brother James, who died in infancy, 1814; also her sister, Isabella, who died 30th January 1826, aged 10 years; also her mother, Isobell Mellis, who died 11th January, 1864, aged 84 years.

45. Erected by Ann Lawrence in memory of her husband, William Milton, who died at Aultmore, 2nd Aug. 1877, aged 78 years.

46. Erected by the family in memory of their parents, William Milton, who died 20th October, 1872, aged 63 years, and Ann Nicholson, his wife, who died the 16th May, 1881, aged 67 years; also two of their children, Isabella and George, who died in infancy

> Our parents here lies underground
> The dearest friends we ever found.
> But through the Lord's unbounded love,
> We'll meet again in realms above.

47. Hope. Erected by George Sutherland, farmer, Bloomfield, in memory of his father, John Sutherland, who died at Craighead, 2nd may 1856, aged 59 years; and of his mother, Margaret Hay, who died at Bloomfield 4th Aug. 1881, aged 83 years; also in memory of his two brothers – John died 1843, aged 21 years; Alexander died 1856, aged 19 years. Sacred also to the memory of his beloved wife, Ann Wilson, who died at Bloomfield 11th January, 1883, aged 44 years.

48. Erected by William Wright, Brooklyn, USA, in memory of his father, Alexander Wright, farmer, Greenhill, who died 27th December 1862, aged 72 years, and his mother, Ann Burgess, who died 31st January 1859, aged 67 years.

49. Erected by Alexander Smith, farmer, Burns, in memory of his father, William Smith, who died the 21st November 1845, aged 80 years.

50. Erected the 25th November 1825 at the desire of Alexander Lawtie, late tenant in Upper Skeith, in memory of his father and mother, also his sisters Janet, and Elizabeth, and an infant son, whose bodies are interred here.

51. Erected by Charles Shepherd in affectionate remembrance of his father, William Shepherd, crofter, Cottartown, Ardoch, who died 30th January 1871, aged 75 years; also his mother, Margaret McKenzie, who died 4th April 1877, aged 82 years.

52. Besides the remains of his beloved mother lies all that was mortal of her dear son, the Rev. George Innes, Minister first of Seafield Church, and afterwards of the Free Church of Cannonbie, who died on the 24th of November 1847, in the 29th year of his age and 5th of his ministry, after having been subjected to much hardship in consequence of the refusal of a piece of ground on which to build a house in which he and his congregation might assemble in comfort to worship Him to whom the earth and the fullness thereof belongs. If we suffer with Christ we shall also reign with him. Ii Tim ii. 12.

53. Sacred to the memory of Jane Milne, wife of the Revd. George Innes, Minister of Deskford, who lived beloved and esteemed, and on the 7th March 1836, in the 45th year of her age, departed this life in the blissful hope of being with her ever living and gracious Redeemer. Blessed are the dead who die in the Lord.

54. In memory of the Revd. George innes, born at Huntly, 7th July 1777, ordained as Minister of Cullen 1st Decr. 1808, translated to Deskford 7th August 1829, and since the Disruption in 1843 Minister of the Free Church here, died 1st Octr. 1851, in the 75 year of his age. "Come ye blessed of my father, inherit the Kingdom prepared for you from the foundation of the world" Mat. XXV. 20.

55. Sacred to the memory of Elizabeth Longmore, wife of George Morison in Milltown, who died the 24th Feby. 1840, aged 49; also, to the memory of said George Morison, who died 18th April 1855, aged 76.

56. Sacred to the memory of Margaret Longmore, wife of James Black, farmer in Ardoch, who died the 17th Novr. 1827, aged 56. Here also lie the remains of the said James Black, who died the 8th March, 1849, aged 88 years.

57. Sacred to the memory of Mrs Sarabella Morison, daughter of the Revd. Walter Morison, 49 years Minister at Deskford, married first to the Revd. Harry Gordon, Minister at Ardersier, by whom she had five children, and second to the Revd. Walter Chalmers, the present Minister at Deskford. Pious in heart and benevolent in mind, in person graceful, and in manners affable, a dutiful daughter, an indulgent

parent, a tenderly affectionate wife, a warm and judicious friend. She died the 3rd Jany. 1811, aged 77.

58. Mr . Valtrvs . Ogilvy . verbi . divini . Minister . pivs . nunc . inter . coelites . beat . qvi . fatis . cessit . xv . Kal . Feb. . ano . dv . 1658.

59. W.O. .......M.S. 1669 (This stone stood formerly in the churchyard wall.)

60. Sub hoc cippo condvntur cineres probae mulieris Agnetae Simson Mri Andreae Hendersoni ecclesia Deskfurdiensis ministry coniugis dilectae quae per decennium marito nupta septem que liberos enixa quor. Tres hic partier sepulti sunt placid ac pie morti succubit xvi. Kal. Sep. Ao. Aet. Xxxiv aer Chr. MDCLXIII. Wil. H. Hel. H. Jea. H.

61. Here lyes in hope of a blessed resurrection Mr John Murray, Minister of the gospel at Deskfoord, who departed this life march 1st 1719; also Jean ord, his spouse, who departed the......day of ....17...........; as also Jams Murray, thier son, who departed Meay the 5. 1717.

APPENDIX 11. INVENTORY OF DESKFORD KIRK SESSION PROPERTY AND FUNDS 2004 (WILLIE TAYLOR)

1. One Parish Church
2. One vestry with furnishings
3. Organ, value £200
4. Heating apparatus in Church
5. Solid oak Communion table
6. Sacramental vessels
7. Four silver cups, date 1873
8. Two pewter bread plates, date 1796
9. Four old cups, two large dated 1796 and two small dated 1670
10. One tankard, electroplated, dated 1891
11. Two solid silver bread plates, dated 1906
12. One old pewter bread plate with inscription "Deskford 1711"
13. Two stained glass windows in memory of Rev Dr Mackintosh and Mrs Mackintosh
14. Two Communion Roll books, two Registers of Baptism, five volumes of Session Records, Register of Proclamation of Banns and Register of Cases of Discipline
15. Case of solid silver Communion Vessels for private Communion, with inscription "Parish Church of Deskford 1900"
16. Case containing solid silver trowel with ivory handle, with inscription "To Viscount Reidhaven by the parishioners on the occasion of his laying the Memorial Stone of the Established Church of Deskford, March 13th 1872" (This trowel was handed back to the Earl of Seafield as an heirloom)
17. Proctor's legacy. £50 for behalf of the poor of the parish not in receipt of Parochial Relief, and at present in the Post Office Savings Bank. Now in Consols 1915
18. The McWillie Bequest. A sum of £15 left by the late Miss McWillie, Backies, for the upkeep of the family burial ground. Invested in Consols 1915
19. The Mackintosh Trust. A sum of £7 given by Prof Ashley W. Mackintosh, Aberdeen, for the upkeep of the family burying plot. Now in Consols 1915
20. George Duncan Trust. £300
21. George Duncan Educational Legacy. £100
22. Milton Fund £500
23. £10 given by the executors of the late George Duncan for the upkeep of his burial ground. Invested in 2½% Consols.

APPENDIX 12. LIST OF HEADS OF FAMILIES IN COMMUNION WITH DESKFORD CHURCH 1834

James Wright, Clochmacreich
William Gray, Carrothead
William Bidie, Backies
James Lawtie, Upper Skeith
Alex Clark, Mid Skeith
William Black, Broadrashes
James Elder, Broomhaugh
James Elder, Hollybush (sic)
James Lawrence, Broadrashes
Alex Wright, Greenhill
John Nicol, Hoggie
John Watt, Ordens
John Russell Sen, Oathillock
Robert Greenlaw, Knows
John Ingles, Greenhill
Joseph Gairn, Blairock
George Milton, Faichyhill
Andrew Reid, Squaredoch
John Reid, Squaredoch
James McHattie Sen, Squaredoch
James McHattie Jun, Squaredoch
John Milton, Squaredoch
George Taylor, Squaredoch
John Burges, Squaredoch
Wm Grigor, Auldmore
Alex Murray, Auldmore
James Russell, Auldmore
John Howie, Auldmore
Wm Thain, Auldmore
Wm Grant, Auldmore
Wm Longmore, Auldmore
Wm Milton, Auldmore
Abercrombie Wilson, Auldmore
Alex Wilson, Auldmore
Wm Stevenson, Auldmore
Alex Wilson, Auldmore
Wm Reid (mason), Berryhillock
George Duffus, Knappcausey
George Gray, Berryhillock
Alex Reid, Berryhillock
Wm Reid, Berryhillock
James Wilson, Berryhillock
John Lawrence, Berryhillock
Alex Chalmers, Berryhillock
John Shearer, Berryhillock
John Whyte, Berryhillock
James Mitchell, Burnheads
John Reid, Swailend
James Keir, Carrothead
James Forbes, Ramore
George Barclay, Ramore
James Scott, Craibstone
John Mason, Langlanburns
Alex Wilson, Lower Cliff
Wm Reid, Hoggie
Robert Gray, Knows
James Wilson, Knows
James Lawrence, Cultain
George Murray, Ardicow
Andrew McKonnachie, Bleachfield

James Wright, Auldmore
John Milton, Carestown
Wm Skene, Milton
Robert Stephen, Milton
James Whyntie, Milton
Andrew Reid, Milton
Peter Galt, Clunehill
Alex McHattie, Clunehill
George Skinner, Clunehill
George Morison, Milton
Wm Rumbles, Faichyhill
James Black, Ardoch
Alex Bagrie, Ardoch
Wm Smith, Ardoch
Wm Lawrence, Ardoch
John Longmore, Ardoch
Alex Riddoch, Kirktown
James Lorimer, Ardoch
James Smith, Kirktown
John Stewart, Kirktown
Wm Black, Squaredoch
John Sutherland, Auldmore
Andrew Milton, Berryhillock
John Thomson, Berryhillock
Donald Campbell, Auldmore
John Skinner, Kirktown
George Wright, Kirktown
Alex Stephen, Kirktown
James Morrison, Nether Blairock
Alex Elder, Little Skeith
John Anderson, Lichestown

APPENDIX 13. CORDINER'S DRAWING OF THE TOWER OF DESKFORD 1788

APPENDIX 14. LIST OF PROPERTIES IN DESKFORD IN THE BARONY OF OGILVIE, 1747

1. The Town and Kirklands of Deskford Mannor Place, Tower, fortalice and yards thereof.
2. The Town and Lands of Over Blairock.
3. The Town and Lands of Faichyhill.
4. The town and Lands of Swallowhillock.
5. The Town and Lands of Knows.
6. The Milltown of Deskford with the Mills of the same, Mill Lands, Multures, Thirlage, Knaveship, Sucken and Sequalls thereof.
7. That part of the Lands of Clune. John Thom's Land.
8. The Town and Lands of Clockmacreech.
9. The Town and Lands of Over and Nether Tullybreedless called Our Lady's Land.
10. The Town and Lands of Over Skeith.
11. The Town and lands of Middle Skeith.
12. The Lands of Wairds commonly called My Lord's Wairds.
13. The Town and Lands of Craibstoun.
14. The Town and lands of Croftgloy.
15. The Lands of Acres of Squaredoch.
16. The Town and Lands of Ramore.
17. The Town and Lands of Ordins.
18. The Town and Lands of Oathillock.
19. The Town and lands of Airdecow.
20. The Town and Lands of Nether Blerock.
21. The Town and Lands of Airdoch.
22. The Town and lands of Cultain. That part and portion of the Lands of Cultain called Little Cultain as the samen is Meiches and Marches from the rest of the Lands of Cultain and has been possessed by Colonel James Abercrombie of Glassah and his predecessors and their Tenants, with the tiends and pertinents thereof.
23. The Town and Lands of Cairston.
24. The Town and Lands of Inaltry.

25. The Town and Lands of Coattain.
26. The Town and Lands of Meikle and Little Knows.
27. The Town and Lands of Nether Clune.
28. The Town and Lands of Clunehill.
29. The Town and Lands of Smithstown.
30. The Town and lands of Leitchestoun together with the hail Lands of Skeith and all other Lands pertaining and belonging to the said Barony of Ogilvie, as well not named as named with all and whole the other Houses, Biggings, Yards, Orchards, Tofts, Crofts, Mosses, Muires, Meadows, Fishings, Commonties, Common Pasturages, Outsetts, Insetts, Annexis, Connexis, Dependancies, Parks, Wairds, Tenants, Tenandries and service of Free Tenants, parts and pendicles of Over Blairock, Faichyhill, Swallowhillock and Knows, The Milltown of Deskford, mill lands, multures, thirlage, knaveship and sucken and sequalls thereof and that part of the lands of Clune called John Thom's Land, the Towns and Lands of Over and Middle Skeith, the Wairds commonly called My Lord's Wairds.

APPENDIX 15. TENANCIES AND ACREAGES HELD IN DESKFORD, 1771.

(INFIELD, OUTFIELD, MEADOW AND PASTURE, TOTAL)

1. Clochmacreich, Peter Thain, (31, 16, 40, 88)
2. Backies, John Wright, (24, 9, 17, 51)
3. Bognygeith, Mr. Grant, Tochieniel, (11, 9, 23, 44)
4. Upper Skeith, John Reid, (23, 7, 28, 44, plus 21 improveable)
5. Mid Skeith, William Milne, (43, 10, 37,104, plus 14 improveable)
6. Little Skeith, Walter Milne, (11, 14, 19, 57, plus 6 improveable and 5 under wood)
7. Little Skeith, Andrew Black, (0, 9, 3, 13)
8. Little Skeith, John Peterkin, (11, 5, 9, 29, plus 2 under wood)
9. Mains of Skeith, John Peterkin, (21, 9, 17, 57, plus 8 under wood)
10. Broadrashes, James Lawrence, (8, 2, 0, 10)
11. Broadrashes, Alex Reid, (5, 2, 12, 20)
12. Kintywairds, Alex Reid, (0, 4, 5, 9)
13. Hoggie, labourers in lots, (17, 0, 3, 21)
14. Hollandbush, John Nicol, (0, 10, 5, 15)
15. A croft, Geo Taylor, (2, 0, 0, 3, plus 3 improveable)
16. Broom Haugh, John Smith, (3, 0, 2, 6)
17. Mill Lands of Berryhillock, Charles Russel, (6, 0, 2, 9)
18. Croftgloy, James Lawrence, (11, 9, 7, 27)
19. Croftgloy, by sundries, (17, 1, 21, 40)
20. Ordens, Mathew Morison, (41, 18, 45, 110, plus 5 under wood)
21. Oathillock, William Riddoch, (12, 0, 3, 13)
22. Oathillock, Alex Taylor (Kirktown), (0, 20, 3, 23)
23. Oathillock, James Wilson (Ardoch), (14, 13, 13, 41)
24. Park of Kirktown, Alex Taylor, (0, 4, 10, 15)
25. Meikle Knows, Alex Taylor, (4, 6, 5, 16)
26. Meikle Knows, Wm Watt, (0, 8, 1, 9)
27. Meikle Knows, Charles Russel, (0, 8, 3, 12)
28. Meikle Knows, Wm Riddock, (0, 15, 4, 20)
29. Meikle Knows, James Reid, (0, 12, 35, 47)
30. Little Knows, Jas Wilson and Morison, (7, 7, 6, 21)
31. A Loaning betwixt Little and Meikle Knows, (0, 0, 0, 16), (hill and moor 16)
32. Lurghill, lying south from Greenhill of Deskford, (0, 0, 0, 203), (hill and moor 203)

33. Greenhill of Deskford, (0, 0, 106, 491, plus 65 improveable and 119 under wood)
34. Moor on which Sir Robert Abercromby has a tolerance for firing (peat), (0, 0, 0, 204), (hill and moor 204)
35. A loaning betwixt Ardicow and the Greenhill, (0, 0, 0, 18), (hill and moor 18)
36. Ardicow, James Murray, (25, 25, 69, 120)
37. Little Ardicow, Alex Murray, (14, 11, 31, 57)
38. Carestown, Wm Riddoch, (27, -, 13, 40)
39. Carestown, Alex Reid, (28, -, 9, 38)
40. Banks, west from the Greens, (-, 32, -, 32)
41. Inaltry, Wm Grant, (72, -, 25, 111, plus 13 planted in wood)
42. Cottoun, Wm Grant, (22, -, 10, 33)
43. The Bleachfield, Wm Rennie, (0, 0, 0, 9,9)
44. Leechiestown, James Reid, (41, -, 41, 106, plus 23 hill and moor)
45. The Cottown Hill, (0, 0, 0, 0, plus 165 hill and moor)
46. Meikle Cultain, James Murray, (31, -, 57, 148, plus 59 hill and moor)
47. Little Cultain, James Dason, (7, -, 19, 56, plus 29 hill and moor)

APPENDIX 16. FARMS AND THEIR ACREAGES IN THE PARISH OF DESKFORD, 1866

Clunehill Croft 11
Clunehill 62
Burns 65
Nether Blairock 143
Upper Blairock 132
Airdoch 179
Cottartown (6 holdings)
Braidbog 40
Rashiehill 48
Greens of Blairock 76
Briggs 33
Nethertown 60
Braehead 16
Burnside 29
Kemps Croft 13
Badenhannen 36
Backburn 44
Hillhead 46
Rosebank 32
Bogrotten 34
Mosside 100
Squaredoch 87
Burnheads 102
Swailend 62
Leitchestown 110
Inaltrie 167
Carestown 137
Meikle Cultain 170
Little Cultain 52
Ardicows 163
Little Knows 45

Muckle Knows 79
Kirktown 62
Oathillock 81
Ordens 109
Mains of Skeith 162
Greenhill Crofts (11) 10 each
Earlstown (Greenhill) 96
Kintywairds 101
Hoggie 21
Hoggie Croft 9
Holland Bush 4
Lower Broadrashes 31
Upper Broadrashes 29
Little Skeith 86
Mid Skeith 123
Viewfrith 133
Upper Skeith 77
Backies 112
Clochmacreich 111
Langlanburn 234 (inc. Tillybreedless)
Craibstone 190
Bogetra 51
Milton Croft 4
Mill Croft 9
Todholes 42

(In addition there were many un-named crofts on Aultmore plus some which only bore the crofter's name. These were all named individually in the 1860s, just before the first OS map was published).

APPENDIX 17. SELECTED ITEMS FROM A LIST OF SUMS ADVANCED BY THE PROPRIETOR FOR BUILDING AND REPAIRING HOUSES AND FARMS.

(The main purposes for these loans were drainage, new offices, new dwelling houses, new steadings, turnip sheds, granaries, mill houses, implement sheds, dairies and cottages. There were many other loans in addition to those shown below)

1. 1858. Leitchestown, Wm Proctor, £150 @ 5%. £7:10/- interest added to rent.
2. 1860 and 1861. Braidbog, John McGregor, £60 @5%. £3 interest
3. 1860. Bogrotten Croft, Wm Muggoch, £40 @5%. £2 interest
4. 1860, 1861 and 1864. Carestown, Wm Stevenson, £400 @ 5%. £15 interest, but none on £100
5. 1863. Inaltrie, John Cowie, £100 @5%. £5 interest
6. 1863. Bleachfield Croft, Mrs Garden, £19:12:2d @ 5%. 19/7d interest.
7. 1863. Bleachfield, Wm Grant, £38:19:9d. No interest
8. 1864. Marchbanks, Jas Sellar, £50 @5%. £2:10/- interest.
9. 1864 and 1865. Mosside, H Wood, £243:12:11d @ 5%. £7:3:7d interest including a deduction for taking in new land.
10. 1865 Nether Blairock, Jas Smith, £196:17:7d. No interest.
11. 1868. Burns, Jas Main, £303:14/-. Interest restricted to £5
12. 1868 Burnside, John Allan, £463:6:1d @5%. £23:3:3d interest.
13. 1868 and 1869. Ardoch, Robert Proctor, £72:2:4d. No interest.
14. 1869 and 1870. Berryhillock Mill Croft, Robert Cruikshank, £152:17/- @5%. £7:12:10d interest.
15. 1869. Craibstone, John Sutherland £172:19:6d @5%. £8:12:11d interest.
16. 1870 and 1874. Burns, James Main, £343:4/- @4%. £13:12:6d interest.
17. 1870. Burnheads, Charles Milne, £60 @ 5%. £3 interest
18. 1870. Mains of Skeith, Jas and Wm Thomson, £287:4/-. No interest.
19. 1871. Ramore, L A Milne, £50. No interest.

APPENDIX 18. DRAWING OF, AND INDIVIDUAL OX POSITIONS ON, A "TWAL OWSEN PLOUGH"

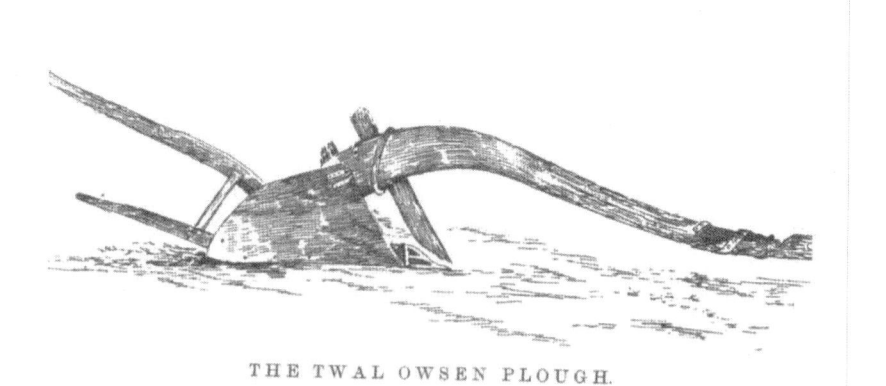

THE TWAL OWSEN PLOUGH.

Wyner Ox	Steer Draught	Fore Throck in fur	Mid Throck in fur	Hind Throck in fur	Fit (foot) in fur
On Wyner Ox	On Steer Draught	Fore Throck on land	Mid Throck on land	Hind Throck on land	Fit (foot) on land

APPENDIX 19. A GAMRIE FARMER'S MONEY TRANSACTIONS, 1760 – 1769

1 sheep, 2/6d -3/-
1 cow, £2 - £3
1 horse, £4:4/-
pease, 6/- a peck
beans, 8/- a boll
butter, 7d a pound
manservant (winter), 12/-15/-
manservant (summer), 5/-
female servant (6 months), 1/8d
1 heuk, 6d
hired labourer, 4d a day
1 pair muck creels, 1/6d
same from a roup, 2d
smith for coulter and sock, bridle,
   nails and four shoes
   on two horses, 4/-
lime, 7d a boll
peats, 6d a load
Scots coal, 10d a barrel
18lb red clover, 2½ lb white
   clover, 2½ bushels rye grass
   and ½ peck lint seed, £1:10:10d
1oz turnip seed, 2d
kale, 2d per 100
potato, 5d per peck
turnip, 3d per peck
12 china cups and flats, 14/-
mutchkin of whisky, 4d

loaf sugar, 9d a pound
½lb soap, 4d
10lb rushes, 10d
1lb candle, 7d
1 mutchkin lamp oil, 4d
10 doz speldings, 2/6d
10 doz haddocks, 2/-
midwife at christening, 6d
Dr, 1/6d for prescribing and 6d for pills
to son for St John's fair, 1/-
school fees, 9d repeating
music dues, 3d
dancing lessons, 1/-
newspaper, 2/- a year fly band, hesp and
1 pair farmer's shoes, 4/6d
1 pair farmer's wife's shoes, 3/-
1 pair child's shoes, 1/3d
2 doz tackets, 2d
black breeches, 2/-
man's bonnet, 1/11d
child's bonnet, 1/4d
to make a pair of stockings, 3d
for dressing 2st 14lb lint, 2/8d
scarlet plaid for daughter, £1
1 or 2 bottles of ale, 3d to 1/-
6 table knives, 2/8d
18 pewter spoons, 1/-
tea, 3d per oz

APPENDIX 20. INVOICE FROM WILLIAM DUNCAN, BLACKSMITH TO MR A WRIGHT, UPPER SKEITH, 1927

DESKFORD. Nov 28th 1927
CULLEN

Mr A Wright, Upper Skeith

TO WILLIAM DUNCAN,
GENERAL BLACKSMITH.

1927				
May	26	To marles of D.B. Plough mended		6
June	11	1 cock ship'd 3/-, 25 cartridges 3/3	3	6
	13	new tramp for spade		3
	14	Shim repd 5 tynes laid grubber	5	
	"	new axle to wheel	1	6
	15	2 new shoes toed 6/-, 2 rem 2/9	8	9
	24	3 new hoe blades	1	6
July	27	2 new shoes toed	6	
Aug	5	2 new shoes 5/6, 2 rem 2/9	8	3
	"	1 bolt 1½ x ½		2
	29	2 shoes rem & toed	3	6
	"	1 new Unbreakable scythe blade & set	8	6
	30	1 scythe set	1	
Oct	6	2 shoes rem 2/9, 1 new girdle 4/-	6	9
	8	1 new sickle 10, 2 bolts 3" x ½ 6	1	4
Oct	3	2 shoes rem & toed	3	6
	10	1 shoe rem	1	3
Nov	8	2 new shoes toed 6/-, 4 cogs 3"	6	3
	"	4 frost nails = 2 = 8		8
	15	4 shoes rem 5/9, 8 brunts 6	6	3
	"	8 holes @ 2 = 1/4	1	4
			£3	15 9

Paid   Wm Duncan

APPENDIX 21. INDIVIDUALS IN DESKFORD PAYING CLOCK TAX AND FARM HORSE TAX, 1797/98

Clock and Watch Tax
Rev Chalmers, 7/6d

Farm Horse Tax	No of Horses	Total Duty
Alex Anderson, Leitchestown	3	6/-
Wm Beedie, Backies	2	4/-
Alex Bennett, Deskford	1	2/-
Alex Clark, Mid Skeith	1	2/-
James Clark, Raemore	2	4/-
Rev Chalmers, Minister	2	4/-
John Duffus, Cnapcasied (Knappycausey)	2	4/-
James Morrison, Longlonbyron	2	4/-
Alex Lawtie, Upper Skeith	2	4/-
James Lawrence, Cotton	2	4/-
John Longmoor, Milntown	3	6/-
James Lawrence, Crathglow (Croftgloy)	2	2/-
Andrew Littlejohn, Tulochbreadels	2	4/-
Alex Murray, Little Ardicow	2	4/-
James Murray, Ardicow	3	4/-
James McHatty, Skerevdoch (Squaredoch)	1	2/-
Alex McHatty, Natry (Inaltrie)	3	6/-
James Mitchell, Berryhillock	2	4/-
James Nicolson, Cnowls (Knows)	2	4/-
John Peterkin, Skeith	2	4/-
Alex Piper, Deskford	2	4/-
James Reid, Ardoch	6	8/-
James Reid, Fachie (Faichyhill)	2	4/-
William Ruddach, Kerstown (Careston)	2	4/-
James Black, Neither Blairock	3	6/-
Walter Sim, Berryhillock	1	2/-
James Scott, Craibston	1	2/-
George Smith, Upper Blarie (Blairock)	2	4/-
John Smith, Mosside	2	4/-
George Taylor, Cullen of Deskford	2	4/-

Farm Horse Tax	No of Horses	Total Duty
George Wright Windiehill	1	2/-
William Wilson, Craibston	1	2/-
James Wilson, Kirktown	2	4/-
James Wilson, Little Cnowls (Knows)	2	2/-
Alex Watt, Ordens	2	4/-
James Mitchell, Berryhillock	1	2/-
Alex Couper, Deskford	2	4/-
George Skinner, Cloverhill	2	4/-

APPENDIX 22. SELECTED INTERNAL REVENUE SERVICES PROPERTY VALUES 1910

Blackhillock with Bogetra	£ 705
Barone Croft	£ 353
Mid Skeith	£2,860
Hoggie Croft	£ 218
Gateside Croft	£ 104
Inaltry, Cottartown and Smithtoun	£2,940
Berryhillock Mill	£ 836
Upper Craibstone	£ 88
Mains of Skeith	£3,066
Todholes	£ 452
Hollanbush	£ 213
Ardoch	£4,476
Comb's Croft	£ 119
Craibstone	£1,669
Craibstone Quarry	£ 22
Craigie Croft	£ 182
Nether Blairock	£2,675
Little Skeith	£ 423
Ardiecow	£1,162
Church and ground	£1,030

APPENDIX 23. ASSESSMENT FOR ALLOWANCES TO WIVES AND FAMILIES OF MILITIAMEN, 1806 – 1812

John Peterkin, Mains of Skeith	£1/5/5d
John Lawrence, Broadrashes	3/7d
William Black, Broadrashes	3/-
Geo Reid, Hollandbush	2/5d
John Nicol, Hoggie	1/2d
Geo Black, Hoggie	1/2d
Janet Sim, Hoggie	1/2d
James Stewart, Hoggie	2/5d
16 crofters and Lord Seafield, Kintywaird	2/8d
Geo Duffus, Knappiecausway	12/8d
James Clark, Raemore	14/6d
Geo Reid, Feichyhill	7/3d
James Wilson, Kirktown	19/4d
John Smith, Mosside	15/10d
James Black, Blairock and Ardoch	15/8d
James Black, Nether Blairock and Milntown	16/10d
Alex Smith, Mousehillock	5/5d
Geo Skinner, Clunehill	16/4d
Wm Rannie, Clune, Bleachfield and Oathillock	£1/11/6d
Alex Anderson, Leitchestown	19/4d
Wm Riddoch, Carestown	18/2d
James Lawrence, Cultain	9/8d
James Murray, Ardicow	12/1d
Alex Watt, Ordens	11/2d
James Lawrence, Croftgloy	12/10d
Wm Elder, Little Skeith	8/5d
Alex Lawtie, Upper Skeith	9/8d
Wm Bidie, Backies, Bognagight and Tillybreadless	16/11d
Geo Wright, Clochmacreich	14/6d
Wm Taylor, Kirktown	1/9d
James Wilson, Knows	7/3d
James Wilson, Knows	4/10d
James Wilson, Little Knows	1/2d

James Clark, Mid Skeith	15/9d
John Smith, Oathillock	3/-
Wm Rannie, Inaltrie	17/-
Wm Rannie, Cotton	9/9d
Wm Rannie, Smithstown	10/9d

APPENDIX 24. LIST OF THE POOR IN DESKFORD 1846

	Age	Name	Money	Bolls	Firlots	Pecks
1.	53	Janet Reid	£3:18/-	2		
2.	67	Elspet Buie	£3:18/-	3		
3.	31	Elspet Gray	£3:18/-	2		
4.	62	John Raffan	£2:12/-			
5.	83	Janet Milne	£2:12/-	1	2	2
6.	76	Elspet Longmore	£1:10/-	1	2	2
7.	74	Jane Bremner	£2:12/-	1		
8.	34	Margaret Clark jun	£3:18/-	3		
9.	74	Mary Taylor	£2:12/-	1		
10.	61	Mary Strachan	£2:12/-	3		
11.	65	Margaret Clark sen	£2:12/-	3		
12.	64	Margaret Lawrence	£3:18/-			
13.	77	Ann Ewan	£3:18/-	1		
14.	74	Elspet Milton (d. 01/05/1846)	£2:12/-	3		
15.	49	Margaret Skinner	£1:12/-	1	2	2
16.	66	Margaret Donald	£2:12/-	2		
17.	23	Elizabeth Elder	£2:12/-			
18.	60	Jane Merson	£7:16/-	1	2	2
19.	74	George Reid sen	£3:18/-	1	2	2
20.	56	Isobel Shepherd	£2:12/-	1		
21.	93	Helen Fraser	£5:4/-	1		
22.	61	Janet Munro	£2:12/-	3		
23.	66	Janet Russell	£2	2		
24.	90	Isobel Cumming	£5:4/-	1	1	
25.	70	Elspeth Lawrence	£2:12/-	3		
26.	67	Isobel Lawrence	£2:12/-	3		
27.	64	Catherine Kemp	£5:14/-			
28.	83	John Anton	£2:12/-			
29.	9	George Reid jun	£3:18/-			
30.	87	Margaret Taylor	£2	1	3	3
31.	74	James Fraser (d. 01/11/1846)	£2:12/-			
32.	8	Robert Raffan	£1:6/-			
33.	9	George Reid jun	£1:6/-			
34.	2	Alexander Forbes	£1:12/-			
35.	19	Elizabeth Smith	£2:12/-			

36.	75	Ann Russell	£2:12/-
37.	55	Ann Milton	£1
38.	71	Isobel Smith	£1:6/-
39.	73	Alexander Murray	£2:12/-
40.	40	Mary Geddes	
		(d. 04/04/1846)	£3:18/-
41.	59	John Smith	£2:12/-
42.	52	Ann Berry	£3:18/-
43.	79	Janet Cruikshank	£5:4/-

APPENDIX 25. WORLD WAR 1 DESKFORD ROLL OF HONOUR

1. Benzies, George. Private No 316451, B Company, 13th(SH) Black Watch; killed in action, 17th October 1918; son of Mr W. Benzies, Barone.
2. Brown, Alexander, Sergeant, M.M., D.C.M., No 23311. No 2 Section, R.E. 13th Infantry Brigade Headquarters. B.E.F. France; grandson of Mrs Howie, Berryhillock.
3. Cooper, William, Private, No 197, D Company, 4th Battalion, 1st Infantry Brigade, Australian; wounded and discharged; son of Mr C Cooper, Knowes.
4. Cruickshank, Alexander, Private, No. 9252, E Company, 2nd Battalion Gordon Highlanders; quarryman, Cottartown; killed in action, 22nd April 1917.
5. Cruickshank, George, Lance-Sergeant, No. 267205, B Company, 1/6th Black Watch, miller, Berryhillock. (killed in action 1915?)
6. Cruickshank, Robert, Lance-Corporal, No 7323, B Company, 2nd Battalion Seaforth Highlanders; wounded and discharged; son of late Mr Cruickshand, Inspector of Poor.
7. Cruickshank, Milton, Private No 24816, A Company, 4th Gordon Highlanders; ditto.
8. Cruickshank, James, Private, No 24183, C Company, 3rd Gordon Highlanders; son of Mr James Cruickshank, Backies.
9. Dalgarno, Henry, Private, No 21316, 1/7th Battalion Gordon Highlanders; grandson of Mr James Spence, Craigie Croft.
10. Davidson, Robert, Private No 13321, A Company, 15th Battalion H.L.I.; stepson of Mr John McCulloch, Ardoch.
11. Duncan, Charles, Driver, No 85818, 19th M.G. Squadron, Egypt; son of Mr James Duncan, Cottartown.
12. Duncan, James, Private No 79231, 14th Canadian Machine Gun Company; ditto.
13. Duncan, John, Sapper, No 352228, I.W. and D., R.E.; ditto.
14. Duncan, Peter, Private No 61714, E Company, 13th Royal Scots Fusiliers; ditto.
15. Duncan, William, Corporal, No 679, 1st Battalion Gordon Highlanders; died of wounds, 19th March 1915; son of Mr James Duncan, Faichyhill.
16. Farquhar, George, R, Lance-Corporal, No 266125, A Company, 2nd Battalion Gordon Highlanders; son of Mr James Farquhar, Muir of Squaredoch.

17. Farquhar, Robert, Lance-Corporal, No 10999, 1/6th Battalion Gordon Highlanders; died of wounds, 7th January 1917; ditto.
18. Findlay, Alexander, Private, No 265818, Q.M.'s Stores, 6th Battalion Gordon Highlanders; Kirktown.
19. Fordyce, James, Private, No 2122, 3/1st Highland Field Ambulance; brother of Mr John Fordyce, Rosebank.
20. Forsyth, Robert, Private No 51085, 6th Cheshire, 9th Corps Training School, B.E.F, France; Greenhill.
21. Fraser, William, Lance-Corporal, No 402222, No 5 Army Workshop Company, R.E., France; son of Mr Alexander Fraser, Rottenhillock.
22. Garvock, James, Private No 40171, A Company, 2/6th Battalion Gordon Highlanders; son of Mr George Garvock, late of Backies.
23. Geddes, John, Marine Engineer, H.M.'s Patrol Boat; stepson of Mr John McCulloch, Ardoch.
24. Gordon, Robert L, Private No 11202, 2/6th Battalion, Gordon Highlanders; demobilised; stepson of Mr Alexander Ingram, Stripeside.
25. Gray, George, Sapper, No 17493, Seaforth Battery, Seaforths, Liverpool; son of Mr James Gray, Knowes.
26. Gray, James, Private No 268122, B Company, 5th Battalion Canadians, died of wounds 10th November 1917; ditto.
27. Gray, John, Driver, No 116985, C Company Transport, 2nd Battalion M.G.C.; ditto.
28. Harper, William, Private, B Company, 13th (S.H.) Black Watch; Combs Croft.
29. Henderson, George, Private, No 436, 35th Labour Group; son of Mr George Henderson, Kentywards.
30. Henderson, Robert, Trooper, 1/2nd Scottish Horse; discharged as result of an accident; ditto.
31. Inglis, James, Sergeant, No 2208361, 41st Company Canadian Forestry Corps; stepson of Mr Alex. Jamieson, Blackhillock.
32. Inglis, Alexander T, Private, No 230121, K.O.S.B.; Demobilised; son of Mr W. Inglis, Wardleys.
33. Ingram, Alexander, Private, No 315634, C Company, 13th (S.H.) Black Watch; son of Mr A. Ingram, Stripeside.
34. Ingram, James, Private, No 58948, 3/6th Gordon Highlanders, M.G.C.; died of wounds, 22nd August 1917; son of Mr James Ingram, Upper Craibstone.
35. Ingram, John McKenzie, Private, No 20101, No 1 Company, 4th Battalion Grenadier Guards; brother of Mr A Ingram, Stripeside.

36. Lawrence, John, Farrier, No 316244, Divisional Headquarters, Anzacs, Palestine; son of Mr John Lawrence, Hillhead.
37. Longmore, Herbert, J, Private, S/24006, D Company, 7th Battalion Seaforth Highlanders; son of Mr John Longmore, Cottartown.
38. Longmore, William, A, Corporal, No 204592, A Company, 6th Battalion, Dorsets; ditto.
39. Maitland, James, Private, No 25283, D Company, 4th Battalion Gordon Highlanders; son of Mr James Maitland, Raemoir.
40. Masson, Alexander, Private, No 340118, Motor Tractor Transport; son of Mrs Masson, Berryhillock.
41. Masson, Alexander, jun, Private No 6998, G Company, Grenadier Guards, M.G.C.; grandson of Mrs Masson, Berryhillock.
42. Milne, Rev Frank, B.D., Chaplain, Australian E.F., France; brother of Mr A Milne, Burns.
43. Milne, James, Corporal, No 316658, C Company, 13th (S.H.) Black Watch; son of Mr Milne, Burns.
44. Milton, Charles, Private, No 241507, 5th Gordon Highlanders; wounded and discharged; nephew of Mr A Milton, Weston.
45. Moggach, Henry, Trooper No 2052, 1/2nd Scottish Horse; demobilised; son of Mr A Moggach, Whiteknowes.
46. Moggach, William, Bombardier, No 645677, No 1 Section, 51st Highland D.A.C.; ditto.
47. Morrison, George, W, Private No 24966, C Company, 3rd Battalion Gordon Highlanders; son of Mr John Morrison, Clunehill.
48. Murdoch, Alistair, I, Second Lieut., 7th Gordon Highlanders; son of Mr W Murdoch, Kirktown.
49. Murdoch, James, M.M. with Bar, Sergeant, No 315526, C Company, 13th (S.H.) Black Watch; ditto.
50. Murdoch, William, Lance-Corporal, No 31107, A Company, 14th Battalion, H.L.I.; died of wounds, 12th January 1917; ditto.
51. Murray, Alexander, Private, No 59526, A Company, 24/27th Battalion Northumberland Fusiliers; killed in action, 24th October 1917; son of Mr William Murray, Hollandbush.
52. McCulloch, Alexander, Private, No S/23140, A Company, 2/14th London Scottish, France; son of Mr John McCulloch, Ardoch.
53. McGregor, Alexander, Sapper, No 420753, Canadian Expeditionary Force; wounded; son of Mr W McGregor, Kirktown.
54. McGregor, William, Sapper No S/11788, D Company, 1st Battalion Black Watch; killed in action, 19th July 1918; ditto.

55. McKay, George, Sergeant, No 151852, D Company, 4th Canadian Railway Troops; son of Mr John McKay, Berryhillock.
56. McKay, Robert, Lance-Corporal, No 6313, 77th M.G. Section, 77th Brigade, Salonika; ditto.
57. McKay, William, Lance-Corporal, No12219, 6th Battalion Gordon Highlanders; wounded and discharged; ditto.
58. Ogg, Lawrence, Private, No 17270, C Company, 1st Battalion Seaforth Highlanders, Egypt; son of Mr W Ogg, Berryhillock.
59. Paterson, John, S, Private, No 266512, G Company, 6th Battalion Gordon Highlanders; son of Mr A Paterson, late of Nether Blairock.
60. Quinn, William, Private No 220675, 10th Battalion H.L.I.; tailor in Berryhillock.
61. Raffan, Alfred, Private, No 290, A Company, 61st Battalion Australian E.F.; nephew of Mr Robert Raffan, Combs Croft.
62. Raffan, George, A, Private, No 315692, C Company, 13th (S.H.) Battalion Black Watch; ditto.
63. Reid, Herbert. W, Rifleman, No 20232, Headquarters, 3rd Battalion, 3rd N.Z.R.B., France; son of Mrs Reid, Berryhillock.
64. Ross, Alexander, Driver, No 083079, 28th Division, A.S.C. Salonika; drowned 2nd June 1917; son of Mr Ross, Kirktown.
65. Ross, James, Bombardier, No 645996, V Battery, Heavy Trench Mortars, 51st. Highland Division; ditto.
66. Rumbles, Charles, Private, No 398201, 3rd Lewis Gun Detachment, France; son of Mr A Rumbles, Muir of Squaredoch.
67. Rumbles, George, Private, No 60238, Y Company, 17th Royal Scots, France; ditto.
68. Rumbles, Frank, M.A., Corporal, No 200673, 3rd Seaforth Highlanders; son of Mr F Rumbles, Milton.
69. Rumbles, Charles, Driver, No 2977, Transport Section, 51st Gordons; son of late Mr P Rumbles, Faichyhill.
70. Rumbles, John, Sergeant, No 265904, 1/6th Gordon Highlanders; ditto.
71. Rumbles, Peter, Private, No 68131, 3rd Reserve Battalion, Wellington Regiment; ditto.
72. Rumbles, William, Private, No 427882, A Company, 15th Reserve Battalion, Canadians; ditto.
73. Russell, George, Engineer, No 3545, H.M.'s Patrol Boat Andrew King; crofter, Greens of Blairock.
74. Sim, George, Private, No 2448414, 4th Canadian Battalion; severely wounded; son of Mr George Sim, Ardoch.

75. Smith, Alexander, Corporal, No 2040, Mounted Military Police, 28th Division Headquarters, Salonika; son of Mr James Smith, Corner Croft.
76. Smith, Alexander, Lance- Corporal, D.C.M., No 9541, 76th Infantry Brigade Headquarters, France; nephew of Mr A Milton, Weston.
77. Smith, Joseph, Private, No 71311, C Company, 27th Battalion, 2nd Canadians, France; ditto.
78. Smith William, Private, No 204889, 36th Company, Canadian Forestry Corps, France; ditto.
79. Smith, Francis, Private, No 242560, Transport, 1st Gordon Highlanders; son of Mr John Smith, Poolside.
80. Smith, James, Private, No 18766, C Company, 6th Gordon Highlanders, France; ditto.
81. Smith, George, B.Sc., Lieutenant, Royal Engineers; grand-nephew of Mr George Smith, late of Upper Blairock.
82. Spence, Alexander, Private, No 14702, B Company, 3rd Gordon Highlanders; son of Mr James Spence, Craigie Croft.
83. Spence, William, Lance-Corporal, No 13367, 15th Battalion, H.L.I., France; ditto.
84. Stephen, George, Driver, No 718017, A Company, 2nd Battalion, Canadian Engineers, France; son of Mr John Stephem, Berryhillock.
85. Stephen, John, Private, No 17241, A Company, 1st Seaforth Highlanders, Egypt; son of Mrs Stephen, Kirktown.
86. Stephen, James, Mine Sweeper, drowned 13th April 1915; son of late Mr James Stephen, Berryhillock.
87. Stewart, Alexander, Private, No 1472, G Company, 1/6th Gordon Highlanders; wounded and discharged; son of Mr James Stewart, Cultain.
88. Stewart, Donald, private, No 1470, G Company, 1/6th Gordon Highlanders; killed in action 6th May 1915; ditto.
89. Stewart, George, Private, No 1473, G Company, 1/6th Gordon Highlanders; wounded and discharged; ditto.
90. Taylor, Alexander, Private, No S/8399, C Company, 1st Battalion Gordon Highlanders; died of wounds 5th April 1918; son of Mr James Taylor, Bellcroft.
91. Taylor, Alexander, J, Private, No 31719, No 5 Company, 3rd Battalion Scottish Rifles; demobilised; son of Mr A Taylor, Little Skeith.
92. Taylor, Joseph, R, Gunner, C Battery, 108th Brigade, R.F.A., B.E.F., France; ditto.

93. Taylor, Charles, Private, No 242475, A Company, 1/7th Gordon Highlanders, B.E.F., France; son of Mr Taylor, Swailend. (killed in action 14th April 1918?).
94. Taylor, George, Private, No 24707, A Company, 3rd Battalion Gordon Highlanders; son of Mr George Taylor, Backburn.
95. Thom, James, Corporal, 100th Siege Battery, R.G.A., B.E.F., France; son of Mrs Thom, Berryhillock.
96. Topp, John, Private, No 20632, B Company, 7th Battalion Gordon Highlanders; son of Mr John Topp, Berryhillock.
97. Wilson, John, Private, No 808111, 137th Battalion Canadian Expeditionary Force; wounded and discharged; son of Mrs Wilson, Kirktown.
98. Wilson, Alexander, Private, No 18402, 1st Troop, 7th Dragoon Guards, D Squadron, France; son of Mr A Wilson, Braehead.
99. Wilson, William, Private, No 3668, G Squadron, Fife and Forfar Yeomanry; ditto.
100. Wiseman, Charles, Private, No 37887, 3rd Battalion Somerset Light Infantry; son of Mrs Masson, Berryhillock.
101. Wood, Alexander, Private, No 242044, D Company, 5th Battalion Gordon Highlanders; nephew of Mrs Rumbles, Milltown.
102. Wood, Robert, Lance-Corporal, No 14018, 8th Otago Company, 2nd Brigade, N.Z.R., France; died of wounds, 30th October 1917; son of Mrs Wood, Cottarclump.
103. Wright, Walter, Lance-Corporal 1/6th Gordon Highlanders; brother of Mr W Wright, Croftgloy.

APPENDIX 26. BRIEF DESCRIPTION OF DESKFORD WORLD WAR 2 WAR DEAD

1. John (Jock) Urquhart Burns. Private. His parents lived in Mid St Keith, and he was the husband of Elsie McLean, Milton Mills. He was killed in action aged 31 when he stepped on a land mine on 28/11/44. His wife remained a widow for 60 years.
2. Alexander Rennie McConnachie. Private. He was the eldest of the 10 children of his parents, who farmed Bloomfield. He had been a Territorial while working as a joiner in Berryhillock. He was evacuated from Dunkirk, but was killed in action in North Africa, aged 23, on 30/04/43. He is remembered on his parents' gravestone.
3. William Ogilvie. Company Sergeant Major. He was born at Badenhannen and had served between 1925 and 1933 in the Gordons, including in the Khyber Pass. He re-enlisted for a 21-year term in 1937, and died in Holland, aged 37, on 25/09/44. He was in charge of 50 German POWs when more came forward under Red Cross flags which they dropped and began firing automatic weapons. CSM Ogilvie allowed his comrades to regroup by advancing alone with a Bren gun till fatally wounded. He was mentioned in dispatches. In addition to the Deskford War Memorial he is also remembered on the Fordyce one and on his parents' gravestone in Grange. His wife, Netta was not informed till 01/11/44, but already knew from Elsie, the wife of Jock Burns, who had gone to console her on hearing the news from her husband who had written home about it.

This scroll commemorates
Company Serjeant-Major W. Ogilvie
Gordon Highlanders
held in honour as one who
served King and Country in
the world war of 1939-1945
and gave his life to save
mankind from tyranny. May
his sacrifice help to bring
the peace and freedom for
which he died.

4. John (Ian) Cruikshank. Flying Officer. He was born at Little Mosside, had obtained a BSc in Agriculture and had joined the RAF Volunteer Reserve. He was killed in action, aged 22, on 19/06/44, has a military grave, and is remembered on his parents' grave in Deskford.
5. George Fordyce. Private. Lived in Drybridge, and died on 11/09/44, aged 25.
6. Marshall Simpson. Able Seaman. He had been a boarded out boy at Combs Croft. He died on 08/06/40, aged 18, when his ship, the destroyer HMS Ardent was sunk by the Gneisenau and Scharnhorst
7. James Wilson. Corporal. He was born in Aultmore and died at Hong Kong, aged 36, on 15/12/41.

APPENDIX 27. LIST OF PRIZEWINNERS AT DESKFORD SCHOOL - INCOMPLETE. (EVELYN E SHIRREN AND M EDITH BEVERIDGE)

DATE	BRANDER/DUX PRIZE	JIM MORRISON PRIZE
1911	Janet Cruikshank	
1916	Edith Cruikshank	Agnes Reid/John Morrison
1917	Agnes Reid/John Jamieson	Edith Reid/Donald Duncan
1918	Jessie Jamieson	Ella Gray/Willie Rumbles
1920	William J Scott	Helen Watson/Arthur Edwards
1921	Annie S Jamieson	Peggy Brown/George Topp
1922	Isabella Currie	
1924	Pat Gordon	
1925	Duncan Nicol	
1927	Nettie Gordon/George McIntosh	
1928	Lawrence Morris	
1930	Jessie B Inglis	
1931	Helen Currie	
1932	Janet Smith	
1933	William Robertson	
1935	Helen Ettles	May Henderson/Gordon Coull
1936	May Henderson	
1937	Margaret Davidson	
1938	George Clark	
1939	Isa McConnachie	Jeannie McLean/Ian Davidson
1940	Kenneth Fordyce	
1941	Sheila Morrison	Rosie Davidson
1942	Jessie Cumming	Jessie Cumming/George Crawford
1943	John Reid	Annie Robertson/John Taylor
1944	Louis Geddes	Edith Beveridge/William Reid
1945	William Masson	Jean Leslie/William Taylor
1946	William Reid	Sheila Coull/Donald Main
1947	Allan Milton/Leslie Boyne	Margaret Coull/James Boyd
1948	Sheila Boyne	Margaret Murray/Samuel Miller
1949	not awarded	Phyllis Ewen/James Boyd
1950	James Boyd	Elsie Smith/Alexander Rough
1951	Mary Main	Ella Smith/James Legge
1952	Ella Smith	Betty Thomson/Robert Kelman
1953	Elis Thomson	Sheila Scott/Stanley Smith
1954	Robert Kelman	Margaret Currie/Ian Sandison

1955	James Duncan	Janet Rumbles/James Duncan
1956	Anna Rumbles	Isobel Thomson/William Murray
1957	John Brown	Gladys Milne/Edwin Morrison
1958	Anne B Ewen	Anne Ewen/Colin Miller
1959	Anne B Ewen	Nora McConnachie/Raymond Murray
1960	Margaret McKenzie	Margaret E McKenzie/Peter Christie
1961	Kathryn Mitchell	
1963	Marjorie Addison	
1967	Jean Milton	

APPENDIX 28. POPULATION OF DESKFORD 1755 – 2011

Year	Population	Notes
1755	940	
1780	600	
1792	752	(male 359, female 393)
1801	610	
1811	634	
1821	693	
1831	828	
1841	860	
1851	917	(60% born in Deskford, the rest in the North East)
1861	1031	
1871	972	
1881	849	
1891	746	(147 families)
1901	714	(40% born in Deskford, the rest in the North East)
1911	696	
1921	584	
1931	541	
1951	415	
1961	349	
1971	269	
1981	196	
1991	158	
2001	183	
2011	198	

APPENDIX 29. LIST OF POST REFORMATION MINISTERS AND READERS

(Joined with (B) Banff, (C) Cullen, (F) Fordyce, (O) Ordiquhill)

Established Church Ministers
William Lawtie, 1563 – 1568 (B)
Gilbert Gardyne, 1568 – 1589 (C) (F) (O)
Alexander Hay, 1590 – 1594 (C)
Gilbert Gardyne, 1594 – 1599 (C)
George Douglas, 1601 -   (C)
Patrick Darg,   - 1627
Walter Darg, 1627 – 1650
Walter Ogilvie, 1654 – 1658
Andrew Henderson, 1659 – 1679
Patrick Innes, 1679
Alexander Gellie, 1680 – 1684
James Henderson, 1684 – 1694
John Murray, 1698 – 1719
Alexander Philip, 1720 – 1730
Walter Morrison, 1731 – 1780
Walter Chalmers, 1780 – 1828
George Innes, 1829 – 1843
James Mackintosh, 1843 – 1890
George Park, 1890 – 1931
William Brown, 1932 – 1945 (union of Established and Free Churches)
William Hamilton, 1945 – 1952
Alfred J Armour, 1952 – 1967
J T Guthrie, 1967 – 1986 (linked with Cullen)
Alexander J Macpherson, 1987 – 1997 (united with Cullen)
Melvyn Wood, 1997 – 2004
Wilma Johnston, 2004 – 2008
Douglas Stevenson, 2010 –

Readers in the Established Church
John Thain or Thom, 1567 – 1574
John Pilmuir, 1576 – 1578
Alexander Forsyith, 1578
David Henryson, 1580 – 1589
George Andersone, 1644

Free Church (and from 1901, United Free Church) Ministers
George Innes 1843 – 1851
W T Ker, 1852 – 1883
Alexander Walker, 1884 – 1887
J Morrison, 1888 – 1931

APPENDIX 30. SOME DESKFORD FARMS NO LONGER IN EXISTENCE AND OF WHICH NO VESTIGE REMAINS OR WHICH ARE RUINOUS (R)

Hellensland
Croft of Forder's Acre
Little Blairock
Wester Blairock
Cross of Ardoch
Smithyhillock
Swallowhillock
Smithstown
Malthouse Croft
Nether Clune
Bogs of Ordens
Little Ramore
Mousehillock
Burns
Nether Skeith
Harder
Tillybreedless
Little Tillybreedless
Blairock Croft
Brigend
Blackheath
Broomhaugh
Hollanbush *
Knows of Careston
Rathillock
Bognagight (Bognygeith)
Woodside
Upper Craibstone
Bogetra
Blackhillock
Upper Broadrashes
Netherseat of Aichries
Acres(Aires)of Squaredoch

Backies Croft (R)
Poolside
Poolhead
Crofthead
Upper Braeside
Braehead
Duffushillock
Lornachburn
Rottenhillock
Stripeside (R)
Todside
Craighead
Bloomfield (R)
Greystone (R)
Bellcroft (R)
Gateside
Comb's Croft
Cotter Clump (R)
Craigie Croft (R)
Bogside (R)
Wellcroft
Faichyhill X 2 (R)
Little Mosside
Upper Squaredoch
Wairdleys
Carrothead
Swailend (R)
Nether Echinaltry
Easter Skeith
Shepherd's Croft
Saughtertown
Upper Mosside

NB In addition, before agricultural improvements there were many small crofts, as small as half an acre, sub-let from tenant farmers.
*What is now known as Hollanbush was originally Hoggie Croft. The original Hollanbush was 200m downhill from the present Hollanbush

APPENDIX 31. TOTAL ACREAGE OF CROPS AND NUMBERS OF ANIMALS IN BANFFSHIRE IN 1883

<u>Acreage</u>

Wheat	166
Barley or Bere	7,432
Oats	54,415
Rye	344
Beans	152
Peas	3
Potatoes	2,534
Carrots	3
Turnips	25,072
Tares	986

<u>Animals</u>

Agricultural horses	6,392
Breeding horses	1,585
Cows or heifers in milk or calf	12,943
Cattle, two years and above	6,748
Cattle under two years	22,766
Sheep, one year and above	30,494
Sheep under one year	18,537
Pigs	4,180

APPENDIX 32. MONEY EQUIVALENTS AND WEIGHTS AND MEASURES

Money
£1 sterling	= £12 Scots
1 merk	= 13/4d Scots (⅔ £ Scots)
1 guinea	= £1:1/-
£1	= 20/- (shillings) or 240d (pennies)
1/-	= 5p
2/6d	= 12½p
5/-	= 25p
10/-	= 50p
15/-	= 75p
2.4d	= 1p

Length
1 ell	= 37 inches (37")
1 foot (1')	= 12 inches
1 yard (yd)	= 36 inches

Weight
16 ounces (oz)	= 1 pound (lb) (with some exceptions)
14 pounds	= 1 stone (st) (with some exceptions)
8 stones	= 1 hundredweight (cwt)
20 hundredweight	= 1 ton

Volume
4 lippies	= 1 peck
4 pecks	= 1 firlot
4 firlots	= 1 boll
16 (8) bolls	= 1 chalder

Area
4 roods	= 1 acre
13 acres	= 1 oxgang
8 oxgangs	= 1 ploughgate
4 ploughgates	= 1 davoch

NB Prior to the above-standardised measures, these varied enormously from place to place and for different items. Commonly used were Paris Measure, Amsterdam Measure and Linlithgow Measure amongst others, all of which were different.

APPENDIX 33. CUSTOMS OWED BY TENANTS TO LANDLORD IN DESKFORD, 1780

PROPERTY	NAME	A	B	C	D	E	F	G
LEITCHESTOWN	Jas Reid	2			10			
½ of SMITHSTOWN	Jas Reid	½			2½			2
½ of SMITHSTOWN	Robert Grant	½			2½			
INALTRY, SMITHSTOWN of COTTON	Robert Grant	4			16		3	
LITTLE CULTAIN	John Mellis	1						
½ of CARESTOWN	Wm Riddoch	1				5		1
½ of CARESTOWN	Wm Riddoch	1			12	4	21	1
Part of MEIKLE KNOWS	Wm Riddoch				1¾	4		
Part of MEIKLE KNOWS	John Reid					4		
Part of MEIKLE KNOWS	John Longmoor					3		
LITTLE KNOWS	Janet Allan	1						
ARDICOW	James Murray	1						
LITTLE ARDICOW	Alexander Murray	1		1				
MEIKLE CULTAIN	John Mellis	2			8			
Part of CROFTGLOY	James Lawrence				6			
OATHILLOCK	William Milne	1						
OATHILLOCK	James Smith				2½			
OATHILLOCK	Alexander Taylor	1			2½			
HOLLAND BUSH	John Nicol		8lb					
MAINS of SKEITH	John Peterkin	1	8lb					
BROADRASHES	Alex Reid & J Lawrence		20lb					
UPPER SKEITH	John Reid	1			5			
BACKIES	John Wright	1			5			
BOGNAGIGHT	Mr Grant, Tochieneal	1						
CLOCHMACREICH	Peter Thain	1						
UPPER TILLYBREEDLESS	Murray & Littlejohn	2	2					
NETHER TILLYBREEDLESS	James Muirson	1			15			

PROPERTY	NAME	A	B	C	D	E	H	I
CRABSTON	John Brebner	1			12			
RAMORE	James Clark	2			10			
CARROTHEAD & BROOM of SKEITH	Alex. Andrew	2	13					
BURNHEADS	James Robertson		2					
BURNHEADS	James Dougal	½	2					
BERRYHILLOCK	James Dougal		2					
BERRYHILLOCK	James Robertson		4	1				
BERRYHILLOCK	John Robertson		8	1				
KNAPPY CAUSEWAY	John Duffus			1	5			
SQUAREDOCH	William Chalmers						16	1
SQUAREDOCH	Walter Reid						16	1
SQUAREDOCH & HOUSE	George Taylor						13	
SQUAREDOCH	William Morrison			2				
SQUAREDOCH & PUBLIC HOUSE	W Taylor			1				
KIRKTOWN	Alexander Taylor	2			10	10		
FAICHYHILL	William Reid	1			5			
UPPER BLAIROCK	Thomas Duncan	3			15			
CLUNEHILL	William Watt	1						
MILL OF MILLTOWN	John Longmoor	1		1	10			
UPPER CLUNE	William Watt	1			10			

A = lambs
B = pounds of butter
C = stones of tallow
D = ells of linen
E = sheaves of straw
F = windlings of straw
G = loads of dung
H = heers (?) of yarn
I = dozen eggs

APPENDIX 34. SCOTS LAW MEANINGS IN C15th AND C16th LAND OWNERSHIP TRANSACTIONS

1. ALIENATION. The legal transfer of title of ownership to another party.
2. ASSIGNATION. Transfer of rights, eg to debts or tenancies.
3. BACK BOND. A deed qualifying, defining or amending the terms of a previous deed.
4. BOND of MANRENT. An Instrument in which a weaker man pledges to serve a stronger lord in return for protection. "He shall be friend to all his friends and foe to all his foes".
5. CHARTER. A grant of authority or rights.
6. DECREET ARBITAL. A decision or award made by an arbiter, perhaps about land ownership.
7. DE EODEM. The same.
8. DISPONE. To transfer ownership of land.
9. DISPOSITION. Formal document transferring ownership or title to land.
10. MORTIFICATION. The leaving of land to another on death.
11. PRECEPT of CLARE CONSTAT. A deed in which a superior recognises the title of the heir of a deceased vassal or tenant to enter upon the superior's land.
12. REDDENDO. A legal clause specifying what particular service is due from a vassal to a superior.
13. RETOUR. A renewal or a replacement.
14. SASINE. The delivery of feudal property, especially land.
15. TACK. A lease.
16. TACK of TEINDS. A lease of the tithe derived from the produce of land.
17. TEIND. Tithe derived from the produce of land.
18. TAILZIE. An entailment or deed by which the normal legal course of succession is replaced by one decided upon and recorded in advance.
19. WADSET. The act by which land is pledged by its owner to a creditor as security for a debt.

SOURCES

BOOKS

1. Adams IG. "Directory of Former Scottish Commonties". Scottish Records Society, Edinburgh. 1971.
2. Adams, Norman. "Hangman's Brae". Black and White Publishing. 2005.
3. Aitchison, Peter and Cassell, Andrew. "The Lowland Clearances. Scotland's Silent revolution 1760 – 1830". Tuckwell. 2003.
4. Alexander, William (ed Ian Carter). "Rural Life in Victorian Aberdeenshire". The Mercat Press, Edinburgh. 1992.
5. Alexander, William. "Notes and Sketches Illustrative of Northern Rural Life in the Eighteenth Century". David Douglas, Edinburgh. 1877.
6. Alexander, William. "The Placenames of Aberdeenshire". 3rd Spalding Club 1952.
7. Allan, John R. "North East Lowlands of Scotland". Robert Hale and Co, London. 1952.
8. Allan, Norman. "The Celtic Heritage of the County of Banff". The Moravian Press. Undated.
9. Anderson, AO. "Early Sources of Scottish History". Edinburgh. 1927.
10. Bannerman, William, AM, MD. "On the Extinction of Gaelic in Buchan and Lower Banffshire". Banffshire Journal. 1895.
11. Barclay. "The Schools and Schoolmasters of Banffshire". Banffshire Journal/EIS. 1935.
12. Barrett, John R. "The Making of a Scottish Landscape". Fonthill. 2015.
13. Barrow, GWS. "Kingship and Unity. Scotland 1000 – 1306". Edward Arnold, London. 1981.
14. Bell, Robert. "Dictionary of Scots Law". Unknown publisher. 1826.
15. Bennet, Margaret. "Scottish Customs From the Cradle to the Grave". Polygon. 1992.
16. Brown, NA. "The Ruin of Craibstone Limekilns, Deskford" Scottish Vernacular Buildings Working Group. 1996.
17. Buchan, David (ed). "Folk Tradition and Folk Medicine in Scotland: The Writings of David Rorie". Canongate Academic. 1993
18. Buchan, Jim. "A School History of Aberdeenshire". Aberdeen County Council. 1961.
19. Buchan, Jim. "In School Board days 1872 – 1919". Aberdeenshire County Council. 1972.

20. Burns, Lawrence R. "A Scottish Historian's Glossary". Scottish Association of Family History Societies. 1997.
21. Cameron, David Kerr. "The Ballad and the Plough". Victor Gollancz. 1978.
22. Cameron, David Kerr. "Willie Gavin. Crofter Man". Victor Gollancz. 1980.
23. Cameron, David Kerr. "The Cornkister Days". Victor Gollancz. 1984
24. Chalmers, Rev Walter. (ed Sir John Sinclair). "The Statistical Account of Scotland" 1791 – 1799.
25. Chamberlain, John. "Magnae Britaniae Notitia". Unknown publisher. 1716.
26. Childe, VG. "Guide to the Ancient Monuments of Scotland". Unknown publisher. 1961.
27. Clarke, George Anderson. "Deskford Parish". National Museums of Scotland. 1993.
28. Cochran, Patrick, RW. "Mediaeval Scotland". James Maclehose. 1892.
29. Cordiner, C. "Remarkable Ruins of North Britain". Peter Mazell, London. 1788.
30. Cormack, Dr AA. "Crop Failures in Scotland in 1782 and 1789" Banffshire Journal. Undated.
31. Cowan, Ian B. "The Parishes of Mediaeval Scotland". Scottish Record Society. 1967.
32. Craigie, James. "A Bibliography of Scottish Education Before 1872". University of London. 1972.
33. Cramond, W. "Reminiscences of the Old Town of Cullen. 1812 – 1818".
34. Cramond, W. "The Annals of Cullen 961-1904". WF Johnston, Buckie. 1904.
35. Cramond, W. "Annals of Banff, Vol 1". New Spalding Club. 1891.
36. Cramond, W. "Annals of Banff, Vol 2". New Spalding Club. 1893.
37. Cramond, W. "The Presbytery of Fordyce". Banffshire Journal. 1885.
38. Cramond, W. "The Church and Churchyard of Deskford". Banffshire Journal. 1885.
39. Cramond, W. "The Church of Grange". John Mitchell, Keith. 1898.
40. Cramond, W. "Illegitimacy in Banffshire". Banffshire Journal. 1892.
41. Cramond, W. "On Scots Drink". Courant and Courier, Elgin. 1896.
42. Crawford, OGS. "Topography of Roman Scotland North of the Antonine Wall". Publisher and date unknown.
43. Cunliffe, B. "The Ancient Celts". Oxford. 1997.

44. Darling, W Fraser, "The Story of Scotland". Collins. 1945.
45. Dawson, James Hooper. "New Issue of the Statistical History of Scotland". WH Lizars, London, and Samuel Highley, London. 1855.
46. Devine, TM. "The Scottish Nation 1700 – 2000". Allen Lane. 1999.
47. Dixon, Piers. "Puir Labourers and Busy Husbandmen", Birlinn/Historic Scotland. Undated.
48. Dobson, EB. "The Land of Britain. Part 6. Banffshire". Geographical Publications Ltd. 1941.
49. Donaldson, D. "A Bibliography of the Works of W Cramond MA, LLD, Schoolmaster and Antiquarian 1844 – 1907". Elgin Library. 1965.
50. Donaldson, James. "A General View of the Agriculture of the County of Banff". Thomas Ruddiman, Edinburgh. 1794.
51. Donnachie, Ian and Hewitt, George. "The Birlinn Companion to Scottish History". Birlinn. 2007.
52. Dorward, David. "Scotland's Place Names". Birlinn. 2009.
53. Duncan, AA. "Scotland: The Making of the Kingdom". Unknown publisher and date.
54. Ewing. "Annals of the Free Church, Vol 2". Unknown publisher. 1914.
55. Fenton, Alexander. "Country Life in Scotland. Our Rural Past". Birlinn. 2008.
56. Findlay, Donald. "Banffshire Churches". The Banffshire Field Club. 1994.
57. Fleet, Christopher; Wilkes, Margaret; and Withers, Charles J. "Scotland: Mapping the Nation" Birlinn/NLS. 2011
58. Gibson, Rosemary. "The Scottish Countryside". John Donald. 2007.
59. Glendinning, Miles and MacKechnie, Aonghus. "Scottish Architecture". Thames and Hudson. 2004.
60. Gordon, JFS. "Book of the Chronicles of Keith". Glasgow. 1880.
61. Gordon, Pryse Lockhart. "Personal Memoirs or Reminiscences of Men and Manners at Home and Abroad, During the Last Century". London. 1830.
62. Gordon, Mary. "John Ross of Pluscarden" Moravian Press. 1986.
63. Goring, Rosemary. "Scotland the Autobiography". Overlook Press. 2008.
64. Gouldesbrough, Peter. "Formulary of Old Scots Legal Documents". Stair Society. 1985.
65. Graham, Henry Grey. "The Social Life of Scotland in the C18th". Adam and Charles Black. 1899.

66. Grange, RMD. "A Short History of Scottish Dress". Burke's Peerage. 1966.
67. Grant and Stringer (eds). "Uniting the Kingdom? The Making of British History". Routledge. 1995.
68. Grant, Alison. "Scottish Place Names". Richard Drew Ltd. 2010.
69. Grant, James (ed). "Seafield Correspondence 1685 to 1708". Scottish History Society. 1912.
70. Grant, James LLB. "Records of the County of Banff 1660 – 1760". Aberdeen University. 1922.
71. Grant, James. "Agriculture in Banffshire 150 Years Ago". Banffshire Journal. 1902.
72. Grant, James. "Banffshire Roads". Banffshire Journal. 1905.
73. Grant, John. "The Penny Wedding". Grant and Co, London. 1836.
74. Gregor, Rev Walter. "Dialect of Banffshire". The Philological Society. 1866.
75. Gregor, Rev Walter. "An Echo of Olden Times From the North of Scotland". Unknown publisher and date.
76. Gregor, Rev Walter. "Notes on the Folklore of the North East". PFLS, London. 1881.
77. Haldane, ARB. "New Ways Through the Glens". Thomas Nelson and Sons Ltd. 1962.
78. Haldane, Elizabeth S. "The Scotland of Our Fathers". Alexander Maclehose and Co. 1933.
79. Hamilton, Rev William. "Third Statistical Account of Scotland". Collins. 1961.
80. Hay Shannon. "Boundaries of Counties and Parishes of Scotland". William Green and Co. 1892.
81. Holmes, Heather (ed). "Scottish Life and Society: Education". Tuckwell Press. 2000.
82. Horsburgh, Davie. "Gaelic and Scots in Grampian". Private. 1994.
83. Houston, R and Knox, W. "The New Penguin History of Scotland: From the Earliest Times to the Present day". Penguin. 2001.
84. Hunter, Fraser. "Beyond the Edge of Empire – Caledonians, Picts and Romans". Groam House Museum. 2007.
85. Inglis, Harry RG. "The Contour Road Book of Scotland". Gall and Inglis, Edinburgh. 1899.
86. Innes, C. "Origines Parochiales Scotiae: The Antiquities, Ecclesiastical and Territorial, of the Parishes of Scotland". Lizars. 1854.
87. Innes, Ewan J. "Scotland c1000 – 1200: The Shire, The Thane, The Sheriff and the Sheriffdom". Publisher unknown. 1994.

88. Innes, Rev George. "The New Statistical Account". Blackwood. 1845.
89. Jervaise, Andrew. "Burial Grounds and Old Buildings in the North East of Scotland with Historical, Biographical, Genealogical and Antiquarian Notes". David Douglas, Edinburgh. 1879.
90. Jillings, Karen. "Scotland's Black Death". Tempus. 2003.
91. Johnston, JKF and Robertson AW. "Bibliographica Aberdonensis". Spalding Club. 1929/30
92. Johnston, James B. BD, FR Hist S. "Place Names of Scotland". John Murray, London. 1934.
93. Johnston, Tom. "Our Scots Noble Families". Forward Publishing Co Ltd. 1909.
94. Keillar, Ian. "Romans in Moray". Moray New Horizons. 2005.
95. Larner, C, Lee,CH and McLachlan,HV. "A Source Book of Scottish Witchcraft". 1977.
96. Larner, Christina. "Enemies of God. The Witch Hunt in Scotland". Chatto and Windus. 1981.
97. Lauder, Sir Thomas Dick. "The Great Floods of August 1829". R Stewart, Elgin. 1873.
98. Lawrence, Robert Murdoch. "In Coaching Days". Banffshire Journal. 1927 (reprint)
99. Lindsay, Jean. "The Scottish Poor Law". Arthur H Stockwell Ltd. 1975.
100. Livingstone, Sheila. "Scottish Customs". Birlinn. 1996.
101. Love, Dane. "Scottish Kirkyards". Amberley. 1989.
102. Lynch, M (ed). "The Oxford Companion to Scottish History". Oxford University Press. 2001.
103. MacCannell, Daniel. "Lost Banff and Buchan". Birlinn. 2012.
104. Macdonald, James. "Place Names of West Aberdeenshire". Spalding Club. 1899.
105. Marsden, John. "Kings Mormaers Rebels". John Donald 2010.
106. Maxwell Stuart, PG. "Satan's Conspiracy: Magic and Witchcraft in C16th Scotland". Tuckwell. 2001.
107. McCaffrey, John F. "Scotland in the C19th". McMillan. 1998.
108. McGibbon and Ross. "The Ecclesiastical Architecture of Scotland From the Earliest Christian Times to the Seventeenth Century". O and T, Edinburgh. 1896/7.
109. McPherson, JM, BD. "Primitive beliefs in the North East of Scotland". Longmans Green and Co. 1929.
110. McNeill, PGB and MacQueen HC (eds). "Atlas of Scottish History to 1707". Edinburgh. 1996.

111. Menzies, Fletcher Norton. "Transactions of the Highland and Agricultural Society of Scotland, Fourth Series, Vol XV1". Blackwood. 1884.
112. Menzies, Gordon (ed). "The Scottish Nation". BBC. 1972.
113. Menzies, G (ed). "In Search of Scotland". Edinburgh. 2001.
114. Michie, Mary. "Cottar and Croft to Fermtoun". Ardo Publishing Co. Undated.
115. Mitchison, Rosalind. "Lordship to Patronage: Scotland 1603 – 1745". Edward Arnold. 1983.
116. Miller, James. "Swords for Hire. The Scottish Mercenary". Birlinn. 2007.
117. Miller, Joyce. "Myth and Magic: Scotland's Ancient Beliefs and Sacred Places". Goblinshead. 2000.
118. Murray, Harold Morrison. "Farm Life 1900 – 2000". Private. Undated.
119. Neill, AS. "A Dominie's Log". Hogarth. 1969.
120. Nicol, Norman. "Life in Scotland Until 1603". Adam and Charles Black, London. 1975.
121. Nicolaisen, WFH. "Scottish Place Names". John Donald, Edinburgh. 2001.
122. Oliver, Neil. "A History of Ancient Britain". Weidenfield and Nicolson. 2011.
123. Paton, H (ed). "Register of the Privy Council of Edinburgh". HM General Register House. 1933.
124. Payne, ML and Slater, TR. "The Making of the Scottish Countryside". Croom Helm. 1980.
125. Pennant, Thomas. "A Tour in Scotland". W Eyres, Warrington. 1774.
126. Pryde, GS. "The Burghs of Scotland: A Critical List". Unknown publisher. 1965.
127. Rennie, John. "A History of Findlater Castle". Private. 1995.
128. Robertson, J. "Collections for the Shires of Aberdeen and Banff". Unknown publisher. 1843.
129. Robertson, Rev WG, MA DD. "The Church Annals of Cullen". David Waldie, Stonehaven. 1938.
130. Scotland, James. "The History of Scottish Education, Vol 1". University of London Press. 1969.
131. Scott, Patrick W. "The History of Strathbogie". Private. 1997.
132. Seebohm, Frederic. "Tribal Customs in Scotland". Longmans Green and Co. 1902 and 1911.

133. Sellar, WDH. "Moray: Province and People". Scottish Society for Northern Studies. 1993.
134. Shepherd, Ian. "Grampian". HMSO. 1986.
135. Shepherd, Ian. "Aberdeen and North East Scotland". HMSO. 1996.
136. Simpson, Eric. "Moray Banff and Nairn" John Donald, Edinburgh. 1992.
137. Skene, William Forbes. "Celtic Scotland. A History of Ancient Alban, Vol 2". Edmonston and Douglas. 1877.
138. Skene, William Forbes. "Celtic Scotland. A History of Ancient Alban, Vol 3". Edmonston and Douglas. 1890.
139. Smith, John S and Stevenson, David (eds). "Fermfolk and Fisherfolk". Aberdeen University Press. 1989.
140. Steel, Tom. "Scotland's Story". Collins. 1984.
141. Smout. TC. "A Century of the Scottish People". Collins. 1986.
142. Smout, TC. "A History of the Scottish People 1560 – 1830". Collins. 1969.
143. Smout, TC (ed). "Scotland Since Prehistory. Natural Changes and Human Impact". Scottish Cultural Press, Aberdeen. 1993.
144. Souter, David. "General View of the Agriculture of the County of Banff". Mundell, Doig and Stevenson, Edinburgh. 1812.
145. Spence, James. "Ruined Castles: Monuments of Former Men in the Vicinity of Banff". Edmonston and Douglas. 1873.
146. Sutherland, Elizabeth. "The Pictish Guide". Birlinn. 1997.
147. Tayler, Alistair and Henrietta. "Jacobites of Aberdeenshire and Banffshire in the Forty Five". Milne and Hutchison, Aberdeen. 1928.
148. Tayler, Alistair and Henrietta. "The Ogilvies of Boyne". Aberdeen University Press. 1933.
149. Taylor, Ian. "Placenames of Scotland". Birlinn. 2011.
150. Turnock, David. "The Making of the Scottish Rural Landscape". Scholar Press, Aldershot. 1995.
151. Undesignated. "Heritage Tales". Cullen, Deskford and Portknockie Heritage Group. 1997.
152. Undesignated. "More Heritage Tales". Cullen, Deskford and Portknockie Heritage Group. 1999.
153. Unknown author. "An Act for Making and Repairing Certain Roads in the Counties of Banff, Elgin, Aberdeen and Inverness, etc". Unknown Publisher. 1804.
154. Unknown author. "Cramondiana". County Library, Elgin. 1965.
155. Unknown author. "Glossary of Gaelic Origins of Placenames in Britain". Ordnance Survey. Undated.

156. Unknown author. "Glossary of Common Gaelic and Scandinavian Elements on Maps of Scotland". Ordnance Survey. 1973.
157. Unknown author. "Antiquities of the Shires of Aberdeen and Banff". Spalding Club 1846.
158. Unknown author. "Antiquties of the Shires of Aberdeen and Banff". Spalding Club. 1847.
159. Unknown author. "Illustrations of the Topography and Antiquities of the Shires of Aberdeen and Banff". Spalding Club. 1849 and 1862.
160. Unknown author. "Illustrations of the Topography and Antiquities of the Shires of Aberdeen and Banff, Vol 2" The Spalding Club. 1867.
161. Unknown author. "Trials for Witchcraft 1596 – 1597". Spalding Club. Undated.
162. Unknown author. "Gazeteer of Scotland". Fullarton and Co, Glasgow. 1842.
163. Unknown author. "Gazeteer of Scotland, Vol 1 ". Fullarton and Co, Edinburgh, London and Dublin. 1853.
164. Unknown author. "Ordnance Gazeteer of Scotland, New Edition, Vol 2". Unknown publisher. Undated.
165. Unknown author and publisher. "Slater's Directory" 1852 – 1915.
166. Unknown author. "Banffshire Yearbook and County Directories". Banffshire Journal. 1875 – 1880.
167. Unknown Author. "Scoti Monasticon. The Ancient Church of Scotland". Unknown publisher and date.
168. Unknown author. "Regesta Regum Scottorum" Edinburgh University. 1988.
169. Unknown author. "Banffshire Yearbook 1899". Banffshire Journal. 1899.
170. Unknown author. "Banffshire Yearbook 1912". Banffshire Journal. 1912.
171. Unknown author. Index to Surnames in the 1851 Census for Banffshire, Vol 4". Unknown publisher and date.
172. Unknown author and publisher. "IRS Field Book, Deskford". 1910.
173. Unknown author. "Census 1971. County Report. Banff". HMSO. 1973.
174. Unknown author. "Northern Scotland". Centre for Scottish Studies, Aberdeen University. 1972 – 2004.
175. Unknown author. "RCAHMS National Monuments". Records of Scotland. 1997.
176. Unknown author. "The Portsoy Manuscript of 1843". Portsoy Community Council. 1993.

177. Unknown author. "Fordyce. The Garden Village". Fordyce Community Association. c 2010.
178. Unknown author. "In the Shadow of Bennachie". RCAHMS/Society of Antiquaries of Scotland. 2008.
179. Unknown author. "Libreties and identities in Mediaeval Britain and Ireland". The Boydell Press, Woodbridge. 2008.
180. Urquhart, Christine. "Mither o' the Meal Kist: A Pictorial History of Fordyce". Private. Undated.
181. Watson, Fiona. "Macbeth. A True Story". Quercus. 2010.
182. Watson, WJ. "The History of Celtic Placenames of Scotland". Blackwood. 1926.
183. Watt, William. "A History of Aberdeen and Banff". Blackwood and Sons. 1900.
184. Westwood, Jennifer and Kingshill, Sophia. "The Lore of Scotland" Random House. 2009.
185. Whittington, G and Whyte, ID (eds). "An Historical Geography of Scotland". Academic Press. 1983.
186. Whyte, Ian. "Agriculture and Society in C17th Scotland". John Donald, Edinburgh. 1979.
187. Wickham-Jones, CR. "Landscape of Scotland: A Hidden History". Tempus. 2001.
188. Wightman, Andy. "The Poor Had No Lawyers". Birlinn. 2011.
189. Wilson, Graeme (tr). "Protocol Book of George Duncansone, Notary Public, Cullen". 1558 and 1587.
190. Wilson, James. "Journal of My Life and Everyday Doings, 1879 – 81 and 1885 – 92". Scottish History Society. 2008.
191. Wooll, A. "From Pictland to Alba". Unknown publisher and date.
192. Wormold, Jenny. "Court, Kirk and Community. Scotland 1470 – 1625". Edward Arnold, London. 1981.

PAMPHLETS AND PAPERS

TBFC = Transactions of The Banffshire Field Club

CDPHG = Cullen, Deskford and Portknockie Heritage Group

1. Barclay, W. "Old Farming Conditions". TBFC. 21/12/1932.
2. Brander, Ron. "The Deskford Carnyx: Resemblance of a Swine's Head". Private. 2005.
3. Bulloch, John Malcolm. "Old Banffshire Volunteers". TBFC. 26/11/1914.
4. Cramond, W. "Excursion to Deskford". TBFC. 13/09/1884.

5. Cramond, W. "A Walk in the Churchyard of Cullen" TBFC.
6. Cramond, W. "Court Books of the Regality of Ogilvie". TBFC. 18/03/1886.
7. Cramond, W. "Tumuli in the Cullen District". TBFC. 28/03/1895.
8. Cramond, W. "Notes on Tumuli in Cullen District". Proceedings of the Society of Antiquaries in Scotland. 04/12/1897.
9. Cramond, W. "Old Scots Land Measures". TBFC. 28/06/1901.
10. Cramond, W. "Relics of the Poll Book of Banffshire". TBFC. 18/12/1903.
11. Cramond, W. "The Barony Courts of Banffshire". TBFC. 18/12/1903.
12. Davidson, B. "Hydro Electricity in Scotland". CDPHG. 1995.
13. Forbes, Mr, Macduff. "A Gamrie Farmer's Money Transactions 1760 – 1769". TBFC. 28/03/1895.
14. Grant, James. MA LLB "Agriculture in Banffshire 150 Years Ago". TBFC. 1902.
15. Grant, James. "Banffshire Roads During the First Half of the C18th" TBFC. 16/10/1905.
16. Grant, Major. "Seven Banffshire Ministers in the Revolution". TBFC. 18/04/1918.
17. Gray, Isobel M. "Churches in Cullen and Deskford". CDPHG. 1994.
18. Gregor, Rev Walter. "The Goodman's Croft". TBFC. 16/10/1884.
19. Hall, Len. "Extinct Limestone Quarry and Limekilns etc at Craibstone". CDPHG.1991.
20. Hall, Len. "Extinct Tochieneal Tileworks". CDPHG. 1991.
21. Hall, Len. "Power of the Deskford Burn". CDPHG. 1991.
22. Hall, Len. "Heritage Tales". CDPHG. 1997.
23. Huie, AC. "A Forgotten Hero". Banffshire Journal Christmas Annual. 1974.
24. Hunter, Fraser. "Excavations at Leitchestown, Deskford, Banffshire 1994". National Museums of Scotland. Privately circulated. 1995.
25. Hunter, Fraser. "Excavations at Leitchestown, Deskford, Banffshire 1995". National Museums of Scotland. Privately circulated. 1996.
26. Hunter, Fraser. "Excavations at Leitchestown, Deskford, Banffshire 1996". National Museums of Scotland. Privately circulated. 1997.
27. Innes, Alexander. "Tales From Thistleflat". Private. Undated.
28. Innes of Learney, Thomas. "The Regality of Strathisla" TBFC. 15/05/1935.
29. Johnston, Tom. "Deskford Castle".

30. Ker, Dr Alice. "Scottish Country Life 50 Years Ago". Birkenhead Literary and Scientific Society. 21/03/1910.
31. Macdonald, Mr, Buckie. "Celtic Placenames With Special Reference to Names in Banffshire". TBFC. 12/12/1882.
32. Macdonald. "Celtic Placenames in Banffshire". TBFC. 26/03/1885.
33. McPherson, Rev Dr. "Folk beliefs in North East Scotland". TBFC. 19/04/1932.
34. McPherson, Dr CS. "The Famine Years in The North East". TBFC. 11/04/1933.
35. Meneer, John. "Notes on the Moral Dissipation During the late C19th in the Parish of Deskford". CDPHG. 1996.
36. Milne, John, Atherb, Maud. "The Making of a Buchan Farm".
37. Rennie, John. "Davy's Castle, Deskford"
38. Rennie, John. "Discovery of an Old Gibbet"
39. Rennie, John. "Inaltry, Deskford"
40. Rennie, John. "TheSecret Army Bunkers at Deskford and Grange"
41. Rennie, John. "Days of Yore"
42. Rennie, John. "The Clune Gallows Site and Well"
43. Runciman, Mr. "Old Roads". TBFC. 23/03/1887.
44. Runciman, John. "Some Changes During the Century". TBFC.24/11/1892.
45. Sanderson, Margaret HB. "The Feuing of Strathisla. A Study in C16th Social History". Unknown publisher. 1974.
46. Scott Moncreiff, Sheriff. "Serfdom in Scotland". TBFC. 10/02/1882.
47. Shirran, Evelyn E and Beveridge, M Edith. "Deskford Public School". Private. 1997.
48. Smith, Alison. "Guerilla Units of the North East". Knock News. 2011.
49. Smith, W. "Deskford Now and As It Was 65 Years Ago". CDPHG. 29/01/1991.
50. Smith, W. "Clearances". CDPHG. 1991.
51. Smith, William, "Deskford". TBFC. 24/04/1884.
52. Summers, Douglas. "Interview with Mrs Beveridge". CDPHG. 04/02/1992.
53. Sutherland, Rev. G "Thanages and Their Lands". TBFC. 23/02/1888.
54. Sutherland, Rev George FSA. "Thanages". Northern Scientific Society Transactions. 1887 – 1891.
55. Sutherland, Rev. G "A Small Farm 100 Years Ago". TBFC. 31/10/1899.

56. Unknown author. "Certificate of Sheriff Under the Church of Scotland (Property and Endowment Act), 1925".
57. Unknown author, publisher or date. "Notes on the Resignation of Rev W Ker, Free Church".
58. Unknown author. " Deskford Parish Statutory List". Moray Council. Undated.
59. Unknown author. "Family Titles". Seafield and Strathspey Estates. 2008.
60. Unknown author. "The Schools Within the Presbytery of Fordyce 45 Years Ago". Education News 29/01/1887.
61. Unknown author, publisher and date. "Clay Buildings in the Lower Spey Valley".
62. Unknown author. "Application by Hugh Shearer, Ardoch, re Emigration to Canada". CDPHG. 1929.
63. Unknown author. "History of Deskford Castle". Cullen and Deskford Church. 2011.
64. Unknown author. "History and Heritage-Deskford". Cullen and Deskford Community Council. 2011
65. Unknown author. "Placenames in the Parish of Deskford". Genuki.
66. Unknown author. Invoice from Blacksmith to Mr Wright, Upper Skeith". CDPHG. 1929.
67. Unknown author. "Farm Valuation. Ordens". CDPHG. 18/05/1936.
68. Various authors. "Deskford Church Newsletters". CDPHG. 1906 – 1956.
69. Watson or Forbes, Margaret. "Deskford". CDPHG. 1975.

NEWSPAPERS

Aberdeen Free Press
Aberdeen Journal
Aberdeen Press and Journal
Banffshire Advertiser
Banffshire Herald
Banffshire Journal
Northern Scot
People's Journal
Scots Magazine

MAPS

1. 1st edition OS 25" to 1 mile 1866
2. 1st edition OS 6" to 1 mile 1867
3. Plan of Deskford Churchyard Extension 1885
4. Sketch Map showing the lines of the turnpike roads in the County of Banff 1866. Alexander Duncan County Roads Trustees. NAS.
5. Plan of the East Side of Deskford. 1771. J Burges. NAS.
6. Plan of the West Side of Deskford. 1771. J Burges. NAS.
7. Plans of the Farms of Shirralds and Ellyside with Upper and Lower Pattenbringan 1794. NAS.
8. Sketch Plan of the East side of Deskford Including the Land of Windyhills. Late C18th. NAS.
9. Sketch Plan of the West Side of Deskford. Late C18th. NAS
10. Plan of the Part of The Greenhill, Deskford Intended For Improvements 1776. NAS.
11. Plan of the East Division of the Lordship of Deskford. John Murray, Portsoy. 1858. NAS.
12. Plan of the West Division of the Lordship of Deskford. John Murray, Portsoy. 1858. NAS.
13. Reduced Plan of the Parishes of Deskford and Part of Rathven and Grange. John Murray, Portsoy. 1886. NAS
14. Sketch of Ground Between Ardoch and Baronsmill. 1839. NAS.
15. Sketch Map of Road From Summertown to Ardicow. 1839. NAS.
16. Excambion Betwixt Deskford and Birkenbog. 1829. NAS.
17. Proposed Excambion Betwixt Birkenbog and Deskford. 1860. NAS.
18. Proposed Turnpike Betwixt Lintmill and Brodiesord. 1824. NAS.
19. Sketch Plan of Area Round Clashmadin Hill. Early C18th. NAS.
20. Plan of Upper and Nether Blairock, Clunehill, Squaredoch etc. George McWilliam. 1841/42. NAS.
21. Plan of the Improvements in Aultmore. George McWilliam. 1824. NAS
22. Plan of the Farms of Inaltry, Clune and Leitchestown. George McWilliam. 1839. NAS.
23. Aberdonia and Banfia. Blaeu. 1654. NLS
24. Aberdeen, Banf, Murrey and to Inverness. Gordon. 1636. NLS
25. Strathbogie and Aenzie. Gordon. 1580. NLS

26. Topographical and Military Map of the Counties of Aberdeen, Banff and Kincardine. James Robertson. 1822. NLS.
27. Northern Parts of Aberdeen and Banffshire. John Thomson. 1832. NLS
28. Inland Revenue Maps. 1910. NAS.
29. Land Use Farm Maps. 1950s. NAS.
30. Map of Scotland. Laurence Nowell. 1561 – 1566.
31. Map of Scotland. Mercator. 1595

MISCELLANEOUS

1. Valuation Roll 1878
2. Valuation Roll 1901/2
3. Valuation Roll 1931/2
4. Valuation Roll 1961/2
5. Valuation Roll 1985
6. Cess Books 1727, 1732, 1747, 1791, 1835, 1925
7. Minutes of Parochial Board 1845 – 1895
8. Minutes of Parish Council 1895 – 1931
9. Minutes of Deskford Kirk Session 1720 onwards
10. Deskford School Log 1899 – 1970
11. Minutes of School Management Committee, District No 2 (Cullen, Deskford, Fordyce, Ordiquhill) of the Education Committee of the County of Banff 1919 – 1938
12. Minutes of Cullen Area School Management Committee 1939 – 1947
13. Accounts of the Roads Commissioners of Banffshire 1805 – 1830
14. Clock Tax Records 1798
15. Horse Tax Records 1798
16. Deskford Parish Census 1841 – 1901
17. Talk to Banffshire Field Club by Moray Burial grounds Research Group 10/09/11
18. Talk to Banffshire Field Club by John Barrett on Scotland's Rural Heritage 08/10/11
19. Banff County Freeholders book 1754 – 1830
20. Accounts of Deskford Turnpike Road Trustees 1835 – 1867

21. List of Sums Advanced by Proprietor for Building and Repairing 1856-1884
22. Assessment for Allowances to Wives and Families of Militiamen 1806-1812
23. Assessments for Commutation Act 1812
24. Book of Conversions and Customs 1780
25. Letter from William Morrison minor to the Clerk of the Society for the Propagation of Christian Knowledge, answering survey. 1755
26. Letter to Kirk of Forgue from Mr Morison
27. Documents relating to Deskford Farmers' Supply Association. c. 1915
28. Sheriff Court submission by John Clark, Hoggie
29. Accounts and triennial return of Deskford Agricultural Cooperative Society. 1924
30. Minute Book of Deskford Free Church Deacons' Court. 1885 – 1823
31. Session Register of Deskford Free Church. 1843 – 1914
32. Documents re sequestration of Robert Henderson, Oathillock. 1932
33. Documents re closure of Deskford Primary School
34. Ordnance Survey Original Name Books Scotland: Banffshire. 1866
35. Witness statements and other court documentation re the alleged attempted rape by Charles McHardy, Kirktown of Deskford. 1833
36. North Circuit Sheriff Court minutes. 1871 – 1873
37. Documents relating to the guardianship of Deskford Old Parish Church by the Ministry of Public Building and Works. 1938
38. Valuer's Field Books. Deskford. Late C19th
39. Papers and letter to the Press and Journal regarding the proposed supply of water to Cullen from Leitchestown
40. Papers and correspondence between Rev Morrison, Free Church, and the Chief Inspector of Income Tax
41. Application for exemption from Income Tax by the Deskford Parish Council. 1929
42. Parochial Minutes. Cullen, Deskford and Boyndie. 1861 – 1911
43. Application by Deskford Public Hall Committee to the Carnegie United Kingdom Trust for a grant
44. Legal papers regarding an action by the Church of Scotland General Trustees and the Minister of Deskford against the Heritors of Deskford, and others. 1927
45. Leges Inter Brettos et Scottos. C12th codification of laws by King David 1st

46. Register of Sasines. Index for Banff 1600 – 1780
47. Scottish War Memorials Project. Ann Marr
48. Register of the Great Seal of Scotland. 1306 – 1424. Vol 1
49. Registrar General. Log of Examiner's Annual Visits to Deskford. 1912 – 1959
50. 1715 charter of the Burgh of Regality of Deskford, the Barony of Findlater and the Thanedom of Boyne
51. Signatour of Resignation of the Barony of Ogilvie in favour of James, Lord Deskford. 27/04/1750
52. Seafield Inventory of the Regality of Ogilvie. c1768
53. Diary of Mrs Ethel McCombe nee Raffan, Combs Croft. 1928 – 1944
54. Diary of William McWillie, Backies. 1881 – 1888
55. Memorial for Alexander Smith in Hogie. 1755
56. Minutes of Deskford Community Association
57. Deskford Women's Guild accounts.1932 – 1950
58. Sketch of turf fence built at Greenhill of Deskford. Late C18th
59. Minutes of Deskford Mutual Improvement Society (Association). Vol 1 1856 – 1929. Vol 2 1922 – 1953
60. Detailed specification for building new farmhouse at Inaltrie. 1880
61. Autobiography of Alexander Donaldson Jr of Auchip 1838 – 1902

WEBSITES
www.rps.ac.uk
www.rcahms.gov.uk
www.scotlandsplaces.gov.uk
www.abdnet.co.uk/genuki
www.angelfire.com
www.stairsociety.org
www.workhouses.org.uk/deskford
www.stravaiging.com/places/parish/deskford
www.visionofbritain.org.uk
www.ukniwm.org.uk
warmemscot.s4.bizhat.com
www.oldroadsofscotland.com
genegenie-scotland.blogspot.com

www.cullen-deskford-church.org.uk
www.buckieheritage.org.uk
www.ndhm.org.uk
www.britishlistedbuildings.co.uk

INSTITUTIONS

Aberdeen City Archive
Aberdeen University Library
Aberdeenshire Library and Information Service
Banffshire Field Club
Cullen, Deskford and Portknockie Heritage Group
Moray Council Library Service
Moray Heritage Centre
National Library of Scotland
National Library of Scotland. Maproom
National Records of Scotland
National Archive of Scotland. Local History Collection.
Seafield Estates
Thomas Thomson House. NAS Map Repository

INDIVIDUALS

Jean Allan (nee McLean)
Stuart Black
Ian Currie
Bill Davidson
Tommy and Cathie Davidson
Willie Fordyce
Bill and Mabel Gauld
Louis Geddes
Sandy Henderson
Rachel Horberry
Alistair Mason
Alex McKay
Duncan Mclean
Ian McLean
Roy Milligan
Billy Murray
Arnold Pirie
John Rennie
John and Pamela Robertson
George Sinclair
Alison Smith
Geordie Smith
Jackie and Gladys Smith
Margaret Smith (nee McHattie)
Jimmy Stewart
Laura Stewart
Sandy and Margaret Strathdee
Willie and Jean Taylor

....and many, many more, too numerous to mention.

RECORDS NOT LOCATED

1. Deskford School Registers of Attendance and Register of Entry and Withdrawal.
2. Deskford School Log Book 1875 – 1899 (lost in the fire of 1899).
3. Deskford Turnpike Trust Minutes.
4. Deskford School Board Minutes.
5. Poor Law Registers for Deskford.
6. 1695 Poll Records for Banffshire.
7. Deskford Parish Church Communion Roll Books.*
8. Deskford Parish Church Registers of Baptism.*
9. Deskford Parish Church Session Records.*
10. Deskford Parish ChurchRegister of Proclamation of Banns.*
11. Deskford Parish Church Register of Cases of Discipline.*

* All known to have been in existence in 2004

Index

A

Aberchirder 21,39
Aberchirder School 258
Aberchirder, Thanage of 306
Abercrombie 13,14,32,78,109,164,414,480
Abercrombie of Birkenbog 414
Abercrombie of Skeith 179,180,203,213,279,303,315
Abercrombie, Alexander, Berryhillock 302,326,358
Abercrombie, Alexander, Birkenbog 302
Abercrombie, Alexander, elder, Skeith 297,304,315,316
Abercrombie, Alexander, Nether Skeith 296,302,303
Abercrombie, Alexander, Skeeth 279,329,359,360
Abercrombie, Anne, Craibston 375
Abercrombie, Col James, Glassah 278
Abercrombie, Elizabeth 296
Abercrombie, General 304
Abercrombie, George, Inaltry 296
Abercrombie, George, Pitmedden 297
Abercrombie, George, younger, Skeith 281,304,352
Abercrombie, James, Skeith 281,386
Abercrombie, James 279
Abercrombie, Janet, Little Skeith 302
Abercrombie, Janet, Nether Clune 298,299
Abercrombie, Jean 302
Abercrombie, John, Glassa 301
Abercrombie, John, Skeith 297,299,300,301
Abercrombie, Marrion, Little Skeith 302
Abercrombie, Mill of 298
Abercrombie, Sir Alexander, Birkenbog 302
Abercrombie, Sir James, Birkenbog 352
Abercrombie, Sir Robert, Birkenbog 304
Abercrombie, Thomas, Skeith, elder 187
Abercrombie, Thomas, Skeyth 164,301,352
Abercrombie, Walter, Berryhillock 302

Abercrombie, William, Over Skeith 298,300,301,352
Abercrummy, Alexander, Ardecow 300
Abercrummy, Alexander, Skordiaicht 300
Abercrummy, Hector, Arddecow 300
Aberdeen 54,106,137,146,173,176,183,219,237,262,376,386,390,432,517
Aberdeen Cathedral 151,178
Aberdeen Grammar School 383
Aberdeen Infirmary 352,353,363,379,399,447,452
Aberdeen Journal 59,63,70,312,351,466
Aberdeen Lunatic Asylum 399
Aberdeen Railway Male Voice Choir 452
Aberdeen University 217,219
Aberdeen University Bursary Competition 387
Aberdeen, Bishop of 151
Aberdeen, Bishopric of 79
Aberdeen, Catholic Church in 194
Aberdeen, Diocese of 435
Aberdeen, King's College 465
Aberdeen, Old 219
Aberdeen, Synod of 161,179,240,339,370,463,484
Aberdeenshire 39,104,228,468
Aberlour 452,481
Abernethy, Margaret 328
Abernethy, Peter, Durn 326
Act Anent the Poor 368
Act for Abolishing Heritable Jurisdictions 311
Act of Indemnity 281,386
Adam, Isobel 489
Addison, Chrissie 454
Addison, George, schoolmaster 235,239
Addison, Mr, plumber 254
Adomnan 24,318
Aedan Mac Gabrain 23
Africa 432
Aged Ministers Fund 365
Agricultural Rates Grant 357
Agricultural Unemployment Scheme 223
Aikenhillock 91
Alba 383

Alford, Presbytery of 493,494
Alice in Wonderland 264
Allan, James, schoolmaster 235
Allan, Jean (nee Mclean) 52,101
Allan, Walter 46
Allardyce family 346
Allardyce, Thomas, Alvah 346
Allardyce, C 237
Alloway 376
Alton Burn 6
Alves, Robert, schoolmaster, later Rector of Banff Academy 235,388
Alves 376,386
American War of Independence 387
Ames, Mr College of Agriculture 242
Amsterdam Measure 72
Anderson, Alexander, Crabstoun 359,372
Anderson, Alexander, Milntown of Noth 359
Anderson, Alexander 328
Anderson, Elspet, Broomie Knowe 499
Anderson, George, Leitchestown 285
Anderson, James 374,379
Anderson, James's Croft, Raemore 113
Anderson, John, Aberdeen 203
Anderson, John, Nether Blairock 270
Anderson, John, sailor 203
Anderson, Mr, Boyndie 440
Anderson, Walter, blind and lame 373,375
Anderson, William 50
Andersone, George, Cottone of Enaltre 178,324
Andrew, Alexander, Carrothead 344,489
Andrew, Ann, Carrothead 202
Andrew, Walter, Carrothead 113
Andrews, George, Carrothead 497
Angler, Mr, watchmaker, Buckie 445
Angles 267,383
Angus, Earls of 308
Angus, Minnie 174,454
Animals Act 280
Annachy 360
Anton, John 469
Antoninus Pius 21

Arbroath 290
Arbroath, Abbot and Convent of 295
Archibald, Isobel, farm servant, Darbreich 330
Ard, Alexander de, Earl of Caithness 307
Ard, Christian del 307
Ard, de, family 307
Ardicow 4,6,14,34,86,87,88,140,269,278,295,296,297,300,303,330,475
Ardicow, Little 86
Ardoch 9,13,32,34,40,44,56,58,86,87,107,261,278,295,299,307,308,321,329,332,359,415,426,453,457,476
Ardoch Cottage 91
Ardoch, Back Park of 91
Ardoch, Cross of 91
Ardoch, Cottartown of 36,39,44,148,418
Ardoch, Cottartown of, Smithy 66,137,138,147
Ardoch, Manor House of 36,412,416
Argentina 350
Argyll 267
Armour, Miss, The Manse 192
Armour, Rev Alfred J 184,254
Arnolds, Messrs 254
Association of Total Abstinence 170
Auchindoun 297
Auchinhove 21,47,48,51
Auchip, Fordyce 44,406
Auld John, Shoemaker, Berryhillock 64
Auld, George & Sons 136
Aultmore 5,11,19,28,31,34,35,36,46,58,61,70,108,113,117,118,119,123,124,140,283,288,289,326,329,330,348,380,407,432,446
Aultmore Crofts 35,90,417
Aultmore Lodge 8,44,52,143,275,311,425
Aultmore Wood 90
Aultmore, Burn of 348,427
Aultmore, Burnside of 9,91,142
Aultmore, Common of 316
Aultmore, Moss of 328,389
Australia 350
Aven, John, Pittenbringand 326
Awards for All 456

B

Backburn 91,124
Backies 4,9,34,41,46,51,63,64,85,94,120,141, 168,194,316,350,397
Backies Bridge 51
Backies Croft 41,43,92,141
Backies Mill Dam 120
Baden Powell, Col 270
Badenhannen 91,124,270
Badenyouchers 45,139
Badenyouchers, Barnyards of 101
Badminton Club 392,450,452,459
Bagrie, John, elder 187
Baillie 85
Baillie Court 200
Baillie, Katharin 373
Bain, Janet, Cottartown 492
Bain, Janet, Squaredoch 373,378
Bain, Louis, Provost, Cullen 254
Bainzie surname 382
Bainzie, Alexander, kirk officer 190,342,362
Baird, James, Banff 315
Baldwin, Stanley, miller, Berryhillock 433,438
Ballachulish 142,423
Balvenie Castle 263
Banchory 286
Banff 70,81,154,170,179,237,241,264,269, 275,327,348,350,417,438,476,491,517
Banff Academy 237,258
Banff Dean of Guild 325
Banff Egg Packing Station 126
Banff Harbour 361
Banff Links 262,264,267
Banff Lunatic Asylum 285,290
Banff Museum 29
Banff Sheriff Court 114,332,492
Banff Tolbooth 477,485
Banff, Church of 295
Banff, John George, 5th Lord 312
Banff, Lord 342
Banff, Mercat Cross 319
Banff, Sheriff of 368
Banff, Sheriffdom of 279
Banff, Summeruiftis Fair 326
Banff & Buchan Nurseries 147
Banffshire 40,44,97,104,118,122,136,150,250, 275,279,306,308,313,315,350,369,384,408, 418,468,474,483
Banffshire Advertiser 290
Banffshire Analytical Association 280
Banffshire County Council 38,44,52,294,358, 424,473
Banffshire Educational Committee 223,229, 244,253,263
Banffshire Horticultural Association 280
Banffshire Journal 207,225,290,338,353,466, 478
Banffshire Local Authority 280
Banffshire Reporter 81,289
Banffshire Sheriff Substitute 490
Banffshire, Lower 19,107,384,460
Banffshire, Mid 384
Bank of Credit and Commerce International 163
Bankhead 91
Bannockburn, Battle of 307
Barbary Pirates 360
Barber, Mr, Lanarkshire 227
Barber, Robert, farm servant, Mid Skeith 427
Barclay, George, Craibstone 285
Barclay, Gilbert, Swalbog 298
Barclay, Graham 431
Barclay, Ina 174
Barker, Alexander, Tillybreadless, elder 187, 205,329,339
Barnet, Alexander, Ardoch 343,364,376
Barnet, Alexander, Cottartown 492,496
Barnet, Alexander, Squaredoch 166
Barnet, James 487,492
Barone 91
Barons of the Exchequer 364
Baronsmill, Fordyce 476
Barony Courts 26,85,109,281,320
Bartlet, Mr, Leitchestown 377
Bass, Mr, worker, Versatile Windows 430
Battle of the Bauds 23,29,267
Bauds 20

Bay of Biscay 432
BBC Schools Broadcasts 254
BBC Wireless Station, Glasgow 238,433
Beattie, Alison 225
Beattie, W, Jr 94
Beattie's Band, Aberchirder 450
Beauly 438
Bedfordshire 388
Beidie, Helen 342
Beidie, William, Ordains 326
Bell, Adrian 456
Bell, Debbie 456
Bellcroft 35,90,91
Bellie 22,40,180
Bennett or Geddes, Mary Ann 289
Bennett, Charlie 227
Bennett, Wendy, elder 188
Benzie, George 247
Benzie, John, Shoemaker 64
Benzie, Lizzie 265
Benzie, Mr, blind lecturer, Banff 441
Benzie, William, Barone 283,468
Benzies, Alexander 286
Benzies, George 221
Benzies, Mr, Blackhillock 106
Bernard, Abbot of Arbroath, Chancellor of Scotland 307
Berryhillock 8,41,42,46,48,49,54,55,56,57,58, 63,64,65,68,69,113,123,126,131,139,193,204, 216,229,247,289,302,304,329,334,362,353, 366,416,417,418,457,482,489,502,509, 517
Berryhillock Blacksmith's Shop 446
Berryhillock Mill 9,58,59,66,93,103,133,134, 135,143,144,388,346,498
Berryhillock Mill Dam 429
Berryhillock Village 36,37,38,39
Berryhillock William & Annie Milton Fund 373
Best Kept Village Competition 456
Bethune(Beaton), Mary 201,308,385
Beveridge, J A, headmaster 54,187,220,223, 224,226,235,237,238,239,244,260,391,433,450
Beveridge, Mrs 119
Bidie, Ann, General Merchant, Backies 64
Bidie, George, Muttonbrae, Fordyce 290

Bidie, George, Surgeon General, CIE, Backies 388
Bidie, Mr, merchant, Backies 287
Bin Hill 58,75,136,260,306,462,517
Binhill Covens 517
Birkenbog 13,302
Birkenhill 14
Birlay Courts 24,25,83,109,276,277,320
Birlaymen 83,85,276,277
Birnie 20
Bishop Davie Stewart 31
Black Banks 11
Black Cairn 14,28
Black Death 77,108,109,152,268,349,392,395, 404
Black or Benzies, Bell 285
Black Rocks, Cullen 312
Black Watch 271
Black, Andrew, Little Skeith 116
Black, Barbara 284,285
Black, Betty 480
Black, Elizabeth, widow, Greenhill 490
Black, Isobel 286
Black, James, Ardoch 49,475,476
Black, James, Nether Blairock 114,200
Black, John 221
Black, Mary 469
Black, Stuart, Cultain 19
Black, Willie, Broadrashes, fiddler 388
Blackgutter Moss 11
Blackheath 91
Blackhillock 44,90,93,106,107,114,124,425,471
Blackspot Burn 6
Blairmore House, Glass 275
Blairock 9,11,34,87,108,110
Blairock Croft 89
Blairock Wells 59
Blairock, Easter 89
Blairock, Greens of 9,13,51,68,89,90,101,123, 124,140,276,428,457
Blairock, Little 89
Blairock, Nether 13,43,49,52,56,77,89,114, 140,172,269,278,303,329

Blairock, Upper 13,44,51,59,77,88,89,93,138, 143,277,285,295,298,303,329
Blairock, Wester 89,135
Blairock, Wester Greens of 68
Blanch, Doreen 443,455
Bleachfield 39,45,52,55,57,90,138,143,144, 147,256,349,416,424
Blindwells 59
Blinshell, Robert, Regality Court Clerk, Cullen 321
Bloomfield 8,35,44,68,89,90,91,93,425
Boat o' Brig 331
Boer War 249
Bogetra 90,93,124
Boggie Strype 6
Bogmuchalls 11,13,45,61,69,81,101,108,139, 242,295,303,306
Bogmuchalls Pic-Nic 439
Bognabrae 88
Bognageith 34,85,88,116,303,329
Bogrotten 9,34,57
Bogrotten, Lower 68,90,124
Bogrotten, Upper 35,90,124
Bogside 91
Boharm 376,466
Bossie's Moss 11
Bossy Hillock 7,426
Botriphnie Secondary School Badminton Club 266
Bowes, Mary, Kirktown 487
Bowie, Alf 237
Bowie, Ann 226
Bowie, Catherine 226
Bowie, Ella, Briggs 251
Bowie, Ian, Private, Secret Army, Briggs 251, 275
Bowie, Sheila 225
Boyd Neill String Orchestra 264
Boyd, Ernest, farm servant 427
Boyndie 21,154,180,269
Boyne 22,306,308
Boyne, Deanery of 152
Boyne, Forest of 306
Boyne, Mrs, audiometrician 401

Boyne, Thanage of 268,305,306,308,315
Brabner, Andrew, Crabstonne 300
Braco, William, Lord 304
Braco, William, Master of 304
Braehead 35,52,90,124,425,430
Braeside 90,148
Braeside, Upper 90
Braibner, James 300
Braidbog 9,13,30,35,43,51,52,55,59,68,90,93, 124,129,136,275,427
Brandane Fair 80
Brander Prize 237
Brander, Alexander, Shoemaker, Berryhillock 64,475
Brander, James, blacksmith 146
Brander, James, schoolmaster & session clerk 189,230,235,237
Brander, Mr, Kirktown 471
Brankanentham 29
Brannan, Mr, Lanarkshire 227
Brazil 264
Brebner surname 382
Brebner, Agnes, Oathillock 298
Brebner, George 299
Brebner, Jane 488
Brebner, John, Easter Blairock 298
Brechin 386
Bredemannschen Palace, Dresden 313
Brember, Walter, Milntoun 326
Brember, Walter, Over Pittenbringand 326
Bremner, James, Backies 339
Bremner, Jane 469
Bremner, John, Goukstone 113
Bremner, Mr 70
Bremner, W, blacksmith 445
Bremner, Walter, Berryhillock 362
Bremner, William, Braidbog 114
Bremner, William, moss grieve 61,75
Brigend 91
British Legal and United Provident Assurance Company 458
British Railways 254
Broadrashes 68,301,302,352
Broadrashes, Lower 6,43,51,89,121

Broadrashes, Upper 89,92,136,425
Brobner, Viliam, Over Skeith, elder 187
Brobner, Walter, Deskfoord, elder 187
Brodie, Janet 374
Bronton 305
Bronze Age 12,17,18,19,22,27,84,87,305,318
Brooks, D 237
Broom 304
Broomhaugh 34,91
Broomlea, Cullen 353
Brora 60
Brose Day 259
Brown, James, advocate 310
Brown, Mary 454
Brown, Mr, Newmill 130
Brown, Rev William R 176,184,211,261,294,391,451
Brown, Rev William, Chaplain, Leith Hall 494
Browster, Mr, Ardoch 114
Broxy Burn 9,34,46,275
Bruce, butcher, Cullen 67
Bruce, Elsie, Kirktown 455
Bruce, George 225,427
Bruce, Margaret 362
Bruce, Mr, farmer 334
Bruce, Mr, plant hire Ardicow and Kirktown 147
Bruce, Sheila 431
Bruce, William, merchant, Cullen 490
Bryson, William, Factor, Seafield Estate 169,191,206
Buchan 12,19,22,305,306
Buchan, Alexander, Earl of (Wolf of Badenoch), Seneschal 305,308,324
Buchan, Comyn Earls of 383
Buchan, Deanery of 152
Buchan, Earl of 152,267,305,306
Buchan, Earldom of 22
Buchan, Mormaer of 305
Buchanan, Neil, teacher 239
Buchanan-Miller, Rev R G 176
Buckie 51,66,67,103,145,147,193,219,242,253,261,264,401,438,448,452
Buckie Area School Sports 263,266

Buckie High School 219
Buckie Music Festival 260,265
Buckie Oratorio & Operatic Society 450,451
Buckie, Laird of 364
Buckie, Shore of 376
Buie, Alistair, joiner, West Manse Steadings 147
Buie, Elspet 469
Buie, Walter, Regality Court Fiscall 321
Burges, John, Kirktown 114
Burgess, Ann, lunatic pauper 284,285
Burgess, Frank, insurance agent, Slatehaugh 458
Burgess, John 284,285
Burgess, Linda, Lintmill 456
Burghead 23 267
Burn of Aultmore 9
Burn of Blairock 9,13,90
Burn of Cullen 304,306
Burn of Skeith 6
Burnheads 76,95,97,124,131,204,299,301,302,304,352,407
Burnheads, Upper 91
Burnlevnit 136,298
Burns 88
Burns Supper 441
Burns, John, Cullen 333
Burns, Robert 435
Burnsford 9,92,115,121,257,285
Burnside 13
Burnside Cottage 141
Buthergask, Ade 308

C

Cadbury's Ltd. 264.
Cain 77
Cair or Care surname 382
Cairnie, 189,237
Cairnley, Croft of 90
Caithness 376
Callander, Lt Col, SSPCA 264
Calvi, Count 390
Calvi, Roberto, Banco Ambrosiano 390

Cameron, Alexander, Darbreich, moss grieve in Old More (Aultmore) 329
Cameron, James, fisherman, Buckie 291
Cameron, James, Oathillock, elder 159,340,372
Cameron, Lewis 286
Cameron, Margaret, Little Knows 280
Cameron, Nina 174,454
Campbell, Dr Sir James, Old Cullen, factor 220, 249,292
Campbell, George, schoolmaster 235,239
Canada 389,390,490
Canadian Railway Troops 271
Carestown 6,17,19,34,44,45,86,88,94,108,113, 278,303,324,390,440
Carestown Lodge 390
Carnegie United Kingdom Trust 210,354,449
Carnyx 16,19,26,30
Caroline Cottage 42,59
Carrothead 44,46,86,89,124,140,302,304,352
Carroty Sandy 69,388
Casey, Nan 454
Castelfeild 297,305,306
Castle Albrechtsberg, Dresden 313
Castle Hill, Cullen 18,416
Cat Cairn 14,28
Cattenach, Mrs, teacher 228
Cattle Diseases Rate 354
Ce 22
Celts 22
Cenel Loairn 267
Cenel nGabrain 267
Centenary Flower Show 444
Central Banffshire Agricultural Society 280
Cess Books 280
Chaddo Moss 11
Chalmer, James 179
Chalmeris, Janet 298
Chalmers Memorial Hospital, Banff 288,353, 427,429,447
Chalmers, Alexander, Tillybreadless 270
Chalmers, George, author of "Caledonia" 388
Chalmers, George, murderer 339
Chalmers, James, roadman, Bogside 427,465
Chalmers, John, murderer 339

Chalmers, Mr, Fordyce 254
Chalmers, Mrs, Bogside 429
Chalmers, Rev Walter 33,119,165,181,198, 214,279,349,372,463
Chalmer, Walter 339
Chalmers, William John 175,465
Chalmers, William, Squaredoch 114,216
Chapel Haugh 193,194
Chapel Hill 4,194,238
Chapman, Mrs, Mid Skeith 468
Charity Meal 284
Cheddar Gorge 15
Chelsea Pensioner 431
Cheshires 271
Christian Fellowship 170
Christian Instruction of Youth 365
Christian Life & Work 365
Christie, John 143
Christie, Kathleen 174,454
Christie, Lorna 226,227
Christie, Mary, midwife 476
Christie, Mr, Ardoch 446
Christie, Mr, Smithfield, Bogmuchalls 429
Christie, Mr 253
Christie, Norman 226
Christie, Peter, engine driver 358
Christie, Sandy 443,456
Christie, William, Berryleys, headteacher, Skene school 230
Chronicler of Moray 319
Church Badminton Club 459
Church Defence Committee 168
Church Interests 365
Church Social 466
Church Youth Club 453,465
Church of Scotland Army Huts 273
Church of Scotland General Trustees 337,338
Church of Scotland, Property & Endowment Act 175
Civil Magistrate 488
Clapperton, James, schoolmaster 235,240
Clark, Agnes 221
Clark, James, Mid Skeith 220

Clark, John, Hoggie 445
Clark, Katherine 299
Clark, Margaret, Jr 469
Clark, Margaret, Sen 284,285,469,490
Clark, Miss, Backies 347
Clark, Mrs, Kirktown, school cleaner 225
Clarke, John, Hoggie 400
Clarke, Sandy, Mid Skeith 391
Clarkly Hill 20
Clashmadin 5
Claudius Gothicus 21
Clay Strype 6
Claypots 305
Clayton, Mr, heavy athlete 444
Clean, Over 35
Cleanhill 35
Cleanhill, Drybridge 384
Clerk of Works 252,254
Clerk, James Raemore, 344
Clerk, James, Jr, Raemore, 344
Clerk, Jannet, Raemore 344
Clerk, Margaret, Cullen 517
Clochan, 275
Clochmacreich 4,5,27,33,34,41,86,87,88,94, 142,143,168,194,204,277,278,295,296,297, 302,303,313,329
Clock & Watch Tax 279
Clune 6,34,43,52,56,87,93,108,110,129,143, 147,256,278,301,328,329,427
Clune Croft 89
Clune Hill 4,13,28,35,40,42,43,60,89,100,121, 137,269,278,295,299,321,325,327,329, 384,523
Clune, Mid 89
Clune, Nether 86,88,89,269,278
Clune, Over 35
Coal Fund 366,372
Coastal Main 58
Coats, James, Jr, Paisley 439
Cobane, Manis, Skordiaicht 299
Cobban, George hangman 327
Cobban, William 374
Cochrane, Miss, speech therapist 401
Cock, George, Aultmore 330
Coke, George, 114
Colonial Mission 364
Colville, Mr, Hon Sheriff Substitute, Banff 332
Comb's Croft 91
Combe, Bobby, gravedigger 390
Comfort Fund 453
Commercial Bank of Scotland, Keith 284
Commission of Supply 280,323,396
Commissioners of Supply 40,279,281,409
Commonwealth Day 263
Community Association 381,455,456
Community Fund 456
Community Hall & Centre 217,229,230,449, 454,456,457,459
Comyn Earls of Buchan 305,306,308
Congregational Soiree 465
Connell, Mrs, Domestic Science & Meals Supervisor 252
Consols 373
Constabulary Committee 280
Conveth 77
Conveth (Inverkeithney), Thanage of 306
Cook, Margaret 341,342
Cooper Park, Elgin 264
Cooper, Charles, Knows, elder 187
Cooper, John, Knows, elder 187
Cooper, Mr, inspector 107
Copland, Alexander, Craibston 113,364
Copland, Robert 373,374
Corbiecraig 13,91
Corcubion, Spain. 432.
Cordiner, C. 153,413.
Cormack, Angus, servant, Cross of Ardoch. 343.
Cornhill 54,242
Cornhill Station 441
Corrydown 13
Cottar Clump 35,44,68,90,91,92,425
Cottar Croft 90,116
Cotton Hill 4,12,29,44,45,61,75,107,136,204, 272,278,429
Coull, A 46
Coull, Alexander, Kirktown 428
Coull, Edith 237
Coull, Elizabeth 373

DESKFORD
A LOWER BANFFSHIRE PARISH
by JOHN AITKEN

SUPPLEMENTARY LIST OF SUBSCRIBERS

The Bond family, Rothes
Aileen Brown, Whyalla, Aus
Colin Brown, Scone
John Brown, Lintmill
Maria Byron, Buckie
Alisdair Campbell, Fort William
Mrs. J Christie, Portsoy
Tracey Connor, Ottaway, Aus
Elizabeth Cooper, Insch
Heather Eddie, Aberdeen
Elsie Ewen, Macduff
Gordon Hay, Dufftown
Margaret Horne, New Elgin
Meryl Ives, Deskford
Ken Kite & Dot Parley, Cullen

Lewis McConnachie, Windermere
Henry Milne, Whitehills
Margery Naylor, Edinburgh
Stef & Graeme Paton, Boston, USA
Stuart Paton, Dundee
William Peterkin, Cullen
Dawn & John Riddoch, Alton
Janet & William Riddoch, Grange
Margaret S Rumbles, Buckie
Stewart Rumbles, Mosstodloch
Joan Stewart, Fordyce
Maggie Symon, Spey Bay
The Wiseman family, Eshowe, SA
The Wiseman family, Mfolozi, SA

1880

website: www.banffshirefieldclub.org.uk
e-mail: bfc.1880@gmail.com

Coull, Elspet, Ramoir 375
Coull, George, Pattenbringan 298
Coull, Mrs, Kirktown 57
County Architect 254
County Assessments 354
County Clerk 356
County Library 253,454
County Licensing Committee 280
County Sports 260
Courage, Barbara 454
Court of Session 172,332
Coutts & Morrison, Solicitors, Banff 491
Cowgate, Edinburgh 359
Cowie, John 51
Cowie, M 237
Cowie, Miss 263
Coyll Moss 11,34,45,60
Craib, Alec, blacksmith & fabricator, Muir of Squaredoch 147,149
Craib, George, Nether Blairock 114
Craib, James, Mosside & Cottartown, elder 54,87,211
Craib, Mrs, Bankcroft 210
Craibstone 7,8,34,46,49,52,61,86,88,94,108, 124,141,278,280,303,303,305,311,316,329, 352,419,430
Craibstone Cottages 8,141
Craibstone Quarry & Lime Works 6,113,138, 139,140,141,142
Craibstone, Lower 6,41,46,48
Craibstone, Upper 76,90,92
Craig, Margaret, teacher, evacuees 275
Craigellachie 452
Craighead 68,90
Craigie Croft 90,91,92,124
Craigloy 91
Craigmyle, A D, headteacher 223,236,238,438
Cramond, Dr William 155,201
Cramond, Edinburgh 179
Cranloch Moss 11,13,34,44
Craufurde, Elizabeth 324
Creichy Burn 8
Crimean War 270
Cro 25

Croft of the Tack, Craibston 113
Croftgloy 45,84,86,87,88,90,108,113,278,303, 457
Crofthead 90
Croftriddoch 92
Crooked Roadie 43,52
Crookeshank, Agnes 374,376
Crookie Burn 204
Cruden Houses 39,55,57,424
Cruickshank family 143
Cruickshank family, Little Mosside 398
Cruickshank, Charles, Cottartown 353
Cruickshank, Eleanor 174
Cruickshank, Isabella, Berryhillock Mill, Interim Inspector of the Poor 472
Cruickshank, James, Ordens Croft 115
Cruickshank, James 344,485
Cruickshank, Janet 221
Cruickshank, Jeannie, Berryhillock 444
Cruickshank, John, Upper Blairock 377
Cruickshank, Johnne 299
Cruickshank, Milton, Berryhillock 447
Cruickshank, Miss 438
Cruickshank, R 443
Cruickshank, Rachel 174,440
Cruickshank, Robert, Berryhillock Mill 388,432, 437
Cruickshank, Robert, Inspector of the Poor 252,291,292,293,457,472
Cruickshank, Robert, Little Mosside, session clerk 90,190,273,355,390
Cruickshank, Miss, M A 222
Cuie surname 382
Cuie, Jean 487
Cullen 1,5,11,13,16,34,39,40,41,42,43,45,47, 51,52,53,54,55,58,59,60,61,66,67,68,69,74,75, 77,94,131,135,141,142,147,151,152,164,177, 178,179,181,184,189,202,215,218,219,220, 228,232,234,237,241,244,248,250,253,256, 258,259,264,269,277,278,285,306,314,319, 320,321,324,329,331,345,350,351,385,389, 401,410,412,427,430,440,451,452,459,463, 468,474,482,489,502
Cullen Area School Management Committee 224

Cullen Burn 9,42
Cullen Fire Brigade 430
Cullen Fishers' Widows 376,378
Cullen Golf Course 312
Cullen Golf Pavilion 450
Cullen Higher Grade School 265
Cullen House 11,20,56,61,281,312,315,359, 413
Cullen House Fete 260
Cullen Jail 327
Cullen Kirk Session 490
Cullen Labour Exchange 224
Cullen Links 260
Cullen Mart 243,246,330
Cullen of Boyne 306
Cullen of Buchan 306
Cullen Police 428
Cullen Policeman 334
Cullen Post Office 331
Cullen Primary School 228,248
Cullen Reading & Recreation Rooms Committee 449
Cullen Savings Bank 352
Cullen Secondary School 228,231
Cullen Square 333
Cullen Tolbooth 345
Cullen Toll Bar 47,48,425,427
Cullen Town Council 279,295,349
Cullen Town Hall 223,449,450
Cullen Water Scheme 58
Cullen, Auld Kirk 198
Cullen, Baillies & Town Council 309
Cullen, Castle Hill 18,416
Cullen, Constabulary of 33,277,278,297,312
Cullen, Old 30,42,60,315
Cullen, Seafield Arms Hotel 182,440
Cullen, Seafirld St 332
Cullen, Town Clerk 166,341
Culloden 161,269,281
Cullykhan 267
Cultain 19,43,75,87,94,120,142,278,296,297, 303
Cultain, Little 62,278,301
Cumberland, Duke of 161,269,386

Cumming, Isobel 469
Cumming, Mr, Upper Blairock 53
Cumming, William 46
Cunningham, John, Auchenharvie 310
Currie family 148
Currie family, Greens of Blairock 458
Currie, A 443
Currie, Alexander 285
Currie, David 226
Currie, DG, Wester Darbreich 333
Currie, George, Greens of Blairock, private, Secret Army 275
Currie, Ian, entrepreneur, President Flower Show Committee 147,232,443
Currie, Isobel 261,262
Currie, James, Clune 452,458
Currie, Mary 174
Currie, Miss, Greenhill, sunday school teacher 192
Currie, Mr, Burnside 444
Currie, Sir George, Principal, University of Western Australia 390
Currie, William, Greenhill, Cllr MBE 54,81, 224,294,390,438
Currie, Willie, Greens of Blairock, private, Secret Army. 275.
Curries of Greenhill. 390.
Cushnie, Laird of. 493,494.
Cycling Proficiency Test. 264.

D

Daier, John & Huiey. 374.
Dakar 432
Dal Riata 23
Dalgarno, George, Craibstone Cottages 252
Dalgarno, Henry, organ blower 466
Dame School 38,216,229,230
Dapple 137
Darbreich 9,13,34,39,43,198,304,331,349,517
Darbreich Burn 9,142
Darbreich, Briggs of 9,13,51,68,142,257
Darbreich, Easter 13,68,142
Darbreich, Wester 13,68

Darchailye 309
Darg, Rev Patrick 178,324
Darg, Rev Walter 178,179
Darling Mr, Conservative candidate 280,281
Dason surname 382
Dason, Alexander, Over Tilliebreidless 326
Dason, James, Upper Tillybreedless 339
Davidson, Agnes 373
Davidson, Alexander, Braeside 429
Davidson, Alexander, Dallachy 298
Davidson, Cathy 442,443,454
Davidson, Ian, Ardoch 458
Davidson, Ian 226,237
Davidson, Isobel, Clun 373,375
Davidson, James, elder 342
Davidson, Janet, Over Skeith 200,328
Davidson, John, elder & treasurer 189
Davidson, John 114
Davidson, Margaret Bella, Burnheads 485
Davidson, Margaret, Berryhillock 376
Davidson, Marjory 328
Davidson, MLF, Cullen 271
Davidson, Mr, electrician, Cullen 211
Davidson, Robert, trapper, Aultmore 333,427
Davidson, Robert 374
Davidson, Tommy, Aultmore 401,443
Davie's Castle 9,18,30,43,275
Davie's Tower 31
Daviot 237
Dawson, Roddy 227
De Ard surname 382
Dean, Mr, contractor, Monymusk 287
Debatable Lands 296
Decius' Fort 21,387
Dempster surname 382
Deskart, Howe o' 3,4,22,87,275
Deskford Agricultural Cooperative 81
Deskford Amateur Dramatic Society 239,449, 450,451,452,453
Deskford Auxiliary Unit 274
Deskford Buffaloes Football Team 457
Deskford Burn 5,6,7,8,9,10,14,15,30,31,51,58, 59,60,86,107,108,115,116,137,138,143,144, 193,199,407,408,415,437

Deskford Estate 13,311
Deskford Ex Servicemen's Association 274
Deskford Farmers' Supply Association 81
Deskford Flower Show 249
Deskford Football Club 457
Deskford Galleries 148,149
Deskford Hill 428
Deskford Horticultural Society 238,250
Deskford Pic-Nic 434,439,440,444,457
Deskford SWRI 455
Deskford Trust 354
Deskford, Barony of 297,299,300,301,308, 324,412
Deskford, Chapel of, 152,153,309
Deskford, James, Lord, elder 187,194,359
Deskford, James, Master of 301,310
Deskford, Kirk of 40,304,308,352,385,422
Deskford, Kirktown of 36,37,123,126,303
Deskford, Lord 144,213,279,281,345,360,261
Deskford, Lordship of 305
Deskford, Miln of 369
Deskford, Moor of 20
Deskford, Newlands or Nearlands of, (Lurgbrae) 116,296,305
Deskford, Patrick, Lord 325
Deskford, Tower of 20,32,36,37,38,97,135, 137,199,277,301,308,310,321,352,412,413, 414,415,416,422
Deskford, Walter, Lord 301,303
Desson, Alexander, slater 209
Desson, Ann 287
Dick Bequest. 234.
Dingwall 438
Director of Education 222,227,254,255,259, 260,265
Disarmament Conference, Geneva 261
Division of Runrig Act, 1695 83
Dominie 37,42,229,415
Donald, Alexander 200
Donald, baker, Portsoy 67
Donald, George, Squaredoch 114
Donald, Janet, Cottartown 342
Donald, John, Skeith 343
Donald, John, Swailend 113,344

Donald, Kate, Kirktown 432
Donald, Margaret 469
Donald, Stuart, joiner, Barone 147
Donald, William, Cairstown 486
Donald, William, Swilend 344
Dorsets, 271
Dougal, James, Burnheads & Berryhillock Crofts 76,113
Dougall, Anne, Squaredoch 375
Dougall, John 359
Dougall, Jon, Squaredoch 326
Dougall, Walter, Cnappicassa (Knappycausey) 326
Dougall, William, Kirktown 375
Douglas, James, Lord 307
Douglas, Mr, peripatetic fiddler & dance teacher 240
Dounans, Aberfoyle 456
Dover 432
Dovern, James 321
Dow, James, Skeith 326
Dowgall surname 382
Dowgall, John 202
Dowgalls, Alexander 202
Dowgalls, Janet 202
Downie, fishman, Whitehills 67
Downie, William, Berryhillock 488,489
Dresden 313
Dresden City Council 313
Dresden, Church of the Three Kings 313
Drimmie, G K, Dufftown 437
Drybridge 68,69
Drysdale, Margaret, E, teacher, evacuees 239, 275
Duff of Boigs 297
Duff of Braco 315
Duff, George, Burgess, Cullen 297
Duff, George 301
Duff, John, Darbruche 309
Duff, John, Maldauid 300
Duff, John Muldavit 296
Duff, R W, Liberal candidate, later MP, 68,280, 281
Duff, Patrick, Darbreich 300

Duff, William, Squaredoch 470
Dufftown 452,466
Duffus, James, farm servant, Ordens 346
Duffus, John, Croftgloy 115
Duffus, John, Knappycausey 114
Duffus, William 114
Duffushillock 35,44,52,90,425
Dugal, John, elder & treasurer 188
Dunbar, Mr, alehouse keeper, Newmiln, Auchindoir, 493
Dunbar, Sheriff Nicolas, Durn 327
Duncan, Alexander, Berryhillock 470
Duncan, Alexander, Kirktown 220,445
Duncan, Alexander 167
Duncan, Ann H, Huntly 355,470
Duncan, Ann 158
Duncan, Anne, Upper Skeith 346
Duncan, Anne 226
Duncan, Charles 247
Duncan, Elsie. 227.
Duncan, Fraser, Treasurer, Flower Show Committee. 232,443.
Duncan, G, 443.
Duncan, George, J.P. Kirktown, Bequest, elder. 280,366.
Duncan, Gladys. 454.
Duncan, J. 227.
Duncan, James, Cottartown, elder. 187.
Duncan, James, Cunningham House Captain. 227.
Duncan, Joan. 431.
Duncan, John, Cottartown. 446.
Duncan, Maggie Bell 472
Duncan, Maggie, Cottartown 444
Duncan, Margaret, Baronsmill, Fordyce 475, 476
Duncan, Mary & Elsie, Kirktown 398
Duncan, Mr, second horseman, Langlanburn 350
Duncan, Mrs, Clochmacreich 53
Duncan, Thomas, Upper Blairock 114
Duncan, W, Woodend Cottage 443
Duncan, William, blacksmith 146
Duncan, William 364

Duncansone, John, Notary Public, Cullen 295
Dunlop, Mr, advocate, Edinburgh 282,283
Dunlop, Mr, dentist 400
Dunn, Miss, College of Education 223,242
Dunne, Walter, Rettie 298
Durn Hill 18
Durness 360,374
Dutch Bulb Garden, Cottartown 147,433
Duthaich 23
Duthie, Lizzie 247
Dyke 376
Dytach 301

E

Earl's Mill, Keith 388
Earlstown 92
Ecgfrith 23
Eclais 23
Edinburgh 147,148,180,181,189,234,236, 275,324,353
Edingight 13,45
Edmonstone family 306
Edmonstone, Margaret 307,308
Edmonstone, Sir John de 306
Education Committee 424
Education Dept Edinburgh 244
Education Rate 354
Education Scheme 364
Educational Institute of Scotland, Banffshire Branch 280
Edward or Russel, Jane, Milltown 205
Edwards, Mr 171
Egyptians (gypsies) 393
EIS Cup, school sports 266
Elbow Doups 45,59,139
Elder, Ann, Muir of Squaredoch 290
Elder, Elizabeth 469
Elgin 54,308,376,452,458
Elgin Burghs Constituency 314
Elgin Castle 31
Elgin Cathedral 324
Ellyside 58,92,144
Ely Burn 8

Empire Day 260,263
Endowment Scheme to Combat Poverty 365
England 84,112,185,207,268
English Annals 267
Enzie, Lordship of 304
Enzie, Thanage of 306
Enzie, The 22,40,75,306,325,430
Episcopal Church 168,177
Eric of the Bloody Axe 267
Espie, Alan 226
Espie, William, headteacher 226,228,235, 238,239,264
Esplin, Miss, music teacher 222
Established Church 171,172,176,212
Ettles, Helen 400
Ettles, Mrs, Blackhillock 472
European Union 95,407
Everett, Christopher, Fl Lieut 428
Ewan, Jean 487
Ewen, Alexander, Kirktown 333,428
Ewen, Ann 469
Ewen, Catherine 227
Ewen, Ethel 174,227,261,266
Ewen, George, farm servant, Bogrotten 333
Ewen, James, Milntown 175
Ewen, Jane 378
Ewin Thomas, 325
Ewin, William, Berryhillock 299
Exchequer Bonds 356

F

Faichyhill 5,13,34,80,278,303,329
Faitch, Isobel, Tillybreedless & Langlanburn 369,376,378
Falkirk Tryst 104
Farmers' Union 294
Farquhar, G 443
Farquhar, George 247
Farquhar, James, Muir of Squaredoch 290
Farquhar, Mrs, Craibstone 468
Farskane 301
Fatal Accident Enquiry 430

Fauchter spade 62
Faustina 21
Feacht 77
Fendy, Christian, converted Turk 376
Fetch, Isabel, Knows 373
Fetch, Patsy 261
Fetchie, Isobel 310
Field, The 145
Fife 234
Fife & Forfar Yeomanry 271
Fife, Earl of 47,50,305,306
File 23
Findlater 34,277,278,295,306,307,308,329 382,413
Findlater Castle 439
Findlater, Earl of 20,80,112,116,117,119,136, 156,158,159,163,164,179,180,181,189,198, 203,204,213,214,228,233,234,267,277,280, 281,301,302,303,304,305,310,311,312,314, 316,320,327,328,345,346,351,359,360,362, 363,364,369,370,371,409,412,414,415
Findlater, Laird of 324
Findlater's Hotel 313
Findlay, Alexander, tailor, Kirktown 66,357
Findlay, George, chemist, Cullen 357
Findochty 258,277,309,438
Findochtie, Broadhythe of 361
Findochty Feild 309
Findochty Good Templars 439
Finlay, Mr, Banff 106
Finnie, Ann, Fleming House Captain 227
Finnie, Mr, shopkeeper, Berryhillock 54,66
First Aid Classes 452
First Book of Discipline 368
First Statistical Account 181,468
Fischer, Johann Georg 314
Fishers' Well 60
Fishwives' Road (Fisher Road) 44,60
Flaith 23
Flake Burn 6,19,59,138
Flaws, Peter, labourer, Muir of Squaredoch 358
Fleming, Miss, Dairying & Poultry Management teacher 223

Fleming, Mr, Keith 210
Flemish Settlers 84
Fletcher, baker, Cullen 67
Fletcher, Kathleen 454
Flower Show 442,451,457
Fochabers 350,452
Forbes, Alexander 283
Forbes, Charles D, Tochieneal 80
Forbes, Isabella, Muir of Squaredoch 290,470
Forbes, Janet, Ardoch 343
Forbes, Janet 488
Forbes, John, Cross of Ardoch 343
Forbes, Miss, Cullen 438
Forbes, Mr, Free Church School teacher 239
Forbes, Mr, Raemore 49
Forbes, Robert, Old Schoolhouse, Kirktown 397,398
Forbes, Sir Christian de 307
Forboiss, Elizabeth 298
Forces Help Society 263
Forces Welcome Home Fund 448
Forder's Acre, Croft of 91
Fordice, William, Knowes 300
Fordyce 1,4,13,14,27,29,33,34,40,43,44,45, 51,52,61,76,136,151,152,153,154,155,164, 173,178,218,219,244,250,266,269,277,278, 280,296,303,304,315,316,324,340,458,475, 476,490
Fordyce & Deskford Young Farmers 122
Fordyce Academy 52,219
Fordyce Academy Sports 266
Fordyce Cemetery 309
Fordyce Church 345
Fordyce Grammar School 234
Fordyce or Raffan, Catherine 417
Fordyce Pic-Nic 439
Fordyce, Alexander, Chaplain of Cullen 178, 309
Fordyce, Hallow Fair 76,126,350
Fordyce, James, church officer 191,482
Fordyce, James, Knowis, elder 187
Fordyce, Kenneth, Flower Show Committee 232,237
Fordyce, Mr, gravedigger 292

Fordyce, Nannie 454
Fordyce, Presbytery of 152,178,182,230,239, 240,335,339,484,485,486,487,488,489,492, 493,497,502
Fordyce, William, Backburn & Rosebank 125
Fordyce, Willie, Mid Skeith 51,93,95,237
Forfar 267
Forglen 452
Forres 438
Forres Castle 31
Forsycht, Alexander, Vindehills 178,300
Forsycht, John, Vindehills 324
Forsyth, Helen 400
Forsyth, James, Regality Court Procurator Fiscall 329
Forsyth, John, farm servant, Squaredoch 333
Forsyth, Marjorie, teacher 239
Forsyth, Mr, cattleman, Backies 350
Forsyth, Nanny 174
Fortriu 22
Fowler, Alexander 494
Fowler, D 443
Fraisser, Alexander 298
France 162,267,345,350,432
Fraser, Alexander, Chamberlain of Scotland 307
Fraser, Alexander, Rottenhillock 175
Fraser, Helen 469
Fraser, James, Ardoch 202
Fraser, James, smith in Banff 202
Fraser, James 469
Fraser, Mr, mason 254
Fraser, Mr, shipwrecked 376
Fraser, Peter 394
Fraser, Pipe Major, Banff 271
Fraser, Robert 247
Fraser, widow, Grange 355,470
Fraser, Willie, postman 69
Fraserburgh 237
Fraserburgh Beach 264
Free Church 66,169,170,171,173,175,181,182, 183,186,187,191,192,193,203,211,212,230, 272,367,429,485,490,491
Free Church Deacons' Court 347

Free Church Manse 68,212
Free Church School 239
Free Church Session 170,172,176
Free Church Soiree 465
Free Church, Manse Building Fund 367
Free Church, School Building Fund 367
Free Will Offerings 366
French Burr Millwheels 134
French, Thomas 325
Fulton, Master, Kirktown 334
Furness, Ann 454
Fyndlater, Mains of 301,310
Fynlater, Galfridius de 307
Fynletter, John of that Ilk 307
Fynletter, Ricardus de 308,324
Fynletyr, Joanna de 307
Fyntie, James, Overskeith 329

G

Gaelic Language 24,87,88,108,383,384
Gairden, Marjorie, Newmill 321
Gallowhill, Grange 31
Gallows Knowe 4,28,42,321
Gallows Well 28,42,60
Gamie, Peter 46
Gamrie 267
Garden, Jim, grocer's vanman 67
Garden, William, Gordon Highlanders, POW 273
Gardiner, R 443
Gardiner, Rev, Rathven 172
Gardiner, William, schoolmaster 234
Gardner, David, Kirktown 298
Gardyne, Rev Gilbert 178,385
Garioch, Earl of 152,306
Garioch, Robert, Ardoch 362,363
Garioch, William, Ardoch 489
Garngad House Asylum, Glasgow 287
Garvock family 397
Garvock, George 247
Garvock, James, Backies 271
Gateside 35,91,124

Gatling (?), Walter 360
Gaul, George 487
Gaulcross 20,27,29,30
Gauld, Mabel 454,455
Geddes, Alexander 46
Geddes, Alexander 287
Geddes, Alexander, post runner 68
Geddes, Alexander, schoolmaster & session clerk 189,200,234,235
Geddes, Ann 287
Geddes, Brenda 225
Geddes, Charles, Daiskford 299
Geddes, Charlie, Lower Squaredoch 458
Geddes, George 488
Geddes Miss, domestic servant, Edinburgh, school cleaner 224
Geddes, Mr 224
Geddes, Mr, athlete 444
Geddes, N 237
Geddes Orchestra, Tynet 450
Gellie, Rev Alexander 179
Gelly, Patrick, Fordyce 325
General Assembly 165,168,171,460,501
General Board for Lunacy in Scotland 399
General Enclosure Act, 1661 83
General Inspector 468
Gentlemen's Magazine 393
George, Col, recruiting officer 271
Georgetown, British Guiana 432
Gerrie, Robert, Ardoch 328
Gerrie, Robert, Cottartown of Ardoch 496
Gerry, Isobel, Ardoch 202
Geytholos 15
Ghana 264
Gib, William 493
Gibb, Mr & Mrs 468
Giese, master builder, Gotha 313
Gilanne, Archibald, Cullen 352
Girl Pat 334,432
Gittings, Mrs, Oathillock 428
Glasgow 238,475
Glasgow & Edinburgh Railway 337,464
Glassaugh 302
Glassaugh, Laird of 325

Glebe Cottage 211
Glendowachie (Macduff), Thanage of 306
Glenglassaugh 105
Glenlivet 364
Glennie, Miss, youth employment officer 252
Glennie's, Newmill 53
Golden Arrow 52
Golspie 376
Goodbrand, John 298
Gordon Castle 269,441
Gordon family 310
Gordon Highlanders 271,272
Gordon John, Crabstoun 200,362
Gordon, Abercromby, schoolmaster 235
Gordon, Alexander, Pattenbringan 281
Gordon, Alexander, schoolmaster 234
Gordon, Duchess of 236
Gordon, Duke of 13,304
Gordon, Elizabeth 197,198,296,297,309,310
Gordon, Harry 299
Gordon, Henry, Auchanassie 301
Gordon, James, Broadrashes 170
Gordon, James 46
Gordon, John, Berryhillock, elder 187
Gordon, John, Corrydowne 299
Gordon, John, Drumwhindle 40,279
Gordon, John, merchant & chapman, Mid Skeith 363,372
Gordon, John, Over Skeith 378
Gordon, John, younger, Thornebauk 301
Gordon, Johnny, carpenter & undertaker, Berryhillock 53,66,147,294,332,357,417,430,471,472
Gordon, Lord George 295
Gordon, Margaret 297
Gordon, Mr, dumb 375
Gordon, Mrs, Ardoch Cottages, school cleaner 224
Gordon, Pat 374
Gordon, Rev Henry, Ardersier 203
Gordon, Rev James, Rothiemay 310
Gordon, Sir John, of Deskford 297,324
Gordon, William, inventor, Broadrashes 149

Gordon, William, schoolmaster, precentor & session clerk 233,234
Gordon, William, session clerk & precentor 188,189
Gordonne, Christian 298
Gordonne, George, Faichiehill, Baillie 300
Gordonne, Margaret 300
Gordonne, Thomas, Merraik 300
Goukstone 13,40,41,48,86,92,304
Gow, Neil 388
GPO Telephone Link 256
Gracie or Wood, Barbara, Berryhillock 287,471
Graham, Mr, sufferer by fire, England 375
Grange 1,4,5,7,13,14,21,27,51,58,61,68,97, 132,167,264,269,275,304,315,321,322,336, 376,384,390,394,472
Grange Crossroads 51
Grange Kirk Session 378
Grange, Kirk of 40,41
Grant Ogilvie, Sir Lewis Alexander 314
Grant or Mitchell, Isabella Henderson 475
Grant, Alexander, factor 304,312,368
Grant, Alexander, Tochieneal 486
Grant, Charles 493
Grant, Col 372
Grant, David, Ramoir, elder 187
Grant, Dr, School Medical Officer 400
Grant, Elizabeth 497
Grant, Francis William, schoolmaster 235,282, 284
Grant, Francis, Bleachfield 333
Grant, James, Ramoir 326
Grant, James, Sheilburn 114
Grant, John, Bellcroft 445,446
Grant, John, Broom 488
Grant, John, elder 159,340
Grant, John, Free Church deacon 186
Grant, John, grieve to Crabstone, Ramore 326,329
Grant, John, Ramore 487
Grant, Laird of 309
Grant, Lewis, schoolmaster 235
Grant, Major, Banff 271
Grant, Margaret 360

Grant, Miss, Huntly, highland dancer 444
Grant, Miss, teacher 397
Grant, Rev, Ordiquhill 172
Grant, William, Bleachfield, woollen miller 145,288
Grant, William 364
Grantown-on-Spey, 314,498
Gray & Sudding, Messrs, musicians 446
Gray (Simpson), draper, Keith 67
Gray, Andrew 300
Gray, Elspet 469,490
Gray, G 237
Gray, George, Durn 326
Gray, Helen 325
Gray, James, Durn 326,327
Gray, James, editor, Morning Chronicle, London 387
Gray, Janet, Berryhillock 375,487
Gray, John, Tilliebreidless 326,327
Gray, Lizzie, Hoggie 463
Gray, Margaret, Carrothead 489
Gray, Margaret 287
Gray, Mr, Knows, violinist 444
Gray, Mr, shoemaker, Berryhillock
Gray, Mrs, Findlater, witch 517
Gray, Mrs, unofficial midwife 400
Gray, R 46
Gray, Robert 491
Gray, William, Inaltrey 187
Gray, William, shoemaker, Berryhillock 65, 355,443,457
Graye, Elspet, witch 517
Graye, Thomas, younger, Ley 298,
Green Castle, Portknockie
Greenhill 4,10,11,28,34,46,59,87,108,115, 118,136,140,147,275,297
Greenhill Farm 45,92
Greenmoss 333
Greenock 173
Greensinks moss 11
Gregor, Mary, teacher 239
Greig, Dr, Portsoy 283
Greig, Mr, linoleum supplier, Keith 211
Grey Cairn 7,27

Greystone 90,91
Grieve, Mr 263
Grimsby 432
Gudbrand, John 298
Gudbrand, Thomas 298
Guidbrand, Isobel 376
Gundestrop Cauldron, Denmark 267
Gunn, J, Chief HMI 252
Gunn, Tom & Sheree, Carestown 149,390
Gushet 86
Guthrie, Betty 174,256
Guthrie, Christian, Berryhillock 369
Guthrie, Miss, Huntly, highland dancer 444
Guthrie, Rev John T 174,177,184,256
Gyb, James 299

H

Ha' Burn 9,31,43,48,49,52,143
Ha' Hill of Minonie 31
Ha' Hillock 9,31,34,48,59,306,333,428
Ha' Hillock, Alvah 31
Hall Extension Fund 450,451
Hall, Doris 443,454
Hall, Len 443
Halyburton, David, Pitcur 310
Hamilton, Rev William 177,184,262,464
Handfasting 460,508
Happisburgh 15
Happy Harry 394
Harder 91,302,352
Harlaw, Battle of 308
Harper & Dow, merchants, Berryhillock 64
Harper, Miss 466
Harper, Mr, Assistant County Librarian 252
Harper, William, Comb's Croft 271
Harper's Croft Cullen 324
Harriet, Mr, Corporation of Glasgow 226
Hay, Alexander, Arnbath 303
Hay, Alexander, Jr, Arnbath 303
Hay, Alexander, Oathillock 115
Hay, Alexander, Over Skeith 302
Hay, Alexander 51

Hay, Andrew, Rannas 304
Hay, Dorothy 227
Hay, Gordon 17
Hay, James, elder 186
Hay, James, Meikle Knows Croft 115
Hay, James 487
Hay, Janet, Nether Clune 280
Hay, John, Bellie 493
Hay, John, Constable of Cullen 309
Hay, John 364
Hay, Miss 226,263
Hay, Mr 439
Hay, Nan 454
Hay, Rev Alexander 178
Haya, John, Pattenbringan, Constable of Cullen 295
Haye, Alexander 299
Haye, Andrew 299
Haye, George, Smychtstonne 324
Head Courts 320
Heidelberg 361
Hellensland 86,91
Hellfire Club, Portsoy 432,478
Hempseid, John, Baillie in Cullen 300
Henderson, Janet, Kirktown 488,489
Henderson, John 492
Henderson, L 443
Henderson, Mr 430
Henderson, Mr 48
Henderson, R, farm servant, Kirktown 332
Henderson, Rev Andrew 179,194,201
Henderson, Rev George, Cullen 172
Henderson, Rev James 179
Henderson, Robert, Oathillock 351
Henderson, supplicant 360
Henderson, WD, technical teacher 239
Hendry, Miss 466
Henry, Isobel 378,488
Henry, Mr, benchwork instructor 248
Henryson, David 178
Herd & McKenzie's Shipyard, Buckie 263
Herd, Andrew 179
Herd, Janet, Craibstoun 377

Herd, Margaret, Clinhill 369
Herd, Thomas, murderer 339
Herd's Burn 6
Hewitt & Co, organ builder 212
Higden, Ranulph 404
High Court, Edinburgh 331
High Glen 137
High Glen Road 330,331
Highland Folk Museum, Newtonmore 93
Highland Light Infantry 271
Highland Society Show, Aberdeen 440
Highlands & Islands Scheme 365
Hill of Inverkindling 4,14,45
Hill of Maud 40,136,315,428
Hill of Summertown 4,14,475
Hillhead 68,91,124
Hillview 35,44,426
Hilton, Alexander, Raemoir 486,492
Hilton, Walter, Ramore 378,492,493,494
Hilton 452
Hiltoun, Robert, Broom 326
Historic Scotland 196
Hitler 177,465
Hoggie 34,43,63,89,115,118,121,140,208
Hoggie Burn 6,45,51,92
Hoggie Croft 35,92
Hogmanseat (Hoggie) 301,302,304
Holburn Church, Aberdeen 272
Hollanbush 6,34,35,89,92
Holland 128
Home Guard, B Coy, !st Banffshire Battalion 223,274,453
Home Guard, Langlanburn Unit 274,453
Home Mission 364
Home, Lady 376
Horne, Robert, blacksmith 445
Horse Tax 279
Horticultural Society 440,447,449,451,452,453,455
House of Lords 172
Howie, Alexander, Grange 320
Howie, Alexander, pauper lunatic 287,399,480
Howie, Alexander 376

Howie, Forbes, Kintywaird 429
Howie, Helen 400
Howie, James, pauper lunatic 287
Howie, Jean, servant, Hoggie 494,495
Howie, John, Faichyhill 270
Huie surname 382
Huie, Alexander, Todholes & Weston 114,495,496
Huie, James, Faichyhill 80
Huie, James, Todholes & Weston 114
Hume, Mr Keith 427
Humphrey, Alexander 132
Hunter, Dr Fraser 16,19,26
Huntly 264,333
Huntly Express 288
Huntly Johnnie 64
Huntly, Erle 324
Huntly, George, Earl of, Lord of Badenoch, Forrester of Aynye(Enzie) & Boyne 309
Hurst Mr, music supervisor 252

I

Ibowe, Michael, Nigerian visitor 264
Imla, Walter 363
Imlach, Elspet, Oathillock 342
Imlach, Janet 373
Imlach, Jean 488
Imlach, William, Langlanburn 113
Inaltry 33,34,35,45,46,56,58,86,87,88,90,94,184,269,278,280,295,296,297,298,303,320,326,329,351,389,413,423
Inaltrie Castle 31,36,51,135,308,319,412,416
Inaltrie, Cottartown of 36,45,114,295,297,298
Inaltrie, Nether 296
Inaltrie, Upper 296,297
Inaltry, Bogs of 91
Inchgower Distillery 145
India 274
India Mission 364
Industrial & Provident Societies' Act, 1893 81
Inglis, James 472
Inglis, Jessie Bell, Miss, Dux, school cleaner 224,265

Inglis, Jessie, Muir of Squaredoch, housekeeper 333
Inglis, John, Berryhillock 491
Inglis, Mr, Braeside 445
Inglis, Mrs, Berryhillock 473
Inglis, Mrs, Stripeside 473
Ingram, James Upper Craibstone 76
Ingram, Jessie 247
Ingram, Jimmy, dairyman, Woodside, Portknockie 458
Ingram, K 443
Ingram, Margaret, servant Ardoch 475,476
Ingram, W 443
Ingram Miss, dressmaker, Kirktown 64
Innes of Edingight 13,40
Innes, Alexander, Pethnik 352
Innes, Cosmo 108
Innes, George, Oathillock & Ordeins 303,377
Innes, Grizel 352
Innes, James, Oathillock 303
Innes, Janet 376
Innes, John, Edingeith 304,352
Innes, Johne, Auchluncart, elder 187
Innes, Margaret, Oathillock 343,369
Innes, Mrs, teacher 228
Innes, Rev George 70,168,169,170,171,172, 181,183,199,202,214,464,490
Innes, Rev George, Jr, Cannonbie 203
Innes, Rev, Fordyce 172
Innes, Robert of that Ilk 298
Innes, Thomas, Muiryfold 40,
Inverboyndie, Church of 295
Inverness 360,438
Inverness Burghs Constituency 314
Inverurie 433
Irish Annals 267
Irish Burser 374
Iron Age 12,18,19,22,30,39,84,107,305,318, 383,404
Ironside, GK, benchwork instructor 222,430
Irowski, Sigi (Geeks), German POW 458
Ives, Meryl 148,149

J

Jacobites 281 Jaffray, Mrs, teacher 232
Jaguar Jet Aeroplane 428
Jamieson, Jane 491
Jamieson, John, MA, Blackhillick 222
Jamieson, Master John, organ blower 191,466
Jamieson, Mrs, Berryhillock 293
Jamieson, William, Drybridge 427
Jamieson, William, Tod's Cottage 355,471
Janet Bare Ars 435
Jenny's Well, Portknockie 59,463,501
Jesson, Bill 456
Jesson, Mary 443,456
Jewish Mission 365
Jim Morrison Prize 251
John Kerr's Croft, Goukstone 113
John o' Groats 431
Johnny Gib o' Gushetneuk 118
Johnson, Dr 75,386
Johnston, Alexander, Todholes 53,76,444
Johnston, Andrew, Inaltry 351
Johnston, Andrew, schoolmaster 235
Johnston, Isabella 491
Johnston, Jon, Crabstoun 326
Johnston, Judith & Tom 413
Johnston, Mr, schoolmaster 156
Johnston, Rev Wilma 184
Johnston, Todholes 482
Johnston, William, Todholes 100,391
Johnstone Miss, Horsebog, Grange 427
Johnstone, Jean 487
Joss, George beadle 191
Jubilee Hall 56,192,218,456
Justices of Peace 40,48,158,281,321,322,341, 345,346,408,482

K

Keills 37,416
Keir, Alexander, farm servant, Little Skeith 114,429
Keir, Andrew, Little Skeith Croft 116
Keir, Anne, Smithyhillock 346

Keir, James, Broadrashes, elder 187
Keir, James, Croftgloy 375,487
Keir, James, Ordens Croft 115
Keir, James, Skeith 340
Keir, Janet 497
Keir, Walter, Nether Blairock 445
Keir, Walter, Ordens 130
Keith 5,28,39,41,42,43,45,47,51,52,53,54,60, 67,70,75,77,126,132,147,177,215,220,232,237, 256,258,263,271,304,321,327,331,334,350, 376,384,401,410,452,472,517
Keith Cattle Show 246
Keith Grammar School 258
Keith Highland games 458
Keith Parish 384
Keith Parochial Board 282,283
Keith School Meals Centre 263
Keith Sports 266
Keith Station 314
Keith, Jane 469
Keith, New 117
Keithmore 295,297
Kelchyn 25
Kelman, Jimmy 121
Kelsall, Moultrie 451
Kemnay 273
Kemp, Catherine 469
Kemp's Croft 91,124
Kempcairn 277
Kempt, Jon, Knows 326
Kennedy, Mr, Director of Education 224
Ker, Dr Alice West Kirk Manse 389
Ker, Rev WT 170,172,173,183,184
Kil Burn 6,296
Kildrummie 492
Kilnhillock 30
Kinbate House, Kirktown 353
King Alexander 1st 268
King Alexander 2nd 26
King Alexander 3rd 151,176,306
King Bede the Pict 305
King David 1st 25,151,276
King David 2nd 307

King Duncan 267
King Edward 1st 24,26,267
King Edward 7th 249,292
King George 5th 249
King George 162,250,262
King Giric 150
King Indulf 33,267
King James 1st 82
King James 2nd & 7th 179
King James 3rd 309
King James 4th 435
King James 6th 185
King James 216
King Malcolm 151,268
King Memorial Hall, Grange 451
King Robert 2nd 305,307,308
King Robert the Bruce 194,306,307,308,383
King William 277
King William's Dear Years 408
King, James 489
King, Pate (Peter) 249
King's College 219
King's Touch 376
Kinkynie 23
Kinloss, Abbot & Convent of 296,297
Kintore 237
Kintywairds 6,10,89,118,328,426
Kirk Session 69,75,165,166,167,179,187,189, 190,191,198,199,200,203,216,228,233,234, 270,281,320,329,336,337,339,340,341,342, 343,344,345,351,352,359,360,361,362,364, 366,368,369,370,371,378,379,399,409,465, 477,484,488,491,492,494,495,499,501,502
Kirk Session Minutes 35,189,338,431,483
Kirkmichael 331
Kirktown 6,31,32,36,38,40,42,44,45,46 ,48, 51,52, 54,56,57,58,59,63,64,65,66,69,152, 193,214, 216,223,229,230,236,257,259,277, 289,298, 319,328,329,331,340,387,407,415, 416,418, 428,432,437
Kirktown Bridge 428
Kirktown Farm 37,45,121,125,254,461
Kitchen, Maggie, Clune 294
Kitchen, WW, Clune 53,81

Kitchener's Army 271
Knappycausey 13,34,86,89,193
Knights Templar of St John 324
Knock Stables 10
Knows 34,86,100,108,109,113,278,295,296, 300,423,429
Knows, Little 6,12,43,45,77,86,90,121,123, 278,460
Knows, Meikle 44,45,77,86,87,88,92,123,140, 209,278
Kwint, Arnaud 433

L

Lady Teachers' House, Kirktown 81,424
Ladyland, Our 194,297
Ladysbridge Asylum 53,264,391,399,472,482
Laidlaw's Mills, Keith 263
Laing, Isobel, Fachiehill 379,399
Lamb, Rev 182
Lamb, Sandy, Fordyce 130
Lanarkshire 237
Lanarkshire Holiday Camp 227
Lang, Mr, optician 401
Langlanburn 7,11,34,44,48,49,85,86,87,93,94, 143,168,316,350,416
Langmure 309
Larie, William 373
Laurence, Alexander, Croftgloy 270
Lauty, Andrew, Innaitry, elder 187
Law Hillock 27,31,34,319,320
Law of Hypothec 79
Law of the Brets & Scots 25,318
Law of the Innocents 24,318
Lawrence, Andrew, Cotton 375
Lawrence, Elspet, Berryhillock 285,469
Lawrence, Isobel, Berryhillock 285,288,469
Lawrence, James, Croftgloy 115
Lawrence, James, murder victim 160
Lawrence, James 339
Lawrence, Jean 495,496
Lawrence, Jhon, smith 359
Lawrence, John, Broadrashes 116
Lawrence, John, farrier, Hillhead 271

Lawrence, John, Free Church elder 170,186
Lawrence, John, pyper, Milntoun 280
Lawrence, Margaret, farm servant, Ardoch 330,475,476,477
Lawrence, Margaret, Swailend 287
Lawrence, Margaret 374
Lawrence, Margaret 469
Lawrence, Mr, merchant, Kirktown 200
Lawrence, Thomas, Oathillock 115,375
Lawrence, William 364
Lawson, Mr, factor 207
Lawtie family 316,413
Lawtie of Inaltry 203,213,303,352
Lawtie of Tochieneal 352
Lawtie, Andrew, Inaltrie 301
Lawtie, Rev James, Fordyce 21,33,46,180,387
Lawtie, Rev William 178
Lawtie, Thomas 325
Lawtie, William, Burgess in Cullen 325
Lawton's, organ builders 210
Ledingham, Dr, Banff 397,398
Legg, George 46
Legg, Thomas 320
Legg, William, second horseman, Backies 350
Legg's Brae 91
Leggat, nurse 398
Legge, Dovey, shoemaker, 10 Berryhillock 66, 391
Leitch, John, carpenter 445
Leitchestown 6,14,16,19,34,45,52,58,86,88, 90,93,147,269,278,295,298,301,304,328,329, 364,416
Lesley, George, schoolmaster 234
Leslie, Jim 431
Leslie, Katherine 324
Leslie, Lady Elizabeth 300,310
Leslie, Mr 180
Leslie, Robert, Findrassie 301
Leslie, William, Blarrack 324
Letterfourie 13
Lewis, Henry 251
Ley Farm 29,502
Ley, Lade of 299

Ley, Moss of 299
Leycht, Henry 299
Liberton, Edinburgh 376
Liley, Steve 28
Limer's Croft, Craibston 113
Linlithgow Measure 72,95
Linn 6
Linn Burn 6
Linny Moss 11
Lintmill 20,43,58,144,147,248,333,427
Lintmill Lodge 9,42
Lintmill Swifts Football Team 457
Littlejohn, Andrew, Tillybreedless 113,200,372
Littlejohn, Mrs, Tillybreedless 373
Livingstone, Col Sir Thomas, Old Regiment of Dragoons 269
Loanhead Wells 58
Lobban, Adam, Rathven 486
Lobban, George, gravedigger, Lornachburn 293
Lobban, James 46,49
Lobban, Miss 446
Lobban, Mr, Greystone 445
Lobban, Mrs, Kirktown, school cleaner 225
Local Authority Under Contagious Diseases 280
Logan, Mr, His Majesty's Inspector of Education 245
Logie Mar 151
Logie, John, Rector of Rathven 301
Lollius Urbicus 21
Lomond Hill 5
London 104,376
Long Wood 136
Longmore Hall, Keith 274
Longmore, Adam, Cottartown, headmaster, Auchterless school 230
Longmore, Andrew, Inaltry Croft 115
Longmore, Andrew, Jr 488
Longmore, Andrew 114
Longmore, Andrew 378
Longmore, Eleanor 221
Longmore, Isabell 471
Longmore, Isabella 355
Longmore, James, Kirktown 270

Longmore, James, Ramore 346
Longmore, John, Cottartown 187
Longmore, John, Springwells Croft, Bauds 208
Longmore, Miss Cottartown, teacher 210
Longmore, Mr 437
Longmore, Mr, Cottartown 119
Longmore, William, elder 187,282
Longmuir, Andrew Ramore of Skeith 326
Longmuir, Elspet 469
Lord Fife 13
Lord Justice Clerk 495
Lord Roberts Memorial Fund 447
Lord Roberts Workshops 263
Lord Roberts Workshops, Inverness Branch 447
Lord Seafield 75
Lords of Secret Council 297
Lords of the Treasury 337
Lorimer, James, shoemaker, Rose Cottage, Kirktown, elder 66,170,288
Lorimer, John, beadle, gravedigger & kirk officer 191
Lorimer, John, merchant, Dundee 310
Lorimer, John, Regality Court Clerk 329
Lorimer, John, shoemaker, Kirktown 64,65,443
Lorimer, Mr, vet & farrier 480
Lorimer, William, Dytach, schoolmaster 234,235
Lornach Burn 8
Lornachburn 8,51,52,91,143,425
Lorne 267
Loschwitzer Church, Dresden 314
Loschwitzer Vineyards 313
Lothians 104
Loutin' Cross, Fordyce 151
Low, John, Bleachfield 387
Lower Banffshire Football League 457
Lower Banffshire Young Farmers' Club 453
Lowson, Andrew, bell founder, Old Aberdeen 198
Lumber Jills 136,175
Lumleys 254
Lumsden 237
Lumsden, Alexander, Birkenbrewl 493

Lunacy Board 280
Lurg Brae, Greens of 92
Lurg Hill 4,5,6,27,45,57,58,61,110,139,275, 304,329,349,407,432,453
Lurg Hill Moss 11
Lurgbrae 13,14,92,116,139,316
Lurgbrae, Greens of 13,14
Lying Horse, Tomb of 14,28,45,139
Lyon, Peter, Cullen 198
Lyon, Valerie, Lintmill 455
Lythe Old Folks Home 44,147

M

Macbeth 267
Macdonald, George 439
Macdonald, Mr, Youth Employment Officer 226
Macdonald, Nelly 454
Macdonald, Rev John Scott, Queensland 184
Macduff 269,306,491
Machatie, Jean 492,493
Machatie, Margaret, Raemoir 486
Machattie, Donald, Broomie Knowe 498,499
Machattie, Elspet 374
Machattie, Peter, Clochmacreich 369
Machine Gun Companies 271
Mackay, Alexander, Free Church elder 186
Mackenzie, Jean 486
Mackenzie, Mary, Squaredoch 487
Mackie, Jane, Muir of Squaredoch 290
Mackie, Janet 378
Mackintosh, Dr Frank Innes 251
Mackintosh, Mrs (Elsey Fraser) 183,209
Mackintosh, Professor Sir Ashley 182,209,273, 388
Mackintosh, Rev James 170,171,182,214,282, 439,464,490
Mackintosh, Miss 210
Macnaughton, Mr, solicitor, Buckie 347
Macpherson, Rev Alexander 177,184
Mafia 390
Magic Ruby, The 262
Magna Carta 250

Mair, Mr, flesher, Buckie 106
Maitland, James, Raemore 389,443,444,446, 458
Malcolm Canmore 306
Malthouse Croft 92
Man, Andro, Darbreich, witch & warlock 517
Man, John, Baillie, Dundee 310
Man, John 360
Manbie, Matthew 489
Manse, The 38,42,213,214
Mantullen de Netherdale, John, Pattenbringan, Constable of Cullen 295
Mar, Earl of 152,306
Marchbank 13,92,94,316
Marischal College 219
Maritime House 149
Marliter, Stone of 28
Marnoch 171,269,275
Marquess, John, Craibstone, moss grieve in Windyhills 329
Marquis, Christian 270
Marquis, George, private, Aberdeenshire Army 270
Marquis, Janet, Tillybreadless 375
Marquis, John, Tillybreedless 113,339
Marr, George, farm servant, Mid Skeith 332
Marshall, Michael, sub-postmaster, Squaredoch 68
Martin, George, Nether Blairock 427
Martin, James, farm servant, Clune 333
Martin, Lily, Ardoch, school cleaner 225
Martin, Miss, dame school teacher 230
Mary Anne's, Kirktown 57,66,425
Mary, Queen of Scots 310
Mason, Chris 212
Mason, Joseph, loon, Langlanburn 350
Mason, Mary Anne, Knowiemuir 444
Mason, Peter 28,212
Masson, A, roadman 457
Masson, Alexander, Berryhillock, church officer, school cleaner 191,225
Masson, Mr, painter, Cullen 212
Masson, Mrs, Muir of Squaredoch 290
Mathieson, Peter, Fachiehill, Todholes & Weston 114,379,399

Maule, Jo 278
Mawer, Marjorie 297
McAllie, Mr, postman 69
McAllister, Gail 225
McAndie, James 341,342
McBain, Donald 364
McBean, Edith, teacher 239,248
McBean, Malcolm 46
McBeath, Jimmy 80
McBeath, John, Inspector of the Poor, Fordyce 288
McBride, K, Headmaster, Cullen 259
McCombie, George, Leitchestown 445
McCombie, Mr, HMI 243
McCombie, Williamina 220
McConnachie, Frank 265
McConnachie, George, Cllr, Ardoch 53,54,81, 130,209,294
Mcconnachie, Isa 237
McConnachie, Lewis 227
McCulloch, Mr, Fordyce, heavy athlete 444
McDonald, Alexander 50
McDonald, Mr, athlete 444
McDonald, Nellie 174
McGill, Dr 168
McGillivray, Mr, Inspector 107
McGregor, Lynn & David 148,149
McGregor, Mr, painter, Cullen 211
McGregor, Mr, roadman 51
McGregors, Kirktown 272
McGruer, Patrick, labourer, Portsoy 291
McHardy, Charles, lawyer, Kirktown 330,331
McHardy, Dr 292,398,400
McHattie family 166
McHattie, Alexander, carpenter, joiner & wright 146
McHattie, Alexander 431
McHattie, Dr, Cullen 429
McHattie, Isabella, teacher 239
McHattie, James, Inaltrie 429
McHattie, James, Squaredoch 270
McHattie, James 225
McHattie, John, Clunehill Croft Free Church schoolmaster 230,239

McHattie, John 46
McHattie, Maggie, Bleachfield 333
McHattie, Robert, Bleachfield 429
McHatty, Margaret 375
McHaty, James, Squaredoch 166,463
McInnes, Mr, young farmer, Australia 264
McIntosh, William 46
McIver, Miss, teacher 239,450
McKandie, William, Netherton 333
McKay, fishman, Sandend 67
McKay, Helen, Berryhillock 428
McKay, James 247
McKay, Keek 148
McKay, Mr, Oathillock 445
McKay, Mr, acting head teacher 228
McKay, Mrs 374
McKay, Sandy, Oathillock, Rector, Rothesay Academy 230
McKay, William Donald, Backburn 125
McKay, William, scourger, Cullen 325
McKenzie, baker, Cullen 67
McKenzie, James, Barone 445
McKenzie, James, Free Church deacon 186
McKenzie, Margaret 227,262
McKenzie, Miss, Wester Darbreich, sunday school teacher 192
McKenzie, Mr, photographer, Portsoy 264
McKenzie, Mr, Stripeside, school cleaner 225
McKenzie, Murdoch, Little Skeith 378
McKenzie, Nellie 220
McKinnon, AHL, architect, Aberdeen 338
McKinnon, Isabella 472
McLaren, Ann 174,455
McLaren, Bruce 443,456
McLaren, Lena, teacher 239
McLaughlan, David 492
McLaughlan, Janet 496,497
McLean, Duncan, motor engineer 36,101,143, 148,416
McLean family, Milton, 143,398
McLean, Ian, Milton Mills 38,177,274,457
McLean, J 237
McLean, John, blacksmith 444
McLean, Johnny 416

McLean, Mr, labourer 417
McLean, Stewart 227
McLean, William, Berryhillock 107,207
McLennan, Daniel, contractor, Fordyce 332
McLon, Elspet 378
McNeill, MB, Her Majesty's Inspector of Education 232
McPherson, Duncan 46
McPherson, James, freebooter 327
McPherson, James Lord Lieutenant 444
McPherson, Mona, Bleachfield 252
McPherson, Mrs, Bleachfield 252
McPherson, Sheila, Bleachfield 252
McPherson, William, Burnheads 77
McQueen, Mary, Marnoch 491
McQueen's Band, Buckie 450
McWilliam 267
McWilliam, Broomhills, Fordyce, land surveyor 206
McWillie, John 490
McWillie, Mr, Sen 194
McWillie, Willie 64,194,350,439,481
Medical Officer 398,400,471,473
Meg Pam 394
Meikleham, James, Free Church School teacher 239
Meldrum, David 180
Meldrum, Eliza, Wester Blairock 222
Meldrum, John, Wester Blairock, elder 187
Meldrum, Rev George, Aberdeen 180
Mellis, Andrew's Croft, Craibston 113
Mellis, Evelyn, school cleaner 225
Mellis, James, Over & Wester Windyhills 113, 116
Melrose, Earl of 324
Meneer, John 456
Mercator 306
Merchet 25
Merson, Jane 282,285,286
Merson, Jane 469
Merson, John Reid 282
Merson, John, Langlanburn 282
Merson, Mr, music instructor 264
Merson, Mr, Ordens 59

Merson, Mrs, Ordens 225
Mesolithic 16,19
Metcalfe, Jean 491
Michaelmas Head Court 322
Michie, C 50
Mid Croft, Goukstone 113
Milestones 48
Military School of Instruction 272
Militia 269
Militia Act 269
Milkwell Moss 11,13,34,44,58,61,70
Mill Croft (Berryhillock) 134
Mill Croft (Milltown) 115,134
Mill, Elizabeth, servant, Croftgloy 487
Mill, James, Mid Skeith 377
Mill, William, Ardoch 335
Miller, Aileen 442
Miller, Colin 147
Miller, John, architect & clerk of works, Cullen House 209
Miller, Sammy, Burnheads 77,95,124
Miller, Winnie 442,443,454
Milligan, William 271
Milltown Farm 86,115
Milltown, William 364
Miln, George, Squaredoch 80
Milne, Alexander, Burnsford 81
Milne, Alexander, Oathillock Croft 115
Milne, Alexander 364
Milne, Charles, Burnheads 77
Milne, George, hangman 327
Milne, George, Todholes & Weston 114
Milne, George 364
Milne, H 443
Milne, Isobel 227,262
Milne, James, Berryhillock Crofts 113
Milne, James, Burnheads 76,113
Milne, Jane 203
Milne, Janet 469
Milne, John, Burnsford 53,81
Milne, John 450
Milne, Miss 449
Milne, Stewart, Clune, private, Secret Army 275

Milne, Walter, Little Skeith 116
Milne, William, Mid Skeith 116,200
Milne, William 247
Milton Fund 372
Milton Mills 9,46,52,60,66,101,102,107,133, 134,135,143,148,303,327
Milton of Breadhaugh 277
Milton or Tough, Ann, Berryhillock 470
Milton, Alexander, mason, Kirktown 292
Milton, Alexander, merchant 445
Milton, Andrew, retired chief constable, Fall River, Mass, USA 366,373
Milton, Ann, Aultmore 282
Milton, Ann, Faichyhill 287,288
Milton, Elizabeth 226
Milton, Elspet 469
Milton, George, Todholls 375
Milton, George 456
Milton, Gladys 226
Milton, Isabella 437
Milton, James 247
Milton, James 379
Milton, Jane 454
Milton, Janet 373
Milton, Jean 226
Milton, Jim 226
Milton, John, servant, Nether Blairock 341
Milton, M 237
Milton, Margaret, Berryhillock 206
Milton, Margaret 226
Milton, Mr, merchant & car hire operator, Kirktown 66,291
Milton, Sandy, Livingston House Captain 227
Milton, Walter, alehouse keeper 341
Milton, Walter, kirk officer 190
Milton, widow, Fordyce 470
Milton, William, farm servant, Duffushillock 333
Milton, William, Free Church deacon 186
Milton, William, Muir of Squaredoch 290
Miltown, Andrew 492
Miltown Village 36,39,43,46,59,278,322, 329,416
Ministry of Labour 224

Ministry of Public Building & Works 199,294
Mitchell E, Mid Skeith Croft 116
Mitchell, Agnes 374
Mitchell, Andrew, slater 417
Mitchell, Ettie 227,262
Mitchell, Forbes 226,237
Mitchell, Jackie 443,456
Mitchell, James, Burnheads 76
Mitchell, James, Knows, elder 169,172,282
Mitchell, James, tailor, Berryhillock 64,481
Mitchell, Jane, Burnheads 77
Mitchell, John, Burnheads 77
Mitchell, John, Free Church School teacher 239
Mitchell, Mr 286
Mitchell, Mr 439
Mitchell, Robert, Croftgloy 430
Moderator of the General Assembly 177, 178,385
Moggach, Alexander 476,477
Moggach, Jane, farm servant, Todholes 76,391
Moggach, Jean 490
Moir, Andrew, Nether Blairock 341,342
Monboddo, Lord 387
Mons Graupius 21
Moonlight Band, Deskford 450
Moor of Balnamoon 13
Moray 12,19,22,118,268,306,384,418
Moray Council 354
Moray Firth 97
Moray Landscapes 147,148
Moray, Earl of 306
Moray, Earldom of 22
Moray, John, Earl of 308
Moray, Mormaer of 305
Morayshire Combination Poor House, Elgin 473
More, John 345
More, Sheriff 332
Morgan, Messrs & Co, Fife Keith 207
Morison, Alexander, Bossyhillock & Nether Windyhills 113,116
Morison, Colin, schoolmaster & session clerk 189,235,369
Morison, James & William, Oathillock Croft 115
Morison, James 489

Morison, John, Kirktown 114
Morison, Rev Walter 21,46,156,180,181,188, 203,234,236,386,387,498,499,534
Morison, Sarabella 203,205,236,499
Morison, Walter, Ordens 115
Mormaer 23
Morrison Educational Fund 252
Morrison or Walker, Janet 287
Morrison, Alexander, Free Church precentor 191
Morrison, Alexander, kirk officer 191,290,291, 357,482
Morrison, Alexander, merchant, Berryhillock 290,355
Morrison, Ann, Nether Blairock,elder 188,455
Morrison, Dorothy 227,261
Morrison, Edwin 222
Morrison, George, Clunehill 81,100,221
Morrison, Ian, Clunehill 100,457
Morrison, James, Carestown 115
Morrison, James, Clunehill 287
Morrison, James, Marnoch 491
Morrison, James, Nether Blairock 372
Morrison, James, School Board member 243
Morrison, Jane 454
Morrison, Jim 173,251
Morrison, John M, Clunehill 81,445
Morrison, John, Ordens Croft 115
Morrison, loon, Keith 430
Morrison, Miss 438
Morrison, Mr, HMI 243
Morrison, Mr, Ordens 432
Morrison, Mrs, Clunehill 223
Morrison, Mrs 251
Morrison, Rev James 53,171,173,175,182, 183,184,220,250,251,272,273,293,294,437
Morrison, Sergeant, Buckie 106
Morrison, Tony 227
Morrison, William, Grange 346
Morrison's Educational Fund 287
Morrison's Orchestra, Portgordon 449
Mortlach 234,267
Morton, Mr, Cullen House 442
Moss Grieve 61,75,329

Moss Marl 61,75
Moss of Bognagight 11
Moss Tolerances 61
Mosside 5,13,44,56,114,143,332,428
Mosside Burn 9,114
Mosside Park 91
Mosside, Little 90,91,122
Mosside, Upper 91
Mossy Park 119
Motor Tractor Transport 271
Motte 31
Mounth 267
Mousehillock 13,92,114
Muckle Hoose 37,42,58,148,206,207,293,413, 414,416
Muckle Spate 10,12
Muet surname 382
Muet, Janet 345
Muiry, James, tailor & grocer, Berryhillock 53, 65,66,177,357,391,427,448
Muiry, Mr, Lintmill 457
Muiry, Sir William, Secretary, Scotch Education Department 252
Mulgrue, John, farm servant, Whiteknowes 333
Mullen, Miss, Berryhillock 468
Mumbre (Montblairy), Thanage of 306
Munich 148
Munro, Alexander 287
Munro, Helen 470
Munro, Hellen, Greens of Blairock 355,470
Munro, Janet, Broadrashes 469,490
Munro, John, medical practitioner 283
Murdoch, James, Kirktown 443,446
Murdoch, M 265
Murdoch, Miss, teacher 222,250,272
Murdoch, Mrs, Berryhillock 373
Murdock, Jessie 471
Murdock, Miss, teacher, Fyvie 471
Murieson, James, Langlanburn 113
Murray, Alexander, Ardicow & Little Ardicow 115
Murray, Alexander, Aultmore 282
Murray, Alexander, Berryhillock, Headmaster, Birnie School 230

Murray, Alexander, Berryhillock 206
Murray, Billy 93
Murray, Donald 114
Murray, George, elder 171
Murray, James, Tillybreadless 363
Murray, James, younger, Ardicow, elder 187
Murray, James 201
Murray, Janet 376
Murray, John 198
Murray, John 486
Murray, Lucky, unofficial midwife, Berryhillock 206,400,504
Murray, Mr & Mrs, Little Skeith 391,450
Murray, Mr, Cultain 115
Murray, Mr, Demerara 372
Murray, Mr, Mosside 284
Murray, Mrs 359
Murray, Peter 375
Murray, Raymond 227,263
Murray, Rev John 180,201
Murray, Rev William 155,180,359
Murray, Robert, Sheilburn 114
Murray, William, elder 159
Murray, William, Jr 94
Murray, William, Kirktown 114,378
Murray, William, Mousehillock 362,364
Murray, William, Todholes & Weston 114
Mury, James, elder 159
Mutch, Georgina, lunatic pauper 288
Mutch, Miss, teacher 239
Mutual Improvement Association (Society) 238,280,353,436,438,439,441,450,451,453,478
Myreside 7,13,27,92,94,316
Myretown 13

N

Napoleon 269
National Farmers' Union 449,453
Nechtansmere 23,267
Neolithic 16,19,135
Netherdole, Thanage of 306
Nethermills 21,40

Nethertown 13,41,92,316
New Orleans 332
New Spynie 237
New Statistical Account 181,468
New Year Ball, Raemore 442
New Year's Day Foxhunt 456
New Zealand 350
Newmill 176,438
News of the World 432
Newtown 91
Nicol, Isobel 486
Nicol, James, Inaltry 115
Nicol, James, Upper Blairock 114
Nicol, John, Hollandbush 115
Nicol, John, Little Skeith 375
Nicol, Miss, College of Agriculture 242
Nicol, W, farm servant, Ardoch 332
Nicolae 306
Nicoll, David, Tullebradless 324
Nightingales Band, Portsoy 450
Niven, Mr, Mosside 446
Noble, Dr Gordon 20,30
Normans 31,84,96
Norse sagas 267
Norse 268
North East 1,10,15,16,21,22,23,40,55,95,105,113,152,155,216,218,268,305,306,318,350,371,380,381,383,384,395,396,407,467,500
North of Scotland Bank, Cullen 366
Northumbrian Annals 267
Northumbrian 268
Nowell, Laurence 306
Nuisances Removal (Scotland) Act 400
Nunnery (Convent) 38,153

O

Oakwood, The 452
Oathillock 45,46,52,84,86,88,89,94,100,108,109,113,136,172,275,278,295,298,300,303,328,423,426,428
Ogg, Lawrence 247
Ogilvie 32,78,109,306,308,310,352,382,413,415,480

Ogilvie Grant, 6th Earl of Seafield, Lord Lieut of Inverness-shire 314
Ogilvie of Boyne 201
Ogilvie of Deskford & Findlater 197,279
Ogilvie of that Ilk 277
Ogilvie, Alexander of Boyne 308,310,385
Ogilvie, Alexander of that Ilk 152,153,198,295, 296,297
Ogilvie, Alexander, Glashaugh 295,296
Ogilvie, Alexander, Reidhythe 296
Ogilvie, Alexander, Windyhills 296
Ogilvie, Andrew, vintner, Cullen 351
Ogilvie, Baillie of the Regality of 335,336,343, 345,488,494,495
Ogilvie, Barony of 277,278,311,320,321,326
Ogilvie, Elizabeth, Fordyce 517
Ogilvie, Elizabeth 310
Ogilvie, Eosabel 324
Ogilvie, George, Cloon 164
Ogilvie, George, Cullen 298,299,300
Ogilvie, George 364
Ogilvie, James, Ardaycht 299
Ogilvie, James, Blairock 187,298,301,324
Ogilvie, James, Cairstoun 300,325
Ogilvie, James, Findlater 310
Ogilvie, James, mason 360
Ogilvie, James, Nether Blairock 164,279,298
Ogilvie, James, Pattenbringan 300
Ogilvie, James, Skeith, elder 187
Ogilvie, James, Viscount Seafield 277
Ogilvie, James 301,303,324
Ogilvie, James 344
Ogilvie, James Registrar, Cullen & Deskford 390
Ogilvie, Janet, Cottartown 342
Ogilvie, John of Dun 296
Ogilvie, John, Glassaugh 325
Ogilvie, John, Miltoun 301
Ogilvie, John, Over Blairock 279,325
Ogilvie, John, Principal of Civil law, Aberdeen, envoy to France 309
Ogilvie, Johne, Berryhillock, elder 187
Ogilvie, Margaret, Berryhillock 343,344
Ogilvie, Margaret 309

Ogilvie, Mr, kirk treasurer 343
Ogilvie, Mr, merchant, Berryhillock 291
Ogilvie, Patrick, Pittenbringand 303
Ogilvie, Regality of 28,277,278,311,320,321, 326
Ogilvie, Rev Walter 179,201
Ogilvie, Robert, Ardoch 359,372
Ogilvie, Robert, Blerok 372
Ogilvie, Sir James of Churchill 164
Ogilvie, Sir James of that Ilk 277,297
Ogilvie, Sir James, 310,315
Ogilvie, Sir James, Deskford & Findlater, Provost of Banff, Constable of Cullen 308,309
Ogilvie, Sir James 180,295,296,297
Ogilvie, Sir Patrick, Inchmartine 310
Ogilvie, Sir Walter, Auchleven 308
Ogilvie, Sir Walter, Findlater & Upper Blairock 298,299,300
Ogilvie, Sir Walter, Lintrathen, High Treasurer of Scotland 308
Ogilvie, Sir Walter 308
Ogilvie, Thomas, Ardoch 358,372
Ogilvie, Thomas, Cottartown 341
Ogilvie, Thomas, Logie 305
Ogilvie, Thomas, schoolmaster & session clerk 189,234,235
Ogilvie, Walter of Ardoch 40
Ogilvie, Walter of that Ilk 295,307
Ogilvie, Walter, Ardauch 164,298,352
Ogilvie, Walter, Ardaycht 299,300,301
Ogilvie, Walter, Ardoch, baillie 321,324,325, 326,329
Ogilvie, Walter, Cairstoun, elder 187,201
Ogilvie, Walter, Jr 307
Ogilvie, Walter, Lord Ogilvie of Deskford 310
Ogilvie, Walter, Overlochan 301
Ogilvie, William, Leitchestounne 164
Ogilvie, William, Newtown 301
Ogilvie, William, Over Blairock & Clunehill, baillie 299,324
Ogilvie, William, tailor 355
Old Age Pension 471
Old Fir Hill, 5,44
Old Moss 46

Old Schoolhouse, The 230
Old Tullybody 315
Orchard Cottage 58,218,439
Orchard, The 38,204,289,328,434,439,440, 444,457
Ord surname 307
Ord, Alexander of that Ilk 297,309,324
Ord, James, Ardaycht 299
Ord, James, Miltoun 326
Ord, Janet, Ardaycht 299
Ord, John, Clochmacreich, then Slains 497
Ord, John, Kirktown 488
Ord, Margaret 298
Ord, Thomas, Mid Skeith 297,300
Ord, Thomas, Revalter 300
Ord, William, merchant, Craighead 359,360
Ord, William, Middle Skeith 300
Ord, William 40
Ordens 59,84,87,88,89,90,109,113,127,138, 228,278,296,303,328,386
Ordens, Bogs of 91
Ordens, Heiress of 358
Ordiquhill, 1,126,150,151,154,163,164,170, 178,182,237,241,242,244,278,363
Ordiquhill Secondary School 258
Ordnance Survey 90
Organ Repair Fund 367
Oriental Bank 366
Orkney 122,440
Osborne, Dod, Girl Pat 432
Osborne, Jim, Girl Pat 432
Otho 20
Our Lady of Pity 116,193,194,208,499

P

P Celtic language 383
Packman, James 491
Packman, John, Craibstone Cottages 252,334
Pagliera, Rora 390
Paris Measure 72
Parish Council 62,207,208,270,290,291,293, 294,314,354,356,358,368,400,414,417,424, 468,471,472,473,482

Parish (Public) Hall 117,147,182,193,223,226, 260,272,367,391,430,438,448,449,452,453, 459,465,482
Park, Mrs 183
Park, Rev George 53,171,175,182,183,209, 220,222,271,272,273,337,381,437,448,457
Parkinson, JTL, Aberdeen 210
Parkmore Limestone Quarry, Dufftown 263
Parliamentary Grant in Aid of Medical Relief to the Poor in Scotland 399
Parochial Board 75,206,282,289,290,354,357, 368,399,400,409,417,469
Pasch Head Court 321
Pasch Roll 315
Paterson, Alexander, schoolmaster & session clerk 189,234
Paterson, Bill 147
Paterson, Dr, Buckie 429
Paterson, Jimmy, farm worker 457
Patronage Compensation 365
Pattenbringan 22,24,28,29,33,42,92,278,305, 306,309,321,329,384,416
Pattenbringan, Over 300
Patterson, grocer, Buckie 67
Patterson, Isobel, elder 188
Pauper Lunatic Fund 352,363
Peach Blossom 262
Pennan Sandstone Millwheels 134
Pennant, Thomas 29,75,386,418,520
Penny Weddings 165,335,337,435,460,461, 504
Perth 147,408
Peter Fair, Rathven 76,126,389,488
Peterkin, Alexander 46
Peterkin, George, Nether Blairock 284,328, 339,341
Peterkin, James, miller, Milton Millls 327
Peterkin, John, Broadrashes & Mains of Skeith 116
Peterkin, Mr, lawyer, Edinburgh 488
Petrie, butcher, Portsoy 67
Petrie, Mr, Gordon Castle 442
Philp, Alexander, schoolmaster & session clerk 156,188,189,235
Philp, James 269,345

Philp, John, Banff, witch 516
Philp, Rev Alexander 180,213,233
Pickwick Cars 148
Picts 18,19,22,23,24,31,33,84,87,94,103,107, 133,150,267,268,276,305,318,348,404
Pictish Hack Silver 20
Pictish Language 24,383,384
Pilmuir, John 178
Piper, George, Kirktown 374,375
Piper, John, Skeith 378
Pirie, Isabella, Bogside 465
Pirie, Johnnie 67
Pirie, W 376
Pirie, William, Bogside, private, Secret Army 275
Pirie, William, Bogside 429
Pirie, William, Jr, Bogside 128
Playing Field 254
Ploughing & Hoeing Association 451
Police Rate 354
Poll Tax 279,280
Pollard, George, railway labourer 287
Poolhead 90
Poolside 35,90,93,425
Poor Fund 372
Poor Law Amendment Act, 1845 74
Poor Law 323,394,467
Poor Rate 354,356,357
Poor's Houses 8,35,68,285,287,288,289,358, 399,417,425,426,468,473,482
Popery 165
Port of London Authority 432
Portknockie 59,183,258,267,401,459
Portknockie Amateur Drama Association 451
Portobello 226,231,252,275,353,365,482
Portsoy 39,41,43,45,46,55,67,68,69,103,116, 258,266,269,272,275,281,350,363,369, 463
Portsoy Secondary School 264
Poseidon Maritime Services Ltd, Carestown 149
Post Office 66,68,464
Post Office Savings Bank 373
Potato Famine 371
Povitic 91,92

Prebendary Lands of Mary Magdalene, St John the Baptist, St Andrew & Holy Cross 301
Presbyterianism 269
Press & Journal 58,70,264,451
Pretoria 249
Priest's Well 6,59
Prince Albrecht of Prussia 313
Princess Elizabeth 250
Princess Margaret 264
Princess Mary 250
Prism of Preston 351
Prison Visiting Committee 280
Prisoners of War Fund 447
Privy Council 179
Proctor, Mr, Ardoch, £50 Bequest 366,373
Property & Works Committee 424
Psalmody & Hymns 365
Public Hall Committee 354
Public Works Loan Board 208
Pum's Pot 10
Purss (?), Johnne 324
Purves, Mr, Director of Education 231,232

Q

Q Celtic language 383
Quaint's Croft 90,116
Quakers 168
Quarryhead 91,92
Quean's Strype 7,27
Queen Anne 309
Queen Margaret 151
Queen Mary 297
Queen of Elfin 517
Queen Victoria 249,291
Queen Victoria, Diamond Jubilee 440
Queen Victoria, Golden Jubilee 353,434
Quern Stone 93,103
Quinn, William, tailor, Berryhillock 271,446, 457
Quoiting Club 450

R

Raeburn, Geordie 386

Raemore 48,49,85,86,87,89,113,124,143,278, 302,303,329,389,419
Raemore, Little 91
RAF Lossiemouth 428
Raffan, Charles, Keith 470
Raffan, Ethel M, Comb's Croft 265,390, 437
Raffan, George, Comb's Croft 271
Raffan, George, Rottenhillock 427
Raffan, John 469
Raffan, Maggie, Cromdale 470
Raffan, Margaret 486
Raffan, Miss KA, Comb's Croft 446,450
Raffan, Miss, teacher 397
Raffan, Mr, Comb's Croft 273
Raffan, Mrs, Comb's Croft 290,471
Raffan, Robert 469
Raggal 277
Raich surname 382
Raich, James, Crabston 343
Raich, William 343
Rainnie surname 382
Rainnie, Mr, Mid Clune 115
Ralston, Mr 351
Randolph, Thomas, Earl of Moray 306,307
Rannas 13,22,39,40
Rannie, James 49
Rashiehill 13,35,90,114,124
Rashy Park 119
Rathillock 92
Rathven 1,9,13,28,76,177,179,180,220,241, 286,305,315,316,517
Rathven Mart 247,249,327
Rathven WRI Hall 451
Rattery, Christine, Cottartown of Ardoch 485, 487
Red Cross 273,454
Red Cross Work Party 452
Redford, George 285
Redhythe 277
Reformed Churches 365
Regality Court 26,61,85,109,281,321,322, 327,328,330,383
Regality, Burgh of 277,320,485
Regiam Majestatum 26

Registrar General 292
Registration Rate, 354
Reid James, Croftgloy, wright 361,362,363, 364
Reid Annie, shopkeeper & postmistress, organist, Berryhillock 64,66,68,191,430,466
Reid family 397
Reid Gate 427
Reid John, Berryhillock, joiner 457
Reid, Alexander, Berryhillock, tailor, Free Church elder 64,170,186,439
Reid, Alexander, Berryhillock 343
Reid, Alexander, Broadrashes 116
Reid, Alexander, tailor, Hollanbush 270
Reid, Andrew, Bognageith 364,372
Reid, Andrew, Burnheads, precentor 77, 186,466
Reid, Andrew, servant, Ramore 487
Reid, baker, Cullen 67
Reid, Barbara, Berryhillock 343
Reid, Billy 226
Reid, Charles, Kirktown 270
Reid, Elspet 489
Reid, George 282
Reid, George 364
Reid, George 469
Reid, Hazel, 227,261
Reid, Helen, Broadrashes 375
Reid, Herbert 247
Reid, Jack, garage proprietor, Cornhill 458
Reid, James, Leitchestown 115
Reid, James, Meikle Knows 115
Reid, James, Mid Skeith 116,489,497
Reid, James, Over Skeith 329
Reid, James 288,289
Reid, James 469
Reid, James Croftgloy 115
Reid, Janet, Squaredoch 489,497
Reid, Janet 288
Reid, Jean, Darbreich 330
Reid, Jean, Ramoir 377
Reid, Jessie Ann, Cullen postmistress 388
Reid, Jessie, MA, teacher 239
Reid, John, carpenter, joiner & wright 146

Reid, John, Darbreich, 330,342
Reid, John, elder 159,171,370,496
Reid, John, grocer & general dealer, Berryhillock 64,284,355
Reid, John, Ramoire 326,359
Reid, John, Squaredoch, Inspector of the Poor 285,290
Reid, John, Squaredoch 170,389
Reid, John, Swailend 128,388
Reid, John Upper Skeith 116
Reid, Katherine, Vindehills 300
Reid, Lizzie 265
Reid, Margaret, Ramore 379
Reid, Miss 391
Reid, Mr, Portsoy 168,464
Reid, Mrs, Kirktown 57
Reid, nurse 398
Reid, Percy 445
Reid, Robert, Archdeacon, Bishop & Abbot of Kinloss 296
Reid, Robert, Craibstone Cottages 334
Reid, Thomas, Cairnstoun 326
Reid, Walter, Ardoch 270
Reid, Walter, Leichistoun 326
Reid, Walter, schoolmaster 235,240
Reid, Walter, Squaredoch 114,363
Reid, William, Cairstoun 485
Reid, William, Demerary, ex Faichyhill 490
Reid, William, Faichiehill 200
Reid, William, Faichyhill 114
Reid, William, wright 285
Reidhaven, Viscount 209,210
Relief of Mafeking 270
Rennie, John 310,443
Rennie, Kathleen 442,443
Rhodes, Greece 432
Riddoch, Alexander, schoolmaster 235
Riddoch, Jane, Poors Houses 470,491
Riddoch, Jane 291
Riddoch, Jessie 287,288
Riddoch, John 114
Riddoch, Lieutenant, Kirktown 270
Riddoch, Thomas, schoolmaster 189,235

Riddoch, William, Oathillock 115
Riddoch, William 46
Rigby, John, Fl Lieut 428
Ring Cairn 29
Ritchie, George, pauper 471
Ritchie, Isobel, 377
Ritchie, James 46
Ritchisone, John, Mains of Bracco 326
River Deveron 58
River Isla 41
Road Trustees 280
Roads & Bridges Rate 354
Rob Roy, Buckie 389
Robertson & Son, monumental masons, Hardgate, Aberdeen 273
Robertson, A, teacher 239
Robertson, Alexander, carpenter, Cullen, ex Berryhillock 489
Robertson, Alexander, Skeith 189,235
Robertson, draper, Cullen 67
Robertson, grocer & hardware merchant, Fordyce 67,126
Robertson, James, schoolmaster & session clerk 189,236,378
Robertson, Jane 174
Robertson, John, Berryhillock Crofts 113
Robertson, John, servant to the Laird of Glassaugh 340
Robertson, Mr, Berryhillock 429
Robertson, Mr, Crossroads School 437
Robertson, Mr, Skeycht 299
Robertson, Mrs, Faichyhill 225
Robertson, Pam & John 6,19,28,59,138,211, 273,432
Robertson, Peter, Ordens 340,487
Robertson, Rev, Cullen 58
Robertson, Rev, Strathdon 492,493
Robertson, Sir John 154
Robertson, Tash 176
Robertson, Walter, Cullen 200
Robertson, Walter, Ordens, wright 363
Robertson's Band, Newmill 450
Robin Hood 435
Roger, Mr, music teacher 222

Roll of Honour, WW1 271,272
Roll of Voters Rate 354
Romans 20,21,81,387,508
Roman Coin Hoard 20,30
Roman Road 45
Rosebank 44,51,52,68,91
Rosebery, Lord 281
Rosehead 91,92
Ross 268 ,306
Ross or Currie, Ann, Glasgow 470,471
Ross, Alexander, Kirktown Farm, elder 81, 187,294
Ross, Alice, assistant registrar 390
Ross, Ann, Berryhillock, pauper 290
Ross, Euphemia Lady 305,308
Ross, Hugh, Earl of 307
Ross, James, registrar, Kirktown 54,292,293, 223,333,389
Ross's Band, Buckie 260
Ross, Mr, Huntly 53
Ross's Band, Buckie 450
Rothiemay 264,269,275
Rottenhillock 11,35,68,91,425
Row, Mary, idiot 375
Roy, Elsie, domestic subjects teacher 222, 239
Royal Highland Show, Aberdeen 263
Royal Navy 263,269
Ruddach, John, merchant 363
Ruddoch, George, Blairock 235
Rumbles, Charles, Muir of Squaredoch 271
Rumbles, Ernie 227
Rumbles, Frank 445
Rumbles, Geddes, Cottarclump 91
Rumbles, George, Mosside 430
Rumbles, Maggie 221
Rumbles, Mr, Muir of Squaredoch 472
Rumbles, Mrs, Kirktown 57
Rumbles, Peter, Tochieneal 463
Rumbles, Tommy, Kirktown, private, Secret Army 275
Rumbles, widow 472,473
Rumbles, William 221,247,248
Rumbling Wells 58
Runcie, Alexander 46
Runcie, D 443
Runcie, Mr, slater 254
Rural Workers' Society 350
Russel, Alex, Rathven 355
Russel, Alexander, elder 171
Russel, Ann, Aultmore 282
Russel, Charles, Berryhillock Crofts 113
Russel, Charles Hollandbush 115
Russel, James, schoolmaster 235
Russel, James Free Church deacon 186
Russel, Janet 469
Russel, Jessie, Rathven 355
Russel, Mr, Elgin, Valuation Roll Assessor 288
Russel, Mr 200,364
Russel, Mr 347
Russell, Alexander 491
Russell, Barbara 490
Russell, Charles, Free Church beadle 191
Russell, Jessie, Rathven 470
Russia 467

S

Sacrament House 197,199,294,310
Sancto Claro, Johannes de, de Deskford (Sir John Sinclair) 308,323
Sandend 67,262,378
Sanderson, Robert, blacksmith 146
Sanitary Inspector 400
Saughtertown or Netherseat of Aichries 305
School Board 220,244,250,251,440,441
School Board Room 353,437,439,440
School Fund 438
School Management Committee, District No 2 244,251,293
School Meals Service 253
School Nurse 398
School of Scottish Studies, Edinburgh University 80
Scone 307
Scota 15
Scotland 1,80,99,105,112,116,118,128,136,145,163, 212,276

Scotland, Church of 82,165,172,175,209,215, 240
Scots 2488,109,267,268,383
Scotston 277
Scott, Dr, Cullen 431
Scott, George, Sen, Upper Blairock 333
Scott, John, Clunehill Croft 115
Scott, John, schoolmaster & session clerk 189, 235,238,241,250,292,389
Scott, Mayor General of the Sheriffdom of Banff 297
Scott, Mr, Upper Skeith Croft 115
Scott, Robert 48
Scott, Sir Walter 248,439
Scott, Sir Walter, Centenary 261
Scottish Christian Herald 436
Scottish Community Drama Association 450
Scottish Community Drama Association Festival, Cullen 451
Scottish Education Department 231
Scottish Land Fund 456
Scottish Parliament 109
Scottish Sunday School Union 176
Scrimgeour, John, Kirktown 325
Sea Dogs 75
Seafield 309,314
Seafield Church, Cullen 203
Seafield Estate 14,57,58,61,75,78,79,94,146, 275,294,316,332,334,351,414,416,423
Seafield Estate Plan, 1771 85,92,112,260,350
Seafield Trustees 337,338,449
Seafield, 13th Earl 315
Seafield, Caroline, Dowager Countess 191,209, 314,389
Seafield, Earl of 13,19,47,50,116,169,172,196, 199,205,209,210,212,215,218,277,279,281, 282,284,303,311,312,314,371,372
Seafield, Ian Charles, 8th Earl 314
Seafield, John Charles, 7th Earl 314
Seafield, Lady 206,207,209,210,471 Seafield, Nina Caroline Studley Herbert, 12th Countess of 76,209,271,315
Seaforth Highlanders 271
Secret Army 275
Seivwright, Mr, stationer 355

Seivwright, Mrs, Portsoy, unofficial midwife 400
Selfridges 389
Sellar, Francis 49
Shand, Mrs, organiser, school reunion 232
Sharp, Archbishop, St Andrews 358,386
Sharp, Hugh, surgeon, Cullen 271,283,385,289, 399
Sharp, Robert, Sheriff Clerk, Bamfe 358,386
Sharp's Mortification 181,186,358,359,386
Shaw, James, ground officer, Leith Hall 494
Shaw, Mr, Inveresk, sufferer of fire 375
Shearer, Frank 430
Shearer, Hugh, Ardoch Cottages 389
Sheilburn 91,177,198,333,475
Sheilburn School 61,246,251,263,271,452
Sheilmuir 69,92,113,125,142,193,349
Sheilmuir Moss 11,61
Shephard, George 303
Shephard's Croft 301
Shepherd family 140
Shepherd, Alexander, Craibstone 81,141
Shepherd, Alexander, Inaltrie 270
Shepherd, Alexander, tailor 64
Shepherd, Andrew, Bogs of Ordens 346
Shepherd, Anne, servant, Nether Blairock 341
Shepherd, George, Squaredoch 114
Shepherd, Isobel 469
Shepherd, James, Crabston 301
Shepherd, James, Jr, Crabston 301
Shepherd, Janet, Squaredoch 361
Shepherd, Janet 373
Shepherd, Jean, Squaredoch 166,463
Shepherd, John, Crabston 301
Shepherd, John 198
Shepherd, Mr, Craibstone 446
Shepherd, Mrs, Craibstone 443
Shepherd, Robbie 444
Shepherd Cllr Ron 177,207,414
Sheriff 48
Shilling Hill, Portsoy 103
Shiphart, George, Fachihill 326
Shipherd, Johne, Crabstoune, elder 187

Shirer surname 382
Shirer, Janet, Berryhillock 369
Shirralds 30,43,56
Shooting Match, Raemore 441
Sim, Jane, dame school teacher 230
Sim, Mr, Cullen 355
Sim, W, Carestown 115
Sim, Walter, Burnheads 76
Simpson family, Milton 140,398
Simpson, A 443
Simpson, Isobel 238,266
Simpson, James 359
Simpson, James Over Skeith 326
Simpson, Jimmy, Craibstone 54,66,130
Simpson, John, Backburn 125
Simpson, Jon, Cloackmacreigh 326
Simpson, Kathleen 67,227,261,262
Simpson, Margaret 67
Simpson, Marshall, Comb's Croft 273
Simpson, Maud 453
Simpson, Mrs, school cleaner 225,431
Simpson, William, Woodend, elder 187
Simpson, William 364
Simson, Agnes 201
Sinclair 32
Sinclair family 307
Sinclair of Deskford & Findlater 307
Sinclair, Alexander 309
Sinclair, George, Burns 363
Sinclair, Ingram 308
Sinclair, James, schoolmaster, session clerk & precentor 188,189,228,233,234
Sinclair, John 308 Sinclair, Margaret 308,309
Sinclair, Richard (Ricardo de Sancto Claro), Roslyn 307
Sinclair, Walter, Little Blairock, later Nether Blairock 341,362,363
Sinclairs of Roslyn 307,413
Singing Together, Keith Grammar School 264
Skeith 34,77,87,108,110,180,204,278,280, 281,295,301,307,308,316,360
Skeith, Barn of 172
Skeith, Castle of 32,36,97,116,135,137,193, 412,414,415,416

Skeith, Easter 88,295,324
Skeith, Little 6,45,62,89,92,93,108,136,302, 303,352,426
Skeith, Little, Cottage 62,425
Skeith, Mains of 6,32,41,44,45,87,169,193, 208,212,302,415,498,517
Skeith, Mid 5,6,13,43,44,45,46,56,60,88,89, 92,94,95,136,139,140,278,303,329,423
Skeith, Mid, Den 90
Skeith, Nether 296,297,299,302,304,352
Skeith, Upper 5,41,43,86,89,92,139,141,278, 302,303,328,329
Skinner, Daryl 426
Skinner, Elspet 202
Skinner, Jane, Milltown 286
Skinner, Jean 475
Skinner, John, Faichiehill 200
Skinner, Margaret 469
Slack of Standingman 14,476
Slackdale 44
Slatehaugh 91,92,142,475
Slateheuch 9,91,92,142
Slater's Directory 64
Sleepy Green 124
Sluaged 77
Sluie, Alexander 377
Sluie, Archibald, Blerock 373
Small Livings 365
Smart, Mr, Fordyce, athlete 444
Smart, Nellie 250
Smiddy Wood 136
Smith, Alex, foreman, Backies 350
Smith, Alexander, elder 171
Smith, Alexander, Hoggie 494,495
Smith, Alexander, Todholls 375,379
Smith, Alison 70,274
Smith, Alister 265
Smith, Annie 454
Smith, Audrey 226
Smith, Betty 286
Smith, Bill, Braidbog, Sgt, Secret Army 275
Smith, Brian 227
Smith, C 237
Smith, E 237

Smith, Edith, farm servant, Upper Braeside 333
Smith, Edith 400
Smith, Elaine 226
Smith, Ella, Poolside 251
Smith, Elsie 286
Smith, fishman, Sandend 67
Smith, Geordie, Easter Darbreich 124,391
Smith, George, Redmoss Croft 455
Smith, George, Squaredoch 326
Smith, George, Upper Blairock, bagpiper 444
Smith, George 227
Smith, George 265
Smith, George 361
Smith, Gladys 61,92,454
Smith, Ian G 266
Smith, Innes, Blackhillock 472
Smith, Isobel, Kirktown 282
Smith, Jackie 54,61,92,456,457,458
Smith, James, Bank of Squaredoch 114,167
Smith, James, Croftgloy 115
Smith, James, Kirktown, elder 340,379
Smith, James, Mosside, elder 187,379,496
Smith, James, schoolmaster & session clerk 189,205,235,237,238,241,243,289,439,457
Smith, Jane, Aultmore, lunatic pauper 283,288
Smith, Janet, Cottartown of Ardoch 488,490
Smith, Janet, Squaredoch 486
Smith, Jessie, later in Keith 289,470
Smith, John, Barnyards of Cullen House, gamekeeper 331
Smith, John, Broomhaugh 116,200
Smith, John, Mosside 166,463
Smith, John, Todholes 282,283
Smith, John 198,364
Smith, Joyce 456
Smith, Lizzie, Little Darbreich 446
Smith, Maggie, Little Darbreich 446
Smith, Margaret, Inaltrie 429
Smith, Mr, Braidbog 256
Smith, Mr, contractor, Portsoy 211
Smith, Peter, Darbreich, private, Secret Army 275
Smith, T Macauley 222
Smith, Thomas, Cairnley 115

Smith, William 46
Smith, William, Burns, dangerous maniac 284, 285,399
Smithstown, 30,86,92,145,278,298,301,304, 305,309
Smithstown, Parks of 90
Smithyhillock 91
Smycht, Katerine, Skordiaicht 299
Social Work, Church 365
Society for the Propagation of Christian Knowledge 156
Soldiers & Sailors Families' Association 270
Solemn League & Covenant 164,269
Somerset Light Infantry 271
Sorners (beggars) 393
Sostad, Odin, exchange teacher 226
Souter, Rev, Cullen 437
South Africa 389
South Lissens Pottery 9,148,149
South West 267
Southern Rhodesia 251
Spain, 162,467
Sparke, James, Kirkcaldy, Original Wheelbarrow Man 431
Spence, Donald, farm servant, Ardoch 332
Spence, Elizabeth 362
Spence, Harie, session clerk 189
Spence, James 38
Spence, Mary A 250
Spence, Walter, Marchbank 113
Spence, William, Backies 329
Speyside 386
Spynie Palace 31
Squaredoch 13,39,40,44,51,57,63,68,69,86, 88,108,113,121,278,295,298,299,300, 303, 305,328,329,427,434,489
Squaredoch, Hill of 298
Squaredoch, Little 426
Squaredoch, Muir of 8,35,37,44,114,285,288, 358,417,425,426,468,471,482
Squaredoch, Upper 35,426
St Ambrose 220
St Clair, Richard of, Grieve of Cullen, Shield Bearer to King Robert 2nd 307

St Columba 23,150,318
St Fumac's Well, Botriphnie 501
St John's Tree 137,205
St John's Tree, Young 137
St John's Well 59,151,199,205,463,501
St John's, New 89,134,169,173,174,176,177, 182,184,186,192,193,196,207,208,211, 212, 215,273,365,367,426,457,485,490
St John's, Old 37,38,134,152,153,154,171,177, 182,192,193,194,196,197,198,199,204,205, 206,208,209,212,236,294,413,513
St Mary's Well, Ordiquhill 59,151,165,463,501, 516
St Mauire 150
St Modan's, Falkirk 176
St Ninian 23,150
Stables, Alexander 343
Stables, Andrew, Squaredoch 375
Stables, Elspet, Kirktown 114
Stables, Elspet, Milntown 486
Stables, Elspet 375
Stables, James, Kirktown 329
Stables, Jean 190
Stables, John, heckler, Cullen 340
Stables, John 492
Stables, Newmill 53
Stalin, 177, 465
Standingmanhill 4,28
Steenson, Janet, Cleanhill 377
Steinson surname 382
Steinson, Captain 387
Steinson, Helen 485
Steinson, Walter, Kirktown 114
Stenson, John 299
Stephen, Howard, Girl Pat 432
Step**hen**, John, Berryhillock Mill 133,443
Stephen, Mr, Milltown 445
Stephen, Mr 283
Stephen, Mrs Kirktown 292
Stephen, widow 473
Stephen, William, elder 187,282,286,290
Steven, George, Burnheads 330
Steven, Messrs, musicians 439
Steven, Robert & William, bakers 146

Stevens, PC 263
Stevenson, baker, Keith 67
Stevenson, Joseph 46,49
Stevenson, Miss 466
Stevenson, Rev Douglas 177,185
Stevenson, Walter 337
Stevenson, William, schoolmaster & session clerk 189,235,374
Steward, Matthew, Ordenis 299
Stewart, B, 237
Stewart, Dodo, Braehead 130,334
Stewart, Dorothy, Meikle Knows 174,454,455
Stewart, E 443
Stewart, Effie, Barone 443,454,455
Stewart, Frances 225
Stewart, G 343
Stewart, G 443
Stewart, George, Braehead 99,105
Stewart, Hamish 226
Stewart, Isobel 377
Stewart, J, Barone? 443,456
Stewart, J 443
Stewart, Jack, Little Knows 52,123
Stewart, James, Chancellor of Assize 517
Stewart, James 283
Stewart, James 46
Stewart, Jean 454
Stewart, Jimmy, Meikle Knows 27,52,93,95, 103,123,272,320,428,456
Stewart, John, Hoggie, merchant 63
Stewart, Linda 225
Stewart, Mary 454
Stewart, Mrs, Cultain 272
Stewart, Patrick, Clochmacreich, elder 187
Stewart, Sheila 238
Stewart, Thomas, Laird of Bog 179,485
Stewart, William A, Nether Blairock 81
Stewart, William, Greens of Blairock, Free Church elder 485
Stewart's Orchestra, Keith 451
Stitchell, John, Clochmacreich, 328
Stitchells, John, Over Clune 326
Stocking School 228,363
Stone Circle 29,30

Stonehaven Poor House 472
Stooky Sunday 100
Stornoway 163
Stotfauld Burn 6,296
Stotfield Beach, Lossiemouth 263
Strachan, Elizabeth 490
Strachan, George 341
Strachan, John, Inaltry 487
Strachan, Margaret, Oathillock 342
Strachan, Mary 469
Strachan, William, Inaltry 487
Strathdee, Alison 225
Strathdee, Margaret 174,454
Strathdee, Sandy 94
Strathisla 13,296,297
Strathisla, Balliary of 277,312
Strathisla, Barony & Regality of 297
Strathlene Glee Party 452
Strathmore, Lord 350
Strathpeffer 438
Stronach, James, Squaredoch 326
Stripeside 8,35,44,90,91
Stuart, boy whooping cough sufferer 397
Stuart, Janet 374
Suddon, John, postman 69
Summers, Douglas, art teacher 239
Sunday Observance 464
Sunday School 66,177,192,216,449,454
Sunday School Library 436
Sunday School Picnic 451
Sunday Schools, Free Church 170
Sunderland Lime 75
Sunnyside 439
Sutherland 306
Sutherland, Elizabeth, Squaredoch 285
Sutherland, George, Bloomfield 353
Sutherland, James 114
Sutherland, John, farm servant, Mosside 334
Sutherland, Johnny 89,93
Swailend 34,44,52,80,89,98,124,140,147
Swailend, Headroom of 91
Swallowhillock 92,278,303
Syme, Alexander, Jr 297

Syme, George 326
Syme, Walter, alehouse keeper, Berryhillock 69,340,363,376
Symon, John, Tillybridles 343
Symon, William, 339

T

Taas surname 382
Taas, Janet 375
Tack Burn 6,7
Taexali 19,22
Tailor, William, Crabstoun 359
Tarlair 59,463,501
Taylor, Alexander 430
Taylor, Alexander & Walter 359
Taylor, Alexander, Free Church deacon 186
Taylor, Alexander, Kirktown, elder 114,187
Taylor, Alexander, Little Skeith, moss grieve 62,94,355,389,429
Taylor, Alexander, Meikle Knows 115
Taylor, Alexander, Squaredoch, smith 379
Taylor, Bella, Bellcroft 81
Taylor, Bert, Buckie 427
Taylor, Brodie, Swailend 80
Taylor, Charles, Swailend 447
Taylor, Colin 225
Taylor, George, Backburn 125
Taylor, George, farm servant, Cultain 492
Taylor, George, Hollandbush Croft 115
Taylor, George, Kirktown 326
Taylor, George, Little Skeith 445
Taylor, George, Mains of Skeith 130
Taylor, George, shoemaker 64
Taylor, George 247
Taylor, George 480
Taylor, James, Bellcroft 429
Taylor, James, foreman, Langlanburn 350
Taylor, Jean 174,454
Taylor, Jean 343
Taylor, Jessie, Bellcroft 81
Taylor, John 46
Taylor, Margaret 469
Taylor, Mary 469

Taylor, Miss, teacher 253
Taylor, Miss 449
Taylor, Mr & Mrs, Berryhillock 429,473
Taylor, Mr, choirmaster 466
Taylor, Mr, Mains of Skeith 53,54,61
Taylor, Mrs, Cultain 169
Taylor, Robert, Swailend 446
Taylor, Sheila 266
Taylor, William, Raemore 446
Taylor, William 49
Taylor, William Squaredoch, Regality Court Officer 321,361
Taylor, Willie, Braidbog 55,443,456
Teacher Training College 222
Telephone 54
Television 54
Temperance Committee 365
Tenant Road Trustees 51
Tenerife 432
Territorial Army 274
Thain or Thom, John, schoolmaster & reader 178,234,278
Thain surname 382
Thain, Alexander, Clochmacreich 116
Thain's Croft, Cullen 299
Thayne, Johne, Clunehill 325
Thom, Lizzie, lunatic pauper, Grange 293,472
Thom, Miss, school cleaner 224
Thom, widow, Berryhillock 290,355,470,473
Thomas, Mrs Captain 432
Thomson, Charlie 225
Thomson, Dr, Cullen 431
Thomson, Isobel, Hillary House Captain 227
Thomson, Jane, Berryhillock 470
Thomson, Jimmy 226
Thomson, John 50
Thomson, Mr, tenant of Chapel Haugh 193
Thomson, William 325
Thomson's Orchestra, Tarrycroys 450
Thorburn, Mr, solicitor, Keith 283
Three Burns meeting 5,8,40,41,51,141,304
Tillybreedless 34,85,88,122,168,277,305
Tillybreedless Bridge 5,7,49
Tillybreedless, Nether 143,302,303,329

Tillybreedless, Upper 142,302,303,329
Tochieneal 43,54,58,87,130,145,297,304
Tochieneal Distillery 145
Tochieneal Station 141,219
Tochieneal Tile Works 10,30,76,129,138,145, 219,422,423
Tochieneal J P, Lord Findlater's Baron Baillie 344
Tod's Cottage 52,425
Todholes 35,52,90,121,124,140,143,391
Toisech 23
Toll Bars 48
Topp, Helen, Faichyhill 484
Topp, John, Berryhillock 221,447
Topp, Mary Ann 133
Topp, Mrs 133
Topp, Robert 247
Tough, Ann, Berryhillock 470
Towie 30,56,304
Towie Mill 13,14,30,43
Transvaal War Fund 270
Troupe, Alexander 494
Trux, German POW, Croftgib 458
Tuath 23
Tulinach 309
Tullywhull 34,150,151
Tumuli 30
Turkey 467
Turner Memorial Hospital, Keith 427
Turner, K 433
Turnpike 10,43,46,50
Turnpike Acts 46
Turnpike Road Debt Rate 354
Twilight Dance Orchestra, Portsoy 450
Tynet, Andrew, Lechistonne 299

U

Union of the Churches 367
Union of the Parliaments 311
Unionist Association 294
United Banffshire Agricultural Society 280
United Presbyterian Church 492
Upstrath 277,305

Urquhart, baker, Cullen 437
Urquhart, John 296
USA 64,322,350,353

V

Vale of Deskford Temperance Society 439
Vale of Deskford Temperance Society Pic-Nic 439
Valuation Roll 315
Vancouver 226
Vat surname 382
Vat, William Garreaucht 299
VE Day 250
Versatile Windows 147,449
Vicomagi 19,22
Viewfrith 91
Vikings 267,387
Volunteer Battalions 269

W

Wagner 313
Waird Burn 8,204
Wairdleys Croft 8,34,49,113
Wairds, The 87,278,302
Wales 142
Walker, Dr 400
Walker, James, Free Church school teacher 239
Walker, Mr 363
Walker, Rev Alexander 184,439
Wallace, baker, Buckie 67
Wallace, John, Tocheneill 301
Walter, Commendator of Kinloss 296
Walter, Seneschal of Scotland 307
Wans, Isobel 341
Walter, Seneschal of Scotland 307
Wans, Isobel 341
War Committees 268
War Memorial 209,210,367
War Memorial Trust 273
War Savings Association 272,356
Wat, William, Clunehill 489

Wat's Rhives 124
Waterloo 270
Watson, Ann, Muir of Squaredoch 470
Watson, Catherine 221
Watson, James, Kirktown, church officer 191, 224
Watson, Mr 437
Watson, Robert, schoolmaster 235,238
Watson's Croft, Carrothead 113
Watt, Elizabeth 343
Watt, J 458
Watt, James, Berryhillock 288
Watt, James, Croftgloy 115
Watt, James, Nether Clune 115
Watt, James, vintner 64
Watt, Jimmy, joiner, Berryhillock 390
Watt, John, elder, 171
Watt, John, Free Church elder 170
Watt, Robert, Sheilburn 114
Watt, William, Meikle Knows 115
Watt, William, Upper Clune 115
Waugh, David, architect, Glasgow 211
Waverley Novels 439
Weakley, Nett, Easter Darbreich 174,454,455
Webster, Messrs, Aberdeen 254
Webster, Mr, synod treasurer 216
Wellcroft 68,90,91
Wellheads 91
Wellington Bomber 428
Wellington Bomber Crash 276
Welsh Annals 267
West Church 211,212
West Church Houses 365
West Church Organ 367
West Manse 8,44,51,212
Western Isles Council 163
Westminster Bridge 390
Weston, 90,114,124,140
White, James 345
Whitehills 67,261,378,431
Whiteknowes 13,35,63,68,87,90
Whitelaw, Nancy 454
Whitestrype Burn 6,140

Whithorn 150
Whyntie, John, elder 187,282
Whyte, James, labourer, Muir of Squaredoch 333
Wier, Ann, Berryhillock 489
Wilkie, Miss, Free Church school teacher 239
Wilkie, Mrs 367
Will, Mr, tailor, Cullen 289
William & Mary 179
William, Bishop of Aberdeen 153
Williams, George, pedlar, Little Skeith 332,473
Wilson family, The Field 398
Wilson, A, Corbie Craig 115
Wilson, Alexander, Briggs 114
Wilson, Alexander 171
Wilson, Andrew, Rashiehill 390
Wilson, Elspet 491
Wilson, George's Croft, Craibston 113
Wilson, Graeme, Moray Heritage Centre 295
Wilson (James) 12
Wilson, James, 90
Wilson, James, Ardoch 144,165,370
Wilson, James, elder 187,282
Wilson, James, Little Knows 92,168,182,291, 429,439,461,481
Wilson, James, Mains of Birkenbog 332
Wilson, James, Oathillock 115
Wilson, James, Parkley, Fordyce 176
Wilson, James 221
Wilson, Joan, Little Knows 168,481
Wilson, John, factor, Seafield Estate 145,198, 282,369,370
Wilson, John, student, Ardoch 270
Wilson, John, Tack of Craibston 373,374,376, 377
Wilson, John 46,49
Wilson, Miss, teacher 397
Wilson, Miss 450
Wilson, Mr, Milltown 389
Wilson, Mrs, Knows 504
Wilson, William Kirktown 114
Wiltshire, 237
Windyhills 142,304,305
Windyhills Moss 329

Windyhills, Over 13,44,86,92,316
Windyhills, Wester 13,92,94,316
Winfre, Marjorie, Over Pattenbringan 300
Wireless 54
Woman's Guild 174,175,177,184,274,367,440, 447,449,451,452,453,465,478
Woman's Guild Garden Fete 452
Women's Jubilee Collection 353
Women's Land Army 275
Women's Timber Corps 136,275
Wood, Alexander, kirk officer 190,361
Wood, Alexander, Mosside 127,342
Wood, Alexander, Nether Windyhills 116
Wood, David, Cottarclump 445,446
Wood, Dr, Cullen 452
Wood, George 449
Wood, James, pauper lunatic 290,468,471
Wood, Jamesina 491
Wood, Janet 285
Wood, Mr, Cottarclump 209
Wood, Mr, Myreton 113
Wood, Mr, West Church Cottage 212
Wood, Mrs, Gateside 128
Wood, Neville 148
Wood, Rev Melvyn 177,184
Wood, Robert, Bognageith 329
Wood, Robert, Milltown 470
Wood, widow, Milltown 471
Wood, widow, Muir of Squaredoch 471
Wood, William 445
Woodend Smithy 8,66,139,143,147,509
Woodside 136
Wordan, James 298
World War I 80,81,95,171,190,191,219,252, 270,272,273,292,400,444,447,448,449
World War II 38,49,53,55,57,65,66,76,106,125,126,130,135, 136,141,147,177,218,223,226,231,250,253, 261,265,273,294,332,350,367,407,416,424, 428,429,432,438,452,453,457,465,475,482
Wright, Alexander, Saughs 170
Wright, Ann 471
Wright, G, session clerk 172
Wright, George, Burnheads 363

Wright, George, Carrothead 202
Wright, George, Ramoir 343,378
Wright, George, schoolmaster 235
Wright, George's Croft, Craibston 113
Wright, James, Free Church school teacher 239
Wright, James 328
Wright, James 471
Wright, James 490
Wright, Janet, Ramore 346
Wright, John, Edinburgh 470
Wright, Margaret 490,497
Wright, Messrs, Millwrights, Portsoy 80
Wright, Mr & Mrs, Upper Skeith 211,481
Wright, Mr, Backies of Over Skeith 116
Wright, Sgt John, Royal Artillery, Banff 269
Wright, William, Ramore 344
Wyvers' 135

Y

York, Duke of 250
Yorstan, Mr, school dentist 400
Young Worshippers' League 176,452,466
Young, Agnes, Skeith 345
Young, Alexander, collector of cess 270
Young, Alexander, Old Rayne 491
Young, Alexander 341
Young, Archibald, Procurator Fiscal 331
Young, baker, Cullen 67
Young, John 517
Young, Joseph 289
Young, Peter, Squaredoch 486
Younie's Band, Keith 260,450
Youth Club 449,454,455,456
Yule, Marion 454

Please note that where individuals are named above, whilst accuracy has been sought, lack of corroboration or proof may mean duplicate entries for the same individual, or two individuals being conflated into the same entry.

LIST OF SUBSCRIBERS

Aberdeen & NE Scotland Family History Society
Angus Aitken, Broxburn
David & Eileen Aitken, Larbert
Peter Aitken, Bo'ness
Audrey Allan, Cullen
Jean Allan, Bucksburn
Norman Allan, Banff
Graham Barclay, Deskford
W & E Barclay, Deskford
Pat Bardill, Deskford
John Barrett, Aberlour
Ella Bell, Aberlour
Edith Beveridge, Aberdeen
Bill & Margaret Black, Balerno
George Brander, Alicante, Sp
Brown family, Lintmill
Alex Cadenhead, Elgin
Elizabeth Campbell, Strathaven
Stuart Campbell, Glasgow
John & Kath Canning, Deskford
Carol & Neil Carlton, Dufftown
Maggie Castell, Deskford
George Christie, Fordyce
Helen Christie, Deskford
George Clark, Portsoy
Andrew Cortis, Drybridge
Alex Coull, Deskford
Alex (Ike) Coull, Deskford
Betty Coull, Bridgnorth
Edith Coull, Deskford
Margaret Coull, Kirktown
Sheila Coull, Keith
Elizabeth Cowie, Buckie
Artemis & James Curran, Uddingston
Katy & Sam Curran, Uddingston
Andrew Currie, Deskford
Bill & Myrna Currie, Halifax
Ian & Mary Currie, Deskford
James & Jo-Anne Currie, Deskford
John & Bev Currie, Queensland, Aus
Bob Davidson, Fordyce
Brian Davidson, Fordyce
Colin Davidson, Fordyce
Ian Davidson, Portsoy
James Davidson, Summertown
James Davidson, Fordyce
Margaret Davidson, Fordyce
Sheena Davidson, Evanton
Tommy & Kathy Davidson, Deskford
Ishbel Dawson nee Rumbles, Portsoy
Moira & Adrian Dawson, Leicester
Norman Defoe, Deskford
Cynthia Dixon, Western Australia
Robert Donald, Banff
Katherine Donnachie, Deskford
Jeff Dugdale, Speymouth
Fraser Duncan, Deskford
Mary Duncan, Cullen
Mary Dyk, Port Coquitlam, Can
Paula Farquhar, Deskford
Carol Featch, Deskford
The Featch family, Deskford
James Findlay, Cullen
Laurence Findlay, Elgin
Christine Foster, Grange
Ethel Fowler nee Ewen, Glenlivet
Edward Fraser, BC, Can
Anne S Garden, Macduff
Mabel & Bill Gauld, Tochieneal
Howard Watson Geddes, Rowlands Castle
Louis BT Geddes, Cullen
Lindra Gentry, Buckie
Brenda Gifford, Cullen
Jill Green, Keith
Gerry Haggerty, Elgin
Len Hall, Fochabers
Keith & Maggie Hancock, Langbank

Keith & Kathy Harry, Northants
Harry Hawkes, Portknockie
Mick Henderson, Deskford
Cameron Henderson, Edinburgh
David Henderson, Inverness
Roddie Henderson, Cork
Roy Henderson, Perth
The Henderson family, Deskford
Pauline Holdway, Sudbury
Keith Ingram, Grange
Bob Irvine, Edinburgh
Mary Jesson, Deskford
Neil Johnson, Rothiemay
Keith Grammar School
John Kemp, Sussex
Peter Laing, Keith
Henry Lawrence, Bradford on Avon
Caroline Leggat, Banff
Steve Liley, Portknockie
Aileen Logan-Tyson, Amherst, USA
Bryan Longmore, Inverness
Christopher Longmore, Surrey
Herbert J A Longmore, Lochmaben
Lynne Longmore, Lochmaben
Derek Maclean, Deskford
Duncan Maclean, Deskford
Gordon L Maclean, Portsoy
John D Maclean, Portknockie
Maureen Maclean, Deskford
Stewart R Maclean, Cullen
Vicki Maclean, Deskford
Patsy Mair, Edinburgh
Margaret & Alan Maloney, Cullen
Alistair Mason, Banff
Peter Mason, Deskford
Glenda Mattes, Boston, USA
Lynne & David McGregor, Deskford
The McHattie family, Deskford
Alex McKay, Scone
Fyvie McKay, Cornhill

George (Doddie) McKay, Muir of Squaredoch
James McKay, Deskford
Bruce & Anne McLaren, Deskford
Rose McLarnon, Port Elizabeth, SA
James McLean, Deskford
Margaret McRitchie, Huntly
Doreen Melville, Glenrothes
Isobel Merson, Deskford
Eileen Miller, Deskford
Lorraine Miller and Iain Grieve, Deskford
Paul Miller, Deskford
Ronald Miller, Cornhill
Samuel Miller, Deskford
Winnie Miller, Deskford
Roy Milligan, Banff
Stephen Millward, Deskford
Isobel Milne nee Currie, Tullynessle
Alexander McConnachie Milton, Fraserburgh
Eric Milton, Aberdeen
Jim Milton, Saskatchewan, Can
Jimmy Milton, Keith
John Milton, Keith
Mamie Mitchell, Deskford
Hilary Morrison, Deskford
James Muiry, Berryhillock
William J Murray, Georgia, USA
Frank O'Byrne, Cork
Colin Paton, Watton at Stone
Marion Paton, Balmullo
Mhari Paton, Balmullo
Steve & Karen Patterson, Deskford
Cathy Piggott, Gourock
Colin Priest, Bogmuchalls
James Reid, Deskford
John Rennie, Portknockie
Margaret Rhynas nee Currie, Mulben
June Roberts, Forfar

John & Pamela Robertson, Deskford
Norman Robertson, Portsoy
Doreen Ross, Cullen
Robin & Annie Ross, Edinburgh
Anna Rumbles, Deskford
Ernie Rumbles, Dufftown
Ian Sandison, Lintmill
Shiela Sellar, Lintmill
Isobel Shanks, Keith
Ron Shepherd, Cullen
Evelyn E Shirran, Cults
Mary Sim, Huntly
Andy Simpson, Banff
Janet Simpson nee Milton, Portsoy
Jean Simpson nee Milton, Aberdeen
Alison Smith, Macduff
George Smith, Darbreich
Jackie Smith, Deskford
Margaret Smith, Deskford
Morag Smith, Deskford
William Watson Smith, Keith
David Stephen, St Albans
Sylvana Stellini, Treviso, It
Jackie Stevenson, Cullen
Tracey Stevenson, Portknockie
Jack Stewart, Deskford
Jimmy Stewart, Deskford
Robert Stewart, Deskford
Sandy & Margaret Strathdee, Deskford
Colin Taylor, Aberdeen
Jean Taylor, Cullen
Kayden Taylor, Deskford
Margaret Taylor, Keith
Isobel Taylor-Vanhulst, Den Haag, Neth
Hilda Thompson, Nairn
David Turnbull, Gourock
Ray Walkington, Deskford
Robert Watt, Macduff
Graham Weir, Perth
Glyn & Monica Wells, Deskford
Alistair Wood, Cullen
Liz & Neville Wood, Deskford